The Economic Development of Europe's Regions

This book is the first quantitative description of Europe's economic development at a regional level over the entire twentieth century. Based on a new and comprehensive set of data, it brings together a group of leading economic historians in order to describe and analyze the development of European regions, both for nation states and for Europe as a whole. This provides a new transnational perspective on Europe's quantitative development, offering for the first time a systematic long-run analysis of national policies independent from the use of national statistical units. The new transnational dimension of data allows for the analysis of national policies in a more thorough way than ever before.

The book provides a comprehensive database at the level of modern NUTS 2 regions for the period 1900–2010 in 10-year intervals, and a panoramic view of economic development both below and above the national level. It will be of great interest to economic historians, economic geographers, development economists and those with an interest in economic growth.

Joan Ramón Rosés is Professor of Economic History at the London School of Economics and Political Science and fellow of the Academy of Social Sciences. He is editor of the *European Review of Economic History*. His research interests are long-term growth, regional inequality and historical economic geography.

Nikolaus Wolf is Professor of Economics and Economic History at the Humboldt University of Berlin and research fellow at CEPR and CESifo. He is editor of the *European Review of Economic History*. His research is focused on the economic development of Europe since 1870, especially international relations in trade and financial markets and long-run economic geography.

Routledge Explorations in Economic History
Edited by ***Lars Magnusson****, Uppsala University, Sweden*

75. Regulating Competition
Cartel Registers in the Twentieth-Century World
Edited by Susanna Fellman and Martin Shanahan

76. European Banks and the Rise of International Finance
The Post-Bretton Woods Era
Carlo Edoardo Altamura

77. The Second Bank of the United States
"Central" Banker in an Era of Nation-Building, 1816–1836
Jane Ellen Knodell

78. War, Power and the Economy
Mercantilism and State Formation in 18th-Century Europe
A. González Enciso

79. The Western Allies and Soviet Potential in World War II
Economy, Society and Military Power
Martin Kahn

80. Money, Currency and Crisis
In Search of Trust, 2000 BC to AD 2000
Edited by R.J. van der Spek and Bas van Leeuwen

81. The Development of Modern Industries in Bengal
Re-Industrialisation, 1858–1914
Indrajit Ray

82. The Economic Development of Europe's Regions
A Quantitative History since 1900
Edited by Joan Ramón Rosés and Nikolaus Wolf

For more information about this series, please visit www.routledge.com/series/SE0347

The Economic Development of Europe's Regions

A Quantitative History since 1900

Edited by Joan Ramón Rosés and Nikolaus Wolf

LONDON AND NEW YORK

First published 2019
by Routledge
2 Park Square, Milton Park, Abingdon, Oxon OX14 4RN

and by Routledge
52 Vanderbilt Avenue, New York, NY 10017

First issued in paperback 2020

Routledge is an imprint of the Taylor & Francis Group, an informa business

British Library Cataloguing-in-Publication Data
A catalogue record for this book is available from the British Library

Library of Congress Cataloging-in-Publication Data
A catalog record has been requested for this book

ISBN 13: 978-0-367-66448-0 (pbk)
ISBN 13: 978-0-415-72338-1 (hbk)

Typeset in Times New Roman
by Swales & Willis Ltd, Exeter, Devon, UK

Contents

Figures

Tables

Maps

Contributors

Marc Badia-Miró is Lecturer in Economic History at the University of Barcelona, Spain.

Erik Buyst is Professor of Economic History at KU Leuven, Belgium.

Kerstin Enflo is Associate Professor in Economic History at Lund University, Sweden.

Emanuele Felice is Associate Professor of Applied Economics at D'Annunzio University of Chieti–Pescara, Italy.

Frank Geary is Emeritus Professor of Economic History formerly at Ulster University, UK.

Jordi Guilera is Researcher at the Institute of Social Sciences, University of Lisbon, Portugal.

Martin Henning is Senior Lecturer and Associate Professor of Economic Geography at the University of Gothenburg, Sweden.

Kari Anne Janisse is an economist in the Kirkeministeriet (Ministry of Ecclesiastical Affairs), Denmark.

Peter Sandholt Jensen is Professor of Economics at the University of Southern Denmark, Denmark.

Herman de Jong is Professor of Economic History at the University of Groningen, the Netherlands.

Alexander Klein is Senior Lecturer in Economics at the University of Kent, UK.

Julio Martínez-Galarraga is Associate Professor in the Department of Economic Analysis at the University of Valencia, Spain.

Jørgen Modalsli is Head of Research, Unit for Microeconomics at Statistics Norway, Norway.

Cristina Victoria Radu is a PhD student at the University of Southern Denmark, Denmark.

Joan Ramón Rosés is Professor of Economic History at the London School of Economics and Political Science, UK.

M. Teresa Sanchis is Professor of Economic History at the University of Valencia, Spain.

Lennart Schön was Professor of Economic History at Lund University, Sweden.

Max-Stephan Schulze is Professor of Economic History at the London School of Economics and Political Science, UK.

Paul Richard Sharp is Professor of Economics at the University of Southern Denmark, Denmark.

Tom Stark is a retired Senior Lecturer formerly at Ulster University, UK.

Dirk Stelder was Assistant Professor in the Faculty of Economics and Business at the University of Groningen, the Netherlands.

Daniel A. Tirado is Professor of Economic History at the University of Valencia, Spain.

Ulrich Woitek is Professor of Economics at the University of Zurich, Switzerland.

Nikolaus Wolf is Professor of Economics at the Humboldt University of Berlin, Germany.

Gabriela Wüthrich is a graduate student of Economics at the University of Zurich, Switzerland.

1 Introduction

Joan Ramón Rosés and Nikolaus Wolf

Where is Europe heading? The project of European integration has hardly ever been so strongly contested since its beginnings in the 1950s. Faced with several political, social and economic challenges on a global scale, some argue for a return of Europe's nation states, while others hope instead for a United States of Europe. But neither a European superstate nor a retreat back to the national level are likely be a good fit for the enormous diversity of Europe faced with the vagaries of globalization. This book is an attempt to describe the economic development of Europe from the perspective of regions in the long run, before the First World War until today. It is the first quantitative description that aims at a comparison of European regions over time, in the cross section and to other parts of the world. This was possible only due to the collaboration of many researchers from all parts of Europe, who contributed their specific knowledge towards a new synthesis.

At the heart of it is a new data set on economic performance in terms of GDP per capita in the boundaries of modern NUTS 2 regions for the period 1900–2010 (which are also the focus of the regular 'cohesion reports' of the EU). While we are aware of the dangers of using modern definitions of regions and focusing on GDP, we see this as an exercise in benchmarking. To understand how national and supranational institutions have affected the European economy in the long run, we need to capture its variation at the regional level in a consistent way. Our approach is a first step in this direction, and we hope that many follow. To this end, the data on regional GDP are made available both in an appendix to this book (see pp. 387–430) and online (see www.ehes.org/resources.html).

A regional perspective on Europe shows, as if by definition, great diversity. Within a general trend of quite dramatic improvement in the standard of living over the last generations, there are regions that forged ahead, some that kept their position compared to others and finally some that experienced a large decline in relative terms. We find that similar to the dynamics of personal income and wealth distributions, the regions of Europe experienced convergence, that is a decline in regional income inequality. This continued until the 1970s, when it came to a halt and started to reverse thereafter. The many efforts to counter such developments with structural funds and other regional policies since the mid-1970s had an effect, but were clearly insufficient to stop this reversal. We address some of these questions in our country chapters and in a general survey. Finally, we add a chapter on the regional development in the US to our book. In a long tradition of comparative history, we hope that this helps to see more clearly where Europe is different, and how both national and European institutions shaped the economy in the past and can do so in the future.

2 Regional economic development in Europe, 1900–2010

A description of the patterns

Joan Ramón Rosés and Nikolaus Wolf

1. Introduction

Over the last four generations, the European economy has gone through turbulent changes. In 1900, the UK was still the leading country of the world in more than one respect, with France, Germany and others following and catching up. The First World War marked the end of a long period of both economic growth and integration. Moreover, if seen from a global perspective, the Great War also marked the end of European dominance and the beginning of a decline of the continent in weight and influence. During the interwar years, the European growth record was rather poor since erroneous policies and coordination failures prevented Europe from fully realizing its economic potential (Rosés and Wolf 2010). After the Second World War, Europe's economy started another long period of rapid economic expansion (the 'Golden Era'), which slowed down in the 1970s but nevertheless continued until today. Again, this expansion was accompanied by a process of integration across states, notably with the formation of the European Economic Community and later the Eurozone. More recently, the project of European integration has been fundamentally questioned, partly in consequence of the global financial crisis and the European debt crisis that followed in its wake. Moreover, it seems that forces of economic and political disintegration are gaining momentum not only in Europe, but also in other major developed economies. These different historical tendencies have been described and analysed by a substantial literature elsewhere (see, for example, Crafts and Toniolo 1996; Eichengreen 2007; Berend 2016; James 2017).

However, most authors have treated the European economy as a group of national economies, stressing the role of national governments and international organizations. Such an approach has several advantages. First, it naturally ties in with the political history of Europe, based on the emergence of territorial national states during the early modern period and their international relations. Second, most quantitative evidence has been collected and described at the level of nation states based on the work of national statistical offices, which developed during the nineteenth century. Yet this approach comes at some costs. It neglects the often-considerable variation within states (sometimes larger than between states) and it tends to attribute differences in development to differences in national institutions or policies without being able to test this. As we will show in this chapter, there are several clusters of regions, which are sometimes highly developed, that transcend national boundaries, such as the enlarged Rhine–Meuse–Scheldt delta. Furthermore, differences of income per capita (and labour productivity) within countries are larger, and sometimes more resilient, than differences across countries. In particular, the process of income convergence across European nations was not always accompanied by a similar process of convergence of regions within countries. We can show that the distribution of activity across regions shifted over time, first until 1980 converging to a more equal distribution, and from 1980 diverging back to a less equal distribution.

In this book, we want to reconsider the economic development of Europe since 1900 from the perspective of European regions, as pioneered by Pollard (1981), and to provide a quantitative basis for more work along these lines. We do this using modern regional units (following the European NUTS classification as far as we can), which we trace back over time with comparable indicators of economic development. We provide a set of new estimates of regional employment structures and regional GDP and GDP per capita in 1990 international dollars, stretching over more than 100 years. These data allow us to compare regions over time, among each other and to other parts of the world. After some brief notes on our methodology, we describe the basic patterns in the data in terms of some key dimensions: variation in the density of population and economic activity, the spread of industry and services and the declining role of agriculture, and changes in the levels of GDP and GDP per capita. We next discuss patterns of convergence and divergence over time, and show how the geography of activity has changed with a long-run decrease in spatial coherence from 1900 to 2010 and a U-shaped development in geographic concentration and regional income inequality. The latter seems to be related to the finding of a U-shaped pattern of personal income inequality, as documented by Piketty and Saez (2003), Piketty (2014) and others.

2. Data and methodology

Our data set contains 173 regions covering 16 European nation states at the level of NUTS 2 (as of 2014) and spans 11 benchmark years between 1900 and 2010.[1] We could not at this stage include the long-run development of states in Central and Eastern Europe because the reconstruction of historical data that would stretch back until 1900 is still under way. Eight of our 173 sample regions are aggregated from two or three NUTS 2 regions in order to trace the regions over time in constant borders. Moreover, some of our regions have belonged to different political entities over time, such as Alsace or Lorraine, which provides us with some interesting case studies on the potential role of national institutions for economic development. One of our regions – Flevoland in the Netherlands – consists mostly of land that has been reclaimed from ocean beds only in the 1950s and 1960s, and therefore enters the data only in 1970. Lastly, for two states, Luxembourg and the Republic of Ireland, we have no further regional breakdown.

To reconstruct regional GDPs, we have resorted to two different types of methods and sources. After 1960, our book has mostly employed official data on the regional distribution of income. Specifically, from 1960 to 1990, national statistic offices provided that kind of information (see each chapter for detailed information on this), and since then regional data are being provided by Eurostat, the statistical office of the EU. For the majority of countries before 1960, authors have employed Geary and Stark's methodology (Geary and Stark 2002). Notable exceptions here are Austria and the Netherlands, where a more direct approach was used, as described in these chapters. Geary and Stark's methodology has two main advantages: (1) it requires readily available data (employment by sector and region, wages by sector and region, and historical national accounts); and (2) it has an easy interpretation within the national accounting framework. The basic principle is that a country's GDP is equal to the sum of all regional GDPs. More specifically, the total GDP of any country (Y_i) is the sum of n regional GDPs (Y_j):

$$Y_i = \sum_j^n Y_j$$

Furthermore, regional GDP (Y_j) can be decomposed into the contributions from all sectors in the economy:

$$Y_j = \sum_k^K y_{jk} L_{jk}$$

y_{jk} being the output, or the average added value, per worker in each region j, in sector k, and L_{jk} the number of workers in each region j and sector k. As we have no direct data for y_{jk}, its value is approximated by assuming that regional differences in labour productivity in each industry are reflected in the regional industry wage level relative to the national industry wage level $\frac{w_{jk}}{w_k}$.

In consequence, we can estimate regional GDP as:

$$Y_j = \sum_k^K [y_k \beta_k (\frac{w_{jk}}{w_k})] L_{jk}$$

where, as suggested by Geary and Stark (2002), y_k is value added per worker in sector k at the national level, w_{jk} is the wage paid in region j in sector k, w_k is the country average wage in each sector k, and β_k is a scalar that preserves the relative region differences but scales the absolute values so that the regional total for each sector adds up to the country totals. So, in the absence of regional output figures, Geary and Stark (2002) suggest a framework for an indirect estimation based on variation in employment and wages, which allows for an approximation of GDP by region at country factor cost. Hence, the basic data involved in this estimation procedure are national estimates of GDP, value added per worker by sector, and nominal wages and employment by sector and region.

However, authors could (and did in some cases) replace indirect estimates with direct ones whenever the data were available. It should be noted that this methodology allows us to compute not only regional GDPs, but also regional figures for the different industries. Authors of the chapters on Sweden, Portugal and Germany, and the same Frank Geary and Tom Stark for the UK and Ireland, have tested the validity of this methodology against government-based estimations, and have shown that differences between two alternative approaches are typically small and within the range of errors commonly accepted in official national accounting estimates. In one case – the Netherlands – the method proved less reliable for the period before 1950, but the authors could use existing regional GDP estimates from van Zanden (1987) for the years 1820–1910, and thereafter estimates from the Dutch Central Bureau of Statistics. For Austria, regional GDP could be estimated with a more direct approach based on existing regional production data.

Our employment data derive until 1990 from a variety of national sources, mainly population and employment censuses (see each chapter for details), but for the last two benchmarks (2000 and 2010) have been taken directly from Eurostat databases. Obviously, employment data have been made homogeneous to originate in the same sectors across countries (broadly speaking, we have reduced employment to the three basic sectors – primary, secondary and tertiary).

To make our data homogeneous and comparable across different countries, we constructed for each country and year a regional breakdown of national GDP aggregates. Next, we used national-level GDP estimates from the Maddison Project (Bolt and van Zanden 2014), which provides data on GDP of European nation states expressed at purchasing power parity in 1990 international dollars. This database incorporated recent updates to national GDP estimates, such as Germany (Burhop and Wolff 2005), Sweden (Schön and Krantz 2012) and Italy (Baffigi 2013). In the case of Germany, we used the corrected data from Broadberry and Klein (2012) for estimates of the national GDP of the GDR and FRG for the years 1950–1980. Most national GDP figures for 1990–2010 in the Maddison Project data are in turn taken from the Total Economy Database of the Conference Board. It should be noted that country-level estimates of GDP at international prices from the Maddison Project differ slightly from alternative estimates such as those from Eurostat. In consequence, our GDP and GDP per capita calculations at the regional level for the years after 1990 are slightly different from those furnished by Eurostat, even though we have employed regional Eurostat data as the base of our regional distribution of GDP within countries. Our main results are robust to the latest Maddison Project Database (2018) with multiple benchmarks.[2]

Our methodology also implies that – similar to estimates provided by Eurostat and the OECD – we have no regional price deflators, but instead we use national deflators. Hence, we assume that all regions have the same prices within countries. This introduces some bias in our results. The first bias is that our calculations (like all official calculations) overestimate regional differences in living standards since, *ceteris paribus*, the richer regions tend to have higher prices than the poorer ones, given that the non-tradable goods (e.g. housing) tend to be more expensive. The second bias is that regional price differentials have probably changed over time: with the integration of goods markets, prices of tradable goods have become more homogenous within countries while differences in housing prices may have increased over time. But our methodology has an important advantage: a substantial part of the price differential across regions of non-tradable goods is due to the monopoly power of real estate owners (Moretti 2013), who can extract rents from producers (workers). Therefore, our price-unadjusted regional per capita GDP is an imperfect measure of 'welfare' differential across regions in the same country, but it more likely reflects the 'true' differences in labour productivity across regions.

A final problem with our estimates of regional shares in national GDP is the fact that these are based on census years that vary across nation states. In the chapters on individual states, we discuss the original data based on these years. Instead, in our survey, we make the data comparable across countries by interpolating regional shares to several common benchmark years (namely 1900, 1910, 1925, 1938, 1950 and decades thereafter). Next, we use these shares together with national-level GDP data from the Maddison Project for these respective benchmark years to construct regional data. We have always avoided interpolation across war periods. Regional shares in national aggregates tend to change very slowly, and we find it unlikely that regions within a state follow different business cycle dynamics.

3. Basic facts on regional economic development: density of population, employment and GDP

Let us start with a look at population density (see Maps 2.1a and 2.1b). As expected, the density of population measured as persons per km^2 shows considerable variation across regions and over time. The average density increased from 150 (1900) to 282 (2010), the median from 84 (1900) to 149 (2010), indicating that a few very densely populated regions have a large effect. These outliers with extreme population density are basically the same now as they were back then, namely London and surroundings (UK1), Berlin (DE30) and Hamburg (DE60), followed at some distance by Bremen (DE50), Düsseldorf (DEA1), Brussels and Brabant (BE10, with BE24 and BE31), the Île-de-France with Paris (FR10), as well as North and South Holland (NL32 and NL33). A few regions with very high density in 1900, however, experienced a dramatic decline over time, including Hainaut in Belgium (BE32), as well as Chemnitz (DED4) and Leipzig (DED12) in Germany, and we will come back to their destiny further below. There was more stability at the bottom of the distribution, with the least densely populated regions both then and now being located in the northern parts of Sweden, Norway and Finland, followed by Alentejo (PT18) in Portugal and regions in central Spain, namely Castile-León (ES41), Castile-La Mancha (ES42) and Extremadura (ES43).

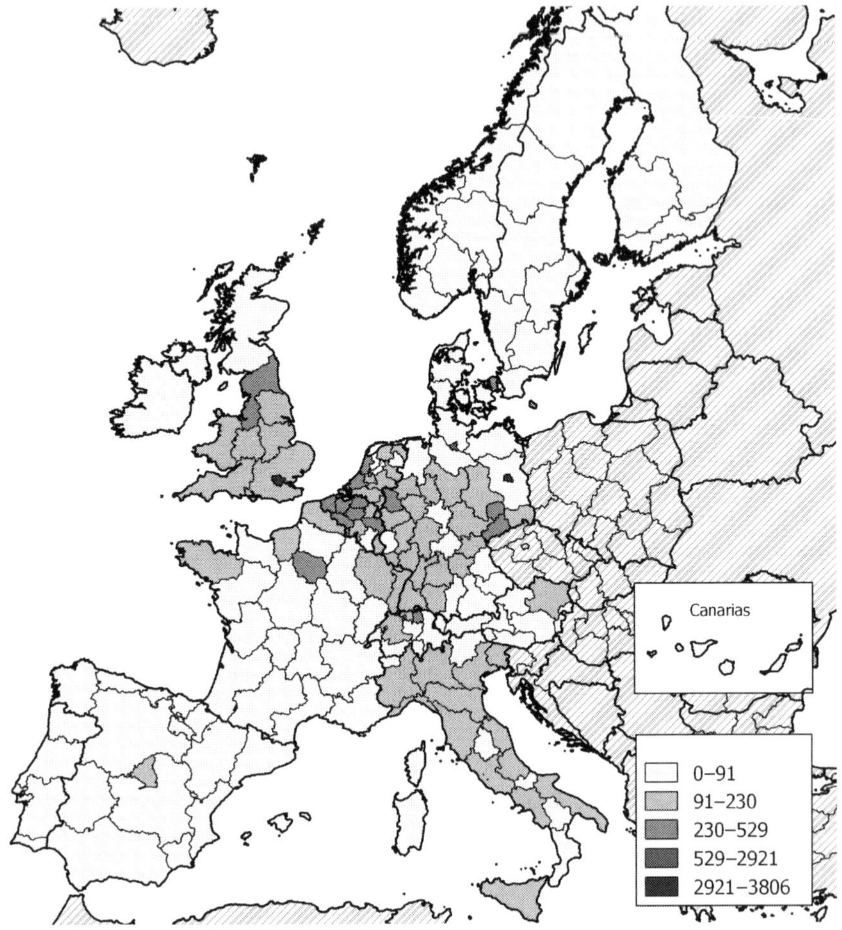

Map 2.1a Population density, 1900

Source: See text.

A simple intuition from these maps is that very low population densities are related to climatic extremes. More generally, natural geography, notably mean temperature, extreme values of average temperature and average precipitation, but also the suitability of soil for agriculture and distance to major sea ports, are indeed very strongly correlated with variation in population density. Moreover, the correlation between the density of population and these geographical variables in 2010 is only very slightly weaker than it was in 1900. Apparently, the impact of natural geography on the location of population across Europe from 1900 to 2010 is strong and persistent. We consider this in more detail in section 6.2.

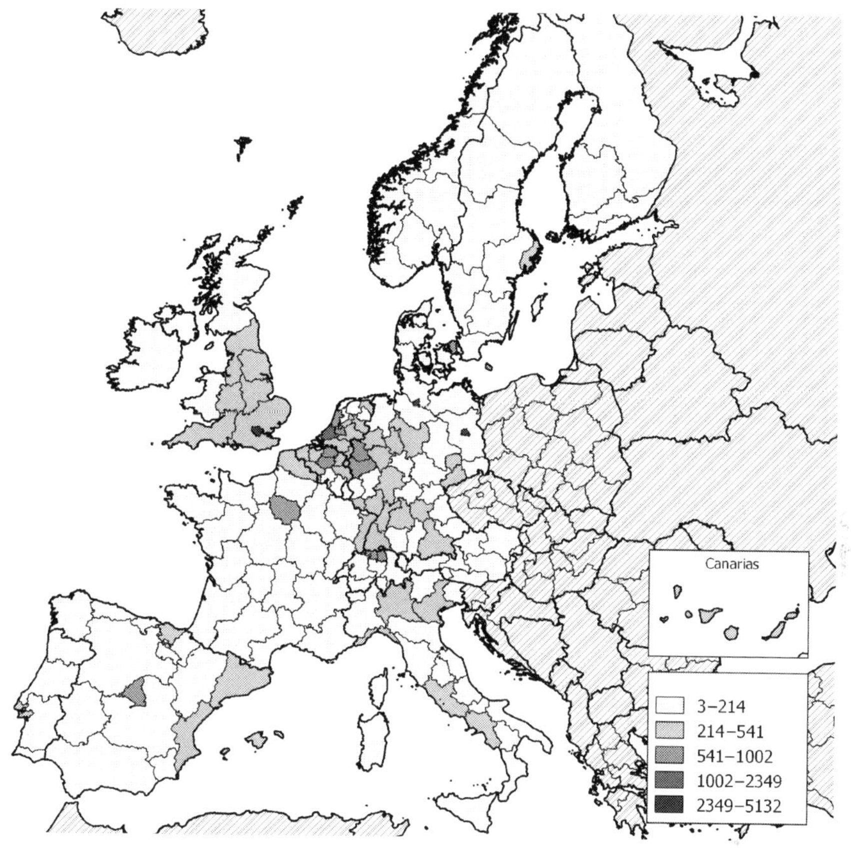

Map 2.1b Population density, 2010

Source: See text.

In a next step, we look at the density of economic activity as measured by total employment per km^2 (see Maps 2.2a and 2.2b). The average employment density roughly doubled from 67 persons per km^2 (1900) to 132 (2010). Not surprisingly, employment density is closely correlated with the density of population. However, population and employment density among regions could differ for several reasons. First, the distribution of dependency rates might be uneven due to different demographic trends (where regions with relatively more children and older people tend to have lower employment). Next, female participation rates could differ, and regions with lower female participation rates also tend to have a lower overall share of their working-age population employed. And third, unemployment rates might vary. These three factors are not independent of each other: thriving regions tend to have lower unemployment rates, but also lower dependency rates, because they attract working-age migrants. Also, they tend to have higher female participation rates, given the abundance of labour opportunities. The contrary holds for poorer regions. Furthermore, the relative importance of these three factors changed over time. Maps 2.2a and 2.2b show how employment density developed between 1900 and 2010.

Finally, the density of GDP, that is GDP per km^2, is again closely related to the pattern of population and employment, but the relationship is changing (see Maps 2.3a and 2.3b). In this case, differences between employment density and GDP density reflect differences in productivity across regions: more productive regions generate more GDP per km^2 with the same employment per km^2 than less productive regions.

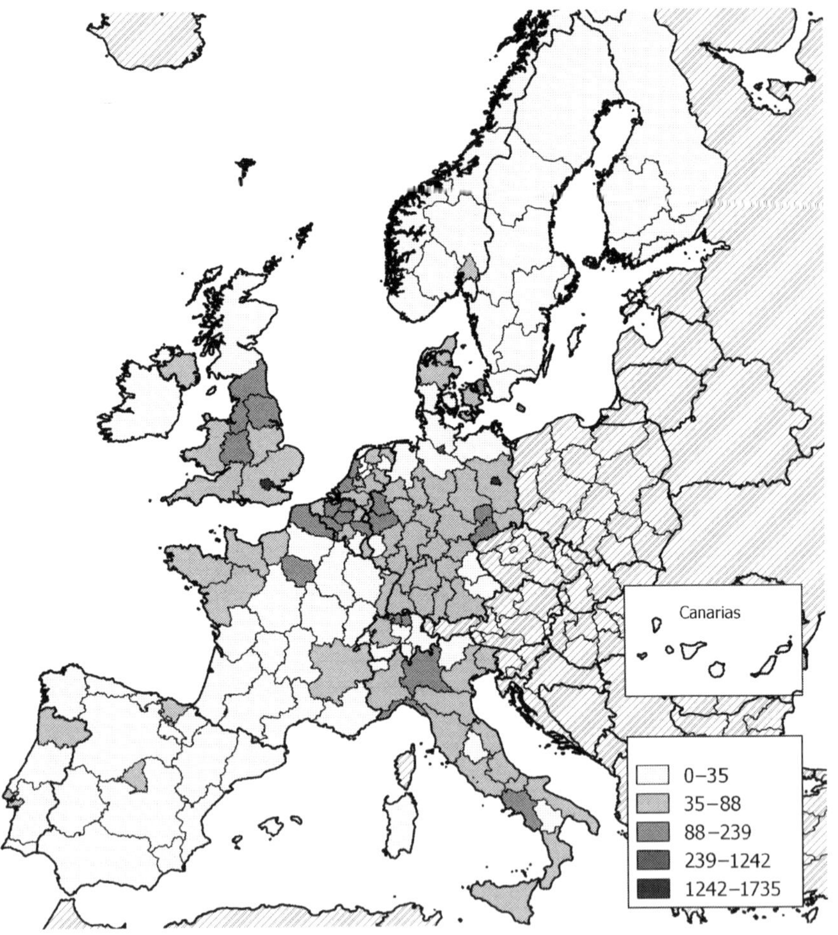

Map 2.2a Employment density, 1900

Source: See text.

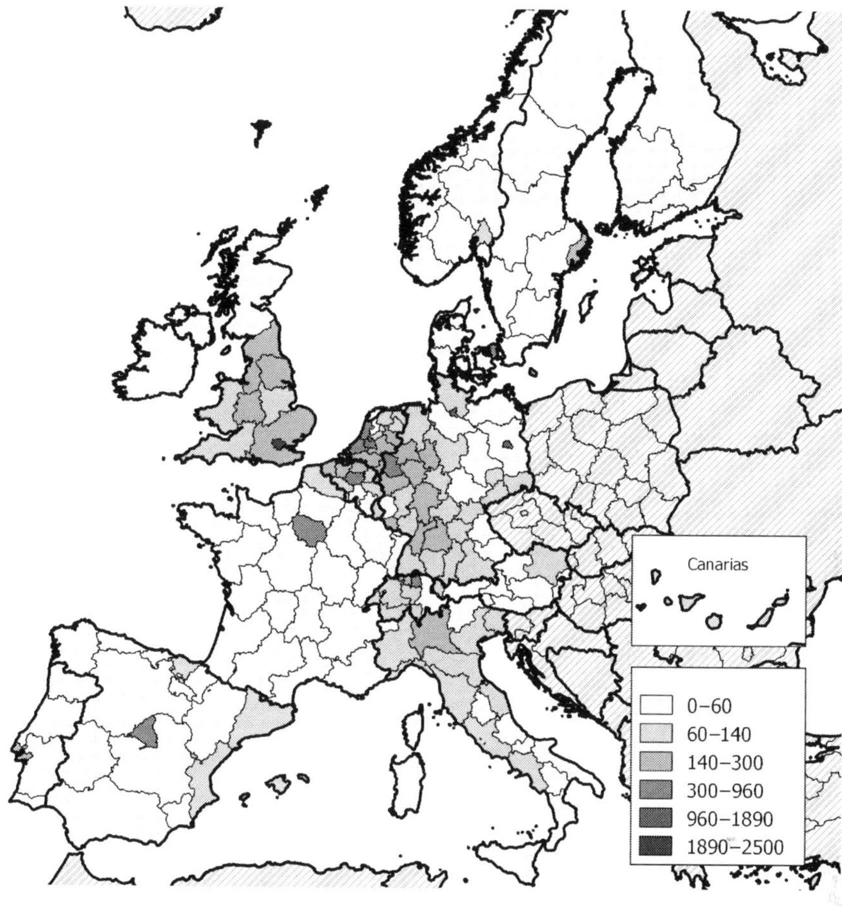

Map 2.2b Employment density, 2010

Source: See text.

Figure 2.1 (p. 14) plots the cross-sectional correlation between population density and GDP density over time. While the correlation between the density of population and GDP is generally high, it clearly declines over time, as reflected in the linear trend (dotted line). Put differently, variation in GDP per area is increasingly due to variation in GDP per capita, and less to variation in population density. Another effect visible in Figure 2.1 is the economic turmoil after the Second World War. In 1950, several densely populated regions have quite low GDP per capita, partly due to destruction such as bombing and partly due to migration of working population. Already by 1960, this effect has largely disappeared, which confirms the resilience of economic activity in certain regions. The drop in correlation in 1990 is due to the collapse of the GDR economy in the wake of German unification, which was followed by a strong recovery thereafter.

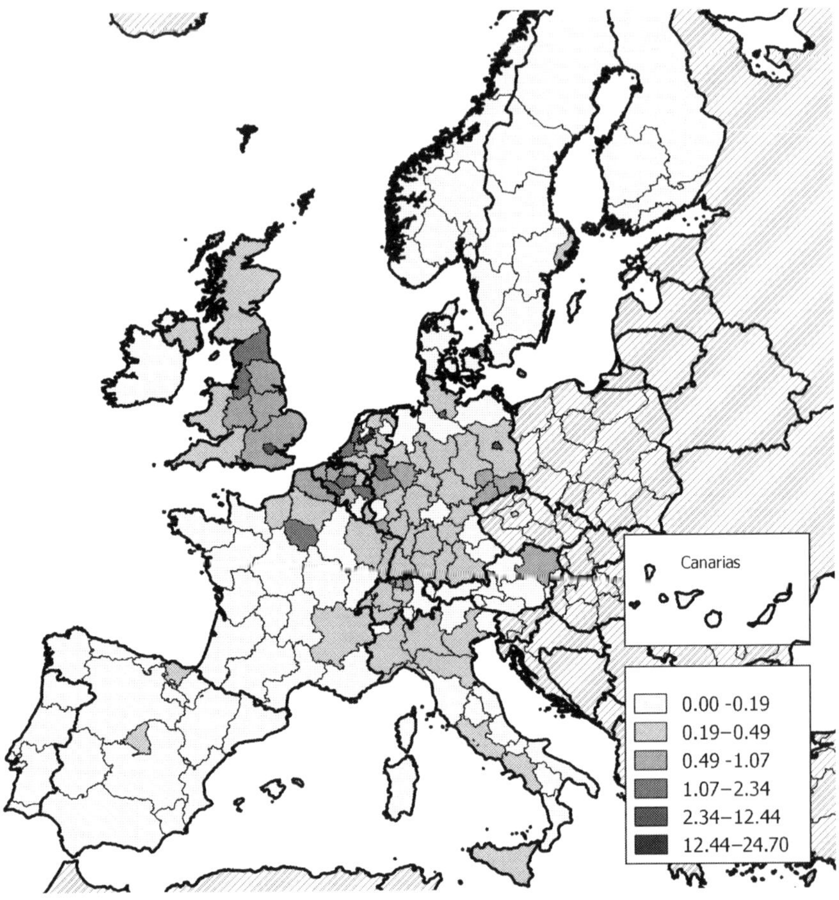

Map 2.3a GDP density, 1900

Source: See text.

4. Changing employment structure: structural change and localization

Before we explore the dynamics of GDP per capita, let us consider changes in employment structures across European regions over the last century. A characteristic of Europe's economic development during the twentieth century – and of economic development more generally – was the continuation of structural change, with labour leaving agriculture to find employment in industry, mining and services (Broadberry 1997; Broadberry et al. 2010). Figure 2.2 shows the evolution of average employment shares across European regions from 1900 to 2010 for three broad sectors: agriculture, industry (including mining) and services. It is evident that the decline of agriculture was due not only to the expansion

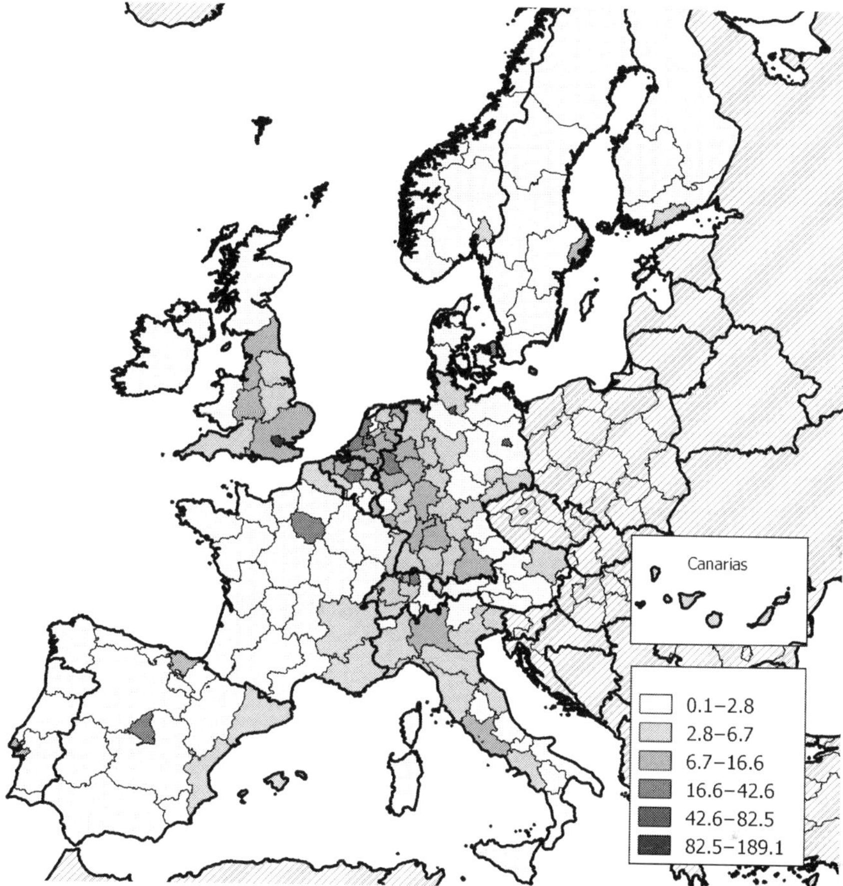

Map 2.3b GDP density, 2010

Source: See text.

of industry, but already early on to an equal expansion of services. After 1960, industrial employment had reached its peak and started a rapid decline, both in absolute terms and as a share of total employment. So, by 2010, the share of industrial employment was about one-fifth less than in 1900.

However, this structural change occurred at very different speeds across European regions. A way to capture the variation in sector-specific employment across regions is to use the location quotient, defined as:

$$lq_i^k = \frac{x_i^k / \sum_k x_i^k}{\sum_i x_i^k / \sum_i \sum_k x_i^k} = \frac{x_i^k / \sum_i x_i^k}{\sum_k x_i^k / \sum_i \sum_k x_i^k}$$

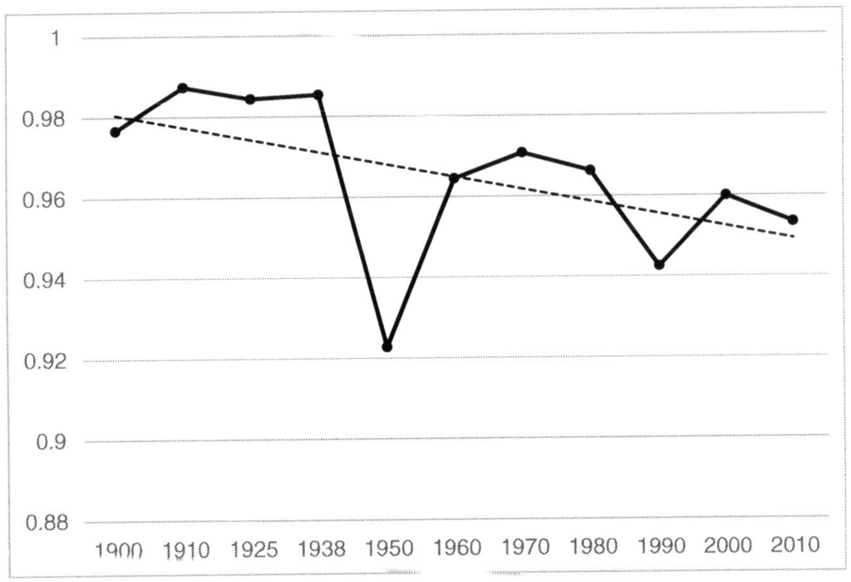

Figure 2.1 Correlation between population density and GDP density, 1900–2010

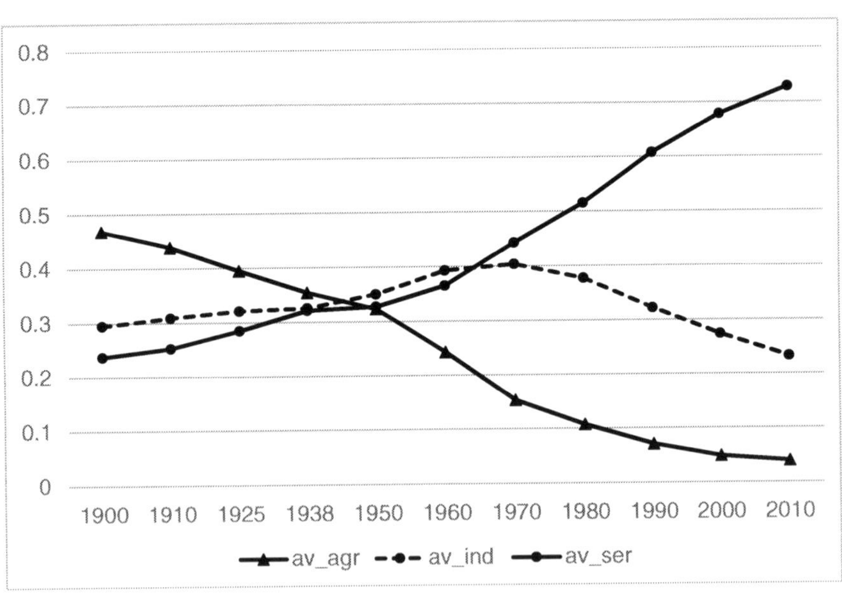

Figure 2.2 Sectoral employment shares across 173 European regions, 1900–2010

where x_i^k is employment in region i in sector k. This can be read as either the specialization of region i in sector k, normalized by the overall share of sector k in total employment, or as the concentration of employment in sector k, normalized by the overall share of region i in total employment. To summarize this evidence on 'localization' for 173 regions, 11 years and three sectors, Figure 2.3 shows the coefficient of variation of lq over the period 1900–2010.

Around 1900, the overall dispersion in agriculture, industry and services was still very similar: most regions have some employment in each sector, typically with the largest share in agriculture. Already, the interwar period is different. We see simultaneously the spread of industry and services and a concentration of agricultural employment. This development is intensified after 1945, with increasing differences in the localization of agriculture across regions and increasing similarities in the localization of both industry and services. From about 1980 onwards, we can observe a stabilization of a new pattern of sectoral localization. A few regions are strongly specialized in agriculture, notably in Southern Europe, such as Galicia (ES11), Alentejo (PT18), Extremadura (ES42) and Basilicata (ITF5). These regions are characterized by their overall remoteness from economic centres, their persistent backwardness in terms of GDP per capita and by the fact that they never developed a significant industrial or service sector. In contrast, many other regions by then have virtually no employment in agriculture.

The localization of industry is much less diverse. Some regions around 1980 are still strongly dominated by industrial employment, often associated with the automobile industry, such as Franche Comté (FR43), Thüringen (DEG0) and

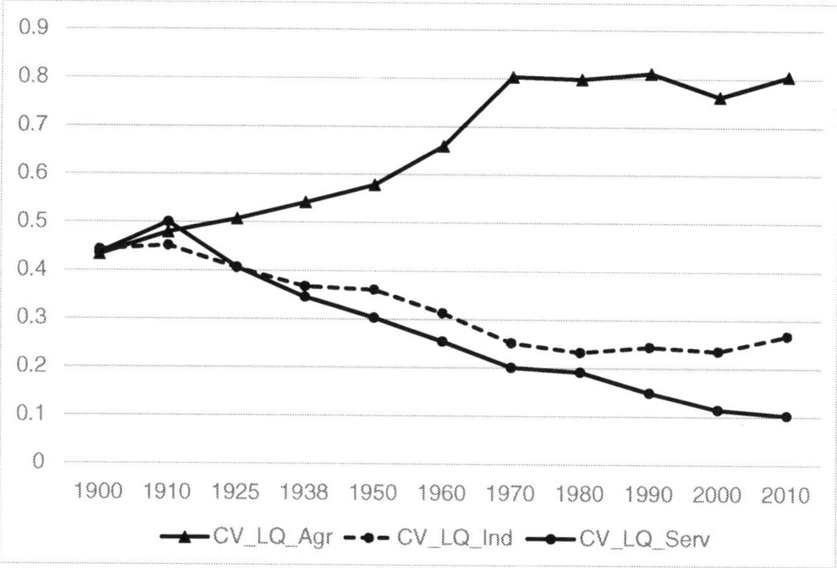

Figure 2.3 The coefficient of variation in localization of agriculture, industry and services, 1900–2010

Stuttgart (DE11). Industry localization is markedly clustered in Germany, eastern France and northern Italy. A notable feature here is that some of those regions that kept a strong localization in industry after the 1970s, and which all used to be economically advanced, were falling back in terms of GDP per capita over the next decades. The correlation between income and industrial localization that had been strongly positive for generations started to disappear in the 1970s and turned weakly negative thereafter. A rather extreme example is the region of Hainaut (BE32) in Belgium, which showed some of the highest industrial employment shares and industrial localization in Europe before the First World War and until the 1950s, accompanied by high levels of GDP per capita. The region experienced a dramatic economic decline afterwards, with the lowest average annual growth rate over the century in our sample (see Table 2.1).

The localization of services in turn was for a long time dominated by capital regions. Not only employment in public services, such as the government was concentrated in the capital, but also many private service providers such as banks had their headquarters and the bulk of their employees there. The institutional framework of the various nation states had a strong effect here, especially until 1950. As expected, capitals of more centralized nation states, such as Paris in France, concentrated a much higher share of service employment relative to their overall employment shares than capitals in less centralized states, such as Bern in Switzerland. However, with the general increase in service employment, due to both outsourcing and growth of the public sector, we observe a spread of service employment over all regions and a strong convergence in overall services localization. To be sure, within the large and growing service sector, there is a strong concentration of more specific types of services such as financial services in large urban agglomerations (Deza and González López 2014; Gallego and Maroto 2015; see also Chapter 3.8 in this book).

5. Growth and variation in GDP per capita

The focus of our interest is on the development of GDP per capita over time and its variation across regions, which summarizes the average level of material living standards. This indicator, and especially its regional dimension, is crucial for a better understanding of the European economy. It shows where income is generated and what scope there is for interregional transfers. It also shows to what extent regional economies have become more or less similar in terms of economic potential over the last century, after wars, disintegration and the stepwise process of European integration. And not least, the variation in income across regions over time complements our knowledge about personal income and wealth inequality. The systematic pattern of regional convergence and divergence that we document here for the first time has far-reaching implications for economic policy.

Over the last generations, all regions experienced a remarkable economic development in terms of GDP per capita. Figure 2.4 shows the change in median GDP per capita, average GDP per capita, as well as the smallest and largest values across regions over the last century.

First of all, we see that the average level of GDP per capita has increased by more than 750 per cent over the last century, in purchasing power parity, expressed in 1990 international dollars. This historically unprecedented increase in material living standards occurred mainly after the Second World War. Next, there was always substantial variation between regions, but until recently the average GDP per capita was rather close to the median. As we see in Figure 2.4, the absolute distance between the poorest and the richest regions has sharply increased over time, but the differences have declined in relative terms. In any case, it is surprising to see that in spite of wars and economic crises, the expansion in levels occurred at a very steady pace. The sudden collapse of industrial activity in regions of the former GDR is visible in the data, as the poorest region in our sample in 1990 is indeed Dresden (DED2). Afterwards, East Germany experienced a strong recovery and convergence to West Germany, yet it is still far behind its pre-war position relative to other parts of Europe or within Germany. On a European scale, in contrast, our data show how the long-run trend of regional convergence came to an end in the 1980s. The small but growing difference between average and median is indicative of growing divergence.

A simple way to show the distribution dynamics in our data is to represent them in the form of a histogram, where we divide for each year the regional GDP per capita data into evenly distributed bins as a simple approximation of the underlying probability density function. Figure 2.5a shows the distribution for the years 1900, 1950 and 1980, and Figure 2.5b for 1980 and 2010.

We see in Figure 2.5a how between 1900 and 1950, and again between 1950 and 1980, the distribution shifted quite systematically to the right, with

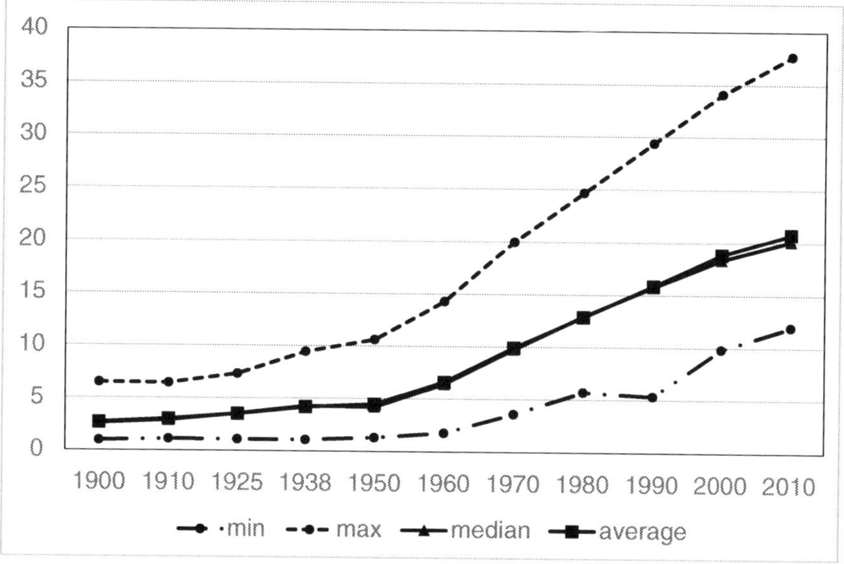

Figure 2.4 GDP per capita across regions, 1900–2010 (GK$1,000)

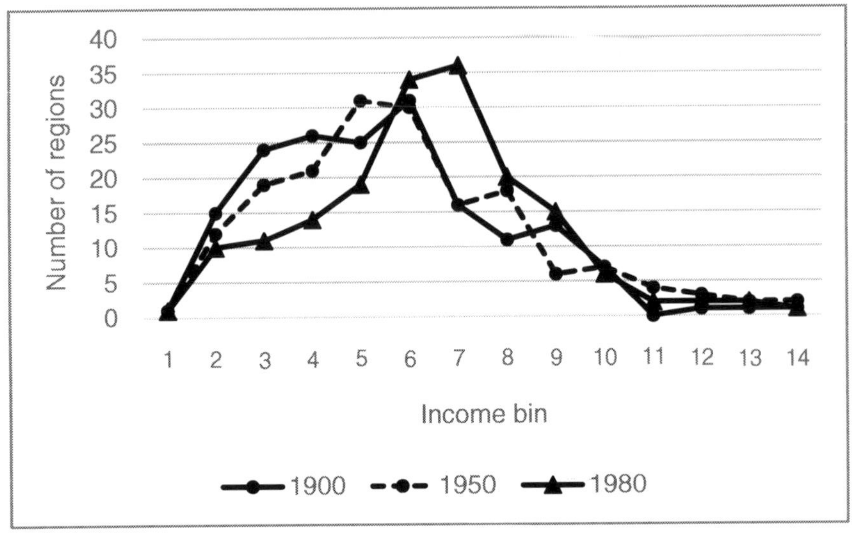

Figure 2.5a Regional income distribution, 1900, 1950 and 1980

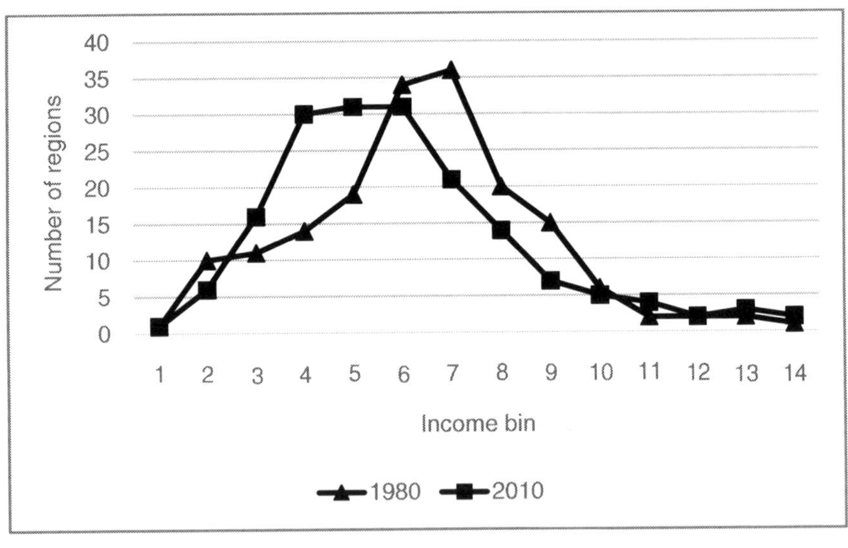

Figure 2.5b Regional income distribution, 1980 and 2010

a growing number of regions positioned around the median. Especially strong is the shift between 1950 and 1980, which will be mirrored in evidence about beta-convergence strong enough to reduce overall dispersion in GDP per capita across regions (compare with Figure 2.8 and Tables 2.3 and 2.5). But this changed around 1980, when convergence weakened and dispersion across regions started to increase again. Figure 2.5b shows that between 1980 and 2010, the distribution shifted back to the left. There was an overall decline in growth rates after the 1970s, but this was clearly very uneven, where some rich regions maintained steady growth rates while others started to fall behind. This emergence of a small club of growth centres has recently been highlighted by Iammarino et al. (2017), who link it to the rise of new economy industries and a new global division of labour.

Table 2.1 adds more detail to this. We see, for example, that some poor regions experienced above-average growth rates, while some formerly rich regions, such as Hainaut (BE32) in Belgium or Berlin (DE30) in Germany, were falling behind. The former is due to structural change and the decline of traditional industrial regions, and the latter is a result of dramatic institutional change in the wake of the Second World War, namely the division of Germany during the period 1949–1990 (see Chapter 3.6 in this book).

Table 2.1 GDP per capita across regions, 1900–2010: cross-sectional variation and growth

Levels in 1990 GK$1,000		1900	1950	2010
	Average GDP per capita (in parentheses: population-weighted average)	2.63 (2.92)	4.44 (4.62)	20.76 (21.39)
	Poorest region	0.96 Galicia (ES11)	1.31 Extremadura (ES43)	11.95 Calabria (ITF6)
	Richest region	6.49 London Counties (UKI)	10.62 Zurich (CH04)	37.68 Luxembourg (LU00)
Growth rates in %		1900–2010	1900–1950	1950–2010
	Average annual growth rates	1.91%	1.02%	2.66%
	Highest growth rates	2.62% Galicia (ES11)	2.55% Västsverige (SE23)	3.99% Extremadura (ES43)
	Lowest growth rates	1.10% Hainaut (BE32)	–0.01% Berlin (DE30)	1.49% Espace Mittelland (CH02)

Source: Own.

Maps 2.4a and 2.4b show more systematically the variation in GDP per capita across regions. The first impression from these two maps is that the pattern of variation was more compact back in 1900 than in 2010. Broadly speaking, it is easy to detect a centre-periphery pattern: some macro-regions such as England and North-Western Europe were richer than the average, the regions of France and Central Europe were close to the average, while several regions in Scandinavia and Southern Europe were poorer than average. In 2010, the picture is more complex. There are islands of prosperity, such as Paris (FR10) in France or Madrid (ES30) in Spain, surrounded by regions with below-average GDP per capita. We will see below that indeed, the degree of spatial correlation has systematically declined over the last century, while the geographical concentration of economic activity has first declined and then again increased since the 1970s. In other

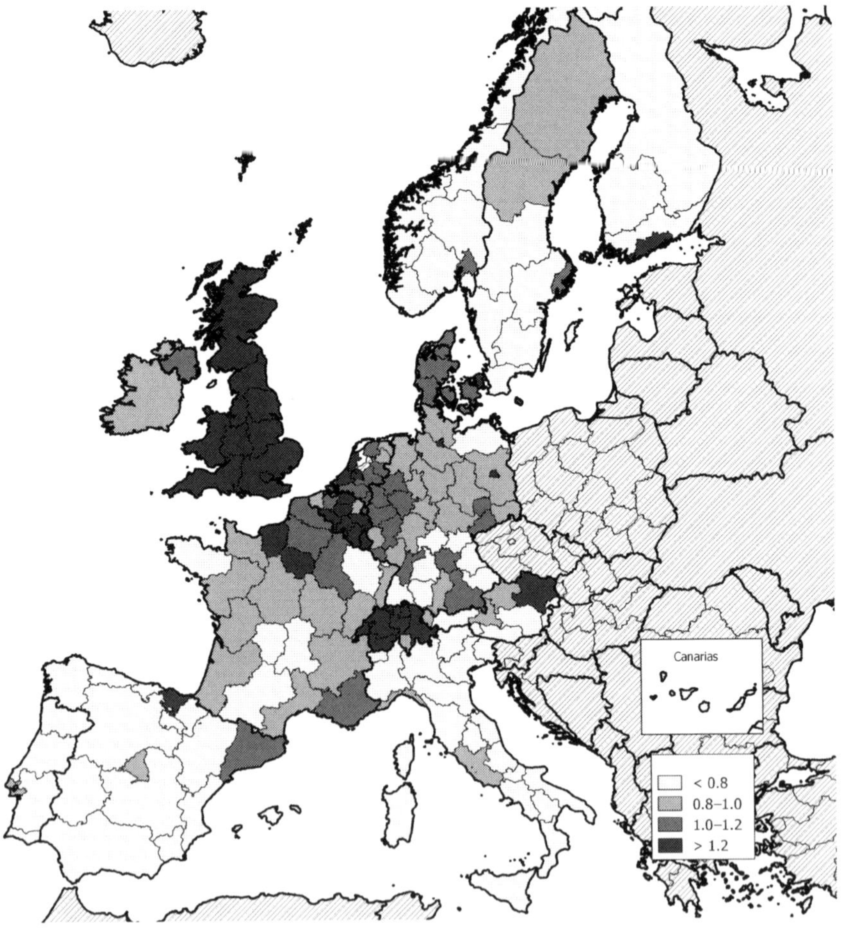

Map 2.4a Relative GDP per capita, 1900 (EU average = 1)

Source: See text.

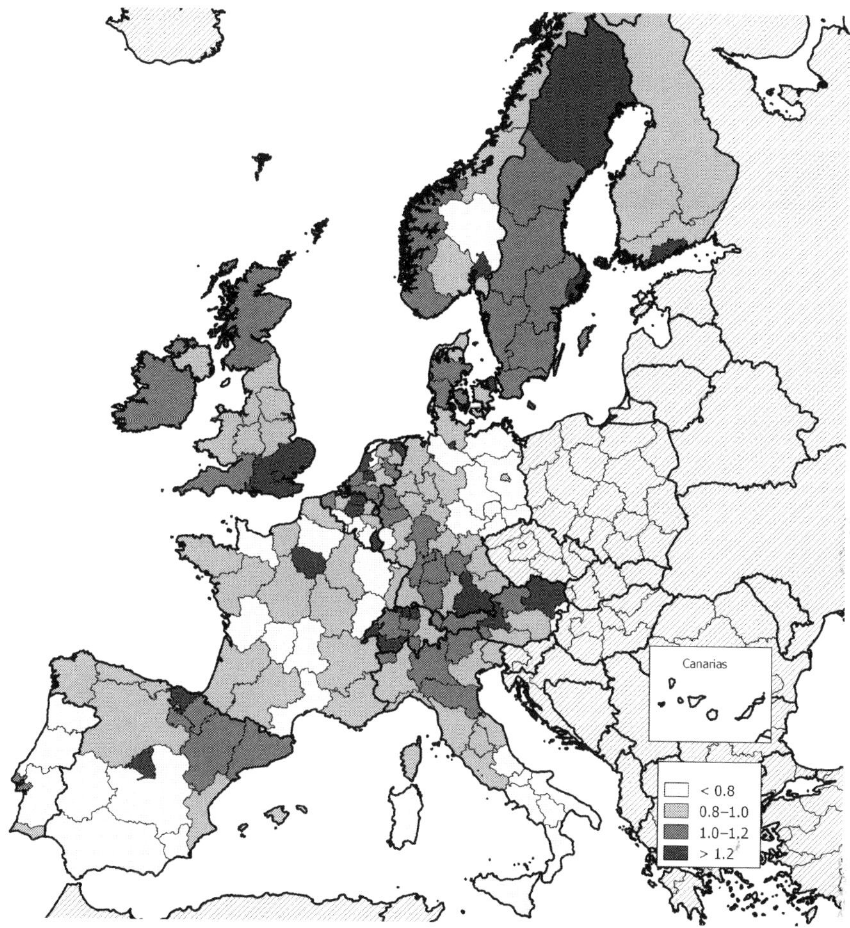

Map 2.4b Relative GDP per capita, 2010 (EU average = 1)

Source: See text.

words, the centre-periphery pattern prevalent in 1900 is vanishing rapidly and is being replaced by a system based on several central regions, which commonly comprise the largest metropolitan areas (see a further discussion of this phenomenon in section 8).

6. Explaining economic growth: adjustment and fundamentals

6.1 Exploring growth dynamics: convergence, structural change and reconstruction

How can we explain the enormous variation in economic activity between regions and their changes over time that is evident from section 5 above? The literature on economic growth distinguishes between factors that shape the short- to medium-run adjustment to a steady state level of growth and factors that shape economic growth in the medium to long run. We will use this as a guidance to describe the growth pattern in our data, but we leave an in-depth analysis of economic growth across European regions for future work.

Let us start with a short-run perspective on growth dynamics. From the perspective of a simple Solow growth model (Solow 1956; Barro and Sala-i-Martin 1992), we expect to find that poor regions tend to exhibit, on average, faster growth rates in GDP per capita. Barro and Sala-i-Martin found for the US a rate of convergence of around 2 per cent per year. The intuition behind this is that we expect a lower capital per labour ratio in poor regions, and hence a higher return to investment in these regions, *ceteris paribus*. This is indeed suggested by Table 2.1. The regions that were initially poorest, Galicia (ES11) and Extremadura (ES43), showed above-average growth rates. The general approach is to regress the average annual growth rate in GDP per capita of a region over some period on the level of GDP per capita at the beginning of the period, or $\hat{y}_{i,t1-t0} = \alpha + \beta \ln(y_{i,t0}) + \varepsilon_i$. In Figures 2.6a–2.6c, we plot the average annual growth rates of regions against their initial level of GDP per capita (in logs). Figure 2.6a shows the result if we consider the entire sample period 1900–2010, while Figures 2.6b and 2.6c distinguish between the period before and after the Second World War.

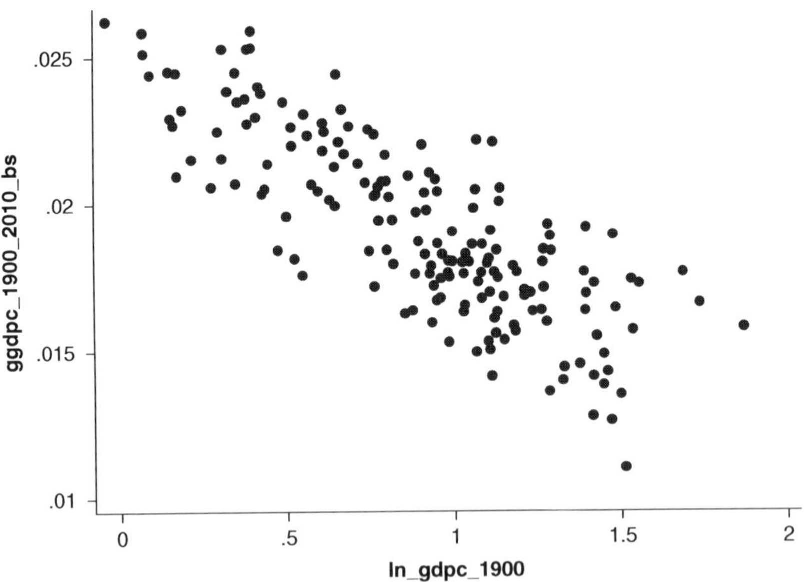

Figure 2.6a Beta-convergence over time (172 regions), 1900–2010

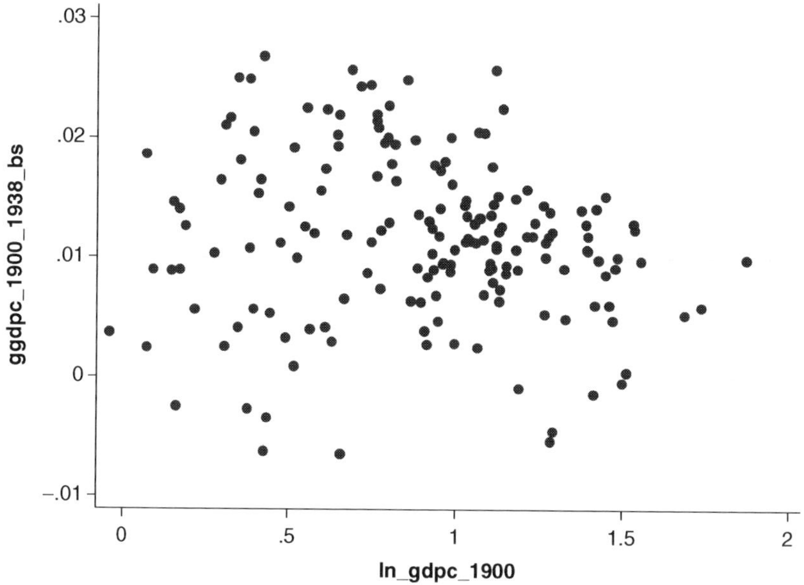

Figure 2.6b Beta-convergence over time (172 regions), 1900–1938

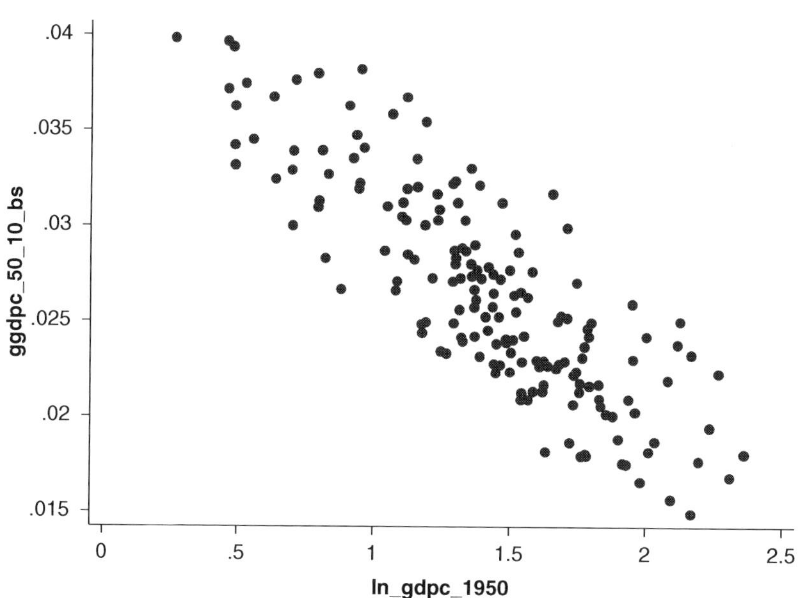

Figure 2.6c Beta-convergence over time (172 regions), 1950–2010

Figure 2.6a suggests that in the long run, regions converged, in the sense that growth rates in GDP per capita were systematically higher the lower the initial level of GDP per capita. However, Figures 2.6b and 2.6c indicate that this view is incomplete. Clearly, convergence was very weak before 1945 (with a beta-coefficient of −0.002, just about significant at 10 per cent) but turned quite strong after the Second World War (beta coefficient of −0.01, significant at 1 per cent). This absence of convergence before the war is remarkable, and it is worthwhile looking into the details of this. In Table 2.2, we show how the beta-coefficients changed over shorter periods of time, notably before and after the two world wars. The final column shows the implied speed of convergence.

While the pattern of convergence changed substantially over time, we find that similar forces were at work in the decade before the First World War and the last decade of our series (2000–2010), with low but highly significant rates of convergence (close to 1 per cent, half of the rate found elsewhere). In contrast, the interwar years were characterized by a divergence of regional incomes. Some regions grew strongly and many others stagnated, but there is no detectable relationship to initial levels of growth, as suggested by a bare-bones Solow model. Elsewhere, we have argued that this very likely reflects the political tensions between European states after 1918 that limited market forces such as trade, migration and capital flows, as well as technology diffusion (Rosés and Wolf 2010). After 1945, there is ample evidence for strong convergence. This was particularly fast during the 1960s and 1970s (well above 2 per cent), before it slowed down during the 1980s, coming back to the fastest rates during the 1990s.

Given that we consider regions and nation states in their modern borders, our data also include the regions of the former socialist GDR as part of modern Germany. One might suspect that this should affect the estimated beta-coefficients because the post-war convergence may have been absent in these regions, while the same regions experienced first a collapse followed by an unusual period of catch-up growth after the fall of the Iron Curtain in 1989 and German unification in 1990. What is more, all GDP estimates for socialist states are questionable, and even more so any regional breakdown of such estimates. An exclusion of the

Table 2.2 Explaining regional growth rates: convergence over time

	$\hat{\beta}_0$ *(t-stat)*	*Speed of convergence (%)*
1900–1910	−0.009 (3.89)	0.94
1925–1938	0.002 (0.44)	−0.20
1950–1960	−0.015 (5.38)	1.63
1960–1970	−0.026 (13.37)	3.01
1970–1980	−0.024 (9.36)	2.74
1980–1990	−0.009 (1.88)	0.94
1990–2000	−0.026 (9.81)	3.01
2000–2010	−0.009 (2.93)	0.94

Source: Own.

GDR regions only affects the results for the decades 1980–2000 somewhat, but does not change the overall pattern. We find that regions converged on average at a rate of between below 1 per cent (1900s and 2000s) and around 2.5 per cent per year during the 1960s and 1970s (not shown here).

Barro and Sala-i-Martin (1995) suggested extending the simple Solow framework to take aggregate shocks into account. Along these lines, Temin (2002) argued to consider the period between 1950 and 1980, often termed the 'golden age of growth' (Crafts and Toniolo 1996), as a period of disequilibrium. The evidence from Table 2.2 suggests that much of this growth was due to a process convergence, where poorer parts of Europe were catching up to the rich. However, some regions had suffered strong destruction during the war, alongside massive population movements, while economic reintegration after 1945 allowed for increased technology diffusion and structural change. From this perspective, some regions in Germany, but also in Austria, Italy, Belgium, the Netherlands and eastern France, should have seen economic growth driven by reconstruction and to some extent structural change, rather than convergence, as suggested in a Solow framework. We apply this idea to our data and construct a variable 'gap', defined as the log difference in GDP per capita in 1938 and 1950 for a region. For example, a region that was strongly negatively affected by the war due to bombing, immigration of refugees or a combination thereof, such as Hamburg (DE6), would show a positive gap. We would expect that such a region would grow faster after the war due to efforts to reconstruct housing and infrastructure. Related, we add a control for the share of agriculture in total employment of a region in 1950 to test for the idea of 'arrested development' (Temin 2002) – the economic reintegration and trade after 1945 might have facilitated structural change and freed up labour in agriculture to move to more productive employment in industry or services. Hence, we re-estimate the relationship between the average annual growth rate of GDP per capita, the initial level of GDP per capita (in logs), controlling for the 'gap' between 1938 and 1950, and the share of agriculture in total employment of a region in 1950, or: $\hat{y}_{i,t1-t0} = \alpha + \beta_0 \ln(y_{i,t0}) + \beta_1 gap_{i,1938\_50} + \beta_2 ag\_sh_{i,1950} + \varepsilon_i$.

We vary the period under consideration, starting with average annual growth rates in 1950–1960, and extending the period until 1950–1990. Table 2.3 shows the results (where we exclude the regions of the former GDR to avoid the distortions caused by economic planning).

Overall, these results are in line with those of Vonyó (2008), who used panel data techniques on a sample of 21 nation states, including Japan, Australia, Canada, New Zealand and the US. Convergence mattered, but it was strongly affected by post-war reconstruction. All results are robust to a modification, where we restrict 'gap' to those cases where GDP per capita in 1938 was actually above the level in 1950 (not shown here). Instead, the contribution of structural change to growth after 1945 is less clear. A closer inspection of the regional data suggests that for regions outside of West Germany, there was some positive contribution of structural change to growth beyond reconstruction and convergence (not shown here). We note however, that all these results are little more than correlations, because

Table 2.3 Explaining regional growth rates: convergence, reconstruction and structural change, 1950–1990

	$\widehat{\beta}_0$ (t-stat) *initial GDP per capita*$_{1950}$	$\widehat{\beta}_1$ (t-stat) *'gap'*$_{1938\_50}$	$\widehat{\beta}_2$ (t-stat) *ag_sh*$_{\_1950}$	*Adj.* R^2	*Observations*
1950–1960	−0.007 (−1.77)	0.045 (7.92)	0.009 (1.01)	0.37	164
1950–1970	−0.017 (−7.25)	0.016 (5.00)	0.002 (0.47)	0.57	164
1950–1980	−0.016 (−9.77)	0.014 (6.08)	0.003 (0.87)	0.72	164
1950–1990	−0.014 (−11.89)	0.009 (5.75)	0.002 (0.71)	0.77	164

Source: Own.

the initial level of income in 1950, the share of agriculture in 1950, as well as the 'gap', are all related to each other and would require a more detailed analysis, which is beyond the scope of this chapter.

6.2 A long-run perspective: institutions and geography

Let us now adopt a long-run perspective with regard to our time span of 110 years of regional development. Which regional characteristics can account for the large variation in growth rates since 1900? Following the literature, we can distinguish broadly between institutional factors and geographical factors, which shape the incentives to invest in and adopt new technologies, and hence economic growth (Acemoglu 2009: 3–25). With regard to the development of European regions, a distinction between national and supranational institutions suggests itself to see how, for example, the process of European integration after 1945 affected growth rates. Specifically, we control for a set of national dummies, varying over time in order to capture very broadly institutional differences between nation states as well as European dummies, whenever a state entered the EEC, the EU or the Eurozone. To capture at least some of the institutional variation within nation states, we add a dummy for capital regions.

When it comes to geographical factors, it is common to distinguish between first and second nature characteristics. The former are factors that can be considered to be exogenous or given by 'nature' (at least over the time horizon considered here), such as climate (captured by extreme values in average temperature and rainfall), soil quality (captured by the average caloric value of crops per hectare), access to coalfields (measured as the proximity to rock strata from the carboniferous era) or the location of main seaports (captured by the distance to the nearest deepwater seaport). Instead, second nature geography refers to factors that result from human intervention, notably the accessibility of markets, which depends on both the economic size of neighbouring regions and access to them (Fujita et al. 1999; Redding and Venables 2004). In a simple first step, we can test for the respective role of each of these factors to explain variation in the level of GDP per capita across our regions and over time. Table 2.4 shows the results of

Table 2.4 Pooled GLS regression with random effects, IV, dep. variable: Ln (GDP per capita), levels 1900–2010

	Coefficients (t-*stat)*
European Community	0.112 (6.16)
European Union	0.141 (2.42)
Eurozone	0.225 (4.43)
Capital region	0.305 (3.70)
National dummies (time-varying)	Yes
Market access (instrumented)	0.280 (1.77)
Distance to deepwater port (ln)	−0.016 (−0.73)
Extreme rainfalls	−0.073 (−0.89)
Extreme temperatures	−0.172 (−2.04)
Soil quality	−0.069 (−1.68)
Coal potential	0.290 (2.33)
Constant	−7.66 (−7.25)
Time dummies	Yes
Observations	1,886
Groups	172
Adj. R^2 within, between, overall	0.96, 0.48, 0.89

Source: Own.

Note: The country time dummies allow for country-specific linear time trends.

a pooled regression that uses all our data. Note that we use the sum of inverted distances to other regions as an instrument for market access.

We have added random effects, clustered standard errors at the regional level and allowed for common time effects. With this rather naïve approach, where we simply pool all data over regions and time, we find that regions with good access to coalfields tend to have higher income levels in the long run, while good soil quality and extreme temperatures are associated with lower income levels. In turn, a good accessibility of markets seems to exert a strong positive effect on income levels (note that this variable has been instrumented in order to deal with endogeneity). After taking geographical factors into account, we also find support for the role of institutions: controlling for unobserved factors at the national level, we find that capital regions always have higher levels of income and that membership in the various European institutions made a positive contribution to income levels, notably after controlling for a full set of time effects. Obviously, this is only a first explorative glance at the data, but it suggests some regularities in line with the idea that a combination of institutional and geographical factors has shaped the economic geography of Europe in the long run. Note also that all results are robust to excluding the regions that were part of the GDR during the period of Germany's division (1949–1989). By closer inspection, we can see that these effects are indeed quite stable over our period of 1900–2010. An interesting exception to this rule is the effect of access to coalfields, which is becoming much weaker after 1945.

This motivates us to consider in a next step the short- to medium-term dynamics of growth rates as a process of adjustment, conditional on more persistent geographical and institutional factors. Table 2.5 gives the results of pooled regressions, where we regress the average annual growth rates of regions each decade on the levels of GDP per capita at the beginning of each decade, the share of agriculture at the beginning of each decade, and the 'gap' defined by the difference in GDP per capita in each region before and after a war. Here, we distinguish between destruction during the First World War and the Second World War and restrict the gap to affect only the immediate decade after the war. In column 1, we repeat the exercise of Table 2.3 for the years 1950–2010, but now exploiting the panel structure of our data. In column 2, we extend the analysis to all decades 1900–2010. In column 3, we include the geographical and institutional factors. In each case, we exclude the regions of the GDR.

The results in column 1 of Table 2.5 are quite similar to those from Table 2.3. For the period after the Second World War, regions did show beta-convergence.

Table 2.5 Pooled GLS regression with random effects, IV, dep. variable: Ln (growth rates), 1900–2010

	Coefficients *(t-stat)*	*Coefficients* *(t-stat)*	*Coefficients* *(t-stat)*
Ln (GDP per capita), t_0	–0.014 (–5.78)	–0.0146 (–7.37)	–0.019 (–9.48)
'gap' (1910–1925)	–	0.035 (3.18)	0.032 (3.40)
'gap' (1938–1950)	0.044 (7.26)	0.044 (3.69)	0.044 (7.58)
Share of agriculture in employment, t_0	0.042 (0.66)	–0.012 (–3.18)	–0.010 (–2.83)
European Community	–	–	0.007 (4.03)
European Union	–	–	0.006 (2.17)
Eurozone	–	–	–0.004 (–1.88)
Capital region	–	–	0.004 (2.96)
National dummies (time-varying)	Yes	Yes	Yes
Ln (market access), instrumented	–	–	0.009 (2.71)
Ln (distance to deepwater port)	–	–	0.001 (1.99)
Extreme rainfalls	–	–	–0.002 (–1.44)
Extreme temperatures	–	–	0.003 (0.32)
Ln (soil quality)	–	–	–0.002 (–4.66)
Ln (coal potential)	–	–	0.001 (0.38)
Constant	0.000 (0.10)	–0.072 (–6.76)	–0.143 (–6.92)
Time dummies	Yes	Yes	Yes
Observations	994	1,650	1,650
Groups	166	165	165
Years	1950–2010	1900–2010	1900–2010
Adj. R^2 within, between, overall	0.66, 0.65, 0.66	0.59, 0.36, 0.57	

Source: Own.

Note: The national dummies allow for country-specific linear time trends.

This result is virtually unchanged if we take various conditioning factors into account, notably reconstruction after the wars, which apparently mattered both after 1918 and 1945, and several geographical and institutional factors. The results in column 3 of Table 2.5 show that most of our findings for the long-run determinants of regional income carry through to a panel analysis of regional growth rates, but with some revealing exceptions.

Regions with a high share of employment in agriculture in time t_0 tend to grow systematically less, and having above-average soil quality tends to be harmful. An explanation for this could be specialization along differences in endowments. Interestingly, the positive effect of coal potential that we found on levels of GDP per capita (see Table 2.4) does not show up in a growth framework. Another result is that membership in the euro was not beneficial for growth, in contrast to strong positive growth 'effects' of the earlier steps of European integration. However, this should be interpreted with caution because our time frame might be too short to test this (our data end in 2010), and for a proper analysis we would have to address issues of selection bias, among other things (see Persson 2001; Ritschl and Wolf 2011).

7. Regional rankings over time

Another way to look at our data is in terms of rankings (compare Figures 2.5a and 2.5b on distribution dynamics). Which regions were on top of the league, and which were at the bottom? And especially, which regions gained relative to others, and which ones were falling behind? This can help to interpret the abstract estimation results and relate them to other evidence on particular regions, as discussed in the country chapters. Table 2.6a shows the 10 richest regions at four points of time: 1900, 1938, 1950 and 2010, each time with the GDP per capita estimate in parentheses. Table 2.6b repeats the same exercise for the 10 poorest regions. In all cases, we exclude Flevoland (NL23), for which we have data only from 1970 onwards.

Obviously, all of these results need to be interpreted with caution because the underlying data for both the historical and more recent periods are incomplete and to some extent uncertain. For example, the difference between Bremen (DE50) and Hamburg (DE60) around 1900 is easily within the margin of error. Nevertheless, there is a clear group of regions that is systematically ahead of the others: London (UKI), Paris – Île-de-France (FR10) and Zurich (CH04) are always among the top 10 regions, and Luxembourg (LU00), Stockholm (SE11) and Helsinki (FI1B) in three of the four years. But there are some remarkable changes. Berlin (DE30) raced up the table between 1900 (position 14) and 1938 (position 3), before it would start a long decline due to the war and its consequences. Hainaut (BE32) in Belgium, in contrast, was a rich region in 1900 (position 7) and still in 1910 (position 9), before it started its decline after the Great War to position 70 (1938), and further down to 153 (2010). While London (UKI) kept its strong position over time, other parts of England and indeed Wales (UKL) declined in the ranking very considerably.

Table 2.6a Ten richest regions, GDP per capita (1990 GK$)

Rank of 172	*1900*	*1938*	*1950*	*2010*
1	London Counties (UKI) $6,489	London Counties (UKI) $9,448	Zurich (CH04) $10,618	Luxembourg (LU00) $37,683
2	Île-de-France (FR10) $5,688	Stockholm (SE11) $8,132	Nordwestschweiz (CH03) $10,100	London Counties (UKI) $36,844
3	Luxembourg (LU00) $5,412	Berlin (DE30) $7,576	London Counties (UKI) $9,672	Île-de-France (FR10) $35,371
4	Helsinki-Uusimaa (FI1B) $4,743	Zurich (CH04) $7,549	Hovedstaden (DK01) $9,365	Hamburg (DE60) $35,123
5	South-East England (UKH + UKJ) $4,653	South-East England (UKH + UKJ) $7,441	Région lémanique (CH01) $9,006	Stockholm (SE11) $34,725
6	Zurich (CH04) $4,630	Oslo og Akershus (NO01) $7,351	Île-de-France (FR10) $8,740	Brabant (BE10 + BE24) $33,393
7	Hainaut (BE32) $4,537	Île-de-France (FR10) $7,106	Espace Mittelland (CH02) $8,739	Groningen (NL11) $33,337
8	North England (UKC + UKD) $4,482	Nordwestschweiz (CH03) $7,083	Luxembourg (LU00) $8,393	Helsinki-Uusimaa (FI1B) $31,705
9	Bremen (DE50) $4,420	Helsinki-Uusimaa (FI1B) $6,871	Stockholm (SE11) $8,319	Zurich (CH04) $31,420
10	Hamburg (DE60) $4,386	West Midlands (UKG) $6,747	Ostschweiz (CH05) $8,112	Hovedstaden (DK01) $30,085

Source: Own.

Table 2.6b shows the bottom end of the distribution. As expected, nearly all of these regions are in Southern Europe (but note that we have no data for Greece), and the differences between them are often too small to have a meaningful interpretation. Our earlier findings suggest that a combination of poor access to markets and poor climatic conditions together with weak national institutions contributed

Table 2.6b Ten poorest regions, GDP per capita (1990 GK$)

Rank of 172	*1900*	*1938*	*1950*	*2010*
163	Abruzzo (ITF1) $1,210	Región de Murcia (ES62) $1,541	Canarias (ES70) $1,879	Sardegna (ITG2) $14,240
164	Calabria (ITF6) $1,191	Centro (PT16) $1,539	Norte (PT11) $1,741	Mecklenburg-Vorpommern (DE80) $14,221
165	Corse (FR83) $1,187	La Rioja (ES23) $1,507	Región de Murcia (ES62) $1,695	Thüringen (DEG0) $14,063
166	Extremadura (ES43) $1,177	Alentejo (PT18) $1,496	Calabria (ITF6) $1,631	Norte (PT11) $13,827
167	Molise (ITF2) $1,167	Andalucía (ES61) $1,357	Castile-La Mancha (ES42) $1,631	Centro (PT16) $13,283
168	Algarve (PT15) $1,159	Castile-León (ES41) $1,319	Basilicata (ITF5) $1,628	Basilicata (ITF5) $12,702
169	Región de Murcia (ES62) $1,097	Castile-La Mancha (ES42) $1,209	Algarve (PT15) $1,618	Puglia (ITF4) $12,458
170	Canarias (ES70) $1,075	Canarias (ES70) $1,178	Andalucía (ES61) $1,589	Sicilia (ITG1) $12,249
171	Nord-Norge (NO07) $1,072	Galicia (ES11) $1,105	Galicia (ES11) $1,586	Campania (ITF3) $11,971
172	Galicia (ES11) $959	Extremadura (ES43) $1,071	Extremadura (ES43) $1,306	Calabria (ITF6) $11,951

Source: Own.

to their relative underdevelopment. If we compare the situation of 1950 to that in 2010, we see that the Spanish regions did relatively better than others in the periphery, and that some parts of the former GDR in Germany have fallen behind in relative terms to levels similar to those in Portugal and southern Italy.

Table 2.7 explores these changes in position more explicitly. The first column shows the ‘winners’, 10 regions in our sample that improved their position most strongly, and the second column shows those that lost most in the ranking over time.

Table 2.7 Ten biggest winners and losers, 1900–2010

Winners		*Losers*	
Improvement in rank	*Name*	*Decline in rank*	*Name*
124	Comunidad Foral de Navarra (ES22)	146	Hainaut (BE32)
114	Provincia Autonoma di Bolzano/Bozen-Provincia Autonoma di Trento (ITH1 + ITH2)	123	Namur (BE35)
113	Agder og Rogaland (NO04)	119	Luxembourg (BE34)
111	Åland (FI20)	115	Liege (BE33)
103	Vestlandet (NO05)	107	Chemnitz (DED4)
92	Tyrol (AT33)	99	Wales (UKL)
88	Stuttgart, Regierungsbezirk (DE11)	91	Leipzig (DED5)
85	Valle d'Aosta/Vallée d'Aoste (ITC2)	89	Haute-Normandie (FR23)
84	Emilia-Romagna (ITH5)	88	Nord-Pas-de-Calais (FR30)
84	Västsverige (SE23)	88	Dresden (DED2)

Source: Own.

The results are revealing and, given the extent of changes we see, they are very likely economically and statistically significant. From the first column, we see that regions in many different countries have improved their position relative to others in Europe. Regions in Italy, but also Scandinavian countries, as well as Stuttgart (DE11) in Germany and Navarra (ES22) in Spain, are in this group. Among the biggest winners are regions that have some autonomy within their country. It would be interesting to analyse if this is a cause or consequence of improvement. On the other side, the second column shows how dramatically some European regions were falling back over the last century. The formerly highly industrialised regions of Wallonia in Belgium, but also Wales (UKL) in the UK and Nord-Pas-de-Calais (FR30) and Haute-Normandie (FR23) in France, that had been reliant on abundant coal resources, and to some extent on the textile industry, were declining with the depletion of resources and changing technology and global competition. The case is different for the three German regions that experienced extreme decline, all of them located in Saxony. While these regions were around 1900 and still in 1938 among the richest in Germany, with a strong

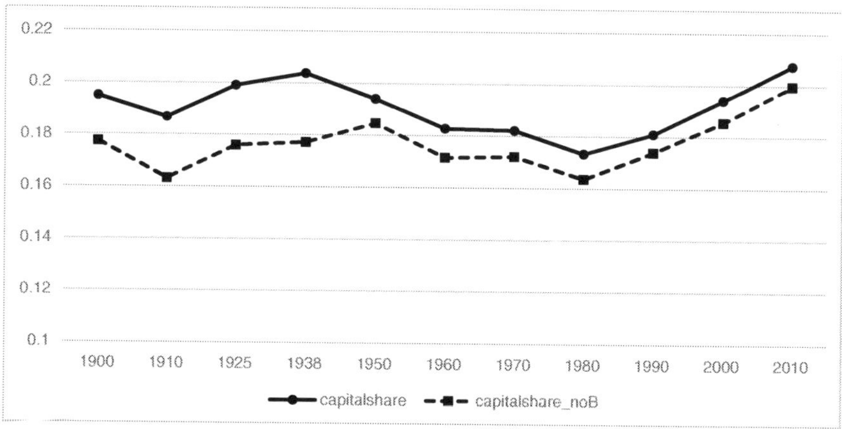

Figure 2.7 Share of capital regions in total sample GDP

industrial sector but also substantial employment in services, they suffered from the combination of division of Germany after 1945 and massive deindustrialization in the wake of unification.

Overall, we see that many regions in Europe do not fit easily into a picture of growth and convergence. Some stayed at the top of the league over more than 100 years and others grew much faster than average, while a third group was quite systematically losing out. Among those who did poorly are several of the former coal-mining regions.

In contrast, the capital regions of Europe did typically rather well, even though their share declined during the 'golden age' of growth and convergence. Figure 2.7 shows how the share of capital regions in total sample GDP developed over time.

We see that the share of capital regions in the GDP of Europe was around 20 per cent, which declined after 1945 in line with our findings of convergence after the Second World War. The findings are unchanged if we exclude Berlin, which is a rather special case due to the division of Germany and the city itself, and the decision to declare Bonn as the temporal capital of West Germany. Around 1980, things start to change, and the capital regions seem to increase their economic size relative to others – a development that is also reflected in population and employment data (not shown). In the next section, we will look more closely into such geographical changes. The decline and rise of capital regions are reflected in broader trends of spatial divergence and concentration over the last century.

8. Back to space: dispersion, spatial correlation and concentration over time

Given the evidence on beta-convergence after 1945 from Tables 2.3 and 2.5, one might expect to find that the overall dispersion of GDP per capita across regions should have declined. A simple measure to capture this is the coefficient of variation (the cross-sectional standard deviation divided by the mean), often referred to as a 'sigma-convergence'. Following Williamson (1965), we use a weighted version of this, where each region enters with a weight according to its population share. Figure 2.8 shows the result of this for all regions and for regions aggregated to nation states. The difference highlights how much of the variation is typically missed if researchers use national instead of regional data.

According to this measure, dispersion in GDP per capita has declined, at least until about 1990, and stagnated thereafter. It is evident that measures based on regional data show more dispersion, but we also observe some differences in trends. While, on average, for the period 1900–1960, measures based on national figures alone would capture around 70 per cent of all underlying variation, this figure has declined to 60 per cent in 1970 and below 50 per cent after 1990. One reason is the very high degree of variation within Germany, which increased between 1950 and 1980, increased again with unification, and declined only slowly thereafter. Another more general reason was visible from our maps on GDP per capita for 1900 and 2010 (see Maps 2.4a and 2.4b). In spite of strong overall growth and a systematic convergence of backward regions during the 'golden age' period, the coefficient of variation hides a process of declining spatial correlation, namely that many neighbouring regions are actually becoming less similar over time. We have seen above that there was substantial turbulence, in the sense that some regions were improving their relative position while others were falling behind, sometimes even within the same country.

A relatively simple way to capture similarity between neighbours is Moran's *I*. Applied to GDP per capita as our variable of interest, this statistic measures the

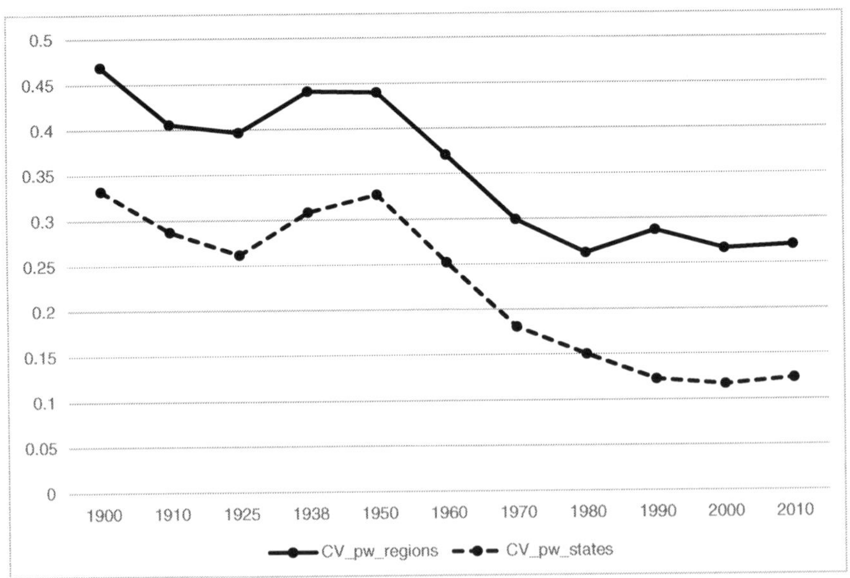

Figure 2.8 Sigma-convergence (population-weighted coefficient of variation), 1900–2010

sum of differences between all pairs of regions in terms of deviations from average GDP per capita, weighted by their distances. For large samples, the expected value under the null hypothesis of no spatial autocorrelation across regions approaches zero. If this measure is large (compared to the expected value), we say that a region shows positive spatial autocorrelation, indicating that nearby regions tend to have similar values of GDP per capita. Instead, if the measure is small (compared to the expected value), this is evidence for negative spatial autocorrelation, indicating that nearby regions tend to have dissimilar values of GDP per capita. Finally, we may find that the measure is not significantly different from the expected value under the assumption of no spatial autocorrelation. In Figure 2.9, we plot a global version of Moran's *I* across our regions over time.

The figure shows standardized values of the measure (*z*-scores), all of which were strongly significant. We see that there is a systematic decline in average positive spatial autocorrelation, especially after 1960 and again after 1990. This shows something that was not visible in the simple measures of sigma-convergence: apparently, the large clusters of neighbouring regions with similar levels of development have started to disappear. Another perspective on this can be gained from Maps 2.5a and 2.5b, where we show local Moran's *I* scores, distinguishing between positive autocorrelation and negative autocorrelation, and excluding the large number of insignificant values.

We see that the old clusters are indeed shrinking and most regions exhibit neither positive nor negative spatial autocorrelation with their neighbours. Note that 'neighbours' here includes all other regions in the sample, weighted by their distance, as well as national data from Poland, the Czech Republic and Hungary.

Finally, let us return to the question of the dispersion of economic activity across regions from the perspective of geographical distribution. In Figures 2.5a and 2.5b,

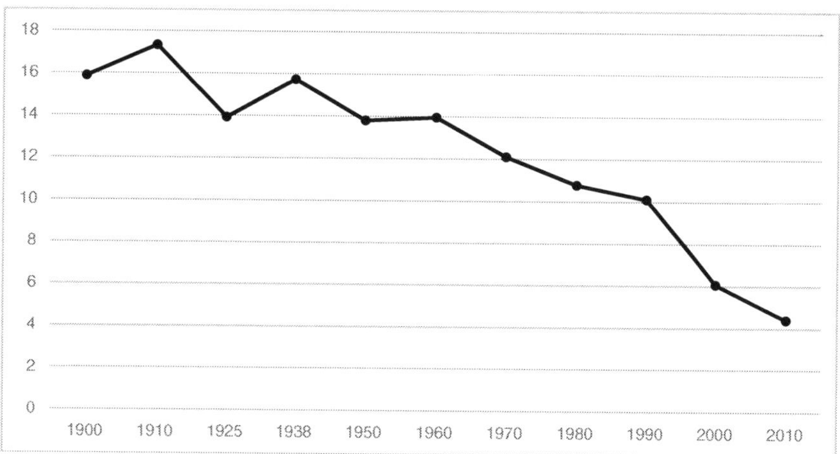

Figure 2.9 Global Moran's *I*, 1900–2010 (*z*-scores)

Source: Own.

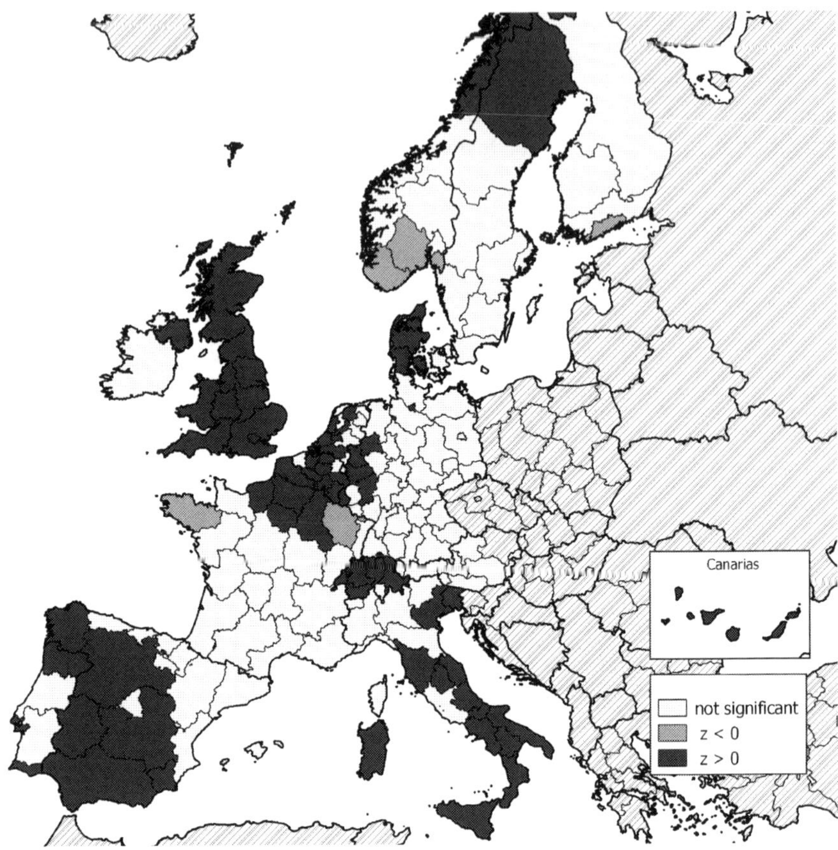

Map 2.5a Local Moran's *I* (*z*-scores), 1900

Source: Own.

we could see that the distribution of GDP per capita across regions had become more equal between 1900 and 1980, but that this process was reversed between 1980 and 2010. Underneath this change is a geographical reconcentration of economic activity, both in terms of population but more so in terms of GDP. The slight but steady decline in the correlation between population density and GDP density (see Figure 2.1) suggested that the latter is increasingly driven by regional variation in productivity. Following Krugman (1991), we constructed a locational Gini coefficient based on the share of each region in total sample population, respectively, the share of each region in total sample GDP. As usual, this coefficient is bounded between zero (all regions have equal shares) and one (all activity is concentrated in one region). Figure 2.10 shows the Gini for population and GDP over time.

We find that the concentration of activity measured in terms of population and GDP followed similar trends. The concentration of population declines slowly

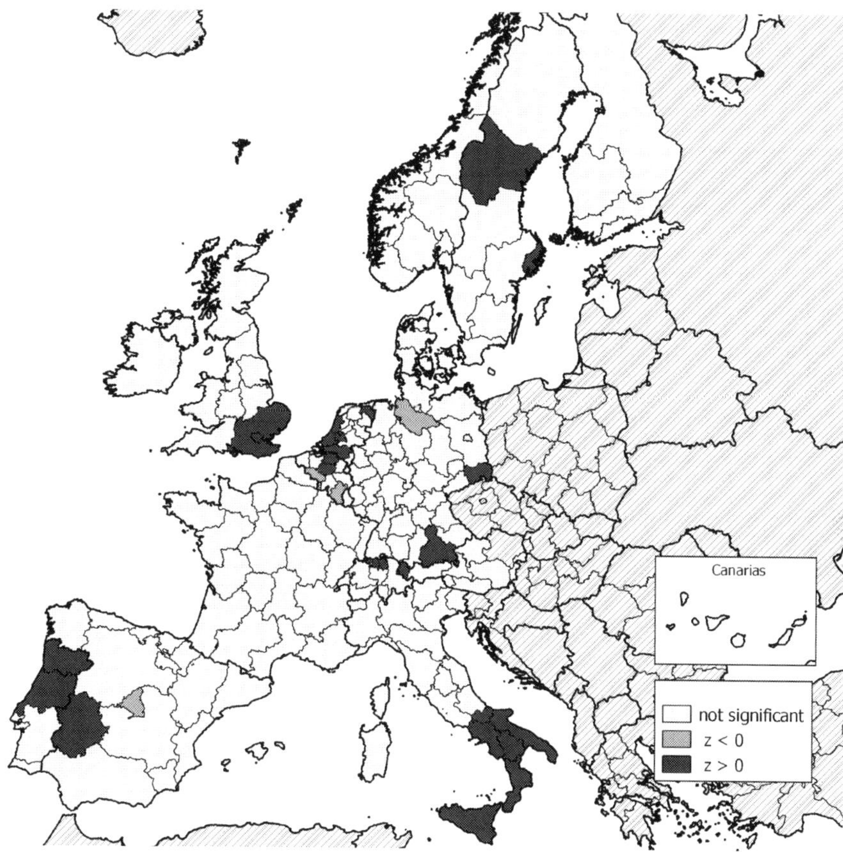

Map 2.5b Local Moran's *I* (*z*-scores), 2010

Source: Own.

after 1900 until 1960, followed by an increase in the 1970s. The pattern is similar but more pronounced for GDP, where we find that concentration declined in the long run, but that this trend was stopped and even reversed around 1980. Alternatively, a simple Herfindahl index of concentration would show a very similar picture, with a decline in the concentration of economic activity until 1980, followed by an increase until 2010. If we would weight each region by area (which is constant over time), we would again find similar pictures.

Other recent research suggests that this phenomenon continues, and is not limited to Europe, but applies to other OECD countries as well (see OECD 2016). In fact, this trend of increasing spatial concentration from around 1980 onwards can also be found for the US, as shown in Chapter 4 in this book. The evidence on sigma-convergence is quite similar for our set of European regions and US states. Starting from a high level, there is no clear change during the interwar years, but a substantial decline in dispersion until about 1980. After this, we find for both the

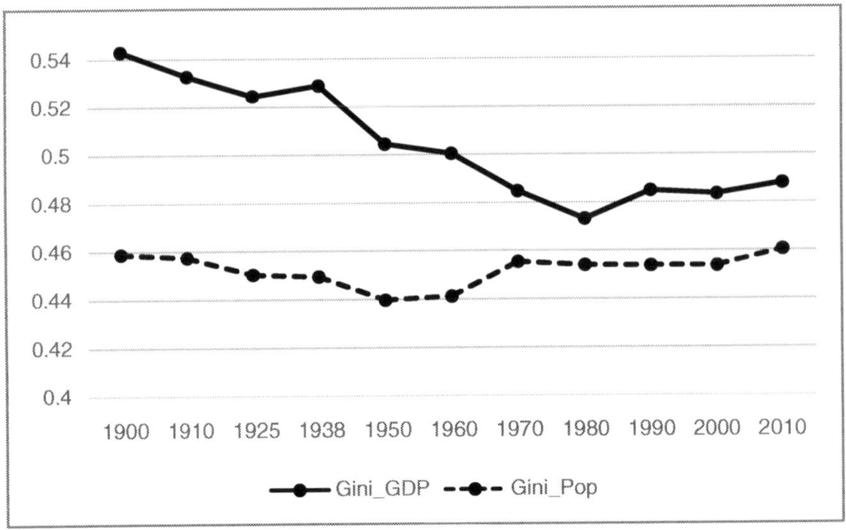

Figure 2.10 Locational Gini coefficients for population and GDP, 1900–2010

US states and European regions a trend reversal, with rising regional inequality due to strong growth in densely populated metropolitan areas (see Figure 2.7).

It is remarkable that the emerging picture on regional inequality in the long run is also similar to the pattern of inequality in terms of personal income and wealth distributions, which has been extensively documented and analysed (Piketty and Saez 2003; Piketty 2014). Regional inequality declined from 1900 but started to increase again around 1980, very much at the same moment when personal income inequality started its dramatic rise. These trends seem to be related to each other, suggesting that we need to rethink the driving forces behind both, as well as their consequences for economic development and political stability. Technological change and a new, deeper type of global market integration favouring high-skilled labour and specific types of services at the expense of traditional low-skill and often resource-intensive industries, have probably contributed to these changes. The combination of rising personal and regional inequality is a major challenge to economic policy for the decades to come.

9. Conclusion

How did European regions do over the last 110 years? We have constructed a new data set at the level of 172 (173) regions to trace their economic development in terms of employment structure and GDP at purchasing power parity in the longer run. The broad trends of growth and stagnation, as well as of convergence after 1945 that earlier studies have found are confirmed by our data. We saw that some regions stayed specialized in agriculture, while employment in industry first spread before it became more concentrated again. The level and growth of GDP per capita can be rather well explained in terms of conditional convergence, taking geographical and institutional factors into account.

But the long-run data allow us to see something more. In the long run, there is remarkable variation within states and some very deep changes that took place from about 1980 onwards. The share of overall variation in GDP per capita that is due to within-country differences has grown from around 30 per cent in 1900 to above 50 per cent in 2010, notably from 1980 onwards. Also, we found a growing disconnection between regions, with the emergence of islands of prosperity out of sync with their hinterland. Perhaps most important is the observation that the pattern of regional inequality over the last 110 years follows a U-shape, just like the pattern of personal income inequality, as documented by Piketty and Saez (2003) and others: after 1900, we find a spread of economic activity across regions and convergence between until about 1980, and divergence as well as geographical reconcentration thereafter.

The following chapters in this book provide a wealth of detail for European countries and a comparison to long-run developments in the US. They show a lot of diversity, but also remarkable similarities between European countries. The major changes in the economy of European regions occurred around the same time, notably the changes in growth rates, convergence and geographical concentration. To what extent are new technologies, and the rise of services, especially financial and business services, driving these changes? What role is there for international trade and capital flows within and beyond Europe? How did European policies affect the dynamics, and what does this imply for issues such as regional cohesion (see Becker et al. 2012)? We hope that our new data will help to analyse these and other questions in a long-run perspective.

Notes

1 We cover Austria, Belgium, Denmark, Finland, France, Germany, Ireland, Italy, the Netherlands, Norway, Portugal, Spain, Sweden, Switzerland and the UK, and also consider newly estimated data for Luxembourg in our empirical work.

2 We use the Maddison Project data with 1990 international dollars to ensure comparability with the bulk of research on long-run development. However, we have recalculated all our main results using the more recent data from the Maddison Project Database (MPD) from 2018 with the new real GDP per capita measures, termed 'CGDPpc', based on multiple benchmark comparisons to improve historical income comparisons across countries. All our results are robust to this, except some minor changes in terms of long-run rankings and a less pronounced change in the locational Gini coefficient for GDP. Notably, the change in distributions (see Figures 2.5a and 2.5b), in the share of capital regions over time (see Figure 2.7) and the development of sigma-convergence (see Figure 2.8) remain the same if we use the MPD 2018 data instead.

References

Acemoglu, D. (2009) *Introduction to Modern Economic Growth*, Princeton, NJ: Princeton University Press.

Baffigi, A. (2013) 'National accounts, 1861–2011', in G. Toniolo (ed.), *The Oxford Handbook of the Italian Economy since Unification, Part II: Sources of Growth and Welfare*, Oxford: Oxford University Press, pp. 157–86.

Barro, R.J. and Sala-i-Martin, X. (1992) 'Convergence', *Journal of Political Economy*, Vol. 100 (2): 223–51.

Barro, R.J. and Sala-i-Martin, X. (1995) *Economic Growth*, New York: McGraw-Hill.

Becker, S.O., Egger, P.H. and von Ehrlich, M. (2012) 'Too much of a good thing? On the growth effects of the EU's regional policy', *European Economic Review*, Vol. 56 (4): 648–68.

Berend, I.T. (2016) *An Economic History of Twentieth-Century Europe: Economic Regimes from Laissez-Faire to Globalization*, Cambridge: Cambridge University Press.

Bolt, J. and van Zanden, J.L. (2014) 'The Maddison Project: collaborative research on historical national accounts', *The Economic History Review*, Vol. 67 (3): 627–51.

Broadberry, S. (1997) 'Anglo-German productivity differences 1870–1990: a sectoral analysis', *European Review of Economic History*, Vol. 1 (2): 247–67.

Broadberry, S. and Klein, A. (2012) 'Aggregate and per capita GDP in Europe, 1870–2000: continental, regional and national data with changing boundaries', *Scandinavian Economic History Review*, Vol. 60 (1): 79–107.

Broadberry, S., Federico, G. and Klein, A. (2010) 'Sectoral developments, 1870–1914', in S. Broadberry and K.H. O'Rourke (eds), *Cambridge Economic History of Modern Europe, Vol. 2*, pp. 59–83.

Burhop, C. and Wolff, G.B. (2005) 'A compromise estimate of German net national product, 1851–1913, and its implications for growth and business cycles', *The Journal of Economic History*, Vol. 65 (3): 613–57.

Crafts, N. and Toniolo, G. (eds) (1996) *Economic Growth in Europe since 1945*, Cambridge: Cambridge University Press.

Deza, X.V. and González López, M. (2014) 'Regional concentration of knowledge-intensive business services in Europe', *Environment and Planning C: Government and Policy*, Vol. 32 (6): 1036–58.

Eichengreen, B. (2007) 'The real exchange rate and economic growth', *Social and Economic Studies*, Vol. 56 (4): 7–20.

Fujita, M., Krugman, P. and Venables, A.J. (1999) *The Spatial Economy*, Cambridge, MA: MIT Press.

Gallego, J. and Maroto, A. (2015) 'The specialization in knowledge-intensive business services (KIBS) across Europe: permanent co-localization to debate', *Regional Studies*, Vol. 49 (4): 644–64.

Geary, F. and Stark, T. (2002) 'Examining Ireland's post-famine economic growth performance', *The Economic Journal*, Vol. 112 (482): 919–35.

Iammarino, S., Rodríguez-Pose, A. and Storper, M. (2017) 'Why regional development matters for Europe's economic future', European Commission Working Papers, WP 07/ 2017.

James, H. (2017) 'Deglobalization as a global challenge', CIGI Paper 135, Centre for International Governance Innovation, Waterloo, Ontario.

Krugman, P. (1991) 'Increasing returns and economic geography', *Journal of Political Economy*, Vol. 99 (3): 483–99.

Moretti, E. (2013) 'Real wage inequality', *American Economic Journal: Applied Economics*, Vol. 5 (1): 65–103.

OECD (2016) *OECD Regions at a Glance*, Paris: OECD.

Persson, T. (2001) 'Currency unions and trade: how large is the treatment effect?', *Economic Policy*, Vol. 16 (33): 434–48.

Piketty, T. (2014) *Capital in the 21st Century*, Cambridge, MA: Harvard University Press.

Piketty, T. and Saez, E. (2003) 'Income inequality in the United States, 1913–1998', *The Quarterly Journal of Economics*, Vol. 118 (1): 1–41.

Pollard, S. (1981) *Peaceful Conquest: The Industrialization of Europe, 1760–1970*, Oxford: Oxford University Press.

Redding, S. and Venables, A. (2004) 'Economic geography and international inequality', *Journal of International Economics*, Vol. 62 (1): 53–82.

Ritschl, A.O. and Wolf, N. (2011) 'Endogeneity of currency areas and trade blocs: evidence from a natural experiment', *Kyklos*, Vol. 64 (2): 291–312.

Rosés, J.R. and Wolf, N. (2010) 'Aggregate growth, 1913–1950', in S. Broadberry and K.H. O'Rourke (eds), *The Cambridge Economic History of Modern Europe, Volume 2*, Cambridge: Cambridge University Press, pp. 181–207.

Schön, L. and Krantz, O. (2012) 'The Swedish economy in the early modern period: constructing historical national accounts', *European Review of Economic History*, Vol. 16 (4): 529–49.

Solow, R.M. (1956) 'A contribution to the theory of economic growth', *The Quarterly Journal of Economics*, Vol. 70 (1): 65–94.

Temin, P. (2002) 'The golden age of European growth reconsidered', *European Review of Economic History*, Vol. 6 (1): 3–22.

van Zanden, J.L. (1987) 'Economische groei in Nederland in de negentiende eeuw: enkele nieuwe resultaten', *Economisch- en Sociaal-Historisch Jaarboek*, Vol. 50: 51–76.

Vonyó, T. (2008) 'Post-war reconstruction and the golden age of economic growth', *European Review of Economic History*, Vol. 12 (2): 221–41.

Williamson, J.G. (1965) 'Regional inequality and the process of national development: a description of the patterns', *Economic Development and Cultural Change*, Vol. 13 (4): 1–84.

3.1 From empire to republic

Regional inequality in Austria, 1870–2014

Max-Stephan Schulze[1]

1. Introduction

This chapter explores the changes in regional inequality in Austria from the 1870s to the present. Drawing on a new data set, it is concerned with the extent and temporal evolution of regional income differentials and their main drivers. The First World War and its aftermath fundamentally reshaped the economic and political context within which regional development in Austria unfolded. Up until 1918, the regions of modern Austria were part of the multinational Austro-Hungarian Empire and its customs and monetary union – a state with a population of more than 50 million people (1913), a territory that shared borders with Switzerland in the west and Russia in the east, and extended from the German border in the north to the Mediterranean. Its total GDP made the country rank among the largest economies on the European continent. Following the empire's defeat, the Treaties of St Germain (1919) and Trianon (1920) sealed its dismemberment and territorial break-up among a number of successor states.[2] 'Austria' in its new republican guise was reduced to a small landlocked country with a population of less than 6.5 million.[3] At a stroke, Vienna, once the political, economic and cultural centre of an empire, became the capital of a country that contained barely more than thrice its own population.

However, the lands within Austria's modern post-1918 borders formed an economic space that in the late nineteenth century was far richer, in per capita income terms, than the Habsburg economy of which it was a part. In 1870, GDP per capita in modern Austria was on a par with (if not as fast-growing subsequently as) that of its northern neighbour Germany. While the aggregate economy experienced pronounced variations in its fortunes over the twentieth century – comparatively modest growth before the First World War, a disastrous performance in the interwar years and a veritable *Wirtschaftswunder* after the Second World War (Klein et al. 2017) – there was considerable convergence in regional incomes that was not subject to major reversals over 144 years. By 2014, income dispersion across Austria's regions was about one-third to one-half the level it was in 1870, depending on the measure used. The evidence would suggest that this was an outcome, first, of structural change associated with interregional factor movements, a decline in both the level and regional differences in agricultural employment, and a broad move into higher-productivity services. Second, the observed gradual shift in economic activity from Lower Austria and Vienna to the western regions since the First World War reflected the changed political map of both Europe and Austria. Lower Austria had, in effect, become an eastern border region in Austria. Vienna had become an over-dimensioned capital that displayed an absolute and relative decline in population after 1918 and into the late 1980s. The division of Europe after the Second World War shifted the balance further in favour of the western regions of Austria. Here it is hypothesized that these changes in the political setting, the consequence of which were severe restrictions on what formerly used to be customs-free access to East Central European markets, had regionally asymmetric effects and imposed a penalty on the eastern regions in terms of their relative market access and relative economic performance. After 1945, the western regions, located between and well-connected to the expanding economies of southern Germany and northern Italy, were better placed to benefit early on from reconstruction and accelerating growth in Western Europe that helped to overcome the constraints of a small domestic market (Butschek 2011: 426ff.). Though the collapse of the Iron Curtain in 1990 reopened access to the economics of the Habsburg successor states in East Central Europe and Austria's accession to the European Union in 1995 enhanced her integration in a continent-wide trade network, so far this has not led to a significant change in the broad, long-run pattern of income convergence within which Austria's west became relatively richer and her east relatively poorer.

2. The data

The extent and temporal evolution of regional inequality in Austria is measured through new estimates of regional GDP for 1870 to 1950 and official and semi-official regional income data for 1961 to 2014. All measures – GDP and population – are fully mapped onto current NUTS 2 region definitions, which in turn correspond with present-day Austrian *Länder* boundaries. For 1870 to 1910 (at 10-year census intervals), GDP at factor cost in current prices for Austria's nine regions – Burgenland, Carinthia, Lower Austria, Vienna, Salzburg, Styria, Tyrol, Upper Austria and Vorarlberg – was estimated in a two-stage process.[4] First, GDP at constant 1913 prices for each of the regions in their pre-1918 borders (Schulze 2007a)[5] has been revised and then fully corrected at sector level for post-1918 borders to reflect the significant territorial and population changes that came with the post-war settlement and to align it with current NUTS 2 regions.[6] The estimates cover eight sub-sectors: agriculture, mining, manufacturing, construction, trade/finance/communications, government/professional services, domestic service and housing. In the second step, regional GDP was converted into current prices, drawing on a wide array of sector- and, to a lesser extent, region-specific price indices. Whenever region-specific price series were not available, and instead average country-wide prices had to be used, these were employed in conjunction with region-specific sector composition weights.[7]

For 1924, 1934 and 1950, total Austrian nominal GDP by sub-sector is given in WIFO (1965). Drawing on aggregate and sectoral employment as documented in the 1934 census, gross value added in each sub-sector was regionally decomposed on the assumption that *relative* output per worker levels *within* sub-sectors across regions in 1934 matched those in 1910.[8] The regional sub-sector outputs so obtained were then aggregated up into regional GDP. With regional *shares* in sub-sector (or industry branch) output thus available for 1910, 1934 and 1961, interpolation yielded region shares at sector level for 1924 and 1950, and finally a regional breakdown of total GDP by major sector.[9] The years 1961–2014 are well covered in the sources and allow for ready computation of nominal regional GDP at NUTS 2 level.[10]

3. Regional inequality in the long run

One way to think about regional inequality is in terms of so-called sigma-convergence, i.e. a reduction over time in the dispersion of per capita income (or output) levels across regions (Barro and Sala-i-Martin 1991; Sala-i-Martin 1996). A typical measure of sigma-convergence is the population-weighted coefficient of variation. A decline in the coefficient is indicative of a reduction in regional income dispersion. Figure 3.1.1 shows two alternative measures: one that covers all years in the range and where Lower Austria includes Vienna (CV); the other where Lower Austria and Vienna are treated as separate NUTS 2 units (CV II). While the two series display slightly different levels of dispersion and a different slope, they tell – in effect – the same story: on both measures, regional inequality in Austria declined without major interruption or reversal between 1870 and 2014.[11] Note the narrowness of the range within which coefficients of variation moved between observation years at least up until the 1930s. There was a gradual decline in inequality throughout the late nineteenth century followed by a relatively modest increase in the interwar period. The latter reflects the regionally asymmetric impact of the First World War, the dislocation of activity following the dissolution of the Habsburg Empire and the Great Depression. It was after the Second World War, though, that regional inequality decreased fairly rapidly, minor fluctuations notwithstanding – a sharp decline across the war period and into the 1950s and 1960s, and thereafter a more moderately paced decrease

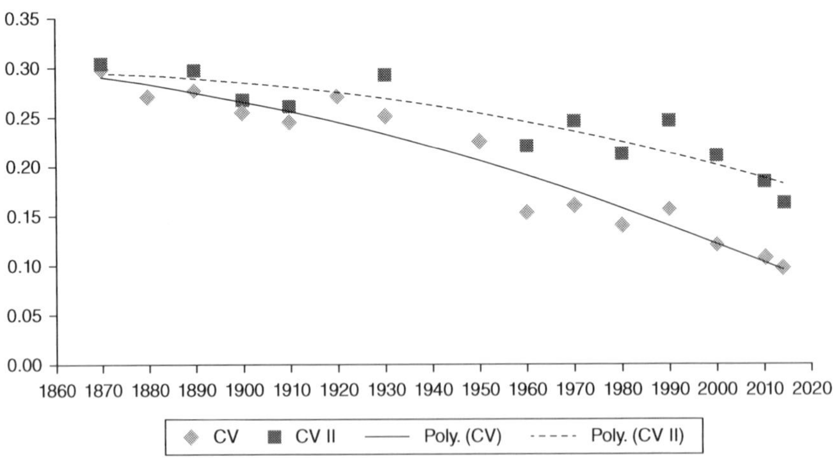

Figure 3.1.1 Sigma-convergence across Austria's regions (weighted CVs)

through to 2014. By that time, the degree of regional income dispersion in Austria had fallen to between one-third (CV) and one-half (CV II) of the level it was in 1870, depending on which of the two inequality measures is being used.

However, the Alpine lands that make up the territory of the post-1918 Austrian Republic were, together with the Czech lands, the richest and economically most advanced regions of the empire. It was here, in the empire's western and north-western parts, where structural change and industrialization first gathered pace and among whose regions income differentials had already become relatively small by the 1870s (Good 1984; Schulze 2007a). Note, too, that by the 1870s, these regions had a significant lead over the rest of the empire in terms of human capital endowments.[12] In comparison to either the former Habsburg Empire as a whole (including *Imperial* Hungary) or its *Imperial* Austrian half (Cisleithania), regional income dispersion in Austria within its modern borders was far less pronounced throughout the late nineteenth century.[13]

A different, albeit complementing, perspective on the convergence issue is provided by the concept of beta-convergence. Here, the hypothesis is that poor regions will tend to catch up with and grow faster than rich regions. This, the argument goes, is an outcome of poorer regions or economies not being faced with as rapidly diminishing returns to capital than high-income and capital-rich economies. Further, poor regions can (potentially) adopt and adapt technologies and institutions characteristic of the leading, rich economies.[14] However, beta-convergence is a necessary but not sufficient condition for sigma-convergence (Young et al. 2008). A basic variant of testing the (unconditional) convergence hypothesis involves regressing the growth rate of per capita income over a given period on the initial income level at the start of the period. An inverse relation between the growth rate and initial income implies poor regions growing faster and catching up with rich regions. Figure 3.1.2 shows this relationship for the Austrian regions, and on this evidence the poor were indeed catching up with the rich over the 110-year period on which this volume focuses (1900–2010).

The implicit rate of beta-convergence, about 0.7 per cent per annum, is low relative to the results of international cross-country comparisons, which are typically in the order of about 2 per cent (Young et al. 2008). The same rate also holds for the longer period from 1870 to 2014.[15] These findings are not surprising: Austria in its modern borders is a small economy in terms of population, area and total GDP. By 1870, regional income differentials were relatively modest in international comparison to start with. At that time, the country disposed already of fairly well integrated labour, capital and money markets, and all of its regions were connected through an increasingly dense railway network facilitating inter-regional trade (Komlos 1983; Good 1984). Further, human capital endowments, for instance in terms of average years of schooling, were fairly similar across the regions of modern Austria and far ahead of empire-wide averages.[16] Likewise, access to domestic and foreign markets was better – especially compared to the eastern regions of the Habsburg Empire – and differed less between the core Alpine regions given their spatial proximity (Schulze 2007a). In short, the scope for more rapid beta-convergence across this set of comparatively homogenous Austrian regions was more limited than for economies characterized by

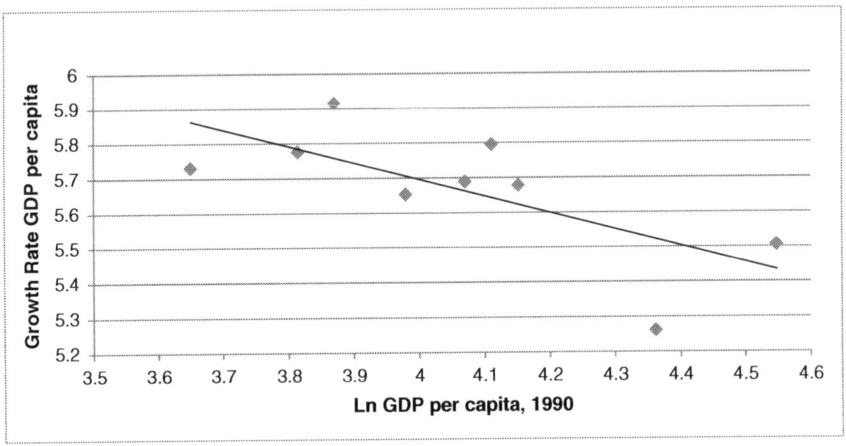

Figure 3.1.2 Beta-convergence across Austria's regions, 1900–2010

higher initial regional income differentials, less well-integrated factor and goods markets, and larger initial differences in human capital endowments.

The outlier is, to some extent, the eastern region of Burgenland, which until 1921 belonged to Hungary. The issue becomes immediately apparent in Table 3.1.1, which documents regions' *relative* GDP per capita over the whole period 1870–2014. Throughout the 144 years under review, and despite some significant catching up in the long run, Burgenland remained considerably poorer than its counterparts. By 2014, its GDP per capita was still below 70 per cent of the Austrian average. Another striking feature is the overall conspicuously dominant position of Vienna, the country's capital. While its relative income remained the highest throughout the period, Vienna's per capita income lead eroded slightly in the late nineteenth century. Though fluctuating, it stayed fairly stable between the 1930s and 1990, and thereafter declined to its lowest level in 2014. The relative decline of Austria's east (bar Burgenland) appears far more pronounced in the data that treat Lower Austria and Vienna as one. The 'capital region' so defined loses its position at the top of the Austrian income league after 1990, a consequence of almost continuous relative decline of Lower Austria proper since 1870. In stark contrast is the record for Salzburg, which by 2000 had become Austria's second richest region after Vienna, and for Tyrol, which moved up to fourth rank. Here, per capita incomes had risen by about 30 percentage points relative to the Austrian average. In comparison, Carinthia and Styria in the south and south-east of the country appear to have made less of the significant initial catch-up potential, as reflected in their comparatively low 1870 per capita income levels. By 2014, incomes there had increased by about 18–21 percentage points, respectively, relative to the Austrian average, but they were still about 10–16 per cent below that average. The cases of Upper Austria and Vorarlberg illustrate that similar starting points in terms of relative incomes do not per se make for similar catch-up outcomes. While Vorarlberg, the most western of Austria's regions, maintained its

Table 3.1.1 Relative GDP per capita (Austria = 1)

	1870	*1880*	*1890*	*1900*	*1910*	*1924*	*1934*	*1950*	*1961*	*1970*	*1980*	*1990*	*2000*	*2010*	*2014*
Burgenland	0.48	0.54	0.52	0.54	0.57	0.54	0.54	0.62	0.57	0.58	0.61	0.62	0.66	0.68	0.69
Carinthia	0.66	0.65	0.59	0.64	0.66	0.62	0.62	0.71	0.82	0.84	0.83	0.79	0.83	0.84	0.84
Lower Austria*	1.32	1.27	1.26	1.24	1.23	1.26	1.24	1.25	1.15	1.15	1.12	1.16	1.10	1.07	1.03
Lower Austria	*1.14*		*1.10*	*1.11*	*1.08*		*0.99*		*0.89*	*0.84*	*0.86*	*0.85*	*0.82*	*0.83*	*0.81*
Vienna	*1.46*		*1.40*	*1.34*	*1.33*		*1.42*		*1.37*	*1.42*	*1.37*	*1.46*	*1.38*	*1.30*	*1.23*
Salzburg	0.85	0.92	0.84	0.86	0.87	0.84	0.82	0.83	1.01	1.08	1.10	1.09	1.12	1.15	1.17
Styria	0.69	0.72	0.73	0.76	0.73	0.73	0.79	0.83	0.85	0.79	0.82	0.80	0.85	0.87	0.90
Tyrol	0.73	0.68	0.62	0.68	0.74	0.71	0.71	0.78	0.93	0.99	1.01	0.99	1.02	1.04	1.07
Upper Austria	0.91	0.92	0.93	0.83	0.82	0.79	0.84	0.86	0.95	0.95	0.98	0.96	0.97	0.99	1.02
Vorarlberg	0.90	0.82	0.80	0.90	0.89	0.95	0.90	0.99	1.05	1.05	1.09	1.01	1.03	1.06	1.08

Sources: GDP: 1870–1910: new estimates based on revisions of regional GDPs from Schulze (2007a) with border adjustments, price indices from SJB (1872–1884), ÖSH (1883–1916), Sandgruber (1978), Mühlpeck et al. (1979), Schulze (1996); 1924–1950: new estimates based on WIFO (1965) and Statistik des Bundesstaates Österreich (1935); 1961–2014: Statistik Austria (2012, 2015b), WIFO (2013). Population: See Table 3.1.3.

Note: * Including Vienna.

rank, it also increased its relative income significantly up to 2014. Upper Austria, in contrast, lost out in relative terms and dropped down the rank order to fifth.

What, then, is the record on changes in the spatial distribution of per capita economic activity? We split the range of relative incomes from Table 3.1.1 (with Austria = 1) into four intervals (≥1.15, 1.14–1.00,.99–.85, <.85) to capture the 'rich', the 'middlings' and the 'poor' (see Maps 3.1.1–3.1.4). Over the long run, the evidence points to pronounced inter-temporal shifts in the regional incidence of high (and low) per capita incomes. There is no *persistent* development gradient across space over the whole period. In the early years, the country's east (bar Burgenland) was significantly richer than its west and south. By the twenty-first century, this pattern had been reversed, and there is some evidence of spatial clustering of regions with higher incomes in the west. Vienna, as the following discussion will show, is an exceptional case.

In 1870, only Vienna was in the top income group defined by per capita incomes more than 15 per cent above the Austrian level (Map 3.1.1). Its surrounding region of Lower Austria in the country's north-east was the only area represented in the 'upper middle' interval. Taken together, then, the richest regions were situated in the country's east. Salzburg (central-west), Upper Austria (north-west) and Vorarlberg (in the west bordering Switzerland) make up the next group, with per capita incomes ranging between 85 and 99 per cent of Austria's overall level. Burgenland (east), Carinthia (south), Tyrol (west) and Styria (south-east) fall into the group with less than 85 per cent of average income. By 1910 (Map 3.1.2), the pattern had gradually changed as Upper Austria had moved down in the income distribution. While some relatively minor variations occurred in the interwar period (cf. Table 3.1.1), the post-Second World War era saw far-reaching changes in the spatial distribution of income. Simply put, the 'rise' of Austria's west, whose early phase is visible in Map 3.1.3, had by 2010 advanced to a point where Salzburg joined Vienna in the richest income group, while Tyrol's relative income had risen to a level placing it in the next income band with Vorarlberg. The story that emerges is a complex one: the long-run relative decline of Lower Austria and the failure of Burgenland to raise its income at a (higher) rate commensurate with its initial income level meant that – despite Vienna's continuing income lead – Austria's east became progressively poorer in comparative terms while the country's west grew richer after 1945. The impression of an east–west shift in per capita levels of activity is not fundamentally altered once we account for the performance of Upper Austria, Carinthia and Styria, and their position in the income distribution (Map 3.1.4).

The question that now arises is to what extent the observed regional differences and changes in per capita incomes corresponded with changes in the centre of gravity in economic activity across the country. Or: what proportion of Austria's GDP was produced in each region? Table 3.1.2 documents the evidence on this measure of regional inequality, which is, of course, strongly influenced by population size. The data tell a story of rapid and profound changes in the location of activity. The most striking case is that of the capital region, Lower Austria and Vienna. Between 1870 and 1910, their combined share of total Austrian GDP rose from 58 to about 65 per cent. This was fuelled by a dramatic increase in Vienna's population from less than 1 million to more than 2 million inhabitants, which in turn was driven by

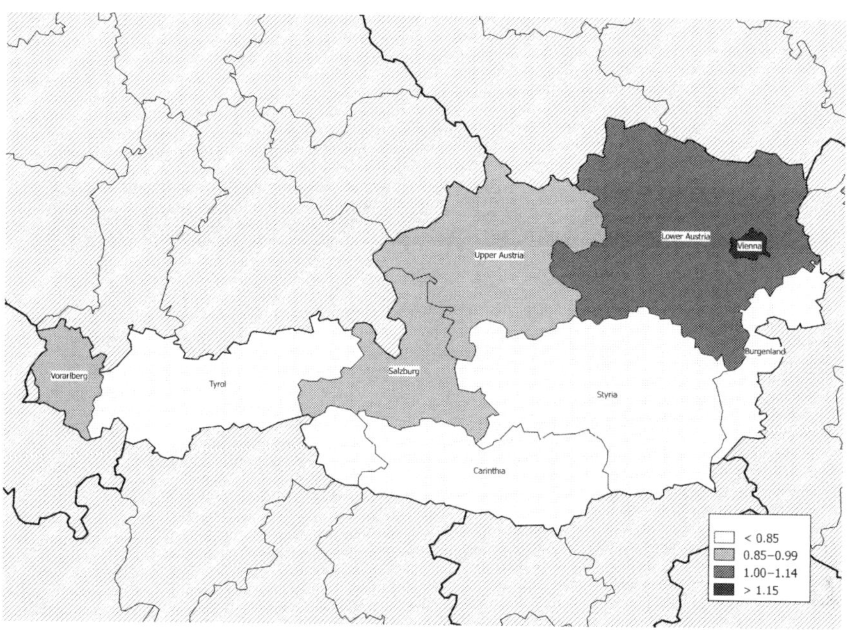

Map 3.1.1 Spatial distribution of GDP per capita, 1870 (Austria = 1)

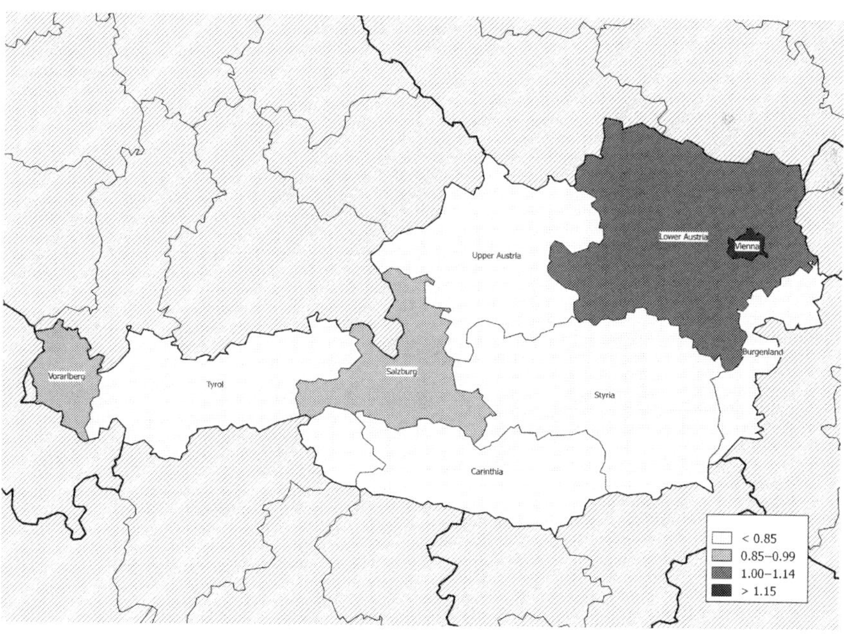

Map 3.1.2 Spatial distribution of GDP per capita, 1910 (Austria = 1)

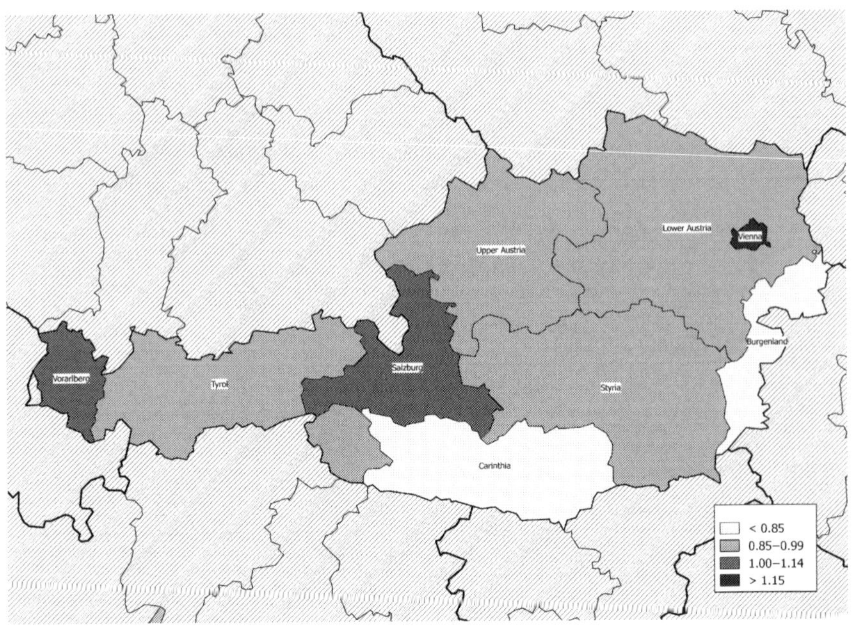

Map 3.1.3 Spatial distribution of GDP per capita, 1961 (Austria = 1)

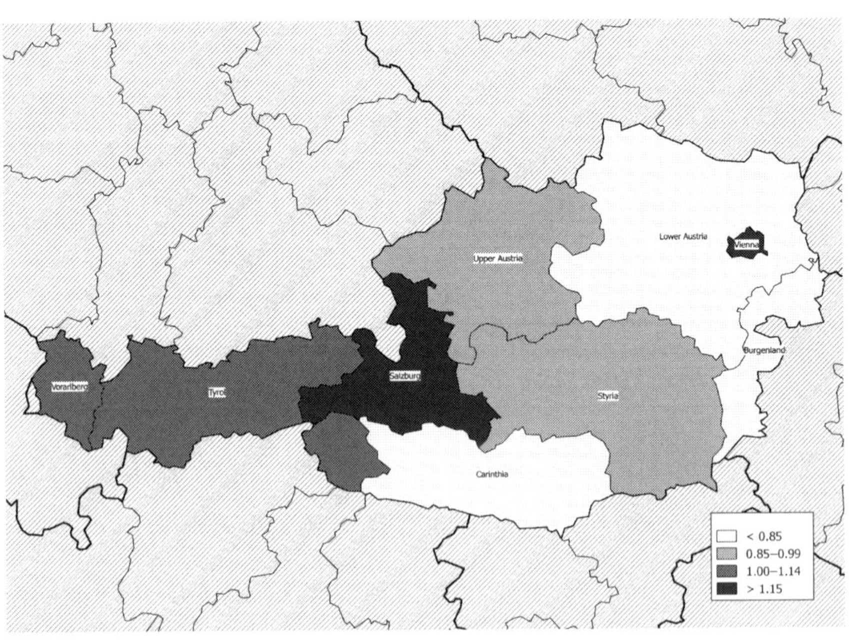

Map 3.1.4 Spatial distribution of GDP per capita, 2010 (Austria = 1)

Table 3.1.2 Regional shares in Austrian GDP (per cent)

	1870	*1880*	*1890*	*1900*	*1910*	*1924*	*1934*	*1950*	*1961*	*1970*	*1980*	*1990*	*2000*	*2010*	*2014*
Burgenland	2.7	2.9	2.7	2.7	2.5	2.3	2.4	2.5	2.2	2.1	2.2	2.2	2.3	2.3	2.3
Carinthia	4.7	4.3	3.7	3.7	3.7	3.6	3.7	4.8	5.7	5.9	5.9	5.6	5.8	5.6	5.5
Lower Austria*	57.9	59.3	61.7	63.6	64.7	64.3	62.1	54.3	48.7	46.9	44.1	44.6	42.6	42.2	41.1
Lower Austria	*28.0*		*24.7*	*24.2*	*23.1*		*21.3*		*17.2*	*15.9*	*16.2*	*16.2*	*15.8*	*15.9*	*15.5*
Vienna	*29.9*		*37.1*	*39.4*	*41.5*		*40.8*		*31.6*	*31.0*	*27.9*	*28.4*	*26.7*	*26.4*	*25.6*
Salzburg	2.9	3.0	2.7	2.8	2.8	2.9	3.0	3.9	5.0	5.8	6.4	6.7	7.2	7.3	7.4
Styria	11.1	11.3	11.2	11.2	10.5	10.9	11.9	13.2	13.7	12.7	12.9	12.1	12.6	12.5	12.8
Tyrol	3.8	3.3	2.9	3.0	3.4	3.4	3.7	4.8	6.1	7.2	7.8	8.1	8.6	8.8	9.1
Upper Austria	14.9	14.1	13.5	11.2	10.5	10.6	11.2	13.7	15.2	15.7	16.4	16.4	16.6	16.7	17.1
Vorarlberg	2.1	1.8	1.7	1.9	2.0	2.0	2.1	2.8	3.4	3.8	4.4	4.3	4.5	4.7	4.8

Sources: See Table 3.1.1.

Note: * Including Vienna.

Table 3.1.3 Regional population shares (per cent) and total population ('000s)

	1870	*1880*	*1890*	*1900*	*1910*	*1924*	*1934*	*1950*	*1961*	*1970*	*1980*	*1990*	*2000*	*2010*	*2014*
Burgenland	5.7	5.4	5.2	4.9	4.4	4.4	4.4	4.0	3.8	3.7	3.6	3.5	3.4	3.4	3.4
Carinthia	7.0	6.5	6.2	5.7	5.6	5.7	6.0	6.8	7.0	7.0	7.1	7.1	7.0	6.7	6.5
Lower Austria*	44.0	46.6	48.8	51.3	52.8	51.2	50.1	43.5	42.4	40.7	39.3	38.6	38.6	39.5	39.9
Lower Austria	*24.0*	*23.2*	*22.4*	*21.8*	*21.4*	*21.8*	*21.4*	*20.2*	*19.4*	*19.0*	*18.9*	*19.1*	*19.2*	*19.2*	19.1
Vienna	*20.0*	*23.4*	*26.4*	*29.5*	*31.3*	*29.4*	*28.7*	*23.3*	*23.0*	*21.7*	*20.4*	*19.5*	*19.4*	*20.3*	20.8
Salzburg	3.4	3.3	3.2	3.2	3.2	3.4	3.6	4.7	4.9	5.4	5.8	6.2	6.4	6.3	6.3
Styria	16.0	15.7	15.3	14.8	14.4	15.0	15.0	16.0	16.1	16.0	15.7	15.2	14.8	14.4	14.3
Tyrol	5.3	4.9	4.6	4.4	4.6	4.8	5.2	6.2	6.6	7.2	7.7	8.1	8.4	8.4	8.5
Upper Austria	16.4	15.3	14.5	13.5	12.8	13.4	13.4	16.0	16.0	16.4	16.8	17.0	17.1	16.9	16.8
Vorarlberg	2.3	2.2	2.1	2.2	2.2	2.1	2.3	2.3	3.2	3.7	4.0	4.3	4.4	4.4	4.4
Total population ('000s)	4497.9	4963.5	5417.4	6003.8	6648.3	6562.0	6755.3	6935.0	7086.3	7467.1	7549.4	7677.9	8011.6	8361.1	8546.4

Sources: Statistik Austria (2014, 2015c).

Note: * Including Vienna.

large-scale net immigration from other, poorer parts of the Habsburg Empire (Good 1984). However, while the collapse of the empire in the First World War and its dissolution led initially only to a modest decline in the capital's and its surrounding region's GDP and population shares (see Tables 3.1.2 and 3.1.3), the Second World War and its aftermath fundamentally altered the situation.[17] Lower Austria and Vienna's combined share in GDP fell continuously to 41 per cent in 2014. At its peak, Vienna alone generated more than 41 per cent of Austrian GDP just prior to the First World War – by 2014, this contribution had declined to less than 26 per cent. Clearly, these are still very high proportions, and Vienna retained the highest regional share in Austria by a significant margin, yet this share is far lower now than it was a century earlier. In contrast, the less populous regional economies in the west – Salzburg, Tyrol and Vorarlberg – expanded rapidly, with all of them almost doubling their (initially low) GDP shares between 1934 and 2014, while they saw little change in their contribution to total Austrian GDP in the decades before. Table 3.1.2 shows further that, with some fluctuations, the other regions' share in total GDP either declined (Burgenland) or increased only slightly over the long term (Styria, Upper Austria).

The results so far indicate that regions' changes in relative GDP per capita and their shares in overall GDP tended to go hand in hand, with the partial exception of Vienna. The next section will ask to what extent these changes were associated with structural change, interregional population shifts in favour of the more rapidly advancing regions and what role the seismic events of the two world wars played in altering the conditions under which regional development in Austria occurred.

4. Accounting for changing regional inequality in Austria

Unlike many other economies in the nineteenth and twentieth centuries, Austria after 1870 did not experience an inter-temporal pattern of regional inequality that conforms to an inverted U-shape, i.e. a pattern characterized by an initial increase in inequality followed by a subsequent decrease (Williamson 1965). As shown in Figure 3.1.1, regional inequality, as measured by the population-weighted coefficient of variation, gradually declined between 1870 and 2014 without major interruptions or reversals. We hypothesize that this had to do with the timing of modern economic growth and industrialization.

In the west of the Habsburg Empire, modern economic growth and its associated changes in the economy's structure began in the late eighteenth and early nineteenth centuries. By 1870, industrialization in the Habsburg domains adjacent to Western Europe, i.e. 'modern' Austria and the Czech lands, was well into the 'machine-industrial phase' proper and had diffused first across these regions as distinct from the rest of the empire (Komlos 1983; Good 1984; see also Pollard 1986). At the time, the share of *industry* (manufacturing, mining, construction) in total employment in the core Alpine lands had already increased to overall 27 per cent, i.e. to a level similar to Germany's.[18] Across the regions, industry's employment share ranged between 15 (Styria, Tyrol) and 38 per cent (Vorarlberg), while it stood at 7 per cent in Burgenland, then part of the economically far less developed Hungary. The shift in employment out of agriculture and into industry was to continue throughout the late nineteenth century and into the second half of the twentieth century (see Table 3.1.A.1.). By 1870, then, Austria's regions (with the exception of Burgenland) had in the main moved beyond the initial stages of modern growth when, typically, early industrial advances in the leading regions and specialization led to widening structural differences between them that served to increase regional income differences.[19] This is, of course, not to say that regional income differentials at that time were trivial. Evidently, they were not. Yet there is evidence of both beta-convergence (see Figure 3.1.2), however modest in pace, and decreasing income dispersion (see Figure 3.1.1) since the 1870s. Irrespective of whether they had actually still imposed significant constraints on economic activity at that time, the major institutional and legal restrictions on the movement of goods, people and capital had been removed by the 1850s (Komlos 1983). Aided by falling transport costs and a rapidly expanding and increasingly dense nationwide railway and communications network, the post-1870 period saw reductions in the interregional dispersion of commodity prices, interest rates and wages (Good 1984: 110–24, 148–61; Schulze and Wolf 2012).[20] Not only had Habsburg internal goods markets become better integrated by 1913 than they had been, say, 30 or so years earlier (see also Eddie 1989), but so had factor markets. There was a discernible increase in interregional labour and capital flows from regions with relatively abundant factors to those characterized by relative factor scarcity, be it labour or capital (Good 1984: 108–24). Up to a point, then, the pattern for the pre-First World War period is broadly consistent with the tenets of standard neoclassical trade models, a tendency towards factor price equalization and the associated reduction in interregional income differences. However, Vienna's trajectory does not easily fit in with this general picture. While its per capita income lead diminished slightly over 1870 to 1910, its share in total income and population increased to an all-time peak right on the eve of the First World War (see Tables 3.1.2 and 3.1.3), driven largely by high rates of immigration from other parts of the empire. Throughout the period 1870–1910, the city was not just the administrative and political centre of the empire, but also its premier location of distribution and financial services, as well as its most industrial area in terms of manufacturing output per capita:[21] on the eve of the First World War, Vienna alone accounted for half of (modern) Austria's industrial and service sector output. The structure of its output was geared towards the higher productivity secondary and tertiary sectors, and significantly more so than elsewhere in Austria or, for that matter, the empire (see Table 3.1.4). The other case standing out is that of Vorarlberg, where as early as 1870 more than half of GDP originated in industry, and which remained more committed to industrial production than Austria as a whole throughout most of the period under review. Butschek (2011: 423) views the early advances in Vorarlberg's dominant textile industry as an 'overspill' of industrial development in adjacent Switzerland. The structural differences between Vienna and Vorarlberg, on the one hand, and the rest of the country, on the other, are also evident in the employment data (see Table 3.1.A.1).

The case of Vienna illustrates the potential importance of agglomeration effects within an integrating national economy. Here, one can reason, market integration aided the spatial concentration of economic activity rather than its diffusion across

Table 3.1.4 Sectoral composition of regional GDP (per cent)

	1870			*1910*			*1934*			*1961*			*1990*			*2010*		
	prim.	*sec.*	*tert.*	*prim.*	*sec.*	*tert.*	*prim.*	*sec.*	*tert.*	*prim.*	*sec.*	*tert.*	*prim.*	*sec.*	*tert.*	*prim.*	*sec.*	*tert.*
Burgenland	52.1	15.1	32.8	52.7	22.3	25.0	54.2	20.7	25.1	39.2	27.9	32.9	9.2	29.3	61.5	3.7	29.0	67.3
Carinthia	42.1	27.9	30.1	29.2	32.9	37.9	24.7	38.7	36.7	18.1	41.2	40.7	4.3	34.9	60.8	2.0	30.7	67.3
Lower Austria*	13.8	40.9	45.4	8.3	42.5	49.2	8.4	41.7	50.0	8.0	44.9	47.1	2.4	33.5	64.1	1.2	22.7	76.2
Lower Austria				*22.7*	*36.2*	*41.0*	*23.6*	*43.5*	*32.9*	*21.5*	*50.7*	*27.8*	*6.2*	*46.1*	*47.7*	*3.0*	*31.6*	*65.4*
Vienna				*0.3*	*46.0*	*53.7*	*0.4*	*40.8*	*58.8*	*0.7*	*41.8*	*57.5*	*0.3*	*26.3*	*73.5*	*0.1*	*17.3*	*82.6*
Salzburg	31.8	25.1	43.1	24.4	30.1	45.4	23.9	32.8	43.3	10.3	40.6	49.0	2.1	30.3	67.6	0.9	25.5	73.6
Styria	40.1	29.4	30.5	27.9	38.3	33.8	22.4	43.0	34.6	15.0	49.8	35.2	4.7	40.7	54.5	2.5	33.7	63.9
Tyrol	32.3	24.1	43.6	27.9	30.3	41.8	22.3	35.9	41.8	10.3	42.7	47.0	2.3	35.8	62.0	0.9	27.6	71.6
Upper Austria	30.8	37.6	31.6	31.8	33.7	34.5	28.1	37.4	34.5	14.9	52.8	32.3	4.8	46.8	48.4	1.9	39.1	59.1
Vorarlberg	18.4	51.7	30.0	13.5	58.0	28.5	13.2	48.3	38.5	6.1	57.4	36.6	1.5	45.5	53.0	0.6	38.6	60.8
Austria	22.9	36.9	40.2	15.9	39.8	44.2	15.0	40.4	44.6	11.5	46.3	42.3	3.3	37.0	59.7	1.5	28.8	69.8

Sources: See Table 3.1.1.

Note: * Including Vienna.

the regions. Agglomeration occurs when and where firms can reap gains from locating near to each other. Further, industries characterized by increasing returns will likely locate in those areas that offer better access to markets (Krugman 1991). In the broader setting of the Habsburg Empire, Vienna, with its central location, communications and historically long-standing population size advantage – in part an outcome of it being the seat of the imperial court, government and central state administration – was, on balance, offering better scope for agglomeration economies of scale and market access than other cities in the realm. This pervasive city size effect is a likely major reason of why regional income inequality in the lands of modern Austria decreased at only comparatively modest pace in the late nineteenth century. Yet the impact of Vienna's absolute and relative rise as a centre of production and consumption before the First World War continued to be felt throughout the twentieth and twenty-first centuries, i.e. long after the conditions that fostered the initial concentration of activity in the capital had more or less disappeared.

These conditions, and the broader context within which Austrian regional development unfolded, were fundamentally altered by the shocks of the two world wars. The dissolution of the Habsburg Empire after 1918 meant that formerly customs-free access to the markets of East Central Europe was henceforth subject to tariff and non-tariff barriers to trade that rose even further in the depression of the 1930s (Resch and Sládek 1996). Thus, long-standing patterns of the regional division of labour were disrupted. This was an outcome not so much of significant shifts in the regional composition of Austrian foreign trade, though these occurred as well, but rather because of a reduction in the overall volume of trade as, unsurprisingly, engagement on Western European markets failed to rise at a rate sufficient to compensate for the decline in the country's eastern and south-eastern trade (Butschek and Průcha 1996: 312). The change in the political map of Europe had profoundly asymmetric effects on Austria's regions, especially over the long term. Lower Austria had become a border region, while Vienna had become the oversized capital of a small country. It was in the interwar years that the broad pattern of a declining east and a rising west began to take hold. Those areas that prior to the First World War benefited the most from their central location within a customs and monetary union, such as the capital region, were now not any longer in a position to make this count. Lower Austria proper experienced a significant decline in both relative per capita income and GDP share that was to continue throughout the twentieth century. While Vienna temporarily increased its per capita income lead between the wars, it did so, in stark contrast to the pre-1914 period, on the basis of an *absolutely* declining population and a *relatively* declining GDP. These were to become characteristic features of the region's development for much of the period after 1945.

However, the overall short-run effect of the post-war border changes on regional income differentials is hard to gauge, as these differentials were likely also conditioned by the sectorially differential impact of the dramatic contraction during the Great Depression. The evidence in Figure 3.1.1 would suggest that this was indeed the case: there is a discernible, if modest, increase in income dispersion in 1934, largely due to Vienna's relative per capita income gain, that cannot be accounted for by border changes (see also Table 3.1.1). During the 1930s, in a world of widespread protectionism and sharply contracting output, employment and foreign trade, the *relative* gains (or losses) to be had from proximity to (or distance from) former empire markets were likely bound to be modest. Following the end of post-war hyperinflation, the stabilization of public finances and the currency in 1923–1924, the Austrian economy grew in real terms at about 3.5 per cent (3.2. per cent per capita) and industrial output by 4.5 per cent per annum to 1929. In the protracted slump thereafter, aggregate output fell by over 6 per cent and industrial production by more than 8 per cent per annum to a 1933 trough. Neither before nor after the great contraction did Austrian real GDP and industrial output reach again their 1913 levels. Even a return to 1929 levels of activity was beyond the Austrian economy's capacity prior to the Second World War (Klein et al. 2017: Table 3.1.A.2). Further consideration of Austria-wide sectoral real output indices (WIFO 1965) would suggest that regions such as, for example, Vienna, with a comparatively high share of activity in services, especially public services, that were thus relatively less affected by the contraction in international trade, tended to do relatively better in terms of per capita GDP over the course of the depression than regions primarily engaged in industry and/or agriculture. However, Butschek (2011: 426–7) suggests that the capital was particularly exposed to the adverse effects of the empire's break-up and economic stagnation as its functions and scale of operations changed. Companies moved headquarters, the reach of a Vienna-based capital and money market shrank, and the size of state administration was reduced to better correspond with lower requirements. However, the point needs clarification. In terms of GDP and population shares, Vienna appears indeed as a region losing out as a result of the post-war settlement (see Tables 3.1.2 and 3.1.3). In terms of GDP per capita, though, this was clearly not the case – at least in the short to medium term (see Table 3.1.1). Here, the still considerable size of a comparatively well-paying public sector may have stabilized output.

Some digression is called for here. In no other region of Austria was the impact of the empire's collapse as pronounced in terms of population size than Vienna. The capital's population more than doubled between 1870 and 1910 to over 2 million inhabitants, experiencing by far the largest absolute increase and one of the highest growth rates among the cities within the territories of both modern and imperial Austria.[22] However, Vienna was Austria's only city over 20,000 residents (in 1870) whose population declined in the immediate aftermath of the First World War (Nitsch 2003: Table 2). In absolute terms, this decline continued to a trough of 1.48 million in 1987, after which population began to rise again to 1.78 million in 2014.[23] The disintegration shock of 1918 meant that Vienna's urban supremacy – the share of the largest city in a country's total urban population – rose by a factor of six between 1910 and 1920 simply by virtue of the reduction in country size brought about by the empire's dismemberment and regardless of the initial post-war population decline. By 1990, this proportion had about halved to 0.34, but that still placed Vienna right at the top of the European urban primacy table. These numbers matter for our study of regional inequality. Following Nitsch (2003), one can think of alternative ways how a shock such as the empire's disintegration may affect city growth. First, a reduction in country size, associated with a sharp rise in urban primacy, offers in itself no a priori reason for the residents of Vienna to move elsewhere. Of course, this needs to be qualified by the extent of the largely one-off effect of outmigration of those who had become citizens of the new nation states, other than Austria, that succeeded the defunct empire. In this view, which stresses path dependence, the break-up would have no significant effect on Vienna's subsequent growth. Second, if, on the other hand, history plays no or only a minor role for the future development of a city, then one would expect Vienna's urban dominance to decline over time: the former imperial capital would likely adjust to a smaller population commensurate with the far smaller size of the new Austrian Republic. Drawing on a cross-country sample of European cities and pooled regressions, Nitsch finds that for 1920–1960, there was indeed a process of city size adjustment at work, which over time led to a statistically significant gradual decline in the capital's disproportionately large population. However, the comparison with the later period, 1970–1990, shows that while Vienna remained considerably over-dimensioned, there was no further significant decline in the capital's urban dominance. These results suggest that after transition to a lower population level, lock-in effects asserted themselves (Nitsch 2003: 407–16). This may be, for example, because individuals, firms or government agencies perceived the costs of switching to other locations elsewhere in Austria as too high relative to the gains to be had from remaining in Vienna's agglomeration. The implications for the question of regional inequality are far-reaching. Whatever the reasons for the observed pattern, the identified stabilization in Vienna's primacy level means that a large proportion of the country's human and material resources remained effectively tied in a still hugely oversized capital city.[24]

The post-Second World War division of Europe shifted the balance decisively in favour of Austria's western regions. The constraints on cross-border exchange with East Central Europe solidified into permanent features with the division of the continent under the impact of the Cold War. The country's political neutrality (from 1955) notwithstanding, Austria's east had, in effect, become the border zone of Western Europe. The Habsburg successor states were now behind the Iron Curtain. After a short recovery in the immediate post-war period, their share in Austria's foreign trade contracted sharply and never regained the relative importance they still had in the late 1930s (Butschek 2011: 187, 402–3). Simply put, the outcome of the First World War raised the cost of trading with countries that were previously part of the common empire market. Formerly domestic trade was turned into foreign trade that was subject to tariff and non-tariff barriers. The outcome of the Second World War was to reduce such trade and, more generally, trade with Eastern Europe to even lower levels, at least in proportional terms.

The proximate causes of post-1945 changes in Austrian regions' relative income positions are, in the main, to be found in structural change. By the early twenty-first century, the output and employment structures were far more similar across the regions than they had been in the mid-1930s (see Tables 3.1.4 and 3.1.A.1). Measured in standard deviations, regional dispersion in output shares declined fairly rapidly and within each of the primary, secondary and tertiary sectors, especially after 1961. Three major factors contributed to this development.[25] First, with the 1938 annexation and Austria's integration into Nazi Germany's war economy, German investment shifted the weight of Austrian industrial production to the west of the country. This included an expansion in Austrian generation of hydroelectric power, accelerating advances made in the interwar republic, which found itself cut off from its former coal supplies mainly from the Czech lands. After the Second World War, the installation of new large-scale power generation capacity was resumed. The western mountainous regions (Salzburg, Tyrol, Vorarlberg) were major beneficiaries of this expansion, with almost one-third of all *additional* generating capacity created between 1948 and 1960 at a time when they counted for less than one-sixth of Austria's total population (SHB 1950, 1961). More than 40 per cent of the Marshall Plan funds allotted for investment in Austrian electricity generation were channelled into the completion of the Glockner-Kaprun storage power plant alone (Sandgruber 1995: 508). Second, the western regions of Austria, though initially relatively poor compared to Vienna and Lower Austria proper, were well placed to benefit from and partake in the economic reconstruction and expansion of Western Europe. They were located at the crossroads between northern Italy and southern Germany – both economically dynamic parts of the newly forming European Economic Community of the late 1950s, and to which access was comparatively easy already from the early 1950s onwards. Third, large-scale international tourism in the western mountainous regions of Austria emerged in the 1960s, i.e. at a time when it 'remained practically non-existent' (Butschek 2011: 428) in the east of the country. This process, just as much as the parallel expansion of manufacturing in the western regions, was aided by an elastic supply of domestic labour that was leaving employment in lower-productivity agriculture. Slow industrial and aggregate growth in the interwar years had been associated with low rates of structural change and demand for industrial labour – in 1934, the employment structure was still remarkably similar to what it was just before the First World War (see Table 3.1.A.1). Thus, the scope for redirecting labour after the end of the Second World War was significant.

These changes stood in stark contrast to development in Austria's eastern regions. Here, Soviet policy in the occupied eastern zone of Austria imposed serious constraints on interregional economic exchange with the rest of Austria and across the country's international borders. While such constraints had been removed with the 1955 restoration of full sovereignty to a non-aligned neutral Austria, and the collapse of the Soviet-led Eastern bloc in 1990 relaxed eastern Austria's position as a region on a 'hard' border, altogether these events did not change the fundamental regional dynamics that came to the fore after the First World War. Neither the opening up of East Central Europe after 1990 nor Austria's entry into the European Union in 1995 nor the EUs eastern expansion in 2004 and 2007 made much of a difference to the bigger picture. Compared to 1910 (1934), the share of Austria's east (Burgenland, Lower Austria, Vienna) in the country's GDP declined from 67 (64) per cent to less than 44 per cent in 2014. Likewise, the eastern regions' average per capita incomes fell from about 17 (18) percentage points above the Austrian total to less than half a percentage point. Even if we were to look only at change since the early 1960s, Butschek's (2011: 428) observation that the post-war west–east gradient is merely a phenomenon pertaining to relative changes in population and (absolute) regional product, but not in per capita output, is not quite borne out by the evidence once the more recent data are taken into account (see Table 3.1.1).

It is the case that the reopening of trade with Central and Eastern Europe left its mark on the regional composition of Austria's foreign trade. In the immediate aftermath of the war, 1946–1947, the eastern Habsburg successor states together accounted for about 20–25 per cent Austrian exports and imports. Though remaining high in comparison with the OECD average during the 1950s to 1980s, these shares declined rapidly with the political and economic division of Europe and then picked up again following the post-1989 political regime change in Eastern Europe. By 2008, trade with the successor states accounted for 19 per cent of Austrian exports and 13 per cent of imports (Butschek 2011: 402–3, Table 76). However, irrespective of Austria's favourable historically and geographically grounded position to benefit from the rapid expansion of trade in goods and services with Eastern and Central Europe after 1990, this has had as yet little, if any, lasting effect on the regional income distribution *within* Austria.[26]

The discussion so far has focused on regional differences in absolute and per capita GDP. However, this measure need not necessarily inform on regional variations in purchasing power. As an addendum, we therefore consider briefly the effects of potentially redistributive tax and social transfer mechanisms, as well as cross-regional commuting to work. These can lead to significant differences in levels, regional rank order and dispersion between regional per capita income relatives measured in terms of disposable income as compared to gross value added (or GDP). In Austria's case, and in the later twentieth and early twenty-first centuries, these effects were powerful indeed. Consider Table 3.1.1. Vienna's per capita output in 2010 was almost twice as high as that of Burgenland. Note that gross valued added is measured at the place of production. Subtracting regions' capital stock depreciation and accounting for interregional net income flows resulting from people living in a region different from their place of work yields regional primary income (which is measured and taxed at the place of residence). Disposable income is finally derived by subtracting tax and social security contributions and adding welfare and other transfer payments received. Table 3.1.A.2 illustrates the extent of interregional income redistribution. In 2010, disposable per capita income in Vienna was a mere 5 per cent higher than in Burgenland. There are three main findings here. First, the dispersion in regional disposable per capita income is far smaller than in regional per capita gross valued added. In other words, purchasing power per capita was regionally far more evenly distributed than output (or income generation). Second, this is due to: (a) regionally different net income flows related to commuting between the place of residence and the place of work; and (b) regionally different net tax and social security burdens.[27] Third, there are 'winners' and 'losers' of regional redistribution in terms of changes to their relative per capita income position, including rank order changes, and the comparative per capita tax burden. Lower Austria moves to the top of the disposable income table ahead of Vienna from near the bottom in terms of gross value added and a middling position in terms of primary income. Burgenland is the other main beneficiary: it is the only region where primary income is actually higher than its output and where disposable income accounts for more than 90 per cent of gross value added per capita. The unweighted average of this latter ratio across the Austrian regions is just under 70 per cent. Vorarlberg in the west, in contrast, loses out in the sense that it carried the highest net tax and social security burden in both per capita terms and as a proportion of its primary income (see Table 3.1.A.2).

The effects of such interregional income redistribution on economic activity in the regions are hard to gauge. It is fair to say, though, that in the late nineteenth century, before the creation of the modern welfare state, the rise in government expenditure as a proportion of national income and the growth in interregional commuting, the issue was of little significance. For the post-Second World War period, however, this is clearly not any longer the case (Butschek 2011: 349, 387). An analysis of the costs and benefits of regional income redistribution and an assessment of its impact on the development of regional output is beyond the scope of this chapter. However, policies that, either deliberately or inadvertently, translate into major interregional income transfers can affect regions' productive activity. For instance, income flows from richer to poorer regions may help raise demand and so encourage local production and employment in poorer areas, region characteristics permitting. Of course, the extent to which such effects might materialize depends, inter alia, on the income elasticity of demand for local goods and services. Yet regional redistribution through the tax and welfare system (as distinct from commuting-related income flows) may have potentially adverse effects, such as reducing incentives to reallocate labour (and other factors of production) to more productive uses across space and/or sectors. This, in turn, may hinder more rapid structural change and faster diminution in regional differences in per capita output. While the evidence on regional labour productivity differentials would suggest that this possibility cannot be excluded,[28] the extent of such adverse effects was not dominating: by the early twenty-first century, the dispersion in output per worker levels across Austria's regions was far lower than in earlier periods.[29]

5. Conclusion

This chapter documents the long-run evolution of regional inequality across Austria in its present-day boundaries. It draws on new estimates of regional GDP at NUTS 2 level for the period 1870–1950 and connects them to (semi-) official data for 1961–2014. The new evidence shows that regional income inequality as measured by the dispersion in GDP per capita declined without major interruptions – albeit at varying speeds – over the last one and a half centuries. By 2014, the coefficient of variation in regional per capita incomes had fallen to between 30 and 50 per cent the level it was in 1870. The long-term reduction in income inequality was associated with convergence in productivity (output per worker), changes in regions' ranking by per capita income, and the country's west becoming relatively richer and its east relatively poorer over time.

Two major factors account for the extent and timing of regional income convergence. First, much of the decline in income and productivity differentials was an outcome of long-term structural change that was sustained by interregional factor movements and gathered pace especially after the Second World War. Second, the political map of Europe and of Austria was redrawn after the First World War. In the long run, this change in the political setting had regionally asymmetric economic effects and affected Austria's eastern regions adversely in terms of their relative market access and relative economic performance. The division of Europe after the Second World War shifted the balance further in favour of the western regions of Austria, enhancing their capacity to catch up with the east.

Appendix

Table 3.1.A.1 Regional employment structure by sector (per cent)

	1870			*1910*			*1934*			*1961*			*2010*		
	prim.	*sec.*	*tert.*	*prim.*	*sec.*	*tert.*	*prim.*	*sec.*	*tert.*	*prim.*	*sec.*	*tert.*	*prim.*	*sec.*	*tert.*
Burgenland	79.3	7.3	13.3	74.2	14.7	11.2	64.9	22.7	12.4	48.8	33.0	18.2	10.7	23.7	65.7
Carinthia	71.5	16.3	12.2	57.4	22.1	20.5	50.5	28.0	21.5	25.7	40.2	34.2	8.8	22.7	68.6
Lower Austria*	32.7	35.2	32.1	20.8	41.6	37.5	19.2	42.3	38.5	15.3	47.2	37.5	3.5	17.6	78.9
Lower Austria				*47.3*	*29.8*	*23.0*	*43.7*	*35.7*	*20.5*	*33.1*	*41.8*	*25.1*	*8.1*	*23.9*	*68.0*
Vienna				*0.8*	*50.6*	*48.6*	*1.1*	*47.2*	*51.7*	*1.1*	*51.5*	*47.4*	*0.1*	*13.0*	*86.8*
Salzburg	60.6	16.8	22.6	47.8	23.9	28.3	42.6	26.7	30.7	22.3	36.1	41.6	4.9	20.5	74.6
Styria	72.2	15.3	12.4	60.2	21.9	17.9	50.2	27.8	22.0	32.2	39.7	28.1	9.0	25.0	66.0
Tyrol	67.7	14.5	17.9	56.1	21.3	22.6	42.6	27.6	29.8	25.3	36.3	38.5	5.6	22.2	72.1
Upper Austria	58.4	23.1	18.6	55.5	24.8	19.6	50.0	29.7	20.3	28.9	43.6	27.5	6.7	29.8	63.5
Vorarlberg	46.9	37.6	15.4	34.5	46.4	19.1	30.9	44.7	24.4	14.6	56.7	28.7	3.2	30.4	66.4
Austria total	51.7	25.5	22.8	38.3	32.9	28.8	33.8	35.6	30.6	23.0	43.5	33.5	5.6	22.4	71.9

Sources: 1870–1910: new estimates based on regional data underlying reconstruction of sectoral labour force data for Imperial Austria and border adjustments; for sources and methods, see Schulze (2007b: Appendix A); 1934–1961: Statistik des Bundesstaates Österreich (1935), Österreichisches Statistisches Zentralamt (1963–1964); 2010: Statistik Austria (2015a).

Note: * Including Vienna. 1870–1961: proportions of the labour force; 2010: proportions of gainfully employed.

Table 3.1.A.2 Comparative per capita income measures, 2010 (euro)

	Gross value added	*Capital stock depreciation*	*Net regional income flows*	*Primary income*	*Disposable income*	*Net tax and social security burden*
Burgenland	21,069	*4,241*	*4,988*	21,816	19,973	*1,843*
Carinthia	26,023	*4,720*	*−65*	21,238	19,685	*1,553*
Lower Austria	25,579	*4,926*	*3,337*	23,990	21,208	*2,782*
Vienna	40,407	*6,934*	*−9,747*	23,726	20,891	*2,835*
Salzburg	35,774	*6,865*	*−4,918*	23,991	20,879	*3,112*
Styria	26,851	*4,298*	*−846*	21,707	19,781	*1,926*
Tyrol	32,154	*6,251*	*−2,883*	23,020	20,053	*2,967*
Upper Austria	30,592	*5,053*	*−2,226*	23,313	20,529	*2,784*
Vorarlberg	32,825	*5,267*	*−3,041*	24,517	20,688	*3,829*
Unweighted CV	0.185			0.048	0.025	

Source: WKO Tirol (2014: Tables 1–3, 5, 7–8).

Notes

1 This chapter draws on research supported by the Economic and Social Research Council (Grant RES-000-22-1598). This support is gratefully acknowledged.
2 In East Central Europe, the Habsburg successor states included Czechoslovakia, Hungary, Poland, Romania and Yugoslavia.
3 For syntheses and interpretations of the long-run economic development of Austria in its modern – as distinct from Habsburg – boundaries, see Sandgruber (1995) and Butschek (2011).
4 The sources available for reconstructing pre-1945 regional GDP typically treat Vienna as part of its surrounding region of Lower Austria. Basic regional decompositions are provided, though, for 1890–1910 and 1934 using labour force data at major sector level to differentiate output between Lower Austria proper (AT-12) and Vienna (AT-13). The implicit assumption is that *within* each sector, there are no significant output per worker differentials between the two regions. This assumption is fairly unproblematic: the sectoral employment structures between Lower Austria and Vienna were different to such an extent that even stark interregional differences in *within*-sector labour productivities would make no material difference to estimated regional GDP and GDP per capita (for sources, see Table 3.1.A.1). For 1870, with known regional populations, *joint* GDP and *joint* GDP per capita, per capita income for Lower Austria *proper* and Vienna has been approximated on the simplifying assumption that, *proportionally*, 1890 per capita income differentials between the two also prevailed in 1870. This yields indicative values for gauging whether differentiation between the two regions makes a difference to the assessment of regional inequality over time.
5 Rather than drawing on a Geary and Stark (2002)-type procedure, the constant price regional GDPs in Schulze (2007a) have been built up from sector and industry branch-level output 'direct' estimates, reflecting the specific and detailed primary source materials available and corresponding with the historical national accounts-type approach used in the reconstruction of statewide GDP aggregates in Schulze (2000, 2007b). The latter provide the national-level 'frame' of sectoral gross value added.
6 The territory of Burgenland belonged to Hungary's Danube Right Bank region before the First World War and was formally transferred to Austria only in 1921. While drawing on Hungarian sources, GDP for Burgenland was estimated in the same manner as for the other Austrian regions and population adjusted. Styria lost about one-third of its pre-war population and more than a quarter of its territory to Yugoslavia. The Tyrol's provinces of South Tyrol and Trentino were ceded to Italy, implying a reduction to less than half of its pre-war area size and less than 28 per cent of its pre-war population, respectively.
7 The sources for the underlying price data are SJB (1872–1884), ÖSH (1883–1916), Sandgruber (1978), Mühlpeck et al. (1979) and Schulze (1996).
8 This assumption is reasonable: further analysis of the data shows that it is not changes in intra-sector output per worker differentials that drive regional inequality, but rather differences in the sectoral composition of output.
9 Seidel et al. (1966) provide a regional breakdown of Austrian GDP for 1952, 1957, 1961 and 1964, albeit without distinction between sectors. Their aggregate and regional GDP reconstructions depart widely from the evidence in WIFO (1965) and, more significantly, the WIFO regional data for 1961–1964. Though theirs is a WIFO study too, their initial regional approximations have not been included in the updated WIFO files on regional product for 1961–2010 (see note 10), and have therefore not been used here. However, apart from level differences, using the regional product shares of Seidel et al. (1966) would make no material difference to the argument put forward here.
10 The files made available by WIFO include: (a) for 1961–1990, WIFO (2013); and (b) for 2000–2010, Statistik Austria (2012). For 2014, the source is Statistik Austria (2015b).

11 Cf. note 4. Even allowing for large margins of error, the data suggest that the coefficient of variation for 1870 (corresponding with CV II) would not be significantly above or below 0.30, i.e. the level observed for the series that subsumes Vienna under Lower Austria (CV).

12 Cf. note 16.

13 There is no evidence of sigma-convergence across the regions of Imperial Austria over 1870–1910 and the population-weighted coefficients of variation across all 22 Habsburg regions, including Hungary, though fluctuating over time, offer only weak support for an empire-wide decline in income dispersion.

14 Cf. Abramovitz (1986) on catch-up growth and threshold levels of social capabilities that must have been attained in order to be able to exploit a country's (or region's) catch-up potential.

15 Note that the representation of beta-convergence is based upon the 1870 regional income distribution that treats Lower Austria and Vienna separately. However, treating them as one would make no material difference (the rate would decline from 0.68 to 0.58).

16 New approximations of regional average years of schooling were derived using regional enrolment data and the coefficients of a regression of aggregate years of schooling on aggregate lagged enrolment (for underlying data, see Schulze and Fernandes 2009).

17 Seidel et al. (1966: 58) report even lower income shares of Lower Austria and Vienna in 1952 than Table 3.1.2 documents for 1950.

18 This is not to imply that Austria (in its modern borders) grew subsequently as fast in terms of GDP, GDP per capita or GDP per worker as her northern German neighbour. On all three measures, Austria performed markedly less well than Germany over the period 1870–1913. Austria's real GDP per capita grew by 1 per cent per annum over the period compared to 1.6 per cent for Germany (for sources, see Tables 3.1.1 and 3.1.A.1; on the German comparison, see Schulze 2007b).

19 Note that the regional dispersion in the employment share of industry declined throughout the late nineteenth century.

20 The evidence on intra-empire nationalism and asymmetric market integration along ethnolinguistic lines is consistent with the argument of relatively high levels of integration within the post-1918 boundaries of modern Austria, whose population composition was far more homogenous than that of the empire as a whole (Schulze and Wolf 2012).

21 Bohemia accounted for most of Imperial Austria's manufacturing output in absolute but not per capita terms (see Klein et al. 2017: Table 4.6).

22 Nitsch (2003: Table 2) reports a threefold increase in Vienna's population for the same period. The difference is due to this chapter's use of standardized population figures based on a consistent and current definition of city area as in Statistik Austria (2014). The differences for the years after 1870 are minor.

23 Vienna's population loss between 1910 and 1923 (164,900 people) was driven by both a sharp fall in fertility (generation renewal −103,900) and outmigration (−61,000). By 1934, the population had increased again by a modest 17,200 due to renewed inward migration that just about outstripped a still negative balance of births (−87,000); this left the population total still 7 per cent below its pre-war level. Spanning across the period of Austria's annexation by Nazi Germany and the Second World War, Vienna's historically largest population loss of almost 320,000 people was recorded between the census years 1934 and 1951. After 1938, 130,000 Viennese Jews were forced to emigrate, and of the 65,000 who had remained in the city until 1942, only 2,000 survived deportation and the Holocaust (Statistik Austria 2014, 2015c; Jewish Virtual Library n.d.).

24 In 2000 (2010), Vienna accounted for 29 per cent (31 per cent) of Austria's total urban population (Statistik Austria 2014; WKO n.d.).

25 The following discussion draws on Butschek (2011: 426–34, 481–2).

26 Mayerhofer (2006) argues that the post-1989 East's opening up and the intensification of cross-border trade and capital flows were not associated with significant changes

in Austrian regions' locational advantage. Drawing on municipality-level data for 1975–2002, Brülhart et al. (2012) find that while post-1990 trade liberalization had a statistically significant positive effect on nominal wages and employment (relative to areas in Austria's interior) within a narrow 25 km band along the country's borders with previously communist economies, no statistically significant impact has been identified beyond a distance of 50 km. This suggests a severely limited spatial reach of trade liberalization effects.

27 For example, the large net outflows for Vienna, Vorarlberg, Salzburg and Tyrol imply that the incomes of those who work there but are resident in other regions are larger than the incomes of those who are resident in these four regions but work elsewhere. The opposite holds for the net inflow regions. The main net beneficiaries are Burgenland and Lower Austria in proximity to Vienna. Note that outflows and inflows are not evenly matched – this reflects the overall larger number of *in*-commuters and seasonal workers from other regions or countries than *out*-commuters and resident Austrians working in neighbouring foreign countries. Region variations in per capita net tax and social security burdens, i.e. the difference between primary and disposable income, are typically an outcome of regionally differential income distributions and those factors that influence them (e.g. employment and unemployment rates, employment status, sector structure or the proportion of pension recipients) (WKO Tirol 2014: 9, 16–17).

28 For example, there was no further significant decline in the regional dispersion of output per worker between 2000 and 2010, and the main beneficiaries in terms of a low net tax and social security burden (Burgenland, Carinthia, Styria) were the regions characterized by the lowest overall productivity levels and the highest agricultural employment shares.

29 The (unweighted) coefficient of variation of regional GDP per worker declined from .29 (1870) and .22 (1934) to .09 in 2000 and 2010 (for sources, see Tables 3.1.1 and 3.1.A.1).

References

Abramovitz, M. (1986) 'Catching up, forging ahead and falling behind', *Journal of Economic History*, Vol. 46 (2): 385–406.

Barro, R. and Sala-i-Martin, X. (1991) 'Convergence across states and regions', *Brookings Papers on Economic Activity*, Vol. 1991 (1): 107–82.

Brülhart, M., Carrère, C. and Trionfetti, F. (2012) 'How wages and employment adjust to trade liberalization: quasi-experimental evidence from Austria', *Journal of International Economics*, Vol. 86 (1): 68–81.

Butschek, F. (2011) *Österreichische Wirtschaftsgeschichte: Von der Antike bis zur Gegenwart*, Vienna: Böhlau.

Butschek, F. and Průcha, V. (1996) 'Einkommensniveau und Wirtschaftsstruktur in der Zwischenkriegszeit', in A. Teichova and H. Matis (eds), *Österreich und die Tschechoslowakei 1918–1938*, Vienna: Böhlau, pp. 309–28.

Eddie, S. (1989) 'Economic policy and economic development in Austria-Hungary, 1867–1913', in P. Mathias and S. Pollard (ed.), *The Cambridge Economic History of Europe, Vol. 8*, Cambridge: Cambridge University Press, pp. 814–86.

Geary, F. and Stark, T. (2002) 'Examining Ireland's post-famine economic growth performance', *The Economic Journal*, Vol. 112 (482): 919–35.

Good, D.F. (1984) *The Economic Rise of the Habsburg Empire, 1750–1914*, Berkeley, CA: University of California Press.

Jewish Virtual Library (n.d.) *Virtual Jewish World: Vienna, Austria*, available at: www.jewishvirtuallibrary.org/jsource/vjw/Vienna.html (accessed 15 April 2016).

Klein, A., Schulze, M.S. and Vonyó, T. (2017) 'How peripheral was the periphery? Industrialisation in East-Central Europe since 1870', in K.H. O'Rourke and J.G. Williamson (eds), *Industrialization in the Global Periphery since 1871*, Oxford: Oxford University Press, pp. 63–90.

Komlos, J. (1983) *The Habsburg Monarchy as a Customs Union: Economic Development in Austria-Hungary in the Nineteenth Century*, Princeton, NJ: Princeton University Press.

Krugman, P. (1991) *Geography and Trade*, Cambridge, MA: MIT Press.

Mayerhofer, P. (2006) 'Veränderte Lagegunst durch die Ostöffnung?', *WIFO Monatsberichte*, No. 3: 173–87.

Mühlpeck, V., Sandgruber, R. and Woitek, H. (1979) 'Index der Verbraucherpreise 1800–1914', in *Geschichte der amtlichen Statistik in Österreich 1829–1979*, Vienna: Österreichisches Statistisches Zentralamt.

Nitsch, V. (2003) 'Does history matter for urban primacy? The case of Vienna', *Regional Science and Urban Economics*, Vol. 33 (4): 401–8.

ÖSH (1883–1916) *Österreichisches Statistisches Handbuch, 1882–1914*, Vienna: K.k. Statistische Central-Commission.

Österreichisches Statistisches Zentralamt (1963–1964) "Census 1961". *Volkszählungsergebnisse 1961*, Heft 2 to Heft 11, Vienna.

Pollard, S. (1986) *Peaceful Conquest: The Industrialization of Europe, 1760–1970*, Oxford: Oxford University Press.

Resch, A. and Sládek, Z. (1996) 'Integrations- und Desintegrationstendenzen. Die Handelsbeziehungen 1921–1937', in A. Teichova and H. Matis (eds), *Österreich und die Tschechoslowakei 1918–1938*, Vienna: Böhlau, pp. 255–308.

Sala-i-Martin, X. (1996) 'Regional cohesion: evidence and theories of regional growth and convergence', *European Economic Review*, Vol. 40 (6): 1325–52.

Sandgruber, R. (1978) *Österreichische Agrarstatistik 1750–1918*, Munich: Oldenbourg.

Sandgruber, R. (1995) *Ökonomie und Politik. Österreichische Wirtschaftsgeschichte vom Mittelalter bis zur Gegenwart*, Vienna: Ueberreuther.

Schulze, M.S. (1996) *Engineering and Economic Growth: The Development of Austria-Hungary's Machine-Building Industry in the Late Nineteenth Century*, Frankfurt: Peter Lang.

Schulze, M.S. (2000) 'Patterns of growth and stagnation in the late nineteenth century Habsburg economy', *European Review of Economic History*, Vol. 4 (3): 311–40.

Schulze, M.S. (2007a) 'Regional income dispersion and market potential in the late nineteenth century Habsburg Empire', LSE Working Papers in Economic History, No. 106.

Schulze, M.S. (2007b) 'Origins of catch-up failure: comparative productivity growth in the Habsburg Empire, 1870–1910', *European Review of Economic History*, Vol. 11 (2): 189–218.

Schulze, M.S. and Fernandes, F.T. (2009) 'Human capital formation in Austria-Hungary and Germany: time series estimates of educational attainment, 1860–1910', in K. Halmos et al. (eds), *A felhalmozás Míve. Történeti Tanulmányok Kövér György Tiszteletére*, Budapest: Századvég Kiadó, pp. 275–89.

Schulze, M.S. and Wolf, N. (2012) 'Economic nationalism and economic integration: the Austro-Hungarian Empire in the late nineteenth century', *Economic History Review*, Vol. 65 (2): 652–73.

Seidel, H., Butschek, F. and Kausel, A. (1966) *Die regionale Dynamik der österreichischen Wirtschaft*, Vienna: Österreichisches Institut für Wirtschaftsforschung.

SHB (1950, 1961) *Statistisches Handbuch für die Republik Österreich*, Vienna: Österreichisches Statistisches Zentralamt.

SJB (1872–1884) *Statistisches Jahrbuch der österreichischen Monarchie, 1870–1882*, Vienna: K.k. Statistische Central-Commission.

Statistik Austria (2012) 'Bruttowertschöpfung zu Herstellungspreisen nach Wirtschaftsbereichen und Bundesländern', *Regionale Gesamtrechnungen* [Erstellt am 18.12.2012], Vienna, file provided by WIFO, personal communication (December 2013).

Statistik Austria (2014) *Statistisches Jahrbuch 2015*, Vienna.

Statistik Austria (2015a) 'Erwerbstätige nach Wirtschaftsbereichen und Bundesländern', *Regionale Gesamtrechnungen* [Erstellt am 14.12.2015], Vienna.

Statistik Austria (2015b) 'Bruttowertschöpfung zu Herstellungspreisen nach Wirtschaftsbereichen und Bundesländern', *Regionale Gesamtrechnungen* [Erstellt am 14.12.2015], Vienna.

Statistik Austria (2015c) *Statistisches Jahrbuch 2016*, Vienna.

Statistik des Bundesstaates Österreich (1935) *Ergebnisse der österreichischen Volkszählung vom 22. März 1934*, Heft 2 to Heft 11, Vienna.

WIFO (1965) 'Österreichs Volkseinkommen 1913 bis 1963', *Monatsberichte des Österreichischen Instituts für Wirtschaftsforschung*, 14, Sonderheft, Vienna.

WIFO (2013) 'Beitrag zum BIP in laufenden Preisen (Mio. ATS)', Vienna, file provided by WIFO, personal communication (December 2013).

Williamson, J.G. (1965) 'Regional inequality and the process of national development', *Economic Development and Cultural Change*, Vol. 13 (4): 1–84.

WKO (n.d.) *Länderprofil Österreich*, available at: http://wko.at/statistik/laenderprofile/lp-oesterreich.pdf (accessed 11 April 2016).

WKO Tirol (2014) *Österreichs Bundesländer im Profil*, Innsbruck: Wirtschaftskammer Tirol.

Young, A.T., Higgins, M.J. and Levy, D. (2008) 'Sigma convergence versus beta convergence: evidence from U.S. county-level data', *Journal of Money, Credit and Banking*, Vol. 40 (5): 1083–93.

3.2 Changing spatial inequality in a divided country

Belgium, 1896–2010

Erik Buyst[1]

1. Introduction

During the last decades or so, the annual publication of regional accounts in Belgium has become something of a special event. Although the database contains many figures at various NUTS levels, the public arena is usually focused on one basic question: Which of the country's three regions performed best in terms of economic growth – the northern Dutch-speaking part (Flanders), the southern French-speaking part (Wallonia) or the bilingual area of Brussels? To add even more flavour to the competition, some commentators give the regional growth figures an explicit political turn by presenting them as indicators of the relative success or failure of the economic policies of the respective regional governments.

But the interregional rivalry does not stop there. Similar to countries such as Spain or the UK, the policies of the federal government are also put under scrutiny. Do they favour a certain region at the detriment of another one? Since the 1970s, mistrust in the Belgian federal government, together with socio-linguistic quarrels, has provoked a gradual devolution of economic and other important competences from the federal to the regional level, a process that continues until today.

Although being a small country, Belgium has always been characterized by large spatial inequality. Perhaps because of the persistence of the problem, there is neither among policymakers nor researchers a consensus on the necessity or effectiveness of public transfers of resources from rich to poor regions (e.g. Capron 2007 versus Persyn 2010).

Despite these controversies, few data are available to analyze the long-term development of spatial inequality in Belgium. Official regional and provincial GDP figures are available from 1955 onwards, but we will demonstrate that until the 1990s, these data are of doubtful quality. For an overview of the whole of the twentieth century, we depend on provincial employment data. Olyslager (1947) pioneered this type of research for several manufacturing branches, but it was De Brabander (1981) who presented the first systematic account of the long-run dynamics of provincial employment for all sectors of the Belgian economy.

In this chapter, we add a new perspective by presenting estimates of provincial GDP per capita for certain benchmark years using the method proposed by Geary and Stark (2002). These estimates, covering the period 1896–1991, are linked to the official provincial GDP figures from 1995 onwards. Belgium's nine provinces, the European Union NUTS 2 level, are used as a geographical unit[2] to take a broader and more nuanced view than the traditional Flanders/Wallonia/Brussels controversy. The maps show that the borders of the provinces remained largely unchanged during the period under consideration.

2. Unreliable official provincial GDP data before 1995 ESA?

A major problem concerns the *official* provincial GDP figures that are available from 1955 onwards. At the turn of the century, the introduction of the 1995 ESA gave rise to a major revision of the sources and estimation procedures. The old top-down approach used in the 1979 ESA and before, which per sub-sector distributed Belgian gross value added at factor costs over the nine provinces by applying a broad range of indicators, was abandoned. Instead, a new bottom-up method was launched that usually started from data at the level of the individual company or institution, which should produce more reliable results (INR 2001).

For the overlapping year of 1995, Table 3.2.1 shows the effects of the introduction of new sources and methods on *official* provincial GDP per capita. First, the difference between the two series is often quite substantial: for almost half of the provinces, it reaches more than 10 per cent. Second, the ranking of certain provinces was shaken up. Suddenly, Brabant became by far the richest province at the detriment of Antwerp, and four other provinces won or lost one spot. Although the population-weighted coefficient of variation – an indicator of spatial inequality – only went from 0.73 to 0.67, it is clear that a break of such magnitude impedes any serious analysis of long-term trends. Therefore, we decided to revise the 1979 ESA and older official provincial GDP figures. Then the question becomes: Is the Geary and Stark (GS) method able to replicate the 1995 ESA data?

Table 3.2.1 Relative provincial GDP per head in 1995 (current prices, Belgium = 1), 1979 ESA versus 1995 ESA

	1979 ESA	*1995 ESA*	*Difference (in %)*
Antwerp	1.22	1.17	–4.1
Brabant	1.12	1.40	24.5
West Flanders	1.04	0.91	–12.8
East Flanders	0.94	0.87	–6.9
Hainaut	0.72	0.67	–7.1
Liège	0.88	0.78	–11.1
Limburg	0.99	0.85	–14.0
Luxembourg	0.86	0.81	–6.7
Namur	0.76	0.71	–7.6

Source: Official 1979 ESA: INR (2000). Official 1995 ESA: INR (2001).

Table 3.2.2 compares the official and GS provincial GDP per capita for 2001, the next year in which a population census was organized. The GS ingredients, an employment and relative wage matrix by sector – agriculture, industry, services – and per province, are taken from Belgostat. Most deviations between the two series are very small, and even the somewhat larger ones remain very much in line with those of a similar test reported by Geary and Stark (2002) for England, Northern Ireland, Scotland and Wales. The ranking of the provinces remains intact and the population-weighted coefficient of variation also barely changes. So, we conclude that the GS method is a reliable instrument to estimate provincial GDP per capita in Belgium for the pre-1995 ESA period.

3. Estimating provincial GDP of the 1896–1991 period

Table 3.2.3 provides an overview of the sources used to nurture the GS method in the period between 1896 and 1991. The starting point is the various censuses that give information on employment per sector and per province.

We did not use the population census of 1920, however. In that year, the Belgian economy was still suffering badly from the extensive devastations during the First World War. Using these figures would produce highly distorted results, especially on a provincial level. Moreover, the 1920 total employment figures per sector and per province were far less detailed than those in other censuses. It illustrates not only the post-war dislocation, but also makes it impossible to calculate data that are consistent with the other benchmark years. Even more importantly, no provincial wages are available for 1920.

Concerning employment, it is important to point out that late nineteenth-century Belgium disposed of a very dense railway network. In addition, the government provided cheap railway tickets to workers in order to avoid a rural exodus to the already overcrowded big cities (Mahain 1910). This policy proved a success: until today, Belgium is a country of relatively high rural population densities. The other side of the coin is that by the early twentieth century, mass commuting had

Table 3.2.2 Relative provincial GDP per head in 2001 (current prices, Belgium = 1)

	Official 1995 ESA	*GS*	*Difference (in %)*
Antwerp	1.15	1.11	–3.4
Brabant	1.44	1.44	0.3
West Flanders	0.94	0.91	–2.4
East Flanders	0.87	0.88	1.7
Hainaut	0.66	0.67	1.4
Liège	0.75	0.78	4.8
Limburg	0.84	0.85	1.0
Luxembourg	0.68	0.70	2.5
Namur	0.69	0.72	5.4

Source: Official 1995 ESA: www.belgostat.be, domain 799, table 285. GS: see text.

Table 3.2.3 Overview of sources used, 1896–1991

Census	*Employment*	*Wages*
1896	De Brabander (1981)	Agriculture: MATP (1900) Mining and industry: MIT (1901) Services (transport only): MIT (1901)
1910	De Brabander (1981)	Agriculture: Vliebergh (1911) Mining: Annales des mines (1911) Industry: Extrapolation from 1896 Services: MIT (1901)
1930	Agriculture and services: CDS (1934) Mining and industry: MTPS (1935)	Agriculture: CDS (1939) Mining: Annales des mines (1931) Industry: Extrapolation from 1937 Services: CDS (1940)
1937	De Brabander (1981)	Agriculture: CDS (1939) Mining, industry and services: CDS (1940)
1947	De Brabander (1981)	Agriculture: Ministerie van Landbouw (1948) Mining, industry and services: NIS (1951–1952)
1961	NIS (1965)	Agriculture: Vertriest (1963) Mining: Annales des mines (1962) Industry and services: RMZ (1961)
1970	NIS (1975)	Agriculture: Vertriest et al. (1972) Mining: Annales des mines (1971) Industry and services: RMZ (1970)
1981	NIS (1986)	Agriculture: Landbouw-economisch Instituut (1983) Mining: Annales des mines (1982) Industry and services: RSZ (1981)
1991	Belgostat	Belgostat

become a way of life. So, from a provincial GDP perspective, it is necessary to have employment figures per province where people are working, not where they are living. From 1961 onwards, the censuses fulfil this requirement for all sectors. The earlier censuses contain only mining and industry employment data according to the municipality where people are working. Services sector employment, however, is registered according to the municipality where workers reside.

The censuses of 1896, 1937 and 1947 collected detailed provincial wage data, but not those of 1910 and 1930.[3] For 1910, we extrapolate the provincial wages of the industrial sector in 1896, taking into account shifts in the provincial employment structure (15 sub-sectors) and relative changes in national wages per sub-sector. Concerning 1930, we apply the same method, starting from the 1937 census. Needless to say, the provincial GDP figures per capita of 1910 and 1930 are less reliable than those of the other benchmark years. For the post-1947 period, we usually take the provincial wage statistics as published by the Social Security Agency (e.g. RMZ 1961).

4. Long-term patterns of spatial inequality

What picture emerges from this exercise? Figure 3.2.1 shows the long-term evolution of the population-weighted coefficient of variation of provincial GDP per capita, which can be considered as a proxy of sigma-convergence. The first decades of the twentieth century were characterized by a gradual reduction in spatial inequality, but from 1930 the trend was reversed. In the 1960s, provincial income divergence reached even a somewhat higher level than in

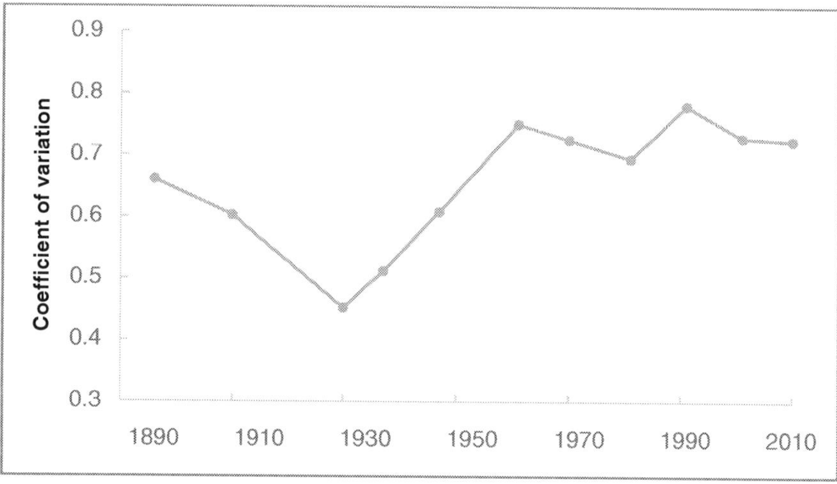

Figure 3.2.1 Sigma-convergence among Belgian provinces, 1896–2010

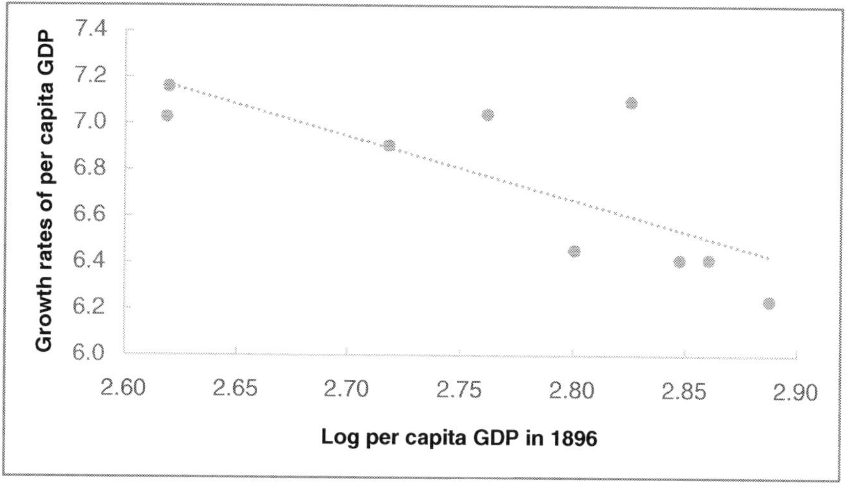

Figure 3.2.2 Beta-convergence among Belgian provinces, 1896–2010

the late nineteenth century. Thereafter, the process of divergence stopped and was followed by a 50-year period in which spatial income inequality remained virtually unchanged.

The absence of sigma-convergence in the long run, however, is not incompatible with the possibility of beta-convergence. Figure 3.2.2 shows that poor provinces in 1896 grew faster during the twentieth century than richer ones. But the implied rate of beta-convergence was a little less than 1 per cent. Although backward provinces grew above average, this was too little to reduce overall dispersion.

Table 3.2.4 demonstrates that the general convergence indicators mask brutal changes on a more detailed level. The ranking of the various provinces in 1896 is completely different from that at the beginning of the twenty-first century. For instance, Hainaut, in 1896 the richest province, had become the poorest one by 2010. This is, of course, the most extreme case, but with few exceptions it can be stated that the relatively poor provinces at the beginning of the period became the richer ones 110 years later, and vice versa. But there is also some stability in the shake-up: when Brabant and Antwerp became the richest provinces in 1930, they never gave up that position in the later decades.

Not surprisingly, the impressive changes in relative per capita income coincided with dramatic shifts in the spatial localization of economic activity (see Table 3.2.5). Between 1896 and 2010, the share of Hainaut in Belgian GDP fell by almost two-thirds, while that of Liège, Luxembourg and Namur halved. By contrast, the part of Limburg doubled, and that of Antwerp and Brabant increased by somewhat more than 50 per cent. At the same time, the spatial concentration of economic activity went up considerably. In 1896, the province with the largest share accounted for 21 per cent of Belgian GDP; in 2010, it had risen to 33 per cent. A similar tendency appears when looking at the three provinces with the largest shares: in 1896, they were responsible for 56 per cent of Belgian GDP; 110 years later, they controlled 64 per cent. These changes were not only caused by differences in economic growth, but by differentials in population development

Table 3.2.4 Relative regional GDP per head, 1896–2010 (current prices, Belgium = 1)

	1896	*1910*	*1930*	*1937*	*1947*	*1961*	*1970*	*1981*	*1991*	*2001*	*2010*
Antwerp	0.93	1.03	1.16	1.15	1.12	1.08	1.12	1.16	1.11	1.15	1.15
Brabant	1.08	1.12	1.25	1.26	1.26	1.42	1.37	1.33	1.40	1.44	1.41
West Flanders	0.67	0.69	0.77	0.78	0.75	0.79	0.87	0.95	0.94	0.94	0.94
East Flanders	0.84	0.82	0.86	0.86	0.85	0.79	0.82	0.79	0.88	0.87	0.90
Hainaut	1.24	1.17	0.96	0.96	0.97	0.84	0.80	0.77	0.71	0.66	0.65
Liège	1.17	1.18	1.11	1.09	1.10	1.06	1.00	0.97	0.81	0.75	0.74
Limburg	0.67	0.64	0.62	0.64	0.69	0.66	0.74	0.81	0.86	0.84	0.82
Luxembourg	1.02	0.87	0.62	0.62	0.75	0.68	0.63	0.69	0.77	0.68	0.67
Namur	1.13	1.05	0.80	0.81	0.87	0.83	0.77	0.76	0.74	0.69	0.72

Source: For 1896–1991: GS-method (see text). For 2001–2010: www.belgostat.be, domain 799, table 285 and domain 812, table 115.

Table 3.2.5 The share of the provinces in Belgian GDP, 1896–2010 (per cent)

	1896	*1910*	*1930*	*1937*	*1947*	*1961*	*1970*	*1981*	*1991*	*2001*	*2010*
Antwerp	11.2	13.5	16.9	17.0	16.8	17.0	17.8	18.4	17.9	18.5	18.5
Brabant	20.1	22.2	26.0	26.6	26.6	30.7	30.9	30.0	31.4	32.9	33.4
West Flanders	8.1	8.1	8.6	8.9	8.8	9.2	9.5	10.4	10.4	10.3	10.0
East Flanders	13.0	12.4	12.2	12.2	12.2	10.9	11.2	10.6	11.7	11.5	11.9
Hainaut	21.1	19.4	15.0	14.4	13.9	11.5	10.9	10.2	9.1	8.2	7.8
Liège	14.7	14.2	13.3	12.7	12.4	11.6	10.4	9.8	8.2	7.4	7.3
Limburg	2.4	2.4	2.8	3.1	3.7	4.2	5.0	5.9	6.5	6.5	6.3
Luxembourg	3.4	2.7	1.7	1.6	1.9	1.6	1.4	1.6	1.8	1.7	1.7
Namur	6.0	5.1	3.5	3.5	3.6	3.3	3.0	3.1	3.1	3.0	3.1

Source: For 1896–1991: GS method (see text). For 2001–2010: www.belgostat.be, domain 799, table 285 and domain 812, table 115.

as well. Rising provinces became simultaneously richer and more populated. How can we explain these remarkable shifts?

5. The resource-based economy of the late nineteenth and early twentieth centuries

As was often the case in (late) nineteenth-century Europe, the localization of coal mines largely determined where modern industrial centres would flourish (Pollard 1982). Map 3.2.1 demonstrates that Belgium was certainly no exception to this rule. The provinces with the highest per capita GDP in 1896, Hainaut and Liège, fitted very closely the areas containing rich coal deposits. The abundance of relatively cheap energy attracted iron and steel plants, machine-building facilities and glass industries. As a result, the area belonged to one of the most important manufacturing centres of nineteenth- and early twentieth-century Europe (Broadberry et al. 2010). But resources and technical skills do not suffice. A small country is only able to grow in a sustained way if entrepreneurs can sell their products abroad in large quantities. And Walloon business people succeeded in doing so on a remarkable scale. They participated vigorously in the first global economy and exported, for instance, locomotives and other transport equipment to all corners of the world (Wautelet 1995).

The densely populated north-west of Belgium, however, was an example of failed mechanization. In the mid-nineteenth century, the large export-oriented Flemish rural linen industry did not manage to transform itself from traditional hand spinning and weaving into modern factory production. Blown away by British competition, the age-old cottage industry collapsed. As a result, the densely populated countryside of East and West Flanders suffered from massive structural underemployment for decades to come. Emigration to Wallonia, France and the New World did happen, but many preferred to stay in their impoverished small towns. They found poorly paid jobs in sweatshops producing baskets, brooms, clogs, shoes and other low-value-added goods (Verhaegen 1961).

Brabant, located in the middle of the country, took an intermediary position between 'poor Flanders', on the one hand, and the thriving Walloon manufacturing belt, on the other. It benefited strongly from the presence of Brussels. The rapidly growing capital city provided an interesting market for horticulture, luxury industries – paper and printing, haute couture, specialized food processing – and tertiary activities (Bogaert-Damin and Marechal 1978).

Table 3.2.4 indicates that Hainaut's leadership in GDP per head did not last for long. Already in the first decade of the twentieth century, the province suffered from a relative decline. Exhaustion of the coal mines led to rising costs and stagnating production. It necessitated increasing imports of coal from overseas, which stimulated the construction of new coke smelting plants along Belgium's waterway system. The by-products of these facilities – gas, tar, ammonium, benzene, etc. – often attracted chemical and other industries. Especially the canal linking the river Scheldt with Brussels and Charleroi developed into a highly diversified manufacturing axis (Olyslager 1947).

The port of Antwerp benefited from the rising imports of coal as well. But the volume of trans-shipment was boosted even more by Antwerp's excellent railway connections with the rapidly growing Ruhr area in Germany. The employment of dock workers grew vigorously together with that of port-related industries – food processing and ship repair – and services such as logistics, wholesale and finance (Loyen et al. 2003).

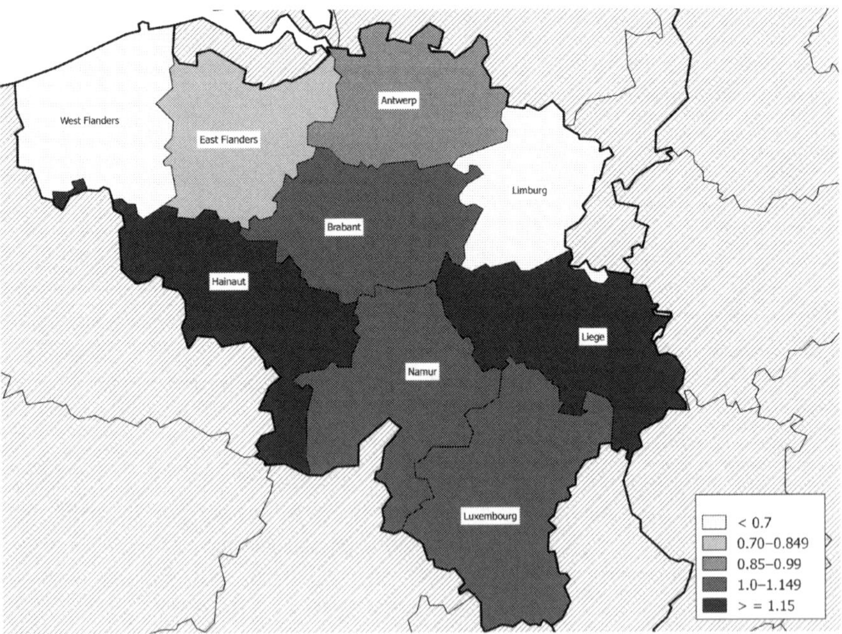

Map 3.2.1 Relative regional GDP per capita in 1896 (current prices, Belgium = 1)

Source: Table 3.2.4.

6. The interwar period and the 1950s: decline of the resource-based economy

The spatial tendencies that were already visible during the first decade of the twentieth century continued during the interwar period. As the exhaustion problems in coal mining got worse, Hainaut's relative position weakened further. Table 3.2.4 shows that its GDP per capita even fell below the national average. Liège, the other coal-mining province, could resist the downward pressure somewhat better as its economy was more diversified. The chill winds of interwar protectionism and import substitution dealt another blow to Wallonia's economic structure. Exports of locomotives and rolling stock took a hit, so that the area became mainly an exporter of semi-finished steel and metal goods (Maizels 1963).

The growing structural difficulties in the Walloon manufacturing belt had serious consequences for neighbouring Luxembourg and Namur. In the late nineteenth century, these sparsely populated provinces were characterized by high wages. It was the only way to prevent workers from moving to neighbouring Charleroi or Liège. As the employment opportunities in these cities dried up during the interwar period, the relative wages in Luxembourg and Namur fell back considerably (MATP 1900; MIT 1901; CDS 1939, 1940). Moreover, the absence of even medium-sized cities deprived both rural provinces from the stimulus given by the continuously expanding services sector (De Brabander 1981).

The opposite was true for the provinces of Brabant and Antwerp. Their big cities acted as magnets for all kinds of tertiary activities. Moreover, the port of Antwerp managed to attract new promising industries, such as the production of telephone equipment (Bell Telephone), photographic paper and car assembly (e.g. Ford and General Motors). The discovery of rich copper, radium and other deposits in the Belgian Congo gave rise to a rapidly expanding non-ferrous metals industry (e.g. Métallurgique de Hoboken). In Brabant, the canal zone linking the port of Antwerp with Brussels kept on expanding, especially in the field of metal processing (Baudhuin 1946; Buyst and Lefebvre 2007). Not surprisingly, the provinces of Brabant and Antwerp became the richest areas in per capita income during the interwar period.

In the early twentieth century, substantial coal deposits were discovered in Limburg, until then a poor and peripheral province in the north-eastern corner of Belgium. In the 1920s and 1930s, coal production took off, but Table 3.2.4 shows that the impact on Limburg's relative economic performance was negligible. The rise of coal mining indeed developed few linkages with the rest of the Limburg economy (Hogg 1986). In sharp contrast to the Walloon coal-mining areas a century earlier, no heavy manufacturing or related sectors emerged. The Dutch-speaking province of Limburg remained a supplier of energy mainly to the French-speaking industrial basin of Liège. In a linguistically divided country, this peculiar situation created political tensions. Some Flemish academics and policymakers blamed the Belgian government and the (French-speaking) steel barons for lack of initiative (e.g. Pinxten 1939).

Table 3.2.4 shows that the continuous relative decline of Hainaut and Liège came to a sudden standstill between 1937 and 1947. Was there a revival of the old resource-based model (see Map 3.2.2)? Not really. The post-war reconstruction effort in Belgium and elsewhere in Europe provided an artificial stimulus to the demand for coal, steel, glass and cement, which fitted almost perfectly the production structure of the Walloon manufacturing belt (Baudhuin 1958). By the late 1940s, however, these extraordinary favourable conditions were fading away and the old structural problems re-emerged.

In the late 1950s, the breakthrough of oil as a major source of energy dealt a heavy blow to the resource-based economy. Dozens of mines had to be closed down, and as the Walloon manufacturing belt was hit disproportionally hard, frustration grew. Many intellectuals and labour unionists in Wallonia felt abandoned by the Belgian establishment. They demanded economic autonomy for the Walloon provinces so that they could develop their own strategies to tackle the severe restructuring problems (Bismans 1992).

7. The emergence of regional policies: solution or failure?

Table 3.2.4 shows that Hainaut and Liège were not the only provinces that faced structural difficulties. In the 1950s, densely populated East and West Flanders

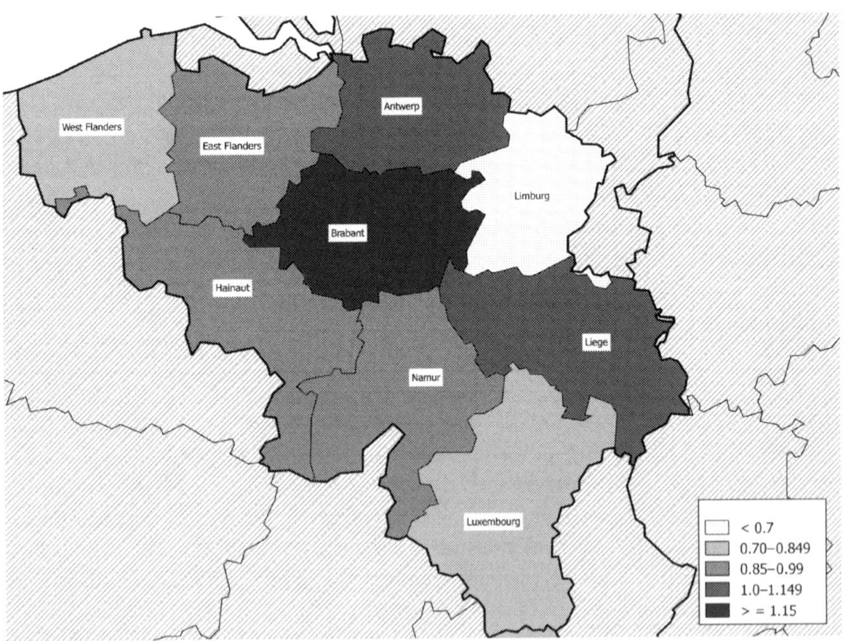

Map 3.2.2 Relative regional GDP per capita in 1947 (current prices, Belgium = 1)

Source: Table 3.2.4.

also boasted low per capita income figures. They suffered from relatively high unemployment rates as a result of the decline of agriculture and of labour-intensive industries such as textiles, shoemaking and clothing (Leroy 1962; De Brabander 1981).

The only big winner was Brabant. In a highly centralized country, the expansion of the welfare state caused public and semi-public sector employment in Brussels to grow rapidly. Trade, finance and other commercial services expanded vigorously as well, and more than compensated the relative deindustrialization of the capital city (Kirschen 1962). Consequently, commuting to Brussels became a way of life for many workers living in Flanders, and increasingly so in Wallonia. But the perceived over-concentration of economic activity in Brussels also provoked criticism that the capital city was draining resources away from the rest of the country (Verheirstraeten 1970).

In 1959, the government responded to the spatial inequality problems by launching the so-called expansion laws, the Belgian variant of regional policy. Various forms of tax incentives and the development of well-equipped industrial sites should lure (foreign) investments to areas struck by unemployment or other structural difficulties, but to little avail for Hainaut and Liège: the historically high wages prevailing in coal mining had pushed up labour costs in other industries too. It proved very difficult to adjust these wages after the collapse of coal mining due to labour market rigidities. The resulting competitiveness problem and militant labour unions often deterred potential (foreign) investors (Baudhuin 1970; De Grauwe 1980; Brion and Moreau 1998).

If the breakthrough of oil was a nightmare for the southern provinces, then the opposite was true for the north. In the 1960s and early 1970s, massive transshipments of the 'new black gold' attracted oil refineries and petrochemical plants to the Flemish ports. Moreover, the area benefited strongly from the process of European economic integration. After the Treaty of Rome (1957), many multinational firms were looking for locations to set up additional production facilities in the newly formed EEC. They often settled in the northern provinces, with their relatively low wages, and easy access to the sea and to a densely populated hinterland. As a result, metal processing and the production of consumer durables expanded rapidly. It more than compensated for the decline in textiles, clothing and – in Limburg – coal mining (Van der Wee 1997).

The oil shocks of the 1970s and their aftermath again hit southern Belgium particularly hard. The emergence of low-cost producers in newly industrialized countries and worldwide overcapacity forced Wallonia's important steel industry through a phase of radical downsizing (Nagels 2002). In contrast with, for example, Glasgow or Bilbao, reconversion to commercial tertiary activities made very little headway. Consequently, high unemployment rates pushed the provinces of Hainaut and Liège deeper into the economic mire. Massive subsidies since the 1980s, also from EU funds, could not prevent Hainaut becoming Belgium's poorest province. One reason is that the Belgian system of national wage bargaining became more and more rigid over time, and ultimately made regional wage rate divergence virtually impossible. In the context of a declining relative labour

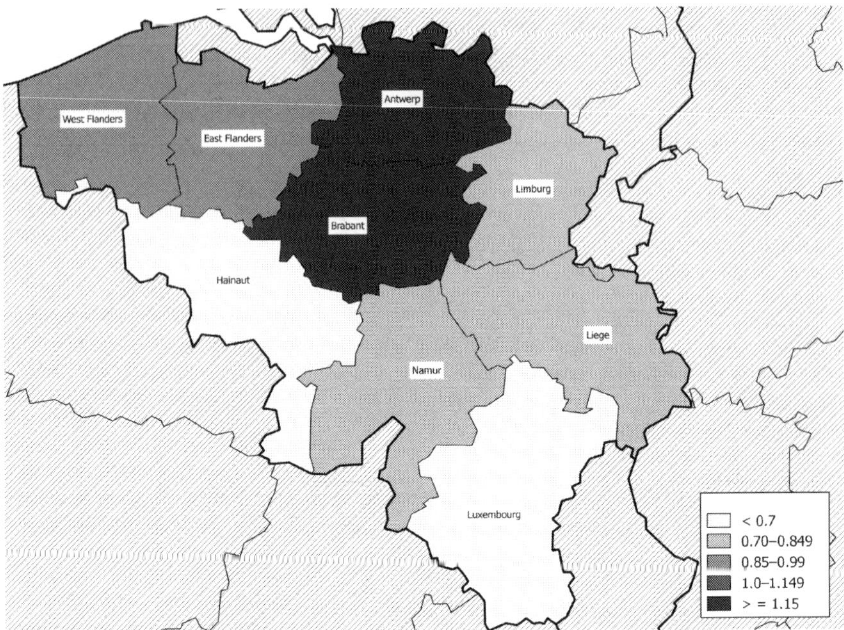

Map 3.2.3 Relative regional GDP per capita in 2010 (current prices, Belgium = 1)

Source: www.belgostat.be, domain 812, table 115.

productivity performance, it undermined further the area's competitive position (Estevão 2003; Bassilière et al. 2008).

Belgium's northern provinces also experienced tough times during the late 1970s and early 1980s. The traditional textile and clothing industries and shipbuilding literally disappeared from the economic scene. But afterwards, the area managed to take part in a general European recovery. Antwerp became one of the world's major chemical clusters. The textile and non-ferrous metals industries found new niche markets, such as carpets, protective clothing, recycling and composite materials (Loyen et al. 2003).

Another important development was the revival of the process of European integration from the mid-1980s onwards. Brussels, the seat of the European Commission and the European Council, positioned itself more and more as 'the capital of Europe'. In doing so, Brussels became a magnet for European headquarters of many multinational companies. This stimulated other high-value-added services, such as finance, law firms and consultancy – including lobbying, etc. (see Table 3.2.4). Northern Belgium participated in the bonanza by attracting several distribution centres of multinational companies (Buyst 1997).

Figure 3.2.1 shows that regional policies – first by the Belgian government, and from the mid-1980s increasingly by European funds – did not succeed in favouring convergence. The sustained economic gap also generated serious political difficulties as the linguistic border became more or less the dividing line between relatively successful and declining areas (see Map 3.2.3). Consequently, cultural-linguistic quarrels easily mixed up with social-economic frustration (Buyst 2011). Walloon public opinion blamed the central government for neglecting its vital economic interests (Yerna 1989). And in Flanders, complaints rose that the central government's massive subsidies only went to agonizing companies and other bottomless pits (Heremans 1983).

To accommodate for the mounting political tensions between the two linguistic groups and to allow for different social-economic strategies in both areas, the 1980 reform of the Belgian state transferred some economic competences to the newly established Flemish and Walloon regions. In subsequent state reforms, the Brussels region became operational (1989), and ever-more economic and other competences were devolved to the regions.

8. Conclusion

In this contribution, we provide a long-term view on the evolution of spatial inequality in Belgium. We demonstrated that the *official* provincial GDP estimates available from 1955 until the 1990s are of doubtful quality. The problem was only resolved with the introduction of new sources and methods when the 1995 ESA framework became operational. Therefore, we produced a new database of provincial GDP per capita for the period 1896–1991 that links up with the official 1995 ESA figures.

The data reveal dramatic changes in the relative position of the various provinces. Hainaut boasted the highest per capita income in 1896 but entered the twenty-first century as the poorest one. Conversely, the relatively poor provinces in the late nineteenth century often became the richer ones 110 years later. An important cause of the reversal of fortune was the demise of the resource-based economy. At the end of the nineteenth century, coal mining still largely determined the location of energy-intensive industries such as steel, glass and machine-building. But in the following decades, this model came under serious pressure. Exhaustion became a major issue for the Walloon coal mines, and the successful exports of locomotives and rolling stock proved very vulnerable to interwar protectionism. The relatively poor northern provinces, on the other hand, started capitalizing on their easy access to the sea. Growing imports of coal from overseas and of copper from the Belgian Congo gave rise to new manufacturing plants in the ports and along major waterways.

The breakthrough of oil in the 1950s accelerated the decline of Wallonia's resource-based economy. After a long death struggle, all coal mines were eventually closed down. In the 1980s, the southern provinces were hit again by a substantial downsizing of the steel industry and related sectors. Many old industrial areas in the Western world shared a similar fate, but in the Walloon case rigid labour costs stifled most attempts at reconversion.

Most northern provinces, however, benefited from the massive shift of coal to oil as the Flemish ports became focal points of refining and petrochemicals. In the

1960s and early 1970s, the area attracted large flows of foreign direct investment, which gave another boost to the modernization of its industrial structure. In more recent times, the setting up of several distribution centres of multinational companies further strengthened its transit function.

Brabant, located in the middle of the country, took full advantage of the continuous economic expansion of Brussels. In the decades following the Second World War, the city and its surroundings benefited from the rapidly growing Belgian state bureaucracy and related sectors. From the mid-1980s, Brussels managed to profile itself as 'the capital of Europe', and in that role it managed to attract many high-value-added services.

As the linguistic border became more or less the dividing line between relatively successful and declining provinces, social-economic frustration easily fuelled political and cultural antagonisms. To alleviate the tensions between the two linguistic groups, the 1980 reform of the Belgian state devolved some economic competences to the newly established Flemish and Walloon regions. It was the first in a series of state reforms continuing until today that transferred evermore powers to the regional level.

Notes

1 The chapter benefited from comments during conferences and workshops at Warwick, Florence, Colmenarejo, Barcelona, Utrecht and Berlin. We thank Roel Helgers and HISGIS for their help with the historical maps.
2 In 1995, the province of Brabant was split up in Flemish Brabant, Walloon Brabant and Brussels-Capital Region. In order to preserve consistency over time, we present figures after 1995 that add up the results of the three new entities.
3 A more elaborate discussion on the wage data of 1896, 1937 and 1947 is found in Buyst (2010).

References

Annales des mines de Belgique, 1896–1994.
Bassilière, D. et al. (2008) 'Vingt-cinq ans d'évolutions régionales. Un aperçu au départ de la base de données du modèle HERMREG', Planning Paper, No. 104, Bureau fédéral du Plan, Brussels: 37–8.
Baudhuin, F. (1946) *Histoire économique de la Belgique 1914–1939*, Vol. 2, Brussels: Bruylant.
Baudhuin, F. (1958) *Histoire économique de la Belgique 1945–1956*, Vol. 3, Brussels: Bruylant.
Baudhuin, F. (1970) *Histoire économique de la Belgique 1957–1968*, Vol. 4, Brussels: Bruylant.
Bismans, F. (1992) *Croissance et regulation: La Belgique 1944–1974*, Brussels: Académie royale de Belgique.
Bogaert-Damin, A.-M. and Marechal, L. (1978) *Bruxelles: développement de l'ensemble urbain 1846–1961*, Namur: Presses Universitaires.
Brion, R. and Moreau, J.-L. (1998) *La Société Générale de Belgique 1822–1997*, Antwerp: Fonds Mercator.

Broadberry, S., Federico, G. and Klein, A. (2010) 'Sectoral developments, 1870–1914', in S. Broadberry and K. O'Rourke (eds), *Cambridge Economic History of Modern Europe*, Cambridge: Cambridge University Press, pp. 59–83.

Buyst, E. (1997) 'The decline and rise of a small open economy: the case of Belgium (1974–1990)', in H. Van der Wee and J. Blomme (eds), *The Economic Development of Belgium since 1870*, Cheltenham: Edward Elgar, pp. 67–76.

Buyst, E. (2010) 'Reversal of fortune in a small, open economy: regional GDP in Belgium, 1896–2000', *Rivista di Storia Economica*, Vol. 26 (1): 75–92.

Buyst, E. (2011) 'Economic aspects of the nationality problem in nineteenth- and twentieth-century Belgium', in A. Teichova, H. Matis and J. Pátek (eds), *Economic Change and the National Question in Twentieth-Century Europe*, Cambridge: Cambridge University Press, pp. 33–47.

Buyst, E. and Lefebvre, W. (2007) 'Enkele verklaringsfactoren voor de regionale gedifferentieerde industriële ontwikkeling van Vlaams-Brabant tussen 1896 en 1961', *Belgisch Tijdschrift voor Nieuwste Geschiedenis*, Vol. 37 (1–2): 41–77.

Capron, H. (2007) 'Fédéralisme, transferts interrégionaux et croissance régionale', *Reflets et perspectives de la vie économique*, Vol. 46 (1): 45–63.

CDS (1934) *Bevolking. Algemeene telling op 31 december 1930, Vol. V*, Brussels: Centrale Dienst voor de Statistiek.

CDS (1939) *Economische en sociale telling van 27 februari 1937, Enquête nopens het arbeidstelsel en de loonen in den landbouw*, Brussels: Centrale Dienst voor de Statistiek.

CDS (1940) *Economische en sociale telling van 27 februari 1937, Vol. IV–V*, Brussels: Centrale Dienst voor de Statistiek.

De Brabander, G.L. (1981) *Regional Specialization: Employment and Economic Growth in Belgium between 1846 and 1970*, New York: Arno Press.

De Grauwe, P. (1980) 'Aspecten van de economische achteruitgang van Wallonië', *Tijdschrift voor Economie en Management*, Vol. 25 (2): 225–43.

Estevão, M. (2003) 'Regional labor market disparities in Belgium', *Reflets et Perspectives*, Vol. 42 (1): 95–114.

Geary, F. and Stark, T. (2002) 'Examining Ireland's post-famine economic growth performance', *Economic Journal*, Vol. 112 (482): 919–35.

Heremans, D. (1983) 'Financieringsaspecten van een gewestelijke industriepolitiek', *Tijdschrift voor Economie en Management*, Vol. 28 (3): 295–331.

Hogg, R.L. (1986) *Structural Rigidities and Policy Inertia in Inter-War Belgium*, Brussels: Koninklijke Academie.

INR (2000) *Regionale Rekeningen. Economische groei van de gewesten, provincies en arrondissementen – periode 1985–1997*, Brussels: National Accounts Institute.

INR (2001) *Regionale Rekeningen. Toegevoegde waarde en lonen, 1995–1998*, Brussels: National Accounts Institute.

Kirschen, E.S. (1962) 'L'économie bruxelloise face au fédéralisme', *Cahiers économique de Bruxelles*, Vol. 14: 159–66.

Landbouw-economisch Instituut (1983) *De rendabiliteit van het landbouwbedrijf in 1981–1982, Schriften Nr. 232*, Brussels: Landbouw-economisch Instituut.

Leroy, R. (1962) *Signification du chômage belge*, Brussels: Office belge pour l'accroissement de la productivité.

Loyen, R., Buyst, E. and Devos, G. (eds) (2003) *Struggling for Leadership: Antwerp-Rotterdam Port Competition between 1870–2000*, Heidelberg: Physica-Verlag.

Mahain, E. (1910) *Les abonnements d'ouvriers sur les lignes de chemins de fer belges et leurs effets sociaux*, Brussels: Misch et Thron.

Maizels, A. (1963) *Industrial Growth and World Trade*, Cambridge: Cambridge University Press.

MATP (1900) *Agriculture. Recensement général de 1895. Partie analytique*, Brussels: Ministère de l'Agriculture et des Travaux Publics.

MIT (1901) *Recensement général des industries et des métiers (31 octobre 1896), Vol. IX–XIV*, Brussels: Ministère de l'Industrie et du Travail.

Ministerie van Landbouw (1948) 'Lonen in de landbouw', *Landbouwtijdschrift*, Vol. 1: 54.

MTPS (1935) 'Le recensement de l'industrie et du commerce au 31 décembre 1930', *Revue du Travail*, Vol. 36: 1329–497.

Nagels, J. (2002) 'La situation économique de la Flandre et le mouvement flamand', *Cahiers économiques de Bruxelles*, Vol. 45 (4): 95–136.

NIS (1951–1952) *Algemene Volks-, Nijverheids- en Handelstelling op 31 december 1947, Vol. XI–XII*, Brussels: Nationaal Instituut voor de Statistiek.

NIS (1965) *Volkstelling op 31 december 1961, Vol. VIII-2*, Brussels: Nationaal Instituut voor de Statistiek.

NIS (1975) *Volkstelling op 31 december 1970, Vol. VIII*, Brussels: Nationaal Instituut voor de Statistiek.

NIS (1986) *Algemene volks- en woningtelling op 1 maart 1981, Vol. III*, Brussels: Nationaal Instituut voor de Statistiek.

Olyslager, P.M. (1947) *De localiseering der Belgische nijverheid*, Antwerp: Standaard.

Persyn, D. (2010) *Transfers en regionale groei*, Leuven: VIVES Briefing.

Pinxten, K. (1939) *Het Kempisch steenkolenbekken: een economische studie*, Brussels: Standaard.

Pollard, S. (1982) *Peaceful Conquest: The Industrialization of Europe 1760–1970*, Oxford: Oxford University Press.

RMZ/RSZ (1961, 1970, 1981) *Jaarverslag*, Brussels: Rijksdienst voor Maatschappelijke/Sociale Zekerheid.

Van der Wee, H. (1997) 'The economic challenge facing Belgium in the 19th and 20th centuries', in H. Van der Wee and J. Blomme (eds), *The Economic Development of Belgium since 1870*, Cheltenham: Edward Elgar, pp. 52–66.

Verhaegen, B. (1961) *Contribution à l'histoire économique des Flandres, Vol. 2*, Leuven: Nauwelaerts.

Verheirstraeten, A. (1970) 'Vlaams-Brabant en Brussel: elementen voor een economische ordening', Working Paper 86, Centrum voor Economische Studiën, Leuven.

Vertriest, W. (1963) *Overzicht van de gemiddelde boekhoudkundige resultaten van 165 landbouwbedrijven. Boekjaar 1961–1962, Schriften Nr. 5*, Brussels: Landbouw-economisch Instituut.

Vertriest, W. et al. (1972) *Overzicht van de gemiddelde boekhoudkundige resultaten van 1111 landbouwbedrijven. Boekjaar 1970–1971, Schriften Nr. 146*, Brussels: Landbouw-economisch Instituut.

Vliebergh, E. (1911) *Etudes d'économie rurale*, Leuven: Bibliothèque Choisie.

Wautelet, J.-M. (1995) *Structures industrielles et reproduction élargie du capital en Belgique (1850–1914)*, Louvain-la-Neuve: Academia.

Yerna, J. (1989) 'Fédéralisme et réformes de structure', *CRISP Courrier hebdomadaire*, Vol. 1234, Brussels.

3.3 Regional GDP in Denmark, 1850–2010

Kari Anne Janisse, Peter Sandholt Jensen, Cristina Victoria Radu and Paul Richard Sharp

1. Introduction

This chapter presents new estimates of income per capita and examines subregional convergence for Denmark between 1850 and 2010 based on the method from Geary and Stark (2002). Going back to 1850 enables a view of regional economic activity that starts well before the Second Schleswig War of 1864, when Denmark lost the duchies of Schleswig and Holstein, and which is often considered to be a turning point in Danish (economic) history. Moreover, the new data allow us to both estimate regional income convergence and divergence patterns in the long run. As stipulated by new economic geography, a decline in transportation can lead to agglomeration. Since there was only one railroad in Denmark before 1850, and the road network was limited, starting in 1850 also helps to explore the effects of decreasing transportation costs in the context of Danish growth.

Denmark represents an interesting case because, unlike other rich European nations, agriculture represented the most important sector of the economy up to the middle of the twentieth century, with employment in industry surpassing that of agriculture only in the 1950s (Henriksen 2006). The remarkable success of Danish agriculture on the international market in the second half of the nineteenth century led to an accumulation of wealth in the countryside and was the driving force behind the development of improved transportation links and industry.

One of the factors that influenced this development was the higher land-to-labour ratio compared to other European countries, which enabled the emergence of a wealthier peasantry. The proximity to the rich nations in Western Europe such as the UK, the Netherlands and Germany also contributed to the economic growth of the country, coupled together with the good access to sea transport (no place in Denmark being further away than 30 km from the sea). Another factor shaping the economy was the general lack of mineral resources. Only relatively small deposits of oil and gas were being found in the North Sea at the beginning of the 1970s.

2. Historical background

Following Henriksen (2006) and Pedersen (1995), the economic history of Denmark covered in this chapter can be divided into five periods. The first, up to

1870, was one of agrarian reforms and international market integration, notably with the UK. For much of the eighteenth century, the Danish rural population was subjected to a form of serfdom commonly termed 'adscription'. But towards the end of the century, the situation started to change, as the rural population increased mainly due to lower mortality rates. This meant that landlords did not need to bind labourers to the land anymore, so, with support from the monarch, serfdom was gradually abolished, and a new class of landless peasants developed. These peasants rented the land from the owners, which meant that during periods of strong inflation, the value of the rent in real terms decreased. This was one factor that pushed landlords into selling large amounts of land to their tenants in the beginning of the nineteenth century and in the 1840s and 1850s. By 1870, two-thirds of the land was being farmed by owners of mid-size farms, compared to only 10 per cent in the middle of the eighteenth century. These reforms, together with the introduction of new technologies, led to an increase in agricultural production per capita and meant that farmers no longer practised subsistence farming, but also had produce available for export in good harvest years. During this time, conditions for external trade improved as a liberalization of import tariffs at the beginning of the eighteenth century marked the end of mercantilism in Denmark. After losing the Norwegian market for grain in 1814, Danish exports started to target the British market. Trade was boosted when the UK Corn Laws were repealed in 1846. In these conditions, agricultural exports increased from 10 per cent in 1800 to 30 per cent of production in 1870.

Next, the period from 1870 to 1914 was one of rapid modernization and convergence with other rich nations. Although grain prices increased in the middle of the nineteenth century, export conditions for grains deteriorated from the 1870s due to increasing competition with New World producers. Danish farmers thus turned increasingly to animal production, with the Danish dairy sector being an early beneficiary of innovations in technology (especially the automatic cream separator) and institutions (cooperatives), which allowed peasants to produce more and better-quality butter and to organize themselves at a higher level of efficiency than their competitors of the day (see, for example, Henriksen et al. 2011). This diversification from grain to animal-based agriculture meant that Denmark was less exposed to the downturns in grain markets during the 1870s (Hansen 1984). The increasing export trade with England meant that the Danish and British economies mostly fluctuated together during the last half of the nineteenth century (Hansen 1984: 19–25).

The success of Danish agriculture was such that by the early 1870s, Denmark was a creditor country with over 200 million krone in assets; this success made possible a series of public investments for the improvement and support of the infrastructure to support the marketing of Danish agricultural goods (Hansen 1984). The improvements to infrastructure are particularly evident in the kilometres of railroad in the Danish realm: in the late 1840s, the monarchy had one railroad in the duchies of Schleswig and Holstein, but by 1900 the railroad network included 3,047 km of track covering the main areas of Funen and Zealand, as well as the Jutland peninsula (Koed 1997). In the period from 1894 to 1914, improvements in shipping and an increased capacity of the railroads made higher levels of exports possible. The shipment of heavy machinery, further industrialization and a second phase of railroad expansion generated further economic growth. Before 1894, Danish industry had been primarily focused on the domestic market; however, increasing demand and the profits from agriculture fostered the first phase of industrial expansion (Hansen 1972: 24; Pedersen 2010). By 1914, the share of agricultural product that was exported had increased to 60 per cent, while 10 per cent of domestic industrial production was being exported.

The outbreak of the First World War marks the beginning of the third period, from 1914 to 1950, which was one of stagnation. Here, as elsewhere, the war caused a significant disruption to the industrialization process by limiting the import of raw goods such as seed and fertilizer, as well as the export of agricultural products to England. During the war years, a trade surplus imbalance went unchecked, leading to a depreciation of 60 per cent in the value of the krone in 1920. A failure to address this problem properly led to a deterioration in Denmark's competitive position, which only improved after 1931 when the country renounced the gold standard, following the UK as its main trade partner. This development, together with trade barriers during and protectionism after the war, meant that growth rates fell to pre-1890s levels and agriculture was hard hit by the disruptions, although protection also insulated and fostered growth for new Danish industries (Hansen 1984) by limiting external competition.

After the Second World War, the period from 1950 to 1973 was one of liberalization, international market integration and growth of the welfare state. Pedersen's description of events fits closely with the expectations of a neoclassical growth model: technological change made much of the agricultural labour redundant, while the industrial centres benefited from relatively inexpensive and abundant labour, together with technology imported relatively cheaply from innovative countries. After the Second World War, Danish women entered the workforce, increasing demand for the Danish public sector services that enabled women to work. The widespread support for the introduction of the welfare state played a large part in the high demand for public goods and services, which fuelled the employment growth of the public sector during the 1960s and 1970s. A change in government policy favoured public spending, and as the public sector increased, many women entered the labour force. In spite of this boost to the workforce, the growth of the 1950s was slower than that of other European nations (Hansen 1984; Christoffersen 1999; Pedersen 2010). Also, a process of regional convergence arising from substantial economic transition had begun. This phase continued throughout the 1960s, although the massive expansion in government services came at the cost of the Danish balance of payments, so that by the time of the oil crisis in the early 1970s, high wages in Denmark constituted a loss of competitiveness for Danish firms in international markets (Christoffersen 1999; Pedersen 2010).

The period from 1973 onwards was one of slower growth. The shocks of the oil crisis were exacerbated by automatic wage indexation, which caused a sharp increase in real wages, leading to negative growth and an increase in unemployment. During the years up to 1980, the economic policy reactions were inappropriate and institutional changes happened too slowly, leading to a permanent shift to a regime with high unemployment and continued slow growth. A period of recovery followed from 1980, but ended in 1986 as the foreign debt position had grown too large and required more fundamental policy changes. Since then, the country has had a good record regarding inflation and current accounts, but growth has been slow. In this time, the oil crisis of the 1970s and the oil discovery in the North Sea led to non-agricultural growth in western Jutland. Additionally, a substantial growth of the service sector saw the north of Zealand emerge with larger shares of per capita income than other regions. Part of the dominance of northern Zealand in terms of the share of income may be due to the developments in the housing market, with a dramatic increase in home ownership (Christoffersen 1999). However, by 2010, the region with the highest GDP per capita was once again Copenhagen.

With the prominence of agriculture and the public sector, the industrial era of the Danish economy was indeed rather brief, in part due to a prolonged period of agricultural dominance and in part due to the early prominence of the service sector. The gradual shifts between sectors are echoed by Pedersen (2010: 16), where he justifies his critique of the idea that Denmark remained a backward agricultural country until well into the twentieth century. The sector shares of total employment show that by 1850, industry was already a significant source of employment, but that in 1890 a substantial increase in industrial employment occurred. Whether or not industrialization began in 1850 or 1890, it was not until 1950 that industry became the largest sector of employment, and its prominence lasted only around two decades.

3. Data and estimations

In order to give a picture of the evolution of regional inequality in Denmark, regional GDP per capita figures were estimated using the Geary and Stark methodology, every 10 years starting from 1850 to 2010 at a regional (NUTS 2) and subregional (NUTS 3) level. While most of the data required, including employment data, were relatively easy to find, the availability of wage data necessitated some deviations from the standard methodology. Data on population by region can be found in the Danish census statistics, while gross factor income is available from established sources such as Hansen (1984).

Data on employment are available from the Danish censuses. However, before 1970, the statistics were compiled in terms of households, counting the number of people that were dependent on a certain job, instead of just the number of employees. This means that in some cases, employment appears to be above 100 per cent because of families where more than one person worked. For this reason, GDP per capita, instead of GDP per worker, was computed, which in turn might affect the estimates for counties with a larger number of people outside the workforce.

The most difficult challenge, however, was finding sectoral wage data at the local level. While for the period 1850–1940, agricultural wages at the county level can be found, for the other sectors and periods, only wage by sector at a national level was found. To overcome this obstacle, instead of sectoral hourly wages, taxable income was used as a measure of productivity, as data on income earned per person were more readily available.

In order to test the validity of these assumptions, the estimated values are regressed against the official estimates, which start from 1993.[1] The tests yield a statistically insignificant difference in values (*t*-stat 0.8631). Performing the same test against the estimates of regional GDP presented by Molle et al. (1980), and Maddison (1982) for the 1970s, also results in failure to reject the null hypothesis at the 5 per cent level. Hence, we think that our new estimations provide a credible approximation of the regional distribution of GDP for the period of the study.

One source of distortion in the data before 1900 is that Copenhagen City, Greater Copenhagen and Roskilde are closely linked, although they are separated in two NUTS 2 regions (and three NUTS 3 regions). This means that Copenhagen appears to start with a smaller share of GDP in the beginning, although the Copenhagen-Roskilde area was probably the most developed at the time. Another issue faced when performing the estimations was the subregion of Southern Jutland, which historically belonged to the duchy of Schleswig and was conquered by Germany in 1864. The territory was returned to Denmark after the First World War. This creates a gap in the data from 1864 to 1921. The problem was solved by doing an interpolation for the missing years. However, this is likely to overestimate the GDP for those years.

4. Descriptive analysis

Our new estimates of total and per capita GDP allow analysing the evolution of inequality between Danish regions. Figure 3.3.1 shows the regional shares of

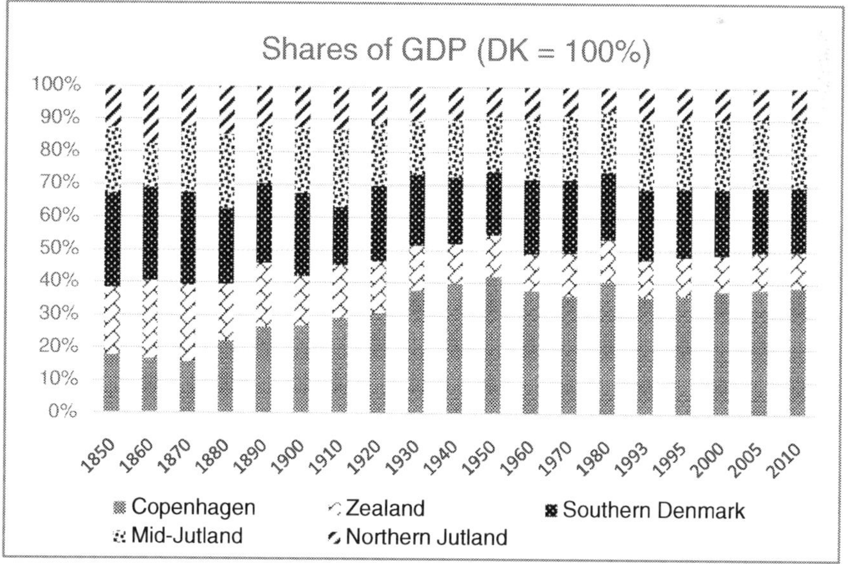

Figure 3.3.1 Regional shares of GDP, 1850–2010

GDP of the NUTS 2 regions for 1850–2010; the remarkable growth of the share of income in the capital region is especially prominent.

In terms of absolute GDP, Copenhagen does not emerge as the largest region until the 1890s, with 26 per cent of national income for that year, and by 2010 the share had reached 37 per cent, thus growing substantially from a starting point of 17.7 per cent in 1850. In the most general terms, the regions with the largest shares of agriculture in 1850 are the regions that are smallest today, such as Northern Jutland and Zealand, with 10 per cent and 9 per cent of absolute GDP in 2010, respectively. Both were heavily reliant on shipping and agriculture prior to 1900, and appear to have benefited less in absolute terms from the economic growth over the last 160 years than Copenhagen.

Figure 3.3.2 shows GDP per capita of Denmark's regions relative to the national average and gives us a similar picture. Copenhagen diverges more from the rest of Denmark in the latter part of the twentieth century than any other region. In the late nineteenth and early twentieth centuries, regional per capita GDP appears to have converged, followed by a period of divergence between 1920 and 1950. After that, during the economic boom that lasted until the early 1970s, inequality in GDP per capita decreased to its lowest level, but has been increasing since then until today.

However, we need more disaggregated data to understand at least some of the driving forces behind these long-term patterns of growth. As we will see, it is especially important to distinguish between the more and less urbanized parts of those five regions. In consequence, the remainder of our chapter will deal with the smaller NUTS 3 regions. Table 3.3.1 shows GDP per capita relative to the national average at the subregion level.

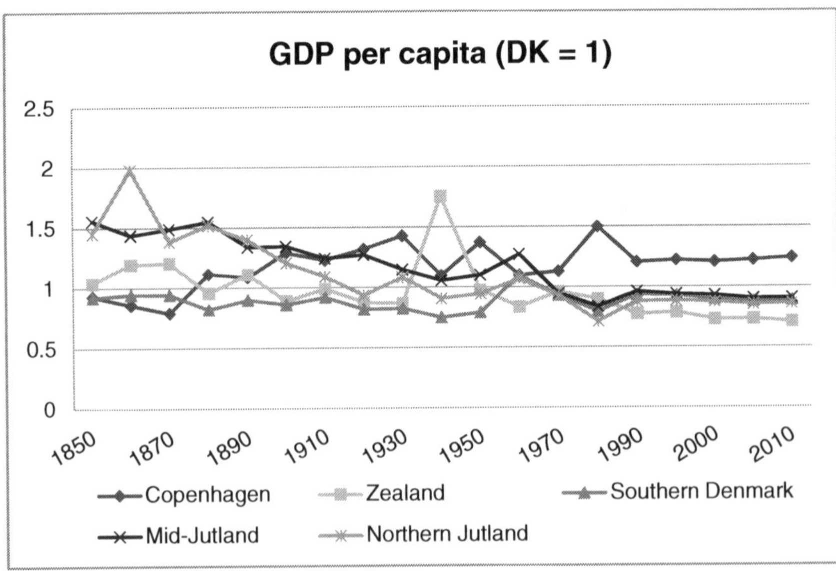

Figure 3.3.2 Danish regional GDP shares

Table 3.3.1 GDP per capita for NUTS03 regions, Denmark = 100

	Copenhagen City	*Greater Copenhagen*	*North Zealand*	*Bornholm*	*East Zealand*	*West and South Zealand*	*Funen*	*South Denmark*	*East Jutland*	*West Jutland*	*North Jutland*
1850	113.65	92.75	77.30	38.90	51.02	104.50	100.46	86.98	101.77	140.78	103.61
1860	107.51	80.47	67.80	34.37	38.32	124.59	95.51	93.78	88.40	92.74	141.04
1870	92.49	56.33	71.38	39.25	51.20	128.09	108.43	85.50	94.69	144.39	77.34
1880	114.88	91.16	87.29	60.34	24.13	109.07	85.08	80.41	75.55	154.19	104.52
1890	126.12	75.92	96.67	49.43	101.00	112.15	72.63	100.92	88.42	118.01	105.62
1900	146.99	126.72	82.08	63.14	92.62	88.52	93.46	80.84	144.23	114.97	95.84
1910	131.96	125.67	91.38	72.90	92.22	99.63	94.83	89.89	141.76	107.37	86.35
1920	144.53	117.40	91.83	73.18	86.80	87.70	85.50	79.01	118.09	90.73	73.13
1930	155.72	119.91	102.36	74.98	82.54	87.00	84.71	80.73	108.11	97.51	87.53
1940	134.95	126.71	106.89	74.27	83.12	86.21	91.72	85.00	144.25	94.50	86.92
1950	149.28	119.62	103.17	79.56	96.85	98.29	82.98	76.08	114.18	91.62	76.78
1960	113.30	117.74	110.89	73.63	106.69	81.80	109.35	94.82	144.22	101.73	91.10
1970	127.93	120.02	110.64	88.76	86.62	93.68	87.86	90.04	87.51	80.60	89.57
1980	132.71	105.50	108.88	83.97	103.98	102.53	80.81	91.76	85.27	91.53	75.59
1990	129.71	103.45	130.35	90.23	101.41	89.61	88.11	94.30	86.10	80.90	87.45
1995	192.96	83.84	92.86	84.44	92.85	75.61	85.91	96.18	85.00	76.88	89.54
2000	210.49	78.78	93.40	73.63	94.45	80.66	82.43	98.05	81.55	75.95	84.47
2005	181.21	80.71	93.74	70.31	92.02	83.59	83.60	100.74	84.69	73.78	86.68
2010	169.41	73.60	89.00	72.77	109.33	93.41	108.59	124.34	79.32	55.82	83.86

Source: Own data.

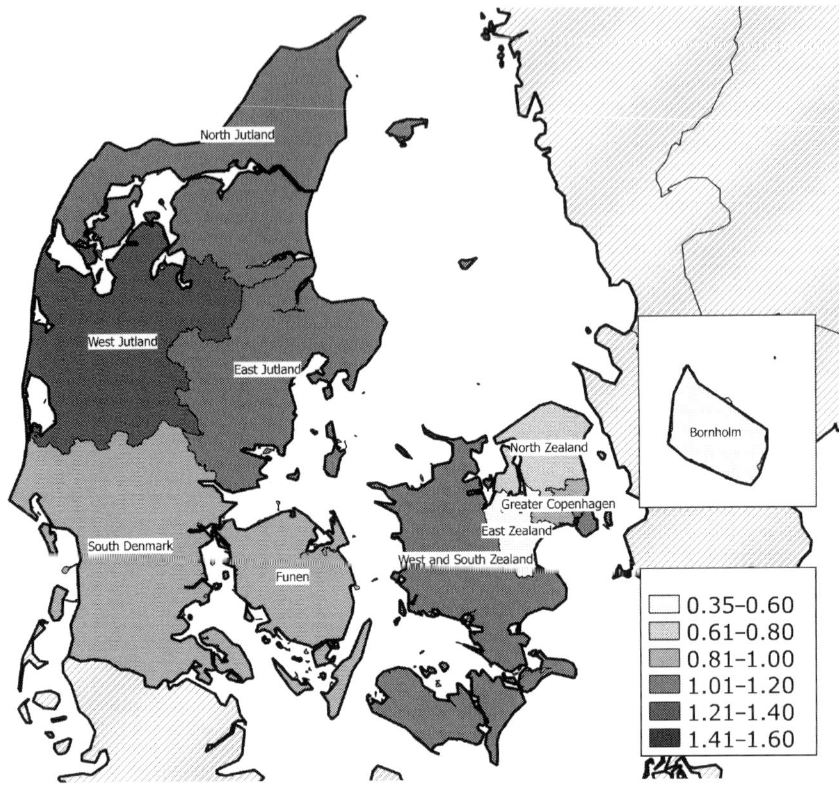

Map 3.3.1 Relative GDP per capita, 1850 (Denmark = 1)

Source: Own data.

To help explain how regional GDP evolved, the results for GDP per capita are plotted on a map of the NUTS 3 regions.

Map 3.3.1 depicts relative GDP per capita at Danish NUTS 3 regions for the year 1850. Our estimates reveal that agricultural areas such as West Jutland or West and South Zealand were already wealthy at that time. As the shift from serfdom to owner-occupied farming took place, better productivity, coupled with increased exports, led to an increase in the wealth of agricultural regions. It should also be noted that Copenhagen City had above-average GDP per capita because it was the administrative and trade center of the kingdom. But outside the capital, the economy was still agrarian and the modern industrial centers had yet to take shape.

Examining Table 3.3.1, we can observe that the trend of increasing GDP per capita for the agricultural centers continued up to the 1880s. This was a consequence of the success of Danish agriculture on the international market as it reoriented itself from grain to the more profitable animal produce. This in turn increased the demand for industrial goods, such as machines that improved productivity and better transport links, to get the goods faster to the market (Hansen 1984).

Table 3.3.2 Net migration into cities ('000s)

	1840–1845	*1845–1855*	*1855–1860*	*1860–1870*	*1870–1880*	*1880–1890*	*1890–1901*	*1901–1911*
Capital	4	14	8	21	52	68	38	35
Other cities	4	17	7	6	20	41	61	18

Source: Boje and Hyldtoft 1977: 212, Table 5) – net migration into urban areas in '000s of people.

Table 3.3.2 presents the cumulative effect of migration into cities. The data show urbanization started slightly earlier in Copenhagen, but by the end of the century both the capital and the other cities showed strong population growth. These figures for the urban population size support the theory that as the transportation of food and people became less costly and agriculture more productive, city growth and industrial agglomeration started to set in. Indeed, the urbanization

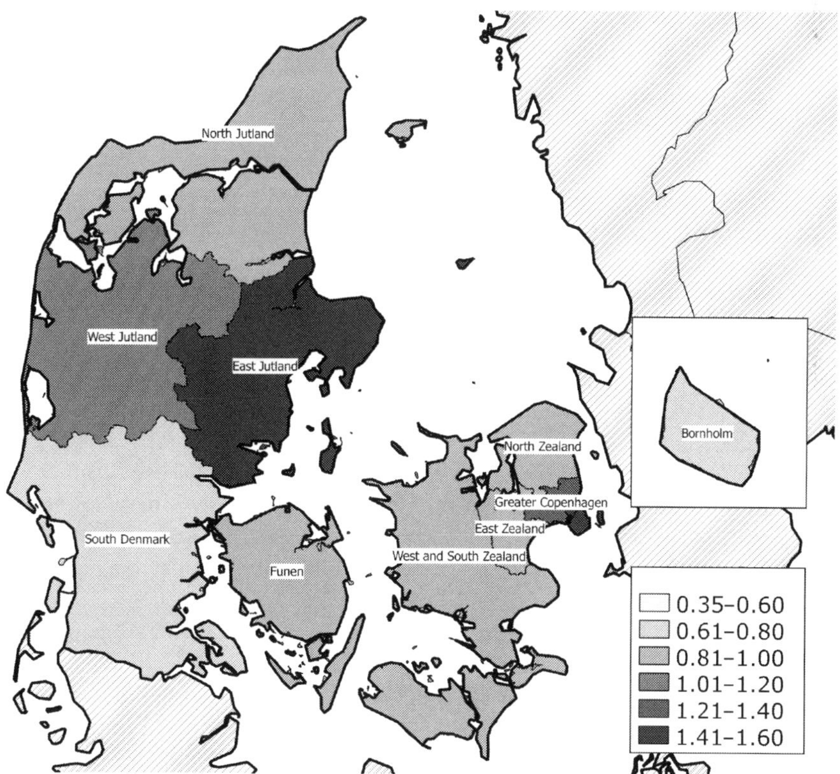

Map 3.3.2 Relative GDP per capita, 1900 (Denmark = 1)

Source: Own data.

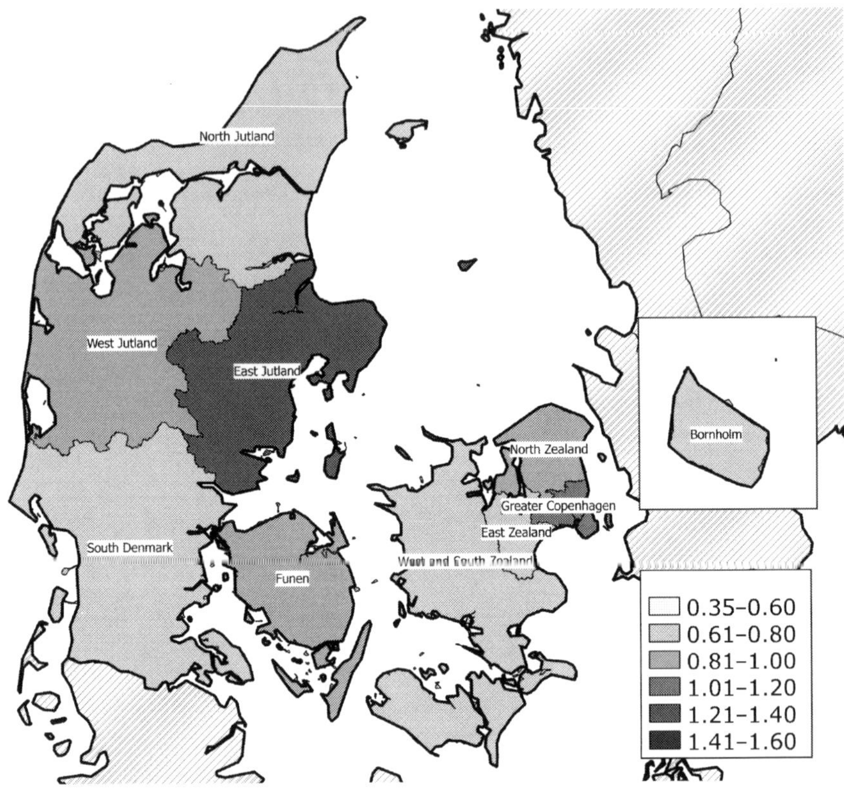

Map 3.3.3 Relative GDP per capita, 1940 (Denmark = 1)

Source: Own data.

process described by Boje and Hyldtoft (1977) coincided with the creation of the Danish rail network. For example, by 1880, as industrial development was beginning to take hold, the cities with deep ice free harbours had also been connected by rail to other cities in Denmark (Koed 1997). In 1850, only 9 per cent of the Danish population lived in urban areas, by 1900 this had increased to 21 per cent, and by 1940 the share had reached 64 per cent. After 1940, urbanization increased at a slower pace but attained a value of 84 per cent in 2010.

As a result of increasing population and industrialization, the GDP per capita figures for the subregions started to overtake those of the agricultural regions. Map 3.3.2 shows that overall variation in relative GDP per capita has decreased since 1850 and the richest regions are now Copenhagen City and East Jutland (where the second largest city in the country, Aarhus, is located)

With the onset of the First World War, Denmark entered a period of significant disruption to the industrialization process that lasted until after the Second World War. Both industry and agriculture were hampered by problems such as

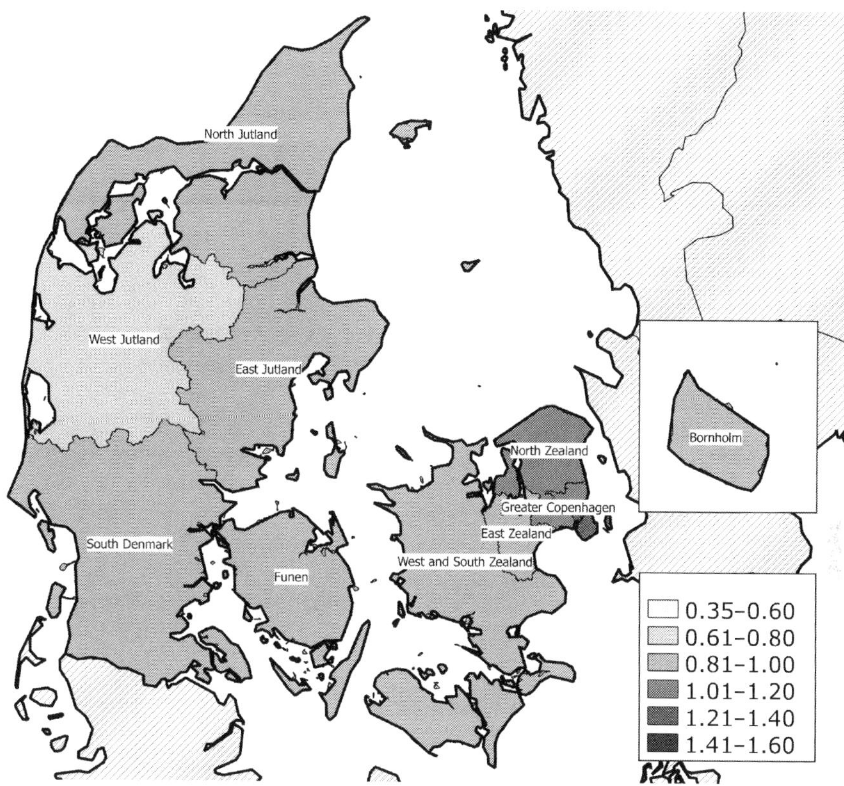

Map 3.3.4 Relative GDP per capita, 1970 (Denmark = 1)

Source: Own data.

reduced availability of raw materials, such as seeds and fertilizer, barriers to trade, protectionism, and a financial policy that failed to contain inflation at the end of the First World War, but turned very restrictive afterwards (Henriksen 2006). On the other hand, protection also insulated and fostered growth for new Danish industries (Hansen 1984) by limiting external competition. The result was that the regional pattern of GDP per capita did not change much from 1900 to 1940. There was only a small increase in relative GDP per capita for urban counties and an opposite effect for the agricultural regions, as is presented in Map 3.3.3.

In the period of strong economic growth that followed the Second World War and lasted up to 1970, the gap between the richest and the poorest counties decreased, reaching the smallest value in the year 1970, as presented in Map 3.3.4. As more women entered the job market, home ownership in the cities became affordable for Danish families with two incomes, and urbanization increased. These urban centres dominate in terms of GDP per capita. However, we note that high levels of income redistribution in this period limited the income gap between regions.

After 1970, the oil crisis brought a recession that was followed by more sluggish growth. During this time, the gap between the richest and the poorest counties started to increase once again, which is also visible from a comparison between Maps 3.3.4 and 3.3.5.

Around 1990, the county of North Zealand overtook Copenhagen to be the subregion with the highest GDP per capita in Denmark. This remarkable development was fuelled by a boom in the services market and an increase in the demand for housing in the area. Two decades later, as shown in Map 3.3.5, the situation has changed again, with Copenhagen City emerging as the top-earning subregion. The Danish economy went through a number of phases, which we see reflected to a certain extent in our data. Gains from agricultural advances in the nineteenth century accrued to rural counties, but gains from urbanization accrued to the capital region, as did the expansion of the public sector after the Second World War.

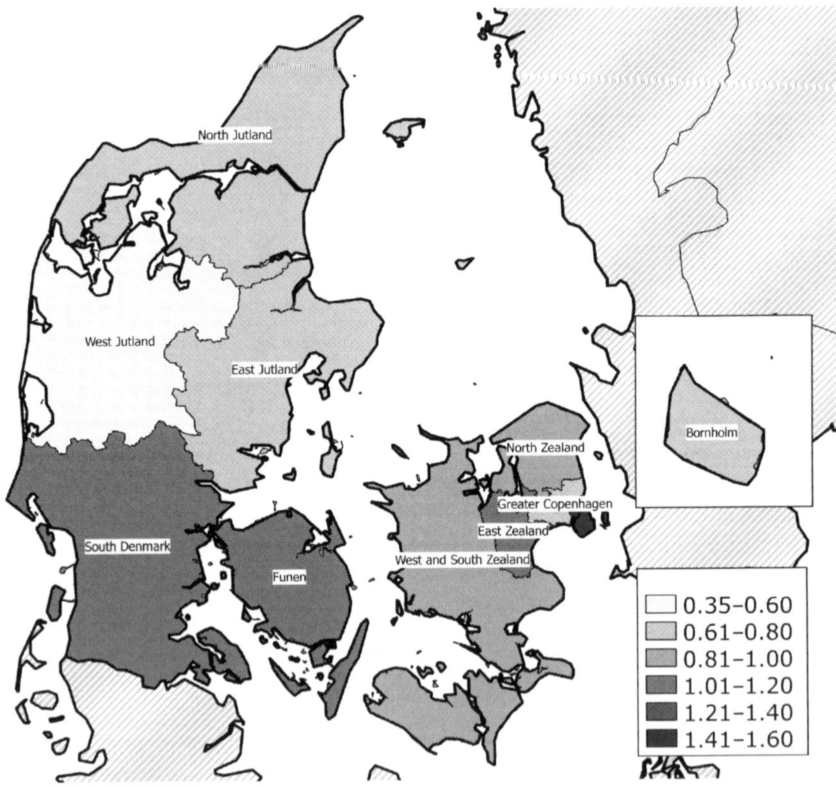

Map 3.3.5 Relative GDP per capita, 2010 (Denmark = 1)

Source: Own data.

The next section uses our estimates to take a closer look at regional convergence over time.

5. Stylized facts and analyses

To measure whether or not poorer areas grew faster than rich ones in Denmark, unconditional sigma- and beta-convergence equations are estimated using the GDP per capita data presented in the previous section.

Indeed, the poorest subregion in 1850 – the island of Bornholm – had a mean growth rate of 4.26 per cent per year over the period 1850–2010, well above the national average of 3.22 per cent. However, other fast-growing regions are Greater Copenhagen and East Jutland (possibly reflecting the aforementioned effects of urbanization), with mean growth rates of 4.26 and 4.65 per cent, respectively. These two subregions include the two biggest cities in Denmark (Aarhus and Copenhagen), thus pointing away from traditional theories of convergence and towards theories of agglomeration and urbanization. Hence, the regions with the highest growth rates are not just 'backward' regions, as some would suggest (Jensen-Butler and Madsen 2005; Dam 2015).

The gap between the wealthiest and the poorest subregions in Denmark is described next. A simple neoclassical growth model would suggest that the variation in GDP per capita across regions should decrease over time, or 'sigma-convergence'. To test this assumption, we calculate the coefficient of variation (CV) and the population-weighted coefficient of variation (also known as the Williamson index, WI). The results of these calculations are presented in Figure 3.3.3.

Both indicators tell a similar story. Denmark saw considerable sigma-convergence between 1850 and 1970, which reflects the narrowing of the gap between the richest and poorest counties evident in the maps of the previous section. The income inequality during the late nineteenth century was driven by the demand for Danish (agricultural) exports. In the period up to 1880, income inequality rose as agricultural regions grew richer than the other regions. Once industrialization took hold, inequality decreased, as the urban regions caught up and then overtook the agricultural ones, which is a remarkable difference to the experience in other parts of Europe. During the world wars and the interwar period, inequality rose once again as difficult conditions for trade led to stagnation in the economy.

By the end of the Second World War, Danish industry had developed enough to absorb the excess workforce that was no longer needed in agriculture and the many women who joined the workforce after 1950.

From 1940, there is a significant decrease in inequality, which reflects the extensive societal and cultural reforms of the 1950s and 1960s. In the 1950s, Danish society was in the midst of a fairly extensive process of determining what well-being meant and what the government's role in fostering that should be. Increased government spending and strong economic growth in the years up to 1970 saw income inequality decrease to its lowest levels for the analysed period.

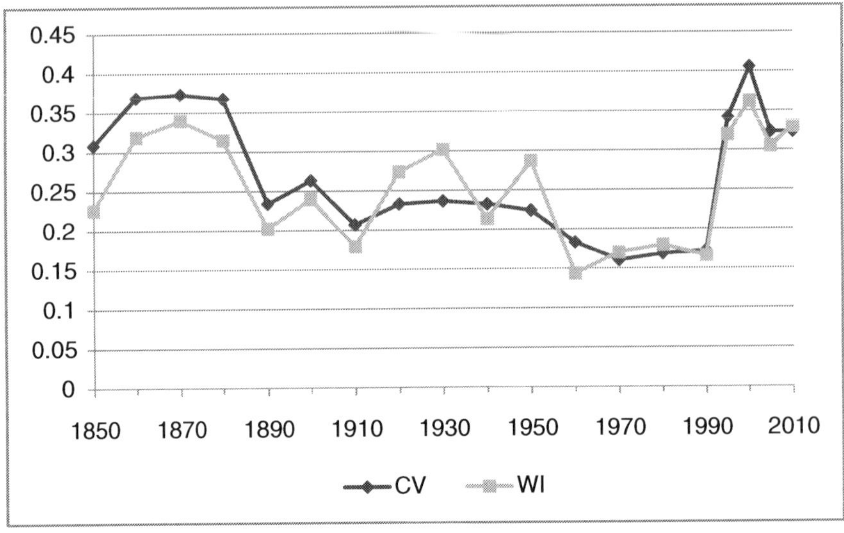

Figure 3.3.3 Coefficient of variation (CV) and population-weighted coefficient of variation (WI)

The increase in the size of the labour force and the cultural demand for greater equality is reflected in the sharp drop in inequality, which persisted until the late 1990s. By the late 1970s, the labour force had stopped increasing, probably also because the focus of trade unions during wage negotiations was on maximizing wages rather than employment.[2] This made the cost of Danish goods uncompetitive compared to foreign goods, thus stunting growth. Without income from the sale of goods domestically and abroad, the growing costs of the public sector proved to be unsustainable and the Danish model came under pressure (Pedersen 2010). The upside of public interventions was, of course, the dramatic decrease in inequality. It should be noted, though, that the trend lasted only until the economy started to have troubles in the late 1970s. After 1990, inequality between regions increased once again, as urban regions such as Copenhagen City continued to grow richer, while agricultural regions such as West Jutland declined in relative terms.

Let us proceed to test formally for 'beta-convergence' between the Danish NUTS 3 regions. This would mean that regions with a lower value of per capita GDP in 1850 should have experienced higher average growth rates from 1850 until today. In order to test for this, the growth rates of per capita GDP are plotted against per capita GDP in 1850 (see Figure 3.3.4).

The figure clearly shows a negative relationship between initial GDP per capita and long-run growth rates. Moreover, it might also lend support to the idea that the government's policy of investing in infrastructure had the desired effect

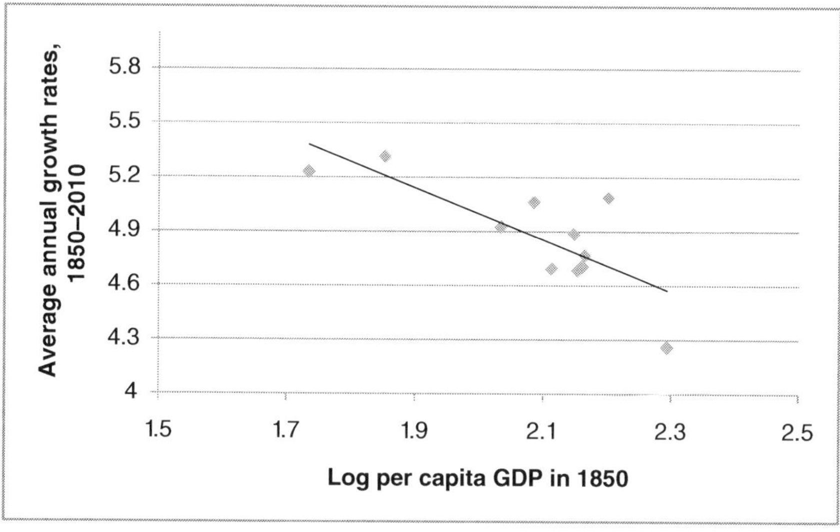

Figure 3.3.4 Beta-convergence for the Danish subregions, 1850–2010

of moving capital and technology from richer to poorer regions, as has also been suggested for Sweden by Enflo and Rosés (2015).

A closer look at the growth rates in Table 3.3.1 reveals that in 1850, the richest subregion was West Jutland, a region without large cities and heavily focused on agriculture. Checking the values for 2010, we can observe that this region has become the poorest one. While the cities of Denmark are without doubt the wealthiest parts of the country today, in 1850 the areas surrounding large cities such as Copenhagen and Aarhus were not the most productive in terms of agriculture. Because this sector in the late nineteenth century was labour-intensive and remote agricultural regions competed for labour, wages there were comparatively higher, and thus less attractive to early industrialists. Although there were concentrations of wealth in the cities (evident in absolute GDP), the per capita GDP of city regions was not necessarily higher than in rural Denmark.

Without the railroads, Danish transportation was by rural (mostly unpaved) roads and by boat. With the arrival of trains, a passenger in 1910 could take a train from Aarhus to Odense without ever leaving the vehicle (Koed 1997). The cost of a journey declined both in terms of time required to make the journey as well as in terms of effort required by travellers. Hence, with railways, relatively lower wages were needed to attract labour into industry. After the establishment of the railroad system at the end of the nineteenth century, urban regions showed strong growth, catching up and eventually overtaking the agricultural ones in terms of GDP per capita. In the years after the Second World War, the high growth and the social welfare policies led to a decrease in inequality between regions, pushing it

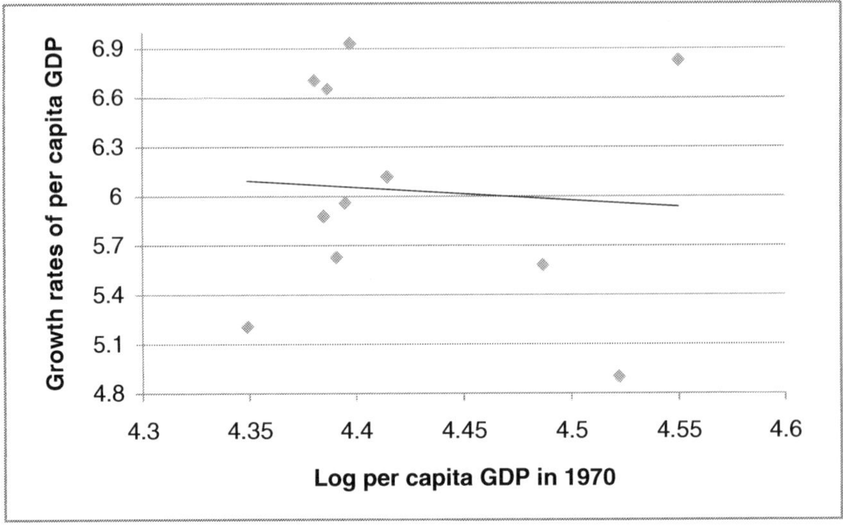

Figure 3.3.5 The end of beta-convergence? Evidence for 1970–2010

to its lowest value in the 1960s and 1970s. Since then, inequality between regions has increased again, especially after the year 2000. To show this, we plot again the initial level of GDP per capita in 1970 against average annual growth rates thereafter, shown in Figure 3.3.5.

The results show that even though the coefficient is still negative, there is little evidence of beta-convergence after 1970. Some of the more developed regions did indeed have above-average growth. For example, South Denmark developed as oil was discovered in the North Sea and the City of Esbjerg grew to become the hub of Danish oil exploitation. In contrast, the adjacent region of West Jutland failed to capitalize on this development because it did not have a port of the same size on the west coast, and became the region with the lowest per capita GDP in the country. Overall, economic growth in this period appears to be concentrated on urban regions, with Copenhagen diverging away from the rest of the country.

6. Conclusion

The analysis of long-run regional growth in Denmark presented here provides a picture of the quite remarkable Danish path to modern economic growth. In the middle of the nineteenth century, as land reforms and new technology increased agricultural productivity, the success of Danish farm exports caused an increase in GDP per capita in the agricultural regions of Denmark. As demand from agriculture led to an improvement in transport links and the development of local industry, the income of urban regions started to grow fast in the period up to 1910 and inequality between regions decreased. In the period between the two world wars, bad trading conditions hurt the economy, but protectionism did help the development of some local industry, causing a small increase in the GDP per capita share of urban counties. After the wars, a period of high economic growth and development of the welfare state followed, which decreased regional inequality. But after the oil shocks of the 1970s, economic growth slowed down and favoured large cities such as Copenhagen, leading to an increase in inequality between regions, especially after 1990.

The analysis of growth rates provides evidence of sigma-convergence in the period from 1850 until 1970, and a reversal thereafter. A similar picture is painted by the analysis of beta-convergence. Looking back from 1850 until today, the calculations show clear evidence that poor regions grew faster. However, our calculations show very weak evidence of beta-convergence from 1970 until today. As the country moved from an agricultural economy to an industrial and then to a service-based economy, the link between inequality and income followed a U-shaped pattern.

One interesting note is the effect of railroads on development. As transaction costs fell in connection with the establishment of railroads, the improvement of transportation increased mobility, which led to high rates of migration. This migration was accompanied by a significant reallocation of wealth and employment from rural to urban areas. This had a mixed effect on the regional distribution of inequality, causing first a decrease in inequality, as cities caught up with rural areas, but rising inequality afterwards, when further development of industry and the rise of services widened the income gap.

In conclusion, based on the evolution of Danish subregions, the convergence analysis and the development of inequality, the evidence presented here suggests that neoclassical features of growth that predict convergence are present. Our results imply that rather than rural Denmark experiencing poor growth, there is evidence of rural areas converging towards Copenhagen, especially in the high growth period up to 1970. On the other hand, there seems to be a distinct lack of advantages for firms and citizens to locate in these areas and evidence of a divergence afterwards. Future research should explore the dynamics of convergence and divergence, and the driving forces behind this, in more detail.

Notes

1 The majority of the work presented here treats growth in 10-year intervals; however, to provide a basis of comparison, the GS estimates are compared to official statistics from the Danish Statistical Bank at five-year intervals from 1990 to 2010.

2 Christoffersen (1999) and Pedersen (2010).

References

Boje, P. and Hyldtoft, O. (1977) *Økonomiske, geografiske og demografiske aspekter. Urbanisering i Norden, Vol. 3*, edited by G.A. Blom, Oslo-Bergen-Tromsø: Universitetsforlaget.

Christoffersen, H. (1999) *Danmarks Økonomiske Historie efter 1960*, Aarhus: Forlaget Systime.

Dam, M. (2015) *The Rotten Banana: Rural Challenges in Denmark*, BEAHS Environmental Leadership blog post, available at: https://beahrselp.berkeley.edu/blog/the-rotten-banana-rural-challenges-in-denmark/ (accessed 13 August 2018).

Enflo, K. and Rosés, J.R. (2015) 'Coping with regional inequality in Sweden: structural change, migrations, and policy, 1860 to 2000', *The Economic History Review*, Vol. 68 (1): 191–217.

Geary, F. and Stark, T. (2002) 'Examining Ireland's post-famine economic growth performance', *The Economic Journal*, Vol. 112 (482): 919–35.

Hansen, S.A. (1972) *Økonomisk vækst i Danmark bind I: 1720–1914*, Copenhagen: Akademisk Forlag.

Hansen, S.A. (1984) *Økonomisk vækst i Danmark bind II: 1914–1983*, Copenhagen: Akademisk Forlag.

Henriksen, I. (2006) 'An economic history of Denmark', *EH.Net Encyclopedia*, edited by Robert Whaples, October 6, 2006, available at: http://eh.net/encyclopedia/an-economic-history-of-denmark/ (accessed 13 August 2018).

Henriksen, I., Lampe, M. and Sharp, P. (2011) 'The role of technology and institutions for growth: Danish creameries in the late nineteenth century', *European Review of Economic History*, Vol. 15 (3): 475–93.

Jensen-Butler, C. and Madsen, B. (2005) 'Decomposition analysis: an extended theoretical foundation and its application to the study of regional income growth in Denmark', *Environment and Planning A*, Vol. 37 (12): 2189–208.

Koed, J. (1997) *Danmarks Jernbaner i 150 år*, Kunst & Kultur, Aalborg: Nordjyllands Bogtrykkeri A/S.

Maddison, A. (1982) *Phases of Capitalist Development*, Oxford: Oxford University Press.

Molle, W., van Holst, B. and Smit, H. (1980) *Regional Disparity and Economic Development in the European Community*, Farnborough: Saxon House.

Pedersen, J. (1995) 'Postwar growth of the Danish economy', in N. Crafts and F. Toniolo (eds), *Economic Growth in Europe since 1945*, Cambridge: Cambridge University Press.

Pedersen, J. (2010) *Danmarks Økonomiske Historie 1910–1960*, Copenhagen: Multivers.

3.4 Balancing east and west

Evidence from Finland's regional GDPs, 1880–2010[1]

Kerstin Enflo

1. Introduction and historical background

During the last two centuries, Finland has undergone a dramatic transformation: from one of Europe's poorer and more peripheral countries, to a fast-growing high-tech economy. Finland has proven successful in reaping the benefits of openness to trade by moving up the value-added ladder. The country went from being a supplier in furs and tar in the pre-industrial era, to industrializing by exporting sawn goods, pulp and paper. In the post-war period, a definite transition to high-value-added exports took place, with companies such as UPM (bio- and forest industries), Kone (elevators and escalators) and Nokia (mobile telephony) reaching world recognition.

This chapter will explore Finland's remarkable growth trajectory from a geographical perspective. There exist excellent accounts of Finland's development from industrialization and onwards (for example, Heikkinen and Hjerppe 1986, 1987; Hjerppe 1989; Ojala et al. 2006), but much less has been written about its geographical evolution. A related study by Kangasharju (1998) documents beta-convergence in 88 Finnish small-scale subregions from 1934 to 1993 by using taxable incomes as an indicator of regional income levels. Taxable incomes need not correspond to values of productions, since the geographic distance between the location of production and the location where associated incomes were taxed might be large in the presence of capital mobility. In addition, the period covered by Kangasharju (1998) is too short to cover the entire industrialization process. There is only one previous study that has attempted to measure regional production accounts, but it is focused on the interwar period only (Kiiskinen 1958). Other regionally oriented historical studies have either focused on the spatial allocation of population (Tervo 2010) or income formation (Kiiskinen 1961).

From roughly around the twelfth century until 1809, Sweden and Finland were joined as one country. Constitutional laws and judicial, religious and government authorities developed in parallel in Sweden and Finland, and lay the ground for a rather egalitarian society of freeholders. Swedish-speaking settlements in the archipelago and on the coast of Finland have existed since the Middle Ages, and Finland is still a bilingual nation with Finnish and Swedish as national languages.[2] Following King Gustav III's *coup d'état* in 1772, Sweden-Finland adopted an absolutist yet liberal constitution. Gustav III introduced laws of religious toleration, humanization of the criminal law, reduced export tolls and attempted to free the trade of grain. Gustav III also reduced the tax burden of the Finnish peasantry. The constitution of 1772 remained in place in Finland until 1919.

Geographically, Sweden-Finland was a circular country, surrounding the Gulf of Bothnia almost as an interior lake. This meant that the western parts of Finland flourished due to superior market access through water transportation. Consequently, the capital of the Finnish part (Turku) was conveniently situated on the west coast to facilitate communication with the eastern capital (Stockholm) across the Archipelago Sea.

In 1809, Finland was annexed by Russia and became a Grand Duchy of the Russian Empire, with the Czar as Grand Duke. In fact, many of the institutions set up during the Swedish period remained untouched, and Finland enjoyed a large degree of autonomy in terms of domestic policies. Most importantly, the Finnish peasantry remained free (unlike the Russian serfs), as the old Swedish law, including the relevant parts from Gustav III's constitution of 1772, remained effective. In terms of development into democracy, Finland was a forerunner. A unicameral parliament with general suffrage was initiated as early as 1906. Thereby, Finland was one of the first countries in the world to grant women the right to vote. Finland also enjoyed relatively large autonomy in issues concerning trade and monetary policy and had her own state finances. Between 1877 and 1914, Finland was part of the classical gold standard.

Even though the Russian annexation had relatively little impact on Finland's institutional structure, it meant more in terms of influencing its geographical structure. In order to facilitate connections with St Petersburg, the Czar moved the capital of Finland from Turku in the western part of the country to the more centrally located Helsinki, and market access began to change towards the east. From the 1830s, regular steamship connections were established between Helsinki and St Petersburg. Even more important for market integration was the domestic railroad network. Surveys for a rail link between Helsinki and St Petersburg had been made in 1857, but it took until 1870 before the line was opened. The rail was the responsibility of the Finnish railroads, and it was not until 1912 that the Finnish and the Russian networks became connected properly. It is said that the gradual expansion of the Finnish railroad network was a compromise between the political and military interests of the Russian Empire and the industrial need for transportation (Kirby 2006: 109). Studies have shown that the railroad network has influenced the geographical long-run evolution of the Finnish population (Kotavaara et al. 2011). The railroads were largely state-directed and state-owned.

Finland's industrial take-off is said to have taken place in the latter half of the nineteenth century, and is often described as an export success story. During this period, exports consisted mainly of raw materials and little-processed goods (Hjerppe 1989: 159). There was, however, a clear division of export markets between east and west. Timber products were exported to Western Europe, especially to markets in the UK, whereas a wide range of manufactured and industrial handicrafts found markets in Russia, especially in the province of St Petersburg. Finnish exports to Russia were encouraged since they could be imported duty-free until the 1880s. Thereafter, Russia levied tariffs on Finland, which, however, were low compared to tariffs imposed on other Western European countries. Russia dominated as trading partner by 1880, but the UK increased its share until the First World War. The geographical division of exports had consequences for Finland's internal geographical organization. Kiiskinen (1961: 92) argues that industrializing Finland can be divided into two parts. The south-east, central and northern regions became dominated by timber industries, quite oriented towards export. The western parts and some of the south were rather dominated by different branches of industry producing for the domestic market.

During the late nineteenth and earlier twentieth centuries, Russia started pursuing a policy of "Russification" aimed at limiting the special status of the Grand Duchy of Finland. The Finns opposed this policy, and when the Bolshevik Revolution took place in Russia in 1917, Finland seized the opportunity and declared independence. When Bolshevik Russia subsequently closed its borders, trade with the independent republic of Finland declined to almost nil (Kaukiainen 2006: 148).

After Finland's declared independence in 1917, a grim civil war broke out concerning leadership of the newly independent state. The forces fighting were the Social Democrats led by the People's Deputation of Finland (commonly called the Reds) and the forces of the non-socialist, conservative-led Senate (commonly called the Whites). The Reds were based in the towns and industrial centres of Southern Finland, while the Whites controlled the more rural central and northern Finland. The civil war was fought from 27 January to 15 May 1918, and was eventually won by the Whites.

The interwar period involved intensifying trade relations with the Western markets. Consequently, the UK became Finland's most important trading partner, accounting for 43 per cent of total exports in 1920. Finland's specialization and trading pattern was concentrated towards forest products. During the 1920s and 1930s, about 85 per cent of exports consisted of raw wood and related industrial products. In fact, during some years, Finland was the world's largest exporter of sawn goods and plywood (Hjerppe 1989: 161).

During the Second World War, Finland fought against the USSR, first in the Winter War (1939–1940) and thereafter in the Continuation War alongside Germany (1941–1944). In 1944–1945, Finland also fought their former ally Germany in the Lapland War. Despite losing the war, Finland managed to maintain its independence and stay part of the Western bloc. Yet the peace conditions were tough on Finland's side. In the Paris Peace Treaties of 1947, Finland lost about 10 per cent of its territorial land to the USSR and was obliged to pay heavy war reparations. The war reparations were to be paid in the form of goods and machinery to the USSR. Between 1944 and 1952, a total of 141,490 railroad carriages were delivered to the USSR. But the Finns showed impressive industrial capacity, and by 1952 Finland had repaid its debt, making it the only country to pay war reparations in full.[3] The significance of the war reparations to restructure

Finnish industry and its trade with the USSR has been widely discussed. Riitta Hjerppe (1989: 162) argues that it was Finland's long tradition of manufacturing metal and engineering products, as well as its historical trading relations with Russia, that made it possible to deliver the heavy burden.

After the reparations had finished, demand from the USSR for Finnish industrial products remained high. Thus, by the 1950s, the USSR again became an important trading partner for Finland. Between 1940 and 1980, its share amounted to about 15–18 per cent of Finnish exports, which was the largest share for any Western economy (Paavonen 2005: 153). The post-Second World War Finnish–USSR trade structure built on five-year framework agreements and payments was based on bilateral clearings. Finland exported machinery and ships, and later on also textiles and other consumer goods. In return, it imported oil and some heavy industrial products from the USSR (Kaukiainen 2006: 151). Generally, it has been argued that the system was quite profitable for Finland, which contrasts with the experience of Central Eastern European countries under Soviet influence (see Sutela 2014).

The post-war period involved a time of a remarkable economic catching up for Finland. Only Japan, the South East Asian countries and Ireland experienced higher growth levels during the twentieth century (Hjerppe and Jalava 2006: 45). The post-war period also saw efforts to improve Finnish social security and raise the general standards of education by building a welfare state. The value added of the public sector outgrew the rest of the economy from the end of 1940 and onwards. The result was that its share of GDP had doubled by 1985 (Hjerppe 1989: 131).

During the 1950s and 1960s, the first regional policies were implemented in Finland, with a specific target towards developing the sparsely populated northern parts. Another form of regional policy widely used by the Finnish state was the regionalization of university education. While Finland only hosted universities in Turku and Helsinki by 1950, the location of universities has come to spread over the entire country thereafter. By the end of the 1970s, universities had been founded in Tampere, Jyväskylä, Oulu, Vaasa and Rovaniemi. When Finland entered the EU in 1995, Finnish regional policy came under the influence of EU rules. In tandem with this process, the EU also had to adjust to the regional realities of population-sparse countries such as Finland. Specifically, the EU added a sixth objective to the existing five objectives of European regional policy. This new objective was targeted at counties with a population density of eight inhabitants per km^2 or less, whereby counties in north, central and eastern Finland became eligible. The northern and eastern parts also became specifically targeted for structural funds under Objective 1 (Kinnunen 2004).

The collapse of the USSR in combination with a severe global crisis hit Finland hard during the early 1990s (Hjerppe and Jalava 2006: 46). Between 1990 and 1993, Finnish GDP plunged by 9.5 per cent. Similarly, unemployment surged from 3.2 to 16.6 per cent (Ottaviano and Pinelli 2006: 641). During the crisis, an overvalued exchange rate (strong markka) and a tightened fiscal policy worsened the situation.

However, this heavy structural crisis was followed by an economic boom. Between 1994 and 2000, Finnish average annual growth was about 5 per cent (Hjerppe and Jalava 2006: 46). The upswing was mainly driven by high-tech industries, of which mobile telephone company Nokia alone is estimated to account for 1.5 percentage points of the growth rates. During this period, Finland emerged as one of the world's leading information societies. By 2003, the proportion of households owning at least one mobile phone was about 95 per cent and the proportion with Internet access at home was nearly 45 per cent (Statistics Finland 2005), far ahead of other parts of Europe. Despite Nokia's recent hardships, Finland today has reinvented itself as a high-tech advanced economy and is ranked among the top technology nations in the world.

As seen from this short summary of Finland's economic history, openness to trade and varying degrees of market access have played an important role in the localization of industrial production. In addition, access to means of transportation, first via the sea and later on via railways and roads, has been a key issue for regional development in this vast and sparsely populated country. The history of Finland is full of shocks to market access, being the results of wars and world economic events. Examples are the split from Sweden in 1809, the declaration of independence in 1917, the territorial cessations after the Second World War and finally the collapse of the USSR in 1991. In order to measure the effects on regional GDP per capita of the Finnish counties, we will now turn to the construction, sources and results of these new series.

2. Long-term pattern of regional income inequality: new data and stylized facts

Regional GDPs from 1880 to 2010 have been estimated following the method developed by Geary and Stark (2002). During this period, Finland has seen several regional border changes, both internally and externally. The main results from the chapter will be based on calculations from the 12 administrative counties, in their mid-twentieth-century borders. The reason for working with this regional dimension is twofold: (1) The majority of the Finnish historical data were collected at the level of counties, and therefore allow for maximum time consistency in the estimations; and (2) the regional borders of the administrative counties were formed during the Swedish rule. Thus, the Finnish regional GDPs at historical administrative counties are rather consistent with the available long-run Swedish regional GDPs at the county level (see Enflo et al. 2014; see also Chapter 3.12 in this book). This allows for comparisons with the Swedish data.

Unfortunately, the NUTS system does not correspond well to the Finnish historical counties. While there are 12 historical counties, the NUTS system divides Finland into 20 NUTS 3 regions and 5 NUTS 2 regions. Hence, to ensure maximum international comparability of the regional GDP series, data are presented at both county and NUTS 2 levels.[4]

The Finnish Historical National Accounts (Hjerppe 1996)[5] forms the basis of the calculations. From Volume I of this work, I use series of value added and total hours worked per sector (agriculture, industry, services). Regional data on employment come from Statistics Finland (1979), and wage data are drawn from various sources, such as Arvo Soininen (1981) and Auvo Kiiskinen (1958, 1961). Population data for the 12 historical counties from 1880 to 1970 are taken from the official publication *Population by Industry* from Statistics Finland (1979). Population data for the 20 NUTS 3 regions were kindly provided by Hannu Tervo for 1880–2004, and refer to his publication (Tervo 2010). From 1960 onwards, Statistics Finland provides official estimates of regional GDPs (Statistics Finland 1975). For the period 1960–1990, these estimates correspond to the borders of the 12 historical counties. For 2000 and 2010, the official regional GDP data correspond to the 20 NUTS provinces, but are adjusted to the counties using overlapping population shares.[6]

Figure 3.4.1 displays the long-run decline in regional inequality between 12 counties. The graph shows that the population-weighted coefficient of variation fluctuates between 0.35 and 0.45 between 1880 and 1930. These regional inequality figures during early industrialization are quite large in international comparison. The regional divide can be said to centre around a relatively rich, industrialized and urbanized south and a less developed northern part of the country.

Scrutinizing the period a bit more suggests a broad pattern of convergence between 1880 and 1910 and divergence between 1910 and 1930. After 1930, Finland experienced a remarkably fast drop in inequality rates, down to very low levels (0.15) in 1980. The convergence period after 1930, however, ended in 1980, when regional inequality started to rise again. The shape of the Finnish long-run

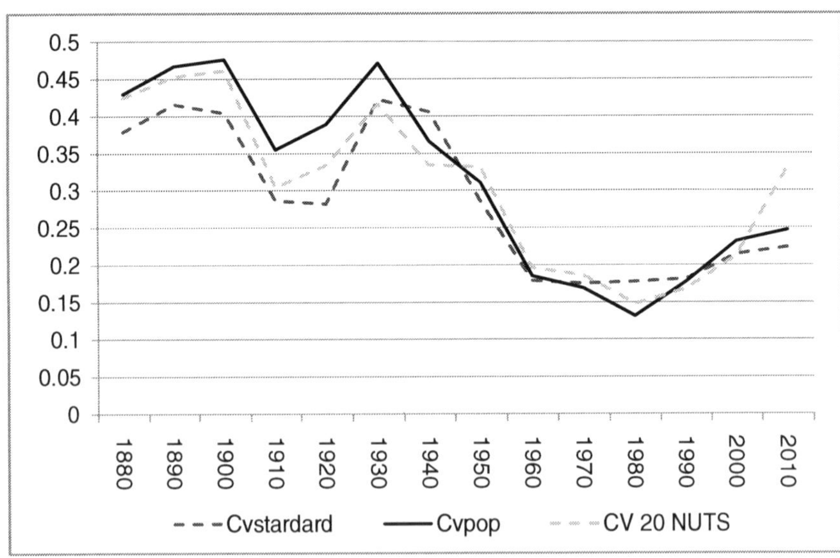

Figure 3.4.1 Coefficient of variation, 12 counties, based on simple averages and population-weighted averages (the CVs for the 20 NUTS 3 regions are also included for comparison)

pattern of regional inequality, with alternating periods of convergence (1880–1910 and 1940–1980) and divergence (1910–1940 and post-1980), is robust to a simple unweighted coefficient of variation, and also to different aggregations of the data (the 12 counties or the 20 NUTS 3 regions). One exception is that the upswing in regional inequality documented after 1980 becomes more pronounced when analysing CVs based on data measured at the more detailed NUTS 3 level. The reason is that NUTS 3 separates the area around the Helsinki region (coded with FI181) more than the county level does, since Helsinki is part of the larger Uusimaa county and Helsinki is the city that has dominated the last decades of diverging growth.

Figure 3.4.2 displays the beta-convergence (i.e. the average annual growth rate of regions) in GDP per capita related to their initial level of GDP per capita. It is clear that the long-run convergence trend identified in Figure 3.4.1 is related to rapid growth of regions with an initially low regional GDP per capita.

3. Explanation of convergence patterns in relative GDP per capita

The broad convergence pattern, described in Figures 3.4.1 and 3.4.2, can be further scrutinized in Tables 3.4.1 and 3.4.2 and supplemented by Maps 3.4.1–3.4.5. For simplicity, the following discussion is organized along the periods 1880–1910, 1910–1940, 1940–1980 and post-1980, which coincide with substantial changes in growth and economic geography.

3.1 The industrialization breakthrough, 1880–1910

As seen from Table 3.4.2, the high initial levels of regional inequality that we observe is mainly a result of Uusimaa's (the capital region) extraordinary high

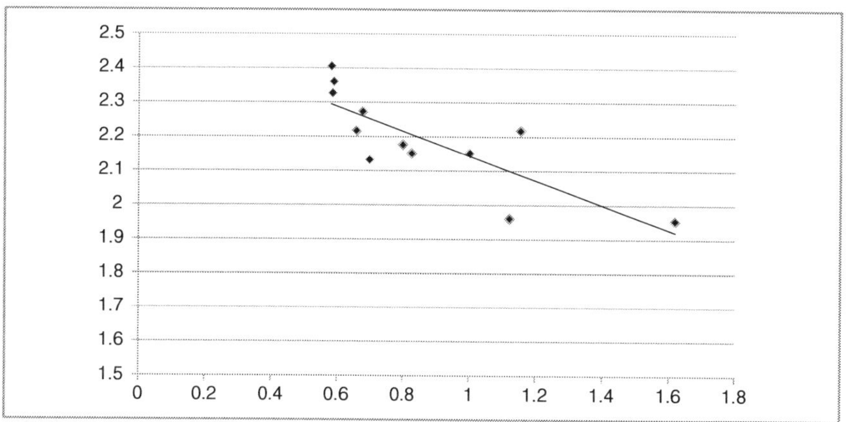

Figure 3.4.2 Beta-convergence: per capita development, 1880–2010 (*y*-axis: annual average growth, *x*-axis: log initial GDP per capita)

relative GDP per capita (2.2 times the Finnish average in 1880). Map 3.4.1 confirms the picture that Uusimaa remained in the top income class, followed by the counties in the south-western part of the country. Over time, inequality was gradually reduced, as seen in Map 3.4.2, partly due to a relative falling behind of Uusimaa and partly due to industrialization spreading to the northern and eastern parts of the country. Earlier research has pointed towards the relative decline in industrial formation of the southern coast between 1890 and 1910 as a driving force of convergence (Kiiskinen 1961: 92). Overall, we observe a reduction in inequality during the industrial break-up, partly due to slow industrialization of the south and partly due to the spreading of agriculture, forestry and forest industry to the peripheral areas of Finland.

3.2 Independence and interwar period, 1910–1940

After Finnish independence, Uusimaa industrialized faster than the rest of the country, and relative GDP per capita levels of this region were again rising inequality until 1930. Despite the closure of the Russian border to trade after the Finnish declaration of independence in 1917, we do not observe any long-run decline of the eastern counties' relative GDP per capita during the interwar period. On the contrary, in 1940, compared to 1910, the regions of Kymi, Kuopio and Northern Karelia appeared to be in relatively better positions. Mikkeli reached an all-time low in 1940. According to Kiiskinen (1961: 68), the regional economy of the mid-south became especially penalized by the 1918 War of Independence, as the most violent battles were fought in this region. From Table 3.4.2, we note a small relative decline in GDP per capita of the Häme county, where the fierce Battle of Tampere was fought in 1918, but a relative increase of Uusimaa between 1910 and 1920.

In general, the interwar period displayed an increasing tendency for divergence, with the capital region forging ahead, the north-western parts of the country falling behind and some weak tendencies for relative improvement in the central parts of Finland, where forestland became exploited thanks to improved transportation investment.

3.3 Post-war period, 1940–1980

As elsewhere in Europe, the post-war period was characterized by rapid convergence. Within 40 years, Finland went from a high-inequality country to one with among the lowest levels of regional inequality in Europe. Regional differences in industrial productivity rapidly levelled out. This was particularly the case in Central Finland, one of the most backward regions in 1880, where relative GDP per capita has converged upwards to the average between 1930 and 1950. In Uusimaa, the opposite was true, as relative regional GDP per capita levels dropped from 2.12 to 1.57 times the average, as seen from Table 3.4.2.

The Åland Islands tell an interesting story. After the League of Nations assigned the islands to Finland in 1921, they became politically neutral, entirely demilitarized and exclusively Swedish-speaking by law. Going from the second richest county in 1880, the islands gradually fell behind and experienced an all-time low in 1930. Table 3.4.2 bears witness to the volatility of the relative position of the islands in terms of GDP per capita, from a quite low position in 1970 to a very high position thereafter.[7] In the post-war period, the islands became successful in shipping, and in 1959 large modern passenger ferries began to operate the route between the islands and Stockholm in Sweden and Turku in Finland. The traffic was made profitable by tax-free sales on goods such as alcohol, perfume and tobacco. Several shipping companies were founded on the Åland Islands, and it is probable that a large part of the islands' GDP can be attributed to value added from the shipping industry. As Finland joined the EU in 1995, the islanders feared that the incomes from tax-free sales would become history. However, the EU granted the islands a special status and an exception to the tax-free rules of the internal market.

By 1980, the relative GDP per capita levels of Finnish regions had converged rapidly, but scrutinizing Map 3.4.5, the relatively richest counties are still today to be found in the south (Uusimaa and Häme) and south-east (Kymi), suggesting that eastern markets probably played a non-negligible role for Finland in 1980. The relative decline of the western region, notably, Turku and Pori, which was the third richest county in 1880, is also notable in relative GDP per capita levels, and visible in Table 3.4.2.

3.4 Post-1980

After 1980, regional divergence has been the trend in Finland. The Finnish weakening of regional convergence also appears to be part of a wider phenomenon documented on an EU-wide basis (Tondl 1999; Enflo 2010; see also Chapter 2 in this book). Finland's economic crisis of the early 1990s has been put forward as a main watershed in long-run regional inequality patterns (Tervo 2005). Although the crisis hit all Finland fairly evenly, with most regions losing about one-fifth of their employment, the post-crisis recovery was highly uneven. The increased labour force mobility[8] and the rise of new non-natural resource-dependent industries[9] have halted the process of regional convergence. Between 1993 and 1996, two-thirds of all newly created jobs were localized in one of the three major cities, Helsinki, Tampere and Turku (Tervo 2005). Post-1990, a new specialization in high-tech, footloose industries interrupted the previous process of long-term convergence, and Finnish agglomeration economies happened in areas with better market and supplier access (Ottaviano and Pinelli 2006). Thus, as can be seen in Table 3.4.2 and Maps 3.4.1–3.4.5, the post-1980s have brought about an increasing concentration of production to the southern part of Finland (Uusimaa). This county has again forged ahead in terms of relative regional GDP per capita, thus fostering the most recent divergence tendency.

4. The spatial allocation of relative shares of GDP, 1880–2010

The broad picture of Finland's regional GDP evolution can be summarized in Table 3.4.3, where the shares of GDP allotted to the five NUTS 2 regions are displayed. From the table, it is clear that regional GDP has become increasingly concentrated to the capital region (Helsinki-Uusimaa), which increased its share from 29 per cent in 1880 to 39 per cent in 2010. Using this very broad spatial definition of a region, we may only observe that the relative strengthening of the capital region has taken place at the expense of the rest of the country. The other three mainland regions (Western Finland, Southern Finland and Northern and Eastern Finland) show equally strong tendencies of decline, between 6 and 8 percentage points from 1880 to 2010. The Åland Islands keep a steady 1 per cent share of Finland's GDP throughout the period. However, the long-run growth experience of Finland offers a richer spatial history than that. In order to properly capture it, we need to go into the level of the counties displayed in Table 3.4.4. From this table, some long-run tendencies can be observed: the western decline, border changes and shifts in market access in the east, and the expansion towards the northern frontier.

4.1 The western decline

Finland's geographical location, skirted by the gulfs of the Baltic, made its southern and western parts relatively more accessible using sea transportation, thus promoting them with superior market access to inland areas. It is generally argued that the south-west, with the province of Turku and Pori (which hosted the Finnish capital, Turku, until 1812) has the oldest business and cultural traditions in the country. Yet it is the western part of the country that shows the steadiest long-run decline in its shares of GDP. While the two provinces on the western coast (Turku and Pori and Vaasa) accounted for 32 per cent of Finland's GDP in 1880, their share in 2010 is down to 19 per cent. This decline was commented on by Eino Jutikkala as early as 1948 in a famous speach where he explained how 'Finland's economic face was turned from the Gulf of Bothnia to the Gulf of Finland' during industrialization.[10] The expansion of the St Petersburg market gave places further east, such as Helsinki and Tampere, leading positions in textile and metalwork industries. These developments were aided by the developments of canals and railroad networks during the mid-nineteenth century. These were, at least partly, set up in the interests of the Russian Empire, and allowed for establishing industry further away from the coasts and helped shift the economic face of Finland further away from the west.

4.2 Border changes and shifts in market access in the east

Finland's annexation into the Russian Empire did not initially result in any change in its destinations for foreign trade. Actually, the trade relations with Sweden continued relatively undistorted until the 1840s, when Sweden received the same treatment as other foreign countries in Finnish trade (Schybergson 1973). Thus, the Western markets remained important, but gradually the economic connections with north-western Russia grew. From the 1830s onwards, cheap Russian grain was imported into Finland, making it easier to supply the populations of the growing industrial centres in the south-east. Similarly, Finnish exports of ironworks and cotton works found new markets in the area around St Petersburg and Estonia. The relative growth of the south-east is manifest in the evolution of Kymi county, where the expanding importance of the St Petersburg market led to an increase in its relative share of national GDP from 6 to 8 per cent between 1880 and 1910.

However, access to Eastern markets proved a volatile virtue for the growing Finnish counties. After the Russian Bolshevik Revolution and Finland's declared independence in 1917, Russia closed its border for Finnish trade. This translated into a small decline in relative GDP shares of Kymi county in 1920, as seen in Table 3.4.4, but the region quickly picked up, thanks to the booming timber and paper industry in the interwar period.

Before the Second World War, Kymi was actually part of the larger province Viipuri that stretched on to Lake Ladoga and incorporated much of the Karelian Isthmus in current Russia. In 1930, Kymi hosted Finland's second largest city, Viipuri (Vyborg). In the territorial cessations after the Second World War, the former province of Viipuri was split into a Russian and a Finnish part and the Kymi county was created. The city of Viipuri and the main part of the area was annexed by the USSR, and the regional distributional effects of the split between Finland and the USSR can be noticed in Kymi's relative share of GDP: Table 3.4.4 shows that it falls from 9 per cent in 1940 to 7 per cent in 1950. The territorial cessations led to the evacuation of the Finnish population living in the annexed area.[11] About 430,000 people (corresponding to about 11 per cent of Finland's population) had to find new homes in Finland. A majority of these people were farmers, who were allotted farmland according to plans designed in the Finnish legislation. The combined regional effects of the territorial cessation and the evacuation after the Second World War are ambiguous. While Finland lost its second largest city, the important port of Viipuri and the markets in the east, it appears that the resettlement policy did not have any specific impact on the rest of the country, as the evacuated population was evenly spread out. Yet we see a drop in the relative importance of the counties close to the lost territories between 1940 and 1950 in Table 3.4.4.

The USSR market became increasingly important for Finnish exports during the post-war period. The Finnish war reparations required a rapid acceleration of industrial expansion in the latter half of the 1940s, which moved the industrial centre of gravity even more in favour of the south (Kiiskinen 1961: 93). After the war reparations had been paid, a lack of competitiveness of the rapidly expanding industries led to continued dependence on USSR orders in the previously favoured areas. Again, we may observe in Table 3.4.4 how the shares of regional GDP of Kymi increased and reached a high in 1960.

4.3 The central and northern parts: expanding towards the frontier

Between 1880 and 1930, cultivation and settlement spread considerably into the north and central parts of the country. Yet the previous literature points towards a great uniformity of regional shares in agricultural output. Although the northern frontier rapidly expanded, it seems that the regions of the south and west have offset their relative smaller changes of expansion by intensification and mechanization (Kiiskinen 1961: 87). The expansion levels off in the 1930s. Taking the example of the northern county of Oulu in Table 3.4.4, it can be found that the share of regional GDP stayed high, around 8–9 per cent between 1880 and 1920, but declined thereafter.

As previously mentioned, forestry and forest-related industries were the dominant factors of income growth in the areas of the south during the late nineteenth century, especially in the rather urban mid-south and south-east. But thanks to advancements in transportation technologies, as well as investment in roads and transport equipment, the forest sector expanded further from the urban centres. This made it possible to put the great forests of central and northern Finland into the sphere of profitable exploitation. As a result, the share of income from forestry fell in Southern and Western Finland but increased in the central and north. With increasing technological sophistication of the forestry and forest industry, central and northern Finland have become heavily specialized in raw-material-intensive and capital-intensive industries.

In Table 3.4.4, we clearly see how the regions of middle Finland (Central Finland and Häme) and the very north (Lapland) experience an increase in the regional shares of GDP from the 1920s and 1930s until the 1980s. These areas benefited from the improved modes of transportation into the inner and northern parts of the country. The state played an active role in industrial policy, for example by the setting up of state-owned manufacturing firms and energy companies, which turned the southern part of Lapland into an area characterized by big industry.

Another form of regional policy is the placement of universities. Notably, the University of Oulu is argued to have had an invaluable effect on the growth of the north-western region (Economic Council 2001). The role of industry–university linkages in the city of Oulu has been much discussed. For example, Waagø et al. (2001) argue that an electronics and telecommunication industry grew out of the long-term planning and close cooperation of regional actors. During its peak of success, Nokia chose to locate its R&D and other departments with about 12,000 employees in Oulu. After Nokia's remarkable fall on the market, the region is still host to a large population of highly skilled programmers and engineers, and is becoming a leading information and communications technology cluster in Northern Europe.

Lately, policies have aimed towards developing tourism in the area. In Lapland today, tourism provides more employment opportunities than any other industry that makes indirect or direct use of natural resources (Saarinen 2003). With the introduction of special efforts into tourism of the north, such as the Santa Claus Village near Rovaniemi or special purpose-built spaces (from glass igloos to luxury suites) to see the Northern Lights, the area is rapidly transforming its economic base.

Despite regional policies and a drive towards developing tourism, Table 3.4.4 indicates that the GDP shares of the provinces in central and northern Finland have stayed rather constant. During the mid-century with the expanding forestry frontier and subsequent industrial policy, the share increased somewhat, but since 2000 it has decreased again. The only exception is Häme, which over the long run has increased its share in relative regional GDP.[12]

5. Discussion and concluding remarks

This chapter analysed the regional evolution of Finland's GDP per capita over more than 130 years. It is shown that Finland's regions were relatively unequal in terms of GDP per capita and in European comparison during early industrialization. Gradually, industrialization was spread to include larger parts of the country, especially thanks to improvements in transportation technologies that made an expanding timber industry possible. Rapid convergence in GDP per capita only took place after the Second World War, but came to a halt in the 1980s and gave way to a new tendency of divergence. When looking at shares of GDP, Finland's spatial evolution can be described as a gradual concentration of GDP in the southern parts of the country. In addition, the historically important western parts have declined, whereas the role of the eastern markets has led to some fluctuations in the share of eastern counties in GDP.

One obvious candidate for the Finnish lack of strong convergence during the early industrialization phase is little internal and external migration. The previous literature supports this idea; for example, Pitkänen (1994) argues that internal migration was fairly modest during the late nineteenth century. As late as the 1920s, about 90 per cent of the Finnish population lived in their home county and 70 per cent even remained in their home municipality. In addition, emigration figures were low: between 1829 and 1929, only 350,000 Finns left for the New World.

The role of regional policies for post-war convergence must also be understood. Finnish regional policy, salient from the mid-1960s onwards, appears to have aimed towards decentralizing industry and spreading it across development areas (Tervo 2010). The outcome is strong regional convergence after the Second World War until 1980. Yet we see similar tendencies in many European countries, and future studies should clarify the role of specific policies for this outcome. A competing candidate explanation for post-war convergence is migration. After the establishment of the Common Nordic Labour Market in 1954, Finland saw a substantial outflow to Sweden, especially in the 1960s and 1970s. Since 1954, as many as two-thirds of the inter-Nordic migrants have been Finnish emigrants to, and Finnish returnees from, Sweden (Fischer and Straubhaar 1996). The 1950s and 1960s have thus been labelled the era of great migrations and involved rapid depopulation of rural areas (Tervo 2005). Some of the underlying reasons for the strong migration wave were the relative income gap between Sweden and Finland and the fast agricultural decline associated with Finland's rapid industrialization. During the 1980s, Finland largely caught up with Sweden in GDP per capita terms and the migration flows slowed down. While emigration led to increasing spatial concentration of economic production and welfare, the effects

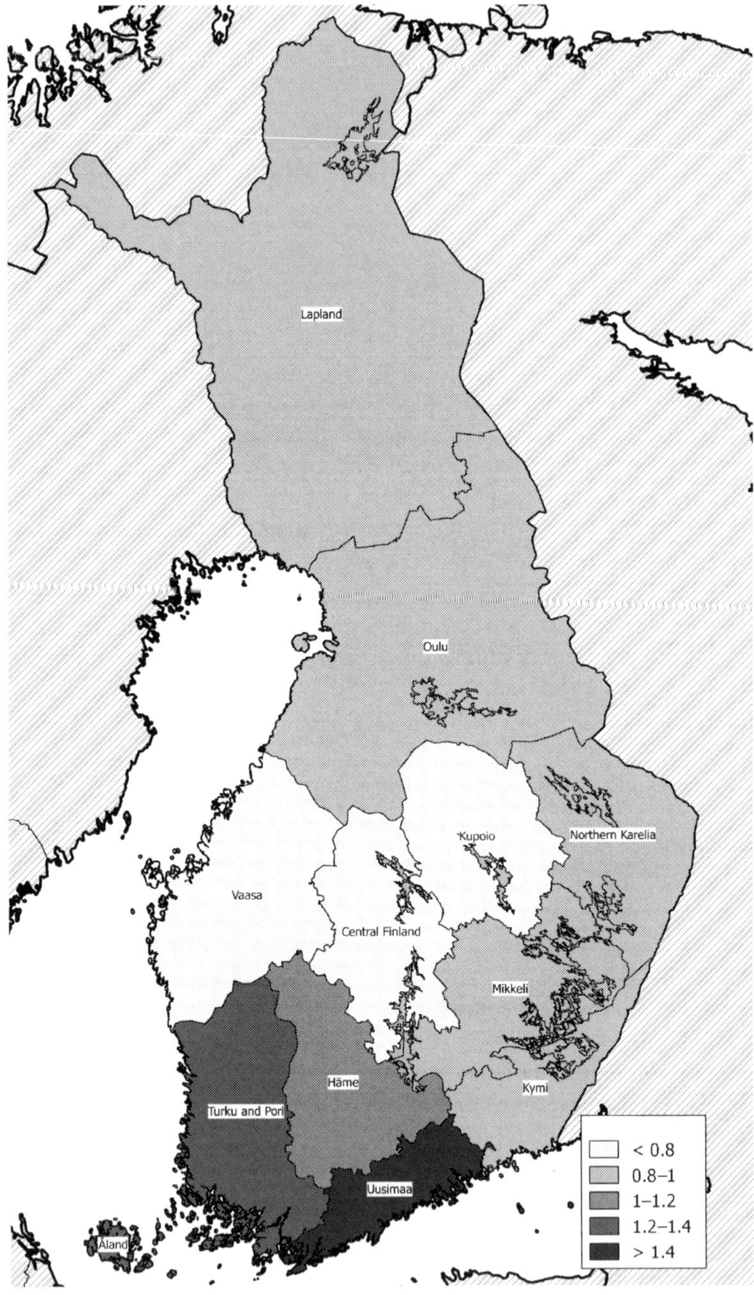

Map 3.4.1 Relative GDP per capita, 1880 (Finland = 1)

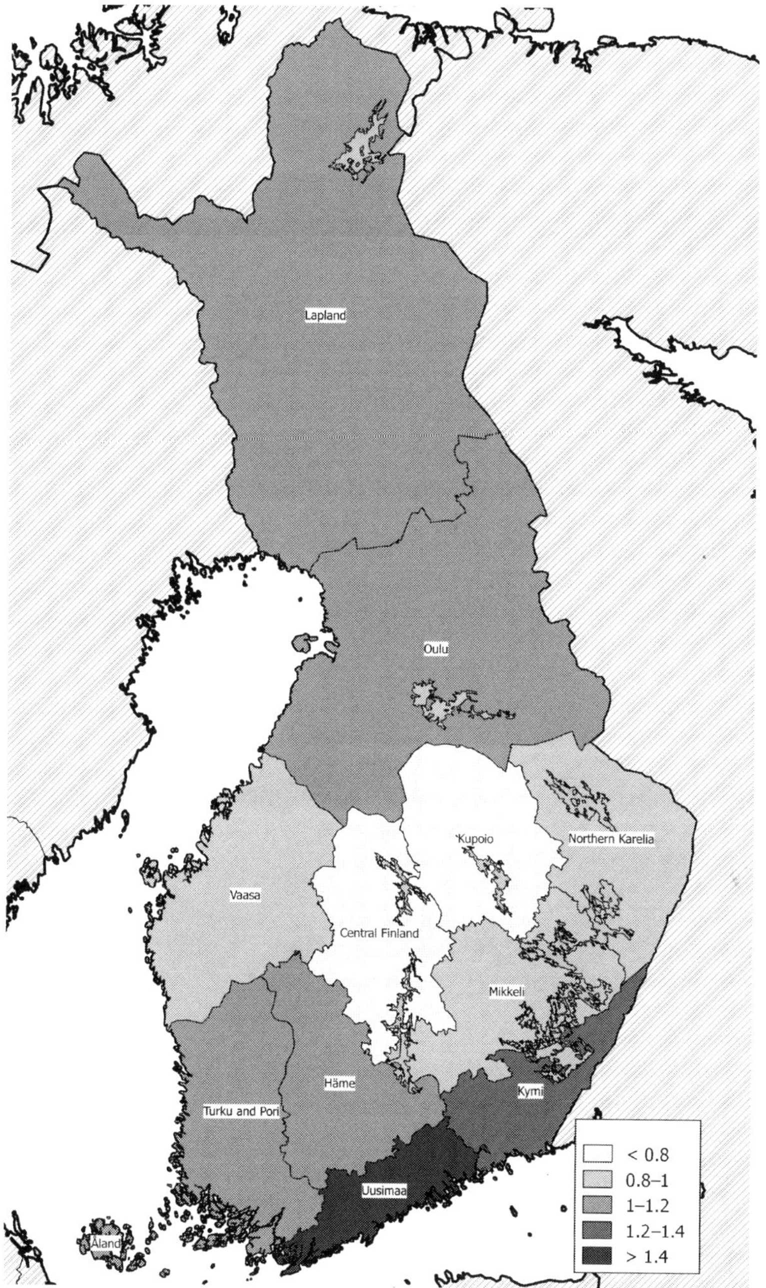

Map 3.4.2 Relative GDP per capita, 1910 (Finland = 1)

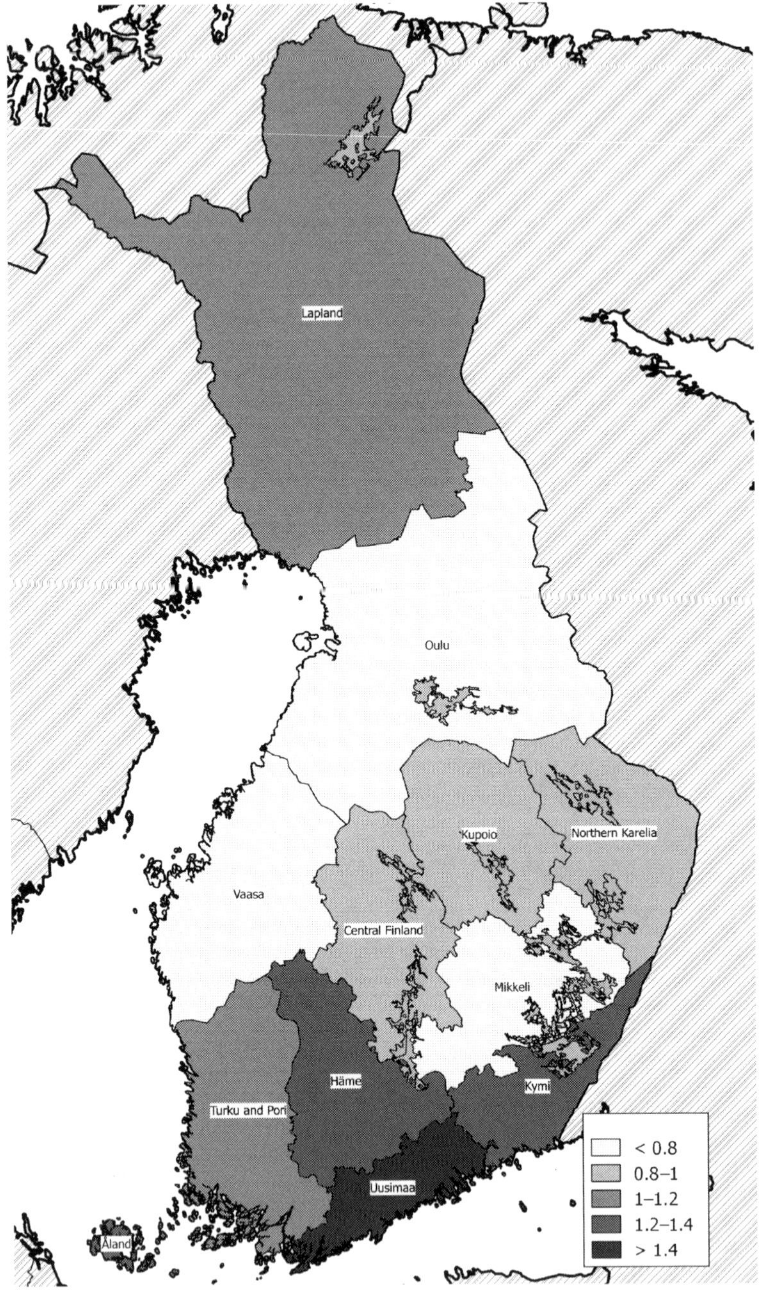

Map 3.4.3 Relative GDP per capita, 1940 (Finland = 1)

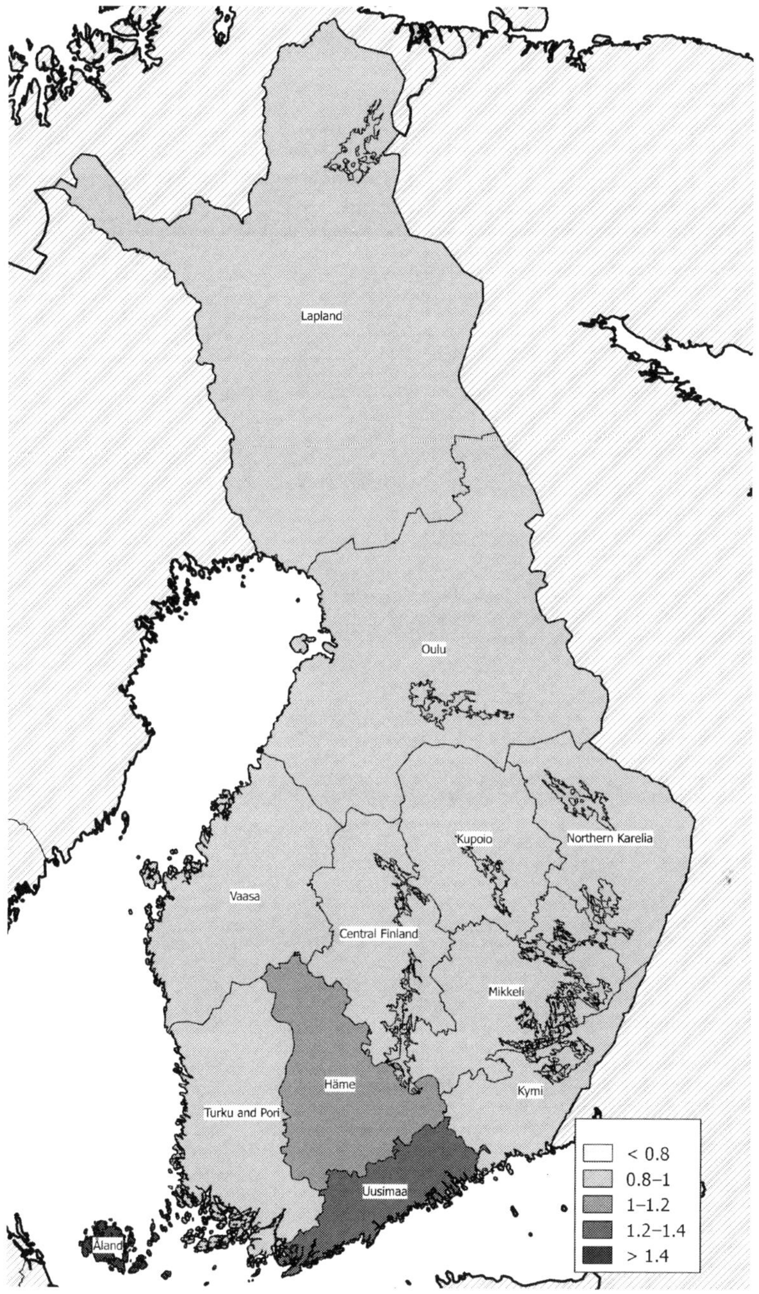

Map 3.4.4 Relative GDP per capita, 1980 (Finland = 1)

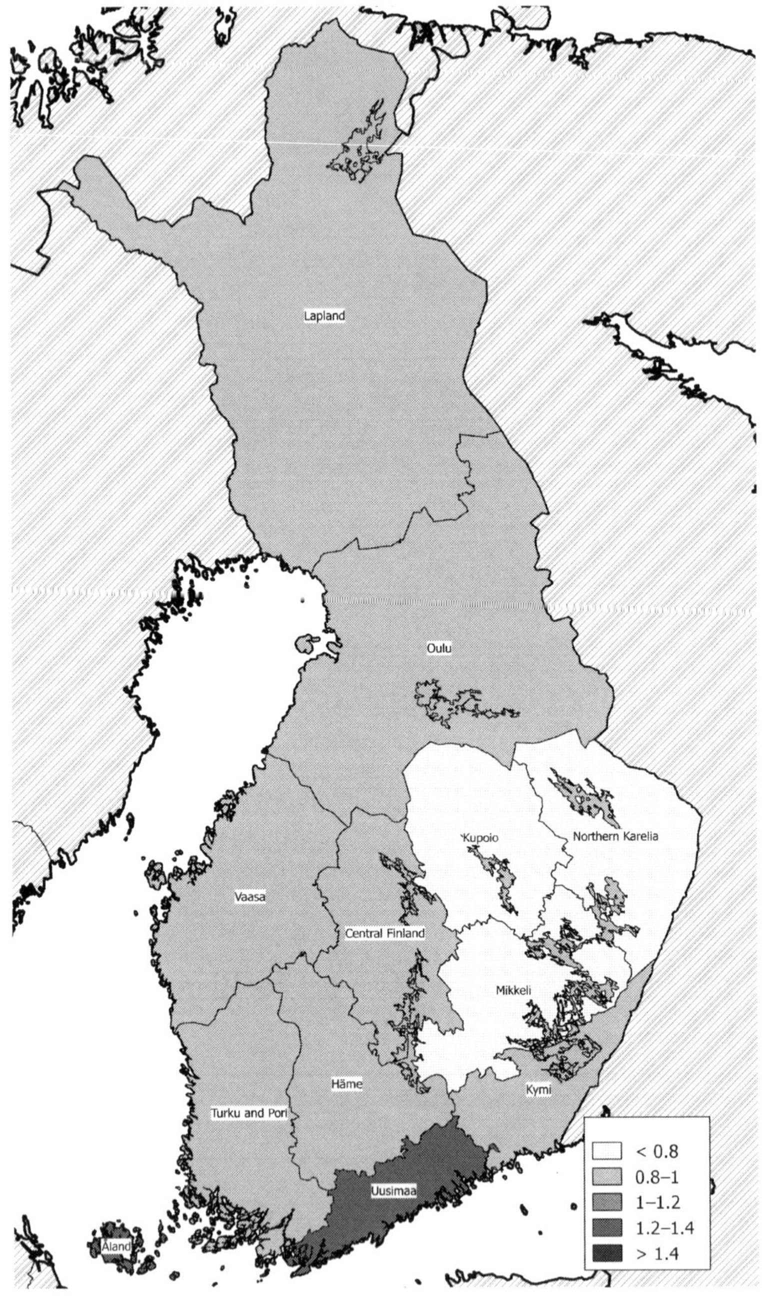

Map 3.4.5 Relative GDP per capita, 2010 (Finland = 1)

Table 3.4.1 Relative GDP per capita, Finland = 1, five NUTS 2 regions

NUTS code	*Official name*	*1880*	*1890*	*1900*	*1910*	*1920*	*1930*	*1940*	*1950*	*1960*	*1970*	*1980*	*1990*	*2000*	*2010*
FI19	Western Finland (Länsi-Suomi)	0.86	0.84	0.76	0.89	0.9	0.91	0.93	0.84	0.86	0.84	0.86	0.8	0.78	0.81
FI1B	Helsinki-Uusimaa	2.63	2.64	2.56	2.04	2.1	2.19	1.73	1.57	1.27	1.23	1.16	1.25	1.32	1.22
FI1C	Southern Finland (Etelä-Suomi)	1.05	1.05	1.03	1.01	0.98	1.01	1.04	0.89	0.9	0.87	0.83	0.82	0.77	0.76
FI1D	East and North Finland (Itä ja Pohjois Soumi)	0.77	0.77	0.77	0.84	0.82	0.76	0.72	0.65	0.73	0.75	0.78	0.74	0.7	0.73
FI20	Åland	1.23	1.21	1.03	0.98	0.91	0.87	1.12	0.82	0.76	0.6	0.99	1.17	1.12	1.08

Source: Enflo (2014).

Note: The regional GDPs were calculated using the Geary-Stark method.

Table 3.4.2 Relative GDP per capita, Finland = 1, 12 counties (*läänit*)

County name	*1880*	*1890*	*1900*	*1910*	*1920*	*1930*	*1940*	*1950*	*1960*	*1970*	*1980*	*1990*	*2000*	*2010*
Uusimaa	2.20	2.27	2.30	1.89	2.01	2.12	1.72	1.57	1.30	1.27	1.21	1.29	1.36	1.38
Turku and Pori	1.34	1.31	1.12	1.14	1.14	1.11	1.20	1.03	1.04	1.02	0.97	0.95	0.92	0.85
Åland	1.38	1.37	1.18	1.11	1.03	0.98	1.24	0.92	0.85	0.67	1.41	1.30	1.24	1.23
Häme	1.19	1.17	1.07	1.07	1.06	1.33	1.28	1.18	1.08	1.02	1.01	0.96	0.92	0.97
Kymi	1.00	1.06	1.20	1.23	1.08	1.13	1.31	0.96	1.12	1.06	1.00	0.97	0.95	0.81
Mikkeli	0.84	0.73	0.83	0.86	0.86	0.79	0.71	0.90	0.80	0.82	0.83	0.80	0.73	0.75
Northern Karelia	0.88	0.81	1.02	0.86	0.95	0.83	0.93	0.77	0.79	0.79	0.82	0.77	0.72	0.70
Kupoio	0.78	0.71	0.68	0.70	0.77	0.97	0.81	0.76	0.81	0.83	0.85	0.87	0.77	0.80
Central Finland	0.78	0.65	0.70	0.76	0.99	1.03	0.98	0.96	0.87	0.87	0.90	0.95	0.89	0.84
Vaasa	0.78	0.78	0.71	0.99	0.94	0.73	0.76	0.66	0.83	0.83	0.95	0.84	0.80	0.88
Oulu	0.97	1.13	0.97	1.19	1.02	0.74	0.66	0.55	0.76	0.83	0.86	0.84	0.80	0.81
Lapland	0.86	0.92	1.05	1.11	1.11	1.15	1.07	0.83	0.93	0.91	0.92	0.89	0.87	0.82

Note: See Table 3.4.1.

Table 3.4.3 Shares of regional GDP, five NUTS 2 regions

NUTS code	*Official name*	*1880*	*1890*	*1900*	*1910*	*1920*	*1930*	*1940*	*1950*	*1960*	*1970*	*1980*	*1990*	*2000*	*2010*
FI19	Western Finland (Länsi-Suomi)	0.29	0.28	0.26	0.28	0.27	0.26	0.27	0.27	0.27	0.25	0.25	0.23	0.22	0.23
FI1B	Helsinki-Uusimaa	0.18	0.19	0.22	0.20	0.23	0.26	0.25	0.25	0.24	0.27	0.28	0.32	0.37	0.39
FI1C	Southern Finland (Etelä-Suomi)	0.26	0.26	0.26	0.26	0.24	0.24	0.25	0.25	0.24	0.24	0.23	0.22	0.20	0.18
FI1D	East and North Finland (Itä ja Pohjois Suomi)	0.26	0.26	0.25	0.26	0.25	0.23	0.22	0.22	0.25	0.23	0.23	0.22	0.20	0.20
FI20	Åland	0.01	0.01	0.01	0.01	0.01	0.01	0.01	0.00	0.00	0.00	0.01	0.01	0.01	0.01

Note: See Table 3.4.1.

Table 3.4.4 Shares of regional GDP, 12 counties (*läänit*)

County name	*1880*	*1890*	*1900*	*1910*	*1920*	*1930*	*1940*	*1950*	*1960*	*1970*	*1980*	*1990*	*2000*	*2010*
Uusimaa	0.20	0.21	0.24	0.22	0.24	0.27	0.26	0.26	0.24	0.28	0.28	0.32	0.37	0.39
Turku and Pori	0.21	0.20	0.18	0.18	0.17	0.16	0.17	0.16	0.15	0.15	0.14	0.14	0.13	0.12
Åland	0.01	0.01	0.01	0.01	0.01	0.01	0.01	0.00	0.00	0.00	0.01	0.01	0.01	0.01
Häme	0.12	0.12	0.11	0.12	0.11	0.14	0.14	0.15	0.14	0.14	0.14	0.13	0.13	0.13
Kymi	0.06	0.06	0.07	0.08	0.07	0.08	0.09	0.07	0.09	0.08	0.07	0.07	0.06	0.05
Mikkeli	0.06	0.05	0.06	0.05	0.05	0.04	0.04	0.05	0.04	0.04	0.04	0.03	0.03	0.03
Northern Karelia	0.04	0.04	0.05	0.04	0.04	0.04	0.04	0.04	0.04	0.03	0.03	0.03	0.02	0.02
Kupoio	0.05	0.05	0.05	0.04	0.05	0.06	0.05	0.05	0.05	0.05	0.04	0.04	0.04	0.04
Central Finland	0.04	0.04	0.04	0.04	0.05	0.05	0.05	0.05	0.05	0.05	0.05	0.05	0.04	0.04
Vaasa	0.11	0.11	0.10	0.11	0.10	0.08	0.08	0.07	0.08	0.08	0.09	0.07	0.07	0.07
Oulu	0.08	0.09	0.08	0.09	0.08	0.06	0.05	0.05	0.07	0.07	0.07	0.07	0.07	0.07
Lapland	0.02	0.02	0.02	0.03	0.03	0.04	0.04	0.03	0.04	0.04	0.04	0.04	0.03	0.03

Note: See Table 3.4.1.

on regional GDP per capita are likely to have been convergence. Thus, it is possible that emigration, in combination with industrialization and structural change, had a converging effect on the regional GDP of Finland in the post-war period.

The role of transportation and infrastructure in sparsely populated countries is often discussed. Theoretical models such as Krugman (1991) predict that increasing investments into infrastructure may lead to further concentration of economic activities. In the case of Finland, improved transportation initially had a de-concentrating effect as inland towns began to form with the growth of forest industries. Future research should clarify the role of the Finnish railroads in shaping local economic conditions and fostering preconditions for decentralized growth and regional convergence. It was not until the 1950s and 1960s that scholars have documented how the infrastructure policy of Finland was deliberately created to lay the foundations for the development of the sparsely populated parts of Finland. Tervo (2005) argues that the policies, for example a major road-building programme that improved the operational preconditions for the manufacturing and service industries, eventually increased the competitiveness of more remote regions.

Let me conclude by pointing towards the recent trend breaks in regional convergence after the 1980s. It appears that the novel high-tech industrial specialization pattern in Finland and elsewhere is fostering agglomerations and industrial concentrations to urban areas. Perhaps these strong diverging forces are even more disruptive in sparsely populated and peripheral countries such as Finland. A future concern for policymakers will be how to combine rapid growth in high-tech industries with regional equality and how societal services will be sustained in sparsely populated areas.

Notes

1 Acknowledgements: The research was carried out in collaboration with the international network Historical Economic Geography of Europe, 1900–2000 (part of GLOBALEURONET, European Science Foundation). Research funding from the Swedish Research Council and the Wallenberg Foundation is gratefully acknowledged. I am thankful for many valuable comments and suggestions from Riitta Hjeppe and Sakari Heikkinen. Björn Enflo provided excellent research assistance. All remaining errors are my own.

2 At present, Swedish is the main language of 5.4 per cent of the population, down from 14 per cent at the beginning of the twentieth century.

3 See House of the Estates (2012).

4 See Enflo (2014) for a detailed description of how the data were calculated using these geographical borders.

5 Riitta Hjerppe's book *The Finnish Economy 1860–1985* includes descriptions of the data.

6 Enflo (2014) provides detailed descriptions about all data sources and methods for estimations.

7 It should be noted that these fluctuating figures after 1970 are not a result of any of the calculations that I made in the chapter: the data are taken from the official publications of Statistics Finland. Since the islands never changed borders, their county and NUTS classifications have remained intact. Rather, the fluctuations are likely a result of the specific economic conditions on the islands.

8 Some 1.5 million people changed their municipality of residence in 1995–2000, while the corresponding figure in 1985–1990 was only 1.2 million (Nivalainen 2003).
9 The significance of high-tech industry rose dramatically, with high-tech products increasing from 12.4 per cent of total exports in 1994 to 20.4 per cent in 1999.
10 The economic development of Finland shown by maps (Jutikkala 1948–1950: 164).
11 The region of Karelia, including Viipuri, in the south-east was the most populous part of the ceded areas. Two other ceded areas, Petsamo and Salla, were located in the sparsely populated northern parts of the country.
12 Häme hosts old cultural traditions and is home to Finland's third largest city, Tampere. The city has old industrial roots, and produces textiles, shoes and metalwares for the Finnish home market.

References

Economic Council (2001) *Regional Development and Regional Policy in Finland: Summary of the Working Group Report*, Helsinki: Prime Minister's Office Publications 2001/2.

Enflo, K. (2010) 'Productivity and employment: is there a trade-off? Comparing Western European regions and American states 1950–2000', *Annals of Regional Science*, Vol. 45 (2): 401–21.

Enflo, K. (2014) 'Finland's regional GDPs 1880–2010: estimates, sources and interpretations', *Lund Papers in Economic History*, No. 135.

Enflo, K., Henning, M. and Schön, L. (2014) 'Swedish regional GDP 1855–2000: estimations and general trends in the Swedish regional system', *Research in Economic History*, Vol. 30: 47–89.

Fischer, P. and Straubhaar, T. (1996) 'Migration and economic integration in the Nordic Common Labour Market', *Nord*, Vol. 1996 (2), Copenhagen: Nordic Council of Ministers.

Geary, F. and Stark, T. (2002) 'Examining Ireland's post-famine economic growth performance', *The Economic Journal*, Vol. 112 (482): 919–35.

Heikkinen, S. and Hjerppe, R. (1986) *Industry and Industrial Handicraft in Finland 1860–1913 (Soumen teollisuus ja teollinen käsityö 1860–1913)*, Helsinki: Bank of Finland Publications.

Heikkinen, S. and Hjerppe, R. (1987) 'The growth of Finnish industry 1860–1913: causes and linkages', *The Journal of European Economic History*, Vol. 16 (2): 227–46.

Hjerppe, R. (1989) *The Finnish Economy 1860–1985: Growth and Structural Change*, 1st English edition, Studies on Finland's Economic Growth, Helsinki: Bank of Finland Publications.

Hjerppe, R. (1996) *Finland's Historical National Accounts 1860–1994: Calculation Methods and Statistical Tables*, Jyväskylä: Kopi-Jyvä Oy.

Hjerppe, R. and Jalava, J. (2006) 'Economic growth and structural change: a century and a half of catching-up', in J. Ojala, J. Eloranta and J. Jalava (eds), *The Road to Prosperity: An Economic History of Finland*, Jyväskylä: Gummerus Oy, pp. 33–64.

House of the Estates (2012) *60 Years after the War Reparations*, Helsinki: House of the Estates, available at: http://vnk.fi/tiedostot/julkinen/pdf/2012/Sotakorvaus_EN.pdf (accessed 13 August 2018).

Jutikkala, E. (1948–1950) 'The economic development of Finland shown by maps', *Proceedings of the Finnish Academy of Science and Letters*, p. 164.

Kangasharju, A. (1998) 'Beta convergence in Finland: regional differences in speed of convergence', *Applied Economics*, Vol. 30 (5): 679–87.

Kaukiainen, Y. (2006) 'Foreign trade and transport', in J. Ojala, J. Eloranta and J. Jalava (eds), *The Road to Prosperity: An Economic History of Finland*, Jyväskylä: Gummerus Oy, pp. 127–64.

Kiiskinen. A. (1958) *Taloudellinen kasvu alueittain Suomessa vuosina 1926–1952 [The Economic Growth by Regions in Finland 1926–1952], series of publications, A:III*, Helsinki: The Economic Research Institute of Finnish Industry.

Kiiskinen. A. (1961) 'Regional economic growth in Finland 1880–1952', *Scandinavian Economic History Review*, Vol. 9 (1): 83–104.

Kinnunen, J. (2004) 'The dynamics of EU cohesion policy: structural funds as a vector of change in Finland', OEUE Phase II, Occasional paper 3.4-09-04, Centre for European Studies, University of Helsinki.

Kirby, D. (2006) *A Concise History of Finland*, Cambridge: Cambridge University Press.

Kotavaara, O., Antikainen, H. and Rusanen, J. (2011) 'Urbanization and transportation in Finland, 1880–1970', *Journal of Interdisciplinary History*, Vol. 42 (1): 89–109.

Krugman, P. (1991) *Geography and Trade*, Cambridge, MA: MIT Press.

Nivalainen, S. (2003) *Where Do Migrants Go? An Analysis of Rural and Urban Destined/Originated Migration in Finland in 1996–1999*, Pellervon taloudellisen tutkimuslaitoksen työpapereita, Helsinki: Pellervo Economic Research Institute.

Ojala, J., Eloranta, J. and Jalava, J. (eds) (2006) *The Road to Prosperity: An Economic History of Finland*, Jyväskylä: Gummerus Oy.

Ottaviano, G.I.P. and Pinelli, D. (2006) 'Market potential and productivity: evidence from Finnish regions', *Regional Science and Urban Economics*, Vol. 36 (5): 636–57.

Paavonen, T. (2005) 'Special arrangements of the Soviet trade in Finland's integrations solutions: a consequence of Finland's international position or pursuit of profit?', in J. Eloranta and J. Ojala (eds), *East-West Trade and the Cold War*, Jyväskylä Studies in Humanities 36, Jyväskylä: Jyväskylä University Printing House.

Pitkänen, K. (1994) 'Historical development patterns of Finnish population' ['Suomen väestön historialliset kehityslinjat'], in S. Koskinen, T. Martelin, I.L. Notkola, V. Notkola, K. Pitkänen et al. (eds), *Finland's Population* [*Suomen väestö*], Helsinki: Helsinki University Press.

Saarinen, J. (2003) 'The regional economics of tourism in northern Finland: the socio-economic implications of recent tourism development and future possibilities for regional development', *Scandinavian Journal of Hospitality and Tourism*, Vol. 3 (2): 91–113.

Schybergson, P. (1973) *Hantverk och fabriker; Finlands konsumtionsvaruindustri, 1815–1870, Bidrag till kännedom av Finlands natur och folk*, Thesis, Åbo akademi, Turku.

Soininen, A. (1981) *Maataloustyöväen palkkakehitys 1800-luvun lopussa ja 1900-luvun alussa ajanjakso 1878–1913, Helsingin yliopiston monistuspalvelu*, Helsinki: Painatusjaos.

Statistics Finland (1975) *Aluetilinpito [Regional Accounting: Production, Employment and Gross Domestic Fixed Capital Formation by Provinces in 1960 and 1970]*, Statistical Surveys, No. 53.

Statistics Finland (1979) *Väestön elinkeino* [*Population by Industry*], Statistical Surveys, No. 63.

Statistics Finland (2005) *Households' Ownership of Consumer Durables, 1996–2003*, Helsinki: Statistics Finland.

Sutela, P. (2014) 'Trading with the Soviet Union: the Finnish experience, 1944–1991', *Kikimora Studies on Russia and Eastern Europe*, Series B39, Aleksanteri Institute.

Tervo, H. (2005) 'Regional policy lessons from Finland', in D. Felsenstein and B.A. Portnov (eds), *Regional Disparities in Small Countries*, Berlin: Springer-Verlag, pp. 267–82.

Tervo, H. (2010) 'Cities, hinterlands and agglomeration shadows: spatial developments in Finland during 1880–2004', *Explorations in Economic History*, Vol. 47 (4): 476–86.

Tondl, G. (1999) 'The changing pattern of regional convergence in Europe', *Jahrbuch für Regionalwissenschaft*, Vol. 19: 1–33.

Waagø, S., Rasmussen, E., Kvaal, T., Gulbrandsen, M. and Trondsen, E. (2001) *The Role of the University in Economic Development: An Analysis of Six European Universities of Science and Technology*, Trondheim: NTNU.

3.5 A long-run perspective on French regional income inequality, 1860–2010

Joan Ramón Rosés and M. Teresa Sanchis

1. Introduction

France is not ranked by foreign analysts among the countries with the most salient regional inequality. However, French geographers, historians and politicians have debated intensely about the extent, nature, causes and remedies of their nation's regional inequality, and the issue has figured prominently in public opinion and economic policy for decades.[1] Contrary to what happens in other European countries, such as Spain, Italy or the UK, the French discussion is not centred on income differences among regions or large parts of the country, but on the role of the country's capital, Paris, in the economic development of the rest of the country. Although the origins of this debate about the economic role of Paris in France can be traced back to the mid-nineteenth century,[2] this issue began to attract considerable attention after the publication of the second edition of Jean-François Gravier's *Paris et le désert français* in 1953. This author forcefully argued that the excessive concentration of French economic activities in Paris damaged the rest of the country, which became increasingly depopulated, deindustrialized and relatively underdeveloped. Furthermore, he pointed out that this process of uneven development was caused by the deliberate action of successive governments that, for example, allocated considerable funds to the modernization of the capital and developed a radial structure of transport. This argument about the role of Paris in French development has had a considerable impact on the early developments of French regional policy[3] and public opinion.[4]

There are also more reasons than the role of the political capital that make French regional inequality interesting for academic research. First, France is a big country, both in terms of surface and population, which is commonly associated with quite large levels of regional inequality and spatial differences in regional specialization. Second, France is one of the European countries with the most stable internal and external political boundaries, which makes this type of long-run analysis much easier. From 1860 onwards, the only territorial losses, and gains, of European France corresponded to the regions of Alsace and part of Loraine, which were part of the German Empire from the end of the Franco-Prussian War (1870) until the Treaty of Versailles (1919). Furthermore, the boundaries and number of French departments, with very few exceptions, have been unaltered from the end of the Napoleonic Wars.[5] France is universally considered as a paradigm of the centralized state, and hence its regions and municipalities have relatively little political autonomy.

Unfortunately, the debate about French regional inequality, and the role of Paris in French economic development, has been hampered by the absence of long-run data on regional incomes.[6] In this sense, this chapter has two main objectives: (1) to present new per capita GDP data at the NUTS 2 level from 1860 to 2010; and (2) to discuss several stylized facts about regional income differences employing this new available information. In contrast to other chapters of this book, we will devote a substantial part of our chapter considering the role of the country's capital on the evolution of regional inequality.

Broadly speaking, our new collected evidence indicates that during the last 150 years, regional convergence has been extremely slow in France, and much slower than in other countries such as Spain or Sweden.[7] More prominently, only during the post-Second World War period, per capita GDP convergence rates were close to the 2 per cent others have found for the US. Our results also point out that income differentials between metropolitan Paris (hereafter, Île-de-France) and the rest of the country are striking and very important in explaining French regional inequalities in the long run. Furthermore, these income differentials showed to be quite resilient. However, our results give little support to the idea that the development of Île-de-France was negative for the economic development of the remaining French regions. Except in the last decade of our database (2000–2010), the GDP expansion of Île-de-France was always accompanied by a similar per capita GDP growth in the rest of the country.

The rest of the chapter is organized as follows. Section 2 discusses the first nature geography of France; therefore, we discuss the morphology, soil quality, climate and natural resources of France. Section 3 describes some basics about the construction of this new data set on French regional incomes. Section 4 presents some stylized facts about the regional distribution of French economic activities in the long run, employing regional data on population, employment and GDP. In section 5, we employ the well-known methodology of convergence analysis to shed light on the evolution of regional GDP per capita. Section 6 concludes.

2. First nature geography of France

The French Republic has a population of nearly 69 million (2017) and an area of about 643,000 km^2. European France,[8] which is located at the western edge of Europe, has a population of 64,860,000 (2017) and covers a land area of 551,695 km^2. By size, it is the third European country, and first of the EU, and the fourth European country, and second in the EU, by population. It shares land borders with Belgium and Luxembourg in the north-east, by Germany, Switzerland and Italy in the east, and by Monaco, Spain and Andorra in the south. France also shares maritime borders with the UK.[9]

In terms of first nature geography, France is one of the most varied countries of Europe. Much of the country is ringed with mountains: in the Spanish border are the Pyrenees; in the Italian and Swiss border are the Alps, the Vosges and the Jura Mountains; in the north-east is the Ardennes Plateau, which extends into Belgium and Luxembourg. The core of France is the Paris Basin, connected in the south-west with the lowland of Aquitaine. The western area is occupied by the Massif Armoricain, with low hills, while the upland of the Massif Central occupies the south-central area. The valley of the Rhône is located between the Massif Central and the Alps, and connects the Paris Basin and eastern France with the Mediterranean.[10]

The country is crossed by four major river systems: the Rhône (813 km), with that of its tributary the Saône (480 km), draining into the Mediterranean; the Seine (776 km), draining into the English Channel; the Loire (1,020 km), which flows through central France to the Atlantic; and the Garonne (575 km), which flows across southern France to the Atlantic. The Rhine forms the eastern boundary of France for 190 km. Waterways connect the major part of French regions and include about 100 canals and rivers, totalling over 8,000 km. Boats (within size limits) can pass through from the English Channel or the Bay of Biscay to the Mediterranean. Furthermore, the northern French waterways are connected to the river Rhine, which in turn is also linked with the main European waterways.

France accounts for about one-third of all EU agricultural land. The country is well endowed in terms of agricultural resources since soils are of excellent value and climate is also generally favourable to cultivation. Broadly speaking, the country can be divided into three major regions: the Oceanic, the Continental and the Mediterranean. The Oceanic climate predominates in the north-west and the Mediterranean in the south, while the rest of the country is under the Continental climate. The Mediterranean has its particular vegetation, but the other two climatic zones share similar vegetal species and soil productivity.

Compared to its agricultural resources, France is far less well endowed with minerals and energy resources. France was an important producer of iron ore and bauxite, principally in Lorraine, but still depended on foreign imports; Lorraine ores were of low quality due to their little metal content and were difficult to agglomerate. Coal production is important, but France has been historically dependent from imports from abroad. Furthermore, French coal suffered from being difficult and expensive to mine and from its mediocre quality. Other energy resources are in short supply: natural gas was only exploited in south-western France from 1957, but reserves were exhausted by the late 1990s; uranium is produced in the Massif Central; and France does not have oil reserves. In sharp contrast, France is well endowed in hydroelectricity given its fast-moving rivers flowing out of highland areas.

3. New data on the long-term patterns of French regional income inequality

In order to analyse the long-term evolution of regional inequality in France throughout the period 1860–2010, we have estimated new regional GDP per capita figures for the years 1911, 1921, 1954, 1962, 1975 and 1982. For the remaining years (1860, 1896, 1954, 1990, 1999 and 2010), the regional data have been collected from different well-known sources but have been rescaled to match with historical national accounts.[11] Consequently, our estimations are homogenous across time and space.[12]

The new figures for the above-mentioned benchmark years have been calculated following the Geary and Stark (2002) methodology.[13] The data necessary for this method are: an estimation of the national output by sector,[14] figures on active population by sector and region, and nominal wages also disaggregated by the same sectors and regions. The data on working population have been drawn from national censuses of population that provide detailed information about active population by sector at different territorial levels (departments, municipalities and districts) for approximately every 10 years.[15] Figures on wages come from different official sources. The main source of wage data has been two wage surveys, which contain detailed information by department and about some municipalities (*chêf de lieux*), for 1911 and 1962. The 1911 wage survey collected data for 34 professions and the 1962 wage surveyed 60 economic activities.[16] This information has been completed with further wage data from the statistical bulletins of 1929 and 1937,[17] which recorded evidence for different working categories disaggregated by departments and the largest cities.[18] Finally, underlining data (wage and employment) for our estimations corresponding to the years 1975 and 1982 have been obtained from several publications of the INSEE collection of regional studies.[19]

For 1860 and 1930, manufacturing and services employment and output levels for each department have been drawn directly from Toutain's estimations,[20] whereas agricultural regional figures have been obtained applying Toutain's (1992) distribution of agricultural output by department. For more recent decades (1990, 1999 and 2010), INSEE has produced official regional GDP per capita estimates following the Eurostat methodology.

4. The regional distribution of French population and economic activities

Our new database contains information on the regional distribution of population, employment and GDP. We will employ these data to consider if French economic activity became increasingly concentrated from 1860 to 2010. Figure 3.5.1 reviews the evolution of three different measures about the dispersion of demographics and employment among French regions (namely the coefficient of variation of population density, population and employment).

These three different dispersion measures delineate a similar pattern: the concentration of population and employment has increased over the last century-and-a-half in France. Furthermore, it is possible to appreciate a similar chronology in these dispersion measures: an initial period, from 1860 until 1930, when concentration grew exponentially; an intermediate period, from 1930 until 1962, in which concentration also grew but at more moderate rates; and the last five decades, when concentration has stabilized at its highest levels. Interestingly, employment and population figures are extremely similar (which implies that population movements have adjusted to employment shocks).

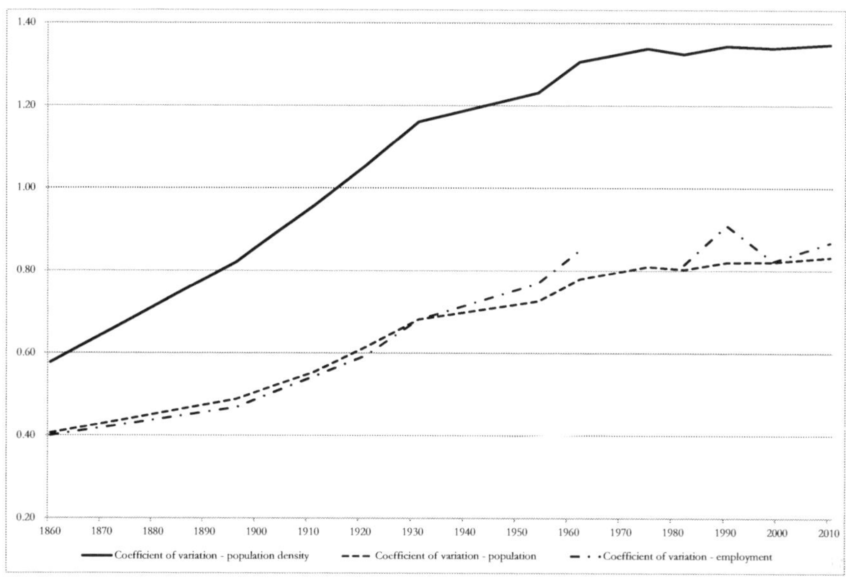

Figure 3.5.1 The distribution of population and employment across French regions, 1860–2010

Table 3.5.1 Population density of French regions (France = 1), 1860–2010

	France = 1	*1860*	*1931*	*2010*
FR10	Île-de-France	3.42	7.26	8.51
FR21	Champagne-Ardenne	0.70	0.58	0.45
FR22	Picardie	1.15	0.91	0.85
FR23	Haute-Normandie	1.41	1.28	1.29
FR24	Centre	0.68	0.57	0.56
FR25	Basse-Normandie	1.24	0.82	0.72
FR26	Bourgogne	0.77	0.58	0.45
FR30	Nord-Pas-de-Calais	2.39	3.40	2.82
FR41	Lorraine	0.97	1.04	0.86
FR42	Alsace	1.86	1.89	1.92
FR43	Franche-Comté	0.87	0.69	0.63
FR51	Pays de la Loire	1.06	0.87	0.97
FR52	Bretagne	1.25	1.14	1.02
FR53	Poitou-Charentes	0.85	0.67	0.59
FR61	Aquitaine	0.79	0.68	0.68
FR62	Midi-Pyrénées	0.82	0.56	0.55
FR63	Limousin	0.77	0.62	0.38
FR71	Rhône-Alpes	1.13	1.09	1.24
FR72	Auvergne	0.83	0.66	0.45
FR81	Languedoc-Roussillon	0.76	0.74	0.84
FR82	Provence-Alpes-Côte d'Azur	0.72	0.99	1.35
FR83	Corse	0.42	0.45	0.31

A more detailed analysis of the population density data shows that only six regions (of 22) have higher population density quotients in 2010 than in 1860,[21] and these same six regions are also the only ones with values higher than 1 in 2010 (see Table 3.5.1). These regions are Île-de-France, Nord-Pas-de-Calais, Alsace, Rhône-Alpes, Languedoc-Roussillon and Provence-Alpes-Côte d'Azur. Interestingly, the population density coefficient of Île-de-France was 3.42 in 1860 and has grown until 8.51 by 2010 (i.e. this region has about 8.5 times the population density of France). Furthermore, this is about 3 times the population density of the following most densely populated region (Nord-Pas-de-Calais) in 2010.

Like all European countries, France has experienced fundamental changes in her employment structure.[22] In 1860, the main source of employment in France was agriculture (about 58 per cent of employment), while its share has decreased to only about 2.5 per cent by 2010. In sharp contrast, the share of services increased from 17 per cent in 1860 to about 76 per cent in 2010. The share of industry was also larger in 1860 (about 25 per cent) than in 2010 (only 21 per cent). By 1931, the share of employment in the different sectors was similar, but the largest employer sector was industry. Therefore, during the last 150 years, France has experienced a genuine process of tertiarization.

Table 3.5.2 Location coefficients of French regions (France = 1), 1860–2010

	1860			*1931*			*2010*		
	Agr.	*Ind.*	*Ser.*	*Agr.*	*Ind.*	*Ser.*	*Agr.*	*Ind.*	*Ser.*
Île-de-France	0.20	1.88	2.41	0.11	1.26	1.70	0.07	0.65	1.13
Champagne-Ardenne	0.75	1.45	1.18	0.89	1.11	0.99	2.27	1.19	0.90
Picardie	0.71	1.70	0.96	0.89	1.13	0.97	1.10	1.13	0.96
Haute-Normandie	0.63	1.53	1.49	0.72	1.15	1.14	0.71	1.24	0.94
Centre	1.15	0.76	0.84	1.47	0.72	0.81	1.22	1.17	0.95
Basse-Normandie	1.09	0.88	0.86	1.52	0.68	0.79	1.88	1.19	0.92
Bourgogne	1.13	0.80	0.85	1.34	0.82	0.84	1.82	1.13	0.94
Nord-Pas-de-Calais	0.71	1.60	1.10	0.43	1.67	0.84	0.58	1.08	0.99
Lorraine	0.88	1.25	1.04	0.61	1.38	0.98	0.69	1.18	0.96
Alsace	0.95	1.19	0.89	0.77	1.23	0.98	0.56	1.34	0.92
Franche-Comté	1.18	0.73	0.79	1.20	1.04	0.73	1.03	1.47	0.87
Pays de la Loire	1.11	0.84	0.85	1.54	0.72	0.72	1.68	1.22	0.92
Bretagne	1.27	0.49	0.83	1.78	0.54	0.66	1.88	1.07	0.95
Poitou-Charentes	1.25	0.57	0.80	1.66	0.61	0.73	1.99	1.08	0.94
Aquitaine	1.24	0.59	0.78	1.48	0.69	0.83	1.93	0.95	0.98
Midi-Pyrénées	1.21	0.83	0.56	1.64	0.67	0.68	1.54	1.00	0.98
Limousin	1.27	0.73	0.50	1.81	0.60	0.56	2.12	1.01	0.96
Rhône-Alpes	0.99	1.09	0.89	1.00	1.15	0.82	0.65	1.16	0.97
Auvergne	1.37	0.51	0.45	1.57	0.75	0.65	2.01	1.15	0.92
Languedoc-Roussillon	1.10	0.81	0.93	1.33	0.75	0.92	1.50	0.80	1.04
Provence-Alpes-Côte d'Azur	0.90	0.86	1.54	0.69	0.92	1.45	0.61	0.79	1.07

Information on the distribution of different economic activities could be obtained by considering the location quotient for each sector (agriculture, industry and services) using regional data on employment. More specifically, we estimated the following equations (see Table 3.5.2):

$$LQ_{EMP} = \frac{E_{ji}}{E_i} \Big/ \frac{E_{jFRA}}{E_{FRA}} \tag{1}$$

Considering the regional specialization in different activities, agriculture was the most evenly distributed in 1860 but the most unevenly distributed by 2010; instead, services have experienced the contrary evolution from the most localized to the most dispersed. Interestingly, industry has experienced the same trend towards dispersion as services. This latter evidence has important consequences since a substantial strand of the literature considers that the spatial concentration of industry is behind the growing regional inequality during the initial phase of modern economic growth.

In each of the three different benchmarks (1860, 1931 and 2010), Île-de-France stands out when compared with the rest of France. In 1860, it was the region with the lowest agriculture location coefficient and the highest in industry and services. This situation remained practically unaltered by 1931, but in the last benchmark (2010), Île-de-France no longer has the highest location coefficient in both industry and services. More prominently, its specialization is strongly based on services, and location quotients in other sectors are below 1 (industry: 0.65, agriculture: 0.07).

The industrial location coefficient could also be employed to delineate the geography of French industrialization. In 1860, all eight regions with coefficients above 1, except Rhône-Alpes, were situated at the north of the country. Note that the reserves of iron and coal were also located there. Seventy years later (in 1931), the situation was similar, with only France-Comté added to the group of industrial regions. Instead, the last benchmark year (2010) shows industry more evenly distributed, with up to 17 regions with values above 1. Now, the two most heavily industrialized regions are situated along the border with Germany (France-Comté and Alsace), which is a testimony of the importance of international (European) markets for French manufacturing.

The evolution of services location is quite different from those of agriculture and industry. In the first year of Table 3.5.2 (1860), only six regions enjoyed values superior to 1, with Île-de-France showing an extraordinary 2.4 location coefficient. By 1931, the number of regions specialized in services decreased to only three (Île-de-France, Provence-Alpes-Côte d'Azur and Haute-Normandie) and the majority of regional values collapsed towards 1. This tendency has been confirmed in the last period, when every region shows location coefficients closer to 1 (the minimum of 0.87 corresponds to the most industrialized region – France-Comté – and the maximum of 1.13 to Île-de-France).

To finish this section, we will consider the evolution of the share of each region in the French GDP. The necessary data for this is collected in Table 3.5.A.1.

The spatial localization of French GDP presents significant changes from 1860 to 2010. The most relevant result is the overwhelming advance of Île-de-France, doubling its share between 1860 (about 15.5 per cent) and 2010 (about 30.1 per cent). Apart from Île-de-France, only two other regions have increased their share in national GDP from 1860 to 2010, Rhône-Alpes, from about 8 per cent to about 9.8 per cent, and Provence-Alpes-Côte d'Azur from 4 per cent to 7.3 per cent. In sharp contrast, the five regions around the Parisian core have halved their participation in the French economy (Champagne-Ardenne, Picardie, Haute-Normandie, Centre and Basse-Normandie). In sum, data on the distribution of regional GDP show an increasingly skewed distribution and a substantial concentration of economic activities in and around Paris.

However, these changes in the share of GDP across French regions were not continuous over the last 150 years. In particular, the expansion of Île-de-France took place between 1860 and 1954, and it was particularly intense during the second half of the nineteenth century. Since then, its share in French GDP has remained broadly constant, with a recent but more modest increase since 1980. In sharp contrast stand the remaining regions. Rhône-Alpes and Provence-Alpes-Côte d'Azur have increased their share in practically every benchmark. The three early industrializing regions (Nord Pas de-Calais, Lorraine and Alsace) experienced an expansion of their share until 1931 and a decrease since then. Finally, the remaining regions have experienced a monotonic decrease in their GDP shares.

5. Long-run income convergence across French regions

A substantial amount of literature approaches the evolution of regional disparities through the analysis of regional GDP per capita convergence.[23] Regional convergence analysis has two main advantages: (1) despite the fact that it is based on an explicit economic model – the Solow model of growth – its results can be interpreted within alternative analytical frameworks; and (2) it can be put in perspective given the substantial amount of previous empirical studies.[24] Convergence across regions in a given country requires both sigma-convergence and beta-convergence. The former consists in a reduction in the dispersion of GDP per capita differences across regions, while the latter takes place when poorer regions tend to growth faster than richer regions. According to the Solow model, regional income convergence is a consequence of diminishing returns of capital.[25] Richer regions, which enjoy higher capital-to-population ratios, tend to grow slower than poorer regions because the latter benefit from higher capital returns, and hence more investment. In the presence of factor movements across regions, the predictions of the model do not change, since capital should flow from poor to rich regions, while labour migration would tend to move in the opposite direction. The direction of factor movements is driven by their relative intensities; capital returns should be higher in the poorer regions, while the contrary holds for wages.[26]

It is important to note that alternative models of regional growth do not necessarily predict monotonic income convergence across different locations. In particular, the Williamson (1965) and Krugman and Venables (1995) models predict an inverted U-shaped curve in regional inequality. Regional economies diverge during the initial phases of modern economic development and converge thereafter. The former model relates this divergence to the unequal spatial distribution of manufacturing activities since the industrializing regions tend to become richer than the agrarian ones. However, when manufacturing spreads across the country, regional inequality tends to peter out. Instead, Krugman and Venables attribute the initial upsurge in regional inequality to the process of commodity market integration as a consequence of decreasing transport costs. In the presence of increasing returns in certain sectors, firms from these sectors tend to locate closest to the larger demand markets, which leads to increasing regional inequality. With further reductions in transports costs, closeness to larger markets become less attractive and firms spread across the country. Indeed, this leads to a reduction in regional disparities.

In order to analyse the evolution of French regional income inequality throughout the whole period 1860–2010, we present different statistics following the convergence methodology. Figure 3.5.2 draws both the population-weighted coefficient of variation of GDP per capita for the French NUTS 2 regions and the same coefficient for all regions except Île-de-France in order to highlight the impact of Paris on French regional inequality. This coefficient captures the idea of sigma-convergence, which studies regional dispersion in GDP per capita.[27]

The indices represented in Figure 3.5.2 do not confirm the U-shaped curve of long-run regional inequality for France,[28] in line with the broad evidence for Europe, but in contrast to the evidence for some other European countries such as

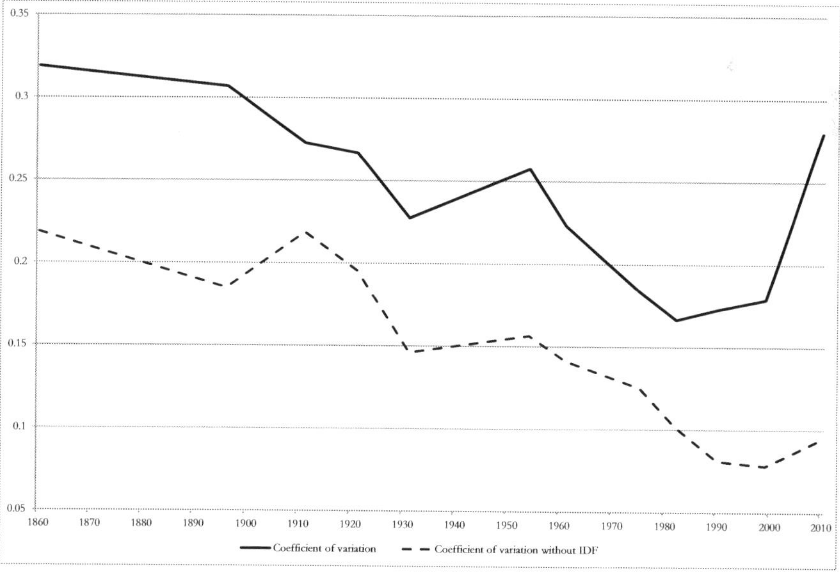

Figure 3.5.2 Sigma-convergence in income per capita across French regions, 1860–2010

Spain.[29] The first index (which includes all French metropolitan regions) points towards a declining trend of French regional inequality from 1860 until 1982 (with the exception of the resurgence during the 1930s and 1940s). For 1982 onwards, the reversal of this process of regional convergence can be easily observed: in 2010, the index reaches a value that is similar to the value observed 150 years before, in 1860. This revival of regional inequality at the end of the twentieth century has also been observed in other advanced European countries such as Sweden, Finland or Belgium. The second coefficient of variation that excludes Île-de-France tells a quite similar, albeit less dramatic, story about the evolution of French inequality.[30]

The startling difference between the two indices is a good indication of the importance of Île-de-France for French regional income dispersion. For example, in 1860, one-third of the overall regional French income inequality is a consequence of the income differences between Île-de-France and the rest of the country. Instead, by 2010, that difference accounts for about two-thirds of total regional inequality. This seems to indicate that the recent increase in inequality might be almost totally explained by the increasing dominance of the Paris metropolitan region in the French economy. This result contrasts with those obtained by Combes et al. (2011), who, with data for 88 French continental departments and comparing two dates (1930 and 2000), conclude that France is more egalitarian than usually presumed, and that the Paris region has not polarized the income distribution throughout the twentieth century.

After considering sigma-convergence, we will analyse unconditional beta-convergence according to the following basic equation:

$$\frac{1}{T} ln\left(\frac{GDP^{i}_{2010}}{GDP^{i}_{1860}}\right) = \alpha + \Theta \ln GDP^{i}_{1860} + \varepsilon \qquad (2)$$

where T is the number of years considered and GDP is the GDP per capita on the designated year for the regions i. This equation can be estimated by pooled ordinary least squares (OLS) with robust standard errors. The results are as follows:

$$\frac{1}{T} ln\left(\frac{GDP^{i}_{2010}}{GDP^{i}_{1860}}\right) = 0.4311 - 0.0037 \ln GDP^{i}_{1860} \qquad (3)$$

Note that the value of Θ is −0.0037 (standard error: 0.0009), which implies convergence among French regions was very slow from 1860 to 2010.[31] Furthermore, the resulting convergence rate of 0.55 per cent per year[32] is significantly lower than the widely observed 2 per cent.[33] We have also run convergence regressions for three sub-periods: 1860–1931, 1931–1982 and 1982–2010. The values of Θ are: −0.005 (implied convergence rate of 0.64 per cent per year) for the first period; −0.012 (implied convergence rate of 1.93 per cent per year) for the second

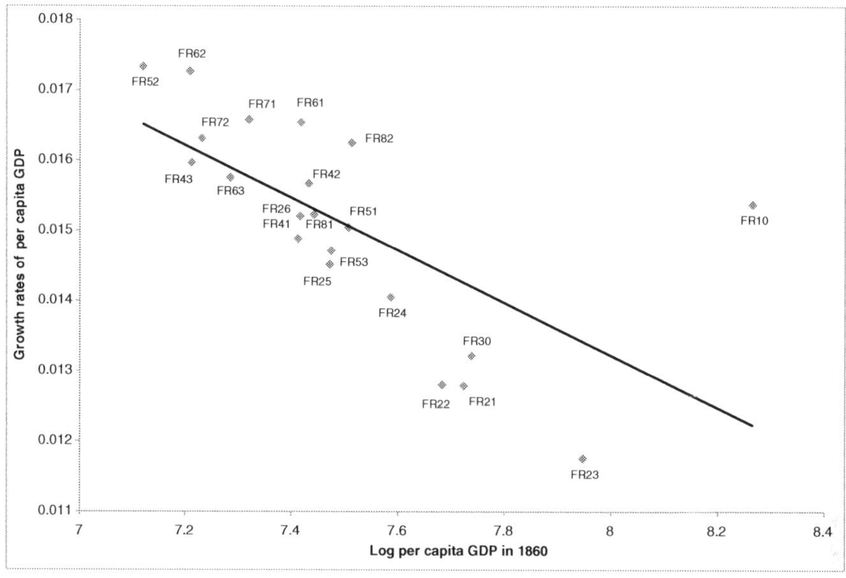

Figure 3.5.3 Beta-convergence in income per capita across French regions, 1860–2010

period; and 0.003 (implied divergence rate of 0.35 per cent per year) for the third period. In sum, only during the second period could French convergence rates be considered within the range of the typical 2 per cent.

Figure 3.5.3 is a graphical representation of Equation 2 (unconditional beta-convergence) that estimates the relationship between the rate of growth of per capita income between two periods (1860–2010) and the initial level of per capita income (1860). This graph clearly shows how the Île-de-France region breaks this relationship between initial GDP per capita levels and subsequent GDP per capita growth rates because its rate of economic growth is far above that expected according to its initial level of development. In the last 150 years, Île-de-France has grown more rapidly than those regions with the closest levels of per capita GDP in 1860 (Haute-Normandie, Nord-Pas-de-Calais, Champagne-Ardennes, Picardie and Centre), and at similar rates to Alsace, which had only 43 per cent of its GDP per capita in 1860. Obviously, this indicates that the process of catching up between the rest of France and its richest region is extremely weak.

Maps 3.5.1–3.5.3 illustrate the spatial perspective of per capita income by regions in 1860, 1931 and 2010. The picture that emerges in 1860 is that of a geographical core represented by the Paris region and the rich belt of regions located in the north of Paris. This belt is made up of Haute-Normandie, Picardie, Champagne-Ardennes and Nord-Pas-de-Calais. The maps divide the distribution of regions into several groups in terms of GDP per capita relative to the French average (i.e. set equal to 1). One can observe that even in the first benchmark

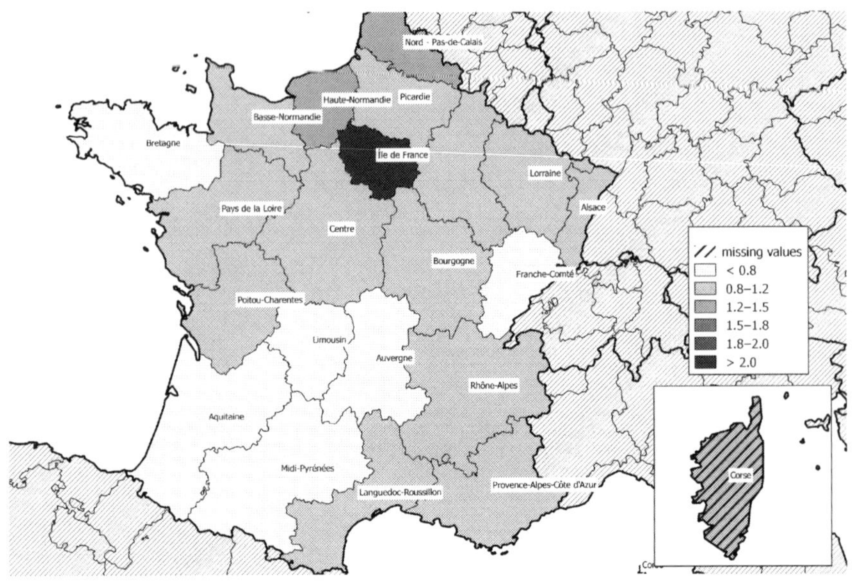

Map 3.5.1 The distribution of income per capita across French regions, 1860

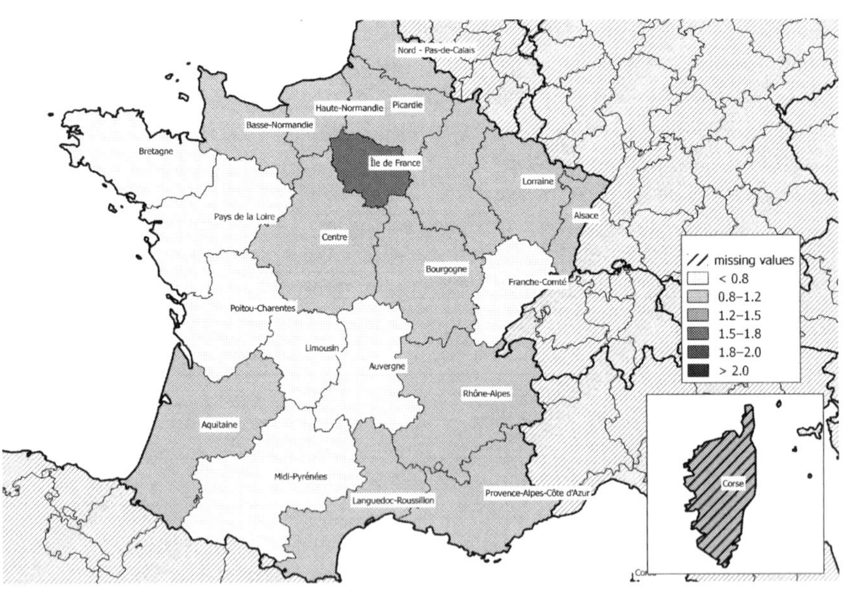

Map 3.5.2 The distribution of income per capita across French regions, 1931

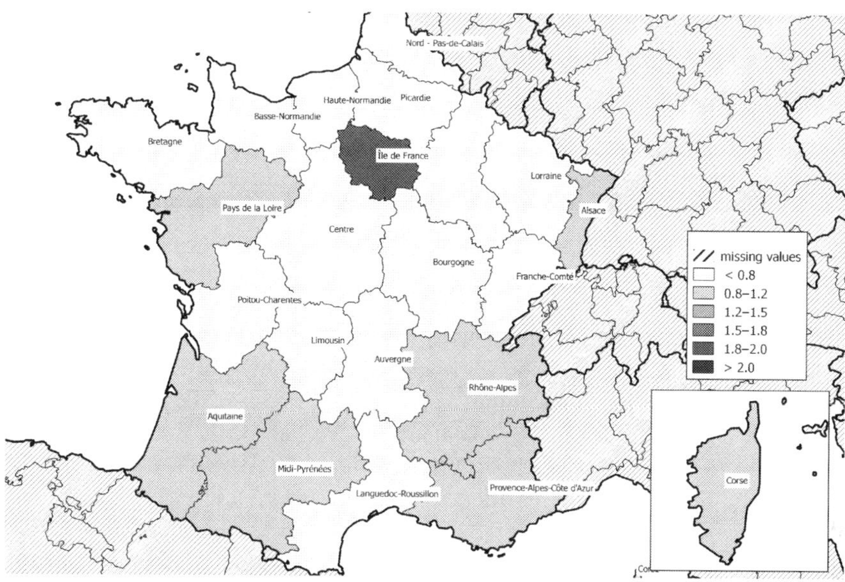

Map 3.5.3 The distribution of income per capita across French regions, 2010

year, the Paris region was far above the second region (Haute-Normandie) and the following ones (Picardie, Nord-Pas-de-Calais and Champagne-Ardennes). The remaining regions are at a big distance from the core, in the first and second groups of the distribution.

Seventy years later (in 1931), the picture shows a bigger belt of rich regions around Paris that now includes also the regions of Champagne-Ardennes and Lorrain. Due to industrial growth, three peripheral regions reached levels of per capita income similar to the rich northern ring. These regions are Alsace, Rhone-Alpes and Provence-Alpes-Côte d'Azur. Hence, two centres of progress emerge in 1930, the Parisian core and the south-eastern regions. The neighbouring regions around these two hubs of development also improved their levels of per capita income, and it is possible to state that in 1930, the middle-east of the country was richer than the western one, with the unique exception of Aquitaine, where the prosperous city of Bordeaux is located.

The final picture in 2010 presents a more egalitarian country, where the belt around the Paris region has vanished as a consequence of two main forces: the process of beta-convergence, where the poorer regions have grown more quickly than the richest ones, and the unstoppable advance of the Paris region, propelled by new forces related to economies of agglomeration and the new knowledge economy. Hence, a new map of France emerges, with Îlle the France as the main hub of economic progress and all the regions located at a big distance from the leader region.

The process of regional income convergence has altered the relative position of the regions throughout the whole century (see Table 3.5.A.2). With the exception of the Paris region, not all the leader regions in the second half of the nineteenth century will stay at the forefront of the income distribution in 2010. The regions with the highest per capita income were in descending order: Île-de-France, Haute-Normandie, Champagne-Ardenne, Nord-Pas-de-Calais, Picardie, Provence-Alps-Côte-D'Azur and Rhone-Alps. With the exception of the two Alps regions, the other ones belong to the prosperous ring around the Paris core, and all of them enjoyed a per capita income above the national average in 1896. Throughout the 150 years analysed, the two regions that lost more positions in the ranking of per capita income were both in the northern borders of the Paris region (Nord-Pas-de-Calais and Picardie). Nord-Pas-de-Calais declined from 1.21 of the national GDP per capita in 1860 (3rd position) to 0.79 in 2010 (13th position), and Picardie from 1.14 (5th position) to 0.75 (21st position). The positions in the poorer extreme of the distribution do not present great changes. The most successful regions are Aquitaine and Rhone-Alpes. Aquitaine occupied the 16th position in 1860 and reached the 6th position in 2010; meanwhile, Rhone-Alpes, where Lyon is located, progressed from the 13th position in 1860 to the 2nd in 2010. However, the main characteristic throughout the different benchmarks is a general tendency of the regions to concentrate around 75 per cent and 100 per cent of the national average, but without surpassing it. Only the Paris region has been over the national GDP per capita level in the 150 years analysed, and has considerably increased its distance to the rest of the country in the last three decades.

6. Conclusions

Using a novel data set, this study explores the long-term evolution of regional income inequality in France between 1860 and 2010. Overall, regional disparities have decreased since the early stages of modern economic growth, but divergence has developed since the 1980s. Our study thus does not provide empirical evidence in favour of an inverted U-shaped pattern for France between 1860 and 1982. In addition, dispersion in per capita income across French regions has steadily narrowed, but the gap between the provinces and Île-de-France persists.

Appendix

Table 3.5.A.1 Regional shares (NUTS 2) in French GDP (per cent), 1860–2010

	1860	*1896*	*1911*	*1921*	*1931*	*1954*	*1962*	*1975*	*1982*	*1990*	*1999*	*2010*
Île-de-France	15.48	21.64	21.57	24.49	26.26	29.01	29.20	27.71	27.07	28.59	28.82	30.95
Champagne-Ardenne	3.95	3.50	2.90	2.64	2.80	2.32	2.35	2.39	2.52	2.20	2.13	1.81
Picardie	4.71	3.91	3.13	2.78	3.17	2.68	2.85	3.08	2.86	2.72	2.58	2.30
Haute-Normandie	4.76	3.56	4.09	2.92	3.00	2.71	2.82	3.02	3.26	2.82	2.74	2.52
Centre	5.09	4.20	3.81	3.64	3.48	3.40	3.32	3.83	3.80	3.88	3.74	3.37
Basse-Normandie	3.71	2.76	2.42	2.16	2.26	2.23	2.26	2.27	2.05	2.02	1.95	1.81
Bourgogne	3.92	3.50	3.16	3.09	2.79	3.04	3.07	2.73	2.60	2.53	2.37	2.13
Nord-Pas-de-Calais	6.58	7.51	6.82	6.30	7.92	6.88	6.93	6.45	6.09	5.45	5.25	5.13
Lorraine	3.69	4.30	4.31	4.24	4.31	4.14	4.53	4.21	3.79	3.40	3.21	2.84
Alsace	2.53	2.42	2.09	2.83	3.18	2.76	2.67	2.81	2.96	2.93	2.92	2.66
Franche-Comté	1.86	1.70	2.32	2.09	1.56	1.86	1.98	1.81	1.73	1.67	1.65	1.46
Pays de la Loire	6.03	4.79	4.94	4.76	4.05	4.31	4.18	4.60	4.69	4.56	4.90	4.96
Bretagne	4.07	3.87	3.43	3.59	3.55	3.95	3.57	4.10	4.13	3.95	4.23	4.12
Poitou-Charentes	3.76	2.91	3.87	2.91	2.40	1.95	1.71	2.40	2.32	2.27	2.33	2.24
Aquitaine	4.78	4.94	5.22	4.62	4.35	4.42	4.15	4.25	4.56	4.31	4.39	4.48
Midi-Pyrénées	4.88	3.96	4.39	3.89	3.61	3.52	3.51	3.49	3.48	3.74	3.80	3.95
Limousin	1.85	1.61	1.97	1.72	1.35	1.26	1.19	1.25	1.04	1.05	0.98	0.87
Rhône-Alpes	7.96	8.30	8.38	8.74	8.54	8.85	9.46	8.85	9.01	9.64	9.74	9.79
Auvergne	2.89	2.86	2.55	2.59	2.51	2.45	2.38	2.15	1.91	1.98	1.84	1.69
Languedoc-Roussillon	3.46	3.32	3.15	3.06	3.28	2.40	2.34	2.73	2.79	2.95	3.02	3.21
Provence-Alpes-Côte d'Azur	4.03	4.45	5.13	6.58	5.62	5.57	5.21	5.59	7.00	7.00	7.07	7.32
Corse	n.d.	n.d.	0.34	0.34	n.d.	0.29	0.31	0.28	0.34	0.34	0.34	0.41

Table 3.5.A.2 Relative GDP per capita of French regions, 1860–2010 (France = 1)

	1860	*1896*	*1911*	*1921*	*1931*	*1954*	*1962*	*1975*	*1982*	*1990*	*1999*	*2010*
Île-de-France	2.05	1.99	1.68	1.69	1.64	1.70	1.60	1.47	1.46	1.52	1.54	1.82
Champagne-Ardenne	1.20	1.13	0.99	0.97	1.03	0.87	0.90	0.94	1.02	0.92	0.93	0.72
Picardie	1.15	1.05	0.89	0.87	0.97	0.83	0.89	0.96	0.89	0.85	0.81	0.69
Haute-Normandie	1.50	1.21	1.41	0.97	1.04	0.91	0.94	1.08	1.07	0.92	0.90	0.77
Centre	1.04	0.89	0.84	0.82	0.85	0.83	0.83	0.94	0.91	0.93	0.90	0.76
Basse-Normandie	0.93	0.88	0.85	0.78	0.85	0.82	0.87	0.91	0.82	0.82	0.80	0.72
Bourgogne	0.88	0.85	0.84	0.85	0.83	0.95	0.99	0.91	0.89	0.89	0.86	0.76
Nord-Pas-de-Calais	1.21	1.11	0.93	0.89	1.02	0.87	0.88	0.87	0.84	0.78	0.77	0.78
Lorraine	0.88	1.01	0.93	0.99	0.96	0.91	0.96	0.95	0.89	0.83	0.81	0.72
Alsace	0.89	0.87	0.71	0.99	1.10	0.97	0.94	0.97	1.03	1.02	0.99	0.83
Franche-Comté	0.72	0.74	1.06	0.98	0.77	0.93	0.99	0.90	0.87	0.86	0.87	0.69
Pays de la Loire	0.96	0.82	0.88	0.86	0.79	0.80	0.79	0.87	0.87	0.84	0.89	0.81
Bretagne	0.65	0.61	0.55	0.58	0.62	0.72	0.69	0.83	0.83	0.80	0.85	0.78
Poitou-Charentes	0.93	0.78	1.09	0.85	0.75	0.60	0.55	0.82	0.81	0.81	0.83	0.75
Aquitaine	0.80	0.87	0.96	0.85	0.84	0.86	0.83	0.88	0.93	0.87	0.88	0.85
Midi-Pyrénées	0.71	0.69	0.85	0.79	0.78	0.76	0.79	0.81	0.81	0.87	0.87	0.84
Limousin	0.77	0.66	0.85	0.79	0.70	0.73	0.75	0.89	0.76	0.82	0.81	0.72
Rhône-Alpes	0.88	0.93	0.97	0.99	0.98	1.04	1.09	0.97	0.98	1.02	1.01	0.93
Auvergne	0.73	0.75	0.73	0.76	0.80	0.84	0.87	0.85	0.78	0.85	0.82	0.74
Languedoc-Roussillon	0.90	0.87	0.85	0.80	0.88	0.71	0.70	0.80	0.79	0.79	0.77	0.78
Provence-Alpes-Côte d'Azur	0.97	1.04	1.10	1.34	0.98	0.99	0.86	0.80	0.96	0.93	0.92	0.98
Corse	n.d.	n.d.	0.48	0.48	n.d.	0.50	0.80	0.51	0.76	0.77	0.76	0.86

Notes

1 See, for example, Vanhove and Klaassen (1980), Burnham (1999), Duranton et al. (2008) and Prager and Thisse (2009).
2 Gravier (1953) summarizes some early contributions to this debate.
3 See, for example, Vanhove and Klaassen (1980) and Burnham (1999).
4 On the influence of Gravier, see, for example, Marchand (2010).
5 Administratively, France is divided into 22 NUTS 2 regions: Île de France, Champagne-Ardenne, Picardie, Haute-Normandie, Centre, Basse-Normandie, Bourgogne, Nord-Pas-de-Calais, Lorraine, Alsace, Franche-Comté, Pays de la Loire, Bretagne, Poitou-Charentes, Aquitaine, Midi-Pyrénées, Limousin, Rhône-Alpes, Auvergne, Languedoc-Roussillon, Provence-Alpes-Côte d'Azur and Corse. The offshore regions (Guadeloupe, Martinique and Guyane) are not taken into account for the analysis that is centred in the European territories.
6 There are some previous studies on French regional income inequality: Combes et al. (2011) analyse long-run trends, but only with three benchmarks (1860, 1930 and 2000); Caruana-Galizia (2013) analyses the period 1872–1911; and Bazot (2014) considers the period 1840–1911. Furthermore, any of these studies include in their calculations German-occupied Alsace and Lorraine and offer information at the NUTS 2 level.
7 For Spain, see Martínez-Galarraga et al. (2015), and for Sweden, see Enflo and Rosés (2015).
8 To simplify the exposition, when we refer to France, we mean European France.
9 All information retrieved from CIA (2015).
10 A complete review of the physical geography of France is available in Koster (2005).
11 French figures in nominal terms have been converted to international (real) PPP dollars with the calculations from the Maddison Project (2015).
12 This methodology is analysed in Geary and Stark (2002).
13 See also Geary and Stark (2002). As we mentioned earlier, after the Franco-Prussian War, France lost Alsace and parts of Lorraine to Germany. These regions came back to France after the First World War. Therefore, their data for 1896 and 1911 are not available in French statistics. Data for the German period have been kindly provided to us by Nikolaus Wolf (see Chapter 3.6 in this book). Furthermore, we have computed the NUTS 2 region of Lorraine in 1896 and 1911 by combining French and German data. Population shares have been employed to weigh per capita GDP from French and German Lorraine. Finally, we have also increased overall (nominal) French GDP to include the regions under German administration.
14 The historical series of national output by sector (agriculture, manufacturing and services) are taken from Toutain (1987) for the years 1860, 1896, 1911, 1921 and 1930, and from the national accounts for post-1950 years available at the Groningen Growth and Development Centre Historical National Accounts Database (http://www.rug.nl/ggdc/historicaldevelopment/na/).
15 The population censuses that we have employed in our calculations are the following: 1911, 1921, 1954, 1962, 1975 and 1982.
16 The 1911 wage survey is *Salaires et coût de l'existence: à diverses époques, jusqu'en 1910* (Ministère du Travail et de la prévoyance sociale/Statistique générale de la France 1911), while the 1962 survey is *Recensement Industriel de 1963. Resultats pour 1962.*
17 The source for wages in 1929 is the *Bulletin de la statistique générale de la France et du service d'observation des prix*, tome XIX, fascicule II (January–March 1930). Wages in 1937 are taken from *Bulletin de la statistique générale de la France et du service d'observation des prix*, tome XIX, fascicule II (January–March 1938).
18 These data have been used to interpolate the relative wages for 1921 and 1954.
19 Muet et al. (1970), Chanut and Trêca (1975), Chauet and Monfort (1978), Mary and Turpin (1981) and Donnellier et al. (1987).
20 These series have been published in the appendix of Combes et al. (2008).

21 These are calculated as the ratio between population density (habitants per km^2) in the corresponding region and the population density of France. Therefore, values above 1 indicate that the population in that region was higher than in France.
22 To maintain consistency in our calculations, we exclude Corse from them, given the absence of data for 1860.
23 The pioneering study in the use of this methodology for regional convergence analysis is Barro and Sala-i-Martin (1991).
24 Convergence methodology is discussed, for example, in Barro and Sala-i-Martin (2003).
25 Furthermore, a simple mathematical derivation of the Solow model predicts that in the presence of diminishing returns to capital, the rate of beta-convergence among different regions (countries) should be about 2 per cent (see Barro and Sala-i-Martin 2003).
26 Barro et al. (1995).
27 We have also calculated other alterative indices of inequality such as the Gini, the unweighted coefficient of variation and the population-weighted Theil index. For space reasons, these indices are not presented here, but are available from the authors.
28 Bazot (2014), who estimates gross domestic product by department for the period 1840–1911 using the *patente*, a tax on non-agricultural value added, concludes that the modernization of the French economy in the nineteenth century is characterized by an increasing inequality between regions that only changed slowly towards a more egalitarian spatial distribution in 1890, whereas wealth concentration increased in the Paris region. Combes et al. (2011), working with data for only three cross sections (1860, 1930 and 2000), conclude that the 1860–1930 sub-period witnesses an increase in spatial concentration, whereas the 1930–2000 sub-period is characterized by dispersion. But as these authors recognize, one of the main fragilities of their analysis is to check the validity of the bell-shaped curve with data for only three years.
29 For Spain, see Martínez-Galarraga et al. (2015).
30 Using another kind of approach, Morrison and Snyder (2000) analyse the evolution of income distribution in France in the eighteenth and nineteenth centuries, and find that when modern industrialization began around 1830, inequality increased until the 1860s, and since then it began to decline towards greater equality.
31 The r^2 of the regression is 0.41 and the F-test is 14.92.
32 Following Barro and Sala-i-Martin (2003), it is straightforward to derive the yearly convergence rate of the regression (2) as $\beta = -(1/T)\ ln(\Theta T + 1)$.
33 The 2 per cent convergence rate is also the prediction of the Solow model.

References

Barro, R.J. and Sala-i-Martin, X. (1991) 'Convergence across states and regions', *Brookings Papers on Economic Activity*, Vol. 22 (1): 107–82.

Barro, R.J. and Sala-i-Martin, X. (2003) *Economic Growth*, 2nd edition, Cambridge, MA: MIT Press.

Barro, R.J., Mankiw, N.G. and Sala-i-Martin, X. (1995) 'Capital mobility in neoclassical models of growth', *American Economic Review*, Vol. 85 (1): 103–15.

Bazot, G. (2014) 'Interregional inequalities, convergence, and growth in France from 1840 to 1911', *Annals of Economics and Statistics*, Vol. 113–114: 309–45.

Bulletin de la statistique générale de la France et du service d'observation des prix, tome XIX, fascicule II (January–March 1930).

Bulletin de la statistique générale de la France et du service d'observation des prix, tome XIX, fascicule II (January–March 1938).

Burnham, J. (1999) 'Contrasts and contradictions in French regional policy: from de Gaulle to Chirac; from the Treaty of Rome to the Treaty of Amsterdam, from central direction to local cooperation', in M. Allison and O. Heathcote (eds), *Forty Years of the Fifth French Republic: Actions, Dialogues and Discourses*, Bern: Lang, pp. 77–94.

Caruana-Galizia, P. (2013) 'Estimating French regional income: departmental per capita gross value added, 1872–1891', in *Research in Economic History*, Bingley: Emerald, pp. 71–95.

Chanut, J.M. and Trêca, L. (1975) 'Analyse régionale et indicateurs regionaux', *Les Collections de l'INSEE*, C3, Institut National de la Statistique et des Etudes Economiques (INSEE).

Chauet, A. and Monfort, J. (1978) 'Les comptes régionaux des branches industrielles en 1975', *Les Collections de l'INSEE*, C3, Institut National de la Statistique et des Etudes Economiques (INSEE).

CIA (2015) *The World Factbook: Field Listing – Area*, Washington, DC: Central Intelligence Agency.

Combes, P.P., Lafourcade, M., Thisse, J.F. and Toutain, J.C. (2008) 'The rise and fall of spatial inequalities in France: a long run perspective', Working Paper No. 2008–54, Paris School of Economics, Paris-Jourdan Sciences Economiques, Laboratoire d'Economie Appliquée-INRA.

Combes, P.P., Lafourcade, M., Thisse, J.F. and Toutain, J.C. (2011) 'The rise and fall of spatial inequalities in France: a long run perspective', *Explorations in Economic History*, Vol. 48 (2): 243–71.

Donnellier, J.C., Maliverney, J. and Montlouis, E. (1987) 'L'appareil productif regional de 1975 a 1984. Un analyse des valeurs ajoutées', *Les Collections de l'INSEE*, C3, Institut National de la Statistique et des Etudes Economiques (INSEE).

Duranton, G., Martin, P., Mayer, T. and Mayneris, F. (2008) *Les Pôles de compétitivité: que peut-on en attendre?* Paris: Editions Rue d'Ulm (ENS).

Enflo, K. and Rosés, J.R. (2015) 'Coping with regional inequality in Sweden: structural change, migrations, and policy, 1860–2000', *Economic History Review*, Vol. 68 (1): 191–217.

Geary, F. and Stark, T. (2002) 'Examining Ireland's post-famine economic growth performance', *The Economic Journal*, Vol. 112 (482): 919–35.

Gravier, J.F. (1953) *Paris et le désert français*, 2nd edition, Paris: Le Portulan.

Koster, E.A. (2005) *The Physical Geography of Western Europe*, Oxford Regional Environments Series, Oxford: Oxford University Press.

Krugman, P. and Venables, A.J. (1995) 'Globalization and the inequality of nations', *The Quarterly Journal of Economics*, Vol. 110 (4): 857–80.

Marchand, B. (2010) 'Le graviérisme aujourd'hui', in J. Salomon Cavin and B. Marchand (eds), *Antiurbain: origines et conséquences de l'urbaphobie*, Lausanne: Presses polytechniques et universitaires romandes, pp. 203–16.

Martínez-Galarraga, J., Rosés, J.R. and Tirado, D.A. (2015) 'The long-term patterns of regional income inequality in Spain, 1860–2000', *Regional Studies*, Vol. 49 (4): 502–17.

Mary, S. and Turpin, E. (1981) 'Panorama économique des régions françaises', *Les Collections de l'INSEE*, C3, Institut National de la Statistique et des Etudes Economiques (INSEE).

Ministère du Travail et de la prévoyance sociale/Statistique générale de la France (1911) *Salaires et coût de l'existence: à diverses époques, jusqu'en 1910*, Paris: Imprimerie Nationale.

Morrison, C. and Snyder, W. (2000) 'The income inequality of France in historical perspective', *European Review of Economic History*, Vol. 4 (1): 59–83.

Muet, P.A., Bolton, P. and Cozin, F. (1970) 'Études de démographie régionale. L'emploi de 1954 a 1968', *Les Collections de l'INSEE*, C3, Institut National de la Statistique et des Etudes Economiques (INSEE).

Prager, J.C. and Thisse, J.F. (2009) *Les enjeux géographiques du développement économique*, Paris: Agence française de développement.

Recensement Industriel de 1963. Resultats pour 1962.

Toutain, J.C. (1987) 'Le produit interieur brut de la France de 1789 á 1982', *Économies et Société. Série AF 15*, available at: www.rug.nl/research/ggdc/data/historical-national-accounts (accessed 13 August 2018).

Toutain, J.C. (1992) 'La production agricole de la France de 1810 à 1990: départements et régions', *Économies et Sociétés*, Série AF, 17 (11–12 and 1–2 and 3–4), pp. 1–334, 352–723 and 733–1078.

Vanhove, N. and Klaassen, L.H. (1980) *Regional Policy: A European Approach*. Farnborough: Saxon House.

Williamson, J.G. (1965) 'Regional inequality and the process of national development: a description of the patterns', *Economic Development and Cultural Change*, Vol. 13 (4): 1–84.

3.6 Regional economic growth in Germany, 1895–2010

Nikolaus Wolf

1. Introduction

The economic development of Germany's regions has attracted considerable attention among economists, historians, geographers and political scientists alike. More recent studies in the fields of economics and economic history include Frank (1994), Kiesewetter (2004), Grant (2005), Sleifer (2006), Ziblatt (2006), Redding and Sturm (2008), Wolf (2009), Gutberlet (2014), Hornung (2015), Schöttler (2016) and notably Vonyó (2018) for West Germany after 1945. The topic is of a more general interest for several reasons. First and most obvious, Germany is at the centre of Europe, and bridges the industrial regions in the north-west, regions characterized by crafts and small-scale industry in the south, trade and financial centres in the north and agriculture in the east. With the formation of the German Empire in 1871, this economic and social diversity was unified into one political system under the dominating influence of Prussia. Hence, second, the case of Germany is interesting because it allows the study of economic diversity within a relatively homogenous framework of institutions from 1871 onwards. Third, Germany has experienced – and caused – tremendous economic and political changes and disruptions over the last 200 years.

The country developed from an overall backward net importer of manufacturing goods in the first half of the nineteenth century to become Europe's industrial core. Over this period, the German state changed both its boundaries and political character several times: starting with the divisions after the First World War and Second World War, which resulted in the formation of two German states, the country was unified in 1990. This was accompanied by dramatic institutional changes from constitutional monarchy (1871), to republic (1919), fascist dictatorship (1933–1945), democratic republic and socialist dictatorship (1949–1989), and back to a republic based on parliamentary democracy. In principle, these changes in borders, political system and economic position provide ample material for studies on economic and political change. However, the flipside of this abundance of variation is a scarcity of data that would allow comparisons over time and across regions.

In this chapter, I will focus on the economic development of Germany in the borders of 1990 at the level of NUTS 2 regions, and do this over the period

1895–2010. For the case of Germany, this has several important implications. The development of Alsace and Lorraine, which were part of the German Empire until 1919, is discussed in Chapter 3.5 of this book. North Schleswig in turn is discussed as a part of Southern Denmark in Chapter 3.3 in this book. Instead, the development of Germany's former eastern territories, which were ceded to Poland, Russia and Lithuania after 1919, respectively 1945, are not treated in this book, and left for future work. Recently, Bukowski et al. (2017) have estimated the economic development of Poland at the regional level for 1870–1914. Arguably, the approach to use modern regional units has its drawbacks, but it nevertheless allows adopting a long-run perspective on a consistently defined set of regions. For example, it allows for the first time ever a description of Germany's long-run development in her current borders, including the changing position over the last century of those parts of the country that were split into the socialist planned economy German Democratic Republic (GDR) and the democratic market-oriented Federal Republic of Germany (FRG).

On the following pages, I will start with a brief description of Germany's "first nature" geography (Cronon 1991), including the very basic features of topography and geology of the country. Next, I will describe Germany's "second nature" geography, namely the city system, the most important elements of infrastructure, the development of population density over time and the location of main clusters of economic activity. This description uses the European NUTS classification system for regions, where all historical data have been recalculated for 36 modern NUTS 2 regions of Germany. Of this, 28 regions are in West Germany (hence, the former FRG), seven are in East Germany (hence, the former GDR) and Berlin is treated as one (!) separate region (in moderns NUTS 2 borders) throughout. The list of regions, the sources for employment and population data, for sector-specific labour productivity and regional variation in labour productivity are given in appendix I. I then describe the approach to construct a set of regional GDP estimates and discuss the development of GDP, GDP per area and GDP per capita levels over time and their variation across regions. Finally, I will contrast the results with earlier studies on regional development and conclude with some remarks on their implications.

2. On first nature geography: patterns of topography and geology

Located at the centre of Europe with a population of about 82 million (2015) and an area of about 357,000 km^2, Germany is the most populous and fourth largest state in the European Union (EU). It shares land borders with nine countries, all of which except Switzerland are members of the EU. In terms of first nature geography, the country is characterized in the north by the North European Plain (Schleswig-Holstein, Hamburg, Bremen, Lower Saxony and Mecklenburg-Vorpommern), with a coastline on the Baltic and the North Sea and flat terrain. Towards the centre and south, Germany is hilly in the Central Uplands, reaching higher mountain ranges in Bavaria (Alps) and Baden-Württemberg (Black Forest,

Swabian Alb). Hence, there is a wide range from entirely flat territories in the north to very rugged territories in the south and south-west. The country is crossed by three river systems: the Rhine and tributaries in the West, including the Main (reaching further central and eastwards), which empty into the North Sea; the Elbe and tributaries in the East, which empty partly into the North Sea and partly into the Baltic; and finally the Danube and tributaries in the south, which empty into the Black Sea. Beyond the sea access to the British Isles, Scandinavia and the Atlantic, the rivers Rhine and the Danube have historically provided for connections of central and northern Germany to regions in France and Switzerland in the south and for connections eastwards to Austria (Vienna) and South-Eastern Europe (Budapest and Belgrade).

In terms of geology, Germany has important resources of hard coal and brown coal (lignite), but also iron ores, potash and rock salt. While iron ore can be found in many of the mountainous regions of Germany, the location of hard coal, lignite and salts is more concentrated. Over the nineteenth century, we observe a massive increase in the exploitation of ores and other resources, accompanied by a spatial concentration of production towards regions with coal resources and good transportation facilities (Kiesewetter 2004). Apart from the large mining district in Upper Silesia (today Poland) and Lorraine (today France), the most important mining districts located in modern Germany are the Ruhr area and the Saar area for iron ore and hard coal, the Lusatia and Central German lignite districts and several potash mining districts in Lower Saxony, Saxony-Anhalt and Thuringia. These resources mattered for the economic development of Germany as inputs (see Fremdling 1977; Gutberlet 2014), notably coal as a source of energy, but also due to their by-products such as sulphuric acid, with many uses in the chemical industry. Before technological change made it profitable to use coal as a source of energy, the availability of water power in the rugged territories in southern, south-western and south-eastern parts of Germany determined the location and development of an early iron and textile industry (Kiesewetter 2004: 182). Towards the late nineteenth century, water power and especially lignite started to matter for the electrification of the country. This allowed for a gradual decentralization of economic activity away from the location of natural sources of energy (Salin 1928).

3. Second nature geography: cities, infrastructure and the location of economic activity

Germany was historically fragmented into a multitude of sovereign and part-sovereign territories, which started to be unified during the Napoleonic Wars and Prussia's westward expansion after 1815. The roots of this political fragmentation are subject to a large literature (for recent historical interpretations, see Simms 2013; Wilson 2016; for a new economic perspective, see Huning and Wahl 2017). Not unlike the situation in early modern Italy, fragmentation was accompanied by the existence of many small and medium-sized cities, most of which reach back to the wave of city foundations in the twelfth and thirteenth centuries.

The foundation of the German Empire in 1871 changed the city system, when most notably Berlin emerged as the leading city in terms of size and functions. By 1939, Berlin was not only the political capital; it also hosted the largest number of headquarters, the financial centre with the largest banks and the most important stock exchange, the airport hub of the country, and the largest publishing houses. But Berlin never dominated Germany quite as much as London or Paris dominated the UK and France, respectively. Around 1939, Berlin's share in the population of Germany (in modern borders of the city, which were established in 1920) peaked at just above 7 per cent. With the division of Germany after 1945, Berlin lost its central functions to regional centres in West Germany, such as almost all parts of the federal government to Bonn, many company headquarters to Munich, Düsseldorf or Cologne and several publishing houses to Hamburg, or the airport hub and financial centre to Frankfurt/Main (see Redding et al. 2011). While the Federal Republic of Germany (FRG) was characterized henceforth by a decentralized city system, Berlin stayed the capital and functional centre for the German Democratic Republic (GDR) in the east. After German unification in 1990, Berlin has regained some of its former centrality, and its population share in unified Germany has recovered from a low point of 3.8 per cent in 1980 to just above 4 per cent in 2010. Nevertheless, Germany continues to be characterized by a rather decentralized city system, with many strong regional centres such as Hamburg, Munich, Cologne or Frankfurt/Main and a weak capital.

The fragmented system of cities and regions was to some extent integrated with the construction of transport infrastructure after 1815. Prussia in particular invested in the construction of waterways and paved roads, and from the 1850s onwards facilitated the construction of railways. By 1914, Germany had one of the densest rail networks in Europe (Kopper 2015). While many of the new railway connections followed existing roads and waterways, the growing network provided for a much faster and (in most cases) cheaper communication between waterways and important cities. An important step was the opening of the Köln-Minden railroad in 1847, which connected the rivers Rhine and Weser (up to the seaport of Bremen). This also provided for a link to Hannover, and from there to Berlin, and shortly afterwards in 1848 further via Breslau (Wrocław) to Kraków. The transportation of goods and people between the eastern and western parts of Germany became much easier than ever before. For example, the average travel speed on stagecoach had reached around 10 km/h in 1850 (Beyer 1986: 55), while railroad passengers could travel at up to 90 km/h in 1900 (Holtz 1985: 240). By 1880, there existed a dense network that connected all German cities and regions, as well as their European neighbours.

A main effect of improved transportation was the integration of markets. While still in 1914 some border regions were better integrated across the border than with other parts of Germany (Wolf 2009), the political unification and the improvement of infrastructure from the 1850s onwards had a very substantial effect. Keller and Shiue (2013) showed that both factors helped to integrate, for example, grain markets in nineteenth-century Germany. Hornung (2015) found a causal effect of the expansion of the railroad network on the spatial allocation of population across Germany, where connected cities grew significantly faster than non-connected cities. This probably also increased labour productivity in those cities as it allowed for larger establishments. Moreover, the growth of the railroad network before 1900 had strong backward linkage effects for the development of a modern iron and steel industry and engineering (Fremdling 1977). The transport infrastructure improved again dramatically during the twentieth century. Several new canals extended existing waterways, notably the Nord-Ostsee Kanal connecting the North Sea and the Baltic (opened in 1895) and the Mittellandkanal connecting the Rhine, Weser and Elbe, (opened formally in 1938).[1]

While the 1920s and 1930s saw some first (rather limited) efforts to construct national highways ('Autobahnen'), the age of mass motorization started in the 1950s with a quick expansion of highways and roads in both West and East Germany. However, these networks increasingly diverged after 1945, when the border between FRG and GDR, and GDR and West Berlin in particular, became virtually impenetrable with the Iron Curtain and the Berlin Wall in 1961. Trade, migration, capital flows and communication between both parts of Germany, which had been intense until 1945, collapsed. After unification, the transport networks of waterways, railroads, and highways started to be unified with the construction of several missing east–west connections. But the integration of transport networks was still very incomplete in 2010 as the former division of the country is still clearly visible in patterns of intra-national trade (see Nitsch and Wolf 2013). Another important element of infrastructure is the country's electricity grid, which started to emerge in the 1890s and then rapidly expanded after 1919. While the network obviously grew faster in more developed and resource-abundant regions, over the course of the twentieth century it improved access to energy in all parts of Germany and benefited regions without coal deposits more strongly than others, notably in terms of the growth of energy-intensive industries.

Given the country's first nature geography and infrastructure development, but also given division in 1945 and unification in 1990, where did people live and work in Germany during the twentieth century? Let me first describe the changing pattern of population density before we look at the evolution of employment over time. Based on census data, the average population density of the German Empire in 1913 borders was 95.7 people per km^2 in 1895 and 114.1 people per km^2 in 1907. If we limit our attention to Germany in modern (1990) borders, population density was higher (114.9 people per km^2 in 1895 and 141.6 people per km^2 in 1907), because the territories that Germany lost after 1919 were on average less populous. Over time, average population density in modern post-unification borders has increased from about 115 people per km^2 (1895), over 168.5 people per km^2 (1939), 200.1 people per km^2 (1950), 221.5 people per km^2 (1992), to about 229 people per km^2 (2010). Before 1945, this growth was mostly due to natural population growth; after 1945, it was mostly due to migration. But the averages mask some remarkable regional variation. Figure 3.6.1 shows the development of Germany in modern borders, split into the territories of the former FRG and GDR, and excluding in both cases Berlin.

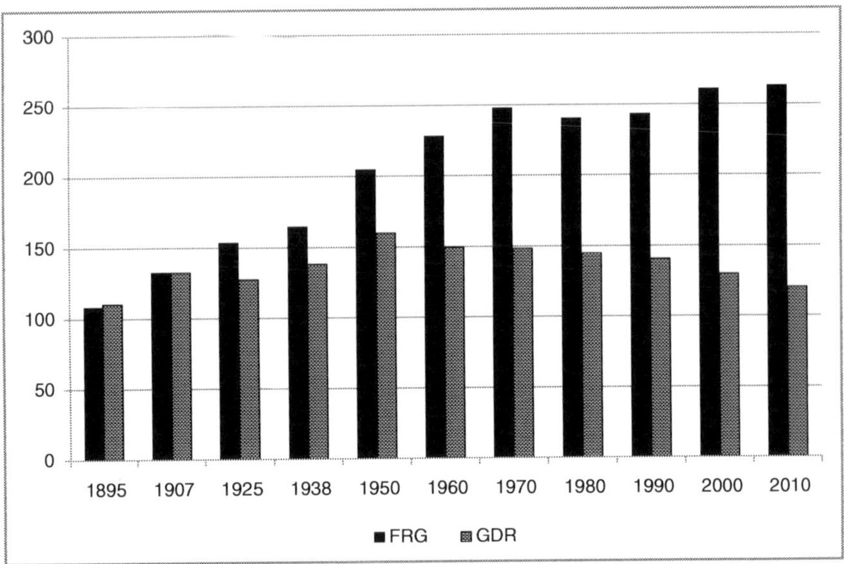

Figure 3.6.1 Population density in the territories of the GDR and FRG, 1895–2010 (people per km^2)

Source: Own calculation, see appendix II; Berlin is excluded throughout.

The figure shows how the two parts of Germany stood at nearly identical levels of population density before the First World War, initially with a small advantage in the east. They started to diverge already after 1919, notably before the division of Germany. After 1945, densities increased in both parts of the country due to a large inflow of refugees and expellees from eastern territories that nowadays belong to the Czech Republic, Lithuania, Poland and Russia. The effects of this migration were rather unequal across German regions (see Hefele 1998; Frey 2003, specifically on Bavaria). However, from 1950 to 1961, population density in the GDR declined from 159.8 people per km^2 to 149.6 people per km^2 due to a substantial outmigration to West Germany in response to political oppression in the East and diverging living standards. This is mirrored by an increasing population density in the FRG. The construction of the Berlin Wall in 1961 'successfully' stopped the outflow of people from the GDR (many of which had escaped to the West via the airport of West Berlin, see Redding et al. 2011). From about 1970 until unification, population density in the FRG and the GDR stayed roughly constant at about 240 and 140 people per km^2, respectively. Unification was accompanied by another wave of substantial outmigration from the former GDR to West Germany. While before 1945 the two least populated German NUTS 2 regions were in the West, Lüneburg (DE93 and Oberpfalz (DE23), after 1990 the two – by far – least populated regions are located in the East, Mecklenburg-Vorpommern (DE80) and Brandenburg (DE40). Also, before 1945, Leipzig (DED5) and Chemnitz (DED4) were always among the most densely populated regions in Germany, while after 1990 they are no longer in the top 10. On average, population density in East German regions declined from 102 per cent of West Germany (1895) to 83.6 per cent (1938), 65.6 per cent (1961), 58 per cent (1992) and 45 per cent (2010) (excluding Berlin). Unsurprisingly, this change in population density was directly related to a relocation of economic activity from East to West, which shaped and distinguished the development of German regions compared to other parts of Europe.

The evidence on population density gives a good preview for the development of employment across German regions. Total employment increased on the territory of Germany in modern borders from about 17 million in 1895 to over 39 million in 2010. As expected, the location of economic activity as measured in terms of employment density followed the pattern of population density closely, but not exactly. While total employment per area on the territory of the (future) FRG and GDR was nearly the same in 1895, it diverged over time, as shown in Figure 3.6.2. This divergence started already after 1914 before it was stopped by the Iron Curtain in the 1960s. Unification led to another decline down to a level of about 40 per cent the employment density of West Germany in 2010 (compared to 45 per cent in terms of population density). Underneath this change is a relocation of people, companies and state institutions, but also a change in demographics and the labour market regime. The employment ratio (total employment relative to total population) increased from about 42 per cent (1895) to nearly 50 per cent (2010). This rate was historically higher in the territories of the GDR compared to the West already before 1945, but especially during the GDR (1949–1989), when the regime supported high female labour market participation and when unemployment was essentially absent. However, after unification, the regions of the former GDR experienced a process of deindustrialization together with fast population ageing that resulted in high unemployment and selective outmigration of young, skilled people. From about 2005 onwards, unemployment rates in the East started to converge slowly to those in the West due to a decline in the supply of labour rather than an increase in demand (Brenke 2014).

Like all other regions in Europe, Germany experienced a fundamental change in occupation structures from the second half of the nineteenth century. Millions of people found employment outside of agriculture in industry and services, accompanied by large-scale migration, the growth of cities and rising levels of productivity. Both increases in labour productivity within sectors and a reallocation of labour away from agriculture to more productive employment in industry and services resulted in higher GDP per capita, albeit with enormous differences across regions. If we look at Germany in modern borders, the share of agriculture in total employment declined from 38 per cent (1895), 28 per cent (1938) and 5.5 per cent (1990) to just 1.8 per cent (2010) (see Table 3.6.1). The share of industrial employment reached a peak around 1960 with 49 per cent and declined thereafter, especially in the last two decades. This aggregate development masks a lot of regional variation, including stark differences between East and West. Note that the regions, which after 1945 constituted the GDR, had on average a *higher* share

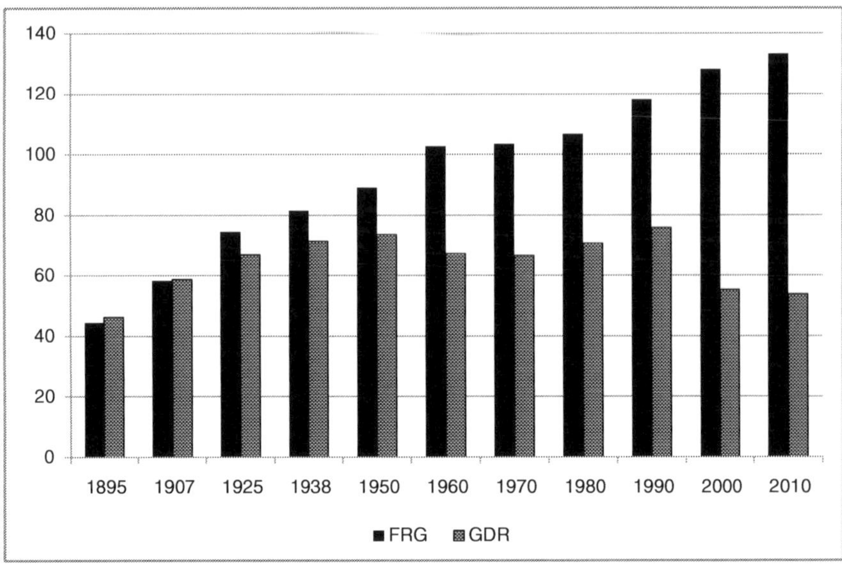

Figure 3.6.2 Employment density in the territories of the GDR and FRG, 1895–2010 (employment per km²)

Source: Own calculation, see appendix II; Berlin is excluded throughout.

of industry than their counterparts in the West. Industrial employment accounted for 44 per cent in 1895 (compared to 35 per cent in the West), and was still high in 1990 (49 per cent compared to 37 per cent) before it declined rapidly.

To see how the economic activity of regions changed over time, I ranked all 36 German regions according to their employment density (total employment per km²).

Table 3.6.1 Sectoral change in Germany, 1895–2010

	Share in total employment	*1895*	*1925*	*1950*	*1970*	*1990*	*2010*
Germany	Agriculture	37.7	33.1	25.5	10.0	5.5	1.8
	Industry	36.8	39.9	42.1	48.5	39.0	25.5
	Services	25.5	27.0	32.4	41.5	55.6	72.7
FRG	Agriculture	40.0	35.7	26.2	9.4	4.3	1.8
	Industry	34.9	37.9	41.3	47.9	36.8	26.1
	Services	25.1	26.4	32.5	42.7	58.9	72.0
GDR	Agriculture	30.2	27.2	25.6	13.8	10.9	2.1
	Industry	44.1	46.7	45.6	51.6	48.8	24.7
	Services	25.7	26.1	28.9	34.6	40.3	73.2

Source: Own calculation. All data refers to Germany in 1990 borders, and the borders of the FRG and GDR as of 1949–1989. Berlin is excluded in both the FRG and GDR.

In 1895, the three city regions (Berlin, Hamburg, Bremen) are followed by regions in the Rhein and Ruhr area, Düsseldorf (DEA1), and in Saxony, Chemnitz (DED4) and Leipzig (DED5). While the latter kept a high industrial density, they nevertheless fall back after 1945 and range in the middle in 2010. Instead, some regions in the centre and south of Germany have improved their position, such as Stuttgart (DE11) and Karlsruhe (DE12). Employment growth in the city regions originated mainly from services – in 1938, more than 50 per cent of all employment in Berlin was in services – whereas the rise of central and southern German regions was due to growth in particular industries.

A remarkable outlier is the region around Munich, Oberbayern (DE21), where already, around 1900, employment in services had been far higher than in any other region in southern Germany, stemming from a combination of industry-related services, tourism and especially public services. The historical centres of German industry had all benefited from abundant energy resources – coal for the beginning of iron- and steelworks in the Ruhr or Upper Silesia (now Poland), water power for the growth of textile factories in Saxony. For Germany in modern borders, textiles and apparel were in 1895 still the largest sector within industry with a share of 24 per cent. But at the turn of the century, industry changed away from textiles towards mechanical engineering and electrotechnical and chemical industries, which together doubled their share in total industrial employment from 17 per cent (1895) to 34 per cent (1938). Some of these industries had their origins in the centres of traditional industry, such as machine making in Saxony, which developed due to the demand for textile machinery and later diversified (for example, Sächsische Maschinenfabrik, founded in 1837). Yet, in general, the location of these new industries was less affected by first nature advantages and more by second nature, notably by the location of demand. A prime example is the rise of Berlin to the world's "Electropolis" after 1900, hosting the large factories of Siemens and AEG. Here, the initial demand for light, power for machinery and public transport determined the location of an essentially "footloose" industry, which by 1914 served global markets (Czada 1969). Another factor that fundamentally changed the geography of employment was the combined effect of improved transport infrastructure with electrification, which made energy available in regions hitherto less endowed with either coal or water power. The rise of southern German regions was accompanied by a strong expansion in the new industries, notably in Württemberg – Stuttgart (DE11), Karlsruhe (DE12) – in Oberbayern (DE21) and in Mittelfranken around Nürnberg (DE25), all regions without coal (Petzina 1994: 106). In the next section, I discuss new estimates of regional GDP that summarize all these regional differences in employment structures and sectoral and regional labour productivities over the last century.

4. Regional GDP for German NUTS 2 regions, 1895–2010

The GDP of a region can be estimated in two ways, 'top-down' and 'bottom-up'. The first method uses standard GDP figures calculated in a national accounting framework at the level of the national economy and breaks them down to the level of regions, using a more or less systematic approach. Instead, the second method uses a national accounting framework at the level of regions, typically based on regional production data. Both methods have benefits and problems. As a rule, a 'bottom-up' approach should be used whenever the data allow us to do so. But the manifold changes in German regional and national boundaries over the twentieth century makes this close to impossible for any consistent set of regions. Hence, I will use a 'top-down' approach for the period prior to the Second World War (1895–1938) and the years 1950 and 1960. I follow the basic methodology developed by Geary and Stark (2002), which has been described earlier (see Chapter 2 in this book). The regional GDP figures for the years 1960 onwards are based on a set of much more detailed 'bottom-up' estimates generated by cooperation between the Statistical Offices of Germany's Laender. This will be complemented by estimates of the GDP in East Germany from Broadberry and Klein (2012), which again were broken down to (very tentative) regional figures. To assess the quality of my approach, I compare my estimation results for 1907 to estimates of regional shares in national income from Hoffmann and Müller (1959) for 1907 based on tax records. Next, I compare my estimation results for 1960 to official 'bottom-up' estimates from the German Statistical Offices of the Länder for West German regions for the same year.

The idea of Geary and Stark (2002) is simply to decompose national GDP estimates into the contributions of regions and sectors using regional sector-specific data on employment and labour productivity. The challenges for Germany are first to deal with the changes in national borders and second to find data on region- and sector-specific labour productivity. The German state lost large territories after 1918 (notably Alsace-Lorraine to France, North Schleswig to Denmark, and West Prussia, Pomerania and parts of Upper Silesia to Poland). After 1945, Germany was divided according to a wartime protocol that organized the country into zones of military occupation. In 1949, two states were founded, the FRG in the west and the GDR in the centre of the former German state, while territories further east became part of Poland, the USSR, Lithuania and Czechoslovakia. Existing estimates of historical national GDP are calculated for the state in respective borders, and therefore need to be adjusted to the borders of modern Germany (1990). Moreover, the external borders of both German states were stable since the Second World War, but internal administrative borders changed significantly. The following estimates decompose national GDP estimates at respective borders down into regions in such a way that they can be aggregated up to the FRG, the GDR and their sum, which is Germany in modern borders. Thereby, the new estimates also provide for the first time consistent estimates of GDP and GDP per capita for Germany in 1990 borders from 1895 to today.

I use employment data from Hohls and Kaelble (1989) for the years 1895–1970, complemented by data from Schöttler (2016) for regions of the GDR (1949–1989) and Ahlfeldt et al. (2015) for East and West Berlin (1936–2006). I distinguish between agriculture, mining, capital goods industries, consumption goods industries and services. For these five broad sectors, I use sector- and time-specific value-added data (see, respectively, Hoffmann 1965: Tables 103 and 76) to calculate sector-specific labour productivities. Regional variation in labour productivity in turn is approximated with regional variation in sector-specific deflated wages (for more details, see appendix I). All data are adjusted for changes in regional borders to fit the modern NUTS 2 classification system for 36 German NUTS 2 regions.[2] Table 3.6.2a shows the contribution of the five sectors to national GDP in Germany, 1895–1960, while Table 3.6.2b shows the resulting labour productivity as sector GDP over sector employment (using GDP data from 1895–1938 from Bolt and van Zanden 2013, and GDP data from 1950 and 1960 from Broadberry and Klein 2012).

As visible in these tables, both the contributions to overall GDP and the sector-specific labour productivities varied significantly over time. Together with regional sector-specific employment data and regional wage data to approximate productivity differences within sectors across regions, we can hope to capture most of this variation and derive consistent estimates of regional GDP as a decomposition of national estimates (Broadberry and Klein 2012; Bolt and van Zanden 2013; Bolt et al. 2018). The latter in turn can be seen as summaries of a large literature on the development of German GDP, including the work by Ritschl and Spoerer (1997) and Burhop and Wolff (2005), to name just a few. When I compare my results using 17 historical regions to the set of estimates from Hoffmann and Müller (1959) for 1907, I find a very high correlation of the implied regional shares in national figures (0.985) with a mean deviation of below 2 per cent. For the years 1960–1961 onwards, I use the official regional shares in national value

Table 3.6.2a Sector-specific GDP shares, 1895–1960

	1895	*1907*	*1925*	*1938*	*1950*	*1960*
Agriculture	0.310	0.253	0.157	0.151	0.113	0.076
Mining	0.027	0.035	0.033	0.032	0.031	0.025
Capital goods industries	0.180	0.200	0.223	0.242	0.241	0.288
Consumption goods industries	0.172	0.192	0.229	0.250	0.248	0.297
Services	0.310	0.321	0.358	0.325	0.367	0.313

Source: Hoffmann (1965: Tables 76 and 103).

Note: 1950 and 1960 refer to the FRG.

Table 3.6.2b Sector-specific labour productivity, relative to average, 1895–1960

	1895	*1907*	*1925*	*1938*	*1950*	*1960*
Agriculture	0.820	0.714	0.511	0.581	0.501	0.564
Mining	1.435	1.366	1.234	1.493	1.076	1.117
Capital goods industries	1.370	1.249	1.207	1.097	1.047	0.952
Consumption goods industries	0.799	0.935	1.135	1.451	1.421	1.843
Services	1.214	1.256	1.281	0.998	1.075	0.828

Source: Own.

Note: 1950 and 1960 refer to the FRG.

added estimated by the Statistical Offices of the Länder, together with estimates from Broadberry and Klein (2012), to derive regional GDP in 1990 international Geary–Khamis dollars. For 1960–1961, I have therefore two sets of estimates, and find again that they correlate very strongly (0.979) with a mean deviation of below 4 per cent.

The economy of Germany in modern (1990) borders represented in 1900 a share of 78.5 per cent of total GDP of Germany in 1913 borders; in 1910, this share was 85.5 per cent. After the loss of various territories in 1919–1922, the share of modern Germany in interwar borders (as of 1922–1938) was 91.4 per cent in 1925 and 91.1 per cent in 1938. Both before and after the First World War, the share of modern Germany in terms of GDP was higher than its share in area or population. Figure 3.6.3 shows the development of GDP per capita for the various benchmark years, 1895–2010, measured in 1990 international Geary–Khamis dollars for Germany in modern borders, and the FRG and GDR (in both cases, excluding Berlin). Table 3.6.A.2 (see appendix II) shows GDP per capita for all 36 regions, 1900–2010.

To start, Germany in modern borders had a slightly higher GDP per capita than Germany in historical borders before 1945. More interesting is the evidence on GDP per capita for the regions in Germany that later would constitute the two German states, the FRG and GDR (excluding Berlin) and Berlin. Similar to our finding on population and employment density, GDP per capita on the territories of the GDR was not lagging behind the level in West Germany before division. In 1938, the regions of the GDR were actually slightly ahead of those in the West. Saxony in particular was a powerhouse of the German economy before 1945.

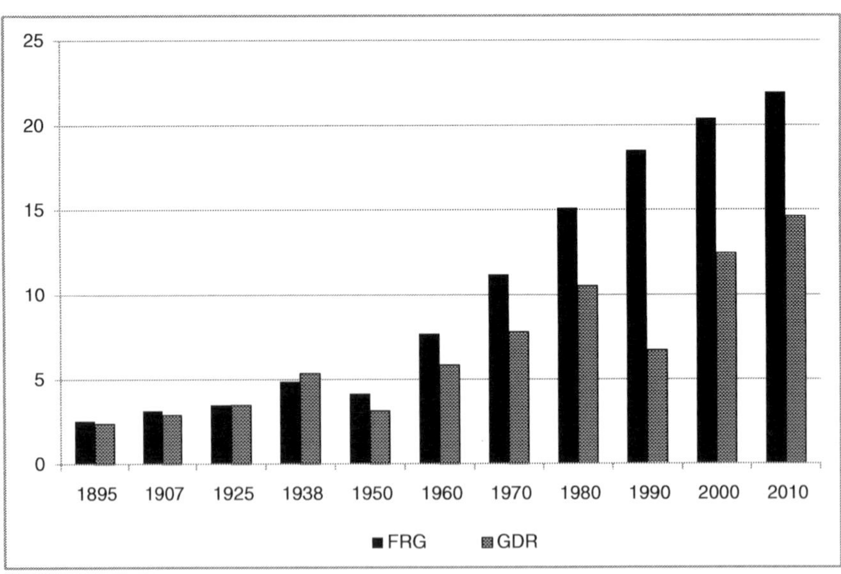

Figure 3.6.3 GDP per capita in modern Germany, 1895–2010 (GK$1,000)

Saxon GDP per capita in 1900 was at 108 per cent the average of Germany in modern borders, and in 1938 112 per cent of the average. Similarly, Thuringia developed quite dynamically between 1925 and 1938.

After division, Saxony was rapidly falling behind as all other regions in the East, reaching a low point in 1990 with just above 40 per cent. By 2010, it has caught up to 73 per cent of the average of unified Germany. Even more dramatic is the development of Berlin over time. In 1907, Berlin was the richest part of Germany, followed by Hamburg and Bremen. In 1938, it was clearly the leading city, with a GDP per capita of nearly 150 per cent the German average. Compared to other capital regions in Europe, however, this lead over the rest of the country was very small. For example, the region of Île-de-France around Paris had in 1938 a GDP per capita of 178 per cent the average of France. Due to the division of Germany after 1945, the city fell quickly behind, in spite of subsidies paid to West Berlin by the FRG and the capital status of East Berlin within the GDR. In 1990, Berlin's GDP per capita stood at around 77 per cent of the German average, a remarkable decline for a capital city. In 2010, Berlin had recovered to about 94 per cent of average German GDP per capita, but is still far behind its historical position.

Maps 3.6.1–3.6.4 in appendix II illustrate the development of GDP per capita across the 36 German regions for four benchmark years, 1900, 1938, 1960 and 2010. Several findings stand out. First, in contrast to other parts of Europe, the map in 1900 shows not one clear economic centre of Germany, but several leading regions. Hamburg (DE60) in the north, Berlin (DE30) and Saxony (DED2, DED4, DED5) in the east, Upper Bavaria (DE21) and Northern Württemberg (DE12) in the south as well as the larger Ruhr area (DEA1, DEA2) all have GDP per capita above the German average. Remarkably, this had not changed much by 1938, in spite of the First World War, hyperinflation and the Great Depression. Only that Berlin was relatively stronger in 1938 compared to 1900, and Saxony and Württemberg were richer than before due to their strategically important industries. This decentralized structure remains characteristic for Germany's economy until today. Second, the maps show clearly how the division of Germany after 1945 led to a strong divergence between East and West that has not been undone after 1990. Saxony and Berlin are the starkest examples for this general decline of all regions of the former GDR from a strong position before 1945.

Beyond this, we can make a third observation from the maps. While in 1900 and still in 1938 several regions not only in the east, but also in the north, west and south of the country, were strong centres of economic activity, the north and the west have fallen behind in the 50 years between 1960 and 2010. Instead, some regions in southern Germany and the region around Frankfurt/Main (DE71) have risen far above the average. The city of Frankfurt/Main and its hinterland represent to some extent the flipside of the relative decline of the GDR as they clearly benefited from the division of Germany. Frankfurt became (temporary) headquarters of the United States European Command, and was seat of the Bizonal Economic Council, the first body of West German self-governance after the war. With this, the city attracted the aviation hub from Berlin to Frankfurt/Main, as well as the seat of the new central bank (Bank Deutscher Länder, later Bundesbank) in March 1948. The new political and economic centrality of Frankfurt/Main determined the decision of large private banks to relocate their headquarters from Berlin, helped the Frankfurt stock exchange (renamed in 1993 to Deutsche Börse AG) to become Germany's most important trading place, and lastly decided about the seat of the European Central Bank in 1998.

The economic strength of Upper Bavaria (DE21), the region around Munich, reaches further back in history, as Munich was already around 1900 a centre of private and public services with a strong industrial sector. But Bavaria – and notably Upper Bavaria – also benefited from division, for example with the relocation of the headquarters of Allianz (insurance) from Berlin to Munich, Siemens (electrics, machinery, equipment) from Berlin to Munich and Erlangen in 1949, and Audi from Saxony to Ingolstadt in 1949. Upper Bavaria developed into one of the most prosperous regions of Germany, with a GDP per capita of 105 per cent the West German average in 1950, to 129 per cent the West German average in 2010, 137 per cent compared to the German average in modern borders. However, if we exclude Upper Bavaria, the remaining regions of Bavaria stayed always slightly below the average level of GDP per capita of the FRG. In contrast, other former economic centres of Germany experienced a decline that was not related to the country's division, but rather to structural change. Notably, the Ruhr region suffered from a degradation of its mining and iron and steel industry similar to other European centres of heavy industry due to intense global competition. Figure 3.6.4 summarizes these changes with a weighted coefficient of variation, where the contribution of each region to overall dispersion is weighted with the region's share in total population.[3]

The figure shows a remarkable development compared to that in other parts of Europe. A relatively low level of dispersion declined further between 1900 and 1938, before it increased after 1945. This increase is not explained by German division alone, but was caused by divergence both between the FRG and GDR and within the FRG.

Within West Germany, the increase in dispersion is due to an early recovery of the northern parts of the country and the centre (Frankfurt/Main) after the war together with stagnation in the south. The decline of heavy industry in the Ruhr and Saar and continuous structural change towards light industries and services in parts of southern Germany combine to explain a tendency of convergence in the 1970s. Stronger than this are the effects of division and unification. The division first contributed to a relative decline of regions located in the GDR and an increase in dispersion between 1950 and 1980. Perhaps more surprising is the peak in dispersion after 1989, which is due to the near collapse of the GDR economy starting in summer 1990 (Akerlof et al. 1991) in the wake of the introduction of the Deutsche Mark and shifting demand. This was followed by a remarkable yet incomplete convergence (for a recent survey of the evidence, see Burda and Weder 2017).

Figure 3.6.5 shows the resulting long-run convergence for the period 1900–2010, measured as the relationship between average annual growth rates over the period and initial (1900) levels of GDP per capita (beta-convergence).

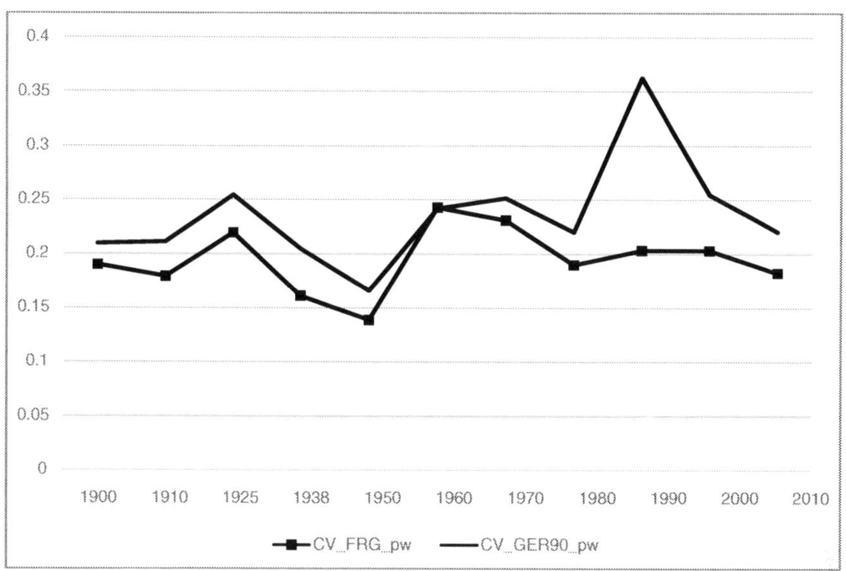

Figure 3.6.4 Population-weighted coefficient of variation, Germany in modern borders and West Germany (FRG), 1900–2010

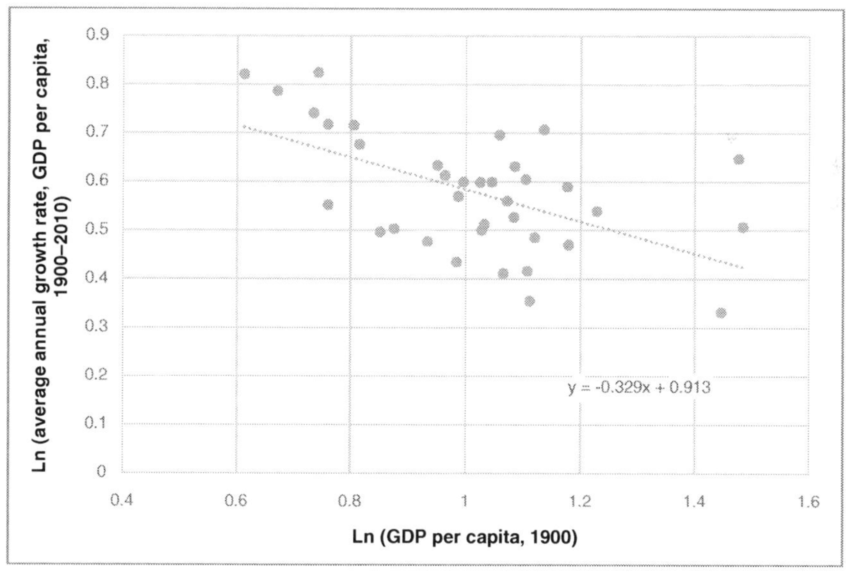

Figure 3.6.5 Beta-convergence, 36 German regions, 1900–2010

Source: Own.

From our historical discussion, we know that this long-run convergence hides more than it actually shows. During the interwar years, some regions were catching up in terms of GDP per capita before division led to a substantial divergence, both within the West and between East and West Germany. More recently, unification allowed the East to reconverge again, but with strong regional differences. Overall, the dispersion across regions in terms of GDP per capita seems to come back down to its level a century ago. But note that the indicator GDP per capita measures average incomes, not economic activity as such. As seen in Figures 3.6.1 and 3.6.2, some regions in Germany face depopulation and a related decline in economic activity. It is a moot point whether such developments call for policy intervention, for example to ensure the viability of public good provision at the local level. The rather coarse data at NUTS 2 level also hide a tendency of agglomeration within regions that was related to the rise of services in the economy. This in turn fits into a much broader development of regional divergence that is visible in other parts of Europe and seems to have started in the late 1970s (see Chapter 2 in this book). But overall, Germany is an outlier in a European perspective, characterized by a strong and decentralized economy with several regional centres and a comparatively weak capital, not unlike in 2010 as it was back in 1900.

5. Comparison to earlier studies and conclusion

How do these new results compare to earlier studies? A notable difference is that no other study has yet constructed GDP estimates covering all parts of Germany for a consistent set of regions over the last century. Earlier studies that produced long-run comparisons of regional income or GDP, such as Orsagh (1968), Tipton (1976), Frank (1994) or Petzina (1994), had a more limited time horizon and often used changing regional units. Others, such as Sleifer (2006), were focused on the East/West comparison. Orsagh (1968) and Frank (1994) both use a simple regression approach, where official estimates of per capita national income from the Imperial Statistical Office for 1913 for 20 regions were regressed on the regional occupation structure as given in the census of 1907, and next projected backwards and forwards with occupational data for other years. Frank (1994) confirms with his earlier results that there was an increase in income inequality over the second half of the nineteenth century, which peaked around 1907 before some convergence set in. Perhaps still the most reliable picture of regional variation across Germany before 1945 comes from Hoffmann and Müller (1959). My new estimates, which decompose national GDP estimates to the level of regions and use a finer sectoral structure, as well as regional variation in labour productivity, modify these results (albeit for the territory of modern Germany). The population-weighted coefficient of variation fluctuated before 1945 and increased thereafter. Another finding in the literature needs to be revised. In contrast to suggestions by Orsagh (1968) and Petzina (1994), regions within West Germany did not converge between 1938 and 1970, but diverged. Not only did regions in the GDR fall behind after 1945, but regions within the FRG also diverged strongly until 1960, before this trend was stopped and then reversed. Compared to the findings of Sleifer (2006), the new estimates suggest that the regions of the former GDR were, if anything, slightly ahead of the West in terms of GDP per capita around 1938, which implies a very strong relative decline relative to the West after 1945.

If we adopt a European perspective, we see that Germany stands out as a country with a relatively equal distribution of economic activity, with a weak capital city and many regional centres. Also, Germany showed an unusual regional divergence after 1945 until the 1960s, even excluding the regions of the former GDR, against a European trend towards convergence.

To be sure, the estimates presented in this chapter should be treated with caution and certainly need further improvement. Nevertheless, they provide a starting point for research into the driving forces behind the long-run development of Germany's regions in a European perspective.

Appendix I: data sources

Employment and population data

The data on sector-specific regional employment and population at the level of Regierungsbezirke is from Hohls and Kaelble (1989). Data on employment and population from 1970 to 2010 are taken from Gemeinschaftsveröffentlichungen (2007) and Gemeinschaftsveröffentlichungen (2012). Data on the employment structures and population in regions of the GDR, adjusted to modern NUTS 2 borders, are taken from Schöttler (2016).

Sectoral value added

Sector-specific value added for the years 1895–1960 is derived from Hoffmann (1965: Tables 76 and 103) on specific industries. For 1950 and 1960, the data refer to the FRG only.

Sector-specific value added for the years 1950–1980 for the GDR is approximated using sector shares in national income (agriculture, industry and mining and services) from Staatliche Zentralverwaltung für Statistik (1989), specifically Chapter 4, p. 100, table 'Nettoprodukt der Wirtschaftsbereiche'.

Regional wage data

Regional variations in labour productivity are approximated using data on average wages across Landesversicherungsanstalten (LVAs), as provided in Hohls (1991). This was extended by data on wages in construction from Zentralverband der Maurer Deutschlands (1906) for 1895 and 1905, and the wage census for 1920 from Statistisches Reichsamt (1921). The wage data are deflated using regional rye prices from Zeitschrift des königlich Preussischen Statistischen Bureaus (var. years), Statistisches Jahrbuch des Deutschen Reichs (var. years), Vierteljahreshefte zur Statistik des Deutschen Reiches (var. years) and Zeitschrift des Königlichen Bayerischen Statistischen Landesamtes (var. years).

Regional GDP, West Germany, 1960–1980, and Germany, 1990–2010

We use estimates of regional GDP at the level of West German counties, 1961–1980, and Germany, 1990–2010, published by Arbeitsgemeinschaft VGR der Länder from 1964 onwards, where we aggregate counties up to modern NUTS 2 levels and use the resulting shares to break down national estimates of GDP from Broadberry and Klein (2012).

Appendix II: regional GDP data

Table 3.6.A.1 shows the share of each region in the total GDP of Germany in 1990 borders, and Table 3.6.A.2 shows GDP per capita for all 36 regions, 1900–2010.

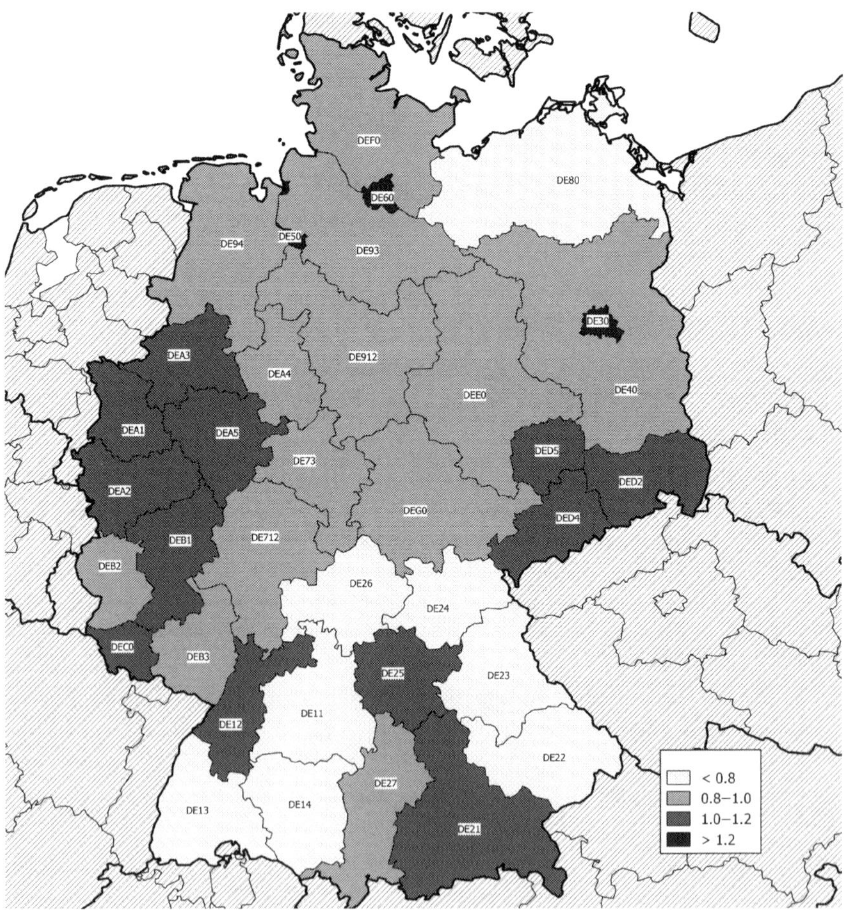

Map 3.6.1 Relative GDP per capita, 1900 (Germany = 1)

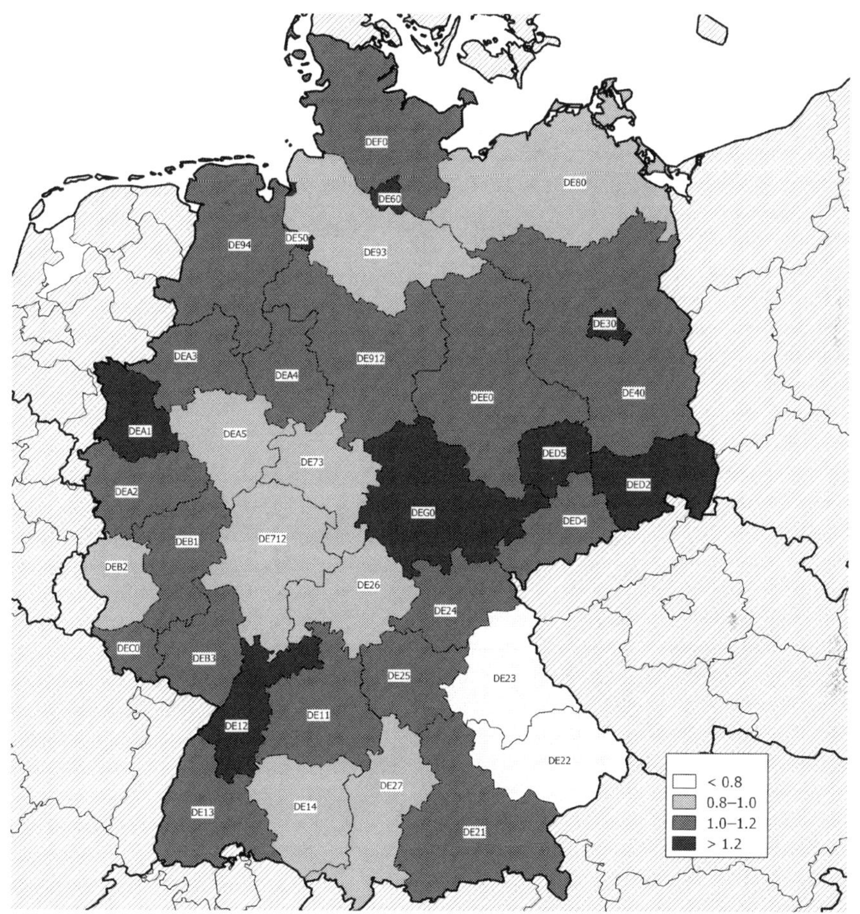

Map 3.6.2 Relative GDP per capita, 1938 (Germany = 1)

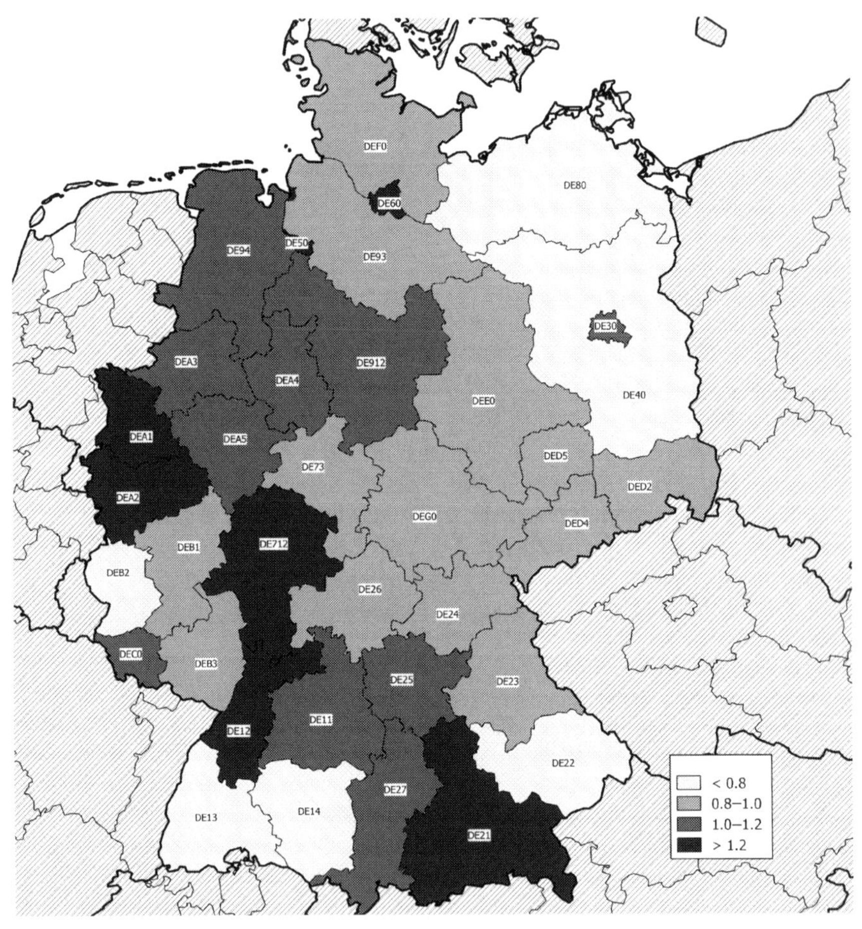

Map 3.6.3 Relative GDP per capita, 1960 (Germany = 1)

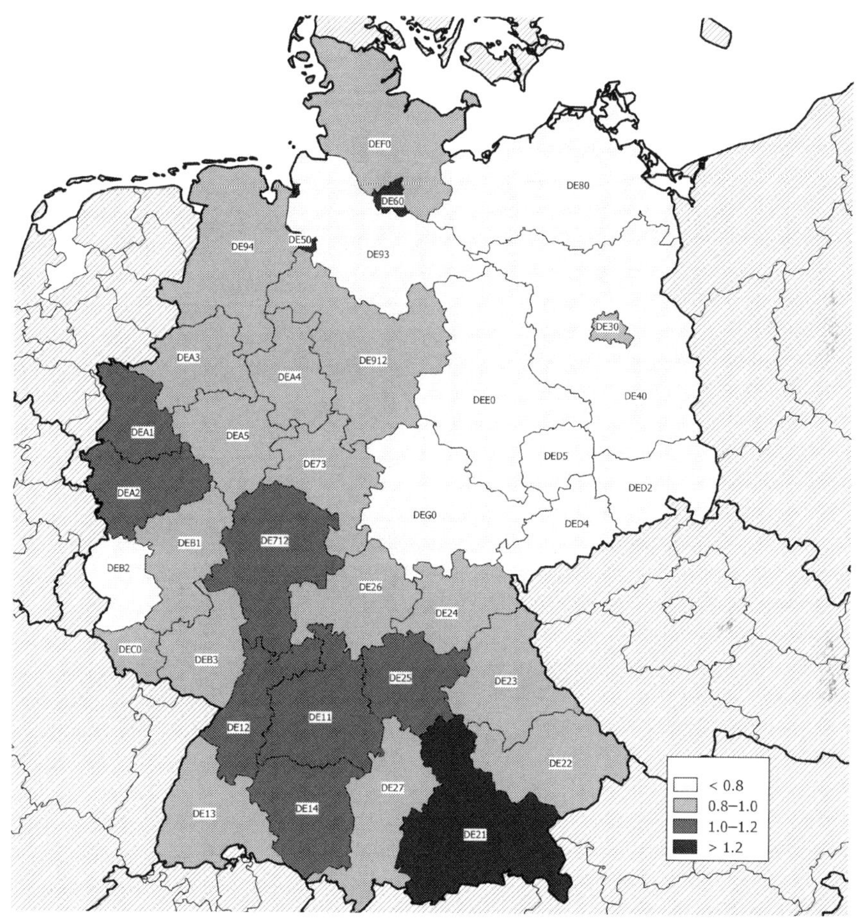

Map 3.6.4 Relative GDP per capita, 2010 (Germany = 1)

Table 3.6.A.1 Regional share in national GDP, 1900–2010

		1900	*1910*	*1925*	*1938*	*1950*	*1960*	*1970*	*1980*	*1990*	*2000*	*2010*
DE11	Stuttgart, Regierungsbezirk	0.0314	0.0307	0.0304	0.0313	0.0428	0.0520	0.0538	0.0545	0.0620	0.0595	0.0594
DE12	Karlsruhe, Regierungsbezirk	0.0283	0.0300	0.0283	0.0268	0.0333	0.0349	0.0388	0.0360	0.0409	0.0372	0.0372
DE13	Freiburg, Regierungsbezirk	0.0219	0.0209	0.0168	0.0188	0.0213	0.0197	0.0220	0.0241	0.0262	0.0258	0.0259
DE14	Tübingen, Regierungsbezirk	0.0168	0.0157	0.0141	0.0146	0.0183	0.0157	0.0180	0.0195	0.0227	0.0224	0.0234
DE21	Oberbayern, Regierungsbezirk	0.0308	0.0271	0.0288	0.0293	0.0383	0.0421	0.0524	0.0604	0.0732	0.0705	0.0729
DE22	Niederbayern, Regierungsbezirk	0.0113	0.0092	0.0070	0.0077	0.0142	0.0085	0.0093	0.0105	0.0130	0.0130	0.0144
DE23	Oberpfalz, Regierungsbezirk	0.0086	0.0080	0.0071	0.0068	0.0123	0.0090	0.0097	0.0096	0.0118	0.0127	0.0136
DE24	Oberfranken, Regierungsbezirk	0.0120	0.0113	0.0112	0.0126	0.0182	0.0134	0.0132	0.0121	0.0142	0.0121	0.0123
DE25	Mittelfranken, Regierungsbezirk	0.0188	0.0191	0.0185	0.0177	0.0200	0.0194	0.0210	0.0207	0.0238	0.0221	0.0225
DE26	Unterfranken, Regierungsbezirk	0.0116	0.0125	0.0114	0.0118	0.0150	0.0123	0.0129	0.0128	0.0154	0.0160	0.0162
DE27	Schwaben, Regierungsbezirk	0.0170	0.0146	0.0130	0.0135	0.0199	0.0173	0.0191	0.0180	0.0214	0.0208	0.0219
DE30	Berlin	0.0876	0.1018	0.1085	0.1050	0.0470	0.0447	0.0419	0.0416	0.0330	0.0398	0.0397
DE40	Brandenburg	0.0514	0.0613	0.0274	0.0350	0.0315	0.0257	0.0225	0.0237	0.0154	0.0214	0.0219
DE50	Bremen	0.0077	0.0075	0.0102	0.0092	0.0092	0.0130	0.0128	0.0127	0.0124	0.0109	0.0106
DE60	Hamburg	0.0336	0.0315	0.0387	0.0338	0.0302	0.0451	0.0408	0.0365	0.0378	0.0373	0.0369
DE712	Regierungsbezirke Darmstadt und Gießen	0.0408	0.0424	0.0402	0.0421	0.0535	0.0562	0.0630	0.0679	0.0842	0.0774	0.0732
DE73	Kassel, Regierungsbezirk	0.0152	0.0156	0.0146	0.0145	0.0137	0.0144	0.0148	0.0147	0.0168	0.0146	0.0143
DE80	Mecklenburg-Vorpommern	0.0230	0.0195	0.0168	0.0231	0.0281	0.0205	0.0169	0.0178	0.0104	0.0143	0.0139
DE912	Statistische Regionen Braunschweig und Hannover	0.0343	0.0304	0.0317	0.0355	0.0458	0.0449	0.0432	0.0475	0.0492	0.0451	0.0449
DE93	Statistische Region Lüneburg	0.0171	0.0143	0.0123	0.0137	0.0210	0.0174	0.0180	0.0136	0.0148	0.0151	0.0145
DE94	Statistische Region Weser-Ems	0.0187	0.0147	0.0166	0.0201	0.0245	0.0238	0.0204	0.0246	0.0268	0.0264	0.0270
DEA1	Düsseldorf, Regierungsbezirk	0.0647	0.0761	0.0820	0.0751	0.0740	0.0934	0.0909	0.0771	0.0741	0.0705	0.0710

DEA2	Köln, Regierungsbezirk	0.0421	0.0428	0.0440	0.0385	0.0399	0.0493	0.0501	0.0543	0.0557	0.0580	0.0575
DEA3	Münster, Regierungsbezirk	0.0187	0.0220	0.0263	0.0251	0.0304	0.0300	0.0277	0.0277	0.0289	0.0274	0.0286
DEA4	Detmold, Regierungsbezirk	0.0168	0.0156	0.0188	0.0178	0.0254	0.0217	0.0228	0.0222	0.0241	0.0252	0.0245
DEA5	Arnsberg, Regierungsbezirk	0.0403	0.0440	0.0474	0.0420	0.0482	0.0528	0.0508	0.0470	0.0467	0.0414	0.0408
DEB1	Statistische Region Koblenz	0.0214	0.0213	0.0184	0.0159	0.0169	0.0137	0.0150	0.0148	0.0156	0.0160	0.0159
DEB2	Statistische Region Trier	0.0078	0.0068	0.0071	0.0061	0.0061	0.0041	0.0049	0.0051	0.0054	0.0051	0.0051
DEB3	Statistische Region Rheinhessen-Pfalz	0.0220	0.0231	0.0246	0.0240	0.0222	0.0202	0.0257	0.0244	0.0248	0.0234	0.0233
DEC0	Saarland	0.0126	0.0145	0.0149	0.0128	0.0126	0.0139	0.0130	0.0126	0.0130	0.0122	0.0119
DED2	Dresden, NUTS 2 region	0.0345	0.0332	0.0396	0.0387	0.0211	0.0207	0.0180	0.0177	0.0104	0.0141	0.0145
DED4	Chemnitz, NUTS 2 region	0.0440	0.0388	0.0430	0.0382	0.0272	0.0232	0.0206	0.0197	0.0084	0.0132	0.0131
DED5	Leipzig, NUTS 2 region	0.0245	0.0237	0.0272	0.0258	0.0168	0.0164	0.0145	0.0134	0.0069	0.0089	0.0093
DEE0	Sachsen-Anhalt	0.0508	0.0428	0.0458	0.0547	0.0385	0.0348	0.0297	0.0297	0.0154	0.0206	0.0203
DEF0	Schleswig-Holstein	0.0269	0.0230	0.0215	0.0232	0.0314	0.0274	0.0279	0.0303	0.0318	0.0308	0.0291
DEG0	Thüringen	0.0349	0.0341	0.0357	0.0394	0.0314	0.0284	0.0241	0.0251	0.0134	0.0189	0.0187

Table 3.6.A.2 Regional GDP per capita (GK$1,000), 1900–2010

		1900	*1910*	*1925*	*1938*	*1950*	*1960*	*1970*	*1980*	*1990*	*2000*	*2010*
DE11	Stuttgart, Regierungsbezirk	2.102	2.643	2.722	5.336	3.633	7.033	9.682	17.459	21.700	23.655	25.084
DE12	Karlsruhe, Regierungsbezirk	2.958	3.684	3.579	6.456	4.673	8.447	12.775	16.733	20.800	21.659	22.950
DE13	Freiburg, Regierungsbezirk	2.138	2.628	2.273	4.842	3.283	4.981	7.401	14.401	17.094	18.878	19.929
DE14	Tübingen, Regierungsbezirk	1.846	2.267	2.203	4.336	3.193	4.610	6.969	14.386	18.081	19.807	21.841
DE21	Oberbayern, Regierungsbezirk	3.113	3.342	3.527	5.036	4.355	8.486	13.732	18.456	24.860	27.226	28.338
DE22	Niederbayern, Regierungsbezirk	2.084	2.333	1.897	2.906	3.654	4.915	7.840	11.740	15.569	17.347	20.449
DE23	Oberpfalz, Regierungsbezirk	1.957	2.473	2.288	3.081	3.820	5.623	8.615	11.089	15.047	18.446	21.328
DE24	Oberfranken, Regierungsbezirk	2.258	2.774	3.003	4.744	4.548	6.822	10.079	12.817	17.052	16.912	19.240
DE25	Mittelfranken, Regierungsbezirk	3.016	3.740	3.786	5.068	4.338	7.848	12.012	15.143	19.204	20.445	22.200
DE26	Unterfranken, Regierungsbezirk	2.236	3.159	3.057	4.413	4.046	6.266	9.278	11.956	15.728	18.626	20.735
DE27	Schwaben, Regierungsbezirk	2.844	3.197	3.015	4.395	4.227	7.058	10.913	13.117	16.973	18.555	20.694
DE30	Berlin	4.248	5.061	5.497	7.576	3.934	7.592	11.095	15.157	12.278	18.303	19.466
DE40	Brandenburg	2.542	3.281	2.875	4.999	3.299	5.426	7.142	9.752	7.396	12.821	14.744
DE50	Bremen	4.409	4.526	5.059	6.478	4.577	10.206	15.074	20.289	23.207	25.484	26.977
DE60	Hamburg	4.376	4.530	5.326	6.207	5.243	13.640	19.333	24.655	29.390	34.090	35.123
DE712	Regierungsbezirke Darmstadt und Gießen	2.880	3.530	3.536	4.424	4.878	8.768	13.272	17.568	23.789	25.184	25.567
DE73	Kassel, Regierungsbezirk	2.706	3.563	3.431	4.070	3.026	6.343	9.338	11.658	17.895	17.967	19.721
DE80	Mecklenburg-Vorpommern	2.139	2.461	2.259	4.059	3.487	5.408	6.847	9.445	6.723	12.406	14.221
DE912	Statistische Regionen Braunschweig und Hannover	2.587	2.888	3.266	5.010	3.902	7.654	10.932	14.332	17.065	18.368	20.171
DE93	Statistische Region Lüneburg	2.674	2.828	2.862	3.840	3.560	6.276	9.049	10.456	12.739	14.126	14.429
DE94	Statistische Region Weser-Ems	2.682	2.638	2.907	4.967	3.637	7.121	8.559	12.999	15.622	17.015	18.446
DEA1	Düsseldorf, Regierungsbezirk	3.244	4.020	4.326	5.734	4.800	9.633	13.742	16.473	18.133	20.839	23.196

DEA2	Köln, Regierungsbezirk	3.415	4.139	4.230	5.356	4.561	8.922	12.417	15.455	17.767	21.189	22.166
DEA3	Münster, Regierungsbezirk	3.249	3.895	3.598	4.890	4.437	7.367	9.819	12.780	14.998	16.329	18.615
DEA4	Detmold, Regierungsbezirk	2.785	3.198	3.950	4.824	4.731	7.497	11.178	13.625	16.486	19.157	20.246
DEA5	Arnsberg, Regierungsbezirk	2.954	3.356	3.849	3.850	4.426	8.145	11.597	14.172	16.009	16.894	18.753
DEB1	Statistische Region Koblenz	3.065	3.953	3.734	4.669	4.143	5.976	9.396	12.070	14.318	16.456	18.037
DEB2	Statistische Region Trier	2.794	3.159	3.482	4.305	3.946	4.936	8.633	12.178	14.391	15.376	16.863
DEB3	Statistische Region Rheinhessen-Pfalz	2.621	3.481	3.810	5.218	4.318	6.637	12.090	15.051	16.967	18.195	19.624
DEC0	Saarland	2.919	3.690	3.765	4.851	3.673	7.181	9.842	13.153	15.418	17.689	19.718
DED2	Dresden, NUTS 2 region	2.901	3.377	4.415	6.353	2.968	6.089	8.156	10.918	5.337	12.759	15.073
DED4	Chemnitz, NUTS 2 region	3.038	3.327	4.052	5.280	3.250	6.092	8.572	11.347	9.025	12.567	14.415
DED5	Leipzig, NUTS 2 region	3.024	3.487	4.244	5.916	2.836	5.999	8.265	10.559	7.001	12.645	15.828
DEE0	Sachsen-Anhalt	2.399	2.644	3.052	5.114	2.953	5.771	7.783	10.656	6.560	12.096	14.565
DEF0	Schleswig-Holstein	2.805	2.998	2.987	4.698	3.378	6.549	9.501	12.928	15.506	17.255	17.348
DEG0	Thüringen	2.342	2.913	3.819	6.045	3.256	6.242	8.030	11.062	6.326	12.007	14.064
GDP in 1990 GK$	Germany, in 1990 borders	2.824	3.385	3.643	5.184	3.906	7.290	10.517	14.193	15.985	18.949	20.661

Source: Own.

Notes

1 However, the Mittellandkanal was not economically usable before the construction of a canal bridge over the Elbe, which was opened only after German unification in 2003.

2 The NUTS 2 regions DE91 Braunschweig, DE92 Hannover, DE71 Darmstadt and DE72 Giessen had to be merged into two new regions, DE921 and DE721, due to data limitations.

3 $CV_{pw} = \frac{\sqrt{\Sigma (y_i - \bar{y})^2 \frac{p_i}{p}}}{\bar{y}}$, where y_i is a region's GDP per capita, $\bar{y}$ is average GDP per capita, and p_i and p stand for population sizes.

References

Ahlfeldt, G., Redding, S., Sturm, D. and Wolf, N. (2015) 'The economics of density: evidence from the Berlin Wall', *Econometrica*, Vol. 83 (6): 2127–89.

Akerlof, G.A., Rose, A.K., Yellen, J.L. and Hessenius, H. (1991) 'East Germany in from the cold: the economic aftermath of currency union', *Brookings Papers on Economic Activity*, No. 22: 1–106.

Beyer, K. (1986) 'Des Reisebeschreibers "Kutsche". Aufklärerisches Bewusstsein im Postverkehr des 18. Jahrhunderts', in W. Griep and H.W. Jäger (eds), *Reisen im 18. Jahrhundert*, Heidelberg: Carl Winter, pp. 50–90.

Bolt, J. and van Zanden, J.L. (2013) *The First Update of the Maddison Project: Re-Estimating Growth before 1820*, Groningen: Groningen Growth and Development Centre.

Bolt, J., Inklaar, R., de Jong, H. and van Zanden, J.L. (2018) 'Rebasing "Maddison": new income comparisons and the shape of long-run economic development', Maddison Project working paper 10, Groningen: Groningen Growth and Development Centre.

Brenke, K. (2014) 'Eastern Germany still playing economic catch-up', *DIW Economic Bulletin*, Vol. 4 (11): 6–23.

Broadberry, S. and Klein, A. (2012) 'Aggregate and per capita GDP in Europe, 1870–2000: continental, regional and national data with changing boundaries', *Scandinavian Economic History Review*, Vol. 60 (1): 79–107.

Bukowski, M., Korys, P., Leszczyńska, C. and Tyminski, M. (2017) 'Rozwój regionalny ziem polskich pod zaborami. Porównanie poziomu produktu brutto per capita na dzisiejszych terenach Polski na przełomie XIX I XX w. (wyniki pierwszych estymacji)', *Roczniki Dziejów Społecznych i Gospodarczych*, Vol. 77: 163–98.

Burda, M.C. and Weder, M. (2017) 'The economics of German unification after twenty-five years: lessons for Korea', SFB 649 Discussion Paper 2017-009.

Burhop, C. and Wolff, G. (2005) 'A compromise estimate of German net national product, 1851–1913, and its implications for growth and business cycles', *The Journal of Economic History*, Vol. 65 (3): 613–57.

Cronon, W. (1991) *Nature's Metropolis: Chicago and the Great West*, New York: Norton.

Czada, P. (1969) *Die Berliner Elektroindustrie in der Weimarer Zeit. Eine regionalstatistisch-wirtschaftshistorische Untersuchung*, Berlin: Colloquium Verlag.

Frank, H. (1994) *Regionale Entwicklungsdisparitäten im deutschen Industrialisierungsprozess, 1849–1939*, Münster: LIT Verlag.

Fremdling, R. (1977) 'Railroads and German economic growth: a leading sector analysis with a comparison to the United States and Great Britain', *The Journal of Economic History*, Vol. 37 (3): 583–604.

Frey, A. (2003) *Die industrielle Entwicklung Bayerns von 1925 bis 1975*, Berlin: Duncker & Humblot.

Geary, F. and Stark, T. (2002) 'Examining Ireland's post-famine economic growth performance', *The Economic Journal*, Vol. 112 (482): 919–35.

Gemeinschaftsveröffentlichungen der Statistischen Ämter des Bundes und der Länder (2007) *Reihe 1/2, Band 1: Erwerbstätige in den alten Ländern der Bundesrepublik Deutschland 1970 bis 1991 sowie in deren kreisfreien Städten und Landkreisen 1980, 1985, 1987 bis 1991 – Korrigierte Fassung, Stand 19. April 2007*, Wiesbaden: Hessisches Statistisches Landesamt.

Gemeinschaftsveröffentlichungen der Statistischen Ämter des Bundes und der Länder (2012) *Reihe 2, Band 1: Erwerbstätige in den kreisfreien Städten und Landkreisen der Bundesrepublik Deutschland 1991 bis 2012*, Wiesbaden: Hessisches Statistisches Landesamt.

Grant, O. (2005) *Migration and Inequality in Germany, 1870–1913*, Oxford Historical Monographs, Oxford: Clarendon Press.

Gutberlet, T. (2014) 'Mechanization and the spatial distribution of industries in the German Empire, 1875 to 1907', *Economic History Review*, Vol. 67 (2): 463–91.

Hefele, P. (1998) *Die Verlagerung von Industrie- und Dienstleistungsunternehmen aus der SBZ/DDR nach Westdeutschland: unter besonderer Berücksichtigung Bayerns (1945–1961)*, Stuttgart: Franz Steiner.

Hoffmann, W.G. and Müller, J.H. (1959) *Das deutsche Volkseinkommen 1851–1957*, Tübingen: Mohr.

Hoffmann, W.G., with Grumbach, F. and Hesse, H. (1965) *Das Wachstum der deutschen Wirtschaft seit der Mitte des 19. Jahrhunderts*, Berlin: Springer.

Hohls, R. (1991) *Arbeit und Verdienst: Entwicklung und Struktur der Arbeitseinkommen im Deutschen Reich und der Bundesrepublik (1885–1985)*, PhD Dissertation, Free University Berlin, Fachbereich Wirtschaftswissenschaften.

Hohls, R. and Kaelble, H. (1989) 'Die regionale Erwerbsstruktur im Deutschen Reich und in der Bundesrepublik Deutschland 1895–1970', in W. Fischer, F. Irsigler, K.H. Kaufhold and H. Ott (eds), *Quellen und Forschungen zur Statistik von Deutschland, Vol. 9*, St. Katharinen: Scripta Mercaturae.

Holtz, H.J. (1985) 'Eisenbahngeschwindigkeiten in der Rückblende', *Technik & Kultur*, Vol. 9 (4): 238–48.

Hornung, E. (2015) 'Railroads and growth in Prussia', *Journal of the European Economic Association*, Vol. 13 (4): 699–736.

Huning, T. and Wahl, F. (2017) 'Lord of the lemons: origin and dynamics of state capacity', Hohenheim Discussion Papers in Business, Economics and Social Sciences 22-2017, University of Hohenheim, Faculty of Business, Economics and Social Sciences.

Keller, W. and Shiue, C. (2013) 'The link between fundamentals and proximate factors in development', *NBER WP* 18808.

Kiesewetter, H. (2004) *Industrielle Revolution in Deutschland. Regionen als Wachstumsmotoren*, Stuttgart: Franz Steiner Verlag.

Kopper, C. (2015) 'Verkehr und Kommunikation', in T. Rahlf (ed.), *Deutschland in Daten. Zeitreihen zur Historischen Statistik*, Bonn: Bundeszentrale für politische Bildung, pp. 224–35.

Nitsch, V. and Wolf, N. (2013) 'Tear down this wall: on the persistence of borders in trade', *Canadian Journal of Economics/Revue canadienne d'économique*, Vol. 46 (1): 154–79.

Orsagh, T. (1968) 'The probable geographical distribution of german income, 1882–1963', *Zeitschrift für die gesamte Staatswisenschaft*, Vol. 124: 280–311.

Petzina, D. (1994) 'Standortverschiebungen und regionale Wirtschaftskraft in der Bundesrepublik Deutschland seit den fünfziger Jahren', in W. Abelshauser et al. (eds), *Wirtschaftliche Integration und Wandel von Raumstrukturen im 19. und 20. Jahrhundert*, Berlin: Duncker & Humblot, pp. 101–127.

Redding, S. and Sturm, D. (2008) 'The costs of remoteness: evidence from German division and reunification', *American Economic Review*, Vol. 98 (5): 1766–97.

Redding, S., Sturm, D. and Wolf, N. (2011) 'History and industry location: evidence from German airport', *The Review of Economics and Statistics*, Vol. 93 (3): 814–31.

Ritschl, A. and Spoerer, M. (1997) 'Das Bruttosozialprodukt in Deutschland nach den amtlichen Volkseinkommens- und Sozialproduktsstatistiken 1901–1995', *Jahrbuch für Wirtschaftsgeschichte*, Vol. 2: 27–54.

Salin, E. (1928) 'Standortverschiebungen der deutschen Wirtschaft', in B. Harms (ed.), *Strukturwandlungen der Deutschen Volkswirtschaft*, Berlin: Reimar Hobbing, pp. 75–108.

Schöttler, R. (2016) *Essays on Germany: Market Access, Industry Location, Price of Land*, PhD Dissertation, Humboldt University of Berlin, Wirtschaftswissenschaftliche Fakultät.

Simms, B. (2013) *Europe: The Struggle for Supremacy, from 1453 to the Present*, London: Basic Books.

Sleifer, J. (2006) *Planning Ahead and Falling Behind: The East German Economy in Comparison with West Germany, 1936–2002*, Berlin: Walter de Gruyter.

Staatliche Zentralverwaltung für Statistik (1989) *Statistisches Jahrbuch 1989 der DDR, Vol. 34*, Berlin: Staatsverlag der Deutschen Demokratischen Republik.

Statistisches Reichsamt (1921) *Die Lohn- und Gehaltserhebung von 1920, Statistik des Deutschen Reichs, Vol. 293*, Berlin: Puttkammer & Mühlbrecht.

Tipton, Frank B. (1976) *Regional Variations in the Economic Development of Germany during the Nineteenth Century*, Middletown, CT: Wesleyan University Press.

Wilson, P. (2016) *The Holy Roman Empire: A Thousand Years of Europe's History*, London: Allen Lane.

Wolf, N. (2009) 'Was Germany ever united? Evidence from intra- and international trade, 1885–1933', *The Journal of Economic History*, Vol. 69 (3): 846–81.

Vonyó, T. (2018) *The Economic Consequences of the War: West Germany's Growth Miracle after 1945*, Cambridge Studies in Economic History, Cambridge: Cambridge University Press.

Zentralverband der Maurer Deutschlands (1906) *Lohn- und Arbeitsbedingungen im Maurergewerbe. Statistik 1905 und Tarifverträge 1905*, Hamburg: Vorstand des Zentral-Verbandes der Maurer Deutschlands.

Ziblatt, D. (2006) *Structuring the State: The Formation of Italy and Germany and the Puzzle of Federalism*, Princeton, NJ: Princeton University Press.

3.7 Regional income inequality in Italy in the long run (1871–2010)

Patterns and determinants

Emanuele Felice[1]

1. Introduction

Italy's regional disparities are renowned throughout the world, in academia and beyond. The unification of the peninsula in 1861, more than 150 years ago, was an event of paramount importance for the history of nineteenth-century Europe. Southern Italy, the former Kingdom of the Two Sicilies, was the most backward part of the country, and has remained so until the present day. What strikes the observer, however, is that it has gained a firm position as a paradigmatic case of a backward society. There is probably no other part of the Western world that can boast such dubious fame. Before unification, in 1851, William Gladstone, who for a time served as the British Prime Minister, had famously defined the southern kingdom as 'the negation of God erected into a system of government' (cited in Acton 1961: 339). With unification, Alexander Dumas, one of the greatest novelists of his time, established himself in Naples for four years, and his regular reports from the former southern capital helped to create the image of a savage south that was prey to organized crime, where "murder is just a gesture" (Dumas 2012: 12). Some years after unification, Italian scholars also began to tackle the *questione meridionale* (the problem of the south), to discuss its origins and the ways to solve it; the debate continued until the fascist dictatorship, and involved an impressive list of prominent figures, among others the prime minister of the late liberal age, Francesco Saverio Nitti (1958), the mathematician Corrado Gini (1914), father of the index of the same name, the liberal philosopher Benedetto Croce (1925) and the most important communist thinker (arguably) of the Western world, Antonio Gramsci (2005), as well as other well-known international scholars, such as the founder of anthropological criminology, Cesare Lombroso (1876). In literary and popular culture, the problem of the south was the subject of some of the most important and successful novels of their times, such as *Fontamara* by Ignazio Silone (1933) or the memoir *Christ Stopped at Eboli* by Carlo Levi (1945). In the first half of the twentieth century, the south's poor reputation even crossed the ocean and reached the US, brought there by millions of southern emigrants – and by the Sicilian Mafia, which travelled with some of them.

In the second half of the twentieth century, as modern economic growth spread from the north-west of the peninsula to the north-eastern and central regions, eventually making Italy one of the great industrial powers of the world, southern Italy remarkably failed to converge and even – more worryingly – to create any significant autonomous industrial enterprise. Since the 1950s, the American political scientist Edward Banfield has probably contributed the most to establishing the Italian *Mezzogiorno* (southern Italy) as the backward society par excellence (Banfield 1958). His view inspired the more recent work by Robert Putnam, who saw the south and the north of the peninsula as two exemplar cases of different settings regarding social capital (and thus institutional performance), which he argued date back to the late Middle Ages (Putnam et al. 1993): as southern Italy remained the paradigm of bad government, another part of the country (the north-eastern and central regions), by contrast, became a symbol of good government and 'civicness', the breeding ground of industrial districts that could embody the alternative to Fordism and big business. Path dependence, the importance of culture and values, the role of local institutions, that of state intervention and even the bi-univocal relationship between democracy and modern economic growth: all these topics central to any economic history reasoning have found in the regional imbalances of Italy – probably more than in those of any other European country – a privileged arena in which to be tested and compared.

The chapter presents up-to-date estimates of Italy's regional GDP, at 10-year intervals spanning from 1871 to 2010, at current national and regional borders. In the light of our broad quantitative picture, the main explanations of the determinants of Italy's regional inequality are rediscussed, and a new interpretative hypothesis – based on long-lasting socio-institutional differences – is proposed.

2. The long-run evolution of Italy's regional inequality

In order to obtain a long-run picture of regional inequality in Italy, regional GDP figures for eight benchmark years, spanning from 1871 to 1951 at regular 10-year intervals (the only exception is 1938 instead of 1941), have been produced; these have been linked to the estimates from 1961 to 2010, in six more benchmarks, available from official sources (Tagliacarne 1962; Svimez 1993; Istat 1995, 2012a, 2012b). As a result, we can now observe the evolution of regional inequality in Italy from around the unification of the peninsula until the present day. For the benchmarks from 1871 to 1951, the estimation methodology is in line with that developed by Geary and Stark (2002): as a general rule, national GDP has been allocated through regional employment, using differences in nominal wages as proxies for differences in productivity. In the case of Italy, however, it was possible to improve Geary and Stark's method in two main respects. First, for most industry in the liberal age (the benchmarks 1871–1911) and for agriculture throughout the period (1871–1951), it was possible to use direct production data by taking advantage of the works by Federico (2003) for agriculture[2] and by Fenoaltea (2004) and Ciccarelli and Fenoaltea (2009a, 2009b, 2014) for industry. Second, the level of sectoral decomposition is here much higher than in the work of Geary and Stark (who estimated three sectors: agriculture, industry and services), and this is partly due to the fact that we have new series for national GDP, which are also highly detailed and reliable (Rey 1992, 2000; Baffigi 2013).[3]

With their historical regional borders, the estimates have been previously published (Felice 2010a, 2011; Felice and Vecchi 2015a) for all the benchmarks minus three (1881, 1901 and 1921). Later on, the three missing benchmarks at historical borders have also been produced (Felice 2015a), and more recently all these estimates have been converted from the historical to the current regional borders, at the NUTS 2 level (Felice forthcoming). This conversion resulted in some non-negligible changes and required us to return to the original sources (population censuses) and work with them at the provincial and even the district level, in order to estimate *ex novo* the GDP of some regions in the liberal age (Aosta Valley, Molise, Trentino-Alto Adige and part of Friuli), which were either included in bigger ones (Aosta Valley in Piedmont, Molise in Abruzzi) or part of the Austro-Hungarian empire, or to recompose the GDP of other regions (namely Latium, but also Friuli-Venezia Giulia and to a more minor degree Emilia-Romagna), which acquired territories from their neighbouring ones (Campania, Abruzzi, Umbria, Veneto, Tuscany, Lombardy). In order to grasp the main border changes at a glance, Map 3.7.1 displays the confines of the Italian regions in three different epochs: the liberal age (before the First World War), the interwar years (after the First World War) and republican Italy (after the Second World War, this being the map of today and of our estimates). As a general rule, the conversion was made via reallocating the population and the employment divided into four sectors (agriculture, industry, construction and services), under the hypothesis that the parcelled-out territories had the same sectoral GDP per worker as their original regional whole.[4] It goes without saying that the new figures have advantages over the previous ones: now, for the first time, we can compare the long-run evolution of regions (i.e. of observations) that are territorially homogeneous throughout the period; the sample does not change, and thus we have removed the variation (of the single regional indices and the aggregate average measures) due to the rearrangement of internal borders and the inclusion of new territories.

What was the pattern of regional inequality in Italy in the long run? To begin with, we can observe Figure 3.7.1, which depicts a population-weighted index of regional dispersion (the coefficient of variation of GDP per capita for Italian NUTS 2 regions),[5] and therefore can be considered as a measure of sigma-convergence.

Regional income inequality was on the rise from around unification until the end of the Second World War. We observe a decrease from 1951 to 1971, during the decades of the most intense growth of the Italian economy. From the 1970s onwards, however, when the national growth slowed down and ultimately came to a halt, the index of regional inequality also remained more or less unchanged; it even increased slightly. In the long run, the pattern has followed the inverted U-shaped curve (Williamson 1965), only up to a certain point. It is true that there was a growth in inequality in the first half (1871–1951), then came a decrease, but this latter was unusual and disappointing at the same time: unusual since it began when the most advanced regions were also growing at their fastest; disappointing

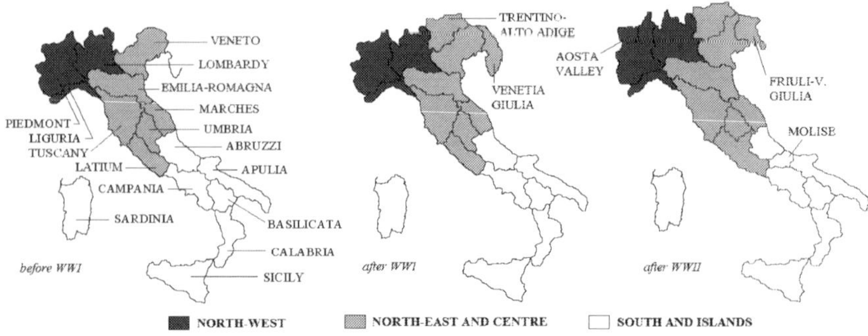

Map 3.7.1 The changes in Italy's regions (1871–today)

Note: Molise was created in 1963.

since it stopped as early as the 1970s. As a result, for the whole period from 1871 until 2010, but also for the entire twentieth century, we register a process of sigma-*divergence*: convergence was the exception, limited to the golden age.

Next, beta-convergence, occurring when the poorer regions grow faster than the richer ones, is measured via growth regressions (see Figure 3.7.2). The correlation between the initial level of per capita GDP and the growth rate over the

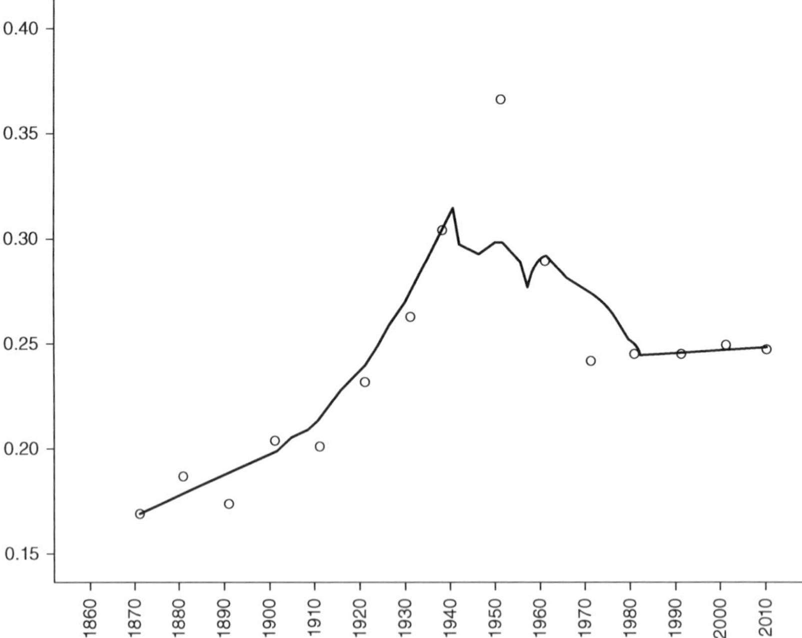

Figure 3.7.1 Sigma-convergence among the Italian regions (population-weighted coefficient of variation), 1871–2010

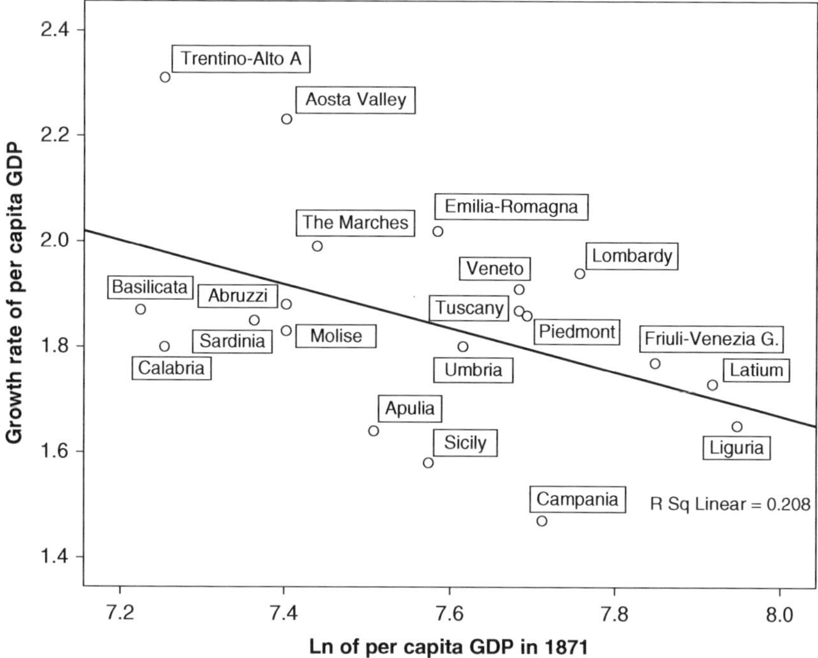

Figure 3.7.2 Beta-convergence among the Italian regions, 1871–2010

whole period is slightly negative, which means that from this perspective, we have a convergence process; but the R^2 is low (0.208), indicating that the linear regression model fits the data badly. Furthermore, the implied convergence rate is barely above 1 per cent, and thus considerably lower than the 2 per cent observed for other countries and periods – and is also the predicted rate of the basic Solow growth model (Sala-i-Martin 1996).

A closer look at Figure 3.7.2 provides us with useful insights into the difference between beta- and sigma-convergence. First, it should be noticed that all the southern regions are below the regression line: thus, given their initial income and their potential for convergence, they grew less than expected. Conversely – and second – the regions that grew the most were those relatively poor regions in 1871 that were part of the centre-north: Trentino-Alto Adige and Aosta Valley, mountainous territories that were 'naturally' backward in an agricultural world, but are now among the richest Italian regions, not least thanks to tourism. By ending up well above the average, in the long run (1871–2010), they have had a remarkable impact upon beta-convergence, but practically none upon sigma-convergence. Third, the opposite has occurred in the most populous southern region, Campania: in 1871, regarding GDP per capita, it was above the Italian average, but in the long run this region grew the least in the entire sample. From 1871 to 2010, its performance contributed to an increase in beta-convergence, but to a decrease

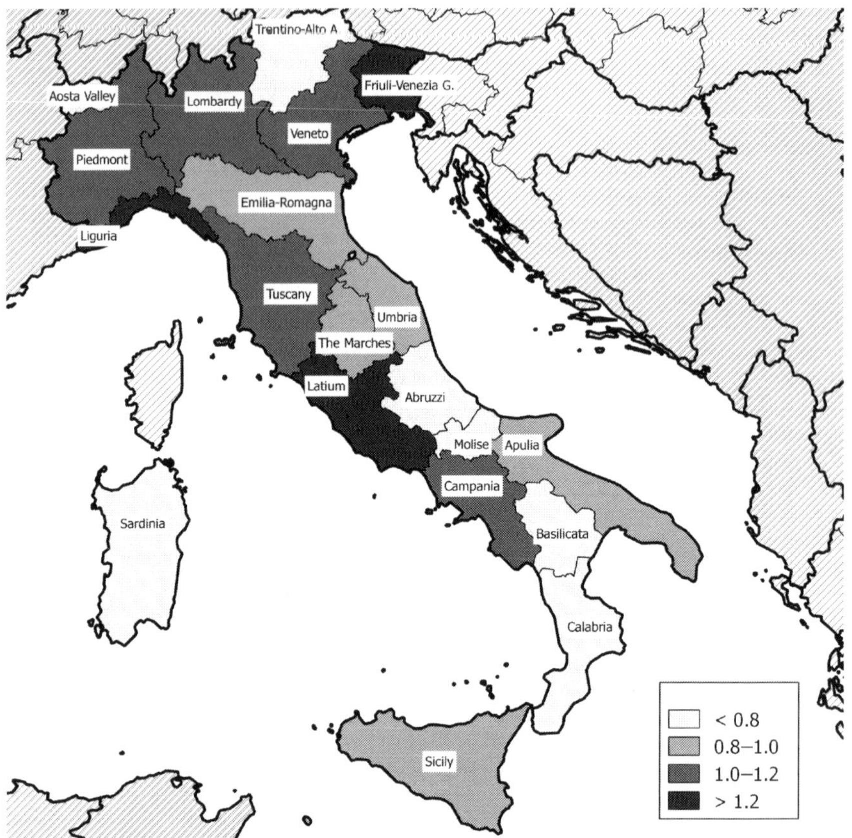

Map 3.7.2 Relative GDP of the Italian regions per capita, 1871 (Italy = 1)
Source: Table 3.7.1.

in sigma-convergence. In short, the discrepancy between beta- and sigma-convergence is due to the disappointing performance of the southern regions, in contrast to the excellent performance of the once poorest regions of the centre-north.

This line of reasoning takes us to Table 3.7.1, which displays the relative per capita income of the Italian regions for each of the benchmarks estimated, and to Maps 3.7.2–3.7.5, which offer a spatial perspective of the regional distribution of per capita GDP in four crucial benchmarks throughout the period (1871, 1911, 1951 and 2010). Around unification, a clear north–south divide still cannot be detected. Although the south was on average below the centre-north, as mentioned, the most important regions in the south were above the average. Campania hosted the ancient capital of the former Kingdom of the Two Sicilies, Naples, which was also the greatest Italian city at that time. Other southern regions were not so far from the average: this is the case for Sicily, which could count on export-oriented agricultural and mining production (citrus fruits, sulphur), but also on a diversified urban structure with several services and manufacturing activities, and even for Apulia, mostly thanks to its diversified agriculture (grain, olive oil, wine). Within the centre-north, the differences were even more pronounced. The richest Italian regions were those that could boast the most developed tertiary sector: Liguria, with its credit and transportation activities, which served also the other regions of the future 'industrial triangle' (i.e. Piedmont and Lombardy); Latium, which hosted the new capital, Rome; as well as Friuli-Venezia Giulia, where Trieste served as practically the only sea harbour of the entire Austro-Hungarian empire. Lombardy and Piedmont were above the average, but it should be noted that the latter was not so much in a better position than Veneto or Tuscany, or Campania in the south. Some regions of the centre-north were very poor: Trentino-Alto Adige and Aosta Valley, the two growth champions of Italian regional development, were still in a position comparable to that of the most backward southern regions (Calabria, Basilicata, Abruzzi and Molise); even the Marches in the centre was only a few points above the neighbouring Abruzzi.

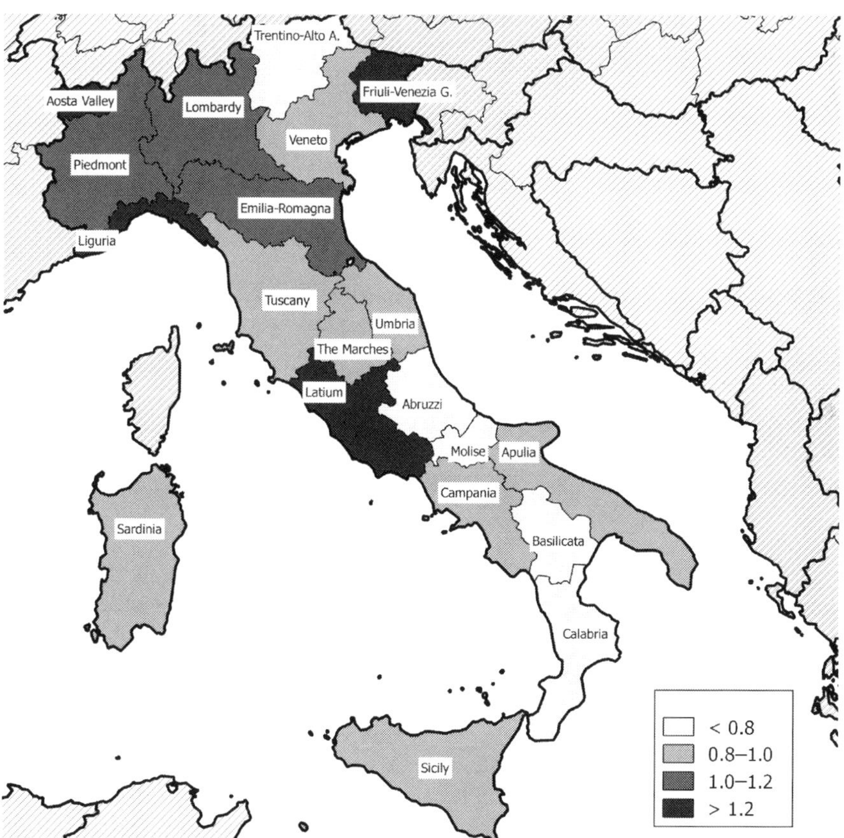

Map 3.7.3 Relative GDP of the Italian regions per capita, 1911 (Italy = 1)

Source: Table 3.7.1.

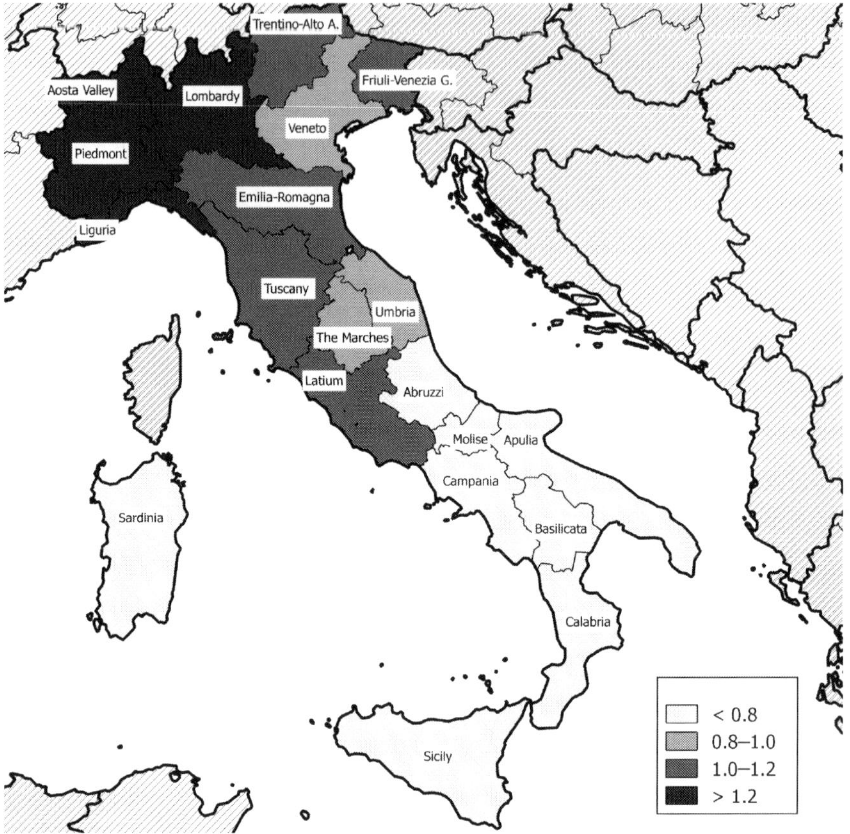

Map 3.7.4 Relative GDP of the Italian regions per capita, 1951 (Italy = 1)
Source: Table 3.7.1.

Things began to change during the liberal age, but slowly. Although regional inequality was on the rise, with the industrial triangle now beginning to take shape and the south falling behind, in 1911 we can still observe great diversification within the three macro-areas displayed: in the south, Campania was only a few points below the national average; in the north-east and centre (henceforth, NEC), Latium and Friuli-Venezia Giulia continued to be richer than Lombardy or Piedmont. It was during the interwar years that the big divide truly emerged. By 1951, the industrial triangle had reached its peak, and Italy was clearly defined into the three macro-areas displayed in Map 3.7.4: all the regions of the north-west were above the regions of the NEC, which were in turn all above the regions of southern Italy. This means that there was an impressive convergence within these three macro-areas, which at the same time continued to diverge from each other.

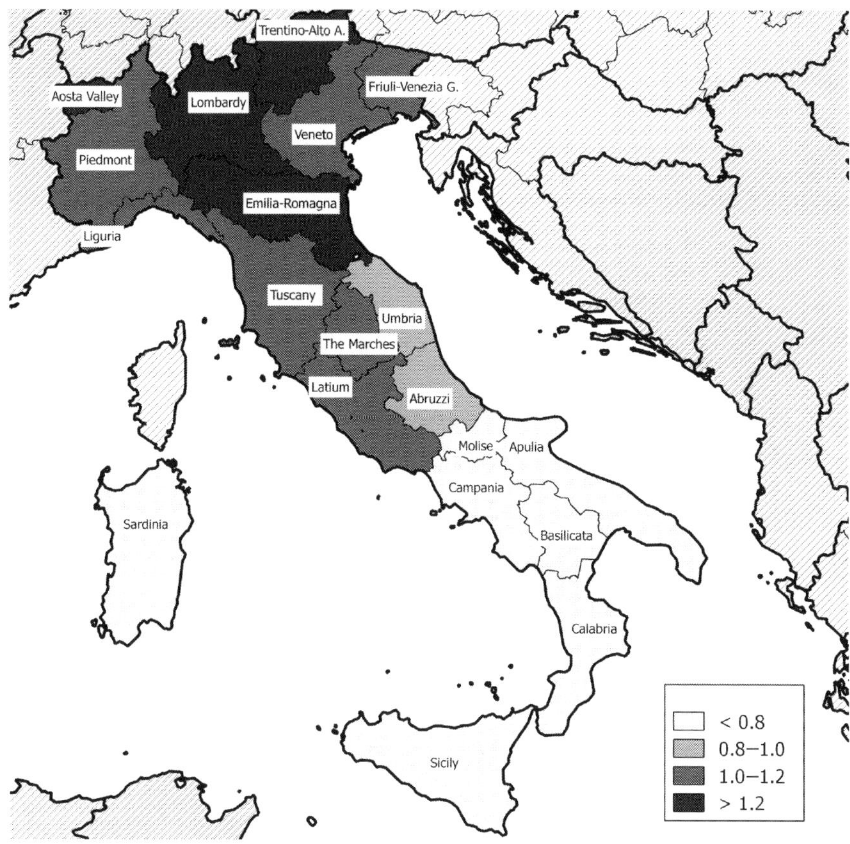

Map 3.7.5 Relative GDP of the Italian regions per capita, 2010 (Italy = 1)
Source: Table 3.7.1.

The years 1951–2010 can be divided into two phases. During the Italian 'miracle', internationally known as the 'golden age', we register some catching up of southern Italy, which significantly contributed to the increase in sigma-convergence (the reduction of dispersion) observed in those years. However, it came to a halt in the 1970s, never to revive. But exactly when southern Italy began to fall slowly back again, in the 1970s, the NEC regions accelerated their rate of convergence with the north-west. As a consequence, by 2010, we no longer have three Italies, as in 1951, but only two: the centre-north, which is now much more internally homogeneous than it was 60 years before, and southern Italy, where even the most 'virtuous' region (Abruzzi) is more than 30 points below the average of the centre-north (Italy settled equal to 100).

When looking at the regional distribution of income (see Table 3.7.2), we receive further confirmation of the above-sketched trends. Around unification, the share of southern Italy out of the total Italian GDP was around one-third. After remaining more or less unchanged during the second half of the nineteenth century, from 1901 to 1951 it fell from 32 to 22 per cent of total Italian GDP: this was an impressive redistribution of income, which moved from the south to both the north-west and the NEC. The share of southern Italy improved slightly during the golden age, but in the last decades of the twentieth century it remained stationary – and declined in the 2000s. In the long run, the south's reduction in the share of the total GDP is even more impressive than that in the relative per capita GDP, since from 1871 to 2010 the south's percentage of the population decreased slightly, from 36.7 to 34.6 per cent, its higher level of fertility notwithstanding: given that the differences in mortality were relatively low, the reason is, of course, a higher level of emigration. On the other side, the big winner is not the north-west, which only gained 2.7 points from 1871 to 2010 (from 29.6 to 32.3 per cent), but the NEC, which in the same period gained 6.8 points (from 37.4 to 44.2 per cent): almost all of this expansion was concentrated in seven decades, the first three of the twentieth century (1901–1931) and the last four of our period (1971–2010); it should also be noted that in the latter four decades, almost all of the NEC increase was made to the detriment of the north-west.

In terms of total GDP, however, by considering the three macro-areas, we cannot see the full story. There are significant differences within the macro-areas that are worth stressing. The Italian region that gained the most, by far, is Lombardy, which from 1871 to 2010 increased its share in Italian GDP by almost 7 points, in sharp contrast to the other two north-western regions, Liguria and Piedmont, which both lost (although Piedmont rose in per capita GDP, it decreased in the share of population, from 10.8 to 8 per cent). Lombardy alone ended up, by 2010, with more than one-fifth of the total Italian GDP, only 2 points below the entire southern part of Italy (!). When compared with those of Lombardy, the gains of the north-eastern regions look only modest. If we look within the centre, we discover that some other winners in per capita GDP are instead losers in total GDP (Tuscany, the Marches). Quite unexpectedly, the NEC region with the largest increase in the total GDP is Latium (+5.1 from 1871 to 2010), a less manufacturing-oriented region, and indeed one that has considerably fallen behind in relative per capita GDP, but it has more than compensated with its faster population growth (within constant present borders, its share of inhabitants rose from 4.2 to 9.4 per cent). The big losers are instead the two most important regions of the south, Campania and Sicily (–3.7 and –3.4 per cent, respectively), and this does not come as a surprise; they are followed by Piedmont (–2.8 per cent). The third most important region of the south, Apulia, still had about the same share in 2010 as it had in 1871, and this is a success relative to the rest of the *Mezzogiorno*.

3. A periodization of regional inequality in Italy

The main periods in the history of Italy's regional inequality can be grasped at a glance by looking at Figure 3.7.3, which displays the evolution from 1871 to 2010 of the per capita GDP of the three Italian macro-regions.

Table 3.7.1 The relative per capita GDP of the Italian regions, 1871–2010 (Italy = 1)

	1871	*1881*	*1891*	*1901*	*1911*	*1921*	*1931*	*1938*	*1951*	*1961*	*1971*	*1981*	*1991*	*2001*	*2010*
Piedmont	1.07	1.08	1.07	1.19	1.16	1.28	1.23	1.38	1.51	1.31	1.24	1.19	1.14	1.15	1.09
Aosta Valley	0.80	0.99	1.06	1.19	1.29	1.43	1.43	1.44	1.58	1.68	1.44	1.40	1.42	1.24	1.35
Liguria	1.38	1.42	1.39	1.48	1.57	1.42	1.64	1.67	1.62	1.25	1.04	1.01	1.06	1.09	1.06
Lombardy	1.14	1.15	1.14	1.23	1.18	1.24	1.23	1.38	1.53	1.45	1.36	1.30	1.32	1.30	1.30
Trentino-Alto Adige	0.69	0.73	0.78	0.82	0.78	0.88	0.92	0.94	1.05	1.01	1.07	1.27	1.30	1.30	1.30
Veneto	1.06	0.89	0.81	0.84	0.88	0.78	0.73	0.83	0.98	0.97	0.98	1.09	1.12	1.13	1.15
Friuli-Venezia Giulia	1.25	1.23	1.22	1.25	1.28	1.06	1.17	1.23	1.11	0.91	0.95	0.97	1.04	1.12	1.13
Emilia-Romagna	0.96	1.07	1.06	1.02	1.09	1.10	1.09	1.04	1.12	1.17	1.14	1.30	1.22	1.23	1.21
Tuscany	1.06	1.08	1.03	0.93	0.98	1.04	1.06	1.01	1.05	1.05	1.08	1.11	1.05	1.09	1.09
The Marches	0.83	0.78	0.88	0.83	0.82	0.78	0.71	0.78	0.86	0.87	0.88	1.00	0.95	0.99	1.01
Umbria	0.99	1.03	1.06	1.00	0.92	0.93	1.00	0.95	0.90	0.93	0.93	1.01	0.96	0.96	0.93
Latium	1.34	1.45	1.37	1.35	1.33	1.36	1.40	1.19	1.07	1.11	1.10	1.06	1.14	1.13	1.15
Abruzzi	0.80	0.77	0.68	0.67	0.70	0.72	0.62	0.57	0.58	0.72	0.79	0.85	0.90	0.85	0.84
Molise	0.80	0.77	0.67	0.65	0.68	0.72	0.64	0.59	0.57	0.67	0.66	0.76	0.78	0.80	0.78
Campania	1.09	1.01	0.99	0.96	0.96	0.88	0.81	0.81	0.69	0.72	0.70	0.65	0.66	0.65	0.65
Apulia	0.89	0.95	1.04	0.94	0.87	0.92	0.85	0.72	0.65	0.71	0.71	0.67	0.68	0.67	0.67
Basilicata	0.67	0.63	0.75	0.73	0.74	0.75	0.70	0.57	0.46	0.64	0.73	0.69	0.67	0.73	0.69
Calabria	0.69	0.66	0.68	0.66	0.71	0.61	0.55	0.49	0.47	0.59	0.66	0.62	0.62	0.64	0.65
Sicily	0.95	0.92	0.95	0.89	0.87	0.72	0.82	0.72	0.58	0.61	0.69	0.72	0.72	0.66	0.66
Sardinia	0.77	0.81	0.97	0.91	0.93	0.91	0.85	0.82	0.63	0.75	0.85	0.75	0.77	0.77	0.77
North-West	1.14	1.15	1.14	1.25	1.22	1.28	1.29	1.42	1.54	1.38	1.29	1.23	1.24	1.24	1.21
North-East and Centre	1.00	1.01	0.99	0.97	0.98	1.01	1.02	1.00	1.04	1.04	1.05	1.12	1.12	1.13	1.14
South and Islands	0.90	0.88	0.90	0.86	0.85	0.79	0.77	0.70	0.61	0.68	0.71	0.69	0.70	0.68	0.68
Centre-North	1.06	1.07	1.06	1.08	1.08	1.12	1.13	1.17	1.23	1.18	1.15	1.16	1.17	1.17	1.17

Source: See the text.

Note: For the composition of the three macro-areas, see Map 3.7.1.

Table 3.7.2 The share of Italian regions in Italian GDP, 1871–2010 (per cent)

	1871	*1881*	*1891*	*1901*	*1911*	*1921*	*1931*	*1938*	*1951*	*1961*	*1971*	*1981*	*1991*	*2001*	*2010*
Piedmont	10.8	11.1	10.7	11.6	10.8	11.1	10.4	11.3	11.1	10.4	10.2	9.4	8.6	8.5	8.0
Aosta Valley	0.2	0.3	0.3	0.3	0.3	0.3	0.3	0.3	0.3	0.3	0.3	0.3	0.3	0.3	0.3
Liguria	4.2	4.3	4.4	4.8	5.3	4.9	5.8	5.9	5.4	4.4	3.6	3.3	3.1	3.0	2.8
Lombardy	14.3	14.4	14.5	15.8	15.9	16.6	16.8	19.0	21.1	21.4	21.6	20.4	20.7	20.7	21.2
Trentino-Alto Adige	1.3	1.3	1.2	1.3	1.2	1.6	1.5	1.6	1.7	1.6	1.7	2.0	2.1	2.2	2.2
Veneto	8.3	6.9	6.3	6.4	7.2	6.7	6.1	6.9	8.0	7.4	7.5	8.4	8.7	9.1	9.3
Friuli-Venezia Giulia	2.2	2.2	2.2	2.2	2.2	2.8	3.2	3.3	2.8	2.1	2.2	2.2	2.2	2.3	2.3
Emilia-Romagna	7.5	8.2	8.1	7.7	8.4	8.7	8.7	8.1	8.4	8.5	8.2	9.2	8.5	8.7	8.8
Tuscany	8.0	8.0	7.7	6.9	7.2	7.5	7.6	7.1	7.1	6.9	7.0	7.1	6.6	6.8	6.7
The Marches	2.7	2.5	2.8	2.7	2.5	2.4	2.1	2.3	2.5	2.3	2.2	2.5	2.4	2.6	2.6
Umbria	1.7	1.7	1.8	1.7	1.5	1.5	1.7	1.6	1.5	1.5	1.3	1.5	1.4	1.4	1.4
Latium	5.7	6.4	6.4	6.6	6.6	7.1	8.3	7.5	7.7	8.9	9.8	9.5	10.5	10.2	10.8
Abruzzi	2.5	2.4	2.1	2.0	2.0	2.0	1.7	1.6	1.5	1.6	1.7	1.8	2.0	1.9	1.9
Molise	1.1	1.0	0.8	0.7	0.7	0.6	0.6	0.5	0.5	0.4	0.4	0.4	0.4	0.4	0.4
Campania	9.9	9.1	8.7	8.2	8.1	7.4	7.0	7.1	6.3	6.7	6.5	6.3	6.5	6.5	6.2
Apulia	4.6	5.2	5.9	5.6	5.3	5.6	5.2	4.5	4.4	4.7	4.6	4.5	4.7	4.6	4.5
Basilicata	1.2	1.1	1.2	1.1	1.0	0.9	0.9	0.7	0.6	0.8	0.8	0.7	0.7	0.7	0.7
Calabria	3.0	2.8	2.8	2.7	2.8	2.4	2.3	2.0	2.0	2.3	2.3	2.2	2.2	2.2	2.1
Sicily	8.9	9.2	9.8	9.4	8.9	7.7	7.9	6.7	5.4	5.7	5.8	6.2	6.2	5.7	5.5
Sardinia	1.8	1.9	2.3	2.2	2.2	2.1	2.0	2.0	1.7	2.1	2.3	2.1	2.2	2.2	2.1
North-West	29.6	30.1	29.9	32.5	32.3	33.0	33.4	36.4	37.9	36.5	35.7	33.3	32.7	32.5	32.3
North-East and Centre	37.4	37.2	36.5	35.5	36.9	38.3	39.1	38.4	39.6	39.2	40.0	42.4	42.3	43.3	44.2
South and Islands	33.0	32.7	33.6	31.9	30.9	28.7	27.5	25.1	22.4	24.4	24.3	24.2	25.0	24.2	23.5
Centre-North	67.0	67.3	66.4	68.1	69.1	71.3	72.5	74.9	77.6	75.6	75.7	75.8	75.0	75.8	76.5

Source: See the text.

Note: For the composition of the three macro-areas, see Map 3.7.1.

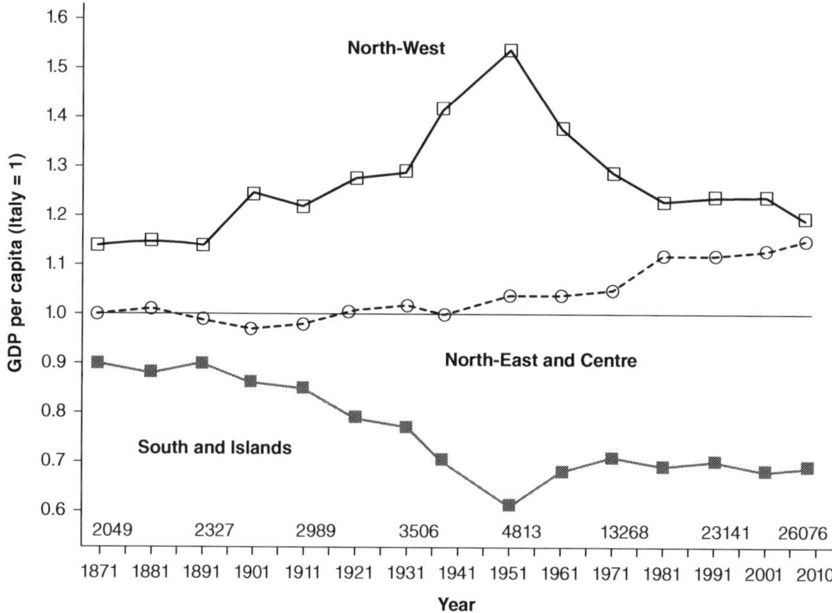

Figure 3.7.3 Per capita GDP of Italy's macro-regions, 1871–2010 (Italy = 1)

We can distinguish four phases: moderate divergence, during the liberal age (1871–1911); great divergence, in the interwar years (1911–1951); general convergence, during the economic miracle (1951–1971); and convergence limited to the centre-north, in the last decades (1971–2010).[6] The attentive reader may notice that these phases also roughly coincide with the periodization of Italy's economic history as a whole – and even with that of its political and social history (Felice 2015b) – which is a sign in itself of how regional inequality in this country is strongly entangled with broader economic and political issues, as well as with modernization and growth at the national level.

3.1 Moderate divergence (1871–1911)

Soon after unification, the regional imbalances increased at a very slow rate. The idea that the south was somehow exploited in order to provide for the industrialization of the north (Romeo 1959: 197 *passim*; Gramsci 2005) does not find confirmation in the estimates presented here. At that time, Italy ranked among the European champions of free trade, the liberal tariff of Piedmont having been extended to the rest of the country: the active competition of the most advanced (and thus cheaper) industrial products from Northern Europe, together with a tight fiscal policy in order to pay down the high public debt coming from the independence wars, contributed to preventing industrial enterprises from developing in the north; in the south, it is true that the new tariff harmed the existing (and highly protected) industrial enterprises, but it is also true that agricultural exports boomed, thus more than balancing the manufacturing crisis, at least in terms of GDP. In those years, the main railways running from north to south were built (Reggio Calabria, in the southern tip of the peninsula, was reached in 1875) (Federico 2007b: 304), yet these had a limited impact, remaining uncompetitive in comparison with coastal navigation (Fenoaltea 1983), and also because the flows of goods and people between the two Italies were still relatively modest (Cafagna 1965). As a result, in terms of regional inequality, little changed from 1871 to 1891, as Italy was growing slowly and failed to industrialize (Felice and Vecchi, 2015b).

In the second half of the liberal age (1891–1911), divergence accelerated. The north-west emerged as the industrial triangle, accounting for around one-third of the Italian industrial employment. In this area, practically all the manufacturing activities were above the national average, from those of the First Industrial Revolution (textiles, food) to those of the Second Industrial Revolution (engineering, chemicals): industrialization was the product of general systemic advantages, rather than sector-specific ones. It was in fact the consequence of several factors, all of which had been able to work at their best since the last two decades of the nineteenth century: richer natural resources, namely hydraulic power, which became crucial following the introduction of electricity in industrial processes (since the 1880s); higher human capital, comparable to the standards of the other European countries that embarked on the Industrial Revolution (well above that of southern Italy at that time), and further reinforced by the creation of technical schools and universities; better transport infrastructures, which in those years were improved via the completion of the secondary rail lines, mostly running through the centre-north (Fenoaltea 1972, 1983); and higher development of the credit sector, which included a tight network of local banks (*Casse di Risparmio, Banche Popolari*) and, from the mid-1890s, the two main universal banks created in the country (mostly with German capital), *Credito italiano* and *Banca commerciale italiana*. The economic policies of the central state also helped, through effective credit reforms (which created the Bank of Italy in 1893 and permitted universal banking) and the implicit adherence to the gold standard, which meant a relatively stable exchange rate favouring the inflows of foreign capital (James and O'Rourke 2013: 51–4; Toniolo 2013: 16–17),[7] but also, it should not be overlooked, via industrial incentives for the navy and military industries, which were concentrated in Liguria. On the other side, our estimates support the view that protectionism harmed exports from southern agriculture, since it reinforced wheat farming to the detriment of Mediterranean products (wine, oil, citrus and other fruits) with higher value added and better comparative advantages.

All this considered, however, the regional divergence was relatively mild. Why? It was the very participation of the country in the first globalization processes that counterbalanced, in the south, the rise of the north-west. To be precise, we should point out the massive emigration outflow, which from 1891 to the First World War resulted in as many as 11.5 million Italians emigrating (including returns), from a population of 30–35 million inhabitants.[8] The majority of these people came from the south (4.8 million) and from Veneto (2.5 million). In the south, the higher rates were recorded from the poorest regions – Abruzzi, Molise, Basilicata and Calabria (Felice 2007: 65–72; Gomellini and Ó Gráda 2013). Not by chance, these were also the regions that slowly converged in per capita GDP from 1891 to 1911 (but not in the total GDP), unlike the other southern regions, where emigration was lower. In the home territories, emigration raised the per capita GDP – at least in the short run – through several channels: the difference between the supply and the demand of labour reduced, and thus the employment rates rose and wages increased; the emigrants sent remittances to their home families; when they returned, the emigrants brought with them human and financial capital that sometimes (not always) was used to start up new business activities. *If* they returned. The point is that in the south, there were fewer return migrants in comparison with Veneto, and thus emigration resulted, in the long run, in a massive draining of the brilliant and the brave.

3.2 Great divergence (1911–1951)

Divergence continued at full speed from the First World War to the Second World War. During this period, the north-west forged ahead for a number of reasons. First, state intervention was now entirely focused on supporting industry in the triangle: the First World War redirected public subsidies towards the existing manufacturers in order to win the conflict; soon afterwards, the reconversion resulted in a crisis of those very industries that had expanded enormously, and thus called for more state funds (Zamagni 2002); the 1929 crisis meant new bailouts and subsidies, again in favour of the northern factories; autarkic fascist policies also contributed to promoting some of the most advanced industrial sectors (chemicals above all), which were concentrated in the north. Second, the north-west continued to benefit from the systemic advantages of the previous period: now in particular, higher human capital and better infrastructures and credit networks helped to concentrate the existing capital flows there; these met with active entrepreneurship and modernizing ruling elites (think of the construction of the Fiat's Lingotto plant in 1922 or, after the Second World War, of the aid from the Marshall Plan used to make the leap towards mass production). Third, protectionism and eventually autarky entailed a reorientation of the national production from international to internal markets, which were much more developed in the north: there, the enterprises could produce at lower costs due not only to the general systemic advantages, but also to the beginning of some economies of scale.

At the other end, some of the conditions that had mitigated the south's falling back of the previous period had been lost. International emigration had come to a halt because of more restrictive immigration laws in the US, but also as a consequence of the new demographic policies of the fascist regime, which actively discouraged it. In agriculture, protectionism was on the rise, and Mussolini's 'battle for grain' (since 1925) further increased cereal production in the south to the detriment of more profitable crops; what is even worse, it provided incentives and protection to the existing, inefficient latifundia. The 'battle for births' (since 1927) promoted fertility, and was undertaken more successfully in the south: given the lack of industrial alternatives (and of the emigration relief valve), it resulted in further worsening of the living conditions of the peasants. Not least, the regime failed to change the existing – and atavistic – agrarian regimes: latifundia were not reformed, neither could they have been, indeed, as the large landowners were among the pillars of the regime (e.g. Bevilacqua 1997: 172–9). From 1911 to 1951, in the south, the share of agricultural employment remained practically unchanged, around 60 per cent, and agricultural productivity declined in relative terms, from around the Italian average to 80 per cent of it (Felice 2011: 937–40). It may be worth stressing that the ruling classes of the south found themselves at ease with the economic stagnation of their territories, as long as their privileges were protected and saved.

3.3 General convergence (1951–1971)

When Italy entered the economic miracle, it also entered a phase of general regional convergence. Industry now spread to the NEC regions as well as – for the first time – to the southern ones. Such convergence is at odds with what is expected from the conventional models, either the inverted U-shape of Williamson (1965), focusing on structural change, or the new economic geography, stressing the size of the market and consequent differences in productivity (Krugman 1991b): the south converged at a time when the centre-north was also growing at its fastest speed; furthermore, this unusual convergence ended in the 1970s, which is precisely when the north-west began to slow down and costs of congestion emerged.

The puzzle is solved once a new actor is introduced: regional policy, as embodied by the state-owned agency 'Cassa per il Mezzogiorno' (henceforth, Cassa). It operated through infrastructural 'direct' works, carried out autonomously by the state agency in a wide range of sectors (but mainly roads and aqueducts), and 'indirect' aid in favour of firms; in addition, state-owned enterprises were obliged by law to locate 60 per cent of their new investments and 40 per cent of their total assets in the south. What resulted was a remarkable channelling of funds to capital-intensive industries, from chemicals to metallurgy to engineering. These were *naturaliter* more financed than light ones, for two reasons: in the Italian economic miracle, the heavy industrial activities were expanding more rapidly; more importantly, state-owned enterprises for the most part operated in those heavy sectors, as a legacy of the bailouts following the 1929 crisis (e.g. La Spina 2003; Felice 2010b). Through this massive public intervention – with no parallels in terms of funds (as a percentage of GDP) in any other western European country (Felice and Lepore 2017) – the Italian state forced the market rules, de facto superimposing upon theoretical predictions an unexpected catching up of the most backward part of the country. Other factors were in favour of convergence, though, particularly massive internal migration, from the south to the north. However, this was less important overall, as proven by the fact that the south caught up in both the industrial productivity and the labour share of industrial employment (Felice 2011).

Nonetheless, the top-down strategy of the Cassa was expensive. A different strategy, which would have paid more attention to the comparative advantages in the south (thus promoting labour-intensive sectors rather than capital-intensive ones) would probably have resulted in slower convergence, but with minor costs and maybe more sound results (Fenoaltea 2007; Lutz 2007). Instead, such 'passive industrialization' of the south (Felice 2013: 107–17) was fragile because it was not based upon market efficiency, but also because, as sharply noted by Zamagni (1978: 216), it was an attempt to change the economy without changing the society (the two weaknesses are interrelated). Here, we come to explain why convergence came to a halt in the 1970s and has never resumed since then. During the crisis of capital-intensive sectors in the wake of the oil crisis, in the 1970s, in Italy it was in the south that the plants closed down, since those were less efficient than their counterparts in the north. Regional policies in favour of the south continued, but they were redirected towards unproductive expenditure, and even came to favour illegal activities (Felice 2013: 156–63). Southern society had not changed in the short-lived age of convergence (in fact, it had begun to change, but slowly, and the 1970s crisis came too soon), and now that state intervention had lost its modernizing strategy, nepotistic rules and political (and criminal) lobbies regained the upper hand, confirming themselves as the norm (Trigilia 1992). With some exceptions (Viesti 2000), southern Italy remained locked in underdevelopment.

3.4 Convergence in the centre-north, or a tale of two Italies (1971–2010)

In sharp contrast to the falling back of southern Italy, it was precisely in the 1970s that the catching up of the NEC increased its speed, and since then it has continued up to the present day. Convergence in per capita GDP has been a consequence of industrialization, and thus of the reallocation of employment from agriculture to industry (and services, to a minor degree): by 2010, some of the NEC regions, namely the Marches and Veneto, had become those with the highest share of the industrial labour force, having overtaken even Lombardy. Now the prediction of the inverted U-shape model was fulfilled: the neighbouring areas of the (former) industrial triangle began to grow faster when the triangle slowed down its pace, with big business relocating plants from the 'core' to the north-eastern and central closest 'periphery', and complementary activities germinating in the latter – although state subsidies were also important (Spadavecchia 2005).

During the course of the 1970s, it became clear that the growth of the NEC was not only due to manufacturers as an accessory or complement to the leading ones in the north-west. Rather, in the NEC, an autonomous industrial morphology was taking place, and even (maybe) a new industrial paradigm, capable of challenging Fordism, by now in decline. The industrial districts were networks of small and medium-sized enterprises that succeeded in light industrial production, strongly export-oriented (this was the well-known 'Made in Italy') and closely linked to their home territory (Becattini 1979). In fact, this link was the key to their success, insofar as the districts took advantage of a wide range of common goods available in their social environment (efficient local institutions and infrastructures, widespread tacit knowledge and a high level of trust that reduced transaction costs) to compensate for their small dimension. Such a peculiar industrial morphology developed from the pre-existing land regimes, the sharecropping that favoured the rise of the entrepreneurial mentality in small family businesses (Bagnasco 1988), and maybe also from the long-run urban tradition of historical autonomy and civicness, which resulted in high social capital and efficient local institutions (Putnam et al. 1993).

The success of the industrial districts in the 1970s led some scholars to talk about a 'third' Italy – the one coinciding roughly with the NEC regions, minus Latium – as something different from both the 'first' Italy (the traditional industrial triangle) and the 'second' one (the *Mezzogiorno*) (Bagnasco 1977). As we have seen, the differences were also in the industrial structure: the traditional big business (or 'first' capitalism) in the first Italy, state-owned enterprises (or 'second' capitalism) in the second one, and the industrial districts (or 'third' capitalism) in the third. In the last two decades, however, the differences between the first and the third Italy have considerably shrunk, not only in terms of average income, but also regarding the industrial structure. On the one hand, the districts spread (or were 'discovered') in the neighbouring Lombardy and Piedmont as well. On the other, more importantly, they went through a deep process of reorganization, as a result of which medium-sized enterprises emerged (sometimes called 'fourth' capitalism), which were able to coordinate the production of small firms in their territories (Colli 2002): some 'hierarchy' returned, making these territories more similar to the traditional industrial triangle.

By contrast, in the south, even the recent convergence of the smallest regions (Abruzzi, Molise and Basilicata) was mainly due to the outsourcing of Fiat's plants in these areas, and thus, again, to investments from the north, which moreover benefited from state subsidies. Nowadays, the regional differentiations notwithstanding, Italy appears to be divided into two halves: the centre-north, home to active industrialization and endogenous growth, and the south and islands, where 'passive' (and incomplete) industrialization prevails; plus Latium, home to the capital. Unsurprisingly, the Italian recent decline and the crisis begun in 2008 affected more heavily the weaker economic fabric of the south.

4. The forces behind regional inequality in Italy

Stemming from an extraordinarily rich debate, which dates back to the late nineteenth century, a number of different explanations have been proposed to account for Italy's regional inequality. Broadly speaking, we can regroup them into a set of 'first nature' causes linked more directly to geography: the characteristics of the territory, the size of the market as a consequence of position and geology, and infrastructures, as long as these too are a consequence of geography (for instance, the tunnels through the Alps, which connect Italy with the rest of Europe, could be constructed only in the north). Among the 'second nature' causes, we can include factors that mostly depend on the human element: of these, we will consider regional differences in social indicators, culture, and economic and political institutions.[9]

4.1 Geography: natural endowments and market potential

Italy is a large country, by European standards. It comprises several environmental settings with marked differences in terms of natural endowments. The four big regions of the north (Piedmont, Lombardy, Veneto and Emilia), plus a fifth smaller one (Friuli-Venezia Giulia), are home to the fertile valley of the Po, the main Italian river, which, together with its affluents, forms a copious hydrogeological basin: as a consequence, water resources are much more abundant in the north than in the south. Important rivers are also present in the rest of the peninsula, such as the Arno in Tuscany (running through Florence and Pisa), the Tiber in Latium (running through Rome) and the Volturno in Campania (running through Capua, now a small town north of Naples, but one of the most important Italian cities in ancient times). Although the Po Valley represents almost two-thirds of the total plain area of the country, fertile plains are also present in the centre-south, namely in Apulia and, to a minor degree, in Latium, Campania, Tuscany and even Calabria. On the other hand, almost 40 per cent of the Italian territory is mountainous, and a portion of this share can be found in practically all the regions. In turn, regions that are prevalently mountainous or made up only of mountains and hills are located in the north (Trentino-Alto Adige, Aosta Valley and Liguria), as well as in the centre (Umbria, Marches) and the south (Abruzzi, Molise and Basilicata). Two more Italian regions – Sicily and Sardinia – are islands, the most important ones of the Mediterranean, both of which can boast a decent variety of geographical and hydrogeological settings, with a good percentage of plain areas and even of water resources (although in both cases, these are below the national average). Italy as a whole is not rich in natural resources, with a few exceptions: zinc, lead and copper in Sardinia; sulphur in Sicily; and iron ores on the island of Elba (Tuscany).

All things considered, we can say that in terms of natural endowments, southern Italy (which also includes the two big islands) could have been a little disadvantaged; nevertheless, it was in a position comparable to that of central Italy. The differences from the north were not dramatic; they were indeed more pronounced *within* the macro-areas than *between* them. We may be right in thinking that in pre- and early industrial times, geographical characteristics had immediate consequences for agriculture, important branches of industries (mining, but also a non-negligible part of manufacturing) and services (transportation and commerce), but precisely because of this, their impact in terms of the regional GDP should not result in a clear north–south divide, but rather in a variety of positions overlapping across the northern and the southern regions. This is what we know beyond any reasonable doubt from the history of pre-modern Italy (some regions of the South – Sicily, Campania and Apulia – were renowned throughout the classical world and later in medieval times for their agricultural products), and this is also what emerges from the estimates of regional GDP in the liberal age: the differences within the centre-north and within southern Italy were as pronounced as those within Italy as a whole, as we have seen, and agriculture played an important part in this result (Federico 2003: 373–5, 2007a; Felice 2007: 133).

If there was a clear geographical divide between north and south, it was in terms of position, the former being closer to the most advanced Northern Europe, at least via land, and thus nearer to the economic 'core'; moreover, the northern regions had better transport infrastructures and a less demanding territory by far, which helped communications. One could infer that the north was favoured at least in terms of market access, both domestic and international. However, even this inference should not be taken for granted. Southern regions were not particularly disadvantaged in terms of sea transportation, which for most of the liberal age remained superior to land transportation, at least concerning international trade (but also in part domestic trade, through coastal navigation). There are indeed competing estimates about market potential in the liberal age, but the latest one (Missiaia 2016) is probably the most accurate, since it is not based on air distances, but tries to calculate the real transport costs: it clearly indicates that Campania and Apulia had market potential above the Italian average, while Apulia was around the average.[10] In particular, Campania appears to have been the third Italian region in terms of market potential, behind Liguria and Lombardy, but it was also the region that in relative GDP fell behind the most in the liberal age (−13 points from 1871 to 1911, Italy settling equal to 100).

Over the course of the twentieth century, market potential increased in the centre-north more than in the south, as the main rail lines and afterwards the big highways were completed, and linked northern Italy more strongly to the rest of continental Europe; in turn, European partners grew in importance, not least because after the birth of the European Community in 1957, trade tariffs and other international barriers were progressively reduced and finally eliminated. In addition, concerning the national market, land infrastructures continued to be by far the most developed in the north, which also enjoyed a higher population density. In fact, the available estimates point out that in the second half of the twentieth century, the north attained a clear advantage in terms of market potential, both domestic and international (A'Hearn and Venables 2013). Nevertheless, not even on this point do our data support the validity of the geographical explanation: first, because in the second half of the twentieth century, the north-west declined in relative terms, while the regions growing at the fastest rate were the NEC ones, which were more distant from the rest of Europe and had lower market potential; and second, because GDP patterns in the south have followed the predictions from the new economic geography only up to a certain point. If it is true that Abruzzi and Molise – the two northernmost regions of the south – are also those that have ended up closer to the centre-north; all the rest have moved in the opposite direction: by 2010, the third southern region in terms of per capita GDP was Sardinia, the most isolated one; from 1951 to 2001, Basilicata, with market potential below that of Apulia and Campania, could boast a performance comparable to that of Abruzzi (+27 points in both cases); above all, the southern region with the highest market potential was still Campania (A'Hearn and Venables 2013: 603), yet it also remained the big loser, even in the second half of the twentieth century. Is market potential the decisive factor? It does not seem so. Rather, it should not pass unnoticed that all the best-performing regions of the south (Abruzzi, Molise, Basilicata and Sardinia) were those that were substantially free of organized crime.

In short, factors related to geography may explain the initial differences we observe among the Italian regions, but not their subsequent evolution – or, if so, only to a very minor degree. From 1871 to 2010, as we have seen, the best-performing Italian region was Trentino-Alto Adige, arguably the one in the north with the lowest market potential (together with Aosta Valley, the second best-performing); the worst-performing region was Campania, the one in the south with the highest market potential.

4.2 The human element: human capital, social capital and institutions

It is not chance, nor fortune or misfortune, but rather the human element, that we must examine to find more convincing (and comprehensive) explanations for Italy's regional inequality. Around the time of unification, the centre-north was ahead of southern Italy in a number of crucial indicators apart from economic ones: the most striking differences were in human capital (literacy, but also the enrolment rate), but there were also imbalances in the level of trust and political and social participation (i.e. in what can usually be defined as social capital) (Felice 2012), as well as – as far as we know – in the personal distribution of income (Felice 2013: 41–9). In all of these dimensions, the differences were indeed much more profound than those estimated for income: a clear north–south divide was already apparent. More importantly, in the long run, it was the pattern of per capita GDP that followed that of these meta-economic indicators, not vice versa (Felice 2018). Recent empirical work suggests that human capital was a significant conditioning variable in the first part of the history of post-unification Italy (1891–1951): in this period, the regions that forged ahead were those of the industrial triangle, which could also boast higher levels of education. Related to this, some authors (Helliwell and Putnam 1995; Lyon 2005) suggest that social capital was an important conditioning variable in the last period: from 1971 onwards, the regions growing faster, those of the NEC, were the ones endowed with more trust and civicness. The discrepancy between the two periods in terms of the role of such conditioning variables may be due to the different requirements of the technological regimes prevailing in those ages: the Fordist firm of the Second Industrial Revolution internalized transaction costs and required low social capital in comparison with human capital (at that time, basic education of the working class and higher education of the white-collar workers and managers), unlike the industrial districts and network economies of the more recent post-Fordist age (Felice 2010a).

The problem with southern Italy was that in each of the periods, it lacked the key conditioning variable. While there was some convergence in human capital over the course of the twentieth century, albeit incomplete (Felice and Vasta 2015), the south continued to fall dramatically behind in terms of social capital, which had become the key conditioning variable during the last stretch of the twentieth century. However, such a lack of 'preconditions' in southern Italy – which, for instance, raised production costs and reduced Marshallian externalities even in Campania, a region with good market potential – was not a product of misfortune, but rather the result of different institutional settings that pre-existed the unification of the peninsula, and persisted and were even reinforced after it. Political institutions were arguably extractive in the former Kingdom of the Two Sicilies, while inclusive in the pre-unification states of the north (Felice 2013):[11] from this divide, the north–south differences in education, in the distribution of income and wealth, and in trust and participation followed. After unification, even though they became formally the same throughout the country, political institutions continued to work differently in the centre-north – where an efficient liberal democracy was progressively set in place – and the south – where power continued to be allocated rather through nepotism and personal loyalty (and even through violence in some cases). Furthermore, the economic institutions (and incentives) were not even formally the same: organized crime, which so patently influenced the social and economic life of the most important southern regions (Campania, Sicily, Calabria, then Apulia) in the liberal age and later on in the second half of the twentieth century, should be regarded as a formal (although illegal) economic institution, which established and enforced economic rules that differed from those applicable in the rest of the country. Among others, it created monopolies that discouraged free-market competition and innovation. Organized crime too – which, however, was only the tip of the iceberg of a more profound *Weltanschauung* – was a legacy of the Kingdom of the Two Sicilies, but its power was also considerably strengthened with the creation of the new unified state (which for the same reason was never capable of fully eradicating it: between the two, there was not only hostility, but also a mutual relationship of power) (Felice 2013: 61–74, 150–63).

In short, in terms of social conditions and institutional settings, and thus of conditioning variables, there were two Italies and – more importantly – such a divide was never bridged: one should not be surprised if in the long run, the pattern of per capita GDP followed that of the pre-existing socio-institutional differences. This is confirmed by what emerges from the sectoral decomposition of our estimates: the north–south divide is nowadays driven by the differences in employment and structural change, rather than by those in sectoral productivity (Felice 2011: 937–41), which might suggest that the problem comes from the extensive margin (people do not enter into new businesses), rather than from the intensive margin (the existing enterprises have more or less the same productivity, and thus economies of scale, as in the north). But why then was the socio-institutional divide never bridged? A full discussion of this point would take us too far from the scope of this chapter. It is only worth noting that institutional settings tend to reproduce themselves over time, along tracks of path dependence, unless some kind of external shock intervenes. The first external shock, unification, actually did not break the path, but rather reinforced it. The other external shock could have been the massive regional policy pursued in southern Italy in the second half of the twentieth century: as we have seen, however, that one too – in part but not entirely due to misfortune – ended up reinforcing rather than weakening the existent extractive institutions.

5. Conclusions

After presenting new regional estimates of GDP in Italy, at 10-year intervals from 1871 to 2010, this chapter discussed the main determinants behind the pattern of Italy's regional inequality. The differences were relatively mild in the second half of the nineteenth century, but since then they have increased, at a slower pace in the last decades of the liberal age and with greater speed from the First World War to the Second World War. As a consequence, in terms of per capita GDP, Italy appeared to be divided into three parts by the time when regional inequality reached its peak, around 1951: the industrialized north-west, the regions of the north-east and centre close to the Italian average and the backward south. Some convergence of the south took place during the economic miracle, mostly thanks to the massive regional policy pursued by the Italian state, but it came to a halt in the 1970s and since then has never revived; at the same time, in the last decades, the convergence of the north-east and centre accelerated remarkably. As a result of these trends, by 2010, Italy was parted into two halves, the centre-north and southern Italy. It is true that we have some confirmation of an inverted U-shape of income inequality – rising divergence until the mid-twentieth century, then convergence – but actually the latter has been limited to the centre-north. As a consequence of the falling back of southern Italy, over the long run (1871–2010), we observe sigma-divergence (i.e. an increase in dispersion) and only a sluggish process of beta-convergence.

The timing and modality of the evolution of Italy's regional inequality suggest that here, geographical factors and the market size played a minor role. Against them are both the fact that most of the differences in GDP are due to employment rather than productivity, and the observed GDP patterns of many regions; for instance, the worst-performing Italian region was Campania, by far the most favoured in the south in terms of market size. Rather, the gradual convergence of regional GDPs towards two equilibria seems to follow the social and institutional imbalances of pre-unification Italy: at the time of unification, there was a socio-institutional divide – in the levels of human and social capital as well as in the nature and functioning of the political and economic institutions – that was transferred to the new state, in different forms, and since then it has not been overcome (indeed, it has even been reinforced). The paramount examples are organized crime in some southern regions regarding economic institutions and the widespread cronyism in the south concerning the working of political institutions; both go along with the renowned differences in social capital. This socio-institutional divide appears to be the ultimate determinant of Italy's regional inequality.

Notes

1 I'm grateful to Anna Missiaia, Luzia Savary and Max Stephan-Schulze for precious help with data and estimates of the Italian territories belonging to the Austro-Hungarian Empire until the First World War. Helpful comments were received by the participants of the Workshop 'The Economic Development of Europe's Regions: A Quantitative History since 1900', Humboldt University of Berlin (13–15 December 2013). I gratefully acknowledge financial support from the Spanish Ministry of Economy and

Competitiveness, project HAR2013-47182-C2-1-P, and the Generalitat de Catalunya, project 2013 SGR 591. The usual disclaimers apply.

2 For four benchmarks (1891, 1911, 1938 and 1951); the others (1881, 1901, 1921 and 1931) have been reconstructed from official sources (the Italian Ministry of Agriculture, Industry and Commerce and later Istat, the National Institute of Statistics), after making their data uniform with Federico's results.

3 In four benchmarks (1891, 1911, 1938 and 1951), the workforce and in part the wage data are allocated through a remarkably high number of sectors, one/four hundreds (Felice 2005a, 2005b). The estimates for 1871, 1881, 1901, 1921 and 1931 are less detailed: a little more than 20 sectors in both cases. Our estimates consider female and child employment separately by assigning them lower weights with respect to adult males (Felice 2009, forthcoming).

4 In the past, current borders figures had also been produced by Daniele and Malanima (2007). They employed regional GDPs that now are partly out of date. Their methodology for conversion was not made explicit.

5 I follow the formula in Williamson (1965): $D = \sqrt{\left(\frac{y_i}{y_m} - 1\right)^2 \times \frac{p_i}{p_m}}$, where y is the per capita GDP, p is the population, and i and m refer to the i-region and the national total, respectively.

6 Iuzzolino et al. (2013) follow a similar periodization, the main difference being that they consider a fifth phase in the last period, which they name the great stagnation (1992–2009).

7 The efficacy of protectionism in favouring industry has been seriously questioned instead (Federico and Tena 1999).

8 There were instead 2.5 million emigrants from 1876 to 1890. Emigration from the territories of the former Austro-Hungarian Empire is not considered.

9 I elaborate on the differentiation between 'first nature' and 'second nature' causes, originally presented by Krugman (1991a).

10 However, the alternative estimate by A'Hearn and Venables (2013) also does not assign a clear advantage to the centre-north in this period.

11 I borrow the basics of the distinction between inclusive and extractive institutions from Acemoglu and Robinson (2012: 74–81).

References

A'Hearn, B. and Venables, A.J. (2013) 'Regional disparities: internal geography and external trade', in G. Toniolo (ed.), *The Oxford Handbook of the Italian Economy since Unification*, Oxford: Oxford University Press, pp. 599–630.

Acemoglu, D. and Robinson, J.A. (2012) *Why Nations Fail: The Origins of Power, Prosperity and Poverty*, London: Profile Books.

Acton, H. (1961) *The Last Bourbons of Naples (1825–1861)*, London: Methuen & Co.

Baffigi, A. (2013) 'National accounts, 1861–2011', in G. Toniolo (ed.), *The Oxford Handbook of the Italian Economy Since Unification*, Oxford: Oxford University Press, pp. 157–86.

Bagnasco, A. (1977) *Tre Italie. La problematica territoriale dello sviluppo italiano*, Bologna: Il Mulino.

Bagnasco, A. (1988) *La costruzione sociale del mercato. Studi sullo sviluppo di piccola impresa in Italia*, Bologna: Il Mulino.

Banfield, E. (1958) *The Moral Basis of a Backward Society*, New York: Free Press.

Becattini, G. (1979) 'Dal "settore" industriale al "distretto" industriale. Alcune considerazioni sull'unità di indagine dell'economia industriale', *Rivista di economia e politica industriale*, Vol. 5 (1): 7–21.

Bevilacqua, P. (1997) *Breve storia dell'Italia meridionale dall'Ottocento a oggi*, III ed., Rome: Donzelli.

Cafagna, L. (1965) 'Intorno alle origini del dualismo economico in Italia', in A. Caracciolo (ed.), *Problemi storici dell'industrializzazione e dello sviluppo*, Urbino: Argalia, pp. 103–50. Now reprinted in Cafagna, L. (1989) *Dualismo e sviluppo nella storia d'Italia*, Venice: Marsilio, pp. 187–223.

Ciccarelli, C. and Fenoaltea, S. (2009a) *La produzione industriale delle regioni d'Italia, 1861–1913: una ricostruzione quantitativa, Vol. 1, Le industrie non manifatturiere*, Rome: Bank of Italy.

Ciccarelli, C. and Fenoaltea, S. (2009b) Private correspondence with the author.

Ciccarelli, C. and Fenoaltea, S. (2014) *La produzione industriale delle regioni d'Italia, 1861–1913: una ricostruzione quantitativa, Vol. 2, Le industrie estrattivo-manifatturiere*, Rome: Bank of Italy.

Colli, A. (2002) *Il quarto capitalismo. Un profilo italiano*, Venice: Marsilio.

Croce, B. (1925) *Storia del Regno di Napoli*, Bari: Laterza.

Daniele, V. and Malanima, P. (2007) 'Il prodotto delle regioni e il divario Nord–Sud in Italia (1861–2004)', *Rivista di Politica Economica*, Vol. 97 (2): 267–316.

Dumas, A. (2012) *La camorra e altre storie di briganti*, edited by C. Schopp, Rome: Donzelli.

Federico, G. (2003) 'Le nuove stime della produzione agricola italiana, 1860–1910: primi risultati e implicazioni', *Rivista di storia economica*, Vol. 19 (3): 359–81.

Federico, G. (2007a) 'Ma l'agricoltura meridionale era davvero arretrata?', *Rivista di Politica Economica*, Vol. 97 (3–4): 317–40.

Federico, G. (2007b) 'Market integration and market efficiency: the case of 19th century Italy', *Explorations in Economic History*, Vol. 44 (2): 293–316.

Federico, G. and Tena, A. (1999) 'Did trade policy foster Italian industrialization: evidence from the effective protection rates 1870–1930', *Research in Economic History*, Vol. 19: 111–38.

Felice, E. (2005a) 'Il reddito delle regioni italiane nel 1938 e nel 1951. Una stima basata sul costo del lavoro', *Rivista di storia economica*, Vol. 21 (1): 3–30.

Felice, E. (2005b) 'Il valore aggiunto regionale. Una stima per il 1891 e per il 1911 e alcune elaborazioni di lungo periodo (1891–1971)', *Rivista di storia economica*, Vol. 21 (3): 83–124.

Felice, E. (2007) *Divari regionali e intervento pubblico. Per una rilettura dello sviluppo in Italia*, Bologna: Il Mulino.

Felice, E. (2009) 'Estimating regional GDP in Italy (1871–2001): sources, methodology, and results', Working Papers in Economic History No. 7, Universidad Carlos III de Madrid, Departamento de Historia Económica e Instituciones.

Felice, E. (2010a) 'Regional development: reviewing the Italian mosaic', *Journal of Modern Italian Studies*, Vol. 15 (1): 64–80.

Felice, E. (2010b) 'State ownership and international competitiveness: the Italian Finmeccanica from Alfa Romeo to aerospace and defence', *Enterprise and Society*, Vol. 11 (3): 594–635.

Felice, E. (2011) 'Regional value added in Italy, 1891–2001, and the foundation of a long term picture', *The Economic History Review*, Vol. 64 (3): 929–50.

Felice, E. (2012) 'Regional convergence in Italy (1891–2001): testing human and social capital', *Cliometrica*, Vol. 6 (3): 267–306.

Felice, E. (2013) *Perché il Sud è rimasto indietro*, Bologna: Il Mulino.

Felice, E. (2015a) 'La stima e l'interpretazione dei divari regionali nel lungo periodo: i risultati principali e alcune tracce di ricerca', *Scienze regionali: Italian Journal of Regional Science*, Vol. 14 (3): 91–120.

Felice, E. (2015b) *Ascesa e declino. Storia economica d'Italia*, Bologna: Il Mulino.

Felice, E. (2018) 'The socio-institutional divide: explaining Italy's long-term regional differences', *Journal of Interdisciplinary History*, Vol. 49 (1): 43–70.

Felice, E. (forthcoming) 'The roots of a dual equilibrium: GDP, productivity and structural change in the Italian regions in the long-run (1871–2011)', *European Review of Economic History*, DOI: 10.1093/ereh/hey018.

Felice, E. and Lepore, A. (2017) 'State intervention and economic growth in southern Italy: the rise and fall of the "Cassa per il Mezzogiorno" (1950–1986)', *Business History*, Vol. 59 (3): 319–41.

Felice, E. and Vasta, M. (2015) 'Passive modernization? The new human development index and its components in Italy's regions (1871–2007)', *European Review of Economic History*, Vol. 19 (1): 44–66.

Felice, E. and Vecchi, G. (2015a) 'Italy's growth and decline, 1861–2011', *Journal of Interdisciplinary History*, Vol. 45 (4): 507–48.

Felice, E. and Vecchi, G. (2015b) 'Italy's modern economic growth, 1861–2011', *Enterprise & Society*, Vol. 16 (2): 225–48.

Fenoaltea, S. (1972) 'Railroads and Italian industrial growth, 1861–1913', *Explorations in Economic History*, Vol. 9 (1): 325–51.

Fenoaltea, S. (1983) 'Italy', in P. O'Brien (ed.), *Railways and Economic Development of Western Europe, 1830–1914*, London: Macmillan, pp. 49–120.

Fenoaltea, S. (2004) 'Textile production in Italy's regions', *Rivista di Storia Economica*, Vol. 20 (2): 145–74.

Fenoaltea, S. (2007) 'I due fallimenti della storia economica: il periodo post-unitario', *Rivista di Politica Economica*, Vol. 97 (3–4): 341–58.

Geary, F. and Stark, T. (2002) 'Examining Ireland's post-famine economic growth performance', *Economic Journal*, Vol. 112 (482): 919–35.

Gini, C. (1914) *L'ammontare e la composizione della ricchezza delle nazioni*, Turin: F.lli Bocca.

Gomellini, M. and Ó Gráda, C. (2013) 'Migrations', in G. Toniolo (ed.), *The Oxford Handbook of the Italian Economy since Unification*, Oxford: Oxford University Press, pp. 271–302.

Gramsci, A. (2005) *La questione meridionale*, edited by F. De Felice and V. Parlato, Rome: Editori Riuniti.

Helliwell, J.F. and Putnam R. (1995) 'Economic growth and social capital in Italy', *Eastern Economic Journal*, Vol. 21 (3): 295–307.

Istat (Istituto centrale di statistica) (1995) *Conti economici regionali: anni 1980–92*, Rome: Istat.

Istat (Istituto centrale di statistica) (2012a) *Sistemi di indicatori territoriali, Contabilità nazionale*, available at: http://sitis.istat.it/sitis/html/ (accessed 1 September 2016).

Istat (Istituto centrale di statistica) (2012b) *Conti economici regionali, 23 novembre 2012*, available at: www.istat.it/it/archivio/75111 (accessed 1 September 2016).

Iuzzolino, G., Pellegrini, G. and Viesti, G. (2013) 'Regional convergence', in G. Toniolo (ed.), *The Oxford Handbook of the Italian Economy since Unification*, Oxford: Oxford University Press, pp. 571–98.

James, H. and O'Rourke, K. (2013) 'Italy and the first age of globalization, 1861–1940', in G. Toniolo (ed.), *The Oxford Handbook of the Italian Economy since Unification*, Oxford: Oxford University Press, pp. 37–68.

Krugman, P.R. (1991a) *Geography and Trade*, Cambridge, MA: MIT Press.

Krugman, P.R. (1991b) 'Increasing returns and economic geography', *Journal of Political Economy*, Vol. 99 (3): 483–99.

La Spina, A. (2003) *La politica per il Mezzogiorno*, Bologna: Il Mulino.

Levi, C. (1945) *Cristo si è fermato a Eboli*, Turin: Einaudi.

Lombroso, C. (1876) *L'uomo delinquente studiato in rapporto alla antropologia, alla medicina legale ed alle discipline carcerarie*, Milan: Ulrico-Hoepli.

Lutz, V. (2007) *Italy: A Study in Economic Development*, Oxford: Oxford University Press.

Lyon, T.P. (2005) 'Making capitalism work: social capital and economic growth in Italy, 1970–1995', FEEM Working Paper No. 70 (05).

Missiaia, A. (2016) 'Where do we go from here? Market access and regional development in Italy (1871–1911)', *European Review of Economic History*, Vol. 20 (2): 215–41.

Nitti, F.S. (1958) *Scritti sulla questione meridionale*, edited by A. Saitta, Bari: Laterza.

Putnam, R.D., Leonardi, R. and Nanetti, R.Y. (1993) *Making Democracy Work: Civic Traditions in Modern Italy*, Princeton, NJ: Princeton University Press.

Rey, G.M. (ed.) (1992) *I conti economici dell'Italia, Vol. 2, Una stima del valore aggiunto per il 1911*, Rome-Bari: Laterza.

Rey, G.M. (ed.) (2000) *I conti economici dell'Italia, Vol. 3, Il valore aggiunto per gli anni 1891, 1938, 1951*, Rome-Bari: Laterza.

Romeo, R. (1959) *Risorgimento e capitalismo*, Bari: Laterza.

Sala-i-Martin, X. (1996) 'The classical approach to convergence analysis', *Economic Journal*, Vol. 106 (437): 1019–36.

Silone, I. (1933) *Fontamara*, Paris: Nuove edizioni italiane.

Spadavecchia, A. (2005) 'State subsidies and the sources of company finance in Italian industrial districts, 1951–1991', *Enterprise and Society*, Vol. 6 (4): 571–80.

Svimez (Associazione per lo sviluppo dell'industria nel Mezzogiorno) (1993) *I conti del Mezzogiorno e del Centro-Nord nel ventennio 1970–1989*, Bologna: Il Mulino.

Tagliacarne, G. (1962) 'Calcolo del reddito prodotto dal settore privato e dalla pubblica amministrazione nelle provincie e regioni d'Italia nel 1961 e confronto con gli anni 1960 e 1951. Indici di alcuni consumi e del risparmio bancario', *Moneta e credito*, Vol. 15 (59): 339–419.

Toniolo, G. (2013) 'An overview of Italy's economic growth', in G. Toniolo (ed.), *The Oxford Handbook of the Italian Economy since Unification*, Oxford: Oxford University Press, pp. 3–36.

Trigilia, C. (1992) *Sviluppo senza autonomia. Effetti perversi delle politiche nel Mezzogiorno*, Bologna: Il Mulino.

Viesti, G. (ed.) (2000) *Mezzogiorno dei distretti*, Corigliano Calabro: Meridiana-Donzelli.

Williamson, J.G. (1965) 'Regional inequality and the process of national development: a description of the patterns', *Economic Development and Cultural Change*, Vol. 13 (4): 3–84.

Zamagni, V. (1978) *Industrializzazione e squilibri regionali in Italia. Bilancio dell'età giolittiana*, Bologna: Il Mulino.

Zamagni, V. (2002) 'La Grande Guerra come elemento di rottura della crescita equilibrata dell'economia italiana', in G. Sanz (ed.), *España e Italia en la Europa contemporánea: desde finales del siglo XIX a las dictaduras*, Madrid: Consejo Superior de Investigaciones Científicas (CSIC), pp. 323–34.

3.8 The comparative development of regions in the Netherlands, 1820–2010

Herman de Jong and Dirk Stelder

1. Introduction

In this chapter, we discuss long-term regional growth patterns in the Netherlands since 1820. In the early nineteenth century, levels of GDP per capita were close to those in England. But the Dutch economy was a latecomer with respect to steam-driven industrial activities. Starting not before the 1860s, modern industrialization was also late when viewed from a continental perspective (van Zanden and van Riel 2004). Growth rates of the economy were well above the long-term rate of the pre-1800 period and increased further in the second half of the nineteenth century and in the twentieth century. The drivers of this growth acceleration were manifold, ranging from major transitions in the structure of the economy, rapid population growth and urbanization, to underlying forces of greater efficiency through falling transport costs, and ongoing industrialization and productivity growth. In the same period, major changes in international trade relations occurred, from free trade before 1913, to de-globalization during the second quarter of the twentieth century, and renewed globalization since the 1970s. The specific nature of regional and urban development in the open economy of the Netherlands can be seen as a net result of these different forces.

From a theoretical point of view, it is not certain what to expect if we look at long-term comparative growth of countries and regions. The neoclassical growth model of Solow (1956) predicts overall convergence of income across countries. New growth theories of both Romer (1986) and Lucas (1988) suggest persisting cross-country differences in development that probably also could manifest themselves on a regional level. The growing body of convergence/divergence literature that has developed since then shows quite different and contradictory results, depending on methods, time frame, stages of development and regional scale.[1] New economic geography (NEG) entered the stage with Krugman (1991), and has drawn broad attention to persisting patterns of agglomeration and core-periphery patterns that show no signs of convergence. As Ottaviano (2008) and more recently the European Commission (2014) have shown, forces of convergence and divergence and their related policy implications are intensively debated today, and there is clearly a need for more empirical research.

One of the long-term trends we observe in this chapter on the Dutch economy is product specialization at the regional level and changes in the regional industrial and occupational structure. Comparative advantages, factor endowments and economies of scale are the standard concepts in the international (new) trade literature at the analytical level of countries, but they are relevant at the regional level as well. We argue that infrastructural improvement and falling transport costs have played an important role in what could be called a first phase of 'globalization' at the national level between 1850 and 1910 that led to increasing trade flows and specialization between regions of a national economy. The inland provinces, where wages were lower than in the urbanized western part of the country, specialized in manufacturing. The expansion of the secondary sector accelerated, however, in a long period of rapid industrialization until the 1960s, arguably strengthened by both world wars and the globalization backlash in the interwar period, and leading to regional wage and income convergence. Deindustrialization and the growth of the service economy reinforced tendencies of divergence, in particular through fast relative income growth in the international services-oriented western provinces.

A more specific reason why the Dutch example is worth analysing is its small geographical size. The models mentioned all originated from the fields of macroeconomics and international trade theory, and refer – implicitly or not – to countries. In the literature, the question whether a general convergence model about countries can also be applied to lower geographical levels such as regions or cities remains unanswered or is often ignored. In theory, however, external economies, spillovers and technology diffusion are the main drivers behind patterns of convergence or forces of dispersion, divergence and agglomeration. It is important to find out on which geographical scales such forces really influence the economy. As will be discussed in more detail in the next section, the Dutch regions we deal with vary in the range of 500,000 to 3 million inhabitants, and the country as a whole (presently *c.*17 million) is comparable with the metropolitan area of Los Angeles (12.8 million). The economic theorist has to make a strong case when claiming that the same forces might be at work in such largely different scales. For example, for the EU, different studies have indicated that there is evidence for convergence at the level of countries and larger regions, but at the same time there are signs of divergence at lower spatial levels.[2] In this study, our main focus will be on the Dutch provinces, which is the NUTS 2 level. In addition, we will also pay attention to the lower level of municipalities for which historical data sets are available since 1840.

2. Dutch historical data sets

A historical analysis of regional development in the Netherlands can be carried out on the basis of population census data from 1830 onwards, combined with reconstructions and estimations of regional income. Most of the census data after 1900 allow for an analysis at lower spatial levels such as municipalities, but regional accounts aimed at estimates of regional GDP need larger spatial units in order to cope with statistical reliability, sample size, border changes over time and effects of local commuting. In this chapter, regional development is studied at the level of

11 provinces for which the administrative borders have remained unchanged since 1813 (see Figure 3.8.1a). At this level, the smallest provinces take up on average 3 per cent of the national population, which amounts to 150,000 inhabitants in 1900 and 500,000 today. Apart from minor border corrections of these provinces over time, the most significant geographical change has been the creation of a new twelfth province, Flevoland (NL23 in the European NUTS 2 classification) in the geographical centre of the country, consisting of three new land reclamations (so-called 'polders') that were completed in 1948, 1957 and 1968 (see Figure 3.8.1b). The province of North Holland was enlarged with two land reclamations already in 1855 and 1934. Flevoland did not become a formal province until 1987, but data on employment, regional GDP and population within the later borders of Flevoland have been available since 1960.

For the period 1820–1950, no official regional GDP data have ever been published, but there are estimations for specific years available from various sources. This chapter aims to connect data for the period before 1950 with published regional GDP accounts from 1950 onwards. The Netherlands was one of the first countries that implemented the system of national accounts (SNA) at the national level, as proposed by the United Nations (1947). This is partly due to the fact that it was not long after the publication of the first input–output table for the US for 1932 by Leontief that Tinbergen created the first input–output table for the Netherlands for 1938 (Leontief 1951; den Bakker 1992). In his pioneering work on SNA, Stone (1961) stressed the importance of a basic input–output table in the process of balancing the various sources of economic information, and by the end of the 1950s Chenery and Clark (1959) reported that 19 countries had prepared basic IOTs, providing the groundwork for including the IO framework into the SNA.

Figure 3.8.1a Provinces and density

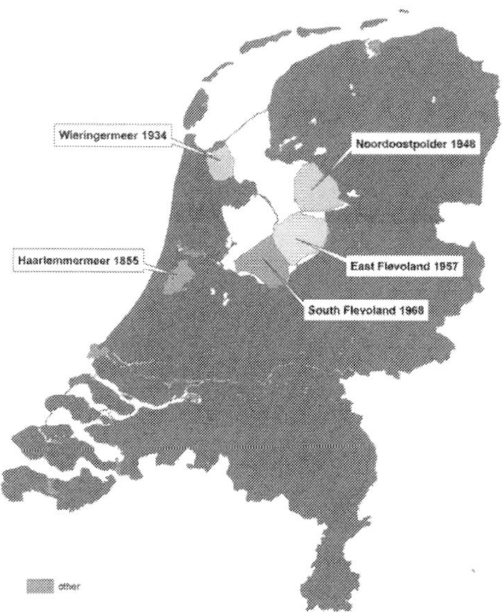

Figure 3.8.1b Transition of water to land

The development of Dutch regional accounts has followed the same path. The earliest study on a consistent set of regional accounts and a regional input–output table was done for the province of Groningen by the statistician Rijken van Olst (1958). Based on his experience with this relatively small part of the national economy (around 3 per cent of national GDP), he concluded that in principle a system of regional accounts (SRA) could outperform the SNA when the regional accounts would be balanced first and then aggregated to the national level. The high costs of such an SRA, however, has prevented the Dutch regional accounts from developing further along this way. A simple set of regional accounts based on input–output tables for all provinces was first published for 1960 (CBS 1968) and later for 1965 (CBS 1970) at a level of five industries/sectors. In 1983, the input–output tables themselves were published for the first time for 30 industries for the year 1970 (CBS 1983). With this publication, a sound basis was formed for the start of the annual Dutch regional accounts, covering an efficient small range of variables such as total output, value added, investment, exports and labour volume at the level of 38 industries, 12 provinces and 42 subregions from 1970 onwards.[3] After 1990, regional income statistics have been published based on information systems of national tax agencies, but these advanced systems do not have any comparable sources in the past. Welfare indicators, which are now widely available, such as disposable income by various income groups and regions as small as zip codes, can only be approximated over longer periods of time at the level of provinces in the form of a one single indicator such as total income or GDP per capita. These results will be discussed further in section 4.

3. Estimation methods

For the early post-war years 1950 and 1960, we have combined census data on employment with provincial GDP data by industry from the regional accounts mentioned above and from an incidental CBS study that has made a consistent comparison of GDP by province and industry for 1950 and 1960 (CBS 1965).

The pre-1950 regional income estimations (1820–1946) in this chapter are based on reconstructions by economic historians and on pioneering work of researchers from the CBS (Central Bureau of Statistics Netherlands) for the inter-war and post-war period. The regional GDP per capita estimates of 1820, 1880 and 1910 have been taken from van Zanden, who used data on regional money wages, rents and other income from capital (van Zanden 1987: 55). We have not made additional estimates for the years between 1820 and 1880. The estimates for 1900 have been linearly interpolated on the basis of the 1880 and 1910 estimations. Regional GDP estimates for the years 1926, 1930, 1938 and 1946 were taken from studies by statisticians of the CBS (Derksen 1942a, 1942b; CBS 1949). We combined these income estimates with official data on population and estimations of regional employment. For the years 1910 and 1930, it was also possible to establish an alternative estimate of regional income levels using wage data only. Provincial wage data by sector were taken from the annual reports of the national Accidents Insurance Bank. Applying the proxy method of Geary and Stark (2002), we combined these wage data by industry with the sectoral employment structure per province. Differences with the previously calculated estimates based on total income levels were large. The reason for this is that wages form only a part of total income. Estimates by Derksen revealed that wages and salaries took up 44 percent of total income, with a lower bound of 34 per cent and an upper bound of 51 per cent across the Dutch provinces in 1938 (Derksen 1942a: 138). Non-wage income varied significantly across provinces. For both 1910 and 1930, we find that the standard deviation of wage levels among provinces was much lower than the standard deviation of total incomes; for 1910, it was 14 against 24.9, and for 1930 16.8 versus 21 (see Table 3.8.1).

There is also a persistent pattern of relatively favourable income levels for the inland provinces Drenthe, Overijssel, North Brabant and Limburg when regional income is estimated on the basis of wage data only. The Geary-Stark procedure thus leads to an upward shift of regional income levels of these provinces to the national average, compressing the 'true' income differences among the provinces. For reasons of consistency, we have decided to use the total income-based measurement of GDP per capita for the pre-1950 period, instead of the method that reconstructs regional income from wage data only.

4. Movements in regional structure and income across time

Here, we present the long-term pattern of regional GDP per capita. Table 3.8.2 and Maps 3.8.1–3.8.5 display the trends. Some provinces show large fluctuations in their relative ranking of GDP/cap levels (e.g. Utrecht). On the whole, however,

Table 3.8.1 Relative GDP per capita, 1910 and 1930 (Netherlands = 100)

	1910	*1910**	*1930*	*1930**
Groningen	87	82	81	81
Friesland	91	78	75	75
Drenthe	73	52	66	61
Overijssel	96	78	99	87
Gelderland	79	88	85	86
Utrecht	86	113	94	111
North Holland	126	130	126	129
South Holland	106	123	112	118
Zeeland	94	87	84	77
North Brabant	94	68	87	77
Limburg	97	62	91	78
Flevoland				
Standard deviation	14.0	24.9	16.8	21.0

Source: See the text.

Note: Columns 1910 and 1930 are based on the Geary-Stark method; columns 1910* and 1930* are based on total income estimates.

the standard deviation of income levels declined between 1820 and 1960, followed by a period of consolidation until 1990. Income divergence increased again during the 1990s. What follows is a short overview of the most characteristic economic developments in the Dutch provinces since 1820.

4.1 General characteristics of the Dutch regional structure since the early modern period until 1900

In the first half of the nineteenth century, market integration within the Netherlands was hampered by spatial restraints in transport systems and different tax regimes across cities and provinces. Although rivers were never far away, the infrastructure in the inland provinces was not as developed as in the coastal provinces and Holland, which boasted an extensive and efficient network of canals (de Vries 1981). Additionally, there were large differences in the cost of living between the coastal and the inland regions. Housing rents in Holland were 10 times higher than in the inland province of Drenthe (van Zanden and van Riel 2004: 61). There were substantial regional variations in local and regional excise duties on, for example, coal and bread, leading to persistent differences in factor costs and nominal incomes across regions and towns. Steam technology in manufacturing developed only slowly in the inland areas, where labour was the cheap production factor and coal relatively expensive. During the first industrialization phase starting from the 1860s, the specialization patterns were not only dictated by existing forces of agglomeration, but also by relative factor costs. Labour-intensive manufacturing activities were concentrated in the inland provinces (such as the textile industry close to the German border, and shoemaking and electrical engineering in North Brabant).

A very rough breakdown of areas with more or less common economic-geographical characteristics would distinguish three clusters of provinces (van Zanden and van Riel 2004: 57). The first group consists of the provinces of Holland (North and South Holland) and Utrecht (see Figure 3.8.1a), which had the highest population densities and urbanization rates in Europe since 1600 (de Vries 1984: 39, 45). The peak of the urban hierarchy in this cluster is represented by the national capital, Amsterdam, once an important global staple market and centre of the international grain trade. For a long time, the urban hierarchy of Holland and Utrecht was characterized by a belt of large and middle-sized cities, later to be known as the 'Randstad'. During the nineteenth century, only 20 per cent of employment in this densily urbanized centre was in the agricultural sector, with high value-added dairying and horticulture. For a long time, the area had a large service sector (44 per cent of GDP in 1800), related to the urban economy and to international (colonial) trade and services such as banking and shipping. The manufacturing sector in the Amsterdam region was specialized in capital-intensive production that was closely related to the international sector, such as papermaking, textile printing, sugar refining, and food processing. The port of Rotterdam greatly benefited from the German industrial expansion in the late nineteenth century. In 1900, 25 per cent of the total Dutch population lived in the four largest cities of this cluster: Amsterdam, The Hague, Rotterdam and Utrecht.

The second cluster of provinces is formed by the coastal provinces of Zeeland, Friesland, Groningen and the eastern part of North Brabant. Agriculture in these regions was a relatively large and well-developed sector, with specialization in crops, livestock and dairy products that were traded internationally. Zeeland and Groningen were characterized by large-scale farming; urban hierarchies were very modest in comparison with the Randstad. Until 1900, the agricultural sector did not decline very much, and the rise of manufacturing employment was relatively modest.

The third cluster was being formed by the inland provinces of Gelderland, North Brabant, Drenthe, Overijssel and Limburg. These areas had lower soil fertility and were less specialized. Grain and milk yields were 20–50 per cent lower than in the other parts of the country during the nineteenth century. Consequently, labour productivity and money wage levels were also much lower than in Holland. These regions show the largest decline of agricultural employment, accompanied by a steady rise of the share of industry, that was larger than the rise in services. Manufacturing employment reaches the highest level in the province of Overijssel because of the growth of its textile industry. The sharp rise of manufacturing in Limburg after 1900 stems from a rapid expansion of the mining industry.

Half of the money wage differences across regions can be explained by price differences. Domestic migration occurred, but it did not result in equalization of money wage levels as life in the cities was more unsure and expensive, which was compensated for by a wage premium. During the nineteenth century, wages in the coastal provinces were 60 per cent higher than elsewhere in the country

Table 3.8.2 Relative GDP per capita, 1820–2010 (Netherlands = 100)

	1820	*1880*	*1900*	*1910*	*1926*	*1930*	*1938*	*1946*	*1960*	*1970*	*1980*	*1990*	*2000*	*2010*
Groningen	90	93	85	82	84	81	92	88	98	88	90	87	89	86
Friesland	101	93	83	78	77	75	81	81	81	82	82	83	83	82
Drenthe	63	60	55	52	61	66	68	83	83	81	80	91	81	76
Overijssel	72	71	76	78	91	99	88	96	94	78	85	89	88	90
Gelderland	76	82	86	88	85	85	87	87	88	96	90	89	86	86
Utrecht	122	117	114	113	113	94	109	95	92	102	105	106	127	122
North Holland	140	138	133	130	130	126	124	117	113	112	109	109	116	118
South Holland	128	126	124	123	116	112	115	114	112	117	116	110	103	102
Zeeland	113	100	91	87	78	84	93	96	95	100	102	110	88	98
North Brabant	65	68	68	68	75	87	78	86	95	95	96	100	103	104
Limburg	57	60	61	62	78	91	80	89	93	80	87	92	90	91
Flevoland											102	79	74	75
Standard deviation	29.1	26.7	25.3	24.9	21.0	21.0	17.1	11.8	10.2	13.4	11.4	11.2	15.3	14.9

Source: See the text.

Note: Data after 1960 excluding incomes from natural gas.

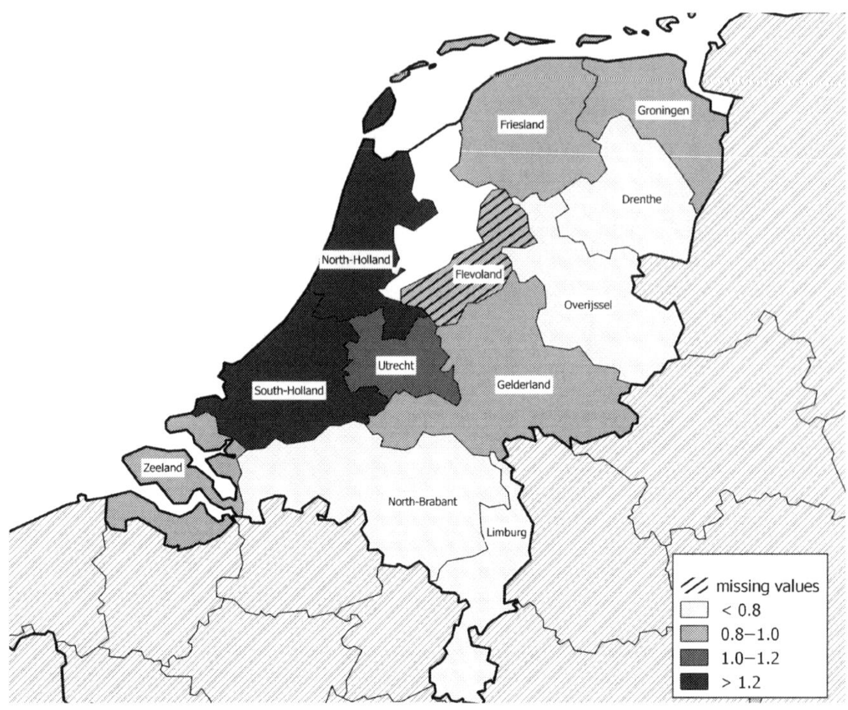

Map 3.8.1 Relative GDP per capita, 1900 (Netherlands = 1)

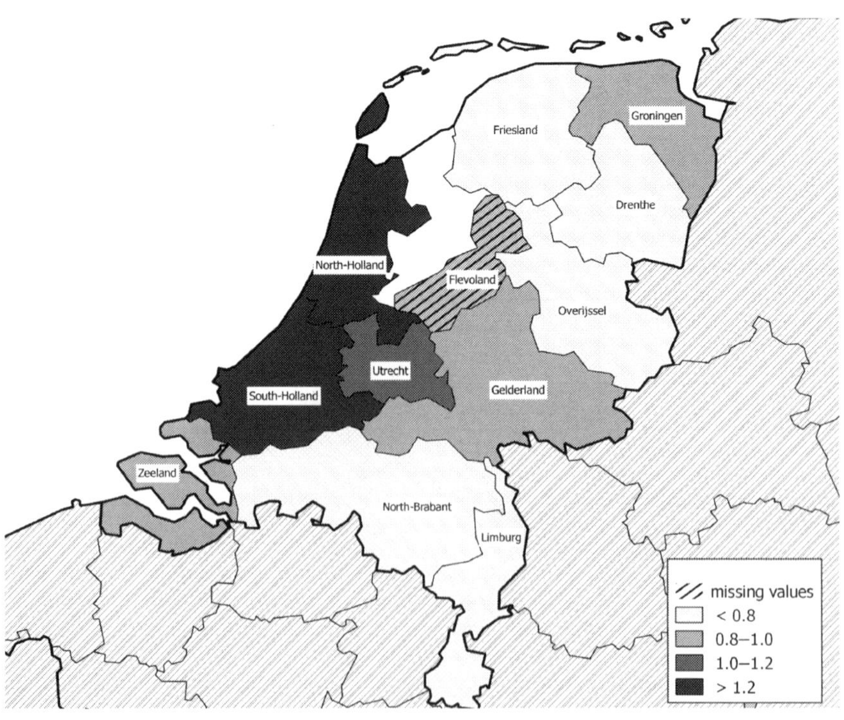

Map 3.8.2 Relative GDP per capita, 1910 (Netherlands = 1)

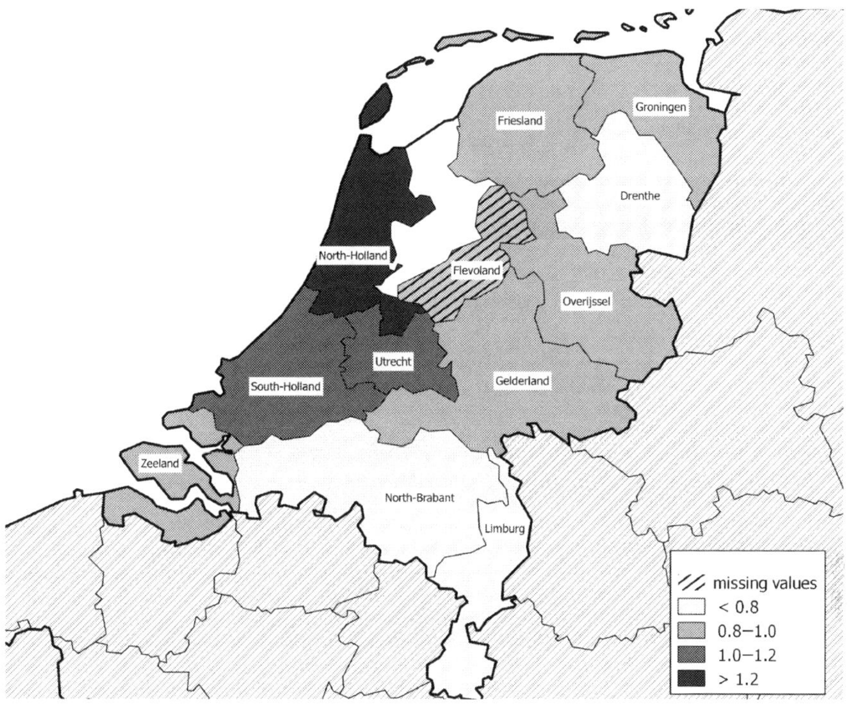

Map 3.8.3 Relative GDP per capita, 1938 (Netherlands = 1)

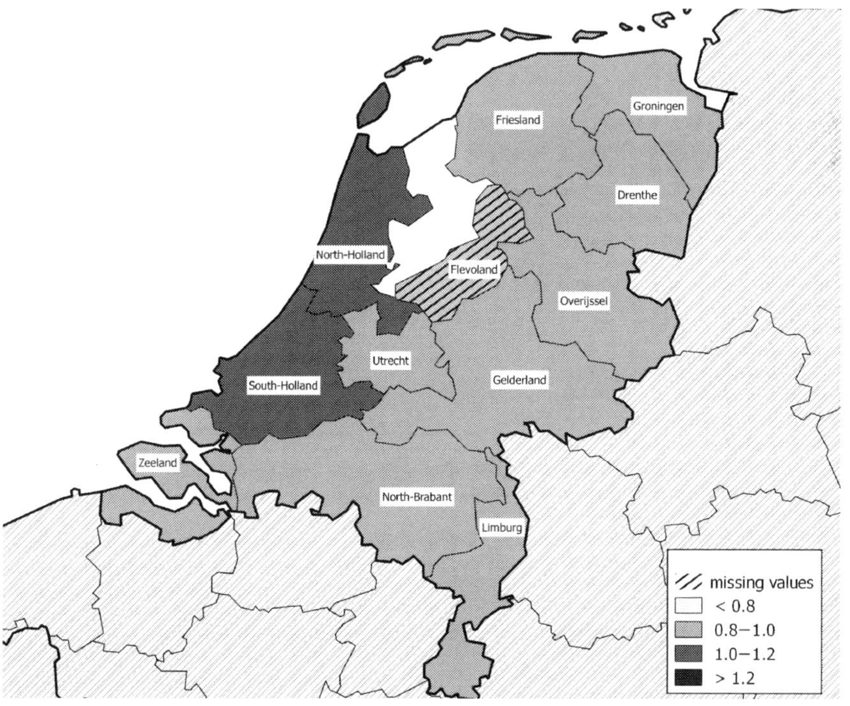

Map 3.8.4 Relative GDP per capita, 1960 (Netherlands = 1)

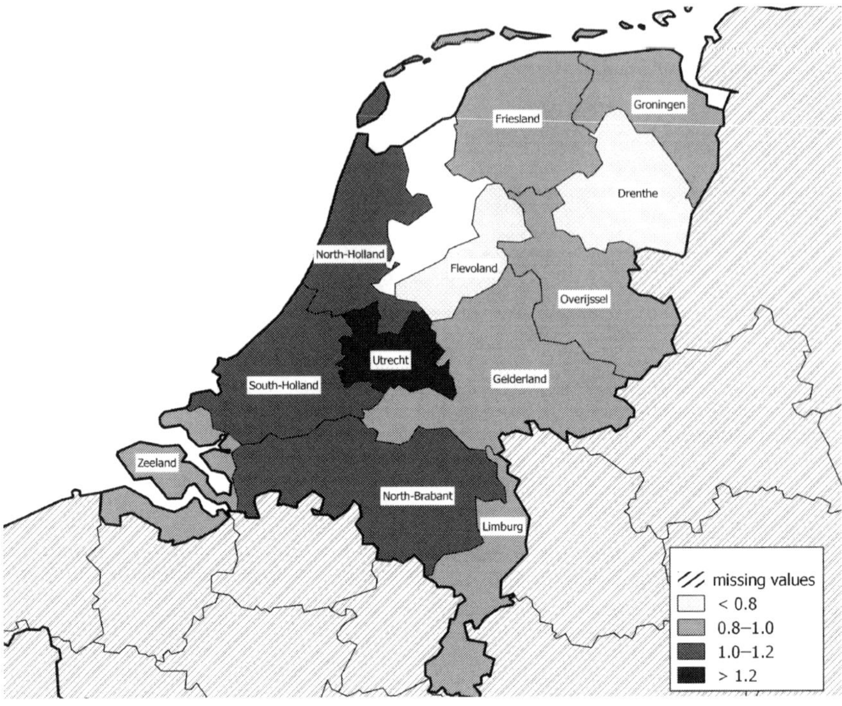

Map 3.8.5 Relative GDP per capita, 2010 (Netherlands = 1)

(van Zanden and Griffiths 1989: 23). Prices equalized in the second half of the nineteenth century with the abolishment of many local taxes and as a result of a first wave of railway building and canal construction (de Jong 1992; Filarski and Mom 2008). Besides high incomes from wages, there were also high levels of capital in Holland, accumulated in the previous centuries. Income inequality across provinces was relatively high, but in real terms it was probably less pronounced. Generally average standards of living were found to be higher in the inland provinces (van Zanden and van Riel 2004: 64).

We can thus characterize three dimensions of the variations in spatial-economic structures across the Dutch provinces since 1820. First of all, there were large income and wage differences between the Randstad and the rest, due to agglomeration economies. Wages and incomes in the Randstad were higher because of physical proximities, scale economies and lower transaction costs. Second, the Randstad enjoyed local non-human endowments in the form of better access to waterways and later on railways, reinforcing existing agglomeration patterns. Third, there were urbanization externalities. The occupational structures in the western provinces were such that skilled labour, high-value-added international services and capital-intensive industries were concentrated there. The inland provinces had relatively more low-skilled labour. During the nineteenth and early twentieth centuries, this broad pattern of occupational structural differences hardly changed (van Zanden and Griffiths 1989: 23). After the 1860s, the movement of labour out of the agricultural sector together with ongoing industrialization, also in the inland provinces, led to a decline in national wage and income differences, resulting in less pronounced income variations across provinces. Two dimensions, urbanization externalities and non-human endowments, also changed through overall population growth and the further expansion of the infrastructural network, respectively. The twentieth century witnessed a further convergence of income levels (e.g. through the spatial spread of institutions for higher education and through ongoing (sub)urbanization).

4.2 1900–1950

Between 1859 and 1960, relative employment in industry increased from 31 per cent to 44 per cent of the Dutch labour force. From the turn of the twentieth century, industrialization broadened with new sectors such as electrical engineering and basic industries such as coal mining, metallurgy and chemicals. Transport infrastructure and facilities developed quickly with the further outlay of railways, local tramways and canals, and later on roads. Trade restrictions and the world wars have stimulated the further broadening of the manufacturing sector, while at the same time putting a brake on the expansion of international services (de Jong 2003). Inland provinces such as North Brabant, Limburg and the eastern part of Overijssel witnessed a fast growth of industrial employment during the first half of the twentieth century. The gap between wage and income dispersion across provinces declined, as well as income per capita variations (see Tables 3.8.1 and 3.8.2). The causes for this decline in functional inequality, and accordingly inter-provincial income inequality, were manifold. During the First World War, industrial workers improved their bargaining position, leading to higher wages and to wage compression between skilled and unskilled jobs. In the province of Limburg, wages went up quickly with the expansion of the coal mines since the Great War. During the German occupation between 1940 and 1945, when wage policies were introduced, variations in wage levels across workers and regions declined even further. This was reinforced during the early post-Second World War period of repair and reconstruction, with an increasing demand for unskilled labour. Although both world wars had differential effects on the agricultural and service sectors, it is safe to say that the agricultural sector has profited more from the war circumstances than the service sector, which was concentrated in the Randstad (Klemann 2002; de Jong 2005). Both wars were thus relatively more damaging for the regional high-wage economy of the west. Our figures show that there was a declining trend in relative income levels in North and South Holland as well as in Utrecht, in particular after 1938. Capital and wealth had become a less important source of income due to wartime inflation, rent control (which lowered the value of real estate), the loss of colonial capital after the Second World War, and progressive taxes on wealth (van Zanden and Griffiths 1989: 24–6).

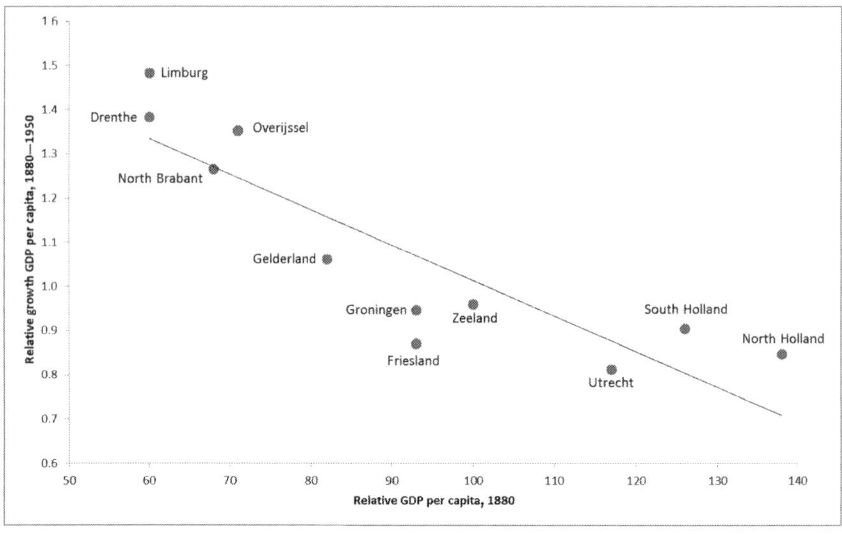

Figure 3.8.2 Beta-convergence, 1880–1946

Figure 3.8.2 shows beta-convergence over the period 1880–1946, illustrated by plotting the initial level of GDP per capita versus GDP growth. The slope is clearly negative, implying that relatively poor regions have grown faster.

4.3 1950–2010

Post-Second World War industrialization and regional cohesion policies maintained manufacturing employment at high levels during the 1950s and 1960s, also in the peripheral parts of the country. But since then, important industries such as shipbuilding and textiles were on a decline. The closing down of the Limburg coal mines in the 1960s had long-lasting effects on income and employment levels in the south. Industrial policies towards declining industries and the creation of new employment opportunities were strongly ambivalent in these days. Shipyards in the western provinces were initially subsidized with state funds, but there was no support for declining sectors such as textiles in the east. During the 1980s, several central government agencies and state-owned companies (such as Dutch Telecom) were relocated to the peripheral areas, but effects of these policies were short-lived.

Together with ongoing decline in agricultural employment and an expanding (international) service sector, the stage was set for a return of the Randstad economy, in particular in banking, finance and business consulting (Amsterdam and Utrecht) since the 1990s (Sluyterman 2005). Deindustrialization changed the nature of Dutch manufacturing. This was strengthened by the discovery of domestic natural gas in the northern part of the country around 1960. 'Dutch disease'

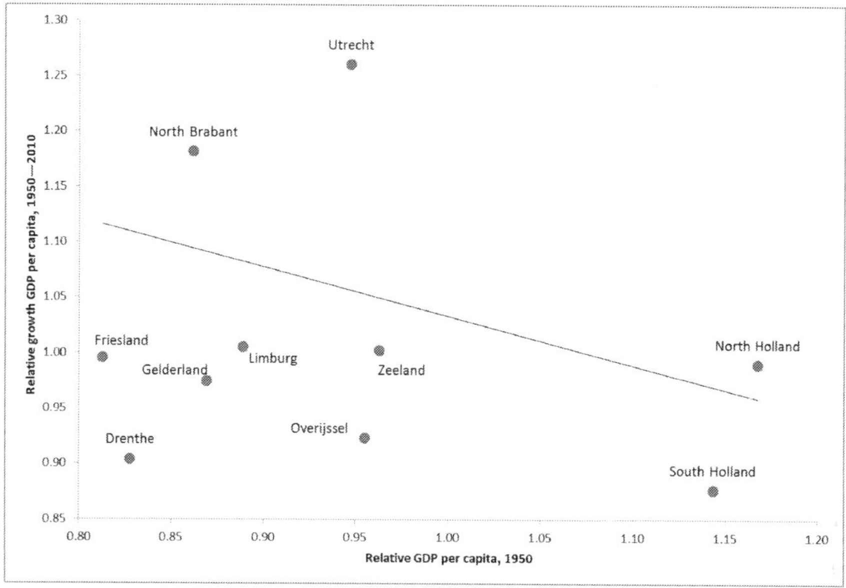

Figure 3.8.3 Beta-convergence, 1946–2010

effects worsened international competitiveness of traditional industries and stimulated capital- and energy-intensive sectors within the economy (Corden and Neary 1982). The exploitation of one of the world's largest natural gas fields in the northern province of Groningen doubled its provincial GDP share from 4 per cent in 1960 to 8 per cent in 1980, but had hardly any effect on local income because the government revenues from natural gas were spent at the national level.

The main reason for the halt in the long-run convergence trend, as shown in Figure 3.8.3, is the transition from a manufacturing to a (return of the) service economy after 1970, which has dominantly taken place in the Randstad regions North Holland, Utrecht and to a lesser extent South Holland. As will be discussed below, these three regions also show up as the only ones with a positive share component for the period after 1970. The standard deviation of the regional GDP per capita distribution indicates that the spread in GDP per capita in 2012 is back at the level of 1946 (see Table 3.8.2). Figure 3.8.3 illustrates how these developments have resulted in a much less pronounced pattern of beta-convergence after 1950. Figure 3.8.4 shows sigma-convergence in the long run, measured as the population-weighted coefficient of variation in GDP per capita.

Clearly, there was considerable convergence across the Dutch regions until 1960 down to a rather low level of dispersion if we compare to other European countries. However, more recently, the discovery of natural resources combined with a strong rise of the service sector stopped this process of convergence and led to a new increase in dispersion after 1990. Still, a return to pre-First World War income variations across provinces is not likely because of national income redistribution policies, such as state old-age pensions, and disablement and unemployment benefits.

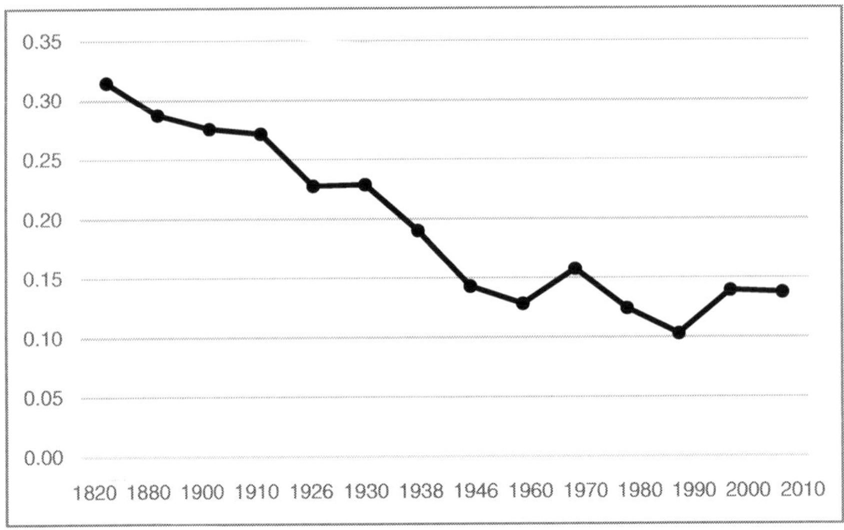

Figure 3.8.4 Sigma-convergence (weighted coefficient of variation), 1820–2010

5. Specialization and industrial structure

The regional shifts in economic development over time have many reasons, but the main explanation is connected to functional changes in sector structure and specialization. Roughly speaking, manufacturing has been dominating production and employment in the central regions and larger cities in the first half of the twentieth century. With the rise of the service sectors and the shift of labour-intensive manufacturing to low-wage countries from 1970 onwards, services have become the dominant sector in central and larger agglomerations, while manufacturing has shifted outwards to second-order agglomerations and peripheral regions. This is a general trend in OECD countries (Henderson 2010). As an illustration, Figures 3.8.5a and 3.8.5b show high sector shares for financial services in the centre and a reverse pattern for manufacturing employment given the spatial distribution of employment in 2011.

Our historical data set enables a simple shift and share analysis for the sectors agriculture, mining, manufacturing and services over the period since 1900. This analysis reveals whether a region: (1) may fall behind others because of a less than average growth at the industry/firm level (shift); or (2) because of an unfavourable industry structure. All regional industries may perform on the average national productivity growth, but some regions may simply have a large share of lesser growing industries (share). For example, the decline of agricultural employment may hit a region harder because it simply has a large agricultural sector (the share component) or because its own agricultural sector has been declining faster than the average national agricultural sector (the shift component). Figures 3.8.6 and

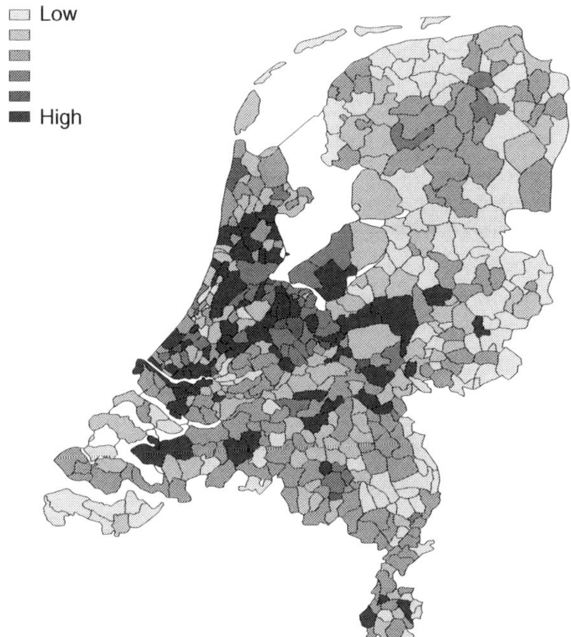

Figure 3.8.5a Sector share financial services

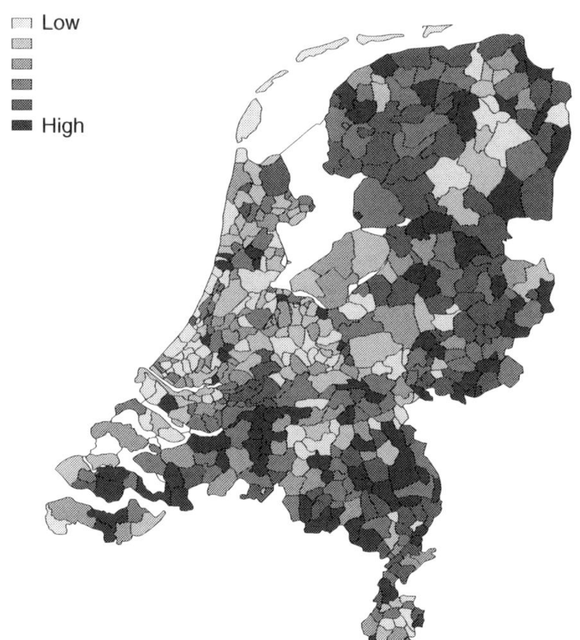

Figure 3.8.5b Sector share manufacturing

3.8.7 show the regional share and shift component, respectively, as the deviation from the national average, which is zero for both components by definition. We have carried out this analysis on employment data for several sub-periods in order to illustrate different phases of transition and because the employment structure by province cannot rely on one uniform definition for all years.[4]

All provinces except the three Randstad provinces, North Holland, South Holland and Utrecht, have substantial negative share components in the first three periods. The main reason for this is the sharp decline of employment in the agricultural sector, which was relatively large in these regions. Later on, the share pattern remains persistent but for a different reason: the growing importance of the service sectors in which the Randstad regions again have a head start. A remarkable result is that the share component declines after 1980. This is due to what could be called the globalization effect on the regional scale: because of increasing specialization at the firm level, we find an increasing 'slicing up the supply chain' (Timmer et al. 2013). Interregional trade, in particular inter-industry trade within the manufacturing sector, is intensifying (Eding et al. 1995). The result of this trend is that regions may increasingly differ in their industry structure at the firm level but show less differences in GDP growth because growth in one region/sector directly induces growth in another region/sector due to closely connected backward linkages. For manufacturing as a whole – but this line of reasoning also applies to services – it implies that regional shares for larger aggregate sectors have tended to converge in the longer run, in particular when globalization and specialization intensified after 1980.

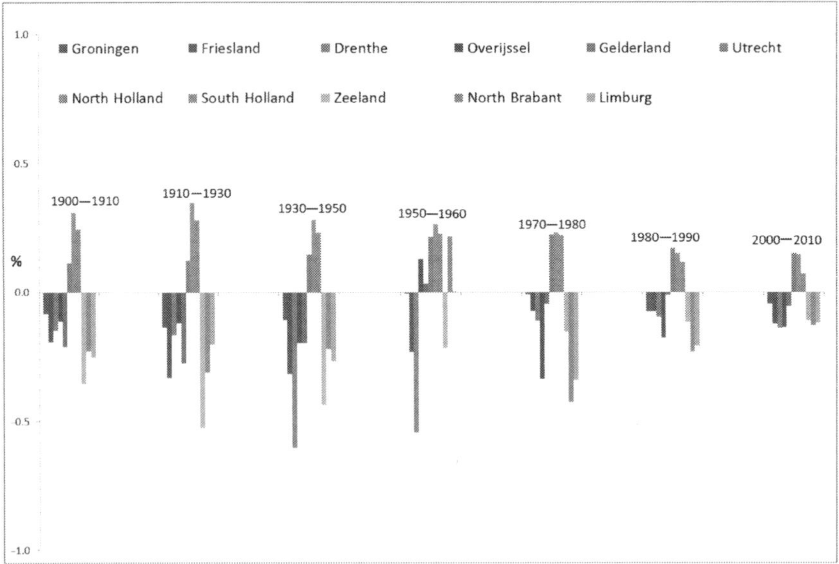

Figure 3.8.6 Annual share component regional employment growth, 1900–2010

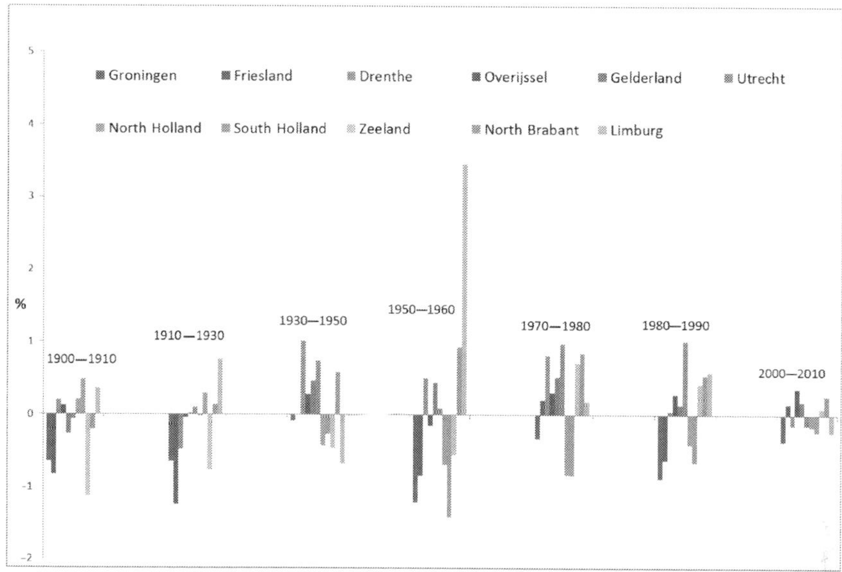

Figure 3.8.7 Annual shift component regional employment growth, 1900–2010

The shift components in Figure 3.8.7 show a more diversified pattern. In the first two periods, the coastal provinces Groningen, Friesland and Zeeland show negative shifts due to slower employment growth in manufacturing. This is also visible in the case of Drenthe in the second period. The largest outlier is a 3 per cent extra growth on top of the national average for Limburg in the first decade after the Second World War, which was characterized by post-war reconstruction of the manufacturing sector that needed large amounts of indigenous coal inputs. The closing of the coal mines in Limburg during 1966–1970 must have caused a large negative shift component, but this cannot be shown because large differences between the employment data of 1960 and 1970 do not allow a growth rate analysis for this period. Another large negative shift that remains invisible is the sharp decline of the relatively labour-intensive textile industry in Overijssel that has almost completely disappeared due to international competition from low-wage countries between 1960 and 1975. Again, the shift component for all regions (positively or negatively) declines after 2000 due to increasing interregional backward linkages.

6. Urban development

It is possible to compare long-run regional development at the level of provinces with population growth and density at a much lower level of municipalities. Figure 3.8.8 shows the distribution of population density for 1840, 1960 and 2012 by municipality. There is some loss of information due to the process of merging into larger municipalities, in particular after 1981, but this does not distort the main trends over the long run.[5] The results show a reverse pattern compared with the development at the provincial level. As discussed above, the rise of manufacturing has led to a general spreading out of economic development from the Randstad to most of the other provinces until 1960. At the same time, within the provinces, manufacturing has been concentrating in the larger urban centres and cities. This is a well-known spatial feature of industrialization that was captured in the first formulation of local externalities and agglomeration advantages by Marshall (1986). It resulted in a slight divergence at the municipality level between 1840 and 1960, as shown in the left panel of Figure 3.8.9.

The result is comparable with more recent studies that show convergence at the national level combined with divergence at the lower regional level (e.g. as a consequence of EU integration) (European Commission 2014). We have seen such regional divergence in Figures 3.8.3 and 3.8.4 for the period after 1960, but surprisingly it has been accompanied by increasing convergence at the lower municipality level, as shown in the right panel of Figure 3.8.9. We can think of two reasons. First, as became clear from Figure 3.8.5b, manufacturing has shifted out of the main urban centres towards less urban areas. This is a general trend that is observed for many modern countries (Henderson 2010). Second, due to rising congestion in the Randstad, population has shifted to neighbouring, less urbanized municipalities within commuting distance. This effect is particularly strong in North Holland and the western part of North Brabant. Typically, these kinds of convergence patterns can be expected at low levels of spatial aggregation when commuting effects become visible, showing relatively more population growth in municipalities with a strong residential function around the main urban centres of employment.

7. Conclusions

This chapter has presented a long-term overview of regional GDP per capita estimates for the Dutch economy on the NUTS 2 level of provinces. The data have been based on a combination of official estimates by the Dutch Central Bureau of Statistics (after 1950), with reconstructions for the pre-1950 period. The most important geographical distinction to be made is that between the urban belt of the west (the so-called Randstad) and the remaining coastal and inland provinces with lower average incomes and lower population densities. Agglomeration economies, local non-human endowments (waterways and railways) and urbanization externalities all have played a role in shaping the nature of regional and urban development of the Netherlands. They interacted with characteristic nationwide developments such as a fast-growing population, a stepwise improvement of the transportation system, and a rather late but strong process of industrialization, which was supported by the international economic and political-military dynamics of the first half of the twentieth century. During this period, the industrialization process has gradually penetrated deeper into the peripheral hinterland of the country. The net result of this was a long-term process of income convergence among the Dutch provinces from the second half of the nineteenth century

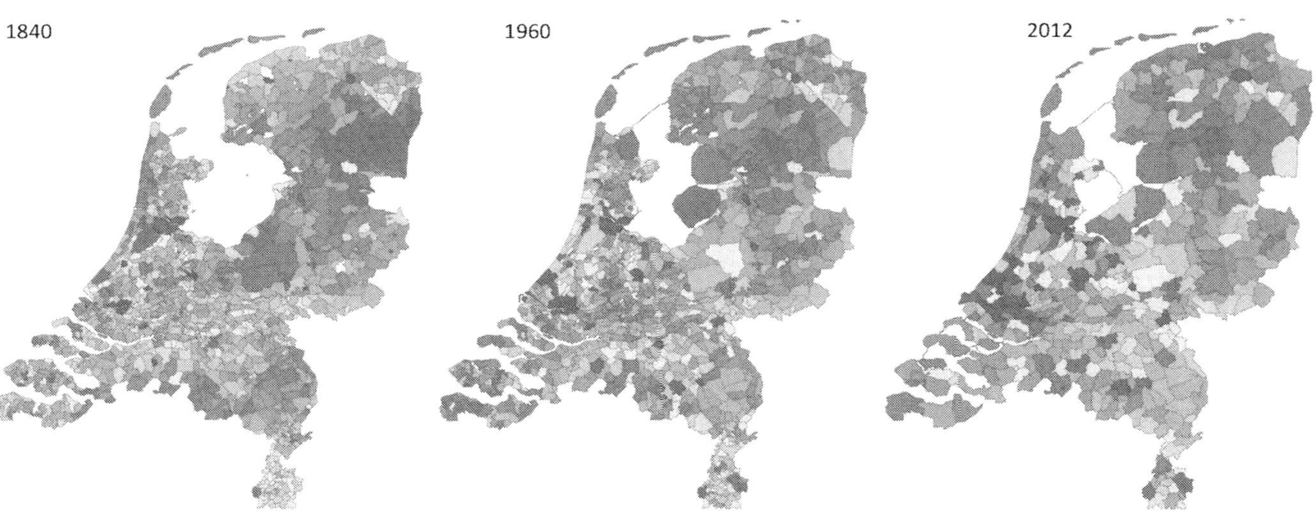

Figure 3.8.8 Population density distribution by municipality, 1840–2012

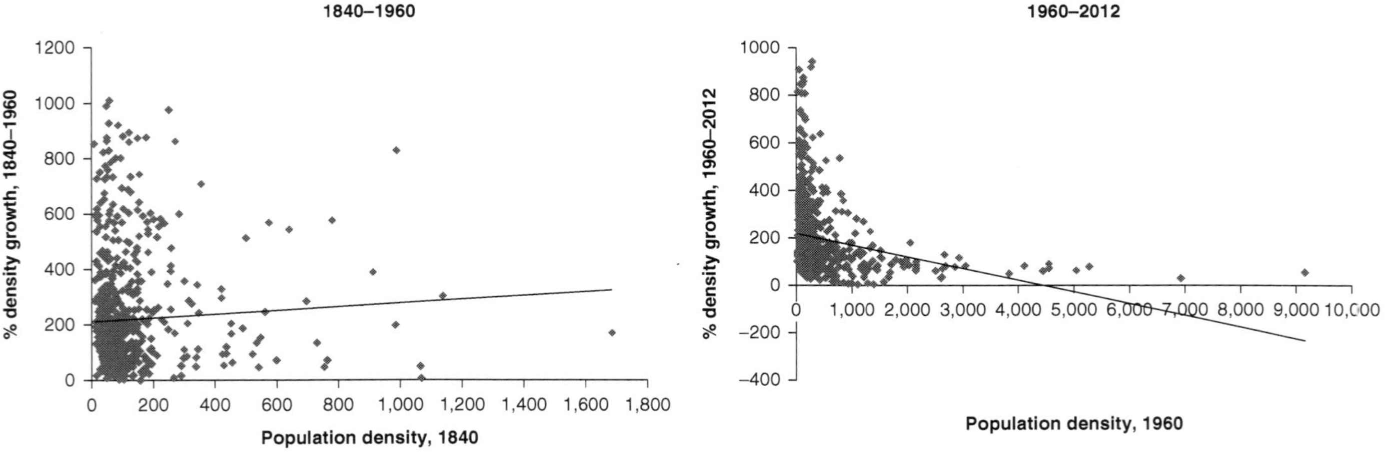

Figure 3.8.9 Beta-convergence population density municipalities, 1840–2012

until *c.*1960. Since the last decades of the twentieth century, a tendency of mild income divergence became visible, being the result of deindustrialization and the rapid rise of the service economy in the western provinces. Due to the small spatial scale of the Netherlands, we can discern opposite tendencies in terms of population development at the level of municipalities. Before 1960, there is divergence due to the concentration of rising manufacturing in the urban centres. After 1960, we find convergence at the municipality level due to the movement of manufacturing out of the urban centres and because of increasing commuting patterns from residential areas to the main urban centres of employment.

Spreading and agglomeration effects may vary according to the spatial level that one wishes to analyse. It therefore may also be helpful to stress a long-term characteristic of Dutch urbanization, and for that matter European urbanization. Since early modern times, the western provinces of the country had an urban density and pattern that was too large in comparison with the territory that needed to be served. The economic historian Jan de Vries noted that the Dutch cities formed part of an urban system that extended beyond the borders of the Dutch Republic. So, in this early modern period, 'the Dutch urban system is so integrated into that of the surrounding countries that it cannot be analysed meaningfully in isolation' (de Vries 1984: 118). Also, for the present period, one could maintain that large parts of the urbanized centre of the Dutch territory belong to the urbanized European 'megalopolis' from north-west England to northern Italy, with a present population of about 100 million people. Seen from this perspective, a further analysis of regional development in the Netherlands would profit from a new transnational approach.

Notes

1 See, for instance, Sala-i-Martin (1996), Boldrin and Canova (2001) and Borsi and Metiu (2015).
2 See, for instance, European Commission (2014: 18) on the development of urban versus rural areas.
3 The 12 provinces (EU NUTS 2 level) are subdivided into 42 COROP regions (EU NUTS 3 level).
4 For 1900–1960, employment is measured as the level of persons employed, but not all years have employment data on mining. After 1960, employment is measured in labour volume of employees. From 2000 onwards, the data measure total labour volume, including the self-employed.
5 The number of municipalities has gone down from 1,076 in 1930 to 982 in 1960, 809 in 1981 and 417 in 2012.

References

Boldrin, M. and Canova, F. (2001) 'Inequality and convergence in Europe's regions: reconsidering European regional policies', *Economic Policy*, Vol. 16 (32): 206–53.

Borsi, M.T. and Metiu, N. (2015) 'The evolution of economic convergence in the European Union', *Empirical Economics*, Vol. 48 (2): 657–81.

Centraal Bureau voor de Statistiek (CBS) (1949) 'De regionale verdeling van het nationale inkomen 1946', *Statistische en econometrische onderzoekingen*, Vol. 4 (1): 36–8.

Centraal Bureau voor de Statistiek (CBS) (1960) *Regional Accounts of the Netherlands*, The Hague: CBS.

Centraal Bureau voor de Statistiek (CBS) (1965) 'De regionale inkomens uit nijverheid, landbouw en dienstenverlening in 1950 en 1960', *Maandschrift van het Centraal Bureau voor de Statistiek*, Vol. 60 (8): 833–40.

Centraal Bureau voor de Statistiek (CBS) (1968) *Regionale rekeningen 1960*. The Hague: CBS.

Centraal Bureau voor de Statistiek (CBS) (1970) *Regionale rekeningen 1965*, Vol. 2, The Hague: CBS.

Centraal Bureau voor de Statistiek (CBS) (1983) *Regionale economische ontwikkeling 1973–1977*, The Hague: CBS.

Centraal Bureau voor de Statistiek (CBS) (1990) *Regionale economische jaarcijfers: tijdreeksen 1970–1985*, Voorburg: CBS.

Chenery, H.B. and Clark, P.G. (1959) *Interindustry Economics*, New York: John Wiley & Sons.

Corden, W.M. and Neary, J.P. (1982) 'Booming sector and de-industrialisation in a small open economy', *The Economic Journal*, Vol. 92 (368): 825–48.

de Jong, H.J. (1992) 'Dutch inland transport in the nineteenth century', *The Journal of Transport History*, Vol. 13 (1): 1–23.

de Jong, H.J. (2003) *Catching Up Twice: The Nature of Dutch Industrial Growth during the Twentieth Century in a Comparative Perspective*, Berlin: de Gruyter.

de Jong, H.J. (2005) 'Between the devil and the deep blue sea: the Dutch economy during World War I', in S. Broadberry and M. Harrison (eds), *The Economics of World War I*, Cambridge: Cambridge University Press, pp. 137–68.

de Vries, J. (1981) *Barges and Capitalism: Passenger Transportation in the Dutch Economy, 1632–1839*, Utrecht: HES Publishers.

de Vries, J. (1984) *European Urbanization, 1500–1800*, London: Routledge.

den Bakker, G.P. (1992) *Origin and Development of the Dutch National Accounts, No. NA-56*, Voorburg: Central Bureau of Statistics, National Accounts Research Division.

Derksen, J.B.D. (1942a) 'De regionale verdeeling van het volksinkomen', *Tijdschrift voor Economische Geographie*, Vol. 33: 133–9.

Derksen, J.B.D. (1942b) 'Enkele schattingen over het volksinkomen der provinciën', *Maandschrift van het Centraal Bureau voor de Statistiek*, Vol. 37: 216–25.

Eding, G., Stelder, T.M., Vos, E.R. and Oosterhaven, J. (1995) *Bi-regionale interactie: nieuwe input-output tabellen voor Groningen, Friesland, Drenthe en Overijssel voor 1990*, Groningen: Stichting Ruimtelijke Economie Groningen.

European Commission (2014) *Investment for Jobs and Growth: 6th Report on Economic, Social and Territorial Cohesion*, Brussels: European Commission.

Filarski, R. and Mom, G. (2008) *Van transport naar mobiliteit, Deel 1: De transportrevolutie (1800–1900). Deel 2: De mobiliteitsexplosie (1895–2005)*, Zutphen: Walburg Pers.

Geary, F. and Stark, T. (2002) 'Examining Ireland's post-famine economic growth performance', *The Economic Journal*, Vol. 112 (482): 919–35.

Henderson, J.V. (2010) 'Cities and development', *Journal of Regional Science*, Vol. 50 (1): 515–40.

Klemann, H.A.M. (2002) *Nederland 1938–1948. Economie en samenleving in jaren van oorlog en bezetting*, Amsterdam: Boom.

Krugman, P. (1991) *Geography and Trade*, Cambridge, MA: MIT Press.

Leontief, W. (1951) *The Structure of the American Economy 1919–1939*, New York: Oxford University Press.

Lucas, R.E., Jr. (1988) 'On the mechanics of economic development', *Journal of Monetary Economics*, Vol. 22 (1): 3–42.

Marshall, A. (1986) *Principles of Economics*, 8th edition, Basingstoke: Macmillan.

Oomens, C.A. and den Bakker, G.P. (1994) 'De beroepsbevolking in Nederland 1849–1990' ['The Dutch labour force 1849–1990'], *Supplement bij de Sociaal-Economische Maandstatistiek*, Vol. 2: 1–43.

Ottaviano, G.I.P. (2008) 'Infrastructure and economic geography: an overview of theory and evidence', *Infrastructure Investment, Growth and Cohesion: The Economics of Regional Transport Investment, European Investment Bank Papers*, No. 13 (2): 8–35.

Rijken van Olst, H. (1958) *De provincie Groningen en overig Nederland*, Groningen: J.B. Wolters.

Romer, P. (1986) 'Increasing returns and endogenous growth', *Journal of Political Economy*, Vol. 94 (5): 1002–37.

Sala-i-Martin, X. (1996) 'Regional cohesion: evidence and theories of regional growth and convergence', *European Economic Review*, Vol. 40 (6): 1325–52.

Sluyterman, K.E. (2005) *Dutch Enterprise in the Twentieth Century: Business Enterprise in a Small Open Economy*, London: Routledge.

Smits, J., Horlings, E. and van Zanden, J.L. (2000) *Dutch GNP and Its Components, 1800–1913*, Groningen: Groningen Growth and Development Centre.

Solow, R.M. (1956) 'A contribution to the theory of economic growth', *Quarterly Journal of Economics*, Vol. 70 (1): 65–94.

Stone, R.A. (1961) *Input-Output Accounts and National Accounts*, Paris: Organisation for European Economic Co-operation.

Timmer, M.P., Erumban, A.A., Los, B., Stehrer, R. and de Vries, G.J. (2013) 'Slicing up global value chains', GGDC research memorandum, No. 135, Groningen: University of Groningen.

United Nations (1947) 'Measurement of national income and the construction of social accounts', *Studies and Reports on Statistical Methods, No. 7*, Geneva: United Nations.

van Ark, B. and de Jong, H.J. (1996) 'Accounting for economic growth in the Netherlands since 1913', *Economic and Social History in the Netherlands*, Vol. 7: 199–242.

van Zanden, J.L. (1987) 'Economische groei in Nederland in de negentiende eeuw: enkele nieuwe resultaten', *Economisch- en Sociaal-Historisch Jaarboek*, Vol. 50: 51–76.

van Zanden, J.L. (1997) *The Economic History of the Netherlands, 1914–1995: A Small Open Economy in the 'Long' Twentieth Century*, London: Routledge.

van Zanden, J.L. and Griffiths, R.T. (1989) *Economische geschiedenis van Nederland in de 20e eeuw*, Utrecht: Het Spectrum.

van Zanden, J.L. and van Riel, A. (2004) *The Strictures of Inheritance: The Dutch Economy in the Nineteenth Century*, Princeton, NJ: Princeton University Press.

3.9 Regional income in Norway, 1900–2010

Jørgen Modalsli

1. Introduction

Norway has experienced substantial economic growth since the early twentieth century. However, until now, no consistent calculation has been made of how the gains from economic growth have been allocated across the country. This article presents, for the first time, a unified estimate of 'gross regional product' from 1900 to 2010, based on existing GDP estimates, census data and contemporary income tabulations.

1.1 The geography of Norway

Norway is one of Europe's largest and most sparsely populated countries, with a total land area of 323,771 km^2. The Norwegian mainland extends north to the 71st parallel, at the same latitude of the northernmost reaches of Alaska or Russia. The southernmost point of Norway is closer to London, Florence and St Petersburg than it is to Kirkenes in the far north-east. In 1900, Norway was a country of 2.2 million people. According to the Maddison database, Norwegian GDP per capita in 1900 was 42 per cent of that in Great Britain and 90 per cent of that in Sweden. By 2010, Norway had grown to become one of the richest countries in the world, with a GDP per capita of US$57,539[1] – higher than all major European countries – and a population of 4.85 million.

In 1900, there was large regional heterogeneity in economic activity across Norway. In the county of Sogn og Fjordane, 80 per cent of the population depended on the primary sector in 1900, compared to only 16 per cent in the capital region. By 2010, all regions had more than two-thirds of the population employed in the tertiary sector. Moreover, communications between regions have greatly improved; in 1909, the railway between eastern and western Norway opened, in 1962 Bodø in northern Norway was connected to the railway network, and from the late 1960s onwards a large network of short-runway airports have been in operation in the far western and northern parts of the country.

It is of central interest to know how economic development and increased integration affected economic growth in the various regions of Norway. Did improved communications and mobility lead to convergence, or did industrial development and agglomeration effects lead some regions to move ahead faster than others? This chapter contributes to the knowledge about Norwegian regional productivity in three ways. First, existing regional GDP estimates from 1965 onwards are collected and harmonized. Second, historical income data are used to extend the estimates back to 1900. Third, a preliminary analysis of the data is conducted. For brevity, the term 'regional GDP' will be used when referring to the gross regional products.

1.2 Availability of historical data

The collection of data on Norway has a long and extensive history. The first full-count census was conducted in 1801, and the statistical agency was established in 1876. Since the mid-nineteenth century, Norway has been divided into 19 or 20 counties (called *Amt* before 1919, *Fylker* thereafter), which have formed the basis for the central government's execution of various policies. In the nineteenth century, governors' reports (*Amtmannsrapporter*) laboriously detailed economic, social and geographic aspects of the various parts of the counties, though mostly in a narrative format that is not amenable to quantitative analysis. Decennial censuses contain detailed information on the population structure and occupations from 1865 onwards, and the reinstitution of the state income tax in 1893 marks the start of a nearly continuous series on income.

Norway first published national GDP estimates in 1952, and regional GDP at the county level was first reported in 1965. As in any reporting of long-run GDP series extending prior to the development of GDP methodologies, the data in this chapter must be based on new applications of historical data, subject to the constraints given by the data that were collected at various times.

A natural starting point for the construction of historical regional GDP series would be the method used by Geary and Stark (2002) for Great Britain and Ireland between 1861 and 1911. Geary and Stark use data on the size of the labour force in the sectors of the economy combined with a data set of regional wages to approximate the level of output in each region. While the rich Norwegian census data easily facilitate an allocation of the labour force in each region to a set of sectors, sectoral wage statistics frequently lack data on the regional composition of wages. As there is no consistent series available for wages by region and sector for the period under study, a direct application of the Geary-Stark method is not feasible. However, it is still possible to construct regional estimates by shifting the focus from wages to income.

The most accurate data on Norwegian incomes come from the tax statistics. The municipality of residence of the individual taxpayer is recorded by the tax authorities, and for most years since 1893, lists of mean income and mean taxes paid by municipality are published. Notably, publication of the data continued uninterrupted through both political independence from Sweden (1905) and military occupation by Nazi Germany (1940–1945). These tax data will form the basis for the construction of regional GDP prior to 1970 presented in this chapter.

Some academic studies exist that describe the regional economic development in Norway in the last four decades. Østbye and Westerlund (2011) use a unified series based on the regional GDP statistics from 1980 to 2000, and find strong signs of convergence across counties in Norway. The only other existing estimates of regional growth known to this author are the income-based convergence measures used by Rattsø and Stokke (2014), where wage incomes from the tax statistics are used to construct a measure of regional productivity at the level of 89 labour market regions. Rattsø and Stokke find convergence in income between these regions from 1972 and 2008.

2. Constructing a regional GDP series, 1900–2010

2.1 Regional units

The division of Norway into regional units has been relatively stable at the county level between 1900 and 2010. There have been two major changes to county borders. In 1948, Oslo was merged with the neighbouring municipality of Aker, transferring 131,000 people from Akershus county to Oslo county. In 1972, the county of Bergen, Norway's second largest city, with a population of 112,000, was merged with the surrounding county of Hordaland, reducing the number of counties from 20 to 19.

When combining income estimates (by residence of the income recipient) and production estimates (based on area of economic activity), high commuting flows can be a challenge, as incomes are then taxed at a different location than where the economic activity takes place. However, with the exception of Oslo and Bergen, the counties are of large geographic extent and there is limited commuting across county borders. This is particularly the case when the data are extended back in time. To alleviate possible mismeasurement of Oslo and Bergen's regional GDP, the following analysis will merge the cities with their surrounding counties: Oslo with Akershus, and Bergen with Hordaland. This gives 18 counties, corresponding to NUTS 3 regions, with the exception of Oslo+Akershus, which is a combination of two NUTS 3 regions. These can further be aggregated to seven NUTS 2 regions, as shown in Table 3.9.A.1.[2]

2.2 Regional GDP estimates

To construct a data series for gross regional product in Norway, the natural starting point is the regional GDP indices produced by Statistics Norway. These were first published in 1965 and later approximately every three to six years, at uneven intervals (Zahirovic and Berge 2013). However, while the national accounts in general have been revised for historical consistency, this is not the case for the regional GDP estimates. In particular, the inclusion and omission of particular industries that are hard to allocate regionally has changed between the publications. In all official estimates, the non-allocated activity is added to a fictional county to maintain compatibility with national estimates.

In 2011, the national accounts for Norway were revised and updated for the entire period 1970–2012 (Gimming et al. 2011). While the main national accounts do not contain a regional decomposition, there is a split of aggregate production between a 'mainland' and 'non-mainland' category. 'Non-mainland' production refers to petroleum activities and ocean transport (Statistics Norway 2012: 10). These activities are sensitive to international price and business cycle movements and are industries of low labor intensity. For this reason, domestic discussion of fluctuations in Norwegian GDP usually refer to 'mainland GDP' only. Non-mainland GDP constituted 8 per cent of GDP in 1970 and 19 per cent in 2010.

Regional GDP estimates do not explicitly refer to mainland and non-mainland activity. As it is not evident to which county the non-mainland activity should be allocated, in this article only the mainland activity will be allocated explicitly to counties.

Existing regional GDP estimates are available for 1965, 1973, 1976, 1980, 1983, 1986, 1990, 1992–1993, 1995 and 1997–2010. In 1980 and earlier, a substantial part of economic activity was not allocated to any specific sector because of data limitations.

In the 1973 and 1980 official regional GDP estimates, the documentation clearly states that the following components were not allocated to counties:

1 Export, imports and inventory changes.
2 Production activities in shipping abroad, petroleum activities, coal mining on Svalbard.
3 Air and railway transport, telecommunications.
4 Parts of consumption and investment in central government, including defence.
5 Redistributive sectors in the national accounts.
6 Parts of the commodity trade sector.

The composition for 1965 is not given in similar detail but it is reasonable to expect the list of omitted sectors to be longer. In 1990 and later estimates, points 3, 4 and 5 are allocated to counties, as well as some of the mainland-based petroleum activities. There were also some changes in definitions between 1990 and 2000. However, these are less important than the 1980–1990 changes, and harder to correct for. For this reason, the ambition of the correction must be restricted to making the 1973 and 1980 estimates comparable to the 1990 estimate. For 1965, a similar exercise is conducted to compare the adjusted regional GDP data to information from the income statistics.

To achieve this objective, data from the 1960 to 1980 censuses were used to obtain data on employment in the industries that were allocated in the 1990 regional GDP estimates, but not in earlier estimates. This was done based on registry files of all individuals in the two censuses. For each county, a tabulation of the total number of people in key industries and occupations was made. A detailed overview of the relevant classification can be found in Vassenden (1987). The key industries are extraction of oil and natural gas, supply of electricity and gas services, or post and telephone communications (codes 22, 41 or

72, respectively), as well as the sub-industries of land or sea transport (codes 711 or 712). In addition, occupations related to railways (codes 63 and 652) and military occupations (code A) were included. This corresponds as closely as possible to the difference in classifications between the 1973 and 1980 regional GDPs, on the one hand, and the 1990 and onwards regional GDPs, on the other. The key assumption for the allocation of the remaining GDP share in the regional GDP estimates of 1973 and 1980 is then that there are no systematic unobserved productivity differences in these sectors across regions, so that the unallocated economic activity is proportional to the share of the population working in the unallocated sectors. In 1990 and later years, the non-allocated activity was not included in the estimates used here; this is equivalent to scaling the allocation of this activity by regional GDP shares.

Table 3.9.1 gives the official and revised estimates of (gross) regional GDP in Norway between 1965 and 2010. The revision of the 1973 and 1980 estimates conducted here scales down the level of activity in the capital region (Oslo+Akershus), while the activity in some coastal counties, in particular in western Norway, is scaled up. To extend the series back to 1900, we turn to the income data. To better be able to evaluate the transition from income-based to GDP-based estimates, 1965 and 1973 shares are calculated using both methods.

2.3 Income-based estimates

For historical GDP values, estimates are based on income data. The income variable reported is that of 'assessed income' (*alminnelig inntekt*), a wider income concept than simply taxable income. Both capital and labour income is included. Total income for counties was digitized from annual reports from 1900 to 1960, as well as for 1965 for comparison to the official regional GDP estimate. For 1973, a similar extract was made from the registry income file held at Statistics Norway (digitized individual incomes are available from 1967 onwards).

For each county, total income was taken as a proxy for total economic activity. The resulting county shares are reported in Table 3.9.2. For 1965 and 1973, adjusted GDP shares are also reported. The discrepancies are in general on the order of a couple of tenths of a percentage point or less, though for the county of Nordland it is as large as 0.7 and 0.6 percentage points. As the documentation for the 1965 official regional GDP estimates is not as detailed as for the later estimates, income data will be used up to and including 1965 and regional GDP data from 1973 onwards.

2.4 National GDP

The main focus of the analysis in this chapter is on the relevant shares of national GDP within Norway rather than comparisons to other countries. However, it is still important to keep in mind how the data should be scaled if used in international comparisons, or to study growth over time. The official GDP series is based on the 2012 revision going back to 1970 spliced with earlier estimates; the version

Table 3.9.1 Estimates of regional GDP shares: official and adjusted estimates

	1965		*1973*		*1980*		*1990*	*2000*	*2010*
	Adjusted	*Official*	*Adjusted*	*Official*	*Adjusted*	*Official*	*Official*	*Official*	*Official*
Østfold	5.5%	5.6%	5.3%	5.4%	5.1%	5.3%	4.5%	4.3%	3.9%
Oslo+Akershus	28.9%	30.4%	28.5%	29.9%	26.4%	28.7%	32.4%	32.9%	31.3%
Hedmark	3.8%	3.8%	3.7%	3.7%	3.9%	3.8%	3.4%	3.2%	2.8%
Oppland	3.3%	3.3%	3.5%	3.5%	3.6%	3.6%	3.1%	3.0%	2.8%
Buskerud	4.9%	5.0%	5.2%	5.3%	5.2%	5.4%	4.9%	4.5%	4.6%
Vestfold	4.5%	4.4%	4.4%	4.2%	4.0%	3.9%	3.7%	3.8%	3.6%
Telemark	4.6%	4.8%	3.8%	3.8%	4.0%	4.4%	3.4%	3.0%	2.8%
Aust-Agder	1.8%	1.6%	1.9%	1.8%	2.0%	1.8%	1.8%	1.9%	1.6%
Vest-Agder	2.9%	2.8%	3.0%	2.9%	3.5%	3.4%	3.2%	3.0%	3.4%
Rogaland	6.1%	5.9%	6.9%	7.0%	7.3%	7.3%	8.3%	8.6%	10.5%
Bergen+Hordaland	8.9%	8.5%	9.0%	8.7%	9.1%	8.5%	9.1%	9.4%	10.0%
Sogn og Fjordane	2.0%	2.0%	2.0%	2.0%	2.6%	2.5%	2.2%	2.2%	2.0%
Møre og Romsdal	4.7%	4.5%	5.0%	4.9%	5.1%	4.9%	4.4%	4.8%	5.1%
Sør-Trøndelag	5.4%	5.3%	5.6%	5.5%	5.6%	5.3%	5.0%	5.3%	5.6%
Nord-Trøndelag	2.2%	2.1%	2.3%	2.2%	2.4%	2.3%	2.2%	2.1%	1.9%
Nordland	5.8%	5.4%	5.3%	4.9%	5.4%	4.7%	4.2%	4.2%	4.1%
Troms	2.7%	2.5%	2.9%	2.7%	3.1%	2.7%	2.9%	2.7%	2.7%
Finnmark	1.8%	1.8%	1.6%	1.5%	1.6%	1.4%	1.3%	1.2%	1.3%

Table 3.9.2 Regional income shares

County	*1900*	*1910*	*1920*	*1930*	*1940*	*1950*	*1960*	*1965*		*1973*	
	Inc	*Inc*	*Inc*	*Inc*	*Inc*	*Inc*	*Inc*	*Inc*	*GDP*	*Inc*	*GDP*
Østfold	7.3%	7.5%	5.8%	6.5%	5.8%	6.6%	6.1%	5.8%	5.5%	5.8%	5.3%
Oslo+Akershus	27.9%	26.6%	32.5%	34.1%	34.2%	30.2%	30.4%	29.3%	28.9%	28.6%	28.5%
Hedmark	4.9%	5.1%	3.6%	3.2%	3.5%	4.0%	4.1%	3.9%	3.8%	4.0%	3.7%
Oppland	3.5%	3.7%	2.8%	3.3%	3.1%	3.6%	3.7%	3.6%	3.3%	3.8%	3.5%
Buskerud	5.4%	5.9%	4.8%	4.9%	4.6%	5.1%	5.0%	5.2%	4.9%	5.4%	5.2%
Vestfold	5.1%	4.8%	4.8%	6.6%	4.8%	5.6%	5.2%	4.7%	4.5%	4.6%	4.4%
Telemark	4.7%	4.8%	4.9%	4.3%	3.9%	4.3%	4.2%	4.2%	4.6%	3.6%	3.8%
Aust-Agder	3.3%	2.8%	1.9%	2.2%	2.1%	1.8%	1.8%	1.9%	1.8%	1.8%	1.9%
Vest-Agder	3.1%	2.8%	2.5%	2.4%	3.2%	2.6%	2.8%	2.9%	2.9%	3.0%	3.0%
Rogaland	4.6%	5.0%	6.1%	5.1%	6.3%	6.1%	6.0%	6.3%	6.1%	6.6%	6.9%
Bergen+Hordaland	8.9%	9.0%	12.5%	9.8%	9.3%	9.4%	8.8%	9.2%	8.9%	9.1%	9.0%
Sogn og Fjordane	2.2%	2.0%	1.3%	1.5%	1.4%	1.9%	1.9%	1.9%	2.0%	2.0%	2.0%
Møre og Romsdal	4.2%	4.2%	3.9%	3.3%	3.1%	4.1%	4.2%	4.5%	4.7%	4.8%	5.0%
Sør-Trøndelag	5.3%	5.8%	5.5%	5.0%	5.7%	5.2%	5.1%	5.3%	5.4%	5.6%	5.6%
Nord-Trøndelag	2.6%	2.5%	1.8%	2.0%	2.1%	2.2%	2.3%	2.2%	2.2%	2.3%	2.3%
Nordland	4.1%	4.3%	2.9%	3.4%	3.7%	4.0%	4.8%	5.0%	5.8%	4.7%	5.3%
Troms	2.0%	2.1%	1.5%	1.4%	1.9%	1.9%	2.2%	2.6%	2.7%	2.8%	2.9%
Finnmark	1.1%	1.2%	0.9%	1.1%	1.3%	1.2%	1.4%	1.5%	1.8%	1.6%	1.6%

as available in February 2014 was used.[3] If one wants to estimate total 'county GDP', the appropriate estimation method would be:

$$GDP_{county} = share_{county} * share_{mainland} * GDP_{Norway}$$

where the regional shares are obtained from the adjusted official regional GDP estimates (1973 and later) and income statistics (1965 and earlier), explained above. The mainland share is taken from the 2012 revision back to 1970; before 1970, no official estimates are available. While petroleum activities were negligible before 1970, international shipping was a major source of employment and income for the Norwegian economy. In lieu of good data on the size of the shipping sector compared to the national economy before 1970, the 1970 share of 7.695 per cent of total GDP was used for all years 1900–1965 (see Table 3.9.A.3). For this reason, the non-mainland portion reported before 1970 should be considered as a scaling factor when comparing Norwegian counties to counties without large-scale international shipping rather than a reflection of economic trends in the offshore economy. Moreover, it is assumed that the regional distribution of domestically reported incomes of seamen in international shipping is proportional to the general level of income in each county.

While estimates of regional GDP give valuable insights in themselves, GDP per capita is usually a more relevant variable for studies of economic development. We now turn to the estimates of population by county.

2.5 Population

The population data are obtained from the Norwegian decennial census, which was conducted every 10 years from 1900 onwards, with the exception of 1940 (postponed to 1946 because of the German occupation) and 2000–2010 (conducted in 2001 and 2011, respectively). Until the establishment of the Central Population Register in the 1960s, there was no attempt by the central statistical authorities to calculate intra-country migration between census years. This could potentially cause problems for the 1940 observation. However, a special population count was conducted in August 1939 for the purpose of coffee and sugar rationing; the results, previously unpublished, are used here as an estimate of the 1940 population.[4] For 2000 and 2010, regional population numbers are available from the Central Population Register.

Sector employment shares (primary, secondary and tertiary) are obtained from official statistics (the census for 1900–1930 and 1950–1990, other sources for 2000 and 2010, no observations for 1940), presented in Table 3.9.A.2. While these are not used directly in the generation of the regional GDP estimates presented here, they are included in the final tabulations for comparison with the industry structure of other countries.

Population numbers are reported in Table 3.9.3. There are large differences in the size of the regions; Oslo and Akershus hold 15 per cent of the population in

Table 3.9.3 Regional population ('000s)

County	*1900*	*1910*	*1920*	*1930*	*1940*	*1950*	*1960*	*1970*	*1980*	*1990*	*2000*	*2010*
Østfold	137	152	160	167	170	185	202	219	232	238	248	272
Oslo+Akershus	344	370	438	490	549	617	698	800	822	873	975	1123
Hedmark	126	135	150	158	161	173	178	179	187	187	187	191
Oppland	116	119	129	138	145	160	166	172	180	182	183	185
Buskerud	113	124	137	143	143	156	168	196	214	225	237	258
Vestfold	105	109	124	134	135	155	172	173	186	197	213	231
Telemark	99	108	125	128	124	136	150	157	162	163	165	168
Aust-Agder	80	76	75	74	70	76	77	80	90	97	102	108
Vest-Agder	82	82	83	81	88	97	108	123	136	144	156	170
Rogaland	128	141	166	173	184	211	237	266	302	336	373	428
Bergen+Hordaland	208	223	248	263	276	311	339	371	391	409	435	477
Sogn og Fjordane	89	90	90	92	92	98	100	101	105	107	108	107
Møre og Romsdal	136	145	159	165	169	191	212	223	236	238	243	251
Sør-Trøndelag	135	148	167	175	182	198	211	232	244	250	263	291
Nord-Trøndelag	83	85	89	96	98	110	117	118	125	127	127	132
Nordland	152	165	174	187	198	222	239	243	244	240	239	236
Troms	74	82	91	97	103	117	127	137	146	147	151	156
Finnmark	33	38	44	53	60	64	72	76	79	74	74	73

1900 and 23 per cent in 2010. The smallest in terms of population is Finnmark in the far north, with around 1.5 per cent of the population both in 1900 and 2010. There are only a few cases of population decline in absolute numbers. Aust-Agder experienced continuous decline between 1900 and 1940. This was a time of substantial overseas emigration and (in the 1930s) low birth rates; some neighbouring counties also had negative population growth in some of the decades. Since 1990, the northern counties of Nordland and Finnmark have also experienced population decline, though the population of northern Norway as a whole has grown.

3. Estimates of regional GDP per capita

With these results, one can proceed to calculate regional GDP per capita shares by dividing GDP shares by population shares. All results are presented scaled (i.e. as a ratio to national GDP per capita).

3.1 Trends

Figure 3.9.1 shows the development of relative GDP per capita by county for all counties, grouped by NUTS 2 regions. In the first panel, we observe that the capital region (Oslo and Akershus) has much higher GDP per capita than any other region. In 1900, the level was 81 per cent higher than the national average; in 2010, this excess was down to 36 per cent. While the inland counties of Hedmark and Oppland have lower-than-average GDP per capita in the entire time period, most of the coastal counties in southern Norway have higher-than-average levels at some point in time. The south-eastern coastal counties (Østfold, Buskerud, Vestfold and Telemark) show a similar trend of moderate secular decrease from higher-than-average to lower-than-average GDP per capita. In the south-west, the trend is flatter; we see an effect of the oil boom in Rogaland after 1980; while offshore oil activities are not allocated to any specific region, there are still spillovers to local economic activities, and much of the administration of the oil extraction takes place in the Stavanger region in Rogaland. Within the three western counties of Hordaland, Sogn og Fjordane and Møre og Romsdal, there is convergence; this is related to the diminishing rural–urban divide between Bergen and the rest of the region. The Trøndelag counties in central Norway have relatively flat trends, with Sør-Trøndelag (including Trondheim) exhibiting higher GDP per capita than Nord-Trøndelag. Finally, while northern Norway is still considerably poorer than the national mean, we see a strong catch-up effect between 1930 and 1970. The population of the county of Finnmark was forced to evacuate by the Germans at the end of the Second World War, and a large portion of the buildings were destroyed; despite this, the estimates show only a minor decrease in Finnmark GDP per capita from 1940 to 1950.

The question of whether levels of GDP per capita across countries have become more equal over time can be studied using the coefficient of variation of the county GDP per capita level (capturing the concept of sigma-convergence). The development of the coefficient of variation is shown in Figure 3.9.2.

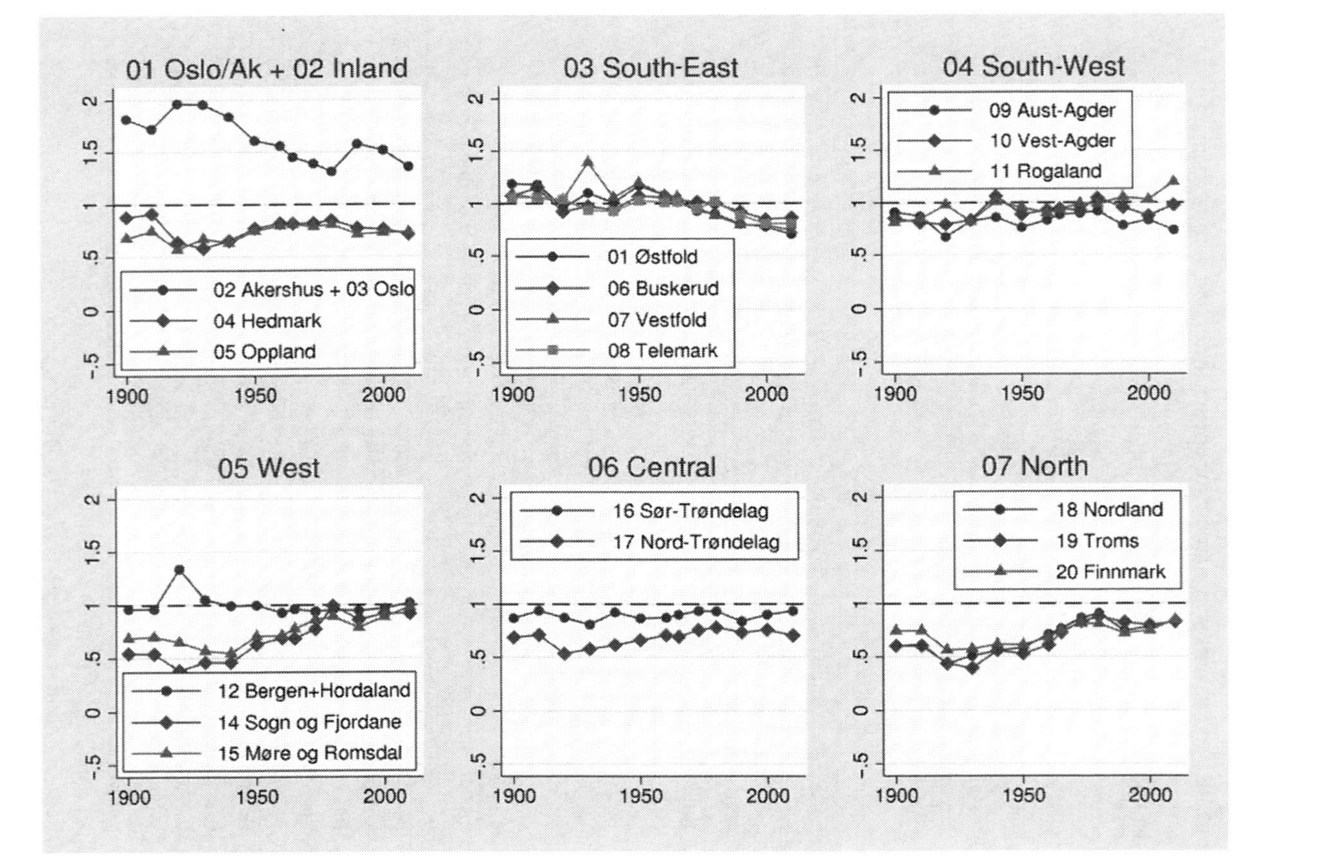

Figure 3.9.1 GDP per capita, relative to national mean

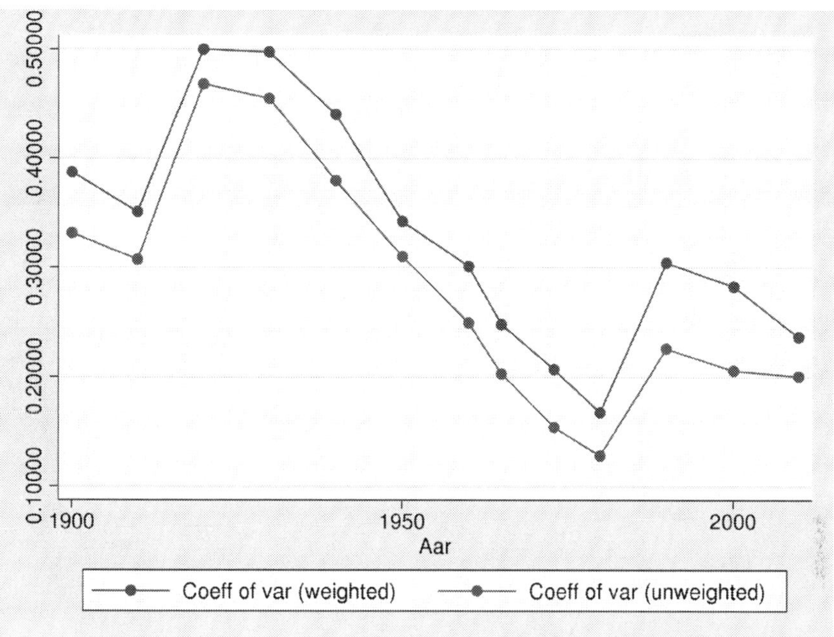

Figure 3.9.2 Between-region coefficient of variation (unweighted and population-weighted)

It is evident that the coefficient of variation has decreased markedly over time. However, there was an increase between 1910 and 1920, and again between 1980 and 1990. The question of convergence can be further investigated using a simple regression approach where economic growth is regressed on the initial productivity level (capturing the concept of beta-convergence). The result of such an exercise is shown in Figure 3.9.3, where the horizontal axis gives log GDP in 1900 and the vertical axis the difference between log GDP in 2010 and 1900.

From 1900 to 2010, there are strong tendencies towards convergence – regions with lower initial GDP levels grow faster. If we split the sample in 1950, there is strong convergence in the latter period but much lower convergence in the initial period (not shown here). In Figure 3.9.2, we observe that the period of strongest sigma-convergence was between 1920 and 1980; this is confirmed by examining beta-convergence over the same period, where we get an R^2 of 94 per cent (compared to 65 per cent for the entire period 1900–2010).

3.2 Divergence, convergence, divergence

When we examine Figure 3.9.2, it is clear that the across-county growth pattern in Norway can be divided into three periods, as marked by two upward jumps

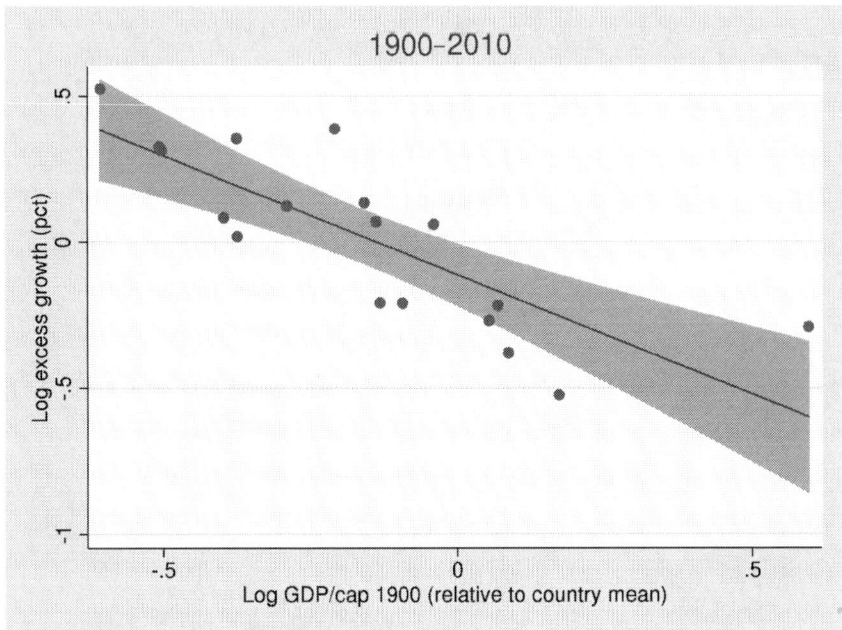

Figure 3.9.3 Convergence, 1900–2010 (average regional growth compared to initial position)

(1910–1920 and 1980–1990) in the coefficient of variation with a more gradual decrease in variation between these jumps.

Interestingly, the first jump coincides with the dramatic changes in Europe identified by Atkinson and Piketty (2007, 2010) and Piketty (2014). These are usually explained by physical destruction and inflationary policies during the First World War. Norway did not actively participate in the war, though there were still many consequences for the Norwegian economy, such as high inflation. The estimates of top income shares by Aaberge and Atkinson (2010) do show an increase in top income shares between 1913 and 1929, suggesting an increase in inequality in this period. If it is the case that top income earners are disproportionately concentrated in regions with higher average incomes, it is reasonable to expect such a co-movement between regional and interpersonal income inequality.

The cross-county inequality increase appears to be driven by income increases in coastal counties. Comparing county growth rates to shipping tonnage per capita in 1920 does show a significant positive relationship between the variables, suggesting a role for shipping in this growth. However, other conditions probably also played a role.

The second jump coincides with liberalization of capital markets in the 1980s, and is largely driven by income growth in the capital region of Oslo. Again, this

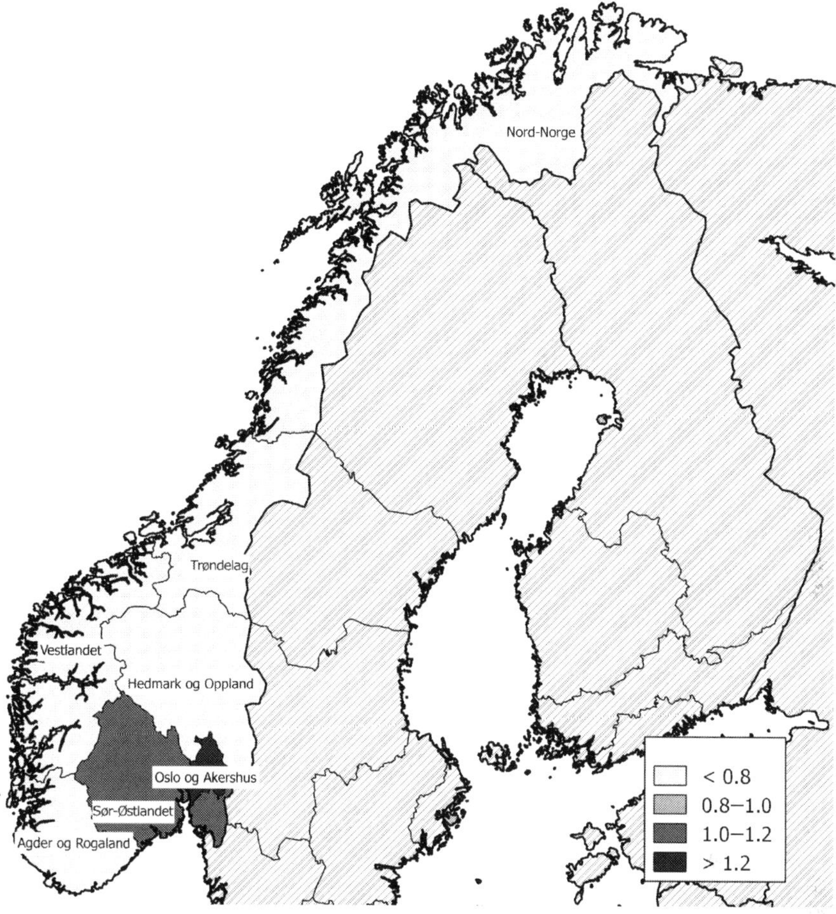

Map 3.9.1 Relative GDP per capita relative to national mean, 1900 (Norway = 1)

coincides with an increase in top income shares and rising income inequality in general. There is also some evidence of an increase in regional GDP in Rogaland following the discovery of oil in the North Sea and the establishment of Stavanger as Norway's 'oil capital'. In this case, the per capita increase is somewhat moderated by a corresponding increase in population. In addition, regions further away from the oilfields also gained substantially from the oil boom through supplier contracts and other related activity, such as finance.

3.3 GDP per capita and employment shares

Employment shares by sector in Norway have followed the traditional development pattern, with the share of the primary sector decreasing from 50 per cent in

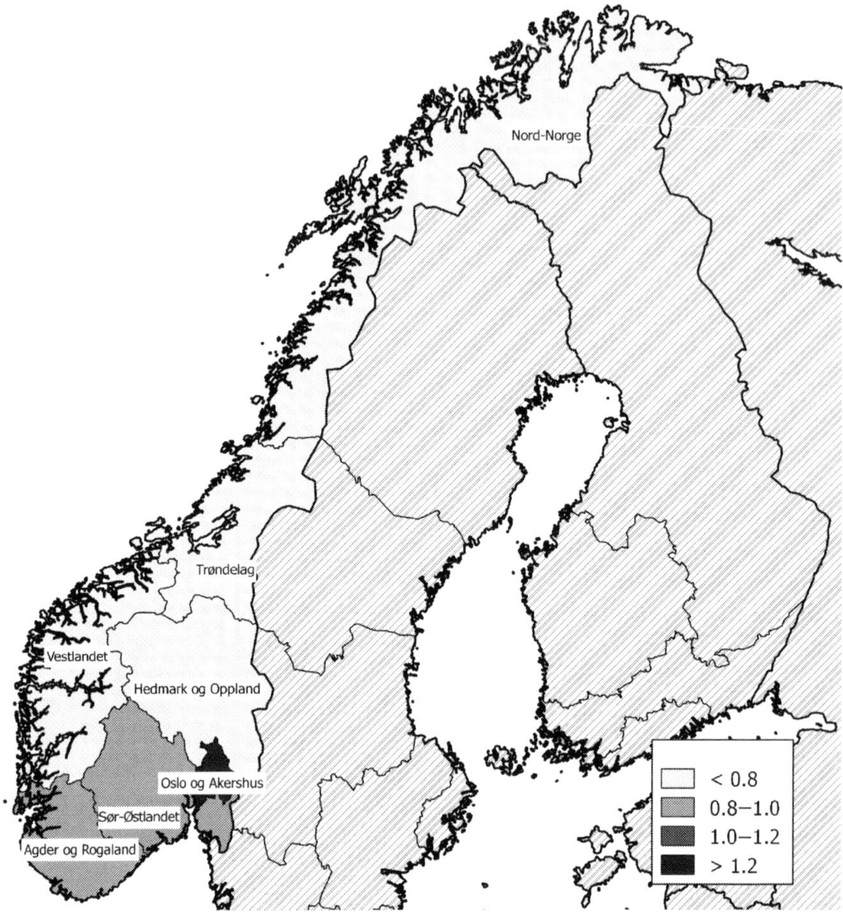

Map 3.9.2 Relative GDP per capita relative to national mean, 1960 (Norway = 1)

1900 to 3 per cent in 2010. Secondary sector employment has increased from 29 per cent in 1900 to 39 per cent in 1960, and further decreased to 20 per cent in 2011, while employment in the tertiary sector has increased in the period studied here. With county data, we can see whether the same relationships hold in the cross section. This was investigated using simple univariate regressions with relative GDP per capita as dependent variable and employment shares as independent variable, for each year separately (except 1940, where there are no census data, and 1960, where there is no regional GDP estimate).

As expected, there is a negative relationship between employment shares in the primary sector and the regional GDP share per year. The relationship is statistically significant for all years except 2010. The point estimate of the coefficient varies between −1.37 in 1910, meaning that a 1 percentage point increase in the

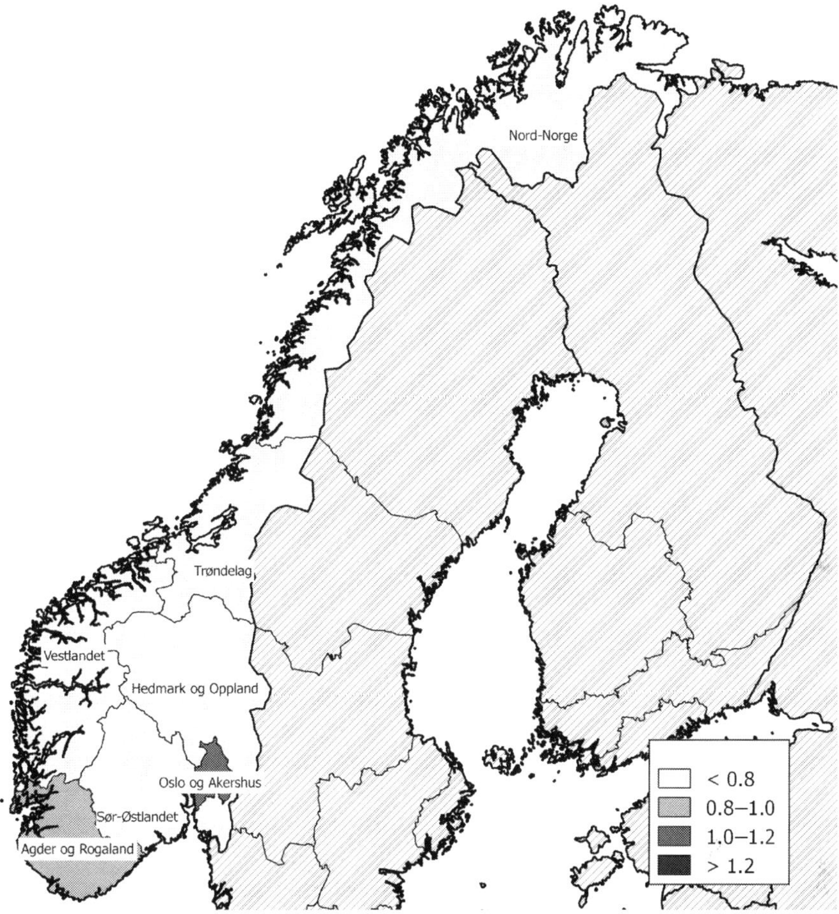

Map 3.9.3 Relative GDP per capita relative to national mean, 2010 (Norway = 1)

employment share of the primary sector is associated with a decrease in regional GDP per capita of 1.37 per cent of the national GDP per capita, and −2.82 in 2000. The coefficient on secondary sector employment is significantly positive for all years until 1960, with point estimates from 3.58 in 1930 to 1.69 in 1960. The coefficient on tertiary sector employment shares is positive and significant in all years except 2010.

It does appear that traditional economic mechanisms contributed to regional growth in Norway. As migration flows are often explained by economic factors, it could be expected that population growth would be positively associated with GDP share growth. However, there is no systematic correlation between the decennial growth rates of population and the growth of regional GDP per capita.

4. Data challenges, interpretations and robustness checks

The data presented here constitute a preliminary view of regional growth patterns, and we should expect more refined estimates to emerge in the future. One limitation of this chapter is that only one data point is provided for each decade; this constraint was largely imposed to fit the scope of this book. However, annual data are available, but would increase the data entry job for the pre-1967 estimates tenfold. There are also some other issues that merit discussion.

4.1 Ownership, income and activity

A concern with the use of the income methodology compared to official regional GDP estimates or the Geary-Stark method is the treatment of income to absentee owners. Ownership of farms, forestry, ships or other assets could be concentrated in cities, while the actual economic activity took place in the countryside. Norwegian counties are large and most contain one or several cities. While we do not observe ownership rates directly, the large geographic distances and (historically) inconvenient communications should alleviate the problem of misallocation of income data. There is one data point supporting this assertion: in a 1915 tabulation of the income statistics, income is split between taxpayers resident within and outside the municipality in which the income is generated. For the tax year 1913–1914, 98 per cent of taxpayers were located in the municipality of taxation, accounting for 96 per cent of income, 88 per cent of wealth, and 92 per cent of taxes paid on income and wealth.[5] It would, however, be reasonable to assume that the problem of cross-regional ownership increases slightly over time.

In the official regional GDP estimates, used here from 1973 onwards, efforts have been made to correct for this problem. However, the issue of absentee ownership and possible over-reporting of productivity of urban areas should be kept in mind while analysing the historical data. One example cited by Sørensen (1997) is the allocation of income from electricity production; in a previous estimate of 1990, all income to individuals in the electricity production sector was allocated proportional to the incomes of individuals working in the sector. In the revised numbers (used in this chapter), some of the activity was instead allocated by the actual location of power generation, leading to an upward revision of activity in counties with large hydroelectric power plants.

There are, however, several arguments for why income data can be preferable to the Geary-Stark method of employment shares and wages. First, the data on service industry wages are often hard to obtain. Indeed, Geary and Stark (2002) use a weighted average of manufacturing and agriculture wages to proxy for service wages. Because the composition of the service sector has changed greatly over time, it is hard to judge the representability of these wages. Second, a substantial share of GDP is income that accrues to capital and land; it is not clear that this should be allocated by wage data. This is an important concern for historical studies of Norway, as the primary sector did to a large extent consist of owner-occupier farmers and independent (non-wage-earning) fishermen.

Crafts (2005) uses income data to allocate regional GDP for Great Britain in the same period as Geary and Stark. As the British taxable income to a large extent derives from capital, Crafts argues that it should be combined with the Geary-Stark wage-based data to arrive at regional GDP estimates that incorporate the regional distribution of both labour and capital income. As regional wage data are missing, this is not possible for Norway; however, 'assessed income' in the Norwegian data includes both labour, capital and self-employment income, and tabulations of income by occupation and social group confirm that substantial income is also allocated to occupation groups such as farmers, servants and factory workers.[6]

4.2 Spikes in the data

There are some spikes in the data shown in Figure 3.9.1 that merit further discussion. This is a problem with decennial data, where it is hard to know whether outliers represent a one-off misreporting or part of a larger trend. The two jumps in the regions of Oslo and Akershus (1910–1920 and 1980–1990) drive some of the national trends. As the 1980 and 1990 regional GDP estimates are not directly comparable, it cannot be ruled out that this jump derives from a change in methodology, though it does coincide with a growth of incomes in the financial sector, which is to a large extent located in Oslo.

There are also large jumps in Bergen and Hordaland (a peak in 1930) and in Vestfold (a peak in 1940). While the large positive jump in Bergen's GDP per capita from 1920 to 1930 could be related to a general trend of higher income growth in cities (there is also substantial income growth in Oslo and Akershus from 1920 to 1930), the high incomes in 1940 remain unexplained here. Income data from 1940 reflect the special circumstances of the year of German invasion, and may not be indicative of the general development of the regional economy in the 1930s.

5. Concluding comments

This chapter has documented the regional development of economic activity in Norway from 1900 to 2010. It shows strong income convergence for the period seen as a whole. The convergence trend is interrupted by divergence episodes between 1920 and 1930 and between 1980 and 1990.

Many characteristics of the modern Norwegian economy are shown to have been more 'extreme' in the historical data. The high level of economic activity in the capital region, for example, was even higher historically. Similarly, all counties in northern Norway have regional GDP per capita below the national average, but in the first half of the twentieth century they were even further behind than they are now.

There is scope for improvement of the data in the future. Income statistics at the county level are in principle available annually, and could be used for a more detailed analysis of the time trends in regional development. There are, however, to the knowledge of this author, not sufficient data to merit a full-scale revision of the official regional GDP data back to 1970 in the same way as has been done for the national GDP estimates.

Appendix: source list

Existing official estimates of regional GDP are listed below. All publications in the NOS series are available in PDF versions at www.ssb.no/a/histstat/nos/.

1965: Regionalt nasjonalregnskap 1965, NOS A376 1970

1973: Fylkesfordelt nasjonalregnskap 1973, NOS A925 1978

1976: Fylkesfordelt nasjonalregnskap 1976, NOS B116 1980

1980: Fylkesfordelt nasjonalregnskap 1980, NOS B486 1984

1983: Fylkesfordelt nasjonalregnskap 1983, NOS B687 1987

1986: Fylkesfordelt nasjonalregnskapsstatistikk 1986, NOS B920 1990

1990: Sørensen, Knut: 'Økonomisk utvikling i fylkene 1990–1992 belyst med fylkesfordelt nasjonalregnskap', Økonomiske Analyser 2, 1997, available at: www.ssb.no/a/histstat/oa/

1992: Fylkesfordelt nasjonalregnskapsstatistikk 1993, NOS C323 1996

1997–2004: Fylkesfordelt nasjonalregnskap 1997–2004, NOS D389 2008

2000–2013: Statistics Norway web pages: www.ssb.no/nasjonalregnskap-og-konjunkturer/statistikker/fnr/aar?fane=arkiv (this page also contains links to regional GDP, 1993–1996, and GDP by county, 1993)

Sources of income data: All numbers are taken from the series on municipal finances or tax statistics, published in the NOS series as:

1900: NOS IV 94
1910: NOS VI 14
1920: NOS VII 107
1930: NOS IX 7
1940: NOS X 42
1950: NOS XI 158
1960: NOS XII 95
1965: NOS A 202

The 1973 income data are obtained from the microdata registry file at Statistics Norway.

Aggregate GDP series can be obtained from:

www.ssb.no/nasjonalregnskap-og-konjunkturer/tabeller/aarlig-nasjonalregnskap-fra-1970-csv-filer, Table 3.9.2 (the 2011 revision, data back to 1970)

www.ssb.no/a/histstat/aarbok/ht-0901-bnp.html (historical series; modern estimate is spliced with earlier data)

Appendix: data tables

Table 3.9.A.1 NUTS definitions, ID numbers and land area, by county

ID (national code)	*NUTS 2*	*Name*	*NUTS 3*	*Name*	*Area (2013) (km^2)*
2 and 3	NO01	Oslo og Akershus	NO011+NO012	Oslo+Akershus	5,372
4	NO02	Hedmark og Oppland	NO021	Hedmark	27,398
5	NO02	Hedmark og Oppland	NO022	Oppland	25,192
1	NO03	Sør-Østlandet	NO031	Østfold	4,181
6	NO03	Sør-Østlandet	NO032	Buskerud	14,911
7	NO03	Sør-Østlandet	NO033	Vestfold	2,225
8	NO03	Sør-Østlandet	NO034	Telemark	15,296
9	NO04	Agder og Rogaland	NO041	Aust-Agder	9,158
10	NO04	Agder og Rogaland	NO042	Vest-Agder	7,277
11	NO04	Agder og Rogaland	NO043	Rogaland	9,376
12	NO05	Vestlandet	NO051	Bergen+Hordaland	15,438
14	NO05	Vestlandet	NO052	Sogn og Fjordane	18,623
15	NO05	Vestlandet	NO053	Møre og Romsdal	15,101
16	NO06	Trøndelag	NO061	Sør-Trøndelag	18,839
17	NO06	Trøndelag	NO062	Nord-Trøndelag	22,415
18	NO07	Nord-Norge	NO071	Nordland	38,482
19	NO07	Nord-Norge	NO072	Troms	25,863
20	NO07	Nord-Norge	NO073	Finnmark	48,631

Table 3.9.A.2 Employment shares Norway, secondary and tertiary sector in total employment, 1900, 1960, 2010

	1900		*1960*		*2010*	
County	*empl_sec1900*	*empl_ter1900*	*empl_sec1960*	*empl_ter1960*	*empl_sec2010*	*empl_ter2010*
Østfold	0.446	0.231	0.553	0.291	0.226	0.753
Oslo+Akershus	0.462	0.370	0.395	0.554	0.111	0.884
Hedmark	0.206	0.121	0.320	0.284	0.192	0.752
Oppland	0.232	0.088	0.353	0.275	0.207	0.733
Buskerud	0.382	0.205	0.505	0.313	0.222	0.756
Vestfold	0.323	0.324	0.448	0.365	0.215	0.766
Telemark	0.315	0.234	0.524	0.293	0.249	0.729
Aust-Agder	0.297	0.319	0.382	0.392	0.241	0.737
Vest-Agder	0.257	0.257	0.437	0.391	0.256	0.725
Rogaland	0.283	0.231	0.405	0.379	0.284	0.684
Bergen+Hordaland	0.303	0.245	0.418	0.434	0.230	0.750
Sogn og Fjordane	0.125	0.074	0.324	0.228	0.247	0.683
Møre og Romsdal	0.172	0.154	0.378	0.316	0.267	0.686
Sør-Trøndelag	0.267	0.197	0.340	0.431	0.184	0.782
Nord-Trøndelag	0.219	0.097	0.324	0.283	0.210	0.708
Nordland	0.148	0.094	0.328	0.355	0.194	0.750
Troms	0.120	0.096	0.260	0.352	0.145	0.814
Finnmark	0.102	0.149	0.343	0.314	0.167	0.769

Table 3.9.A.3 GDP, as well as share of GDP in non-mainland activities, 1900–2010

Year	*GDP (Mill 2005 NOK)*	*Share, non-mainland*
1900	60,878	
1910	75,808	
1920	104,989	
1930	148,103	
1940	173,217	
1950	259,553	
1960	387,237	
1965	491,178	
1970	602,677	7.7%
1973	700,077	8.0%
1980	952,501	17.1%
1990	1,221,175	23.9%
2000	1,756,996	27.1%
2010	2,034,520	19.3%

Notes

1 International dollars from 2011 ICP, source: World Bank.
2 Norway is part of the NUTS scheme despite not being a member of the EU.
3 Downloaded from www.ssb.no/a/histstat/aarbok/ht-0901-bnp.html.
4 I am grateful to Halvard Skiri for providing the 1939 population data.
5 NOS VI 57 (published 1915), p. 6. In addition, a publication from 1876 (NOS C 13) states that in 1870, out of 2,400 industrial establishments (factories), 2,047 were owned by individuals residing in the same municipality as the plant, 333 were owned by domestic individuals residing elsewhere, and 20 by foreigners.
6 See, for example, NOS VI 59, p. 7.

References

Aaberge, R. and Atkinson, A.B. (2010) 'Top incomes in Norway', in A.B. Atkinson and T. Piketty (eds), *Top Incomes: A Global Perspective*, Oxford: Oxford University Press, pp. 448–82.

Atkinson, A.B. and Piketty, T. (eds) (2007) *Top Incomes over the 20th Century: A Contrast between European and English-Speaking Countries*, Oxford: Oxford University Press.

Atkinson, A.B. and Piketty, T. (eds) (2010) *Top Incomes: A Global Perspective*, Oxford: Oxford University Press.

Crafts, N. (2005) 'Regional GDP in Britain, 1871–1911: some estimates', *Scottish Journal of Political Economy*, Vol. 52 (1): 54–64.

Geary, F. and Stark, T. (2002) 'Examining Ireland's post-famine economic growth performance', *Economic Journal*, Vol. 112 (482): 919–35.

Gimming, K., Halvorsen, T., Skoglund, T. and Sørensen, K.Ø. (2011) 'Reviderte nasjonalregnskapstall 1970–2010', *Økonomiske analyser*, Vol. 6: 30–7.

Juvkam, D. (1999) *Historisk oversikt over endringer i kommune-og fylkesinndelingen*, Rapport 99/13, Statistisk sentralbyrå.

Østbye, S. and Westerlund, O. (2011) 'Industrial structure, regional productivity and convergence: the case of Norway and Sweden', *European Urban and Regional Studies*, Vol. 18 (1): 47–61.

Piketty, T. (2014) *Capital in the Twenty-First Century*, Cambridge, MA: Harvard University Press.

Rattsø, J. and Stokke, H. (2014) 'Population divergence and income convergence: regional distribution dynamics for Norway', *Regional Studies*, Vol. 48 (11): 1884–95.

Sørensen, K. (1997) 'Økonomisk utvikling i fylkene 1990–1992 belyst med fylkesfordelt nasjonalregnskap', *Økonomiske Analyser*, Vol. 2: 25–9.

Statistics Norway (2012) *Norwegian National Accounts: GNI Inventory for ESA95*, available at: www.ssb.no/nasjonalregnskap-og-konjunkturer/norwegian-national-accounts-gni-inventory-for-esa95 (accessed 1 December 2014).

Vassenden, K. (1987) *Folke- og boligtellingene 1960, 1970 og 1980, dokumentasjon av de sammenlignbare filene*, Rapport 87/2, Statistisk sentralbyrå.

Zahirovic, E. and Berge, Ø. (2013) 'Fylkesfordelt nasjonalregnaskap 2010, Verdiskapingen i Oslo og Rogaland på topp', *Økonomiske analyser*, Vol. 2: 14–20.

3.10 The evolution of regional income inequality in Portugal, 1890–2010[1]

Marc Badia-Miró and Jordi Guilera

1. Introduction

Portugal is a small and peripheral European economy, and as such its main economic and political developments have been much related to its connection to Europe and to the world economy. First, in the constitution of the Portuguese Empire, then in the efforts done to preserve it, and more recently in the best way to integrate into the European and global economy in order to foster economic growth. The small size of the market has also prompted Portugal to be a relatively open economy for most its history, and particularly since industrialization began, at the end of the nineteenth century. The foreign sector can be seen as the best opportunity to overcome what probably has been the main concern of the Portuguese economy during the last centuries: its relative economic backwardness (Lains 2003, 2007).

Against this background, the low level of human and physical capital investment, the technological gap and institutional underdevelopment, among other factors, have been highlighted by economists and economic historians as some of the crucial elements that hindered Portuguese economic growth in the long term, an issue that also fuelled the emergence of problems of poverty, income inequality and social exclusion, amplified during the recent economic crisis (Alvaredo 2009; Cardoso and Caninas 2010; Guilera 2010, 2014; Lains et al. 2013).

However, most of these debates took place, basically, at the national level, and the geographical component has been broadly neglected, with a few exceptions.[2] Although Portugal may be considered as a united country with a strong cohesion in cultural, linguistic, ethnic and religious terms since medieval times, the economic spatial differences are rather large. As this chapter shows, economic development since the late nineteenth century provoked considerable transformations in the allocation of economic activity at the regional level, which are not depicted in the national histories of Portugal. In fact, the coastal regions, with higher levels of industrialization and better connected to the foreign markets, expanded much faster in the last century, as compared to the backward inner agrarian regions, which lagged behind.

However, the performance of the Portuguese regions was far from being a simple history of prosperity for some regions and stagnation for others. There was an inner-coast history with the stagnation of the regions close to Spain, a history of agglomeration economies in the industrialized regions of Lisbon and Oporto with a diverging path from the 1970s onwards, and a history of a late upswing of some regions linked with the service sector, specifically the transformation led by the tourism sector in the south. As a result, regional inequality increased from the late nineteenth century until the 1970s, to decline thereafter. From 1970 onwards, the spatial distribution of the income changed due to the impact of changes in trade policies, jointly with a crisis in some industrialized regions specialized in labour intensive industries, which were not able to modernize it and to face a stronger market integration with their partners. From 1960, the access to the EFTA, the bilateral trade agreement with Spain in 1980, and the later entrance to the EEC in 1986 started a process towards a more open economy (Costa et al. 2011). It may be highlighted that regional convergence took place relatively late in comparative perspective, which may be related to the backward Portuguese industrialization.[3]

The analysis of regional economic growth may also help to explain the economic performance of Portugal. In this sense, initial regional per capita income levels at the end of the nineteenth century may be closely related to natural endowments, such as soil fertility, weather conditions, mining resources and access to the rivers. Later, over the course of development of the twentieth century, successive technological shocks, the integration of national markets and access to the global economy may have changed those initial conditions.

Industrialization was the main driving force of growth in the Portuguese regions that first took off, namely Lisbon, Porto and Setúbal. The diffusion of industrialization to the other regions and national market integration pushed by the railway diffusion allowed them to catch up after some decades (Justino 1989; Lains 2007; Costa et al. 2011: Chapter 5; da Silveira et al. 2011). However, regional economic development followed different paths with diverse rhythms and characteristics. Those agrarian regions, close to the Spanish border, diverged in economic terms from the average until the end of the 1970s. Finally, during the last decades of the twentieth century, the boom of services sectors and changes in the access to foreign markets introduced another opportunity for some regions to take off. On the other hand, the deindustrialization in some parts of the country was accentuated with the EU integration and reinforced the stagnation of some traditional manufacturing regions, which could not modernize their industrial sector towards higher-value-added activities. In this context, each time the conditions changed, regions were affected by asymmetric shocks that benefited some regions and harmed others. Despite this, there is some stability in the GDP per capita ranking of the Portuguese regions. But there are also both cases of persistent relative economic decline, such as Vila Real and Bragança in the north, and stories of impressive economic success, namely Faro in the south. The analysis of the different regional processes of development may provide a wide illustration of Portuguese economic growth as a whole.

Another important trend to point out is that the tendency to concentrate economic activity in the coastal regions was fuelled by the migration from inner and rural regions towards the main urban and industrialized areas at the Atlantic coast, where more than 80 per cent of the Portuguese population lived in 2010 (de Nunes 1989; Costa et al. 2011). But this long-standing pattern has to be divided in different periods. At the turning point of the twentieth century, improvements in agricultural productivity and rises in wages favoured domestic migration, from inner rural to industrial coastal areas (Justino 1989; Costa et al. 2011). During the *Estado Novo*, intense international migration unequally affected the regions of Portugal. A surplus of rural unskilled workers was channelled towards the richer European countries (Baganha 2003).

This chapter shows the diversity of growth experiences of the Portuguese regions during the twentieth century, which may be partially hidden behind the traditional narratives of Portuguese economic history. The new GDP estimates provided here are also an opportunity to extend the traditional debates and analyses of the Portuguese historiography to encompass all Portuguese regions. The remainder of this chapter is structured as follows: section 2 presents the new data and discusses the stylized facts, and section 3 concludes. The data are provided in the data appendix of this book.

2. Long-term patterns of regional income inequality: new data and stylized facts

2.1 Data

In order to analyse the long-term evolution of regional inequality and its determinants, we have estimated regional GDP figures from 1890 to 1950, which are linked afterwards with data published in official sources, already available from 1960 onwards. The methodology used to perform these estimates is based on sector-specific production data and estimations based on Geary and Stark (2002) when the first one is not available. Direct estimates of regional production are available for the *mining* and *electricity and gas* sectors for 1930, 1940 and 1950. For the rest, we have used Geary and Stark approximation, which is thoroughly described in Chapter 2 in this book.[4] This methodology allows estimating regional GDP based on national GDP per sectors, nominal wages and working population per regions and sectors. For 1960, we have taken the regional GDP shares provided by de Abreu (1969). For 1970, we have considered the data in Corregidor (1975). Estimates for 1980 come from INE (1991). On the other hand, population and EAP data between 1890 and 1980 come from de Nunes (1989).[5]

From 1990 onwards, official data are provided by INE for NUTS 2 and NUTS 3. For the previous period, regional data in Portugal may be presented in two different aggregation levels: Portuguese historical districts and NUTS 2. Unfortunately, we have not been able to also provide those estimates at the NUTS 3 level. Although regional GDP at the NUTS 2 level is essential for comparative purposes in a European context, its economic significance is weaker because it assembles regions with very heterogeneous economic and geographic characteristics. Furthermore, their use prevents an analysis of one of the main topics in the Portuguese spatial economic history, the existence of large differences among inner and coastal regions and their performance in the long run. By contrast, the historical districts, which are in between NUTS 2 and NUTS 3, comprise more economic homogeneous regions.

To provide a long-run analysis, we must spatially homogenize figures of both periods. By taking NUTS 2 as the reference, the economic analysis of the Portuguese regions would be biased. Our proposal is to homogenize all the figures for historical districts. To do that, we have improved the methodology proposed by Tirado-Fabregat and Badia-Miró (2014) based on population shares, and we have considered GDP shares for each Portuguese municipality in order to reconstruct the GDP shares for the historical districts, for 1990, based on the figures of Nogueira Ramos (1998) for 1991. Population and economic active population data came from official sources. For 2000 and 2010 figures, we have used the same shares as in 1990, corrected by population growth for each municipality.

To sum up, we provide data for 18 continental historical districts: eight of them are on the Atlantic coast, three of them are inner regions, five regions are located along the border with Spain, and the remaining two range from the Atlantic to the Spanish frontier, in the south of the country. Their use allows us to illustrate the long-term evolution of regional inequality in Portugal. Notwithstanding that, both NUTS 2 and historical districts figures are provided in the data appendix in this book.

2.2 Stylized facts

In order to analyse the evolution of regional inequality in the long run we have estimated the long-term evolution of the population-weighted standard deviation coefficient of per capita GDP from 1890 to 2010 (see Figure 3.10.1). According to Barro and Sala-i-Martin (1991, 1992), this index may be considered a measure of sigma-convergence (i.e. a measure of how differences among richer and poorer regions change in the long run).

As can be seen in Figure 3.10.1, regional inequality increased with some fluctuations until 1970, it fell steeply during the next decade, and it stabilized with a slight decreasing trend from the 1980s onwards, drawing a sort of inverted U-curve in the long term. Regional inequality was pushed up by the growth of the three main urban areas of Portugal (Lisbon, Porto and Setúbal) due to the industrialization process and the steep decline in agriculture. The 1920 estimate may be partially related to the huge instability of the post-First World War period on Portugal, and particularly on its asymmetric shock at the regional level. Prices and wages were affected by inflation due to a large budget deficit resulting from Portugal's participation in the First World War (Costa et al. 2011: 372–4). Between 1920 and 1970, structural change in the Portuguese economy based on the industrialization of a few regions, and the growth of the service sector around them pushed by domestic demand (Cravinho 1992), reinforced this concentration of economic activity. At the same time, the persistence of a low-productivity agriculture (Lains 2007) prevented an economic recovery of the interior regions. The latter evolution of regional inequality since the 1980s may point to a new period of a reduction of regional inequality, which is something that Spain also

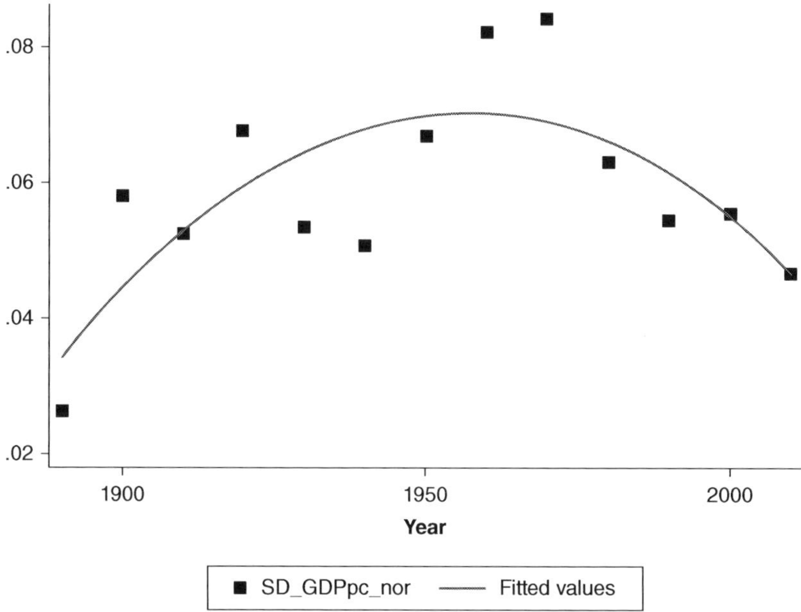

Figure 3.10.1 Sigma-convergence among Portuguese regions, 1890–2010 (coefficient of variation weighted by population)

Source: See Table 3.10.1.

experienced since their entrance into the EEC (López-Bazo et al. 1999; Martínez-Galarraga et al. 2015). The most relevant factors driving this late process of convergence were: (1) the collapse of Setúbal's economy due to the problems with capital-intensive industries in the 1970s (automotive); (2) the slowdown of Porto related to its traditional industry in labour-intensive sectors, which have difficulties to keep their competitiveness in a new international context; and (3) the rise of 'new' regions as Faro jointly with the recovery of other less developed regions (Costa et al. 2011: 393–5). However, what we found for Portugal at the beginning of the twenty-first century is different from what is happening in the rest of Europe. In Europe at large, an increasing inequality started in the 1980s, led by the tertiary sector in larger agglomerations and their linkages to the rest of the economy (Gardiner et al. 2013). In Portugal, as happened in other less developed countries, service sector productivity improved slightly and could not act as a driver of the rise of agglomeration economies based in the tertiary sector (Lains 2008; Pereira and Lains 2012). At the same time, the impact of cohesion funds was limited (Antunes and Soukiazis 2005; Pinho et al. 2015).

Another way to look at the process of regional inequality is based on the concept of beta-convergence. This can be estimated by regressing the rate of growth of the different regions on their initial per capita GDP, in our case applied to the period

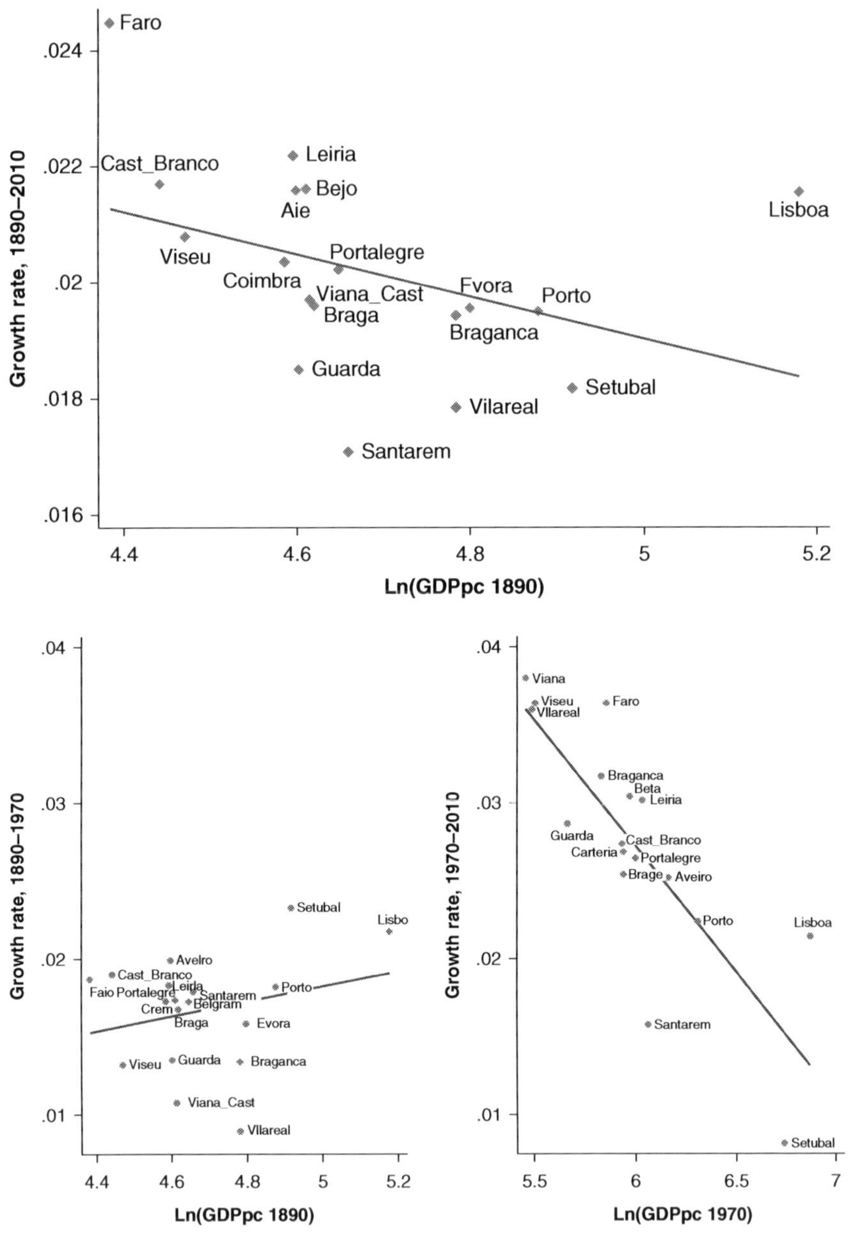

Figure 3.10.2 Beta-convergence among Portuguese regions

Source: See the appendix.

1890 and 2010. A positive correlation would indicate a process of divergence because richer regions would tend to grow faster. On the other hand, a negative correlation would point to a process of catching-up and regional convergence.

The upper panel in Figure 3.10.2 shows the results of the beta-convergence exercise. As may be seen in this figure, there is a slight negative correlation, pointing to a very moderate process of catching up and regional convergence in the very long term between 1890 and 2010. From the perspective of neoclassical economic theory, this finding is rather surprising. The exercise shows that despite a process of some regional catching up in Portugal, this has occurred at a very low pace. It is, however, consistent with the observed late turning point in terms of sigma-convergence, when the diffusion of the modernization of the economy arrived in the most backward regions of the country.

The role played by market integration was especially important during the first decades of the twentieth century. Unlike what we observe in other European countries, in 1890 only 60 per cent of today's total rail mileage of Portugal was in service, and only around 60 per cent of the number of urban agglomerations (but about 90 per cent of the urban population) were connected.[6] In 1910, the rail network was nearly finished, and the interior regions were well connected among each other, with the coast and with the Spanish border. This integration coincided with a divergence in GDP per capita until 1920. Market integration and railway connections pushed the dynamism of the more urban and connected regions such as Porto, Lisbon and Setúbal, driven by this industrialization process and reinforced by rural migration.[7]

Given that the evolution of sigma-convergence reached a maximum divergence around the 1970s, we have repeated the beta-convergence exercise for two subperiods: the first one between 1890 and 1970 when regional inequality peaked, and the second one from 1970 to 2010 (see the lower panel in Figure 3.10.2). The results nuance the conclusions derived from the upper panel in Figure 3.10.2. We observe a slight dispersion in the first period with Lisbon, Setúbal and Porto driving it (the main urban and industrialized cities). However, during the second period, a strong beta-convergence is observed, which coincides with the integration of Portugal into the EU, which may have fostered the growth of the backward regions, together with a strong process of population decline during the 1970s, which already started during the 1960s.[8]

After having looked at the long-term evolution of regional inequality through the concepts of sigma- and beta-convergence, Table 3.10.1 shows the relative per capita income of each Portuguese region throughout 1890–2010. In this table, all regional incomes are expressed in relation to national average. The table shows the evolution in the relative position of each Portuguese region and allows for detection of regional stories of success and failure in terms of economic growth. Clearly, Lisbon and Porto have always been among the richest regions compared to the rest of the country. On the other hand, at the tail of the ranking, the mobility is higher, although Viseu, Guarda and Castelo Branco have remained at the bottom. Some regions, such as Bragança and Vila Real, became worse off, as they were among the richest in 1890 and ended up at the bottom by 2010. Braga and

Viana do Castelo also fell from the middle of the ranking in 1890 to the bottom in 2010. On the other hand, the position of Leiria and especially Faro improved significantly over the period. The case of Faro is worth mentioning as it was the poorest Portuguese region in 1890 and ended up being the second richest region after Lisbon. This economic success is closely related to the explosion of the services sector related to tourism since the 1980s (Soukiazis and Proença 2008). Finally, Porto and Setúbal followed an inverted U-curve, experiencing a golden age of growth until the 1920s and 1970s, respectively, to severely decline afterwards. Porto's decline during the end of the twentieth century and the beginning of the twenty-first century is due to the persistent low productivity levels of its huge industrial sector (see Badia-Miró et al. 2012a). In that sense, the failure of its industry to modernize and overcome the continuous decline of competitiveness explains most of its backwardness in relative terms, compared to the foreign producers, due to European integration and the so-called second globalization (Lains 2003, 2004; Costa et al. 2011: 414; Soukiazis and Antunes 2011; Pereira and Lains 2012).

Setúbal's downfall since the 1970s shared some of the problems suffered by Porto. It underwent a deep industrial crisis but was also affected by the collapse of productivity levels in the services sector (Lains 2004; Costa et al. 2011; Pereira and Lains 2012). Table 3.10.1 also shows that the range of levels of GDP per capita increased substantially between 1890 and 1970 and declined thereafter. In 1890, the level of GDP per capita of the richest region was slightly more than twice that of the poorest; in 1970, the leading region was more than four times richer than the poorest region; and in 2010, this gap has narrowed again to 2.8. This difference is bigger than in other southern peripheral countries, and shows the importance of Lisbon during the decades after the Second World War, leading the transformation of the Portuguese spatial economy.[9]

The allocation of economic activity in Portugal between 1890 and 2010 has an important geographic component as most of the economic activity was concentrated in the coastal regions. Maps 3.10.1–3.10.3 show the relative per capita GDP levels of the Portuguese regions in 1890, 1970 (when regional dispersion peaked) and 2010. As may be seen in these maps, in 1890, the six richer regions were located in two corridors that ranged from Porto and Lisbon (in the Atlantic coast) to the Spanish frontier, including also Vila Real and Bragança in the north, and Setúbal and Évora in the centre. The three northern regions followed the course of the river Douro, an important transport network at that period (da Silva 1997; da Silveira et al. 2011). The rest of the Portuguese regions were in a similar backward position (above 85 per cent), except for Castelo Branco, Viseu and overall Faro, which were at the tail of the rankings in terms of GDP per capita.

In 1970, regional inequality peaked and, as may be seen in Figure 3.10.1, a significant number of regions fell below the 70 per cent income threshold, which was almost empty in 1890. The regions that fell behind were in north-eastern Portugal, with the exception of Faro, which stagnated. As Tirado-Fabregat and Badia-Miró (2014) point out, this pattern is also observed in the neighbouring regions of the north-east of Spain, marking a sort of continuous backward part

Table 3.10.1 The relative per capita GDP of Portuguese regions, 1890–2010 (Portugal = 100)

	1890	*1900*	*1910*	*1920*	*1930*	*1940*	*1950*	*1960*	*1970*	*1980*	*1990*	*2000*	*2010*
Aveiro	88	95	82	81	87	93	96	98	87	96	94	94	90
Beja	89	86	103	73	73	78	89	72	72	73	71	77	91
Braga	90	101	72	98	79	89	78	68	70	78	75	73	73
Bragança	106	93	120	89	87	71	66	58	63	55	78	69	84
Castel Branco	75	64	77	62	73	78	78	67	70	68	74	72	78
Coimbra	87	79	86	77	93	82	65	74	70	84	67	75	77
Évora	108	104	129	101	86	86	97	91	77	95	76	101	87
Faro	71	78	84	70	74	90	96	69	64	91	110	111	102
Guarda	89	78	87	70	81	68	69	54	53	56	59	56	63
Leiria	88	84	84	71	85	81	83	78	77	85	93	98	96
Lisboa	157	175	174	184	163	160	165	186	180	147	171	161	161
Portalegre	93	85	95	80	84	86	115	86	74	87	79	84	81
Porto	117	125	80	133	122	119	108	113	101	102	105	97	93
Santarém	94	91	92	86	88	87	95	79	79	89	76	60	56
Setúbal	121	134	120	121	132	125	122	156	157	121	95	88	83
Viana do Castelo	90	76	95	77	91	88	94	51	43	55	63	66	73
Vila Real	106	88	102	79	81	76	45	56	44	53	70	57	70
Viseu	78	74	88	63	66	74	76	54	45	57	64	68	72

Source: Badia-Miró et al. (2012a) and Tirado and Badia-Miró (2014).

of Iberia on both sides of the northern border. In that sense, the integration of the Iberian market driven by the accession to the EEC just deepened a picture that already existed before. Behind this was probably a lack in infrastructures and the distance to the most important economic centres, which prevented positive effects from integration. Regarding the top of the distribution, in contrast with 1890, the four richest regions are to be found on the Atlantic coast. Unlike in France and Spain,[10] the main industrial region (Porto), apart from the capital, was not able to spread industrialization into the neighbouring regions (with the exception of Braga), and as a result the northern regions stagnated during most of the period.[11] As shown in Badia-Miró et al. (2012a), the reason behind this was that Porto's industry, although being the largest industrial sector of all Portuguese regions, was characterized by low productivity due to its specialization in traditional textiles and manufactured foods, with low added value.

Finally, as may be seen in Map 3.10.3, the trends already detected in 1970 were reinforced even more in 2010. The north-eastern regions consolidated as the most backward Portuguese regions. The Atlantic coast concentrated most of the richest regions: six of the top eight regions. Only Santarem, which is close to Lisbon, and Évora, which is in contact with the Spanish frontier, had no direct access to the sea.[12] It is also worth mentioning the economic decline of Setúbal, which ceased to be among the richest regions, and the success of Faro, which experienced its own golden age of growth during the last third of the twentieth century due to the tourist sector. The picture of the surroundings of Lisbon in 1890s showed a sort of diffusion of the GDP per capita levels, from the capital to the interior regions, with levels above the average in Santarem and Setúbal and slightly below the average in Leiria. At this time, Lisbon and its economic dynamism pulled the hinterland along via demand for their products. These linkages appear to have disappeared over the twentieth century. The differences in GDP per capita levels among Leiria or Santarem and Lisbon grew to 2.3 times in 1970 and to 2.8 times with Santarem in 2010. Moreover, as we have said, Setúbal, another region around the capital, was a leading region around the 1970s due to its industry, but experienced a great collapse starting in the 1980s. As we have seen in the case of Porto's neighbourhood, neither the industry nor Lisbon's home market effect could replace Setúbal's industry as a driver of the economy during the late twentieth century. In consequence, in 2010, it stood at only half the level of GDP per capita of Lisbon. Leiria was the only region around Lisbon that grew and converged to the average, pulled by the dynamism of the tertiary sector and the maintenance of some share of the industry, although the industrial productivity levels in the 1970s were not quite the same as the ones observed in Setúbal and Porto.

Finally, Table 3.10.2 displays the evolution of the relative size of each Portuguese region as a share in total Portuguese GDP. As may be seen in this table, there has been a long-term concentration of economic activity in a few regions. The top four regions contributed 43 per cent of Portuguese GDP in 1890, a figure that increased to 65 per cent in 2010. On the other hand, the bottom half of the Portuguese regions contributed 30 per cent of GDP in 1890, a figure that collapsed to only 13 per cent in 2010. This broad picture is confirmed with the

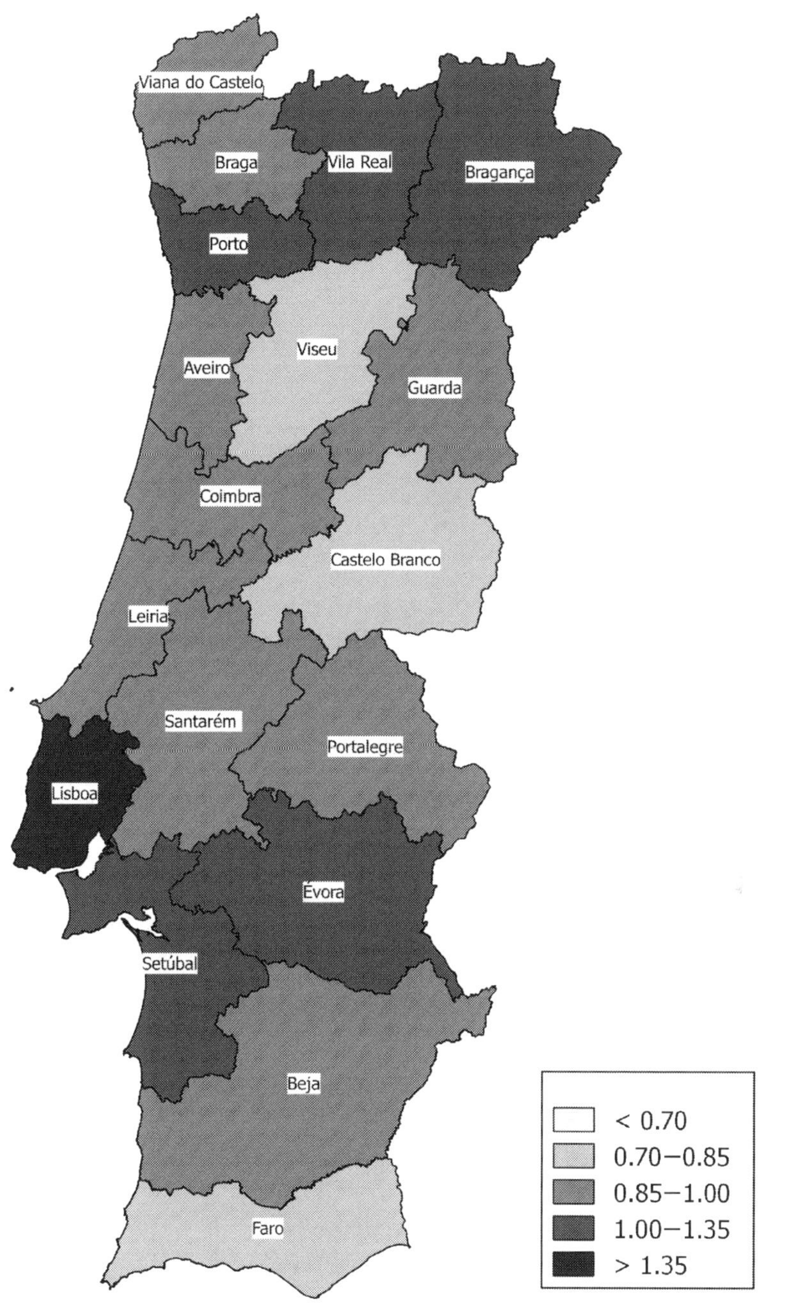

Map 3.10.1 Relative GDP per capita of Portuguese regions, 1890 (Portugal = 1)

Source: See Table 3.10.1.

Note: Own elaboration. Ranges: <0.70 low income, 0.70–0.85 low-middle income, 0.85–1.00 middle income, 1.00–1.35 middle-high income, >1.35 high income.

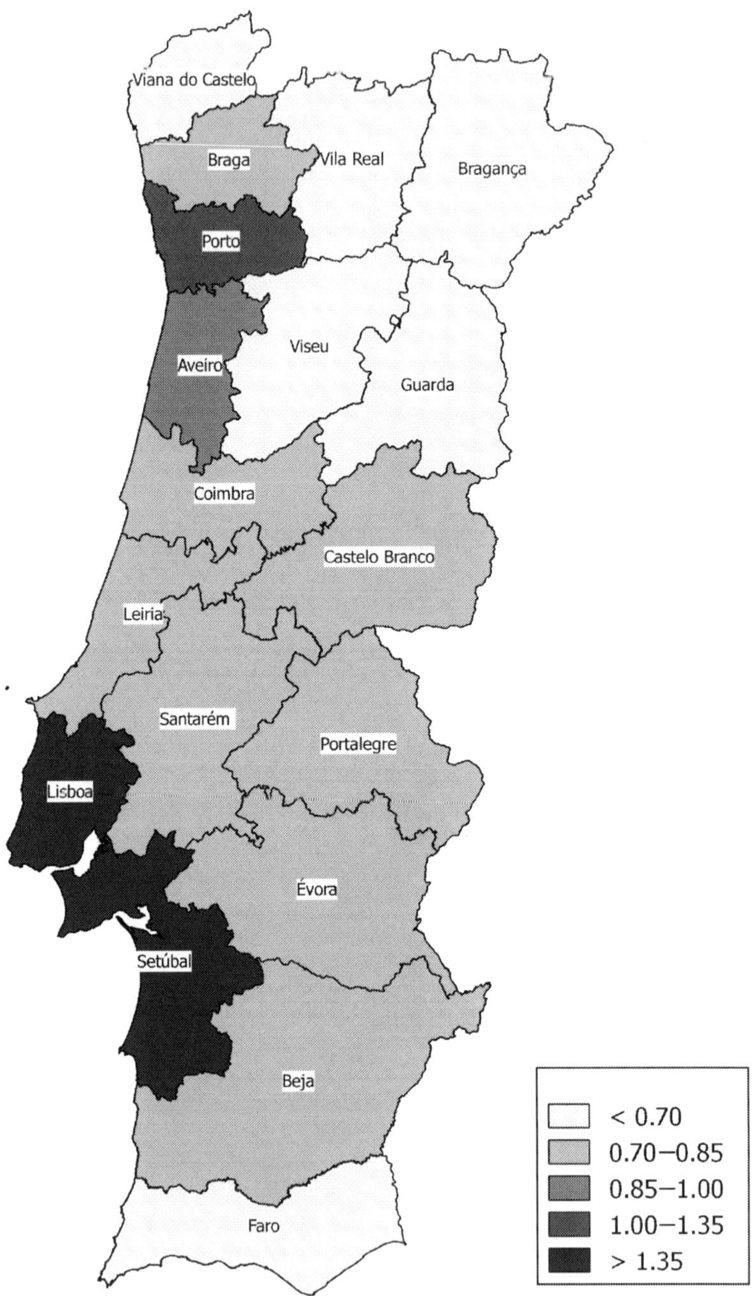

Map 3.10.2 Relative GDP per capita of Portuguese regions, 1970 (Portugal = 1)

Source: See Table 3.10.1.

Note: Own elaboration. Ranges: <0.70 low income, 0.70–0.85 low-middle income, 0.85–1.00 middle income, 1.00–1.35 middle-high income, >1.35 high income.

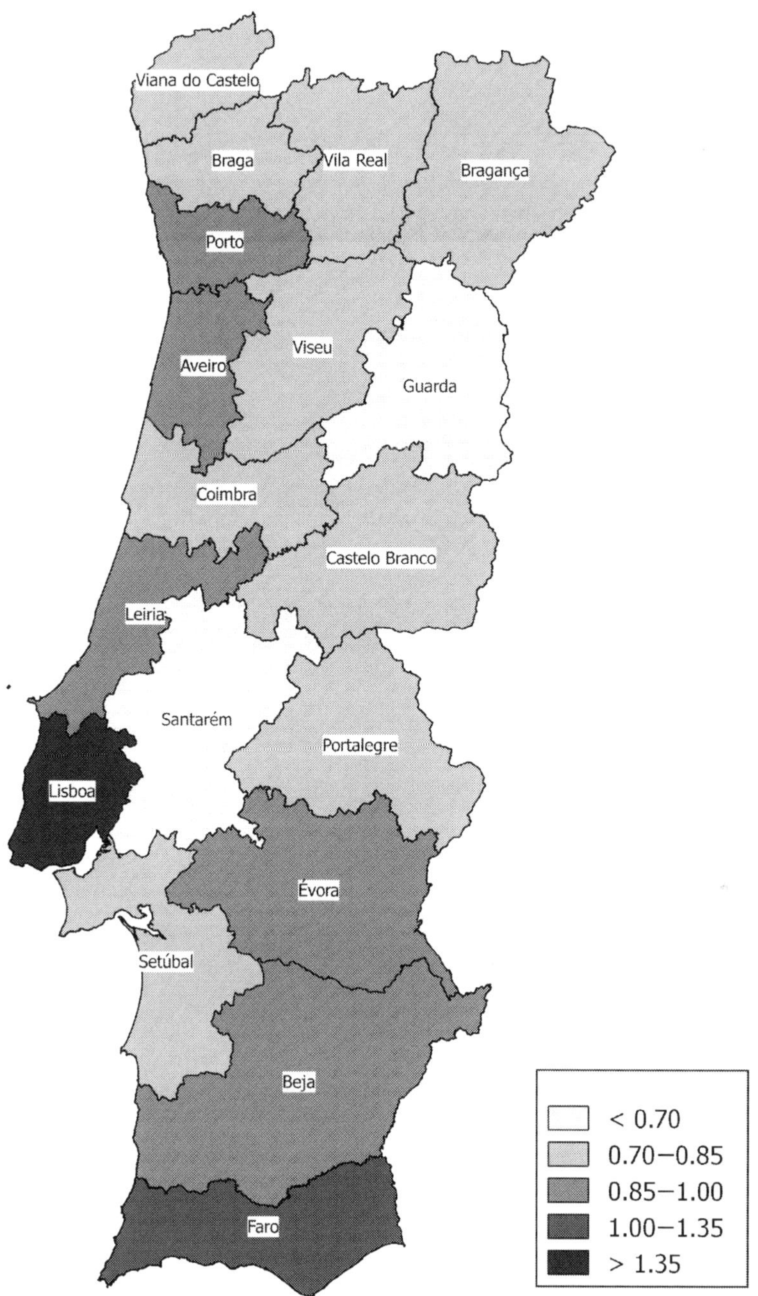

Map 3.10.3 Relative GDP per capita of Portuguese regions, 2010 (Portugal = 1)

Source: See Table 3.10.1.

Legend: Own elaboration. Ranges: <0.70 low income, 0.70–0.85 low-middle income, 0.85–1.00 middle income, 1.00–1.35 middle-high income, >1.35 high income.

Table 3.10.2 The share of Portuguese regions on Portuguese GDP, 1890–2010 (per cent)

	1890	*1900*	*1910*	*1920*	*1930*	*1940*	*1950*	*1960*	*1970*	*1980*	*1990*	*2000*	*2010*
Aveiro	5.5	5.9	5.0	5.0	5.4	5.6	5.9	6.2	5.9	6.4	6.4	6.8	6.4
Beja	3.0	2.9	3.6	2.6	2.8	3.0	3.3	2.4	1.8	1.5	1.2	1.2	1.4
Braga	6.5	7.3	5.0	6.5	5.2	6.0	5.4	4.9	5.3	6.0	6.0	6.3	6.3
Bragança	4.1	3.6	4.2	2.7	2.6	2.1	1.9	1.6	1.4	1.1	1.1	1.0	1.1
Castel Branco	3.3	2.8	3.4	2.7	3.0	3.3	3.2	2.6	2.2	1.7	1.7	1.5	1.5
Coimbra	6.1	5.5	5.7	4.9	5.5	4.7	3.6	3.9	3.5	3.9	2.8	3.2	3.1
Évora	2.8	2.7	3.5	2.8	2.4	2.5	2.7	2.4	1.7	1.8	1.3	1.7	1.4
Faro	3.5	3.8	4.1	3.3	3.5	4.0	4.0	2.6	2.1	3.2	3.8	4.3	4.5
Guarda	4.7	4.2	4.3	3.2	3.3	2.8	2.7	1.8	1.4	1.2	1.1	1.0	1.0
Leiria	4.1	3.9	4.1	3.5	4.1	4.0	4.2	3.8	3.6	3.8	4.0	4.4	4.4
Lisboa	16.6	18.5	21.1	24.1	23.2	23.3	25.5	31.0	35.0	32.5	34.7	34.5	35.5
Portalegre	2.3	2.1	2.4	2.1	2.2	2.3	2.9	1.9	1.3	1.3	1.0	1.0	0.9
Porto	13.6	14.6	9.7	16.6	15.5	15.5	14.4	16.3	16.4	17.1	17.5	16.6	16.1
Santarém	5.1	4.9	5.3	5.1	5.2	5.2	5.5	4.4	4.2	4.3	5.0	4.0	3.7
Setúbal	3.0	3.3	3.5	4.0	4.8	4.7	5.0	7.1	9.1	8.5	6.8	6.9	6.9
Viana do Castelo	4.1	3.4	3.9	3.1	3.3	3.2	3.3	1.7	1.3	1.5	1.6	1.6	1.7
Vila Real	5.4	4.4	4.5	3.3	3.3	3.1	1.8	2.2	1.5	1.5	1.6	1.2	1.4
Viseu	6.6	6.3	6.7	4.6	4.6	4.8	4.8	3.1	2.3	2.6	2.6	2.7	2.7

Source: See Table 3.10.1.

analysis of a Hirschman-Herfindal index, which shows an intense concentration of economic activity until the 1970s, which remained stable until the end of the period. In some regions, those changes were outstanding. Lisbon and Setúbal doubled their participation. Aveiro, Faro and Porto also increased their contribution between 15 per cent and 30 per cent. Leiria maintained its share, whereas the remaining regions lost weight throughout the period; overall, Bragança, Guarda, Vila Real, Viana do Castelo, Beja, Viseu, Portalegre and Castelo Branco that lost more than 50 per cent of their relative size. It may be worth mentioning that an increase in the regional GDP share does not necessarily imply higher levels in GDP per capita, because the effect could be due to population changes. Setúbal might be an example of that, because whereas it more than doubled its relative economic size, its relative GDP per capita fell by 32 per cent.

3. Conclusions

Portugal's regional inequality in the long term followed an inverted U-curve, with a peak around the 1970s, a few decades later than the peak observed in Spain, and later than in other countries. This pattern is related to the limited and slow beta-convergence process observed for the whole period. What really happened was a moderate process of divergence before 1970, due to the growth in the leading industrialized regions. That is, structural change, from the primary to the secondary sector, drove most of the increase in regional inequality. At the same time, this reinforced the differences between coastal and interior Portuguese provinces. It seems that agglomeration economies mattered, along with the specialization process observed in the industrial sector. As a result, there were intense productivity gains in those leading provinces. This pattern changed around the 1970s with the crisis of the traditional manufacture and the integration into the European Common Market. From this point onwards, we observed a convergence due to the leading role of the service sector, albeit accompanied by a process of geographical concentration of activity around Lisbon. This pattern was also reinforced by the intensification of migrations to the most dynamic provinces of the centre and the south of the country.

Notes

1 We acknowledge the support received from 'Globalizing Europe Economic History Network' financed by the European Science Foundation. M. Badia-Miró and J. Guilera acknowledge the financial support from the XREPP, from ECO2009-13331-C02-02 and ECO2012-39169-C03-03 leaded by A. Herranz, ECO2012-39169-C03-02 leaded by D. Tirado, both financed by the Govern of Spain, and 2014SGR1345 (Antoni de Campany Centre of Economy and Economic History). M. Badia-Miró also thanks the financial support of GLOBALEURONET (funded by the European Science Foundation). The chapter was presented at 'Europe's Regions, 1900–2010: A New Quantitative History of the Economic Development of Europe'. We would like to thank several participants for their comments, in particular P. Lains, D. Tirado, J. Martínez-Galarraga, E. Buyst, A. Herranz, J.R. Rosés and N. Wolf.

2 Vieira et al. (2006), Fidalgo et al. (2010), da Silveira et al. (2011, 2013) and Badia-Miró et al. (2012a) are examples of a renovated interest in the spatial dimension of the Portuguese economic performance in the long run.

3 Spain converged earlier and Italy did not converge. In the case of Spain, we could observe the peak around the 1920s, when a process of convergence started until the 1980s (Martínez-Galarraga et al. 2015). The case of Italy is rather complicated. We observe a weak convergence for the whole period that hides a strong polarization between the north and south of the country. Only during the economic expansion during the miracle of the 1960s and the 1970s is a slight convergence of the southern regions observed (Felice 2011).

4 Due to the lack of data for 1900 we have assumed the same regional wage differences as in 1890. For 1910, we assumed 1920 regional wage differences approximated by 1921 shares of EAP for the industry subsectors.

5 For a detailed description of wage data used, see Badia-Miró et al. (2012b).

6 For a comparison between the evolution of the railway network among France, Spain and Portugal, see Mojica and Martí-Henneberg (2011). These figures were very similar to what we found for Spain, but are very different to what we found for France, where, at the end of the nineteenth century, levels reached very close to 100 per cent.

7 A deeper analysis of the relation among railways and population is done in da Silveira et al. (2011). On the urban network before 1940, see da Silva (1997).

8 Some inner and southern regions such as Beja, Bragança, Castelo Branco, Guarda, Portalegre and Vila Real have negative rates of growth of total population from the 1970s onwards.

9 Spanish figures on the difference between richest and poorest regions range from two to four times, and for Italy they range between two and three times (see Chapters 3.7 and 3.11 in this book).

10 See Chapters 3.5 and 3.11 in this book, as well as Rosés et al. (2010), Combes et al. (2011), Caruana-Galizia and Martí-Henneberg (2013) and Martínez-Galarraga et al. (2015).

11 Vila Real and Viseu had more than a half of the economy devoted to the agrarian sector.

12 It may be worth mentioning that between 1970 and 2010, Évora lost population, which could partially explain the increase in its per capita GDP.

References

Alvaredo, F. (2009) 'Top incomes and earnings in Portugal 1936–2005', *Explorations in Economic History*, Vol. 46 (4): 404–17.

Antunes, M. and Soukiazis, E. (2005) 'Two speed regional convergence in Portugal and the importance of structural funds on growth', *4th Annual Meeting of the EEFS*, Vol. 9: 222–41.

Badia-Miró, M., Guilera, J. and Lains, P. (2012a) 'Regional incomes in Portugal: industrialisation, integration and inequality, 1890–1980', *Revista de Historia Económica: Journal of Iberian and Latin American Economic History*, Vol. 30 (2): 225–44.

Badia-Miró, M., Guilera, J. and Lains, P. (2012b) 'Reconstruction of the regional GDP of Portugal, 1890–1980', *Documents de Treball. Facultat Economia i Empresa. Universitat de Barcelona*, E12/280.

Baganha, M.I.B. (2003) 'From closed to open doors: Portuguese emigration under the corporatist regime', *e-Journal of Portuguese History*, Vol. 1 (1).

Barro, R.J. and Sala-i-Martin, X. (1991) 'Convergence across states and regions', *Brookings Papers on Economic Activity*, Vol. 1 (1991): 107–82.

Barro, R.J. and Sala-i-Martin, X. (1992) 'Convergence', *Journal of Political Economy*, Vol. 100 (2): 223–51.

Cardoso, H.F.V. and Caninas, M. (2010) 'Secular trends in social class differences of height, weight and BMI of boys from two schools in Lisbon, Portugal (1910–2000)', *Economics & Human Biology*, Vol. 8 (1): 111–20.

Caruana-Galizia, P. and Martí-Henneberg, J. (2013) 'European regional railways and real income, 1870–1910: a preliminary report', *Scandinavian Economic History Review*, Vol. 61 (2): 167–96.

Combes, P.-P., Lafourcade, M., Thiesse, J.-F. and Toutain, J.-C. (2011) 'The rise and fall of spatial inequalities in France: a long-run perspective', *Explorations in Economic History*, Vol. 48 (2): 243–71.

Corregidor, V.A. (1975) *A populaçao ao Nivel Regional. Tentativa de quantificaçao. Tentativa de identificaçao de áreas prioritarias de captaçao*, Lisbon: Banco de Fomento Nacional.

Costa, L.F., Lains, P. and Miranda, S.M. (2011) *História Económica de Portugal*, Lisbon: A Esfera dos Livros.

Cravinho, J. (1992) 'Sources of output growth in the portuguese economy (1959–1974)', *Estudos de Economia*, Vol. 2 (3): 271–90.

da Silva, A.F. (1997) 'A evoluçao da rede urbana portuguesa (1801–1940)', *Análise Social*, Vol. 32 (4–5): 779–814.

da Silveira, L.E., Alves, D., Lima, N.M., Alcántara, A. and Puig, J. (2011) 'Population and railways in Portugal, 1801–1930', *Journal of Interdisciplinary History*, Vol. 42 (1): 29–52.

da Silveira, L.E., Alves, D., Painho, M., Costa, A.C. and Alcántara, A. (2013) 'The evolution of population distribution on the Iberian Peninsula: a transnational approach (1877–2001)', *Historical Methods: A Journal of Quantitative and Interdisciplinary History*, Vol. 46 (3): 157–74.

de Abreu, A.T. (1969) *O Crescimento regional em Portugal. Análise da sua distribuçao*, Lisbon: Fundado Calouste Gulbenkian/Centro de Estudos de Economía Agraria.

de Nunes, A.B. (1989) *Populaçao activa e actividade economica em Portugal: dos finais do século XIX a actualidade. Uma contribuiçao para o estudo do crescimiento económico portugués*, Lisbon: Instituto superior de economia da Universidade Tecnica de Lisboa.

Felice, E. (2011) 'Regional value added in Italy, 1891–2001, and the foundation of a long-term picture', *The Economic History Review*, Vol. 64 (3): 929–50.

Fidalgo, J.G., Simões, M. and Duarte, A. (2010) 'Mind the gap: education inequality at the regional level in Portugal, 1986–2005', *Notas Económicas*, Vol. 32: 22–43.

Gardiner, B., Martin, R., Sunley, P. and Tyler, P. (2013) 'Spatially unbalanced growth in the British economy', *Journal of Economic Geography*, Vol. 13 (6): 889–928.

Guilera, J. (2010) 'The evolution of top income and wealth shares in Portugal since 1936', *Revista de Historia Económica: Journal of Iberian and Latin American Economic History*, Vol. 28 (1): 139–71.

Guilera, J. (2014) *Income Inequality in Historial Perspective: Portugal (1890–2006)*, PhD Thesis, University of Barcelona.

Instituto Nacional de Estatística (INE) (1991) *1980–1986 Contais Regionais*, Lisbon: INE.

Justino, D. (1989) *A formação do espaço económico nacional. Portugal 1810–1913*, Lisbon: Vega.

Lains, P. (2003) 'Catching up to the European core: Portuguese economic growth, 1910–1990', *Explorations in Economic History*, Vol. 40 (4): 369–86.

Lains, P. (2004) 'Structural change and economic growth in Portugal, 1950–1990', in S. Heikkinen and J.L. Van Zanden (eds), *Explorations in Economic Growth*, Amsterdam: Aksant, pp. 321–40.

Lains, P. (2007) 'Growth in a protected environment: Portugal, 1850–1950', *Research in Economic History*, Vol. 24: 119–60.

Lains, P. (2008) 'The Portuguese economy in the Irish mirror', *Open Economic Review*, Vol. 19: 667–83.

Lains, P., da Silva, E.G. and Guilera, J. (2013) 'Wage inequality in a developing open economy: Portugal, 1944–1984', *Scandinavian Economic History Review*, Vol. 61 (3): 287–311.

López-Bazo, E., Vayá, E., Mora, A.J. and Suriñach, J. (1999) 'Regional economic dynamics and convergence in the European Union', *The Annals of Regional Science*, Vol. 33 (3): 343–70.

Martínez-Galarraga, J., Rosés, J.R. and Tirado-Fabregat, D.A. (2015) 'The long-term patterns of regional income inequality in Spain, 1860–2000', *Regional Studies*, Vol. 49 (4): 502–17.

Mojica, L. and Martí-Henneberg, J. (2011) 'Railways and population distribution: France, Spain, and Portugal, 1870–2000', *Journal of Interdisciplinary History*, Vol. 42 (1): 15–28.

Nogueira Ramos, P. (1998) 'Estimativas do PIB per capita para os concelhos do continente porguês', *Revista de Estadística*, Vol. 3: 29–49.

Pereira, Á.S. and Lains, P. (2012) 'From an agrarian society to a knowledge economy? The rising importance of education to the Portuguese economy, 1950–2009', in G. Neave and A. Amaral (eds), *Higher Education in Portugal 1974–2009: A Nation, a Generation*, Dordrecht: Springer, pp. 109–34.

Pinho, C., Varum, C. and Antunes, M. (2015) 'Structural funds and European regional growth: comparison of effects among different programming periods', *European Planning Studies*, Vol. 23 (7): 1302–26.

Rosés, J.R., Martínez-Galarraga, J. and Tirado-Fabregat, D.A. (2010) 'The upswing of regional income inequality in Spain (1860–1930)', *Explorations in Economic History*, Vol. 47 (2): 244–57.

Soukiazis, E. and Antunes, M. (2011) 'Is foreign trade important for regional growth? Empirical evidence from Portugal', *Economic Modelling*, Vol. 28 (3): 1363–73.

Soukiazis, E. and Proença, I. (2008) 'Tourism as an alternative source of regional growth in Portugal: a panel analysis at NUTS II and III levels', *Portuguese Economic Journal*, Vol. 7 (1): 43–61.

Tirado-Fabregat, D.A. and Badia-Miró, M. (2014) 'New evidence on regional inequality in Iberia (1900–2000)', *Historical Methods: A Journal of Quantitative and Interdisciplinary History*, Vol. 47 (4): 180–9.

Vieira, J., Couto, J. and Tiago, M. (2006) 'Inter-regional wage dispersion in Portugal', *Regional and Sectoral Economic Studies*, Vol. 6 (1).

3.11 The evolution of regional income inequality in Spain, 1860–2010

Julio Martínez-Galarraga, Joan Ramón Rosés and Daniel A. Tirado

1. Introduction

Among the academic controversies regarding economic development, the issue of regional inequality is prominently featured. In the case of Spain, the debate about regional inequalities had superseded academic circles and has a strong influence over politics and the public arena. In fact, public opinion is deeply divided on the issue. Intellectuals and politicians have strongly disagreed about the historical causes of the per capita income differences across regions. Several of them argue that these differences were provoked by the successive governments that pursued deliberate discriminatory policies favouring certain regions, while others blame the culture and institutions of poor regions for their failures. Ultimately, there is no consensus on the necessity and effectiveness of regional cohesion policy and government transfers of resources from rich to poor regions. Unfortunately, the role of academics in these debates has been limited, and the discussion in the public arena has plenty of stereotypes and has been plagued by the absence of good data. In this sense, this chapter has two main objectives: to present new and sound data to analyse regional income inequality in Spain from 1860 to 2010, and to discuss the sources of these regional income differences.

There is an abundant and increasing literature that studies the factors that influence the distribution of regional income within countries. Commonly, scholars differentiate between two groups of factors: 'first nature causes' and 'second nature causes'. The former group is related to natural geographical circumstances, such as the presence of natural resources, rainfall, access to the sea, temperature, roughness of the terrain, or the availability of agricultural land, while the latter is related to human actions and economic incentives, such as interregional trade, scale economies, Marshallian externalities or spillovers (Krugman 1991).

Two characteristics of Spanish geography (i.e. first nature causes) play a major role in explaining the creation of several substantially independent economic regions during the centuries prior to industrialization.[1] However, the size of the country, a continent in miniature, represents substantial agricultural diversity.[2] In the north and the north-west, where there is a relatively mild and humid climate, agriculture follows a pattern similar to those in other north-west European countries. Accordingly, farms are predominantly small and medium family farms, and the principal agrarian products are corn, potatoes and cattle. Because the landlocked centre of Spain is dominated by semi-arid plateaus and mountains subject to temperature extremes, the production of agricultural commodities is particularly difficult, and land productivity is comparatively low. In these interior regions, where irrigation projects are not developed, dry farming is predominant, and the main products are grains, wine and cattle. Finally, in the Mediterranean coast and southern regions, a Mediterranean agriculture prevails. Although the main products of Mediterranean agriculture are wheat, wine and olive oil, several relevant regional differences are observed. For example, in Valencia, irrigated horticulture (orange trees, orchard fruits, rice and vegetables) was more developed than in Andalusia. Just as the agrarian production is heterogeneous throughout the country, the mineral production is also not equally distributed across the country. For example, iron ore is available in the Basque Country but is scarce in other parts of Spain, and coal is produced in Asturias but not in the Balearic Islands.[3]

The shape of the Spanish territory and the distribution of mountain ranges have also strongly influenced the resilience of different economic entities. The territory of Spain is mainly located in the Iberian Peninsula (approximately 85 per cent), but also comprises the Balearic Islands in the Mediterranean, the Canary Islands in the Western Atlantic Ocean off the African coast, and Ceuta and Melilla, two enclaves in North Africa that border Morocco. Spain is certainly a coastal country, with approximately 13,000 km (8,000 miles) of coastline, and of its 50 provinces, only 19 are landlocked. At the same time, the majority of the Spanish peninsular region consists of the Meseta Central, a highland plateau that is rimmed and divided by mountain ranges. The presence of several mountain ranges and other features of physical geography makes communications among the centre and the coastal regions located at its periphery difficult. Similarly, communication between the different coastal regions is also difficult. For example, before the construction of the Spanish railways network, the most efficient and fastest communication between Barcelona and Bilbao was not by land, the shortest Euclidian distance, but by circumnavigating the Iberian Peninsula (a journey of approximately 1,552 nautical miles, the same distance between the ports of Barcelona and Trieste).

As we will show later in this chapter, the distribution of regional income in Spain is influenced by the action of economic forces more than by first nature causes. In other words, these geographical determinants aside, the economic actions of Spaniards, which were sometimes unintentional, had modified the economic geography of Spain and the initial distribution of income and population across the country. If the first nature had been the sole determinant of regional income differences, then the regional distribution of income and population have remained constant throughout history. In retrospect, one observes that several of the richest regions in Spain were among the poorest before industrialization, while several of the regions with abundant natural resources in the past are now among the least developed.

This process was initiated by the reallocation of income through the creation of the national market and the diffusion of the industrialization process, which resulted in a spectacular increase in regional income inequality across Spain. The industrialized regions (in particular, Catalonia and the Basque Country) most benefited from this process of uneven development. Later, the movements of production factors (mainly labour migrations) across regions, the emulation of economic structures, the technological diffusion and the openness of the Spanish economy to foreign trade changed the prevalent distribution of income and reduced regional inequalities. This process of regional income convergence was stopped a few decades ago, after the incorporation of Spain into the European Community. In fact, the data for recent years indicate an incipient upsurge in regional inequalities. This new wave of regional economic inequality is not mainly caused by differences in economic structure across the regions, but by productivity differentials. Therefore, regional income inequality has been an enduring characteristic of the Spanish economy because it has not disappeared, despite more than 150 years of increasing economic and political integration.

2. Long-term patterns of regional income inequality: new data and stylized facts

To analyse the long-term evolution and determinants of regional inequality in Spain, we estimated the regional GDP figures for the years 1860, 1900, 1910, 1920 and 1930, while the data were collected from different well-known sources for the remaining years (every decade from 1940 to 2010).[4] In our estimation of regional GDP, we mainly follow the methodology developed by Geary and Stark (2002), who developed a model that made possible an indirect estimation of the regional GDPs at factor cost in current prices.[5] The data necessary for this type of estimation include Spanish output per worker and sector, as well as working population and nominal wages by the sector and region. In our estimation, however, we improve Geary and Starks' approach in two ways. First, in several industries, we compute direct estimates of regional output. Second, we consider up to five sectors (agriculture, mining, manufacturing, construction and services) for Spain, even though Geary and Stark (2002) only consider three for the British Isles (agriculture, manufacturing and services).[6]

Figure 3.11.1 depicts the long-term evolution of an index of regional income dispersion: the unweighted coefficient of variation of the GDP per capita in Spanish NUTS 2 regions,[7] which could be considered a measure of sigma-convergence.[8]

Regional income inequality in Spain increased between 1860 and 1920. That time was followed by a period of gradual reduction in regional income inequality until 1940. The process stopped during the 1940s and 1950s, which roughly corresponds to the first phase of Franco's regime. Regional per capita income convergence accelerated from 1960 to 1980; conversely, convergence has halted in the years following Spain's ascension to the former European Economic Community (the present-day EU). In the long term, the regional income inequality followed a U-shaped pattern, with a growth in inequality between 1860 and 1920 followed by a long phase of declining regional inequalities that lasted until the 1980s. Since then, the persistence of regional inequalities seems to suggest an end, at least temporarily, of this regional convergence process.

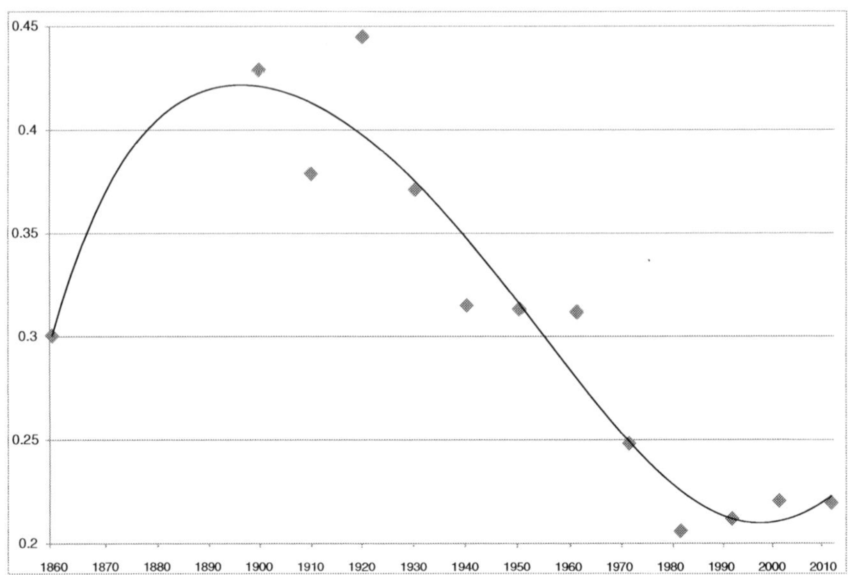

Figure 3.11.1 Sigma-convergence among Spanish regions, 1860–2010 (unweighted coefficient of variation)

Source: See Table 3.11.1.

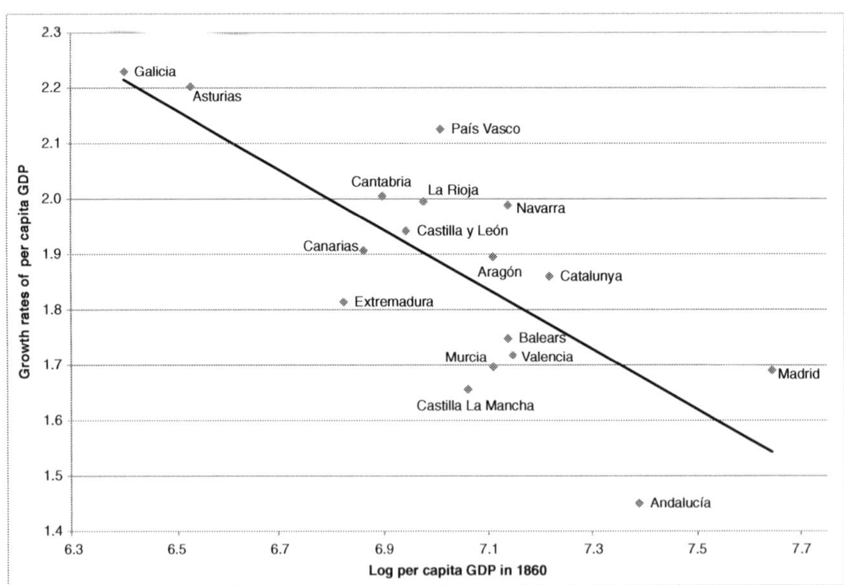

Figure 3.11.2 Beta-convergence among Spanish regions, 1860–2010

Source: See Table 3.11.1.

A complementary approach to the sigma-convergence methodology for investigating the regional convergence process is based on growth regressions, in which the rate of growth per capita income between two periods is explained by the level of initial per capita income. A negative correlation between the growth and initial incomes implies a tendency for poor regions to catch up to the rich ones. The convergence concept associated with these regressions is known as beta-convergence.

This exercise is presented in Figure 3.11.2, which shows how poorer regions in 1860 grew faster over the next 150 years (i.e. from 1860 to 2010) than richer regions. Interestingly, the implied beta-convergence rate, above 2 per cent, is similar for exercises conducted for other countries and periods. It should be noted that this rate is sometimes associated with the predictions of the Solow growth model, and specifically with the action of diminishing returns to capital (Sala-i-Martin 1996).

A more detailed approach to the question of regional inequality is displayed in Table 3.11.1, which contains information on the relative per capita income of the Spanish regions (with the Spanish average set equal to 1). A new interpretation emerges from close observation of this table: regional rankings varied very little during these 150 years. Therefore, the leader and lagging regions maintained their positions despite major changes in overall income dispersion. To be more precise, in almost all of the different benchmarks, the Basque Country, Catalonia and Madrid occupied the first three positions of the regional income rankings. The exceptions to this stability are Andalusia, which was in the second position in 1860, Baleares, which reached the top positions in 1971, 1981 and 1991, and Navarre in 2000 and 2010. Similarly, there is a group of regions that habitually list among the poorer ones. In particular, during these 150 years, Extremadura is ever among the five poorest Spanish regions.

In close connection with the ranking stability described here, few regions experienced relative growth miracles, and few regions also experienced substantial growth failures. The most notable growth miracle is the Basque Country, which was situated in the 10th position (of 17 regions) in 1860 and climbed to be the richest region of Spain in 1900. By contrast, Andalusia lost ground since 1860; it was in the second position in 1860, the ninth position in 1900, in the 15th position in 1950, and remained in the same position in 2010.

Maps 3.11.1–3.11.3 present a spatial perspective of the regional distribution of per capita income in Spain and qualify our previous interpretations. In 1860 (see Map 3.11.1), only two regions were distinguished as the richest (over 20 per cent of Spain's per capita income): Madrid and Andalusia. The remaining regions were clearly ordered following an income gradient from east to west, with the richest regions situated in the eastern part of the country and the poorest in the western part closer to the Portuguese frontier. In 1920 (see Map 3.11.2), the income distribution was substantially altered mainly as a consequence of the growth failure of Andalusia and the growth miracle of the Basque Country. The three richest regions of the country (Catalonia, Madrid and the Basque Country) formed a triangle situated in the north-east part of the peninsula, and the adjacent

Table 3.11.1 The relative per capita GDP of Spanish regions, 1860–2010 (Spain = 1)

	1860	*1900*	*1910*	*1920*	*1930*	*1940*	*1950*	*1961*	*1971*	*1981*	*1991*	*2000*	*2010*
Andalucía	1.36	0.87	0.98	0.76	0.77	0.75	0.72	0.67	0.73	0.73	0.71	0.73	0.74
Aragón	1.02	0.92	0.95	1.08	0.97	1.03	1.00	1.04	1.00	1.05	1.08	1.10	1.09
Asturias	0.56	0.94	0.68	0.87	0.95	1.15	1.14	1.07	1.01	1.00	0.90	0.88	0.95
Baleares	1.05	0.82	1.01	0.82	1.23	1.36	1.17	1.26	1.35	1.34	1.45	1.05	0.90
Canarias	0.79	0.60	0.65	0.72	0.71	0.92	0.85	0.79	0.90	0.97	0.99	0.92	0.86
Cantabria	0.82	0.99	0.90	0.94	1.13	0.97	1.15	1.17	1.09	1.04	0.92	0.97	1.03
Castile-La Mancha	0.97	0.86	0.78	0.72	0.65	0.68	0.74	0.67	0.73	0.77	0.80	0.79	0.72
Castile-León	0.86	0.82	0.80	0.81	0.73	0.85	0.93	0.81	0.83	0.87	0.88	0.92	0.98
Cataluña	1.14	1.84	1.92	2.04	1.67	1.63	1.55	1.54	1.33	1.24	1.24	1.21	1.15
C. Valenciana	1.06	1.05	1.00	1.10	1.20	1.06	1.02	1.12	1.01	1.02	1.03	0.91	0.87
Extremadura	0.76	0.66	0.65	0.53	0 58	0.60	0.59	0.57	0.56	0.62	0.69	0.64	0.72
Galicia	0.49	0.54	0.61	0.49	0.64	0.72	0.72	0.70	0.74	0.80	0.83	0.78	0.86
Madrid	1.77	1.63	1.52	1.64	1.80	1.53	1.49	1.47	1.32	1.30	1.29	1.40	1.39
Murcia	1.02	0.62	0.67	0.69	0.86	0.75	0.77	0.75	0.83	0.82	0.82	0.83	0.81
Navarra	1.05	0.83	0.87	1.13	0.98	1.15	1.17	1.16	1.15	1.11	1.17	1.29	1.29
País Vasco	0.92	2.05	1.55	1.78	1.64	1.67	1.82	1.60	1.38	1.14	1.11	1.28	1.39
Rioja	0.89	1.08	0.88	0.70	0.83	1.22	1.13	1.14	1.09	1.12	1.13	1.16	1.10

Source: Tirado et al. (2015).

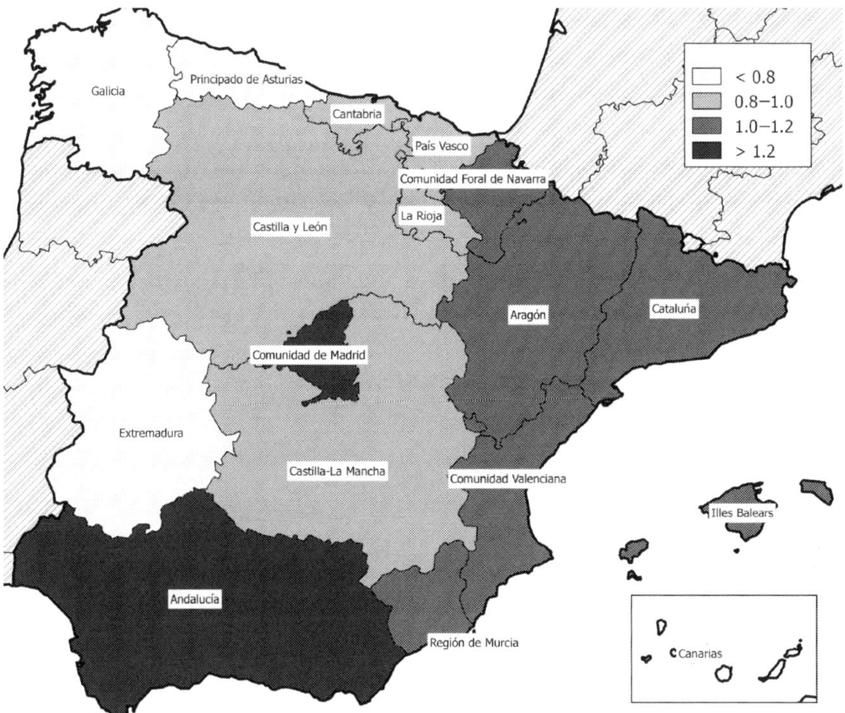

Map 3.11.1 The relative per capita GDP of Spanish regions, 1860 (Spain = 1)

regions enjoyed the subsequent levels of income. The poorest regions were in the western and southern peripheries. As substantial literature observed for recent times, the regions with higher or lower income levels appeared spatially clustered (Magrini 2004). In a comparison of the map for 2000 (see Map 3.11.3) with those for 1920 (see Map 3.11.2) and 1860 (see Map 3.11.1), the changes were much less profound from 1920 to 2010 than in the period 1860–1920. In fact, the income gradient observed in 1920 is also easily observable in 2000. Again, the poorest regions were situated in the western (Galicia) and southern (Andalusia, Castile-La Mancha and Estremadura) parts of the country. Furthermore, five regions (the Balearic Islands, the Canary Islands, Navarre, Murcia and La Rioja) slightly improved their relative positions, while only one (Valencia) lost ground. This improvement translates to the reduction of inequality (sigma-convergence) observed in Figure 3.11.1.

Until now, we have considered the per capita income inequality across regions, but there are other ways to consider the regional distribution of income. One of the most popular methods is the analysis of the relative GDP sizes of the different regions (i.e. the part of Spain's GDP that is produced in each region). This exercise is performed in Table 3.11.2. It is obvious that the spatial localization of Spanish income had been dramatically altered between 1860 and 2010. Five

Table 3.11.2 The share of Spanish regions in Spanish GDP, 1860–2010 (per cent)

	1860	*1900*	*1910*	*1920*	*1930*	*1940*	*1950*	*1961*	*1971*	*1981*	*1991*	*2000*	*2010*
Andalucía	25.8	16.6	18.7	15.0	15.0	14.9	14.5	13.0	12.8	12.5	12.7	13.2	13.3
Aragón	5.8	4.5	4.5	5.0	4.2	4.2	3.9	3.7	3.4	3.4	3.3	3.2	3.1
Asturias	1.9	3.2	2.4	3.0	3.2	3.8	3.6	3.5	3.1	3.0	2.5	2.3	2.2
Baleares	1.8	1.4	1.7	1.3	1.9	2.1	1.8	1.8	2.1	2.3	2.7	2.2	2.1
Canarias	1.2	1.2	1.5	1.5	1.7	2.4	2.5	2.5	3.1	3.6	3.8	3.9	3.9
Cantabria	1.2	1.5	1.4	1.4	1.7	1.5	1.7	1.7	1.5	1.4	1.3	1.3	1.3
Castile-La Mancha	7.5	6.4	6.0	5.6	5.0	5.1	5.4	4.3	3.7	3.4	3.4	3.4	3.2
Castile-León	11.4	10.1	9.5	8.9	7.7	8.9	9.5	7.5	6.5	6.0	5.8	5.6	5.4
Cataluña	12.2	19.5	20.1	22.5	19.8	18.1	17.8	19.9	20.1	19.7	19.4	18.8	18.5
C. Valenciana	8.6	9.0	8.6	9.0	9.6	8.9	8.4	9.2	9.2	9.9	10.2	9.3	9.4
Extremadura	3.4	3.1	3.3	2.6	2.8	2.9	2.9	2.6	1.9	1.8	1.9	1.7	1.7
Galicia	5.6	5.7	6.3	4.9	6.1	7.3	6.9	6.0	5.9	6.0	5.9	5.3	5.1
Madrid	5.5	6.8	6.7	8.2	10.5	9.2	9.7	12.8	14.7	16.3	16.4	18.2	19.2
Murcia	2.5	1.9	2.1	2.1	2.4	2.1	2.1	2.0	2.0	2.1	2.2	2.4	2.5
Navarra	2.0	1.4	1.4	1.7	1.4	1.6	1.6	1.5	1.6	1.5	1.6	1.7	1.8
País Vasco	2.5	6.6	5.2	6.4	6.2	6.0	6.7	7.3	7.6	6.5	6.0	6.6	6.4
Rioja	1.0	1.1	0.8	0.6	0.7	1.0	0.9	0.9	0.8	0.8	0.8	0.8	0.8

Source: See Table 3.11.1.

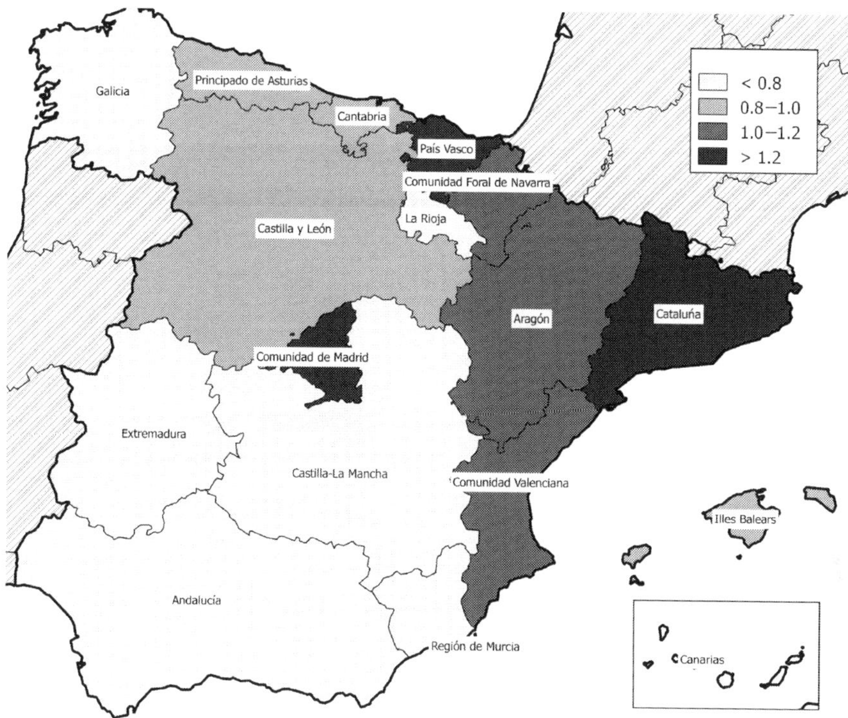

Map 3.11.2 The relative per capita GDP of Spanish regions, 1920 (Spain = 1)

regions (Andalusia, Aragon, Castile-La Mancha, Castile-León and Estremadura) halved their participation in the Spanish GDP, La Rioja and Navarre reduced their participation by about one-fifth, and the participation of Cantabria, Galicia, Murcia and Valencia remained stable (with changes of less than 10 per cent), while the remaining regions experienced notable increases in their participation: Asturias and Baleares increased their participation by one-fifth, Catalonia increased by 50 per cent, the Basque Country more than doubled its share, and the Canary Islands and Madrid more than tripled their shares. As we will show later, these changes in the economic size of the different regions were not only due to differences in GDP per capita, but also to the reallocation of the population across Spain, from the declining to the rising regions, which became simultaneously richer and more populated.

3. The forces behind regional inequality in Spain

In short, the descriptive evidence presented in the previous section for the evolution of regional income inequality in Spain illustrates that its long-term evolution followed an inverted U-shape. The underlying predictions of different theoretical

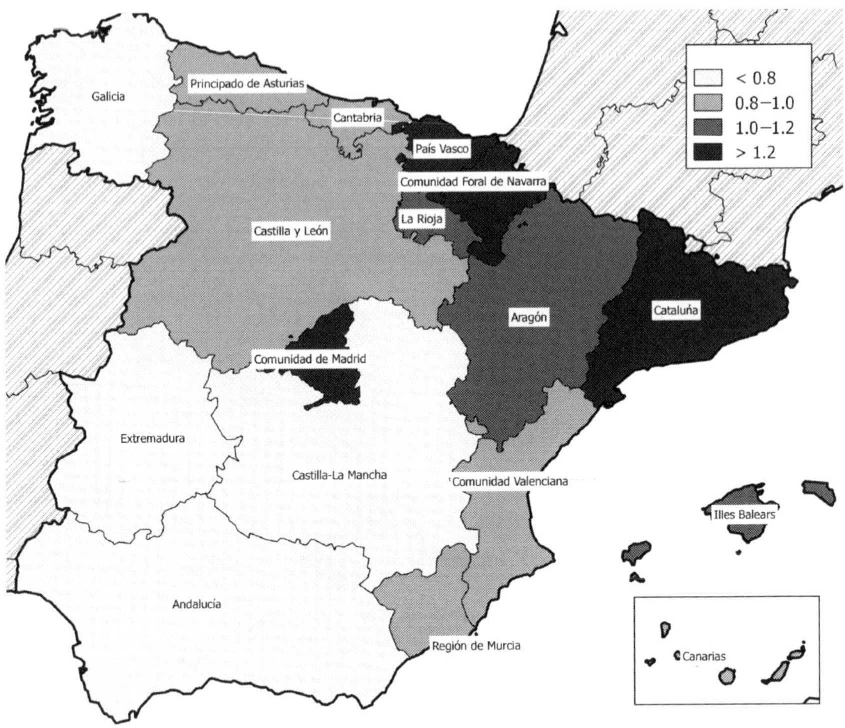

Map 3.11.3 The relative per capita GDP of Spanish regions, 2000 (Spain = 1)

models of trade and growth are compatible with this empirical evidence; however, as we mentioned in the introduction, this changing regional income inequality is not compatible with an explanation based solely on first nature causes, which have resulted in a more stable long-term regional income distribution.[9]

According to neoclassical trade theory, the initial regional income per capita disparities are caused by spatial differences in the distribution of endowments (e.g. natural resources, factors of production and infrastructure) and technology. The increase in trade and factor movements across regions (i.e. the integration of regional markets) may lead to changes in this initial distribution of income. In the optimistic version of the neoclassical trade model, this process produces factor price equalization across regions, and hence per capita GDP convergence. By contrast, in the pessimistic version, the increasing market integration may also point to increasing regional specialization and regional inequality because regions differ in factor endowments. The new economic geography literature is also able to explain this U-shaped evolution of regional income inequality. In these models, market integration can lead to the spatial agglomeration of economic activity in regions with larger markets due to the presence of increasing returns (Krugman 1991). This agglomeration of economic activity produces increasing regional inequality. However, migration and congestion costs counterbalance this process, and eventually generate a process of delocalization of certain economic activities, which may engender regional income convergence.[10] Finally, the models and empirical analyses based on structural change underline that in the first stages of economic growth, structural change and specialization favoured increasing regional inequality. The completion of the structural change process, with associated increases in capital movements and internal migration, spawns a reduction in regional income inequalities.[11]

3.1 The rapid increase of regional income inequality, 1850–1920

Modern Spanish economic growth started in the mid-nineteenth century. This process of economic growth was enhanced initially by the adoption of the classical innovations of industrial production (namely the steam engine and the new textile machinery), the advance in the structural change process, and the integration of national markets for goods and factors of production, as well as the increasingly globalized Atlantic economy.

As we mentioned above, this process of economic development was accompanied by a substantial increase in regional inequality, which lasted until 1920. This upswing of regional income inequality was caused by two concomitant forces: the incomplete process of the national market creation, which was more characterized by trade integration than by factor markets integration, and the uneven process of industrialization. Furthermore, imperfections in the national market and the absence of economic forces that counterbalanced uneven regional industrialization generated the development of a non-optimum currency area, which exacerbated regional inequalities in income and facilitated an extraordinary regional concentration of manufacturing.

From a long-term perspective, the Spanish home market integration received a strong push in the mid-nineteenth century. In fact, prior to the mid-nineteenth century, the Spanish regions had relatively independent economies. The barriers to interregional trade and the movement of capital and labour were ubiquitous: local tariffs and regulations on domestic commerce were widespread; weights and measures differed across regions; transport costs were very high due to low public investment in transportation infrastructure and the particular geography of Spain, which lacked an extensive water transport system; economic information moved slowly across regions; the banking system was underdeveloped; and many regions had their own currencies (although all currencies were based on a bi-metallic monetary system).[12] Furthermore, as we have already discussed in the introduction to this chapter, the regions differed markedly in their agrarian specialization and natural endowments. As a consequence, regional commodity markets were scarcely integrated, although certain interdependencies in commodity prices had existed since the eighteenth century,[13] and the prices of production differed from one region to another (Rosés and Sánchez-Alonso 2004).

Both market liberalization and transport improvements, particularly the completion of Spain's railways network, induced the creation of a national market for most important commodities during the second half of the nineteenth century.[14] According to the calculations of Herranz (2005), the introduction of the railways heralded an enormous 86 per cent reduction in transport prices in 1878. In addition to market liberalization and transport improvements, the successive political reforms of the nineteenth century gave legal support for property rights, eliminated tariffs and local restrictions on home commerce, and assured the free mobility of people and capital (Tedde 1994).

This process of the creation of the national markets for commodities was accompanied by notable progress in the integration of the factor markets for production (capital, land and labour). An examination of regional convergence in short-term interest rates of commercial paper suggests that the integration of capital markets seems to have been accomplished by the latter half of the nineteenth century. More specifically, commercial paper shows a rapid convergence in prices across regions after 1850 (Castañeda and Tafunell 1993). It is not difficult to attribute this decline in interregional short-term interest rate differentials to the developments in Spain's telegraph network and the profound changes in its financial system (Tortella 1973). The first telegraph lines were established in 1855 and rapidly connected all of the Spanish cities during the following decades; however, in comparative terms, the density of the network was low and telegrams were expensive. From the early 1840s onwards, the Spanish banking system experienced notable progress but did not resemble today's structure because the commercial banks had no branches nationwide. For the first time, in 1842, a new legal framework allowed the establishment of private banks that were organized as limited liability corporations. These banks were also granted the right to issue banknotes that were legal tender in the same town in which they were issued but were not accepted elsewhere. Consequently, the transference of capital across the main financial centres was based on a system of bills of exchange and a network of local-based merchant bankers (Castañeda and Tafunell 1993; Maixé-Altés and Iglesias 2009). For this reason, until 1884, short-term interest rates varied from one city to another. However, political reforms dramatically altered this state of affairs. In 1874, the Banco de España became the sole issuing bank (Martorell 2001). Eleven years later, by 1885, the same bank established the first nationwide branch network, allowing the movement of capital across towns at constant and cheap rates, and thus integrating the national capital market and creating a currency union (Castañeda and Tafunell 1993). The development of land markets paralleled this development of capital markets; therefore, a national market for agrarian land was in force in Spain by the early twentieth century (Carmona and Rosés 2012).

The national market for labour was more complex than the capital and land markets. By contrast, substantial evidence indicates that the Spanish labour market became increasingly integrated after the second half of the nineteenth century. In particular, the coefficients of variation of real wages show a significant downward trend, exhibiting the typical behaviour of convergence processes resulting from market integration (Rosés and Sánchez-Alonso 2004). However, this process of wage convergence was not accompanied by dramatic interregional migration processes. Therefore, the number of Spaniards residing outside of their province of origin was relatively small, approximately 9.3 per cent by 1910, especially compared with the number of foreign emigrants residing in the new settlement countries at that time (Silvestre 2003). Despite this reduced number of home migrants, migrations rose appreciably during the second half of the nineteenth century, showing a trend similar to that of other countries in Southern Europe. The most important component of these migration patterns was the movement of populations from the countryside to the cities. Rural migration was often seasonal or to the nearest town, often a first step towards larger towns and the industrial areas (Silvestre 2007). As a consequence, the urbanization rates increased appreciably, and some cities and regions grew rapidly (Reher 1994). However, the impact of these migrations on structural change was relatively modest.[15]

The integration of the Spanish economy into the global Atlantic economy did not follow a similar pattern compared with those observed for the national market. Although the liberal reforms established in the mid-nineteenth century ended the main prohibitions on foreign trade and favoured the free movement of capital and labour across Spain's borders, Spanish foreign trade policy took a protectionist turn in the late 1880s. This protectionism and renouncement of the international monetary system based on the gold standard prevented Spain from taking advantage of the convergence effects generated in the Atlantic economy during the first wave of globalization (O'Rourke and Williamson 2001) and isolated, at least partially, Spanish producers from foreign competition.

In summary, the integration of the Spanish markets had many facets. On the one hand, Spain developed a national market with one currency and unified its laws for the same customs and for the free movement of goods, people and capital. On the other hand, Spain was less integrated in the international economy, and the interregional movements of the population were less intense than the movements of goods and capital. Furthermore, the relatively low taxation and the concomitant small size of the government budget impeded the development of a 'true' fiscal federalism (i.e. the interregional flows of taxes and investment were of little importance). This situation resulted in a non-optimum currency area because the flows of government funds could not be used to counterbalance the presence of spatial asymmetric shocks, and the people and private capital did not move swiftly from one region to another in response to these shocks. As theory predicts, this non-optimum currency area led to an increase in the unequal distribution of economic activity, and hence the regional income inequality across Spain.

The regional distribution of the manufacturing industries during the period 1850–1920 became increasingly unequal, and the levels of manufacturing were comparatively high at the end of the period. In other words, Spanish industrialization was mainly led by Catalonia and the Basque Country, while the rest of the country experienced a substantial process of deindustrialization.[16] Catalonia and the Basque Country produced about 21.5 per cent of Spain's industrial output in 1860. This share doubled over the next 60 years and reached 43 per cent in 1920. Simultaneously, their 14 per cent contribution to the Spanish population remained constant. As a consequence, over the same period, their index of industrial intensity (which divided the relative amount of industrial production by the relative population) grew from 1.6 to 3. Remarkably, a large part of the increasing concentration of manufacturing can be explained by the location of the more modern and sophisticated industries. Thus, by the early twentieth century (1910), Catalonia and the Basque Country accounted for over 61 per cent of the total employment in metallurgy, engineering, chemicals, and textiles.[17]

The creation of the national market was a prime mover of this unequal industrialization. Broadly speaking, when markets became increasingly integrated, regions with a comparative advantage in manufacturing and a potential for increasing returns tended to concentrate their industrial production. Specifically, a combination of comparative advantage forces (particularly the relative abundance of capital, artisans and other skilled labour and the scarcity of agrarian land and professions) and externalities favoured the industrial boom of Catalonia. However, in the case of the Basque Country, without denying the importance of the forces at work in Catalonia and the role played by the national market, the availability of iron ore and the bilateral trade with Britain (iron ore was exchanged for the coal that was used in the Basque metal industries) favoured the localization of the metal industry in the region and the associated process of industrial diversification (Tirado et al. 2002; Martínez-Galarraga 2012).

3.2 The decrease in regional inequality, 1920–1980

Between 1920 and 1980, Spain's real income increased by approximately eightfold, at an average rate of 3.5 per cent. However, economic growth underwent several successive phases and was unstable. Economic growth accelerated in the 1920s, accompanied by substantial total factor productivity (TFP) growth. However, this process was interrupted during the years of turmoil before and after the Civil War. TFP improvements encouraged the explosive growth during the golden age of the 1950s and 1960s, and mitigated the deceleration during the transition to democracy during the years after the first oil crisis (Prados de la Escosura and Rosés 2009).

Figure 3.11.1 shows that the regional inequality decreased, but not at a constant rate, during the period between 1920 and 1980. The process was intense during the 1920s and 1930s (the coefficient of variation fell about one-quarter, from 0.478 in 1920 to 0.348 in 1940), stopped during the early decades of Franco's regime (the 1940s and 1950s) and reassumed its initial intensity during the 1960s and 1970s (the coefficient of variation declined a substantial 37 per cent from 0.356 in 1950 to 0.220 in 1980). This evidence indicates that the period of rapid growth may be associated with periods of decreasing regional inequality.

As mentioned, the first increase in convergence occurred in Spain during the 1920s and the subsequent decade. Several reasons may explain this extraordinary change. On the one hand, the integration of the Spanish market evolved in a novel way because of a substantial increase in paved roads, which complemented the previous development of the railway network, and gave capillarity to the national goods market (Herranz 2008). More prominently, for the first time, the increasing integration of the goods markets was accompanied by mass migrations. Spaniards left declining regions, which were mainly rural and agrarian, and reallocated to the richest regions, which were more urban and specialized in industry and services (Silvestre 2003). This process led to a convergence in unskilled wages, with low-wage regions having a relatively higher increase in wages compared with those in the richer regions (Rosés and Sánchez-Alonso 2004), and a first wave of structural change in which the share of agrarian employment decreased elsewhere, albeit more intensely in the poorest regions (Rosés et al. 2010). Furthermore, the number of industrial locations expanded, and hence industrial employment became increasingly dispersed. There are several likely explanations for this process of extensive industrialization. The same migration that increased wages in the poor locations also increased the demand from local markets, which may have eased the localization of industries with increasing returns. Simultaneously, the notable progress of electrification eliminated many restrictions for industrial location. In particular, factories no longer needed to be located close to energy sources such as coal mines or rivers. Finally, the change of trade policy, which became more protectionist, favoured the development of new industrial centres such as Madrid or Saragossa, which were not located at the frontiers and had better accessibility to the national market due to their central position (Tirado et al. 2003).

The Spanish Civil War and the first years of Franco's regime stopped not only the economic growth, but also the national economic integration. The regulation of markets for goods and factors of production, and the government control of prices and quantities in the final goods, intermediates, energy, capital markets and wages, reduced the mobility of factors and resources. This government intervention created a false impression of price convergence without a significant increase in interregional trade. The movement of capital across regions slowed, and labour migration came to a halt after the first large expansion in the 1920s (Silvestre 2003). Additionally, the absence of infrastructure investment did nothing to reduce the transport costs during the 1940s and early 1950s. The Franco regime's adoption of an autarkic policy implied a substantial isolation of the Spanish economy from the international market. Foreign trade and international capital movements during these years reached their lowest levels in contemporary Spanish economic history (Prados de la Escosura et al. 2011). All of these policies affected the structural change that stopped and even reversed during the 1940s, with a surprising increase in agrarian employment, to the detriment of the industrial and services employment (Prados de la Escosura 2003). Figure 3.11.1 shows that this resulted in a complete interruption of the process of regional convergence.

The economic liberalization and stabilization measures introduced at the end of the 1950s favoured the transition of the Spanish economy towards a new phase of economic development (Prados de la Escosura et al. 2011). This period was characterized by, among other elements, high aggregate growth rates of production and by the lead taken by the industrial sector in the country's economic activity. In association with this growth, the Spanish economic growth in the 1960s was also typified by advances in the construction and services sectors, stimulated by the growing mobility of the workforce that was becoming increasingly concentrated in the big cities. New investments in infrastructures, such as roads, railways, communication networks, and energy supply and distribution, led to further reductions in internal transport costs. These liberalizing policies also affected the Spanish integration into the international economy. Although at a slow pace, Spain started to recover its position in the international markets. Spain's membership in international organizations such as the GATT, the World Bank and the IMF, and its liberal policies regarding the regulation of international commodity and capital movements, marked the starting point for a new wave of growth in the movement of goods, capital and labour across Spanish borders. Nevertheless, the level of integration reached by the Spanish markets for goods and capital during this period cannot be considered that of a truly open economy. The crisis of the 1970s, which in Spain stretched well into the 1980s, drastically slowed these upward trends, and the high average GDP growth rates were not recorded again until the final years of the twentieth century.

The 1960s and 1970s witnessed a new period of rapid decrease in regional inequalities. Again, migrations and structural change seemed to be the prime movers of this process. Several studies argue that the process of convergence in regional structures of production was the major determinant of convergence in labour productivity and per capita income in Spain during 1960–1985.[18] The rural exodus towards cities and also to more developed European countries resulted in a substantial decline in agrarian employment and in an increase in the share of the services sector in all Spanish regions. Tourism, a tertiary sector activity, also became located in many rural areas that were once poor and underdeveloped, and helped the development of many coastal regions such as Andalusia, Valencia, and the Canary and Balearic Islands.

3.3 The recent developments: a new upsurge in regional inequality since the entry into the EU?

A new phase in Spanish economic growth started after the country's entry into the EU in 1986. Until the recent depression, Spain grew faster than its European partners, which resulted in a substantial convergence in income per capita with the most industrialized countries. This new phase was no longer linked to the leadership of industrial production, but rather to that of the services and construction sectors. A new wave of investment in infrastructure helped to reduce further transport costs across Spanish regions and also across national borders. Huge investment programmes in the freeways, high-speed railway and telecommunications were developed during these years, and led to major advances both in the integration of the internal Spanish market and also the integration of Spain into international markets. The ascension of Spain to the EU in 1986 has been a major institutional reform that changed the framework in which the specialization of the Spanish regions occurred.

On a less optimistic note, however, this wave of economic growth was caused by a fast accumulation of production factors but not by productivity increases

(Prados de la Escosura and Rosés 2009). Two complementary explanations exist for the poor performance of productivity in Spain. First, as in most European countries, ICT-producing and -intensive sectors such as wholesale trade, transport and business services have shown weak productivity gains. Second, Spanish specialization was biased towards activities that are labour-intensive and with low added value, such as construction, hotels and restaurants, and personal services. This specialization served to reduce unemployment, but at a cost of sluggish productivity growth.

From a spatial perspective, although the economic growth occurred in all Spanish regions, the differences in growth rates were considerable. As a consequence, the regional disparity regarding income per capita has not only remained, but has also increased. In other words, the process of regional income convergence that occurred since the 1920s has practically ceased. The main mechanism at work in explaining the current increase in regional income inequality is that the differences in productivity across regions have not decreased, but have remained stable or even increased (Tirado et al. 2015). It is also worth noting that during the 1990s and 2000s, productivity variation in the tertiary sector explained most of these differences in regional productivity.

Several reasons serve to explain the resilience of the productivity differences across Spanish regions. The first reason is the end of the process of regional productive structures emulation, which was the main force behind the convergence of productivity during the previous period (Cuadrado et al. 1999). Second, the expansion of services, at the expense of industry and agriculture, contributed to the consolidation of the existing relative differences in income per capita across Spanish regions. Specifically, the different service industries showed remarkably different spatial patterns of concentration (Garrido-Yserte and Mancha-Navarro 2010). Despite an intense process of reduction in the share of agricultural production and employment, regions that traditionally specialized in primary activities have not been able to follow the pattern of development in the most developed regions. The regions historically agrarian have shown low population densities and regressive growth dynamics. Furthermore, they have experienced less dynamism in employment, which resulted in less employment per capita, and they specialized in low productivity services such as construction and the public sector. In contrast, those regions founded on a productive structure with stronger links to industry or services have been able to consolidate their specialization, which has resulted in comparatively higher productivity (Raymond and García Greciano 1994).

4. Conclusions

In this chapter, we have offered a long-term view on the regional inequality in Spain, and we have also explained some of its potential causes. For this purpose, we have assembled a new database on regional GDP per worker (per capita) that links new estimates for 1860–1930 with those existing for 1930–2000. As a result, we analysed the long-term evolution of regional GDP per worker (per capita) inequality across the Spanish NUTS 2 regions. Spanish regional income inequality followed a long-term inverted U-shaped pattern from 1860 to 2000: inequality rose until 1920 and has decreased since then until 1980. However, it is worth mentioning that during the 1980s and 1990s, the increases in inequality have re-emerged.

On the one hand, our new evidence seems to fit well with the explanations for regional inequality proposed by the neoclassical trade and growth theory, in the sense that the advance in the process of national market integration could have favoured the reduction of regional income inequality in the long term. In particular, the mobility of factors of production could have led to a regional equalization of factor endowments and rewards. On the other hand, however, our results could also be interpreted in light of new growth theory and new economic geography models. Despite the long-lasting and intense process of national market integration, differences in productivity have remained. More prominently, these differences were central not only for explaining the upsurge of inequality during the second half of the nineteenth century, but also for the new growth in inequality during the last years of the twentieth century.

The observations and interpretations presented here are confirmed based on particular regional experiences. Factors behind the success or failure of regions in terms of GDP per capita have changed throughout the long-term national experience of sustained economic growth and integration. During the initial phases, structural change (industrialization) was concentrated in a limited subset of regions that also experienced greater increases in productivity, favouring the initial increase of inequality across Spain's regions. Since the beginning of the twentieth century, further advances in the integration of the national market favoured the mobility of factors of production and, with low transport and transaction costs, a fast convergence of regional economic structures that provoked the decline in income inequality. Nevertheless, richer regions remained rich, and productivity differentials did not vanish, preventing further advances in the reduction in income inequality. Finally, in the last years analysed, the productivity differentials were at the forefront for explaining the apparent upsurge of regional inequality in the context of the Spanish integration into the EU.

Notes

1 A particular feature of Spain that is not shared by many European countries is the relative stability of its political boundaries. Perhaps due to its lack of participation in the two world wars, Spain has borders that have been roughly the same since the beginning of the eighteenth century, when the Kingdom of Spain ceded to Britain Gibraltar and Minorca in the Balearic Islands, the latter of which was definitively returned to the Spanish Crown in 1802.

2 Spain, with an area of 504,030 km^2, is the second largest country in Western Europe after France, and is the fourth largest country in Europe after Russia, Ukraine and France. A good analysis of the historical importance of these agrarian regional differences is available in Simpson (1995).

3 On the long-lasting influence of minerals in Spain's regional development, see Domenech (2008).
4 The following sources are used: Alcaide (2003) for 1930–1950, BBV (1999) for 1955–1995 and FUNCAS (2011) for 2000–2010.
5 This methodology is analysed in Chapter 2.
6 The specific methodology employed and data sources are from Rosés et al. (2010).
7 Spain is divided administratively into 17 regions or autonomous communities, which corresponds to the EU NUTS 2 level, and two autonomous cities (Ceuta and Melilla): Andalusia, Aragon, Asturias, Balearic Islands, Cantabria, Castile and León, Castile-La Mancha, Catalonia, Extremadura, Galicia, La Rioja, Madrid, Murcia, Navarra, the Basque Country and Valencia. The two autonomous cities are included in Andalusia in our calculations. A lower administrative level comprises the 50 provinces, which correspond to the NUTS 3 level. The provinces are the basis for the creation of autonomous communities, and interestingly displayed roughly the same boundaries since their creation in 1833. Furthermore, the definition of the Spanish provinces in 1833 was not based on geographic criteria, but rather the Spanish government created provinces following pre-existing historical divisions and the areas of influence of major towns.
8 For a full development of the concept of sigma-convergence and beta-convergence, see Barro and Sala-i-Martin (2003).
9 Readers should not misinterpret this argument: we do not deny that first nature causes have a significant, albeit secondary, role in explaining Spanish regional income inequality.
10 See, for example, Puga (1999).
11 Williamson (1965), Kim (1998) and Caselli and Coleman (2001).
12 See a review of the evidence in Rosés (2003).
13 See, for example, Ringrose (1996).
14 Gómez Mendoza (1983) suggested that the social savings linked to the construction of railways in Spain were significant, and even higher than in other European countries. Nevertheless, Herranz (2002) revised these figures, concluding that the social savings were lower than previously estimated. However, the strong reduction in transport costs that came with the railways is unambiguous.
15 Rosés et al. (2010).
16 There is a vast literature on the regional patterns of industrialization in Spain, including Nadal (1987), Nadal and Carreras (1990), Germán et al. (2001), Parejo (2001), Nadal (2003), Rosés (2003) and Paluzie et al. (2004).
17 Rosés (2003).
18 See, for example, Garcia-Greciano and Raymond (1999) and de la Fuente and Freire (2000).

References

Alcaide, J. (2003) *Evolución económica de las regiones y provincias españolas en el siglo XX*, Madrid: FBBVA.

Barro, R.J. and Sala-i-Martin, X. (2003) *Economic Growth*, New York: McGraw-Hill.

BBV (1999) *Renta nacional de España y su distribución provincial: serie homogénea años 1955 a 1993 y avances 1994 a 1997*, Bilbao: Fundación BBV.

Carmona, J. and Rosés, J.R. (2012) 'Land markets and agrarian backwardness (Spain, 1904–1934)', *European Review of Economic History*, Vol. 16 (1): 74–96.

Caselli, F. and Coleman, W.J. (2001) 'The U.S. structural transformation and regional convergence: a reinterpretation', *Journal of Political Economy*, Vol. 109 (3): 584–616.

Castañeda, L. and Tafunell, X. (1993) 'Un nuevo indicador para la historia financiera española: las letras de cambio a corto plazo', *Revista de Historia Económica*, Vol. 11 (2): 367–82.

Cuadrado, J.R., García, B. and Raymond, J.L. (1999) 'Regional convergence in productivity and productive structure: the Spanish case', *International Regional Science Review*, Vol. 22 (1): 35–53.

de la Fuente, A. and Freire, M.J. (2000) 'Estructura Sectorial y Convergencia Regional', *Revista de Economía Aplicada*, Vol. 23: 189–205.

Domenech, J. (2008) 'Mineral resource abundance and regional growth in Spain, 1860–2000', *Journal of International Development*, Vol. 20: 1122–35.

FUNCAS (2011) *Balance económico regional (autonomías y provincias). Años 2000 a 2010*, Madrid: Gabinete de Estadística Regional.

Garcia-Greciano, B. and Raymond, J.L. (1999) 'Las disparidades regionales y la hipótesis de convergencia: una revisión', *Papeles de Economía Española*, Vol. 80: 2–18.

Garrido-Yserte, R. and Mancha-Navarro, T. (2010) 'The Spanish regional puzzle: convergence, divergence and structural change', in J.R. Cuadrado-Roura (ed.), *Regional Policy, Economic Growth and Convergence*, Berlin: Springer-Verlag, pp. 103–24.

Geary, F. and Stark, T. (2002) 'Examining Ireland's post-famine economic growth performance', *Economic Journal*, Vol. 112 (482): 919–35.

Germán, L., Llopis, E., Maluquer, J. and Zapata, S. (eds) (2001) *Historia económica regional de España, siglos XIX y XX*, Barcelona: Crítica.

Gómez Mendoza, A. (1983) 'Spain', in P. O'Brien (ed.), *Railways and the Economic Growth of Western Europe*, London: Macmillan, pp. 148–69.

Herranz, A. (2002) *Infrastructure and Economic Growth in Spain, 1845–1935*, PhD Thesis, London, School of Economics and Political Science.

Herranz, A. (2005) 'La reducción de los costes de transporte en España (1800–1936)', *Cuadernos Económicos del ICE*, Vol. 70: 183–203.

Herranz, A. (2008) *Infraestructuras y crecimiento económico en España (1850–1935)*, Madrid: Fundación de los ferrocarriles españoles.

Kim, S. (1998) 'Economic integration and convergence: U.S. regions, 1840–1987', *Journal of Economic History*, Vol. 58 (3): 659–83.

Krugman, P. (1991) *Geography and Trade*, Cambridge, MA: MIT Press.

Magrini, S. (2004) 'Regional (di)convergence', in J.V. Henderson and J.F. Thisse (eds), *Handbook of Regional and Urban Economics, Vol. 4: Cities and Geography*, Amsterdam: Elsevier, pp. 2741–96.

Maixé-Altés, J.C. and Iglesias, E.M. (2009) 'Domestic monetary transfers and the inland bill of exchange markets in Spain (1775–1885)', *Journal of International Money and Finance*, Vol. 28 (3): 496–521.

Martínez-Galarraga, J. (2012) 'The determinants of industrial location in Spain, 1856–1929', *Explorations in Economic History*, Vol. 49 (2): 255–75.

Martorell, M. (2001) *Historia de la peseta: la España contemporánea a través de su moneda*, Barcelona: Planeta.

Nadal, J. (1987) 'La industrial fabril española en 1900. Una aproximación', in J. Nadal, A. Carreras and C. Sudrià (eds), *La economía española en el siglo XX. Una perspectiva histórica*, Barcelona: Ariel, pp. 23–61.

Nadal, J. (ed.) (2003) *Atlas de la industrialización de España, 1750–2000*, Bilbao: Fundación BBVA.

Nadal, J. and Carreras, A. (eds) (1990) *Pautas regionales de la industrialización española (siglos XIX–XX)*, Barcelona: Ariel.

O'Rourke, K.H. and Williamson, J.G. (2001) *Globalization and History: The Evolution of a Nineteenth Century Atlantic Economy*, Cambridge, MA: MIT Press.

Paluzie, E., Pons, J. and Tirado, D. (2004) 'The geographical concentration of industry across Spanish regions, 1856–1995', *Jahrbuch für Regionalwissenschaft* [Review of Regional Research], Vol. 24 (2): 143–60.

Parejo, A. (2001) 'Industrialización, desindustrialización y nueva industrialización de las regiones españolas (1950–2000). Un enfoque desde la historia económica', *Revista de Historia Industrial*, Vol. 19: 15–75.

Prados de la Escosura, L. (2003) *El progreso económico de España, 1850–2000*, Madrid: Fundación BBVA.

Prados de la Escosura, L. and Rosés, J.R. (2009) 'The sources of long-run economic growth in Spain, 1850–2000', *Journal of Economic History*, Vol. 69 (4): 1063–91.

Prados de la Escosura, L., Rosés, J.R. and Sanz-Villarroya, I. (2011) 'Economic reforms and growth in Franco's Spain', *Revista de Historia Económica/Journal of Iberian and Latin American Economic History*, Vol. 30 (1): 45–89.

Puga, D. (1999) 'The rise and fall of regional inequalities', *European Economic Review*, Vol. 43 (2): 303–34.

Raymond, J.L. and García-Greciano, B. (1994) 'Las disparidades en el PIB per cápita entre Comunidades Autónomas y la hipótesis de convergencia', *Papeles de Economía Española*, Vol. 59: 37–58.

Reher, D. (1994) 'Ciudades, procesos de urbanización y sistemas urbanos en la península ibérica, 1550–1991', in M. Guàrdia, F.J. Monclús and J.L. Oyón (eds), *Atlas histórico de las ciudades europeas. Península Ibérica*, Barcelona: Salvat – Centre de Cultura Contemporània de Barcelona, pp. 1–30.

Ringrose, D. (1996) *Spain, Europe and the 'Spanish Miracle', 1700–1990*, Cambridge: Cambridge University Press.

Rosés, J.R. (2003) 'Why isn't the whole of Spain industrialized? New economic geography and early industrialization, 1797–1910', *Journal of Economic History*, Vol. 63 (4): 995–1022.

Rosés, J.R. and Sánchez-Alonso, B. (2004) 'Regional wage convergence in Spain 1850–1930', *Explorations in Economic History*, Vol. 41 (2): 404–25.

Rosés, J.R., Martínez-Galarraga, J. and Tirado, D.A. (2010) 'The upswing of regional income inequality in Spain (1860–1930)', *Explorations in Economic History*, Vol. 47 (2): 244–57.

Sala-i-Martin, X. (1996) 'The classical approach to convergence analysis', *Economic Journal*, Vol. 106 (437): 1019–36.

Silvestre, J. (2003) *Migraciones interiores y mercado de trabajo en España, 1877–1936*, PhD Thesis (unpublished), Universidad de Zaragoza.

Silvestre, J. (2007) 'Temporary internal migrations in Spain, 1860–1930', *Social Science History*, Vol. 31 (4): 539–74.

Simpson, J. (1995) *Spanish Agriculture: The Long Siesta, 1765–1965*, Cambridge: Cambridge University Press.

Tedde, P. (1994) 'Cambio institucional y cambio económico en la España del siglo XIX', *Revista de Historia Económica*, Vol. 3: 525–38.

Tirado, D., Pons, J. and Paluzie, E. (2002) 'Economic integration and industrial location: the case of Spain before World War I', *Journal of Economic Geography*, Vol. 2 (3): 343–63.

Tirado, D., Pons, J. and Paluzie, E. (2003) 'Industrial agglomerations and wage gradients: the Spanish economy in the interwar period', 43rd Congress of the European Regional Science Association: Peripheries, Centres, and Spatial Development in the New Europe, 27–30 August 2003, Jyväskylä, Finland.

Tirado, D., Rosés, J.R. and Martínez-Galarraga, J. (2015) 'The long-term patterns of regional income inequality in Spain (1860–2000)', *Regional Studies*, Vol. 49 (4): 502–17.

Tortella, G. (1973) *Los orígenes del capitalismo en España. Banca, industria y ferrocarriles en el siglo XIX*, Madrid: Tecnos.

Williamson, J.G. (1965) 'Regional inequality and the process of national development: a description of the patterns', *Economic Development and Cultural Change*, Vol. 13 (4): 3–84.

3.12 Regional convergence and divergence in Sweden, 1860–2010

Evidence from Swedish historical regional GDP data[1]

Kerstin Enflo, Martin Henning and Lennart Schön

1. Introduction

Since industrialization, Sweden has experienced an amazing growth trajectory. In 1850, Sweden was a quite poor and peripheral country, with GDP levels close to the world's average. One and a half centuries later, Sweden ranks among the richest countries in the world with GDP levels more than three times the world's average (Schön 2013). Yet apart from a few case studies and some industry studies, little is known about the geographical evolution of Sweden's growth process. This chapter will fill in the gap by presenting estimates of Swedish regional GDPs for 24 counties corresponding to NUTS 3 regions from 1860 to 2010. Using this data set, we will present descriptive evidence on processes of regional convergence and divergence and discuss some tentative explanations for these patterns.

We argue that Sweden is an interesting case for long-run studies of geographical production patterns. With an area of 450,000 km^2, it is the EU's third largest and one of the most elongated. From its southernmost point, the distance to the northern border point roughly equals the distance to Rome. Yet population density is low: during the period that we study, population in Sweden increased from 3.8 million inhabitants in 1860, through 5.1 million in 1900, to 9 million in 2010. With scarcely populated but resource-rich regions in the north (especially hydropower, timber and iron ore) and major population centres in the south, the industrialization process induced a locational tension between natural resources and access to markets. Since Sweden's early industrialization was mostly dependent on iron, timber and agricultural products, industrialization had a pronouncedly rural character compared to other nations (Söderberg and Lundgren 1982). This is why Sweden experienced a late but pervasive urbanization process, still continuing to this day. Since the 1970s, Svensson Henning (2009) noted the increasing concentration of manufacturing and services, especially in technologically progressive industries.

This chapter shows that a long-lasting trend of regional convergence characterized Swedish economic growth. However, this long-term trend was interrupted in two periods, between the two world wars and after 1980. During these periods, convergence was replaced by divergence. In fact, the divergence trend of the post-1980s has taken the Sweden of 2010 back to the same overall regional inequality level as in the 1930s. Thus, it is possible that the 1980s mark the end of the long-term convergence trend.

With migration and urbanization forces, a strong concentration of population to certain growth poles is visible. Thus, for policymakers today Sweden's 'regional problem' is not one of unequal distribution of GDP per capita. It is rather one of unequal distribution of population per km^2. In some areas, population is currently so sparse that it is hard to sustain the minimum of public services required for continued economic activity.

There are some previous studies that have covered aspects of regional economic conditions in Sweden. When Andersson (1978) used data on county-level taxable incomes to study the distribution of income shares and population in Sweden between 1920 and 1975, he identified a high degree of stability during the period. Persson (1997) found long-run beta-convergence using similar data and for 1911 to 1993.

While previous studies document convergence in taxable incomes, their period is too short to cover the entire industrialization process. In addition, because of capital mobility, the distance between where production took place and where the incomes were taxed might be large. This is why we in this chapter focus on the evidence from the GDP series from the whole period from industrialization (1860) until today.

A comprehensive overview of Sweden's economic history is provided in Schön and Schubert (2010).[2] They divided the history into four distinct periods of industrial and institutional change. The period 1850–1890 was characterized by the early breakthrough of modern industrialization. Expanding trade was promoted by market integration, and resulted in the export-led growth of agricultural, iron and wood products. Some particular industries with a home-market orientation expanded as well, such as textiles and products from early mechanical workshops. In the period 1890–1910, the major breakthrough occurred in the industries that were closely linked to the core technologies of the Second Industrial Revolution. These industries include mechanical engineering and paper, but also various kinds of service industries, mainly tied to urban locations. An important feature was also the decreased relative cost of electricity transmission, fuelled by the advent of an early electrical power grid system. During 1910–1930, especially new industries such as shipbuilding and car manufacturing experienced growth. Other sectors, such as agriculture, iron and sawmills, were less successful. The great recession of the early 1930s, however, was less pronounced in Sweden compared to many other countries. The 1930s and 1940s were advantageous decades in terms of aggregate economic growth, coinciding with a continued integration of the electrical power grid.

After the Second World War until the crises in the late 1970s, the mechanical and engineering-based manufacturing industries and chemical industries expanded, while food, sawmilling and textile industries suddenly stagnated or even decreased. The public sector expanded, and the 'Swedish model' of economic organization was mainly implemented, including some policies actively promoting structural change in the economy. During the 1960s, the first major applications of electronic process control were also implemented in the capital-intensive industries (e.g. in paper production). An important part of the structural change during this epoch was the transformation of the agricultural sector, with drastically decreasing employment but strongly increasing productivity. The major crises of the late 1970s had a devastating effect on many traditional manufacturing industries in Sweden, such as shipbuilding. The 1980s and 1990s were characterized by diffusion of new innovations linked to microelectronics and the broadened application of these innovations, but also to major institutional reforms on the capital and labour markets. This has by some observers been labelled the Third Industrial Revolution. The implementation of new technologies related to the Third Industrial Revolution were relatively successful in Sweden, and during the last decades growth rates have generally superseded other nations in Europe.

2. Long-term patterns of GDP inequality in Sweden

2.1 Data and estimations

We estimate regional GDP for 10-year benchmarks since 1860 for the 24 Swedish counties (*län*, here referred to as 'counties'). These counties correspond to Eurostat's NUTS 3 level. The regional boundaries of Sweden's counties date back to Chancellor Axel Oxenstierna's Government Act of 1634, and until the early 2000s very few changes in their geographic definition occurred. However, during the last decade, the number of counties has been reduced to 21. To provide the reader with a consistent database, we have made some adjustments to regional boundaries for the 2010 estimate.

For the estimation of Swedish regional GDP, we have used a slightly modified version of the method suggested by Geary and Stark (2002), as presented in Chapters 1 and 2 of this book. Even though our calculations follow this standard as closely as possible, use of historical data often requires a certain degree of adjustments. For Geary-Stark connoisseurs, the exact specification of the estimation and definitions of the variables and statistical sources for the Swedish case can be found in Enflo et al. (2014a) and Enflo and Henning (2016). However, some important peculiarities deserve to be mentioned here as well.

For the estimations, we used regional employment data from the Swedish censuses and wage data from a wide variety of sources, such as published collections of wage series and the wage statistical yearbooks of Statistics Sweden. For the regional wage differentials, we sometimes had to rely on different kinds of proxies, such as regional living expenses adjustments made for public servants' salaries. To adjust our calculations to the known total national GDP, we used the national estimates from the Swedish National Historical Accounts (Krantz and Schön 2007) and regional population figures by Statistics Sweden. All sources for the historical data are tabulated and discussed in detail in Enflo et al. (2014a). From 1993 onwards, Statistics Sweden supply official regional GDP. One problem with these series, however, is that they refer to the new regional classification of NUTS 3. This means that five counties have merged into two new counties, thus resulting in only 21 NUTS 3 regions (during the 1990s, Malmöhus and Kristianstad were merged into Skåne län and Göteborg och Bohus, and Älvsborgs and Skaraborgs län were merged into Västra Götalands län). In order to retrieve the old border definitions, we assigned GDP, employment and population to their relative shares in 2000. Admittedly, the counties are not functional regions, but larger administrative units, and contain within them some degree of heterogeneity in terms of population density and production (normally, one county contains a few cities, a number of villages and considerable rural areas). To the best of our knowledge, the counties are the lowest possible unit of spatial aggregation for estimation of production values covering a broader set of activities than the manufacturing sector only.

Overall, the validity tests we have performed for our estimations indicate that they capture the regional distribution of GDPs quite well (see Enflo et al. 2014a). The data quality, especially the underlying series of regional industrial and service sector wages, increases from the early twentieth century.

2.2 Empirical results

Figure 3.12.1 describes the standard and population-weighted coefficient of variation for regional GDP per capita from 1860 to 2010. Over the period as a whole, we see a clear convergence trend. However, this is notably interrupted by divergence in 1910–1940 and after 1980.[3] We do not know yet whether the divergence observed after 1980 signifies a definite end to the long-run convergence observed since 1860. However, we note that the first period of divergence occurred in the aftermath of the introduction of Second Industrial Revolution and that the second divergence period coincides with the introduction of the Third Industrial Revolution in the late 1970s.

From Figure 3.12.1, we can organize the empirical patterns of the regional distribution of GDP into four periods or 'eras' of economic development. The first is a convergence period from 1860 until 1910. This period covers the Swedish industrial 'take-off' with the early breakthrough of modern industrialization. Expanding trade promoted the export-led growth of oatmeal, iron and wood products, but also of some specific industries directed towards a domestic market, such as textiles and products of simple mechanical workshops. Henning et al. (2011) showed that industrial take-off benefited geographically disparate areas alike. While exports of iron and timber drove growth in the far north and middle areas, oatmeal and butter production benefited exports in the agricultural south. Accordingly, industrial centres did not cluster in one dominant area only, and while industrialization drove divergence in other European countries such as Spain, Swedish industrialization drove convergence. Convergence was also characterized by the county of Stockholm's limited success, if not regress, in this period.

The above-established GDP per capita convergence was paralleled by convergence in real wages. Sweden was one of the largest sending countries of emigrants to the New World in relation to its population size. In combination with dynamic internal labour markets, migration appears to have resulted in substantial wage convergence from 1860 to 1910 (Enflo et al. 2014).[4]

Large migration rates were a consequence of market integration, favoured by improvements in infrastructure. During the early nineteenth century, canals were constructed, but later on the railroad came to dominance in importance. The Swedish railroad network was a construction of peculiar character. In 1853, the Parliament of the Estates (Riksdag) decided that the state should finance the construction of the main trunk lines of the network. Nils Ericsson was appointed to lay out a plan of the network, but was massively criticized by contemporaries for his 'horror of waterways and cities'. The railroad network mostly ran through uninhabited land, and many of the larger cities remained outside of its reach. Berger and Enflo (2016) show that the cities that did get access to the network were given an early advantage in urban growth and industrialization. This seemingly odd way of connecting cities could potentially explain why the growth process became spatially de-concentrated and convergence in GDP per capita the dominant force.

The divergence period 1910–1940 marked a drastic interruption of the previous convergence trend. Stockholm improved its position to the rest of the country, and the northern counties showed signs of weaker regional economies. The Great Depression of the 1930s involved the contraction of important export markets and hit the traditional industrial regions, especially in the north, hard. Since the initiation of the Royal Waterfall Board (Kungliga Vattenfallstyrelsen) in 1909, the national government took an active role in expanding the electrical power grid throughout the country. In the 1910s, it only connected limited production sites with electricity from hydroelectrical power, and access to power remained a natural advantage for industrial location. Gradually, however, the grid expanded, and in the 1930s the northern and southern grid was connected. From then on, the oversupply of hydroelectrical power from the dams in the northern part of the country could be used at any industrial location site in Sweden. Thus, decreased relative costs for electricity and integration of electricity networks in different parts of the country served to facilitate a concentration of production and location closer to the core markets. This period is therefore closer to what we could expect from historical applications of new economic geography models, emphasizing increasing concentration of economic activities in the event of regional market integration as transport costs decrease (Krugman 1991, 2000). Spatial concentration of production to a number of core areas (where external economies of scale could be achieved) was facilitated by regional integration of transports and power supply. Consequently, Berger et al. (2012) document an increasing concentration of manufacturing activity in the interwar period, measured at city as well as regional levels.

Technological progress and rationalization in the agricultural sector during most of the period is also likely to have facilitated and reinforced this concentration process, as labour left the countryside and peripheral regions to seek new employment in expanding sectors in the expanding metropolitan areas. Moreover, increasing integration on a global scale presented capital-intensive activities with competition forces encouraging rationalization and substitution of labour for capital, resulting in a rise in the GDP per capita.

In 1940, a new period commenced with convergence until the 1980s. Swedish manufacturing industries met favourable demand conditions on the important export markets. After the Second World War, Sweden was one of the few countries in Europe with intact infrastructure and industrial production systems. Additionally, this period was characterized by stable institutional conditions, and especially the golden years of the 'Swedish model' and extraordinary growth rates. The Swedish model balanced regulation of some markets, expansion of the public sector, high tax pressure and sizeable social allowance systems with promotion of international competitiveness and structural change. Three aspects of the Swedish model are especially important to the interpretation of the regional patterns (Enflo and Henning 2016). Schön and Schubert (2010) emphasized that the Swedish mixed economy model favoured investment in existing firms, at the expense of new firm foundation and investment. The result was that the model had a reinforcing tendency in terms of the established industry structure, rather than promoting growth of new structures. Second, the market sensitivity of the economy was reduced by the rapid expansion of the public sector. Third, the centralistic wage negotiation policies served to force less competitive firms out of business, as it allowed for limited variances in wages throughout the country within an industry. Enflo and Rosés (2015) show that compression of inter-industry productivity differentials in combination with policies to promote internal migration served to concentrate population in certain areas while compressing differences in regional GDP per capita.

After 1980, regional convergence has been replaced by divergence, a characteristic feature of regional development not only in Sweden, but in many countries. In the Swedish case, the tendency is pronounced. The recent divergence trend takes Sweden's overall inequality level back to the levels of the 1930s, as measured by population-weighted coefficient of variation (see Figure 3.12.1). From the 1980s onwards, wide-ranging institutional and political reforms took place in Sweden. The 'Swedish model' was modified by reducing state intervention in and less regulation of many markets. This period also marks the start of the wide diffusion of computer technologies as tools for daily operations in many industries, facilitating further substitution of capital for labour.

In terms of regional patterns, divergence is most notably driven by the success of the Stockholm county. The cities of Gothenburg and Malmö also expanded rapidly after 2000 (population in greater Gothenburg, for example, increased with a staggering 12 per cent between 2000 and 2010, and greater Malmö, recovering from a disastrous development in the 1970s and 1980s, increased population by almost 30 per cent between 1990 and 2010). A number of potential, and perhaps complementary, explanations could be suggested for these patterns. An overarching tendency is that the most dynamic growth industries, such as advanced manufacturing industries and advanced services, are all predominantly urban activities. They do not, and will perhaps never, primarily seek low-cost peripheral locations. Rather, they depend on access to highly educated and skilled labour, vicinity to universities and research institutes, and access to fast transportation. These are all classical attraction factors of urban economies. The formerly successful, more traditional, manufacturing industries scattered all around Sweden have been increasingly faced with international cost competition, and for some industries weaker demand. This is to some extent also true for many of the localized resource-dependent industries in peripheral locations (such as paper and pulp industries). However, it does not mean that the rest of the country and peripheral locations are left without economic activities. Although urban growth is the strongest trend, many remaining firms and workers do stay productive and internationally competitive in peripheral locations, but plants tend to employ few workers.

Figure 3.12.2 displays the beta-convergence (i.e. the growth rate of regions in reference to their initial regional GDP per capita) in Sweden. It is clear that the long-run convergence trend identified in Figure 3.12.1 is caused by rapid growth of regions with an initially low regional GDP per capita. Indeed, the relation is not far from perfectly linear. The long-term regional growth patterns in Sweden are characterized not by inertia and static standings, but by quite considerable dynamics.

Table 3.12.1 gives a more detailed picture of the individual growth trajectories of the regions, and displays the per capita regional GDP compared to the national average (set to 1). Over the period as a whole, the capital Stockholm had the highest per capital income for most years, but the convergence trend towards the rest of the country is clearly visible, where Stockholm reached almost the national average in 1980 (1.11). Stockholm's relative GDP per capita then increased rapidly to 1.37 in 2010, thus returning to the divergence levels of the early twentieth century. The Göteborg and Bohus region, including the second largest city of Gothenburg as well as Malmöhus county, including the third largest city of Malmö, have

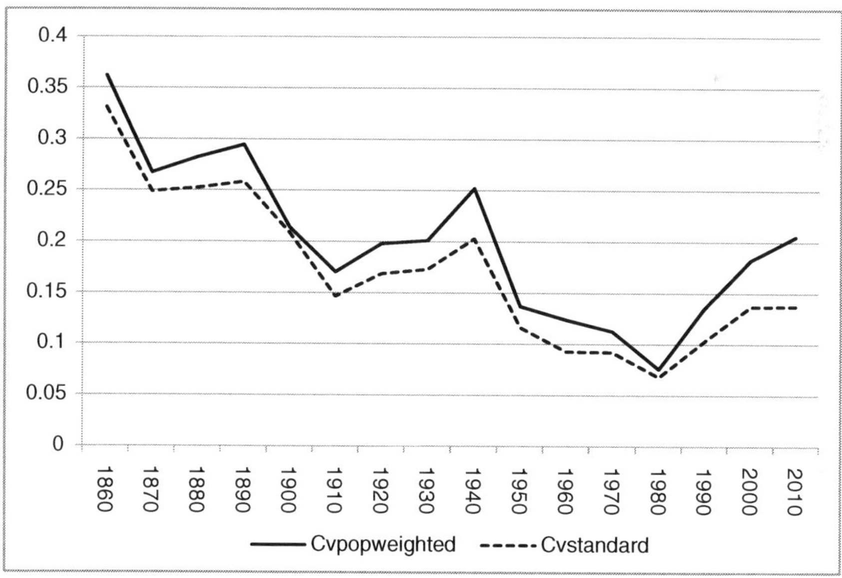

Figure 3.12.1 Population-weighted and standard per capita coefficient of variation (CV)

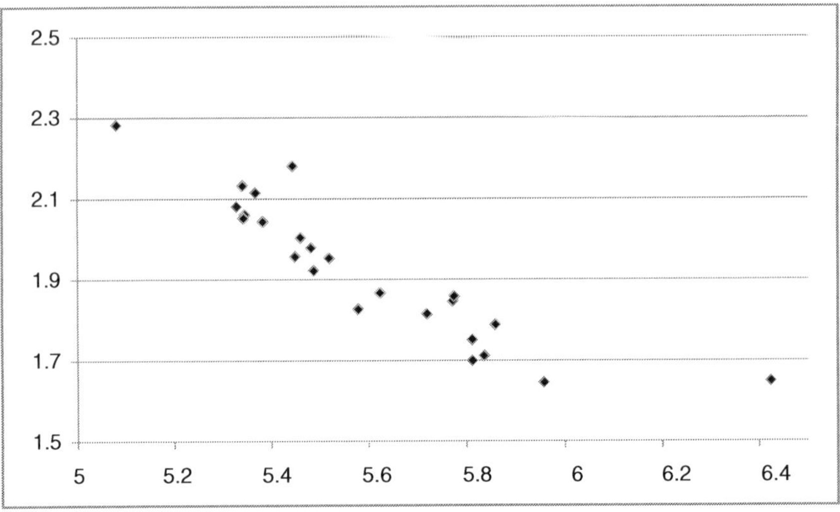

Figure 3.12.2 Beta-convergence: per capita development, 1860–2010 (*y*-axis: annual average growth, *x*-axis: log initial)

also GDP per capita above the national average for most of the time, as could be expected from the main metropolitan regions.

The high mobility of regions in the relative ranking also stands out in Table 3.12.1. The regions of Kronoberg and Jönköping in the southern part of Sweden were among the poorest in the late nineteenth century. These regions were relatively densely populated (by Swedish standards), but the natural preconditions for efficient agriculture were unfavourable due to meager and generally (very) stony soils. As a result, these counties experienced considerable emigration, primarily to the US. In fact, almost 150,000 persons emigrated only from the Jönköping and Kronoberg regions to the US in 1850–1910 (Statistics Sweden 1969). From the Second World War onwards, the Jönköping and Kronoberg regions, however, saw a considerable increase in relative GDP per capita. To some extent, this could be connected to the growth of small-scale entrepreneurship efforts in the region, often with links to local handicraft traditions. In 2000, the Kronoberg and Jönköping regions were the only ones, together with the extreme region of Stockholm, above the national average in regional GDP per capita. In all, the growth journey of these regions during the twentieth-century was spectacular. For some regions in the north of the country, we find the opposite trajectory. During the late nineteenth century, the Gävleborg, Västernorrland and Jämtland regions all had regional GDPs per capita exceeding the national average. One important factor behind this was the success of natural resource connected in industries, such as sawmills. Booming export markets for such products ensured that the coastal regions in the north of Sweden (where sawmills were located) were seen as a 'Swedish Klondike' at the time (see Schön and Schubert 2010). During the course of the twentieth century, the position of these regions in the national ranking deteriorated, and at the end of the twentieth century the regions could be found performing below the national average, even though they were not the least prosperous regions.

One recent exception to the reversal of fortune of the natural-resource-dependent north, however, is Norrbotten county. In 2000, its relative regional GDP was at 90 per cent of Sweden's average, but had climbed to 114 per cent in 2010. This striking performance is explained by international investments in companies related to mining (LKAB), water and wind power (Vattenfall) and information technology (Facebook). Combining increased demand for steel from emerging economies with the demand for reliable power sources by large ICT companies, Norrbotten recently entered a new growth spurt and ranked with the second highest GDP per capita in 2010.

Maps 3.12.1–3.12.5 describe the relative distribution of regional GDP per capita for the years that we have identified as breakpoint years in our convergence–divergence analysis (based on Figure 3.12.1). One striking feature emerges from the maps: a relative instability of the regional relative income per capita. The only county that stands as the richest throughout the period is the county of Stockholm, which is situated in the east. For example, in 1860, the most developed counties (together with Stockholm) were the county of Göteburg in the western part of Götaland and two counties in Norrland (Västernorrland and Gävleborg). In 1910, Malmöhus, the southernmost county, emerged as one of the richest regions together with Norrbotten, the northernmost province and situated above the polar circle. After the interwar period, with its divergence tendency, Norrbotten, like the rest of the counties of the Norrland, dramatically lost ground by 1940, while the richest counties concentrated in the centre of the country made up a relatively rich belt between the two largest cities, Stockholm and Gothenburg. In 1980, both the collapse in regional income inequality and the relative decline of northern counties are immediately observable. Finally, in 2010, Stockholm county stands out as the region with the highest relative GDP per capita, making all other regions look bleak in comparison. The only exception is the far north, which enjoyed remarkably high growth rates due to a boom in iron ore prices and mining activities in 2010.

Table 3.12.2 shows the exact shares of GDP in the Swedish regions. Here, the most striking feature is perhaps the extreme increase in concentration over time to the Stockholm region: from hosting about 13 per cent to 30 per cent of total Swedish GDP during our period. The other regions with metropolitan cities do not show such dramatic increases, but in these regions the cities of Gothenburg and Malmö are surrounded by rural areas of considerable size, which might serve to reduce the impact of urbanization in our indicators to some extent. There could be inner core/periphery dynamics to these regions that we are not able to track. The demise of the northern regions can also be traced in these indicators. Adding the northern counties together, their shares of total regional GDP decreased from 14 per cent in 1900 to 9 per cent in 2010.

Table 3.12.1 Relative per capita income of the 24 counties, corresponding to NUTS 3 regions (national average = 1)

	1860	*1870*	*1880*	*1890*	*1900*	*1910*	*1920*	*1930*	*1940*	*1950*	*1960*	*1970*	*1980*	*1990*	*2000*	*2010*
Stockholms län	2.19	1.68	1.80	1.78	1.39	1.33	1.40	1.37	1.53	1.23	1.24	1.19	1.11	1.22	1.39	1.37
Uppsala län	1.37	1.00	1.00	0.85	0.87	0.91	0.97	0.92	0.92	0.89	0.88	0.90	0.85	0.82	0.88	0.86
Södermanlands län	1.19	0.93	0.98	0.98	0.92	0.97	0.91	0.88	0.95	0.95	0.97	0.97	0.96	0.89	0.79	0.80
Östergötlands län	1.22	1.01	0.99	1.07	0.95	1.03	0.94	0.93	0.94	0.93	0.96	0.96	0.99	0.95	0.85	0.84
Jönköpings län	0.75	0.74	0.91	0.78	0.78	0.92	0.81	0.83	0.85	0.99	0.91	0.96	1.03	1.01	0.99	0.87
Kronobergs län	0.57	0.68	0.73	0.71	0.70	0.80	0.71	0.70	0.68	0.81	0.86	0.95	1.00	0.98	0.94	0.93
Kalmar län	0.74	0.82	0.81	0.83	0.85	0.83	0.84	0.84	0.76	0.86	0.84	0.90	0.97	0.91	0.86	0.85
Gotlands län	0.94	1.06	0.90	0.96	0.84	0.97	0.81	0.78	0.74	0.79	0.83	0.83	0.91	0.80	0.77	0.77
Blekinge län	0.83	0.86	0.86	0.83	0.85	1.01	0.92	0.91	0.89	0.83	0.93	0.95	0.99	0.91	0.92	0.82
Kristianstads län	0.98	0.79	0.79	0.83	0.84	0.97	0.86	0.83	0.80	0.85	0.86	0.94	0.90	0.86	0.89	0.85
Malmöhus län	0.89	1.10	1.19	1.20	1.16	1.27	1.16	1.15	1.11	1.07	1.00	1.04	1.02	1.00	0.92	0.88
Hallands län	0.85	0.96	0.78	0.63	0.81	0.87	0.86	0.84	0.79	0.92	0.85	0.96	0.89	0.87	0.78	0.88
Göteborg-Bohus län	1.25	1.37	1.10	1.09	1.18	1.01	1.28	1.31	1.22	1.18	1.06	1.06	1.09	1.17	1.07	0.96
Älvsborgs län	0.76	0.71	0.68	0.65	0.74	0.79	0.85	0.90	0.93	1.04	0.95	1.01	0.92	0.89	0.88	0.96
Skaraborgs län	0.74	0.77	0.82	0.75	0.76	0.84	0.74	0.72	0.76	0.88	0.85	0.90	0.95	0.90	0.89	0.96
Värmlands län	0.86	0.79	0.76	0.78	0.80	0.81	0.86	0.86	0.83	0.90	0.94	0.91	0.96	0.91	0.84	0.81
Örebro län	0.77	0.93	0.83	0.81	0.89	0.90	0.98	0.99	1.05	1.00	1.00	0.98	0.91	0.93	0.85	0.88
Västmanlands län	1.08	1.00	1.06	0.95	1.00	0.92	0.92	0.90	0.98	0.97	0.99	1.01	1.06	0.98	0.88	0.87
Kopparbergs län	0.73	0.95	0.91	0.97	0.92	1.03	0.90	0.90	0.89	0.95	0.94	0.91	0.97	0.90	0.88	0.88
Gävleborgs län	1.19	1.37	1.42	1.26	1.28	1.05	1.01	1.00	0.89	0.94	0.93	0.93	0.99	0.93	0.87	0.87
Västernorrlands län	1.14	1.17	1.15	1.18	1.17	0.95	0.99	0.98	0.84	0.89	1.00	0.88	0.96	0.94	0.95	0.96
Jämtlands län	1.14	1.15	1.17	1.10	1.20	0.88	0.88	0.82	0.83	0.83	0.95	0.79	0.85	0.83	0.82	0.98
Västerbottens län	0.84	1.02	0.88	0.88	0.96	0.80	0.87	0.85	0.71	0.86	0.96	0.83	0.94	0.91	0.81	0.89
Norrbottens län	0.82	1.44	1.14	1.11	1.35	1.15	1.06	1.04	0.82	0.92	0.97	0.82	0.95	0.90	0.90	1.14

Source: 1860–2000: Enflo et al. (2014a: Table C.2).

Note: The years 2000 and 2010 have been added by adjusting official statistics to the old county borders.

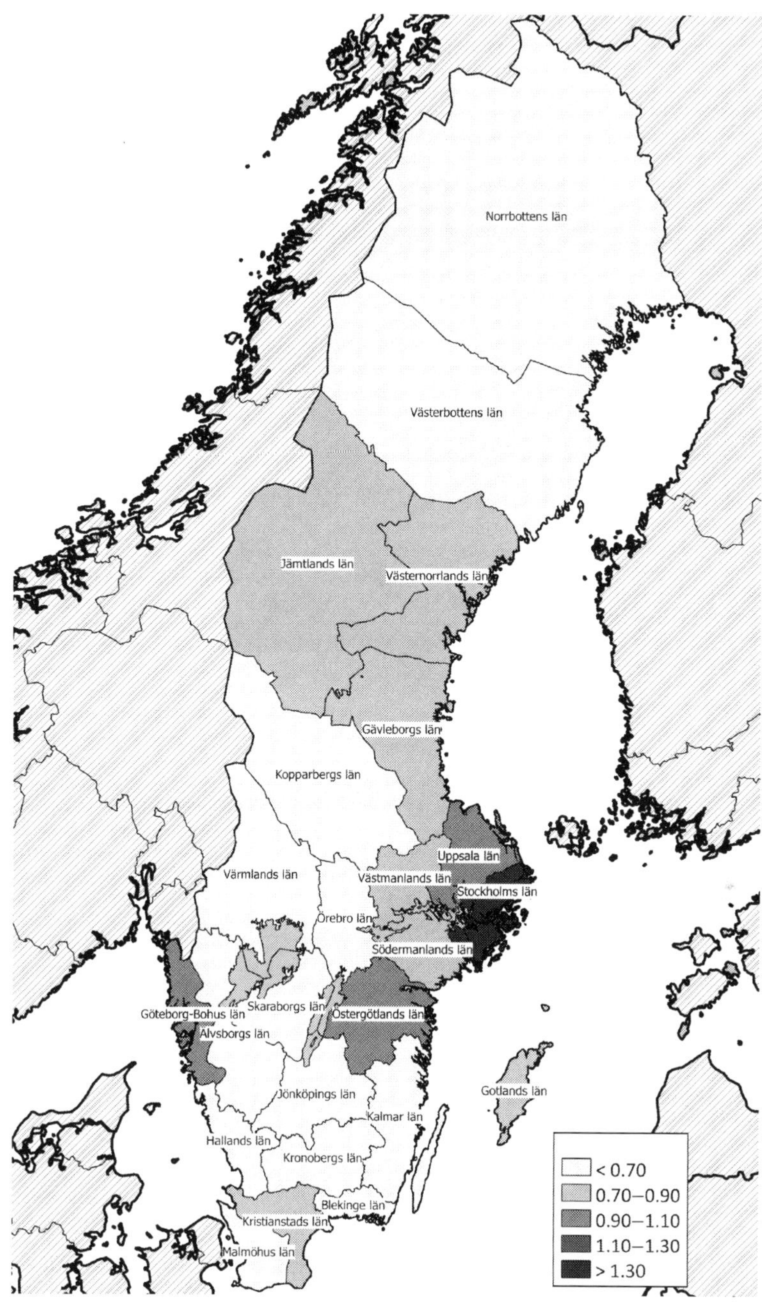

Map 3.12.1 Relative GDP per capita, 1860 (Sweden = 1)

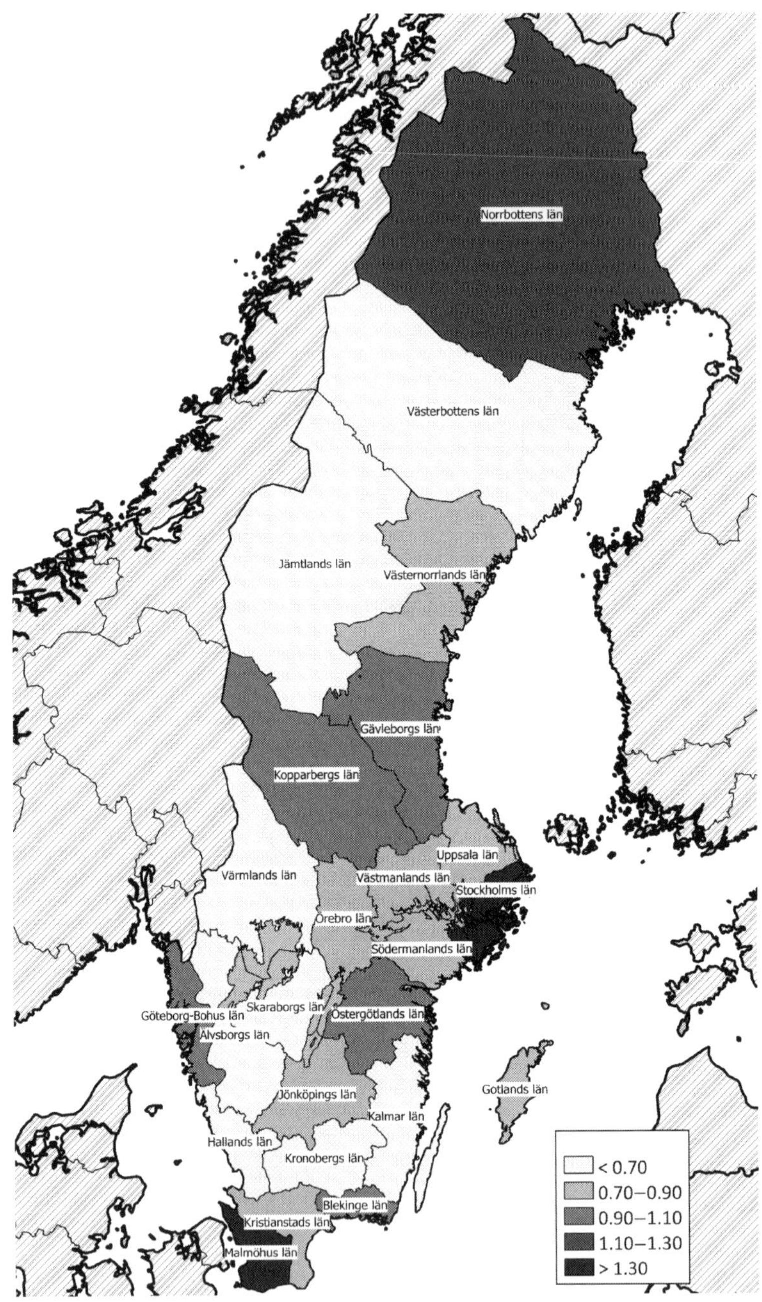

Map 3.12.2 Relative GDP per capita, 1910 (Sweden = 1)

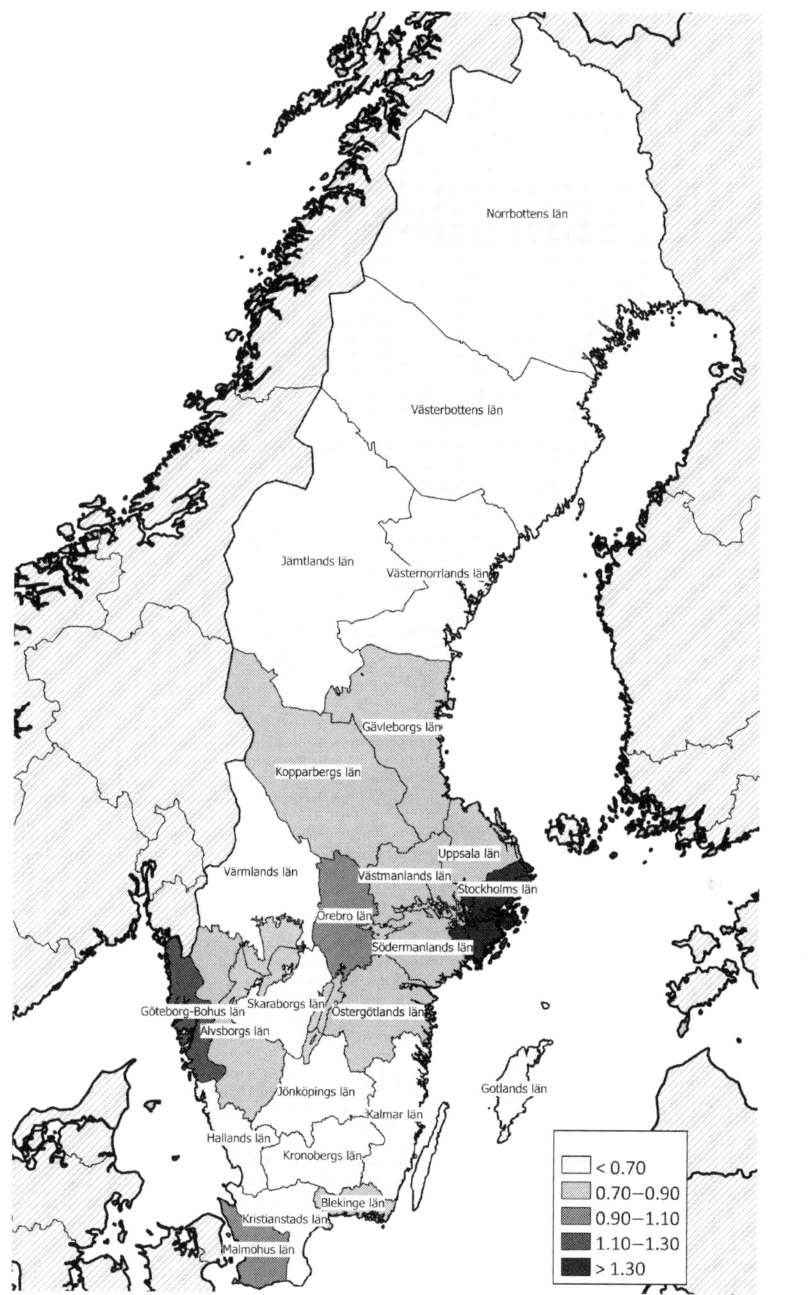

Map 3.12.3 Relative GDP per capita, 1940 (Sweden = 1)

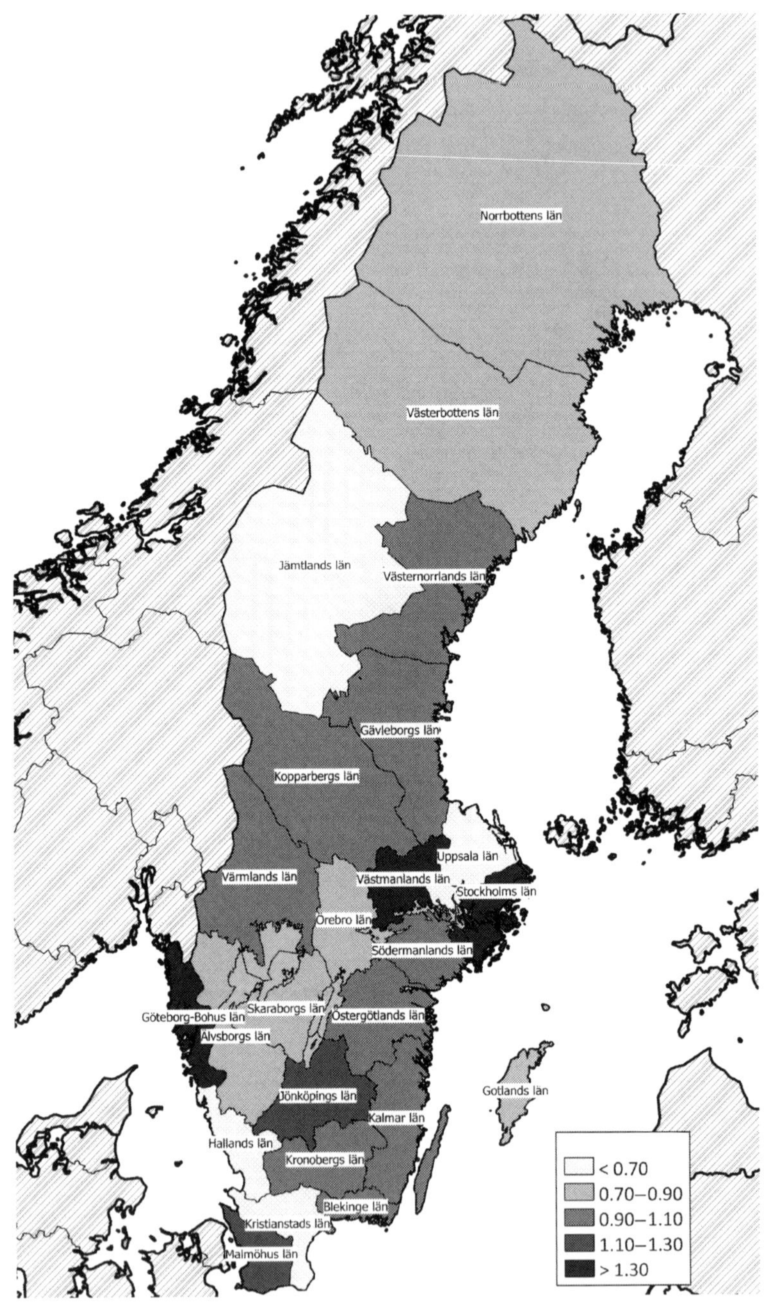

Map 3.12.4 Relative GDP per capita, 1980 (Sweden = 1)

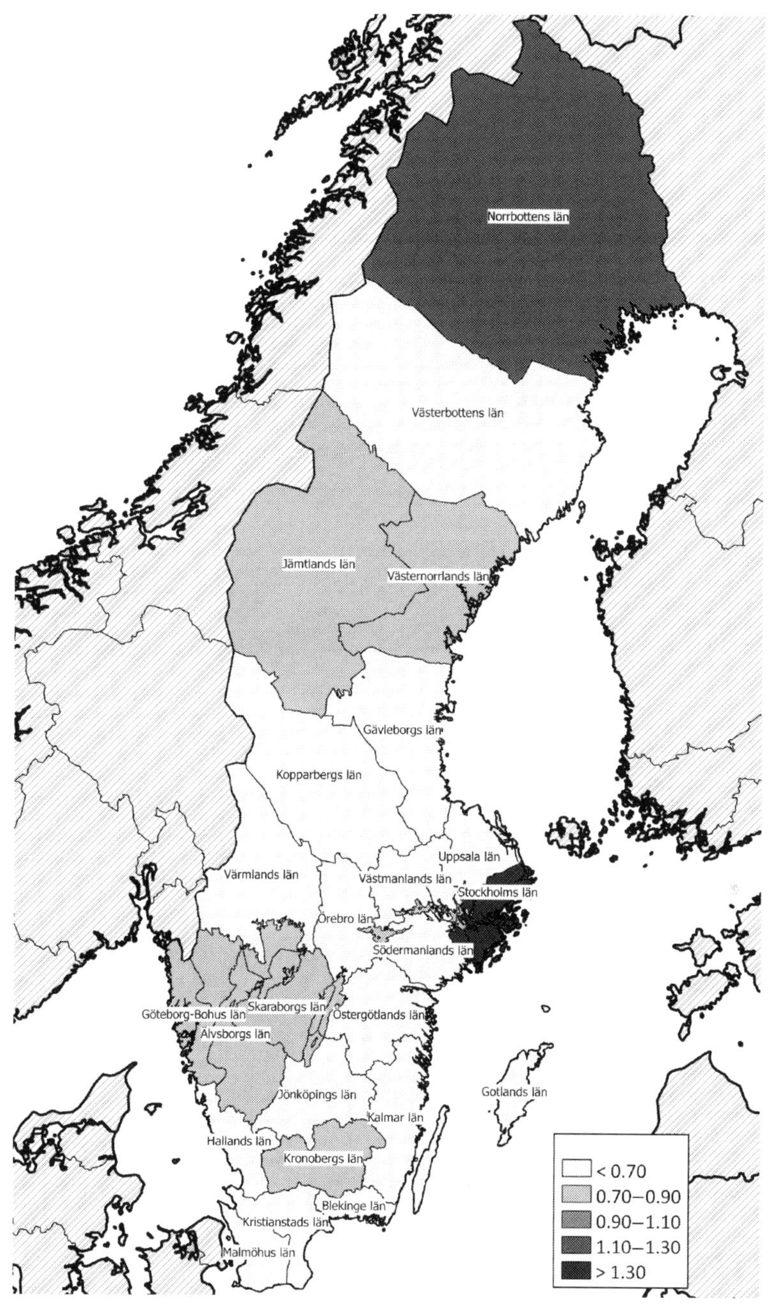

Map 3.12.5 Relative GDP per capita, 2010 (Sweden = 1)

Table 3.12.2 Part of total GDP produced in each region

	1860	*1870*	*1880*	*1890*	*1900*	*1910*	*1920*	*1930*	*1940*	*1950*	*1960*	*1970*	*1980*	*1990*	*2000*	*2010*
Stockholms län	0.13	0.11	0.12	0.15	0.13	0.14	0.16	0.17	0.21	0.19	0.21	0.22	0.20	0.23	0.29	0.30
Uppsala län	0.03	0.02	0.02	0.02	0.02	0.02	0.02	0.02	0.02	0.02	0.02	0.02	0.02	0.03	0.03	0.03
Södermanlands län	0.04	0.03	0.03	0.03	0.03	0.03	0.03	0.03	0.03	0.03	0.03	0.03	0.03	0.03	0.02	0.02
Östergötlands län	0.08	0.06	0.06	0.06	0.05	0.05	0.05	0.05	0.05	0.05	0.05	0.05	0.05	0.04	0.04	0.04
Jönköpings län	0.03	0.03	0.04	0.03	0.03	0.04	0.03	0.03	0.03	0.04	0.03	0.04	0.04	0.04	0.03	0.03
Kronobergs län	0.02	0.03	0.03	0.02	0.02	0.02	0.02	0.02	0.02	0.02	0.02	0.02	0.02	0.02	0.02	0.02
Kalmar län	0.04	0.05	0.04	0.04	0.04	0.03	0.03	0.03	0.03	0.03	0.03	0.03	0.03	0.03	0.02	0.02
Gotlands län	0.01	0.01	0.01	0.01	0.01	0.01	0.01	0.01	0.01	0.01	0.01	0.01	0.01	0.01	0.00	0.00
Blekinge län	0.03	0.03	0.03	0.02	0.02	0.03	0.02	0.02	0.02	0.02	0.02	0.02	0.02	0.02	0.02	0.01
Kristianstads län	0.05	0.04	0.04	0.04	0.04	0.04	0.04	0.03	0.03	0.03	0.03	0.03	0.03	0.03	0.03	0.03
Malmöhus län	0.07	0.08	0.09	0.09	0.09	0.11	0.10	0.10	0.09	0.09	0.08	0.09	0.09	0.09	0.09	0.09
Hallands län	0.03	0.03	0.02	0.02	0.02	0.02	0.02	0.02	0.02	0.02	0.02	0.02	0.02	0.03	0.02	0.03
Göteborg- Bohus län	0.07	0.08	0.06	0.07	0.08	0.07	0.09	0.10	0.09	0.09	0.09	0.09	0.09	0.10	0.10	0.08
Älvsborgs län	0.05	0.05	0.04	0.04	0.04	0.04	0.04	0.05	0.05	0.05	0.05	0.05	0.05	0.05	0.04	0.05
Skaraborgs län	0.04	0.05	0.05	0.04	0.04	0.04	0.03	0.03	0.03	0.03	0.03	0.03	0.03	0.03	0.03	0.03
Värmlands län	0.06	0.05	0.04	0.04	0.04	0.04	0.04	0.04	0.03	0.04	0.04	0.03	0.03	0.03	0.03	0.02
Örebro län	0.03	0.04	0.03	0.03	0.03	0.03	0.04	0.04	0.04	0.03	0.03	0.03	0.03	0.03	0.03	0.03
Västmanlands län	0.03	0.03	0.03	0.03	0.03	0.03	0.03	0.02	0.03	0.03	0.03	0.03	0.03	0.03	0.03	0.02
Kopparbergs län	0.03	0.04	0.04	0.04	0.04	0.04	0.04	0.04	0.03	0.04	0.04	0.03	0.03	0.03	0.03	0.03
Gävleborgs län	0.04	0.05	0.06	0.05	0.06	0.05	0.05	0.05	0.04	0.04	0.04	0.03	0.04	0.03	0.03	0.03
Västernorrlands län	0.03	0.04	0.04	0.05	0.05	0.04	0.04	0.04	0.04	0.04	0.04	0.03	0.03	0.03	0.03	0.02
Jämtlands län	0.02	0.02	0.02	0.02	0.03	0.02	0.02	0.02	0.02	0.02	0.02	0.01	0.01	0.01	0.01	0.01
Västerbottens län	0.02	0.02	0.02	0.02	0.03	0.02	0.03	0.03	0.02	0.03	0.03	0.02	0.03	0.03	0.02	0.02
Norrbottens län	0.01	0.03	0.02	0.02	0.04	0.03	0.03	0.03	0.03	0.03	0.03	0.03	0.03	0.03	0.03	0.03

Source: 1860–2000: Enflo et al. (2014a: Table C.1).

Note: The years 2000 and 2010 have been revised and added by adjusting official statistics to the old county borders.

3. Conclusions

In this chapter, we have used newly compiled estimates to analyse regional convergence and divergence patterns for Swedish regional GDPs for the period 1860–2010. The Swedish experience is interesting not only because of the diverse geographies of the country, but also because of the high average growth rates shown by the country from the nineteenth century until today. High growth rates were followed by low regional GDP per capita differentials, as the industrialization process resulted in long-term convergence. In general, Swedish patterns of regional growth have resulted in a rather high mobility in rankings, compared to other countries. Indeed, many of the previously successful regions experience comparatively sluggish growth during the period that we study, while we also see some quite spectacular regional success stories.

In all, we divide regional convergence/divergence patterns in Sweden in four periods: convergence 1860–1910, divergence 1910–1940, convergence 1940–1980 and divergence 1980–2010. We provide some potential explanations for these patterns, inspired by the literature in the field and previous research that we have performed. For example, the period until 1910 is well known for the rural characteristics of early Swedish industrialization, with both successful industries connected to natural resources and mechanical workshops scattered all around the country. The cities did grow, but important industrial cities could be found in many parts of the country. The divergence after 1910 co-occurred with the crises in several industries characterized by rural location patterns, as well as with a strengthened market integration. The regional markets were no longer isolated islands and integration fostered concentration of economic activities closer to the main domestic markets. The long convergence process from 1940 to 1980 coincided with the consolidation of the Swedish model and a long period of high growth, benefiting most parts of the country (see also Henning et al. 2011). From the 1980s onwards, a period characterized by considerable divergence and take-off of the metropolitan regions (especially Stockholm) began. This period, which marked a new era of more liberal and market-oriented policymaking, as well as growth of new knowledge-intensive and service industries, brought the Swedish regional system back to the same overall regional inequality as in the 1930s.

Since the 1980s, some observers have pointed to a Swedish 'regional problem', with periphery that is increasingly lagging behind. As we can see here, this problem has many facets. On the one hand, we do see a concentration of efficient economic activities to the metropolitan regions, and an extremely forceful new wave of urbanization (or perhaps rather 'metropolization', as not all urban regions are as successful as the three largest metropolitan areas). On the other hand, dispersion among the rest of the regions in terms of GDP per capita is not too disastrous: the remaining economies seem to fare pretty well. Also, Swedes are rather prone to migrate within the country, and peripheral locations are normally not left with large stocks of unemployed workers. To put it crudely, the remaining industries are productive, but not many people work there. One obvious problem is that because of migration of working-age population, a heavier burden is put on the peripheral municipalities to support an ageing population in the long run. Although there is a regional distribution scheme between municipalities, it does not also immediately solve the problem of recruitment into care and healthcare in peripheral locations. An ageing population in rural areas is indeed a geographical challenge for the future.

Notes

1 The research resulting in this chapter was funded by the Swedish Research Council (Vetenskapsrådet) and the Knut and Alice Wallenberg Foundation (KAW).
2 The following two sections are adapted from Enflo and Henning (2016).
3 The variation 1870–1890 is less pronounced, mainly visible in the population-weighted CV. Due to the data constraints discussed above, we do not interpret it too generously.
4 Sweden ranks high in internal and external migration rates compared with, for example, Southern Europe, where low industrialization and income barriers to migration hampered labour mobility (Sánchez-Alonso 2000; Rosés and Sánchez-Alonso 2004; Silvestre 2005).

References

Andersson, Å.E. (1978) 'Demografisk och ekonomisk utveckling', in *Att forma regional framtid. 13 forskares syn på regionala problem*, Rapport från ERU, Stockholm: LiberFörlag.

Berger, T. and Enflo, K. (2016) 'Locomotives of local growth: the short- and long-term impact of railroads in Sweden', *Journal of Urban Economics*, Vol. 98: 124–38.

Berger, T., Enflo, K. and Henning, M. (2012) 'Geographical location and urbanization of the Swedish manufacturing industry, 1900–1960: evidence from a new database', *Scandinavian Economic History Review*, Vol. 60 (3): 290–308.

Enflo, K. and Henning, M. (2016) 'The development of economic growth and inequality among the Swedish regions 1860–2010: evidence from regional national accounts', in J. Ljungberg (ed.), *Structural Analysis and the Process of Economic Development: Essays in Memory of Lennart Schön*, London: Routledge, pp. 126–48.

Enflo, K. and Rosés, J. (2015) 'Coping with regional inequality in Sweden: structural change, migrations and policy, 1860–2000', *Economic History Review*, Vol. 68 (1): 191–217.

Enflo, K., Henning, M. and Schön, L. (2014a) 'Swedish regional GDP 1855–2000: estimations and general trends in the Swedish regional system', *Research in Economic History*, Vol. 30: 47–89.

Enflo, K., Lundh, C. and Prado, S. (2014b) 'The role of migration in regional wage convergence: evidence from Sweden 1860–1940', *Explorations in Economic History*, Vol. 52: 93–110.

Geary, F. and Stark, T. (2002) 'Examining Ireland's post-famine economic growth performance', *The Economic Journal*, Vol. 112 (482): 919–35.

Henning, M., Enflo, K. and F.N.G. Andersson (2011) 'Trends and cycles in regional economic growth: how spatial differences shaped the Swedish growth experience from 1860–2009', *Explorations in Economic History*, Vol. 48 (4): 538–55.

Krantz, O. and Schön, L. (2007) *Swedish Historical National Accounts 1800–2000*, Lund Studies in Economic History, Vol. 41, Stockholm: Almqvist & Wiksell.

Krugman, P. (1991) *Geography and Trade*, Cambridge, MA: MIT Press.

Krugman, P. (2000) 'Where in the world is the "new economic geography"?', in G.L. Clark, M.P. Feldman and M.S. Gertler (eds), *The Oxford Handbook of Economic Geography*, Oxford: Oxford University Press, pp. 49–60.

Persson, J. (1997) 'Convergence across the Swedish counties, 1911–1993', *European Economic Review*, Vol. 41 (9): 1835–52.

Rosés, J. and Sánchez-Alonso, B. (2004) 'Regional wage convergence in Spain 1850–1930', *Explorations in Economic History*, Vol. 41 (4): 404–25.

Sánchez-Alonso, B. (2000) 'Those who left and those who stayed behind: explaining emigration from the regions of Spain, 1880–1914', *Journal of Economic History*, Vol. 60 (3): 730–55.

Schön, L. (2013) *Sweden: Economic Growth and Structural Change, 1800–2000*, available at: http://eh.net/encyclopedia/sweden-economic-growth-and-structural-change-1800-2000/ (accessed 17 August 2018).

Schön, L. and Schubert, K. (2010) *Sweden's Road to Modernity: An Economic History*, Stockholm: SNS förlag.

Silvestre, J. (2005) 'Internal migrations in Spain 1877–1930', *European Review of Economic History*, Vol. 9 (2): 233–65.

Söderberg, J. and Lundgren, N.G. (1982) *Ekonomisk och geografisk koncentration 1850–1980*, Stockhom: LiberFörlag.

Statistics Sweden (1969) *Historical Statistics of Sweden Part 1. Population Second Edition. 1720–1967*, Stockholm: KL Beckmans Tryckerier AB. (Tab. 47. Utvandrare länsvis: summor för åren 1851–1967).

Svensson Henning, M. (2009) *Industrial Dynamics and Regional Structural Change: Geographical Perspectives on Economic Evolution*, PhD Thesis, Lund University.

3.13 Switzerland

Ulrich Woitek and Gabriela Wüthrich

1. Introduction

The public image of Switzerland at the beginning of the twenty-first century is that of a high-wage and high-price island, characterized by considerable geographical, regional and cultural diversity (e.g. lowland and Alpine regions, four different native languages). Throughout the twentieth century, it remained at the top of the per capita GDP distribution of developed countries.[1] Moreover, results from happiness research show a very high level of life satisfaction for Swiss citizens, not mainly due to demographic and economic factors, but to the possibilities of direct democratic participation (Frey and Stutzer 2002, 2002).

To analyse the determinants of this development on a regional level in the twentieth century, macroeconomic data are necessary, which are difficult to obtain before the 1960s. Official national accounting data are not available before 1963, covering the period back to 1948, and an official production index was published as late as 1965, going back to 1958 (Cascioni 2000: 281; Fiala 2000: 447). Official regional GDPs were not published before 2012, going back to 2008 (Bundesamt für Statistik BFS 2013a).[2] This is astonishing, given the promising start of official statistics in the nineteenth century. In 1860, the federal statistical office (FSO) was founded, which was an important step to catch up with the development of official statistics in other European countries (Ritzmann-Blickenstorfer 2000: 62). Despite this relatively late start, the quality and quantity of official data available for the nineteenth century are not different from other European countries. This changed in the first half of the twentieth century, when Switzerland did less than other countries to develop the 'new matrix of economic knowledge' (Tooze 2001: 9) in the form of macroeconomic data. An example is the missing production index: in 1936, the *Statistische Reichsamt* published a data collection for the world economy, containing business cycle indicators for 80 countries available at the time (Statistisches Reichsamt 1936). Fifty-four countries had production statistics, but Switzerland was not among them. This problem led to a debate between statisticians and industry representatives about the pros and cons of constructing such an index,[3] but it needed economic crises such as the Great Depression in the 1930s and the business cycle downturn in the 1970s to initiate improvements in the availability of business cycle indicators (Müller and Woitek

2012: 130). Based on the seminal work of Hansjörg Siegenthaler's group in the 1980s, GDP estimates on the federal level dating back to 1851 became available together with cantonal GDPs covering the years 1890 to 1960 (Ritzmann and David 2012), which are an important part of the data set analysed here.

The chapter draws on the analysis in Müller and Woitek (2012) and Hiestand et al. (2012). The results presented here can be seen as a robustness check of these studies, but the available regional data underlying Hiestand et al. (2012) are only used as a comparison. Instead, following the method proposed by Geary and Stark (2002), we construct a regional data set on the NUTS 2 level. This approach has certain shortcomings. One is the concept of GDP – even if GDP measured economic activity correctly, its use as a welfare measure is debated (e.g. Stiglitz et al. 2010).[4] Given data availability, the regional GDPs presented here are not suited for business cycle analysis because they are based on census information, which typically took place every 10 years. Higher-frequency data spanning the entire twentieth century on a regional level are not available, which restricts the research to the long run. Another weakness is the decomposition into NUTS 2 regions. In the case of Switzerland, they are artificial in the sense that they do not constitute institutional regions and are based on the importance of metropolitan areas, which is a relatively recent phenomenon (Hiestand et al. 2012: 754). Moreover, they do not necessarily reflect economic specialization, a problem that is overcome by the district-level GDPs recently constructed by Stohr (2014b). However, the approach adopted here has a major advantage. It allows comparisons across European regions, which outweighs the shortcomings listed above.

2. Historical background

Switzerland is located at the heart of Europe. With its regional and cultural diversity, it has served as a kind of a laboratory of European institutions for a very long time. Its territorial roots go back to the fifteenth century when it emerged as a loose confederation of rural areas and city states with mutually ruled subject domains, as well as associate members. Its territory has been fixed since the Congress of Vienna in 1815. While common civil rights were already implemented in the cantons by Napoleon's short-lived Helvetic Republic in 1799, Switzerland has been characterized by its federal state organization since 1848. Today, it consists of 26 cantons whose areas practically have not changed since then (Hiestand et al. 2012: 754).[5]

Whereas the federal state was given military, monetary and tariff power in 1848, and has granted civil rights ever since, the cantons have been sovereign states that hold – among other competencies – tax, education and health authority. Thus, the cantons can act autonomously in quite a few political, economic and social matters, but all within the common framework of the federal institutions. The federal state of 1848 accordingly laid the basis for Swiss market integration domestically as well as abroad. However, thanks to the large cantonal autonomy, it did not induce cultural, denominational or language unification, and kept local historical diversity (Maissen 2012: 204).

The latter is especially important with regard to the diverse economic premises. In the first half of the nineteenth century, the textile industry had spread over large parts of the Swiss Central Plateau. In the western French-speaking part, the watch industry had been present for more than 300 years (Fallet and Veyrassat 2015). Central Switzerland, the Alpine areas and the Italian-speaking canton Ticino remained predominantly agricultural for much longer.

Yet one of the main tasks of the new federal state was to improve transport infrastructure, which clearly lagged behind other European countries at the time. As parliament decided to consign the construction and operation of railways to private companies, financing treaties with neighbouring states interested in a fast north-to-south transport line as well as commercial banks had to be established first (Maissen 2012: 211–13).

It was during the second half of the nineteenth century when Switzerland developed into today's successful small open economy, driven by the so-called Second Industrial Revolution. As a consequence of the early diffusion of the textile industry, and the late but large-scale railway construction, support industries such as engineering and chemistry, as well as the water-power-driven electricity sector, turned Switzerland into a contemporary high-tech leader, despite the lack of any basic resources (Veyrassat 2010; Maissen 2012).

An essential factor in this already highly knowledge-based economy was human capital. In classical growth accounting, the so-called residual always contributed most to Swiss economic growth. This fact has been interpreted as an indicator for the importance of technical and organizational progress. Progress in a modern economy is closely related to knowledge acquired by basic, professional and academic education (Gugerli and Tanner 2012: 265–7). This was emphasized as early as the 1870s, and as a consequence of the continuing industrialization and specialization of the Swiss economy. Although the federal state had no competences in the area of education, it tried to supervise its efficiency by testing the conscripts. As Boppart et al. (2013) demonstrate, there were large regional differences in educational performance caused by a combination of religious denomination and other cultural characteristics such as the degree of political conservatism in the respective areas. However, up to the First World War, educational performance shows a clear tendency towards convergence among the cantons, probably at least partially due to increasing financial support by the federal state.

It was also during the second half of the nineteenth century when the first cantons started to adopt direct democratic instruments to control the political elites. On the federal level, this development took a bit longer: the referendum was introduced in 1874, and the initiative in 1891.[6] Regarding the cultural, denominational, economic and political diversity of Switzerland, these instruments can also be regarded as an efficient way to protect minorities' interests in order to keep law and order. They seem to have been motivated mainly by a pragmatism that had marked politics at least since the founding of the federal state, if not even since the times of the old confederation. Fritzsche (2000: 89) condenses this pragmatism as follows:

> Showing consideration for minorities is therefore, in the very first place, an act of political pragmatism since, on the one side, united minorities may easily grow into a majority, and since, on the other side, practically every single Swiss citizen, sometime or other, may well belong to one minority or another, be it religious, political, social or whatever else: this fact makes for the consciousness that, sooner or later and according to circumstances, everyone may depend on the goodwill of other minorities.

During the twentieth century, Switzerland experienced a fast sectoral change, with services becoming the most important sector already in the 1920s in terms of GDP. In terms of employment, it took until the 1970s for the service sector to overtake industry (see Figure 3.13.1). Despite the smoothing caused by the NUTS 2 classification, Figure 3.13.2a shows that the industrial sector in 1900 is concentrated in the northern part of Switzerland, while southern and central Switzerland are dominated by agriculture. The shift towards the service sector affected all regions (see Figure 3.13.2b), but it is especially Zurich (CH04) and Geneva (Lake Geneva region) (CH01) where the service sector clearly dominates.

Political stability proved to be an increasingly important comparative advantage of Switzerland in the twentieth century. The First World War came as a shock, and had some severe economic consequences such as problems with food imports. As a neutral state, Switzerland emerged relatively unscathed, although this was the only time when there existed obvious tensions between the German- and the French-/Italian-speaking parts of the country (Hiestand et al. 2012: 761).

After the post-war recession and the boom phase in the 1920s, the Great Depression in the 1930s especially hurt the export-oriented industry. Because of the regional specialization (see Figures 3.13.2a and 3.13.2b), the cantons affected by the crisis were those with important watch, textile or machine industry sectors, such as Geneva (CH01), Neuchâtel (CH02), Basel-Stadt (CH03) and Zurich (CH04) (Hiestand et al. 2012: 791, Figure 3.3.15). The recovery took longer in Switzerland than in other small open economies, which was mainly due to the decision to stay on gold as long as possible (Bordo and James 2007; Bordo et al. 2007; Straumann 2010; Rosenkranz et al. 2013).

After the turmoils of the Second World War, the Swiss economy saw a long period of extraordinary growth, ending in the 1970s (1948–1973: average annual growth rate of real GDP 4.3 per cent) (Müller and Woitek 2012: 133, Figure 1.1.14). The rest of the century is characterized by a slowdown of economic activity (1973–2005: average annual growth rate of real GDP 1.3 per cent) (Müller and Woitek 2012: 133, Figure 1.1.14). In this period, regions different from those in the 1930s were affected, the construction sector being the one that suffered most. However, even in the cantons most heavily hit – Solothurn (CH02), Neuchâtel (CH02) and Schaffhausen (CH05) – the unemployment rate did not increase above 1 per cent (Hiestand et al. 2012: 791, Figure 3.3.15). The weak growth in the 1990s, characterized by a significant decrease in labour productivity, was accompanied by a controversy about the restrictive monetary policy together with the competitiveness of the Swiss economy in the European context (Müller and

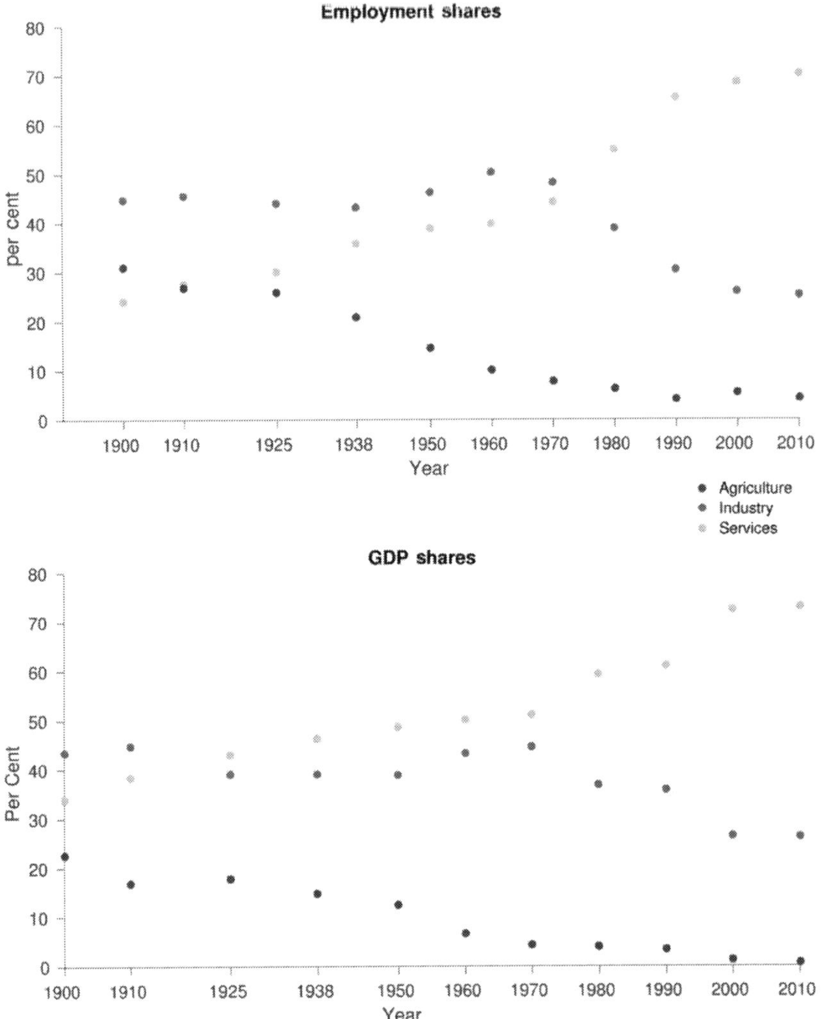

Figure 3.13.1 Sectoral change, 1900–2010

Woitek 2012: 174, 183, Table 1.1.17). The low performance of the Swiss economy since the 1970s led to a debate about the question of whether the period can be classified as a great depression in the Kehoe-Prescott sense (Kehoe and Prescott 2002; Kehoe and Ruhl 2003, 2005; Abrahamsen et al. 2005).

The Swiss economy could cope relatively well with the turbulences in the period 2001–2010 (e.g. financial crisis, EU debt crisis, appreciation of the Swiss franc) (see Rais and Ammann 2013: section 4.1). While the downturn from 2002

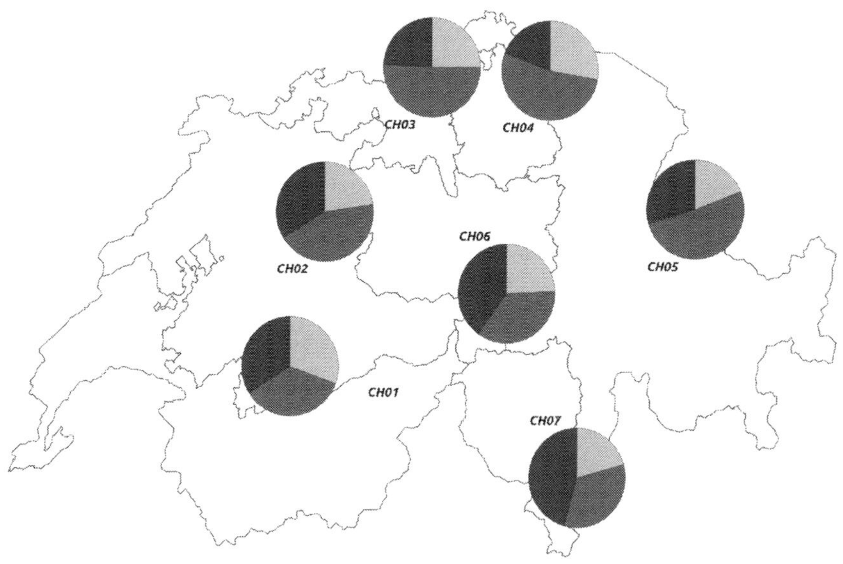

Figure 3.13.2a Regional employment structure, 1900

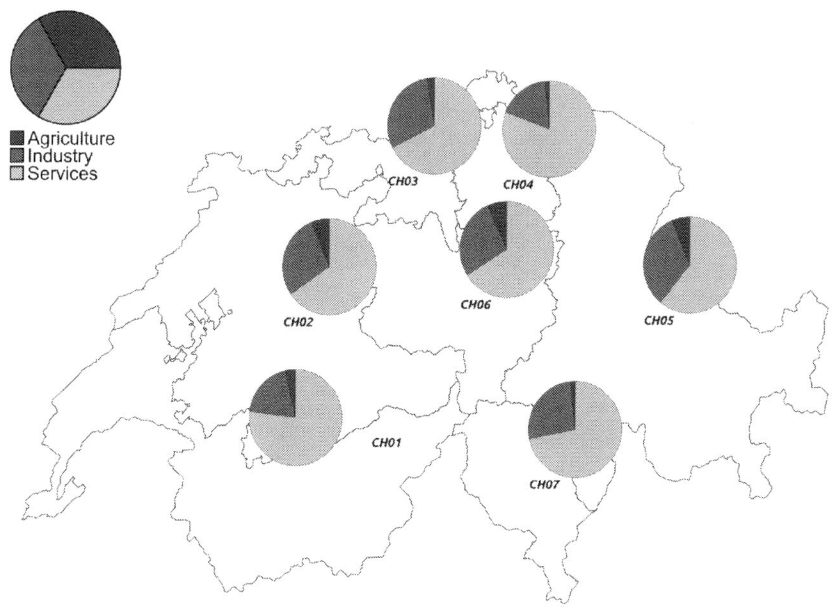

Figure 3.13.2b Regional employment structure, 2010

to 2003 led to an increase in the unemployment rate from 1.7 per cent in 2001 to 3.9 per cent in 2004, the financial crisis led to an increase from 2.6 per cent in 2008 to 3.9 per cent in 2010. Again, these downswings affected the regions differently: compared to the total, Zurich (CH04), Vaud (CH01), Neuchâtel (CH02) and Jura (CH02) showed an increase of the unemployment rate that was higher than the overall rate in both periods (2.2 and 1.3 percentage points, respectively). For other cantons, this was only true for one of the two periods: in 2002–2003, it was Basel-Stadt (CH03) and Geneva (CH01), and in 2008–2010 it was Solothurn (CH02), St. Gallen (CH05) and Thurgau (CH05).[7] All in all, it was the metropolitan area Geneva-Lausanne (Geneva, Vaud) that had the highest unemployment rates in the period 2000–2010, while the unemployment rate in rural regions was relatively low (Bundesamt für Statistik BFS 2013b: 19, Figure G10). Even within these regions, there is considerable dispersion: the Geneva/Lausanne area is also the one with the highest share of highly educated people (30.4/25.8 per cent), hinting at a growing residential segregation that can be observed in other urban areas as well (Bundesamt für Statistik BFS 2005: 23; Bundesamt für Statistik BFS 2012: 17).

Between 2000 and 2010, total population grew by 9.2 per cent (Bundesamt für Statistik BFS 2012: 21), while the number of people employed in the second and third sector increased even more (10.2 per cent) (Bundesamt für Statistik BFS 2012: 7). Due to the 1999 Bilateral Agreements I with the EU, free movement of persons was introduced in Switzerland in 2002.[8] Since then, the relatively stable Swiss labour market has attracted more and more EU citizens. Net migration, which had fallen to less than 2,000 persons in the economic downturn at the end of the 1990s, increased from 25,000 in 2000 to a peak of more than 100,000 in 2008, and stabilized around 70,000–80,000 in 2010.[9] While the Swiss population grew 5.6 per cent between 2000 and 2010, the growth rate of the foreign part of the population amounted to 24 per cent. The share of foreigners accordingly rose from 19.7 per cent in 1990 to 22.4 per cent in 2010, a trend that has continued through to 2013.[10] Regionally, the population grew most in the economically strong metropolitan areas of Zurich and Geneva/Lausanne, as well as in Ticino and along the northern border between Lake Constance and Basle (Bundesamt für Statistik BFS 2012: 21–2).

3. Results

The data set was constructed for the seven NUTS 2 regions of Switzerland: CH01 Lake Geneva region (cantons: Vaud, Vallais, Geneva), CH02 Espace Mittelland (cantons: Berne, Fribourg, Solothurn, Neuchâtel, Jura), CH03 Northwestern Switzerland (cantons: Basel-Stadt, Basel-Landschaft, Aargau), CH04 Zurich, CH05 Eastern Switzerland (cantons: Glarus, Schaffhausen, Appenzell Ausserrhoden, Appenzell Innerrhoden, St. Gallen, Grisons, Thurgau), CH06 Central Switzerland (cantons: Lucerne, Uri, Schwyz, Obwalden, Nidwalden, Zug) and CH07 Ticino. The years under consideration are 1900, 1910, 1925, 1938, 1950, 1960, 1970, 1980, 1990, 2000 and 2010.

Table 3.13.1 Regional GDP shares, 1900–2010

Year	*CH01*	*CH02*	*CH03*	*CH04*	*CH05*	*CH06*	*CH07*
1900	0.16	0.27	0.12	0.16	0.18	0.08	0.03
1910	0.15	0.26	0.12	0.17	0.19	0.07	0.03
1925	0.15	0.27	0.13	0.18	0.17	0.07	0.03
1938	0.14	0.28	0.13	0.20	0.15	0.07	0.03
1950	0.17	0.26	0.13	0.20	0.14	0.07	0.03
1960	0.17	0.25	0.14	0.21	0.14	0.07	0.03
1970	0.17	0.24	0.14	0.21	0.14	0.07	0.03
1980	0.18	0.23	0.13	0.22	0.13	0.08	0.03
1990	0.18	0.23	0.13	0.21	0.14	0.09	0.04
2000	0.18	0.20	0.14	0.23	0.12	0.09	0.04
2010	0.19	0.21	0.14	0.22	0.12	0.09	0.04

Source: See text

Note: CH01: Lake Geneva region, CH02: Espace Mittelland, CH03: Northwestern Switzerland, CH04: Zurich, CH05: Eastern Switzerland, CH06: Central Switzerland, CH07: Ticino.

As mentioned in the introduction, official GDP data for Switzerland are not available before 1948 at the national level, and not before 2008 at the cantonal level. Ritzmann and David (2012) provide new estimates on both the national and cantonal level for the period 1890–1960, and for the period 1965–2005 the FSO published national income data for the cantons. More recently, Stohr (2014b) provides district- and industry-level data, which make a high-resolution analysis of regional growth patterns possible. Here, we follow the methodology proposed by Geary and Stark (2002), and use employment shares and relative wages together with sectoral GDP estimates at the national level to provide a data set consistent with the data from the other projects in this volume. With the exception of the wage data, the main source is the database Historical Statistics of Switzerland Online (HSSO).[11] The sectors considered here are agriculture, industry and services;[12] details can be found in the chapter's data appendix.

The regional GDP shares calculated this way are displayed in Table 3.13.1. Figure 3.13.3 compares the data with the available shares analysed in Hiestand et al. (2012). For this purpose, we recalculated the shares in Hiestand et al. (2012) to follow the NUTS 2 classification. As can be seen, there is no dramatic difference between the shares. The differences are probably caused by the fact that from 1950 to 2005, the results in Hiestand et al. (2012) are based on national income shares. Hence, we are confident that the results reported here can be interpreted as robust.

The most prominent change is for Zurich (CH04), Eastern Switzerland (CH05) and Espace Mittelland (CH02). While the contribution of Zurich increases by 6 percentage points from 1900 to 2010, it decreases by the same amount for Eastern Switzerland and Espace Mittelland. The reduction in the shares is due to the decreasing importance of the textile and watch industry. For the other regions, the shares stay relatively constant.

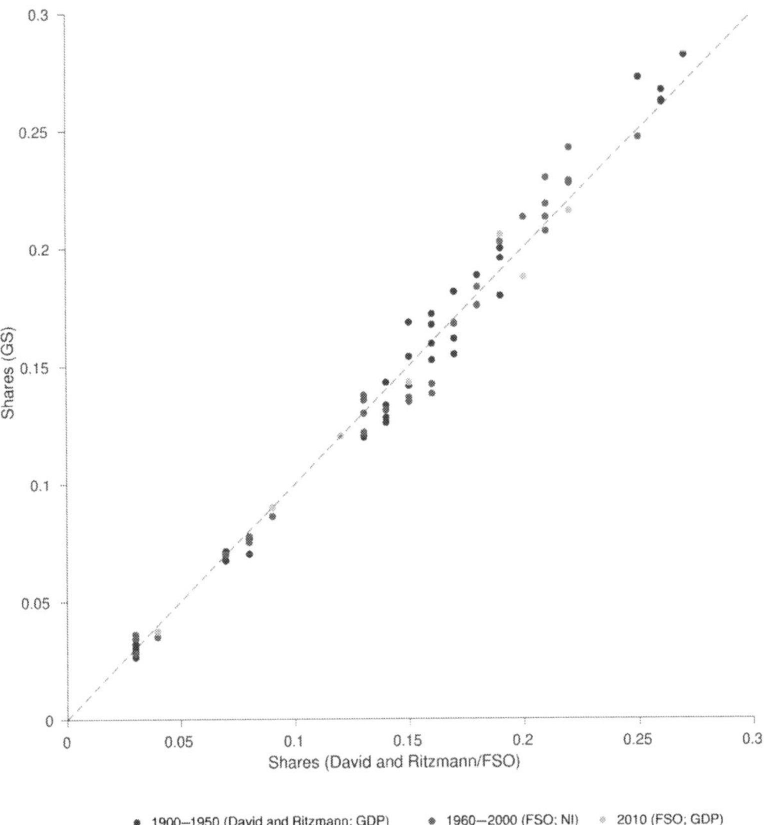

Figure 3.13.3 Robustness check

Regional GDP relative to Swiss GDP can be found in Table 3.13.2 and Maps 3.13.1–3.13.5. Despite small differences (Lake Geneva region) (CH01), the overall picture is the same as in Hiestand et al. (2012: 802, Table 3.3.6, 819, Table 3.3.A3).[13] The contribution of Zurich (CH04) is highest over the entire twentieth century, while it is lowest for Ticino (CH07). The relative GDP for Zurich in 2000 seems very high (1.35), but Hiestand et al. (2012: 819, Table 3.3.A3) report similar figures for 2000 (1.33) and 2005 (1.31). In the following, we focus our discussion on the results for the two obvious 'outliers', Ticino and Zurich.

Over the entire twentieth century, Ticino lags behind the development of the Swiss economy. Around 1900, the agricultural sector was dominating, characterized by small peasant farming not sufficient to keep a family. Because of that, seasonal and permanent emigration of the male agricultural population was still widespread up to the Second World War (Viscontini 2005: 35–42; Marcacci and Valsangiacomo 2015). On the other hand, immigration – as well as cross-border commuting later on of cheap labour from Italy – promoted the establishment of labour-intensive industries such as tobacco processing. Yet, as seen in the employment share, industrial development stagnated in the first half of the twentieth century, partly due to this labour-intensive structure, which inhibited innovation.

In addition, Ticino lacked the financial resources necessary for large-scale investments after important banks went bankrupt in 1914. It was only during the post-Second World War boom that Ticino was finally able to catch up slightly, largely driven by the construction and hydropower sector. Yet, probably due to the large labour force, the Ticinese unemployment rate has always been higher than in the rest of Switzerland (Marcacci and Valsangiacomo 2015). After 1960, structural change accelerated, first supported by an increase in tourist and logistic services, and then by the emergence of a new financial centre in Lugano (Marcacci and Valsangiacomo 2015). The latter suffered from the 2008 banking crisis; however, relative GDP of Ticino is not affected by it, in contrast to Zurich.

Zurich and Geneva are the financial centres of Switzerland. Unfortunately, the decomposition into NUTS 2 regions masks the contribution of Geneva, but the sectoral change towards tertiarization is the cause for the performance of Zurich: as early as 1910, employment in the financial sector was already concentrated in this region (Hiestand et al. 2012: 782). If we look at the period after the Second World War, economic growth after 1970 is mainly due to the service sector, and within the service sector, to the financial sector (Müller and Woitek 2012: 127). But tertiarization not only caused the high per capita GDP of Zurich; it also contributed to its vulnerability during the financial crisis. As stated above, the events starting in 2008 did not have a devastating effect on the Swiss economy as a whole, but different regions were affected differently: for Zurich, the consequence of the financial crisis was a reduction of relative GDP from 1.35 in 2000 to 1.24 in 2010. The effect of the crisis on the banking sector, and on a region with a high specialization in this sector, can also be seen from the decrease in the

Table 3.13.2 Relative regional per capita GDP (Switzerland = 1)

Year	*CH01*	*CH02*	*CH03*	*CH04*	*CH05*	*CH06*	*CH07*
1900	1.01	0.94	1.03	1.23	0.99	0.92	0.82
1910	0.97	0.95	1.02	1.28	1.00	0.86	0.78
1925	0.96	0.98	1.07	1.29	0.93	0.84	0.73
1938	0.91	1.04	1.00	1.26	0.94	0.81	0.69
1950	1.07	0.98	1.04	1.19	0.90	0.78	0.82
1960	1.05	0.96	1.01	1.21	0.91	0.82	0.79
1970	1.00	0.98	0.99	1.21	0.94	0.88	0.72
1980	1.02	0.95	0.98	1.24	0.91	0.89	0.83
1990	0.98	0.97	0.96	1.21	0.94	0.96	0.86
2000	1.01	0.88	1.03	1.35	0.84	0.91	0.84
2010	1.00	0.92	1.05	1.24	0.86	0.95	0.87

Source: See text

Note: CH01: Lake Geneva region, CH02: Espace Mittelland, CH03: Northwestern Switzerland, CH04: Zurich, CH05: Eastern Switzerland, CH06: Central Switzerland, CH07: Ticino.

direct federal tax revenue for corporate bodies (joint stock and limited liability companies) in the crisis year 2008. While the decrease for Switzerland was 15 per cent, it broke down by 29 per cent for the canton of Zurich (Eidgenössische Steuerverwaltung ESTV 2015).[14]

Results on beta-convergence are displayed in Figure 3.13.4. Since with seven observations, the usual approach does not make much sense, we use mean log per capita GDP and the mean growth rate to divide each graph into four quadrants; regional convergence is indicated by the majority of observations lying in the north-west and south-east quadrants. We see that the periods 1950–1980 and 2000–2010 show convergence, while the picture is not so clear for 1900–1950. The period 1980–2000 is clearly characterized by divergence. In all four cases, Zurich stands out, at least in terms of initial GDP per capita.[15] In terms of growth rates, the region is not different from the mean in the period 1900–1950. Zurich shows higher-than-average growth rates in 1950–1980 and 1980–2000, while the growth rate in the period 2000–2010 is clearly below average. Again, this demonstrates the vulnerability of Zurich in the financial crisis.

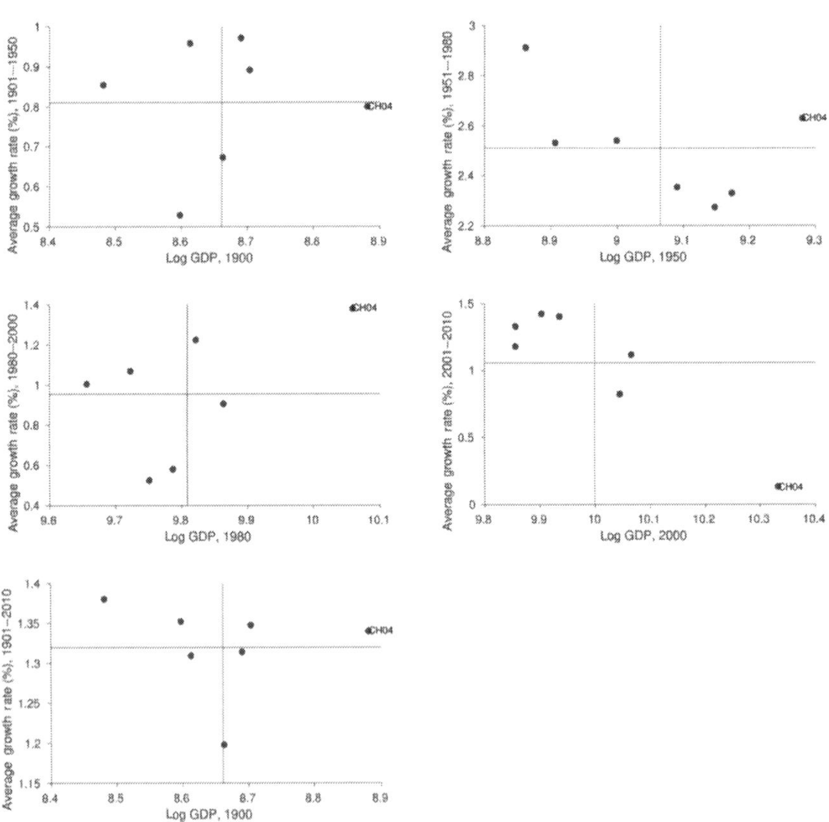

Figure 3.13.4 Beta-convergence

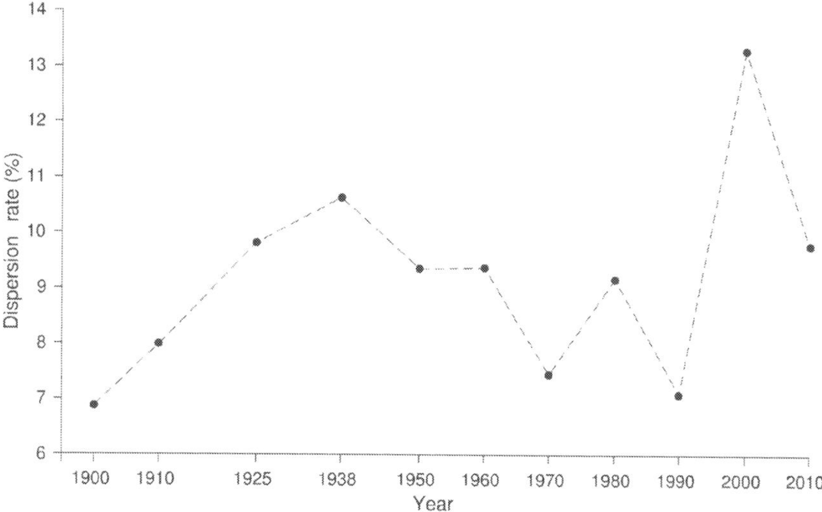

Figure 3.13.5 Regional dispersion

To capture sigma-convergence, we consider the population-weighted coefficient of variation as a measure of dispersion. Figure 3.13.5 shows a pattern of changes in regional disparities comparable to the results reported in Hiestand et al. (2012: 800–2). We see an increase in dispersion until 1938, then a reduction after the Second World War, and a very steep increase in 2000. There are obvious decreases during the business cycle downturn in the 1970s and during the slowdown of economic growth in the 1990s and 2010, while during the growth period in the 1980s, dispersion increased again.

4. Conclusion

The twentieth-century development of Switzerland is characterized by tertiarization. The regions were differently affected by this change: Eastern Switzerland and Espace Mittelland lost in terms of GDP shares, while Zurich gained. In terms of relative per capita GDP, Zurich kept its top position over the entire twentieth century, while Ticino could not catch up.

We already discussed the problems of a decomposition of Switzerland into NUTS 2 regions. However, the advantage of comparability across European regions compensates for the well-known shortcomings of the approach. Stohr's (2014b) study makes district-level GDP data available, offering a decomposition of Switzerland based on the changing economic structure. Moreover, there are alternative measures capturing regional disparities: recently, the FSO started to provide data enabling studying of disparities not only in the economic dimension (Bundesamt für Statistik BFS 2005). The available indices measure social status, individualization, integration and ageing. For 1990–2000, a general profile emerges that, in the past, was characteristic for urban areas.

These measures are certainly also interesting from a historical perspective, providing a more complete picture of welfare changes in the past. There are already studies extending the concept of regional dispersion with respect to the standard of living reflected in average human stature, body mass index, birth weights or mortality (see the overview in Staub et al. 2012). Regional educational performance on the district level before the First World War is studied in Boppart et al. (2013, 2014), and regional income inequality in the late nineteenth century is analysed in Floris et al. (2013). Given the small and diverse geography and the cultural diversity (languages, religion), Switzerland is an ideal subject for deeper regional studies with a broader approach to welfare measurement.

Data appendix

Population

For 1900–1990, regional population data are from HSSO, Table B01 (*ständige Wohnbevölkerung*). For 2000 and 2010, we use FSO data (*Bilanz der ständigen Wohnbevölkerung nach Kantonen*, su-d-01.02.02.01.13). For 1925 and 1939, we take as relevant census years 1920 and 1941.

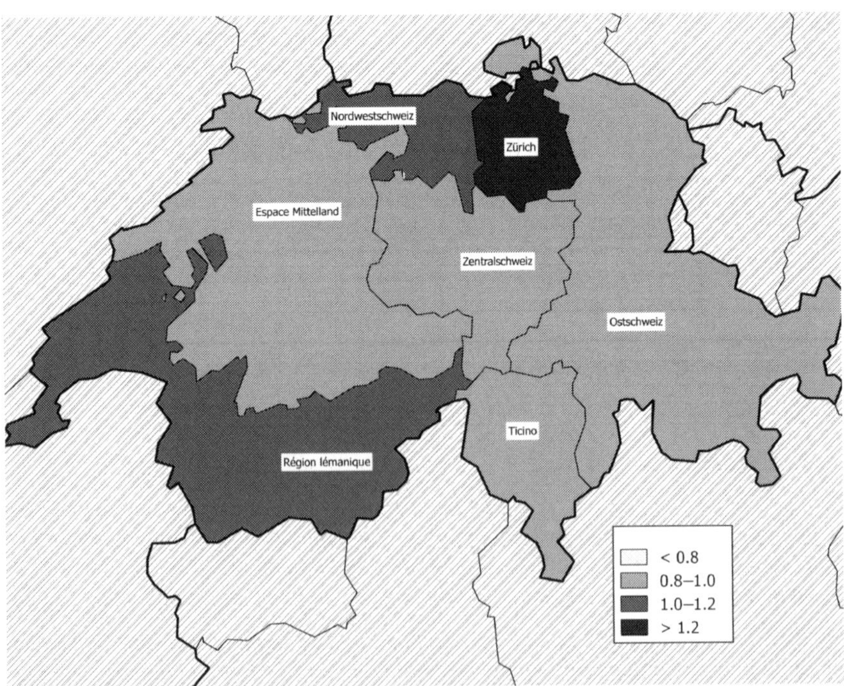

Map 3.13.1 Relative GDP per capita, 1900 (Switzerland = 1)

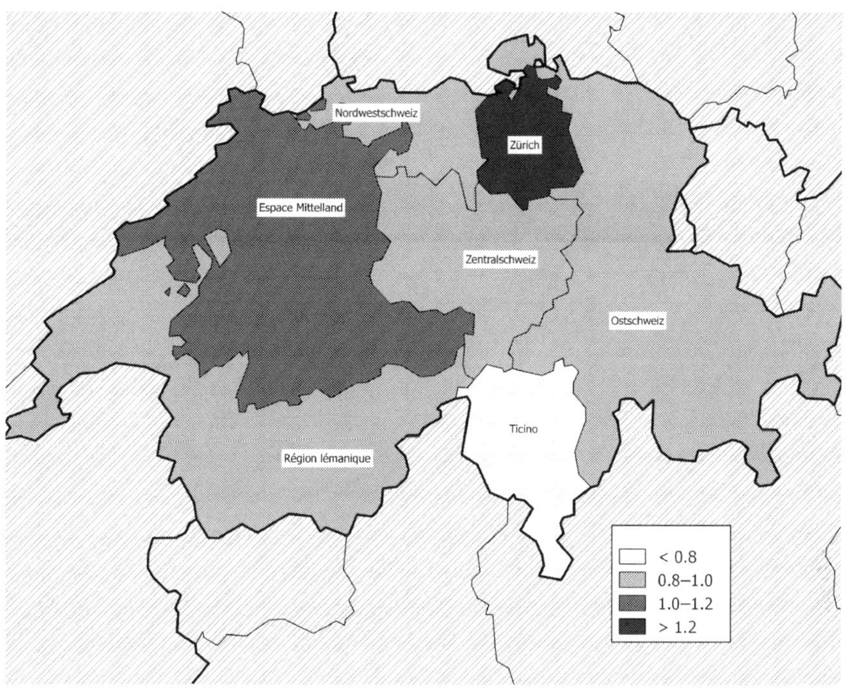

Map 3.13.2 Relative GDP per capita, 1938 (Switzerland = 1)

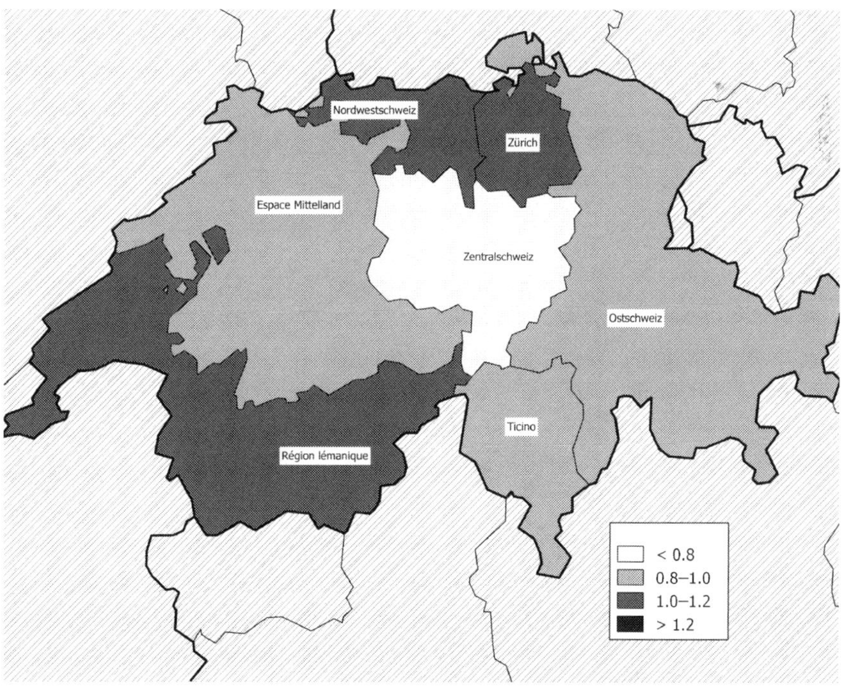

Map 3.13.3 Relative GDP per capita, 1950 (Switzerland = 1)

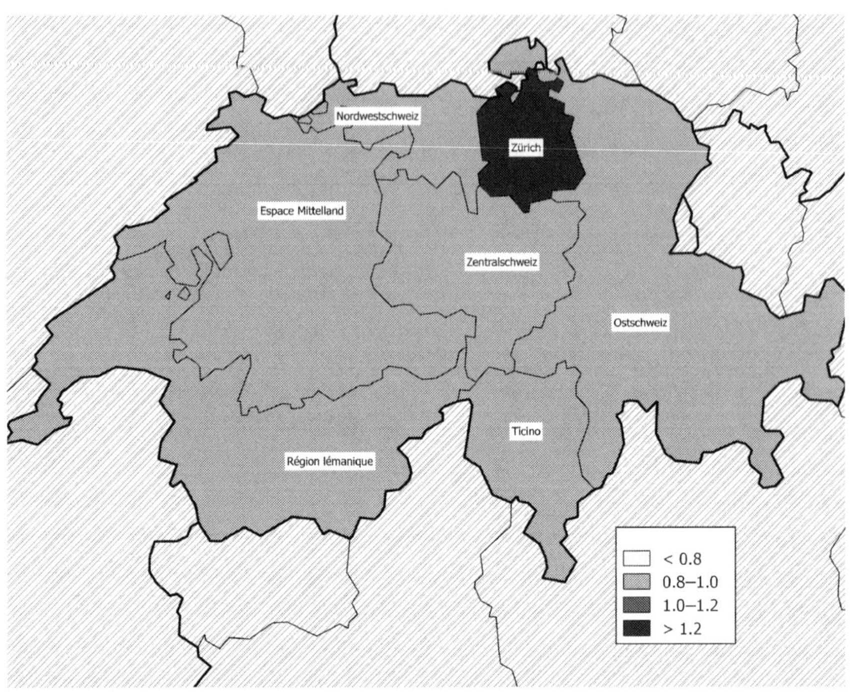

Map 3.13.4 Relative GDP per capita, 1990 (Switzerland = 1)

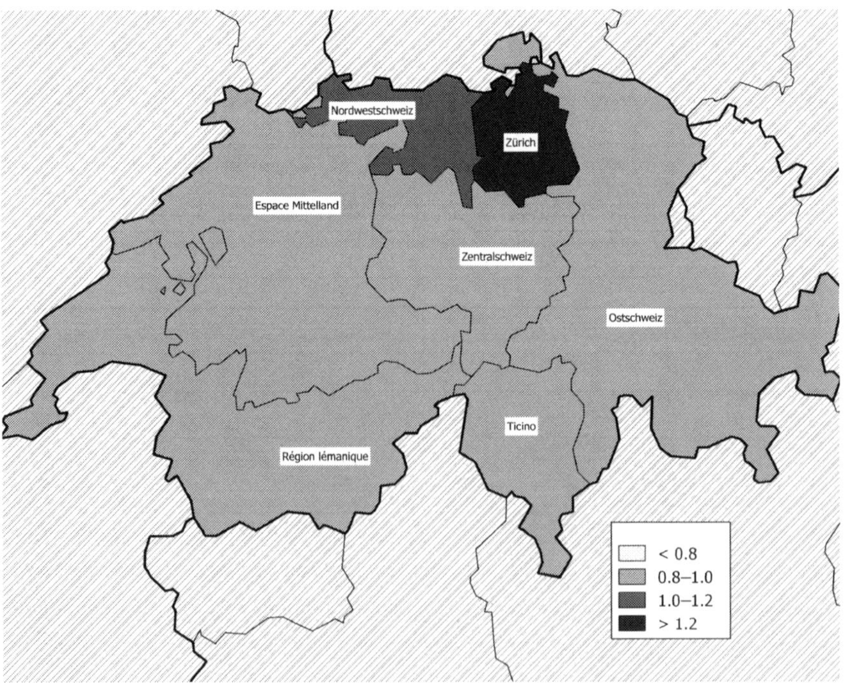

Map 3.13.5 Relative GDP per capita, 2010 (Switzerland = 1)

Employment

1900–1960: HSSO, Table F.10b (Berufstätige im Ersten, Zweiten und Dritten Sektor nach Erwerbsklassen und Kantonen 1860–1960 (exkl. teilzeitbeschäftigte Personen)); 1960–1990: Census (Eidg. Volkszählungen); 2000 (2001) and 2010 (2008): FSO (Arbeitsstätten und Beschäftigte nach Kanton, Wirtschaftssektor und Grössenklasse, www.pxweb.bfs.admin.ch).

GDP

Sectoral GDP (national level): 1900–1960: HSSO, Table Q17a (Ritzmann and David 2012); 1960–1990: HSSO, Table Q2; 2000–2010: FSO, National Accounts, Table T3a.4 (*Produktionskonto nach Wirtschaftssektoren*, je-d-04.03.21).

Cantonal GDP/national income: 1900–2000: HSSO, Tables B.7, B. 43, Q.19 (Ritzmann and David 2012, FSO), Q.5, Q21; 2010: FSO (*Bruttoinlandprodukt (BIP) pro Grossregion*, je-d-04.06.01).

Wages

Agriculture: 1900–1910: milker ("vor dem Krieg"; weekly wages converted to hourly wages using hours worked); 1925–1938 (1939/40): milker (weekly wages converted to hourly wages using hours worked), Schweizerisches Bauernsekretariat, *Statistische Erhebungen* (various issues); 1950–1990 (1985): landscape gardener, minimum hourly wage three years after finishing apprenticeship (NUTS 2 wages are calculated as employment-weighted averages of cantonal wages), collective wage agreements (BIGA *Lohnsätze und Arbeitszeiten in Gesamtarbeitsverträgen* 1949–1952 to 1983–1985, various issues); 2000 (2002)–2010 (2008): monthly gross income by sector, FSO, *Schweizerische Lohnstrukturerhebung*.

Industry: 1900 (1906)–1938 (1939/40): construction workers, hourly wages (CH02, CH03, CH04; CH01, CH05: average; HSSO, Table G.6a), CH07 1900 (1906)–1938: construction workers, hourly wages (1906/09, 1935) (Schneiderfranken 1936: 49); 1950–1990 (1985): mason, minimum hourly wage (NUTS 2 wages are calculated as employment-weighted averages of cantonal wages), collective wage agreements (BIGA *Lohnsätze und Arbeitszeiten in Gesamtarbeitsverträgen* 1949–1952 to 1983–1985, various issues); 2000 (2002)–2010 (2008): monthly gross income by sector, FSO, *Schweizerische Lohnstrukturerhebung*.

Services: 1900–1938: teachers' income 1911 (per teaching hour, regression based on 12,303 individual teachers' incomes on teachers' characteristics and region, data (Huber and Bay 1915);[16] 1950–1990 (1985): CH01, CH02, CH03, CH05, CH06: trade (salespersons with apprenticeship), minimum hourly wage (NUTS 2 wages are calculated as employment-weighted averages of cantonal wages), collective wage agreements (BIGA *Lohnsätze und Arbeitszeiten in Gesamtarbeitsverträgen* 1949–1952 to 1983–1985, various issues); CH04: 1950: average of the relative wages from the above source and the result of a regression of the annual incomes of 104 individuals employed in the service sector on region and individual characteristics 1943 (Freudiger 1943: 62–79; the relative wage is kept constant until 1990); 2000 (2002)–2010 (2008): monthly gross income by sector, FSO, *Schweizerische Lohnstrukturerhebung*.

Notes

1 The exact date of switching from a relatively poor economy characterized by net emigration to a high-performing economy is debated (Studer 2008; Müller and Woitek 2012; Stohr 2014a, 2014b).

2 In betweeen 1965 and 2005, the federal statistical office (FSO) published cantonal national income data.

3 See the opening presentation of Schwarz (1936) at the conference of the Swiss Statistical Society, 'Das Problem einer schweizerischen Produktionsstatistik'.

4 There are alternative approaches, such as the human development index (HDI). With respect to this measure, Switzerland is as well among the best-performing economies (e.g. Baines et al. 2010: 399–410). Other welfare measures from the literature applied to the Swiss case are the already-mentioned happiness research (e.g. Frey and Stutzer 2002) or the biological standard of living (for an overview, see Staub et al. 2012).

5 The canton Jura separated from Berne in 1979.

6 The referendum is a vote against political decisions already taken by the legislators, while the initiative enables citizens to change the constitution (Linder 2002: 110–11).

7 Data: FSO, www.bfs.admin.ch, j-e-d-03.03.01.03.

8 Federal Department of Foreign Affairs, Directorate for European Affairs: Bilateral Agreements (www.eda.admin.ch/dea/en/home/bilaterale-abkommen/inkrafttreten.html).

9 Statistisches Lexikon der Schweiz, Wanderung der ständigen ausländischen Wohnbevölkerung, 1950–2013, Table su-d-1.3.2.1.9. It should be noted that the most recent figures (2016) published by the State Secretariat for Migration point to a reduction of the migration balance by 15 per cent compared to the previous year (Staatssekretariat für Migration 2017).

10 Statistisches Lexikon der Schweiz, Ständige Wohnbevölkerung nach Staatsangehörigkeitskategorie und Geschlecht, am Ende des Jahres, Table su-d-1.1.1.4.

11 www.fsw.uzh.ch/histstat/.

12 We decided not to look at mining because it practically plays no role in the Swiss economy: in terms of employment, the mining share fell from 0.4 per cent in 1930 to 0.01 per cent in 1990 (HSSO Table F02b).

13 As noted above, the regional decomposition in Hiestand et al. (2012) does not exactly follow the NUTS 2 categories: the Lake Geneva region consists only of Geneva and Vaud, while the canton Valais is part of the Alpine region (Grisons, Valais, Ticino).

14 For Ticino, the reduction was below the Swiss average (12 per cent).

15 Zurich becomes less of an outlier if instead of the NUTS 2 classification, the cantonal level is analysed (Fritzsche 2000: 102, Figure 5.5; Hiestand et al. 2012: 796–797, Figures 3.3.18–3.3.20).

16 We could not use the average of agricultural and industry wages, as in Geary and Stark (2002), because it led to unreasonably low relative wages for CH04 (see the discussion of Zurich's relative economic performance in the text).

References

Abrahamsen, Y., Aeppli, R., Atukeren, E., Graff, M., Müller, C. and Schips, B. (2005) 'The Swiss disease: facts and artefacts – a reply to Kehoe and Prescott', *Review of Economic Dynamics*, Vol. 8 (3): 749–58.

Baines, D., Cummins, N. and Schulze, M.-S. (2010) 'Population and living standards, 1945–2000', in S. Broadberry and K. O'Rourke (eds), *The Cambridge Economic History of Modern Europe, Vol. 2*, Cambridge: Cambridge University Press, pp. 391–420.

Boppart, T., Falkinger, J. and Grossmann, V. (2014) 'Protestantism and education: reading (the Bible) and other skills', *Economic Inquiry*, Vol. 52 (2): 874–95.

Boppart, T., Falkinger, J., Grossmann, V., Woitek, U. and Wüthrich, G. (2013) 'Under which conditions does religion affect educational outcomes?', *Explorations in Economic History*, Vol. 50 (2): 242–66.

Bordo, M. and James, H. (2007) 'From 1907 to 1946: a happy childhood or a troubled adolescence?', in Swiss National Bank (ed.), *The Swiss National Bank, 1907–2007*, Zurich: Neue Züricher Zeitung Publishing, pp. 29–107.

Bordo, M., Helbling, T. and James, H. (2007) 'Swiss exchange rate policy in the 1930s: was the delay in devaluation too high a price to pay for conservatism?', *Open Economies Review*, Vol. 18 (1): 1–25.

Bundesamt für Statistik BFS (2005) *Soziokulturelle Unterschiede in der Schweiz. Vier Indizes zu räumlichen Disparitäten 1990–2000*, Neuchâtel: Eidgenössisches Departement des Innern EDI.

Bundesamt für Statistik BFS (2012) *Regionale Disparitäten in der Schweiz*, Neuchâtel: Eidgenössisches Departement des Innern EDI.

Bundesamt für Statistik BFS (2013a) *Bruttoinlandprodukt nach Grossregionen und Kantonen. Methodenbericht und kurze Analyse der Ergebnisse*, Neuchâtel: Eidgenössisches Departement des Innern EDI.

Bundesamt für Statistik BFS (2013b) *Regionale Disparitäten in der Schweiz*, Vol. 21 of *Statistik der Schweiz*, Neuchâtel: Bundesamt für Statistik BFS.

Cascioni, L. (2000) 'Produktion, Umsätze und Wertschöpfung der Unternehmen', in P. Bohley, A. Jans and C. Malaguerra (eds), *Wirtschafts- und Sozialstatistik der Schweiz*, Stuttgart: Haupt, pp. 279–97.

Eidgenössische Steuerverwaltung ESTV (2015) *Direkte Bundessteuer – Juristische Personen – Kantone – Steuerperiode 2008. Tabelle II: Entwicklung der direkten Bundessteuer der juristischen Personen*, Bern: Eidgenössisches Finanzdepartement EFD, available at: www.estv.admin.ch/estv/de/home/allgemein/steuerstatistiken/fachinformationen/steuerstatistiken/direkte-bundessteuer/direkte-bundessteuer---juristische-personen---kantone---steuerpe3.html# (accessed 7 September 2018).

Fallet, E. and Veyrassat, B. (2015) *Uhrenindustrie*, available at: www.hls-dhs-dss.ch/textes/d/D13976.php (accessed 17 August 2018).

Fiala, A. (2000) 'Die volkswirtschaftliche Gesamtrechnung', in P. Bohley, A. Jans and C. Malaguerra (eds), *Wirtschafts- und Sozialstatistik der Schweiz. Eine Einführung*, Bern: Paul Haupt, pp. 443–87.

Floris, J., Woitek, U. and Wüthrich, G. (2013) 'Income inequality of Swiss primary school teachers in the late 19th century', *Jahrbuch für Wirtschaftsgeschichte* [*Economic History Yearbook*], Vol. 54 (1): 57–74.

Freudiger, H. (1943) 'Die Kosten der Lebenshaltung in den Städten Zürich, Basel, Bern, Biel und Neuenburg und in den Kantonen Zürich und Tessin. Haushaltsrechnungen von 104 Familien öffentliche Funktionäre', in Föderativverband des Personals öffentlicher Verwaltungen und Betriebe (ed.), *Die öffentliche Wirtschaft*, Vol. 21.

Frey, B.S. and Stutzer, A. (2000) 'Happiness, economy and institutions', *Economic Journal*, Vol. 110 (446): 918–38.

Frey, B.S. and Stutzer, A. (2002) *Happiness and Economics: How the Economy and Insituttions Affect Human Well-Being*, Princeton, NJ: Princeton University Press.

Fritzsche, B. (2000) 'Unequal regional development in Switzerland: a question of nationality?', in A. Teichova, H. Matis, and J. Pátek (eds), *Economic Change and the National Question in Twentieth-Century Europe*, Cambridge: Cambridge University Press, pp. 85–110.

Geary, F. and Stark, T. (2002) 'Examining Ireland's post-famine economic growth perfomance', *Economic Journal*, Vol. 112 (482): 919–35.

Gugerli, D. and Tanner, J. (2012) 'Wissen und Technologie', in P. Halbeisen, M. Müller and B. Veyrassat (eds), *Wirtschaftsgeschichte der Schweiz im 20. Jahrhundert*, Basel: Schwabe, pp. 265–315.

Hiestand, M., Müller, M. and Woitek, U. (2012) 'Partizipation der Kantone und Regionen', in P. Halbeisen, M. Müller, and B. Veyressat (eds), *Wirtschaftsgeschichte der Schweiz im 20. Jahrhundert*, Basel: Schwabe, pp. 753–819.

Huber, A. and Bay, J.G.A. (1915) *Schweizerische Schulstatistik 1911/12*, Bern: Kommissionsverlag A. Francke.

Kehoe, T.J. and Prescott, E.C. (2002) 'Great depressions of the 20th century', *Review of Economic Dynamics*, Vol. 5 (1): 1–18.

Kehoe, T.J. and Ruhl, K.J. (2003) 'Recent great depressions: aggregate growth in New Zealand and Switzerland, 1973–2000', *New Zealand Economic Papers*, Vol. 37 (1): 5–40.

Kehoe, T.J. and Ruhl, K.J. (2005) 'Is Switzerland in a great depression?', *Review of Economic Dynamics*, Vol. 8 (3): 759–75.

Linder, W. (2002) 'Direkte Demokratie', in U. Klöti, P. Knoepfel, H. Kriesi, W. Linder and Y. Papadopoulos (eds), *Handbuch der Schweizer Politik*, 3rd edition, Zurich: Verlag Neue Zürcher Zeitung, pp. 109–30.

Maissen, T. (2012) *Geschichte der Schweiz*, 4th edition, Baden: hier + jetzt.

Marcacci, M. and Valsangiacomo, N. (2015) *Tessin (Kanton)*, available at: www.hls-dhs-dss.ch/textes/d/D7394.php (accessed 17 August 2018).

Müller, M. and Woitek, U. (2012) 'Wohlstand, Wachstum und Konjunktur', in P. Halbeisen, M. Müller and B. Veyressat (eds), *Wirtschaftsgeschichte der Schweiz im 20. Jahrhundert*, Basel: Schwabe, pp. 91–222.

Rais, G. and Ammann, Y. (2013) 'Überlegungen zur konjunkturellen und strukturellen Entwicklung der Schweizer Wirtschaft', BFS Aktuell, Bundesamt für Statistik BFS.

Ritzmann, H. and David, T. (2012) 'Schätzung des Bruttoinlandprodukts nach Branchen und Kantonen 1890–1960', in P. Halbeisen, M. Müller and B. Veyrassat (eds), *Wirtschaftsgeschichte der Schweiz im 20. Jahrhundert*, Basel: Schwabe, pp. 1185–209.

Ritzmann-Blickenstorfer, H. (2000) 'Historische Statistik der Schweiz', in P. Bohley, A. Jans and C. Malaguerra (eds), *Wirtschafts- und Sozialstatistik der Schweiz. Eine Einführung*, Stuttgart/Wien: Haupt, pp. 58–88.

Rosenkranz, P., Straumann, T. and Woitek, U. (2013) 'A small open economy in the Great Depression: the case of Switzerland', mimeo, Department of Economics, University of Zurich.

Schneiderfranken, I. (1936) *Die Industrien im Kanton Tessin*, PhD Thesis, University of Basle.

Schwarz, A. (1936) 'Bedeutung und Erfassung der industriellen Produktion in der Schweiz', *Zeitschrift für Schweizerische Statistik und Volkswirtschaft*, Vol. 72: 147–58.

Staatssekretariat für Migration (2017) *Migration Report 2016*, Bern: SFBL, Federal Publications.

Statistisches Reichsamt (1936) *Statistisches Handbuch der Weltwirtschaft*, Berlin: Verlag für Sozialpolitik, Wirtschaft und Statistik.

Staub, K., Woitek, U., Pfister, C. and Rühli, F. (2012) 'Überblick über zehn Jahre historisch-anthropometrische Forschung in der Schweiz: Säkularer Trend, soziale und regionale Unterschiede in der mittleren Körperhöhe und -form seit Beginn des 19. Jahrhunderts', *Bulletin der Schweizerischen Gesellschaft für Anthropologie*, Vol. 18: 37–50.

Stiglitz, J.E., Sen, A. and Fitoussi, J.-P. (2010) *Mis-Measuring Our Lives: Why GDP Doesn't Add Up*, New York: The New Press.

Stohr, C. (2014a) 'Lets get this right: Swiss GDP and value added by industry from 1851 to 2008', Geneva School of Economics and Management, WPS 14-09-1.

Stohr, C. (2014b) *Spatial Dynamics of Economic Growth in Switzerland from 1860 to 2000*, No. SES 867, Université de Genève, archive-ouverte.unige.ch/unige:41760.

Straumann, T. (2010) *Fixed Ideas of Money: Small States and Exchange Rate Regimes in 20th Century Europe*, Studies in Macroeconomic History, Cambridge: Cambridge University Press.

Studer, R. (2008) 'When did the Swiss get so rich? Comparing living standards in Switzerland and Europe, 1800–1913', *Journal of European Economic History*, Vol. 37 (2–3): 405–52.

Tooze, A. (2001) *Statistics and the German State 1900–1945: The Making of Modern Economic Knowledge*, Cambridge: Cambridge University Press.

Veyrassat, B. (2010) *Industrialisierung*, available at: www.hls-dhs-dss.ch/textes/d/D13824.php (accessed 17 August 2018).

Viscontini, F. (2005) *Alla Ricerca dello Sviluppo. La Politica Economica nel Ticino (1873–1953)*. Aspetti Cantonali e Regionali, Locarno: Armando Dadò.

3.14 150 years of regional GDP

United Kingdom and Ireland

Frank Geary and Tom Stark

1. Introduction

We present a snapshot of the regional output (GDP/GVA) structure of the British Isles using data for 14 census years between 1861 and 2011. There are fundamental problems involved: between 1800 and 1922, there was one sovereign state in the British Isles – the United Kingdom; since 1922, there have been two – the United Kingdom and the Republic of Ireland; there are no official estimates of UK regional GDP before 1966 and the official designation of UK regions changed in 1994; for Ireland, official estimates of GDP do not appear until the 1950s. In order to overcome the absence of official data and the changing regional structure, we employ the Geary-Stark (hereafter, G-S) method (see Chapter 2) to make estimates of regional GDP for the UK, which we link to official and unofficial estimates for the Republic of Ireland in order to present our picture of the evolution of regional GDP in the British Isles over the last 150 years.

In section 1, we briefly summarize the steps employed to make the estimates of UK regional GDP presented here. Section 2 examines the structure of regional GDP in the UK and its development: a clear pattern emerges. In every period, the region with the largest GDP per head is 'Greater London' or London Counties,[1] exceeding the national average by at least 30 per cent, and in some periods by over 50 per cent. This high GDP per head is also matched by the region's productivity, measured by GDP per employed person (hereafter, worker).[2] Moreover, in most of the census years, the average GDP per head of those who work within 100 miles of Greater London also exceeds the national average (often being the second largest) – a phenomenon generally referred to in UK popular politics as the 'north–south divide'. What happened to the dispersion of regional GDP over the 150 years since 1861 and the north–south divide is the main theme of our analysis.

Between 1800 and 1825, the completion of the union between Britain and Ireland abolished intra-union barriers to trade, established a common external tariff, consolidated the British and Irish exchequers, and Ireland adopted sterling as its currency. The United Kingdom of Great Britain and Ireland existed from 1800 to 1922, after which it became Great Britain and Northern Ireland. Great Britain is a union of two kingdoms (England and Scotland) and a Principality (Wales).[3] The constituent countries of the United Kingdom, however constituted, are culturally distinct and with different resource endowments, but with a common fiscal, monetary and political system. There is, though, from an economic standpoint, a degree of homogeneity in the three countries that make up Great Britain: the Irish economy, especially its relative economic position, has until recently been different from that of the other countries of the UK. Section 3 briefly considers Ireland's performance both within and without the Union.

2. Estimating regional GDP: method and data

The estimates require three sets of data: labour force by sector and region; aggregate GDP and aggregate GDP by sector; and productivity relatives usually (but not always) obtained from wage relatives comparing sector wages in each region with the UK sector wage. Lee (1979) provides data on labour force by industry and region for Great Britain extracted from each census for the period 1841–1971. Irish employment is obtained by reclassifying the Irish census occupation returns to conform to Lee's classification. GDP and sector output are obtained from Feinstein's (1972) estimates of UK GDP at constant factor cost. The wage and other related data used to derive the sector output per head relatives are obtained largely from official returns. The number of sectors employed in the estimation varies with the available data. Often for the services sector, we are reduced to an overall average using the 'Kravis' principle – a weighted average of agricultural and industry wages – or some combination of available service sector wages and the 'Kravis' principle for the remainder.[4] Clearly, direct estimates of output per worker are to be preferred to indirect ones based on wage relatives: censuses of production data enabled the former to be used for the 1931, 1951 and 1961 estimates in industry relatives.[5]

Chapter 2 of this volume sets out the G-S method. Various tests for specific countries that are reported in the country chapters suggest that the method is an accurate predictor of regional GDP, and is robust both with respect to the number of sectors employed and wage coverage, though wider wage coverage within sectors increases accuracy, as does, marginally, increasing the number of sectors (see Geary and Stark 2002, 2015, 2016).

In making the present estimates, we have divided the 150-year period for which data are available into two parts. The first is 1861–1911, when the UK was Great Britain plus Ireland. The estimates are generated using the G-S method with four sectors – agriculture, construction, other industry and services.[6] Employment numbers for Great Britain are from Lee, using his series A classification.[7] The second period overlaps the first, starting in 1901, but refers only to Great Britain plus Northern Ireland, and runs to 2011. The G-S method is used for estimates up to 1961, after which official data are available. The estimates for this period use Lee's employment series B for Great Britain.[8] The Northern Ireland employment figures are obtained by reclassifying the Irish census returns for 1901 and 1911, and the later Northern Ireland census returns to conform to Lee's series for Britain.[9] The 1901 and 1911 estimates are made using four sectors – agriculture, construction, other industry and services; data availability forced us to reduce the number of sectors on which the estimates for 1921–1961 are based to three – agriculture, industry (only manufacturing for 1961) and services. The censuses of production, however, provided both extensive wage and output per employee data for 1931, 1951 and 1961, and wage and turnover data per employee from the census of distribution were available for the 1951 estimates.[10]

The estimates are based on the UK government's regional definition of standard statistical regions (SSRs). In 1996, government office regions (GORs) – since 2011 known officially simply as regions for statistics – became the primary classification for the presentation of regional statistics in England, and subsequently England's NUTS 1 regions.[11] Both classifications involve 12 regions, with seven of them identical under each classification. The main differences are for northern England (other than Yorkshire and Humberside) and the South East, including East Anglia. The definition of London is unchanged. The SSR regions from 1861 to 2011 are therefore as close a consistent approximation as is possible to the NUTS 1 regions for the UK over the 150 years, despite the changing geographical make-up of the UK. In the appendix, Tables 3.14.A.3 and 3.14.A.4 set out the official GOR estimates for 1991–2011, which can be seen to be very close to the SSR estimates for these years.

3. The structure of regional GDP, 1861–2011

3.1 1861–1911

The Industrial Revolution was well established in the UK by 1861. Less than one-quarter of employed persons were engaged in agriculture, with Ireland (49 per cent) and East Anglia (40 per cent) being the only notable exceptions. There were major industrial conurbations in a number of regions – Liverpool and Manchester (the North West), Leeds and Sheffield (Yorkshire and Humberside), Birmingham (West Midlands), Nottingham and Leicester (East Midlands), Glasgow (Scotland), Cardiff (Wales), Newcastle upon Tyne (the North) and Belfast and Dublin (Ireland). For the most part, these regions had one common feature – coal in abundance – and this, combined with producers in the textile, steel, heavy and light engineering, and chemical industries, was the centrepiece of British industrial power. Only Bristol (tobacco), Belfast (textiles and shipbuilding), Dublin (brewing and distilling) and London could lay claim to be exceptions to the rule that regional industrial development was largely energy-resource-determined, though all four of the exceptions were major seaports. Broadly, therefore, two types of region are identified outside London: rural or agricultural regions and industrial regions. This pattern barely changed between 1861 and 1911, though the influence of London expanded beyond Middlesex and Surrey to include neighbouring counties such as Kent and Essex (Lee 1986).

The estimates of GDP presented in Table 3.14.1 confirm this story of London's dominance. Over this period, on average, over 30 per cent of GDP was generated in the South East of England, almost two-thirds of that in London alone. In addition, London's population grew from 3.3 million in 1861 (11 per cent of the UK total) to 6.5 million in 1911 (14 per cent of the UK total). Population growth was not restricted to London: all regions, with the exception of Ireland, experienced

Table 3.14.1 Per cent share in UK GDP

	1861	*1871*	*1881*	*1891*	*1901*	*1911*
South East	28.9	29.2	30.4	30.8	32.8	33.3
London Counties	17.8	20.1	19.6	20.2	21.0	20.0
Rest of South East	11.1	9.2	10.8	10.6	11.8	13.4
East Anglia	3.0	2.6	2.1	2.3	2.3	2.2
South West	8.4	7.3	6.2	5.9	6.0	5.9
West Midlands	6.7	7.2	7.0	7.0	6.4	6.5
East Midlands	4.6	4.9	4.6	4.7	5.3	5.4
North West	11.0	12.6	13.3	14.2	13.3	13.8
North	4.0	5.1	5.2	5.3	5.4	5.3
Yorkshire and Humberside	6.8	7.2	7.3	7.5	7.5	7.7
Wales	4.4	4.3	4.2	4.7	4.1	4.4
Scotland	10.2	9.7	10.4	10.2	10.1	9.6
Ireland	12.0	10.0	9.3	7.6	6.8	5.8

Source: See text.

Note: London Counties = London, Middlesex and Surrey.

population growth. Indeed, some, such as the Rest of the South East and the three northern English regions (North West, North, and Yorkshire and Humberside), grew at a similar pace to London.

London could not be described as an industrial city, nor could it claim to be an originator of the technical and organizational changes that we know as the Industrial Revolution, yet in terms of output per head and per worker and GDP share, it topped the league tables by a substantial margin. London is not a growth pole or an economic core to a rest of UK periphery. Beyond the usual drivers of skills, innovation, enterprise, investment and competition (Dunnell 2009), a possible explanation lies in economies of agglomeration: a clustering of economic activities in an area giving rise to a mix of Marshallian economies of scale, network effects, and economies of both specialization and diversification. Even before the structural and technical changes of the eighteenth century, London was by far the UK's largest city, the capital, financial and commercial centre, home to the London Stock Exchange – an international trading centre and major port. It was also the centre of government, boasting a sizeable political administration. The city had a disparate range of workers supporting a wide range of consumer goods, light manufacturing and service activities. All of this was alongside a national road network – which owed much to the Romans – and by 1861 a highly developed railway system fanning out from the capital such that much, but not all, of the output of the other regions was exported through London – the world's largest and busiest port in the nineteenth century.[12] Servicing a global trading network and empire and its role as the administrative centre of government were contributory driving forces behind the economic prosperity of London.

How does this aggregate dominance translate into measures of average productivity and average prosperity? Ultimately, prosperity depends upon productivity.

However, GDP per worker (average productivity) and GDP per head (average prosperity) are different: participation rates, for example, may drive a wedge between the productivity measure and the prosperity measure. Table 3.14.2 presents the prosperity measure. The corresponding productivity figures are set out in the appendix. Table 3.14.A.1 indicates that the South East managed an average of 33 per cent above the UK average of output per worker over the period, though within this London's advantage averages 47 per cent compared to Rest of South East's 13 per cent. With the exception of East Anglia (14 per cent below) and Ireland (38 per cent below), the remaining regions lie within 10 per cent of the UK average. The output per capita figures suggest that in general, prosperity reflects productivity.

These averages tell us little of the dynamics of changing relative productivity and prosperity. Tables 3.14.2 and 3.14.A.1 indicate that in terms of output per capita and labour productivity, the South East's lead was reduced between 1861 and 1911: the poorer regions were catching up. In the UK, with London always being the richest region, catch-up may be conveniently measured as the gap between London and the rest. Tables 3.14.2 and 3.14.A.1 include a simple arithmetic measure of catch-up based on this proposition: for any year, it is the weighted sum of the differences between the London index (from UK = 100) of GDP per capita or per worker and that of each of the other regions. The differences are weighted for each region according to its share of the non-London UK population. The gap is lower in 1911 than it was in 1861, indicating catch-up of the relatively poorer regions on London over the period: it was closing at a rate of about 0.8 of 1 per cent

Table 3.14.2 GDP per capita (UK = 1)

	1861	*1871*	*1881*	*1891*	*1901*	*1911*
South East	1.45	1.33	1.36	1.30	1.32	1.30
London Counties	1.60	1.67	1.50	1.44	1.46	1.39
Rest of South East	1.26	0.92	1.18	1.09	1.13	1.19
East Anglia	0.87	0.81	0.75	0.83	0.89	0.90
SouthWest	1.07	1.00	0.92	0.93	0.98	0.99
West Midlands	0.98	1.01	0.96	0.98	0.89	0.90
East Midlands	0.93	0.98	0.88	0.83	0.95	0.96
North West	1.09	1.15	1.10	1.12	1.04	1.07
North	0.85	0.98	0.91	0.90	0.88	0.85
Yorkshire and Humberside	1.05	0.99	0.93	0.93	0.90	0.92
Wales	0.96	0.96	0.94	0.99	0.84	0.83
Scotland	0.96	0.91	0.96	0.95	0.93	0.90
Ireland	0.60	0.59	0.63	0.61	0.63	0.60
CV	0.286	0.299	0.249	0.230	0.225	0.218
Catch-up factor (on London)	*67.8*	*72.7*	*57.1*	*49.8*	*53.3*	*45.3*

Source: Table 3.14.1, Lee (1979) and Census of Ireland.

Note: CV in this table and all following tables is population-weighted and treats South East as two separate regions: London Counties and Rest of South East.

per annum. This is not particularly impressive catch-up: at this rate, it would have taken about 90 years for London's lead of 1861 to be halved.[13]

Country and regional convergence is more commonly discussed in terms of beta- and sigma-convergence. The former is a necessary but not sufficient condition for the latter. The simple measure of catch-up outlined above is supported by the standard measure of unconditional beta-convergence. Figure 3.14.1 shows a negative relationship between initial level of GDP per capita and subsequent growth: poorer regions were growing faster than richer ones. Again, the relationship is not particularly strong (annual average convergence of 0.2 of 1 per cent), especially when considered against the commonly held rule that regions tend to converge at a rate of about 2 per cent per year (e.g. see Sala-i-Martin 1996). Sigma-convergence focuses on change in the dispersion of regional GDP. This is indicated by movement in the coefficient of variation of both regional GDP per worker and per person, which in 1911 were noticeably lower than in 1861. The conclusion is that poorer regions were, on average, catching up, albeit not particularly rapidly, on London (and the South East), and that regional dispersion of GDP diminished in the decades leading up to the outbreak of the Great War.

3.2 1901–2011

In 1921, the political boundary of the UK altered with the signing of the Anglo-Irish Treaty. The 26 counties of the present-day Republic of Ireland departed the United Kingdom to become the Irish Free State in December 1922. The remaining

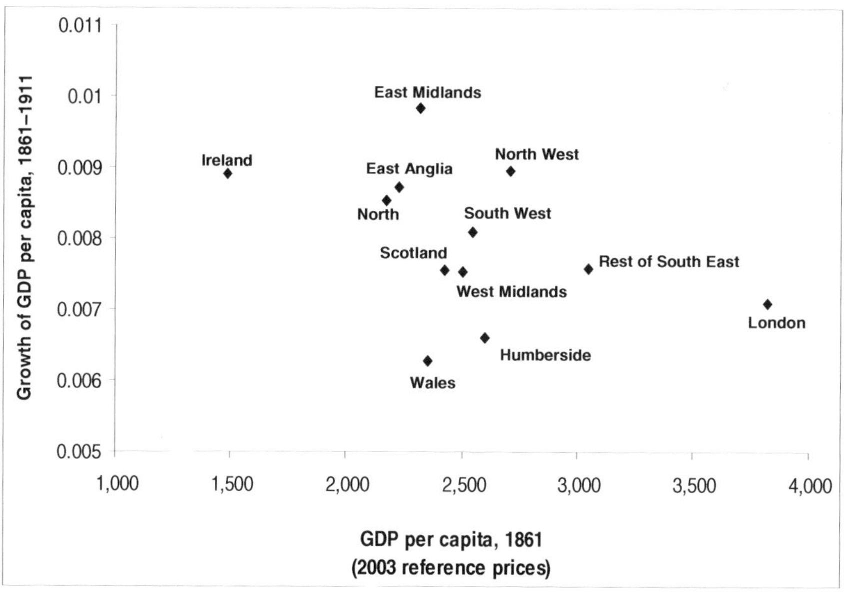

Figure 3.14.1 Regional growth rates in the UK, 1861–1911

six Irish counties opted to remain within the UK as Northern Ireland. We were able to estimate the GDP of these two parts of Ireland for the years 1901 and 1911 such that in Table 3.14.3, we can present the GDP shares for the present UK jurisdiction for 1901 onwards. See also Maps 3.14.1–3.14.11, which show the GDP per capita of NUTS 1 regions of the UK relative to the UK average for 1900–2010. Note that North-West and North-East and East Anglia and South-East had to be merged.

The most notable feature is the relative increase in the share of the midland and southern regions between 1901 and 2011. The South East displays the greatest percentage increase in share of GDP, though note that this has been driven by an increase in the share of Rest of South East rather than London. This gain for the southern regions has been at the expense of the northern English and the Celtic regions. In fact, this pattern really only sets in after 1921.

These changing shares are matched by a population shift to the Rest of South East. In the twentieth century, the population of the South East grew by 77 per cent (10.5 to 18.5 million), compared to 20 per cent (6 to 7 million) by London and 54 percent (38.7 to 58.7 million) for the nation as a whole. This, however, did not represent a decline in London's importance, but rather geographical expansion of its economic presence. The London of the previous section was spreading

Table 3.14.3 Per cent share in UK GDP (UK = GB + NI)

	1901	*1911*	*1921*	*1931*	*1951*	*1961*	*1971*	*1981*	*1991*	*2001*	*2011*
South East	33.4	33.4	34.0	38.3	33.4	35.1	35.4	35.4	35.9	39.1	41.5
London	21.2	20.9	21.0	22.8	20.1	19.9	19.3	15.4	15.0	17.6	20.2
Rest of South East	12.2	12.5	13.0	15.4	13.3	15.2	16.0	19.9	20.9	21.5	21.3
East Anglia	2.3	2.3	2.2	2.1	2.3	2.5	2.8	3.2	3.6	3.8	3.9
South West	6.2	6.0	5.8	5.8	5.9	6.0	6.5	7.3	7.8	7.8	7.7
West Midlands	6.8	7.2	6.6	7.9	9.2	9.5	9.5	8.4	8.5	8.0	7.3
East Midlands	5.7	5.9	5.3	5.3	6.1	6.2	5.9	6.6	6.8	6.5	6.2
North West	14.7	14.7	14.9	11.9	13.3	11.9	11.7	10.8	10.0	9.4	8.8
North	5.7	5.7	5.7	4.3	5.6	5.6	5.2	5.2	4.8	4.0	3.8
Yorkshire and Humberside	8.0	8.2	8.2	7.9	8.5	8.0	8.1	8.0	7.5	7.3	6.8
Wales	4.3	4.8	4.7	4.6	4.4	4.6	4.3	4.2	4.3	3.8	3.6
Scotland	10.7	10.0	10.3	10.0	9.1	8.8	8.7	8.9	8.6	8.0	8.1
Northern Ireland	2.1	1.8	2.2	1.9	2.0	2.0	2.1	2.0	2.2	2.3	2.2

Source: 1901 to 1961: see text; 1971: regional trends 22 T9.1; 1981: regional trends 26 T12.2; 1991: regional trends 30 T12.1; 2001 and 2011: GOR 2001 using NUTS 2 data; 2011: ONS Downloads gvanuts1_tcm77 -388571and census of population 2011(KS101EW and KS605EW).

Note: For 2001 and 2011, 8 of the 12 GOR regions are identical to their SSR equivalents. Using NUTS 2 data, we were able to adjust for three, namely North, North West and East Anglia. The South East was then calculated as a residual and the GOR estimates for London subtracted to derive the Rest of South East.

now into the South East. This can probably be dated to the interwar period, though it is worth noting that between 1901 and 1921, the Rest of South East region was at least keeping pace with or slightly outpacing London in terms of share of GDP. Whether its origins were Edwardian or in the interwar years, the South East became a metropolitan area with a public transport system expanding to meet the growing demand for suburban commuter traffic. The interwar decades saw a well-documented increasing north–south divide characterized by the struggling staple export industries of Outer Britain and the growing new industries of the Midlands and the South East (Scott 2007).

The different regional reactions to the difficulties of post-war reconstruction were as much due to the industrial structure with which the different regions entered the interwar period as any changes in industrial structure they experienced during the period. London and the South East lacked the Victorian specialization in heavy industry and textiles that had served the northern and Celtic regions well before the war, such that in addition to any traditional advantages, their industrial structure was geared towards the new expanding industries of electrical engineering, motor vehicles, aircraft production and their ancillaries. Similarly, the West Midlands had initiated a pre-war transition towards bicycles, motorcycles, motor vehicles and electrical goods that left it well positioned to take advantage of growth in these areas (Aldcroft 1973; Law 1980; Lee 1986). Considering regional reaction to the shock of the Great Depression, Richardson (1967) argues that the South and Midlands did not experience much of a depression and recovered much earlier than the rest of the country. The Great Depression had a much greater impact on the regions of Outer Britain where there was little sign of recovery before the second half of the decade.

To some extent, this experience was reversed by the Second World War: between 1931 and 1951, the South East, including both London and the Rest of South East, lost share. The war years saw a good deal of physical damage to the South East's economy and some strategic industries were moved to other regions. This, together with a revival of the old heavy industry and government measures aimed at encouraging growth in the depressed regions, improved the position of these areas. Although the years between the early 1950s and the early 1970s saw historically high growth rates for the UK, the economy also experienced a competitive decline in many major industries – shipbuilding, coal, iron and steel, and textiles – which again affected the northern regions disproportionately. After the initial fall in the South East's share in GDP to the 1950s, it very slowly recovered share until the 1990s. This, though, masks a fall in London's share. East Anglia, South West, East Midlands and (perhaps surprisingly) Northern Ireland[14] all gained shares to 1991.The shares of the other regions all fell, although other than the North West changes were not large.

From the 1990s, the fall in London's share of GDP was decisively reversed as deregulation of financial markets allowed the city to become the world's largest foreign exchange, banking and financial centre. London and the South East now had their own major industry – a growth centre with built-in agglomeration economies. The South East was heading a financial sector revolution, and a new north–south divide became apparent as all other regions (apart from Northern Ireland) lost share to the South East, though now the big gainer was London. Finally, possibly due to the increasing dominance of the South East in the UK economy, the countries versus regions issue re-emerged: by the end of the century, Scotland, Wales and Northern Ireland had achieved devolved assemblies – re-achieved in the case of Northern Ireland, which experienced a 30-year bitter identity war.[15] Scotland also benefited from North Sea oil, and it is only a quirk of the UK statistical authorities that prevents this impact showing up in regional statistics.[16]

How do these changes in aggregate shares of GDP translate into measures of average prosperity and productivity? These measures are set out in Tables 3.14.4 and 3.14.A.2. Considering the period as a whole, despite two world wars, the difficulties of the interwar years and post-war deindustrialization that impacted severely on the regions of Outer Britain and Northern Ireland, compared to the 50 years preceding 1914, there was some narrowing in the relative productivity gap. The South East averaged about 16 per cent above the UK average, compared to 33 per cent before 1914, though within this London managed a 26 per cent (47 per cent pre-1914) advantage compared to 6 per cent (13 per cent pre-1914) for the Rest of South East. With the exception of Northern Ireland (22 per cent below), the remaining regions lie within 10 per cent of the UK average. The prosperity measure broadly follows the productivity measure, though Wales and the North join Northern Ireland, with GDP per capita more than 10 per cent below the UK average.

Table 3.14.A.2 indicates that the pre-1914 pattern of convergence and catch-up was interrupted by the Great War and the ensuing problems of excess capacity in the Victorian staple export industries that disproportionately affected the old industrial areas of Outer Britain and Northern Ireland. However, some time between 1931 and 1951, the gap between productivity in the South East and the rest of the country narrowed noticeably, then largely stabilized until the 1970s, after which it began to widen again, taking off in the 1990s: the widening of the gap since 1981 has been overwhelming due to productivity growth in London. GDP per capita figures tell a similar tale. After a period in which the gap between the South East and the rest narrowed, by 2001 both London and the Rest of South East had surpassed their 1901 advantage.

Whether measured as SSRs or GORs (see Tables 3.14.A.3 and 3.14.A.4), the trends established in the closing decades of the twentieth century continued through the shock of recession in 2008. The South East region continues to pull away from the rest, driven by London. Despite the impact of prolonged recession and despite the fact that the recession had its roots in the financial sector, the negative impact in London and the Rest of South East was less than elsewhere, other than Scotland. Bearing in mind that the regional make-up of the UK altered with the withdrawal of the Republic of Ireland from the United Kingdom in 1922, per capita GDP in London by 2011 was 50 per cent greater than the UK average, and this has not been the case since the 1870s. Sigma-dispersion in the UK has also returned to the levels of the 1880s (see Tables 3.14.2 and 3.14.4), and there has been no beta-type 'catch-up' for half a century.

These trends are reflected in two of the convergence measures – the catch-up factor and the dispersion measure – both of which, in broad terms, display a U-shape

Table 3.14.4 GDP per capita GDP (UK = 1)

	1901	*1911*	*1921*	*1931*	*1951*	*1961*	*1971*	*1981*	*1991*	*2001*	*2011*
South East	1.22	1.20	1.22	1.31	1.11	1.14	1.15	1.17	1.19	1.24	1.28
London	1.36	1.35	1.38	1.45	1.40	1.46	1.44	1.30	1.21	1.44	1.56
Rest of South East	1.03	1.01	1.02	1.15	0.85	0.89	0.92	1.09	1.18	1.11	1.10
East Anglia	0.82	0.83	0.84	0.83	0.90	0.93	0.95	0.97	1.01	1.11	1.11
South West	0.91	0.92	0.92	0.93	0.90	0.90	0.92	0.94	0.94	0.93	0.92
West Midlands	0.88	0.93	0.83	0.97	1.05	1.05	1.03	0.91	0.93	0.89	0.82
East Midlands	0.96	0.99	0.89	0.87	0.97	0.95	0.9	0.97	0.97	0.91	0.87
North West	1.08	1.08	1.10	0.89	1.05	0.97	0.97	0.94	0.91	0.88	0.85
North	0.88	0.85	0.84	0.66	0.89	0.9	0.87	0.93	0.89	0.79	0.78
Yorkshire and Humberside	0.92	0.92	0.94	0.87	0.98	0.95	0.97	0.92	0.87	0.87	0.82
Wales	0.81	0.83	0.77	0.82	0.86	0.91	0.88	0.83	0.85	0.77	0.73
Scotland	0.92	0.88	0.93	0.95	0.9	0.9	0.93	0.96	0.96	0.93	0.97
Northern Ireland	0.66	0.62	0.78	0.69	0.73	0.73	0.74	0.75	0.79	0.81	0.78
CV	0.178	0.177	0.188	0.231	0.179	0.192	0.180	0.134	0.132	0.194	0.245
Catch-up factor	25.2	28.7	29.8	31.0	16.4	20.6	21.2	24.9	27.3	38.6	46.8

Source: Table 3.14.3, Lee (1979) and Census of Ireland.

Note: For purposes of continuity and comparison, the years 1901 and 1911 refer to GB + NI. The UK in these years was GB + Ireland. Catch-up factor is with respect to the South East.

(see Figure 3.14.2). Considering GDP per worker, the movement in the coefficient of variation indicates a decline in the dispersion of per worker regional productivity between 1901 and the 1970s, with a reversal of this trend in the interwar period.

The catch-up measure is now calculated with respect to the South East (rather than London) and shows general catch-up between 1901 and 1971, with again a reversal of this trend in 1921 and 1931. After 1971, there is no catch-up evident, with substantial reversal after 1991. For both measures, the 1990s decisively reverse any previous trend towards convergence.

Considering the standard measure of unconditional beta-convergence, Figure 3.14.3 indicates no or very little correlation between the pace of a region's growth and its initial level of GDP per head. This is a very broad-brush approach, which of course fails to pick up the trend reversal of 1911–1931 and the dramatic 1931–1951 catch-up, nor does it pick up the subsequent weak then strong divergence as the gap between London and the rest, along with regional dispersion of GDP per head, was restored to levels not seen since the beginning of the twentieth century. What it suggests, though, in terms of the standard neoclassical growth model, is that with no overall relation between level of GDP per capita and its subsequent growth, then UK regions are at or near their steady state. The implication is that the determining elements of the steady state – capital accumulation and total factor productivity widely defined – in the poorer regions are below those of the richer regions. What is required, then, for catch-up in the twenty-first century is a change in these determining factors.

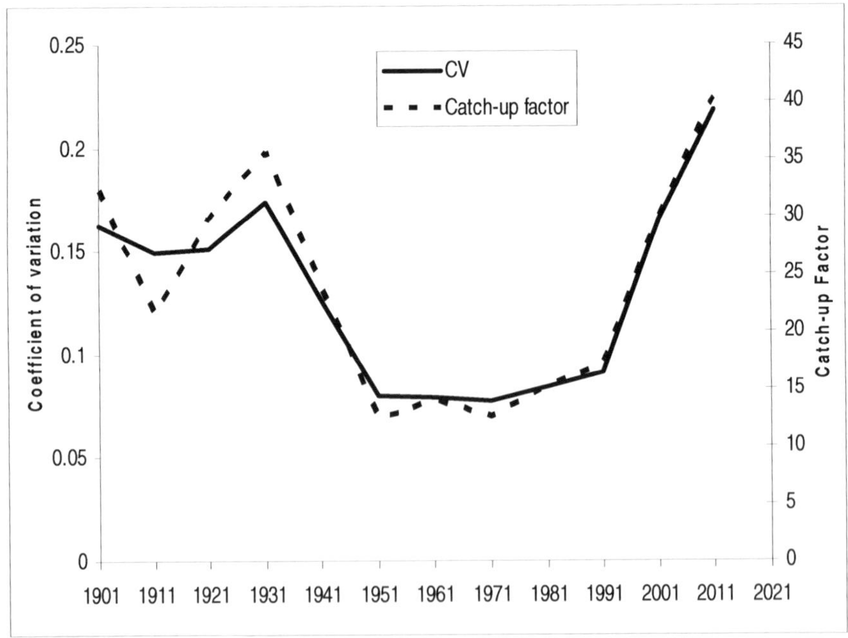

Figure 3.14.2 CV and catch-up factor, 1901–2011 (GDP per worker)

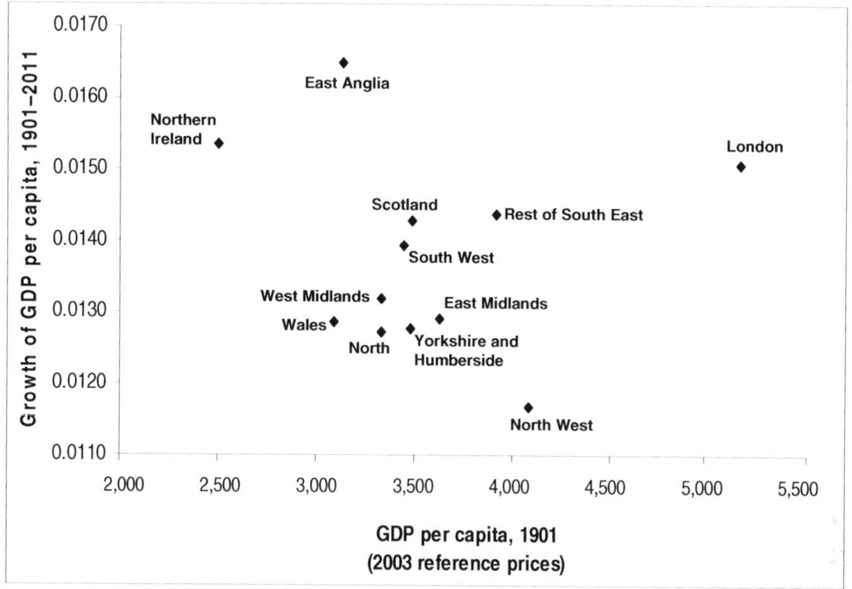

Figure 3.14.3 Regional growth rates in the UK, 1901–2011

What is the likely effect of regional price variation on these estimates? We have considered this in more detail elsewhere.[17] Taking account of regional price differences reduces the shares of the southern regions in almost all years, with the bulk of the reduction falling on the South East. The CVs for regional productivity and output per head fall marginally, but the broad trends identified previously are not affected.

4. Ireland

4.1 Pre-1922

Ireland as a whole was part of the UK between 1800 and 1922. At the time of the Act of Union and subsequently, Ireland was the poorest of the UK regions, with neither GDP per worker nor GDP per capita exceeding 63 per cent of the UK average before 1914, and, of course, Irish population between 1861 and 1911 fell by 25 per cent. However, Ireland was part of the UK, so it can be described as the poorest of the rich. To provide some perspective on Ireland's position, we can ask the question: How poor was Ireland over the half-century before the Great War compared to the rest of Europe?

Comparison requires estimates of GDP per head in Ireland (and therefore also Great Britain) in 1990 international dollars, which can then be slotted into Maddison's (1995) estimates for European and North American economies.

The exercise is completed in three stages. The first is to compute Ireland's price level relative to that of Great Britain in 1912 (see Geary and Stark 2015: Table 9). The second stage is to calculate equivalent Irish and GB price levels for each census year back to 1861 in order to derive Irish/GB PPPs. We did this by scaling the 1912 price index for the two regions by their respective price indices back to 1861. For GB, we assumed that the ONS index of consumer price inflation since 1750 (O'Donoghue et al. 2004) would suffice. For Ireland, we linked Geary and Stark's (2004) price index for 1861 to 1871 to an average of the four indices produced by Brunt and Canon (2004). In stage 3, we took Maddison's estimates for UK GDP in 1990 international dollars and subdivided them according to our estimated Irish and GB shares in UK GDP. These estimates for each of the census years 1861–1911 were then divided by the appropriate price indices for Ireland and GB, and recalibrated to sum to the Maddison totals and GDP per head estimates in 1990 international dollars. The results are set out in Tables 3.14.5 and 3.14.6. In passing, we note that the US can be seen to have overtaken both the UK and GB by 1911, though clearly not the South East of England.

Though Ireland was the poorest region in the UK, it was not the poorest in Europe. In 1861, 7 of the 15 countries above had per capita income levels below that of Ireland. By 1911, this had been reduced to six. Most were catching up Great Britain and a number converging more speedily than Ireland; nevertheless, the Irish performance relative to GB between 1861 and 1911 would not be

Table 3.14.5 GDP per head in 1990 international dollars

	1861	*1871*	*1881*	*1891*	*1901*	*1911*
Belgium	2,310	2,682	3,070	3,395	3,719	4,148
Denmark	1,747	1,993	2,183	2,555	3,104	3,857
Finland	958	1,127	1,110	1,350	1,636	1,939
France	1,769	1,899	2,194	2,432	2,826	3,250
Germany	1,583	1,817	2,025	2,397	2,871	3,408
Italy	1,447	1,506	1,467	1,651	1,890	2,461
Netherlands	2,397	2,734	3,074	3,224	3,440	3,888
Norway	1,104	1,376	1,528	1,712	1,902	2,255
Sweden	1,183	1,406	1,565	1,836	2,248	2,814
Switzerland	1,859	2,225	2,481	2,987	3,745	4,378
UK	2,904	3,315	3,574	3,970	4,459	4,714
Great Britain	3,251	3,625	3,806	4,168	4,618	4,895
Ireland	1,519	1,799	2,237	2,579	3,138	3,028
Portugal	883	933	970	1,099	1,269	1,242
Spain	1,248	1,298	1,679	1,654	1,901	2,017
Canada	1,451	1,755	2,040	2,409	2,911	4,213
USA	2,178	2,503	3,215	3,467	4,091	5,046

Source: See text; see also Brunt and Cannon (2004), Geary and Stark (2004) and Maddison (2015: Tables D1a and D1b).

Table 3.14.6 GDP per head in 1990 international dollars (UK 1911 = 100)

	1861	*1871*	*1881*	*1891*	*1901*	*1911*
Belgium	49	57	65	72	79	88
Denmark	37	42	46	54	66	82
Finland	20	24	24	29	35	41
France	38	40	47	52	60	69
Germany	34	39	43	51	61	72
Italy	31	32	31	35	40	52
Netherlands	51	58	65	68	73	82
Norway	23	29	32	36	40	48
Sweden	25	30	33	39	48	60
Switzerland	39	47	53	63	79	93
UK	62	70	76	84	95	100
Great Britain	69	77	81	88	98	104
Ireland	32	38	47	55	67	64
Portugal	19	20	21	23	27	26
Spain	26	28	36	35	40	43
Canada	31	37	43	51	62	89
USA	46	53	68	74	87	107

repeated for another half-century.[18] As regards the sources of Ireland's growth performance, we have argued elsewhere that contrary to the widespread view, only between 20 and 30 per cent of growth in GDP per worker can be accounted for by emigration, leaving between 70 and 80 per cent to be accounted for by an upward shifting aggregate production function – capital accumulation, structural change and TFP gain (Geary and Stark 2015).

4.2 Post-1922

Unfortunately, there are no statistics available for UK GDP after 1920 that include the 26 counties of Ireland that currently form the Republic of Ireland. Moreover, there are no 1921 wage data for the 26 counties that might enable us to hazard an estimate via the G-S technique. Therefore, our 1911 estimates have to be our point of reference between pre- and post-independence GDP. In Table 3.14.7, we summarize the post-1911 relationships between the Republic of Ireland (RoI) and the UK (now GB + NI) and between the RoI and Northern Ireland (NI).

Cullen (1972) argues that in the 1920s, per capita incomes in the Irish Free State rose more rapidly than they did in Britain, which is consistent with the G-S/Maddison PPP comparison above. Catch-up, however, did not continue after 1931. The emergence of trade barriers and tariffs hit Irish exports, as did the 'economic war' or financial dispute with the UK, and despite increasing industrialization, the Irish economy entered a period of stagnation that continued as a result of 'neutrality' and enforced 'self-sufficiency' through the Second World War and taking in the 1950s (Cullen 1972; Ó Gráda and O'Rourke 1996). Ó Gráda and O'Rourke

Table 3.14.7 Comparisons of Ireland and UK GDP and GDP per capita, 1911–2011

Year	*Current price estimates*			*PPP estimates*		
	Irish GDP as % of UK GDP	*Irish GDP per capita as % of UK GDP per head*	*Irish GDP per capita as % of Northern Irish GDP per head*	*Maddison*	*Penn World Tables*	*Eurostat*
1911	3.9	0.52	0.84	0.542		
1931	3.6	0.56	0.80	0.62		
1951	2.9	0.49	0.67	0.51	0.56	
1961	2.5	0.48	0.65	0.52	0.56	
1971	3.3	0.61	0.83	0.60	0.61	
1981	3.8	0.62	0.83	0.67	0.72	
1991	4.6	0.72	0.91	0.71	0.80	0.78
2001	7.2	1.09	1.38		1.14	1.10
2011	8.9	1.23	1.53		1.15	1.23

Source: National Income and Expenditure CSO Dublin (various); Penn World Tables versions 6.1,7.1 and 8.0; Maddison (1995: Tables D1a and D1b); Eurostat Yearbook 1998/99 and website (https://ec.europa.eu/eurostat/web/national-accounts/data/main-tables); 1931 UK Nat Inc + taxes less subs on exp from Cambridge Key Stats and Ireland from Cullen (1972); and ONS/CSO National Income and Expenditure 'Blue Book' London (various).

Note: (1) The UK in all cases refers to GB + NI. (2) The 1911 G-S estimate is derived from that of table 1.

(1996) show that Ireland was in 'catch-up' mode once again in the 1960s at least on the UK, if not on the rest of Western Europe, and the estimates in Table 3.14.7 confirm this.[19] Macroeconomic policy had focused heavily on industrial development, especially in new and 'high-tech' areas. Generous capital grants and tax relief were directed to the attraction of foreign investment.

The UK's economic (and political) troubles in the following decade adversely impacted on Ireland. Both countries joined the EU in 1973, and Ireland left parity with sterling in 1979 and signed up for the EMS. Despite early problems associated with these major structural changes, a flat-rate 10 per cent corporation tax and the government's Programme for Competitiveness and Work saw the emergence of the 'Celtic Tiger' by the mid-1990s. US and EU multinationals set up plants and headquarters in the Republic, and growth boomed. The population expanded rapidly for the first time in 160 years. Monetary change brought a rapid growth in the financial sector, especially around Dublin, and with it a massive property boom, largely financed by debt (O'Toole 2010; McCann 2011). Inevitably, Ireland fell badly foul of the 2008 crisis, and bank 'bailouts' from a variety of sources were necessary.[20] Nevertheless, the estimates in Table 3.14.7 show that Ireland's 'catch-up' became 'overtake' at the turn of the century and persisted through to 2011. This catch-up, though, is more regionally focused than estimates at NUTS 1 would indicate.

Table 3.14.8 indicates that much of Ireland's income is generated in the Dublin area and to a lesser extent in the Cork area, and for some areas this implies a lower

Table 3.14.8 Regional GDP in Ireland, 2010

Region NUTS level 3	*Per cent share of GDP at market prices, 2001*	*Per cent share of GDP at market prices, 2011*	*GDP per head, Ireland = 100, 2001*	*GDP per head, Ireland = 100, 2011*
Border	6.9	6.5	62.0	57.7
Midland	3.7	3.7	63.7	60.8
West	6.9	7.8	71.3	80.6
Dublin	41.4	41.8	143.9	151.5
Mid-East	8.6	7.9	82.2	67.9
Mid-West	7.1	7.1	81.2	85.4
South-East	8.5	7.3	78.9	67.0
South-West	17.0	17.9	114.2	123.1
CV			0.318	0.374
Catch-up			61.8	72.5

Source: http://ec.europa.eu/eurostat/web/national-accounts/data/main-tables.

Note: GDP is at market prices, as opposed to basic prices/factor cost in all other tables, and "catch-up" is on Dublin.

GDP per head than in the whole NUTS 1 region of Northern Ireland. Overall, there is an even greater regional inequality than in the UK, and like the UK inequality has increased over the decade.

Figure 3.14.4 effectively shows no correlation between initial level of GDP per head and subsequent growth among Ireland's NUTS 3 regions. As with the UK,

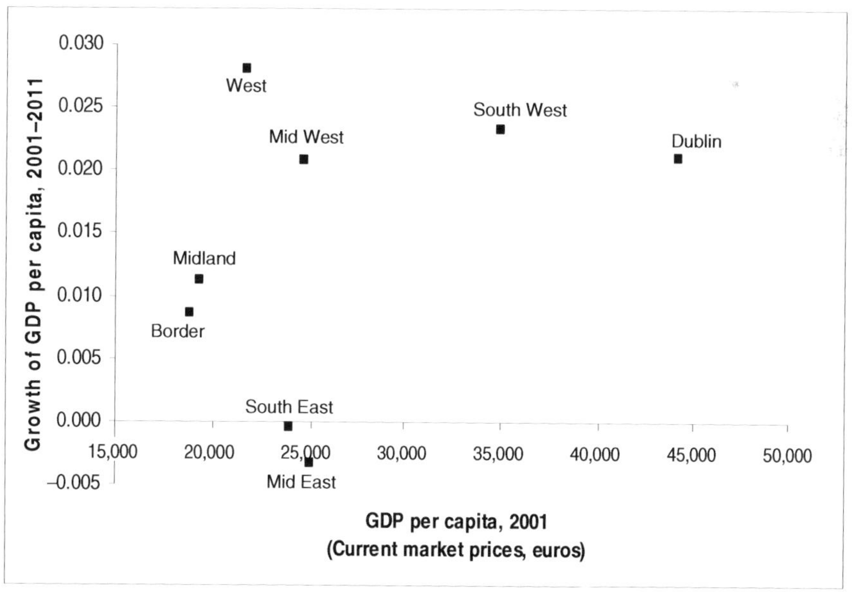

Figure 3.14.4 NUTS 3 regional growth rates in RoI, 2001–2011

the implication for the poorer regions in the Republic of Ireland is that achieving catch-up requires a fundamental change in the determining factors of their steady states – capital accumulation and TFP.

Dublin's GDP per head is clearly on a par with London, and both cities have much in common – financial centres (14 per cent of employment in Dublin), administrative centres, major tourist attractions and cosmopolitan populations. However, the fact that Irish GNP is only 80 per cent of the size of its GDP – a result of the outflow of the profits of foreign companies – whereas in the UK GNP is 2 per cent higher on average, implies that even a PPP-adjusted comparison of GDP per head as a rough measure of living standards overstates the relative Irish position.

5. Conclusion

Between 1861 and 2011, the measure of inequality for the regions of the UK displays, broadly speaking, a U-shape. It appears that the Industrial Revolution and the so-called Great Specialization[21] enabled the regions of Outer Britain to catch up on London and the South East during the second half of the nineteenth century. Nevertheless, the South East remained by some distance the dominant region. The increase in trade of the pre-1914 regime benefited not just the regions of Outer Britain, but also Ireland, which also caught up on the rest of the UK. Nor was this catch-up based solely on the export of people: the great bulk of Ireland's growth performance is attributable to TFP growth, capital accumulation and structural change. Reports of Ireland's then poverty may be exaggerated: while Ireland was the poorest region in the richest economy in the world, it was by no means the poorest region in Europe.

The convergence of UK regions (now excluding 26 Irish counties from 1922) was brought to a halt by the Great War, the subsequent excess capacity of the Victorian staples located in Outer Britain, and the difficult trading conditions of the 1920s and 1930s. Some time between 1931 and 1951, possibly due to rearmament and the emergence of regional policy, the convergence process picked up again.

Although convergence stalled between 1951 and 1971, the measure of dispersion of regional incomes remained at historic lows, and the regions of Outer Britain experienced their fastest growth of the twentieth century between 1931–1951 and 1971 (Geary and Stark 2016). All of this has gone decisively into reverse since 1991. London is at least 50 per cent richer per capita than any other region, and this has not been the case since 1861 and 1871. Sigma-dispersion has also returned to the levels of 150 years ago, and there has been no beta-type 'catch-up' now for half a century. In the meantime, the 26 counties of the Republic of Ireland may have gone from being the poorest region of the British Isles in the nineteenth century to the second richest in the twenty-first century, with Dublin on par with London, though with regional inequality greater than that of the UK.

Appendix

Table 3.14.A.1 GDP per worker, 1861–1911 (UK = 1)

	1861	*1871*	*1881*	*1891*	*1901*	*1911*
South East	1.43	1.35	1.34	1.28	1.29	1.27
London Counties	1.56	1.60	1.51	1.40	1.41	1.33
Rest of South East	1.25	1.00	1.11	1.11	1.13	1.19
East Anglia	0.91	0.82	0.75	0.84	0.91	0.91
SouthWest	1.07	0.98	0.93	0.93	0.99	0.99
West Midlands	0.97	1.03	0.99	0.99	0.89	0.89
East Midlands	0.90	0.96	0.88	0.88	0.96	0.95
North West	0.99	1.06	1.05	1.06	0.99	0.99
North	0.94	1.06	1.02	0.99	0.98	0.96
Yorkshire and Humberside	1.02	0.98	0.94	0.91	0.90	0.90
Wales	1.04	1.01	0.99	1.00	0.89	0.88
Scotland	1.00	0.95	1.00	0.96	0.93	0.94
Ireland	0.60	0.58	0.61	0.61	0.66	0.68
CV	0.274	0.280	0.249	0.213	0.214	0.190
Catch-up factor (on London)	64.8	68.9	58.6	46.2	47.8	38.3

Source: Table 3.14.1, Lee (1979) and Census of Ireland.

Table 3.14.A.2 GDP per worker, 1901–2001 (UK = 1)

	1901	*1911*	*1921*	*1931*	*1951*	*1961*	*1971*	*1981*	*1991*	*2001*	*2011*
South East	1.22	1.19	1.23	1.23	1.08	1.09	1.08	1.10	1.12	1.17	1.23
London	1.31	1.28	1.26	1.31	1.15	1.14	1.15	1.18	1.20	1.41	1.51
Rest of South East	1.08	1.07	1.19	1.13	1.00	1.03	1.01	1.05	1.06	1.03	1.05
East Anglia	0.87	0.86	0.89	0.89	0.95	0.97	0.97	0.96	0.97	1.07	1.09
South West	0.94	0.93	1.00	0.97	0.96	0.96	0.98	0.96	0.96	0.91	0.90
West Midlands	0.88	0.93	0.86	0.96	0.99	0.98	0.98	0.90	0.92	0.91	0.86
East Midlands	0.96	0.98	0.94	0.86	0.96	0.94	0.90	0.94	0.94	0.89	0.86
North West	1.00	1.00	0.98	0.93	1.00	0.95	0.97	0.98	0.95	0.93	0.88
North	0.97	0.95	0.92	0.81	0.96	0.99	0.93	0.98	0.96	0.86	0.82
Yorkshire and Humberside	0.89	0.90	0.86	0.89	0.96	0.94	0.97	0.94	0.90	0.89	0.84
Wales	0.86	0.88	0.86	0.99	0.97	1.02	0.98	0.93	0.94	0.85	0.78
Scotland	0.91	0.92	0.91	0.87	0.95	0.96	0.98	0.99	0.99	0.94	0.96
Northern Ireland	0.63	0.64	0.77	0.64	0.75	0.78	0.82	0.90	0.96	0.90	0.84
CV	0.162	0.149	0.151	0.174	0.080	0.079	0.077	0.084	0.091	0.165	0.218
Catch-up factor (on South East)	32.3	21.6	29.9	35.7	12.3	13.9	12.5	15.1	17.1	29.9	40.3

Source: Table 3.14.3, Lee (1979) and censuses of population.

Table 3.14.A.3 Per cent share in UK GDP, GOR regions residence-based (workplace-based in brackets)

GOR regions	*1991*	*2001*	*2007*	*2011*
South Eastern England	40.3	42.9 (44.6)	43.9 (44.8)	45.4 (46.0)
East	*9.6 (8.5)*	*9.8 (8.6)*	*9.5 (8.7)*	*9.5 (8.6)*
London	*16.2 (18.5)*	*17.6 (20.8)*	*18.9 (21.5)*	*20.2 (22.7)*
South East	*14.5 (13.4)*	*15.5 (15.2)*	*15.4 (14.6)*	*15.7 (14.7)*
South West	7.5	7.8 (7.6)	7.7 (7.6)	7.7 (7.5)
West Midlands	8.3	8.0 (7.9)	7.6 (7.5)	7.3 (7.3)
East Midlands	6.6	6.5 (5.9)	6.4 (6.0)	6.2 (6.0)
North East	3.8	3.4 (3.1)	3.3 (3.1)	3.2 (3.1)
North West	10.8	10.0 (9.9)	9.8 (9.8)	9.5 (9.6)
Yorkshire and Humberside	7.7	7.3 (6.9)	7.2 (7.3)	6.8 (6.9)
Wales	4.1	3.8 (3.5)	3.6 (3.6)	3.6 (3.5)
Scotland	8.7	8.0 (8.1)	8.1 (8.0)	8.1 (7.9)
Northern Ireland	2.1	2.3 (2.3)	2.3 (2.4)	2.2 (2.2)

Source: ONS Downloads gvanuts1_tcm77 291856 and 345463.

Note: South Eastern England is the former South East of England plus East Anglia. The new region of East comprises East Anglia plus the counties of Bedfordshire, Essex and Hertfordshire, which formerly were in the Rest of South East region. These regions accounted for 34 per cent of population in 1991 and 36 per cent in 2011. The 1991 shares for the seven identical SSR/GOR regions in Tables 3.14.3 and 3.14.4 differ slightly at the first decimal point. Both sets of data are from official ONS sources.

Table 3.14.A.4 GDP per worker and per capita, GORs (UK = 1)

	Per worker			*Per capita*		
	1991	*2001*	*2011*	*1991*	*2001*	*2011*
South Eastern England	1.12	1.17	1.21	1.19	1.23	1.26
East	1.03	1.01	0.99	1.12	1.07	1.03
London	1.30	1.41	1.51	1.31	1.44	1.56
South East	1.03	1.06	1.10	1.13	1.16	1.15
South West	0.91	0.91	0.90	0.91	0.93	0.92
West Midlands	0.91	0.91	0.86	0.91	0.89	0.82
East Midlands	0.91	0.89	0.86	0.93	0.91	0.87
North East	0.92	0.87	0.82	0.84	0.79	0.77
North West	0.95	0.92	0.88	0.91	0.87	0.85
Yorks and Humber	0.92	0.89	0.84	0.9	0.87	0.82
Wales	0.91	0.85	0.78	0.82	0.77	0.73
Scotland	1.01	0.94	0.96	0.98	0.93	0.97
Northern Ireland	0.91	0.90	0.84	0.75	0.81	0.78
CV	0.122	0.165	0.216	0.153	0.195	0.247
Catch-up (on London)	34.2	46.8	58.9	35.4	50.1	64.4

Source: Table 3.14.A.3 and censuses of population.

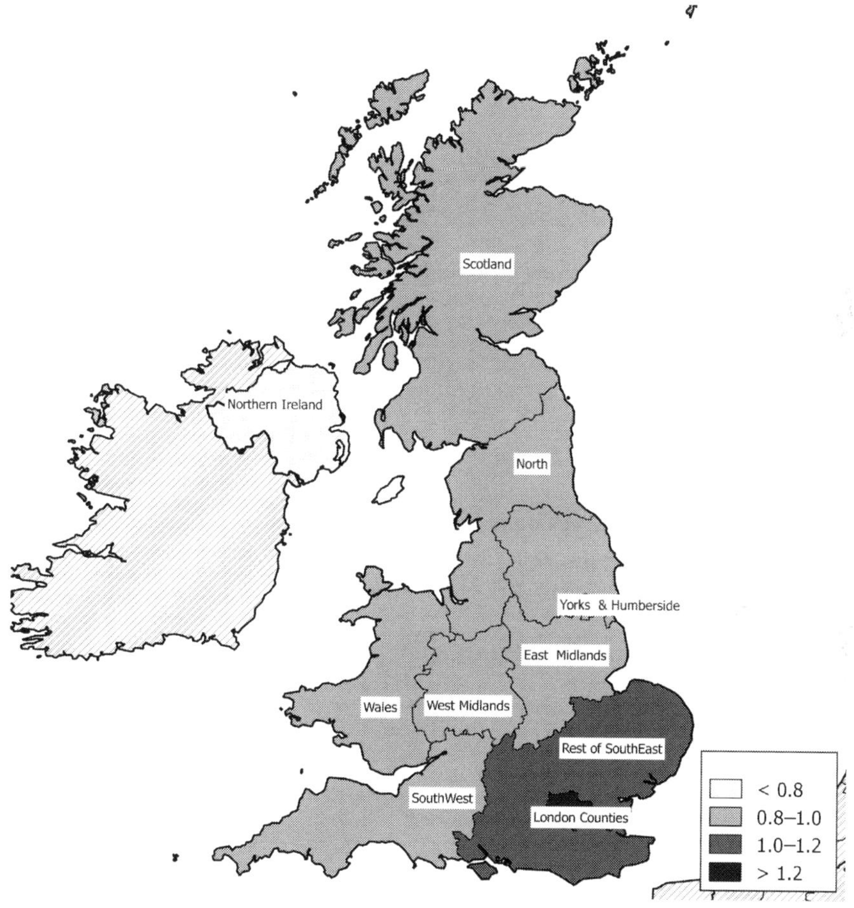

Map 3.14.1 Relative GDP per capita, 1900 (UK = 1)

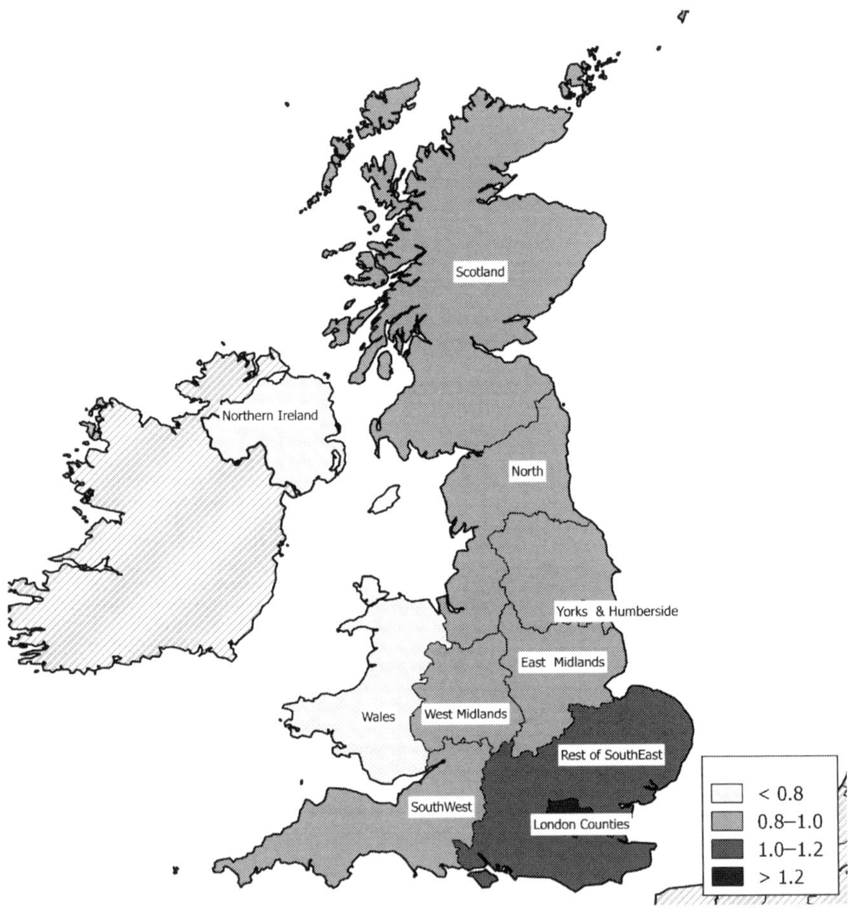

Map 3.14.2 Relative GDP per capita, 1910 (UK = 1)

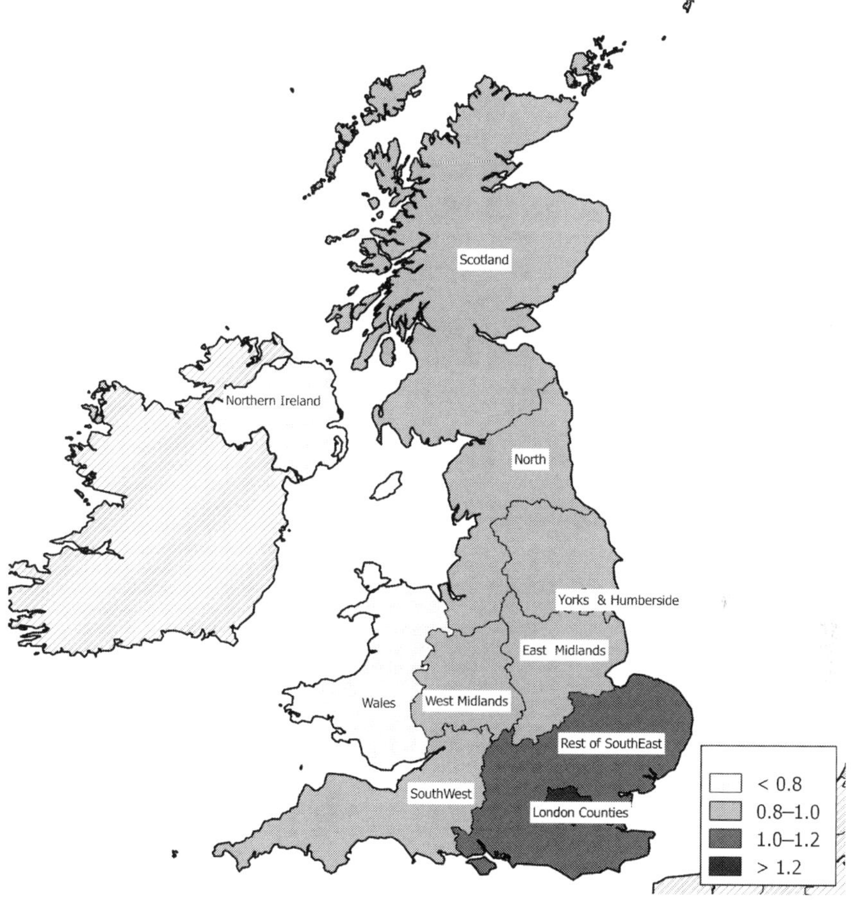

Map 3.14.3 Relative GDP per capita, 1925 (UK = 1)

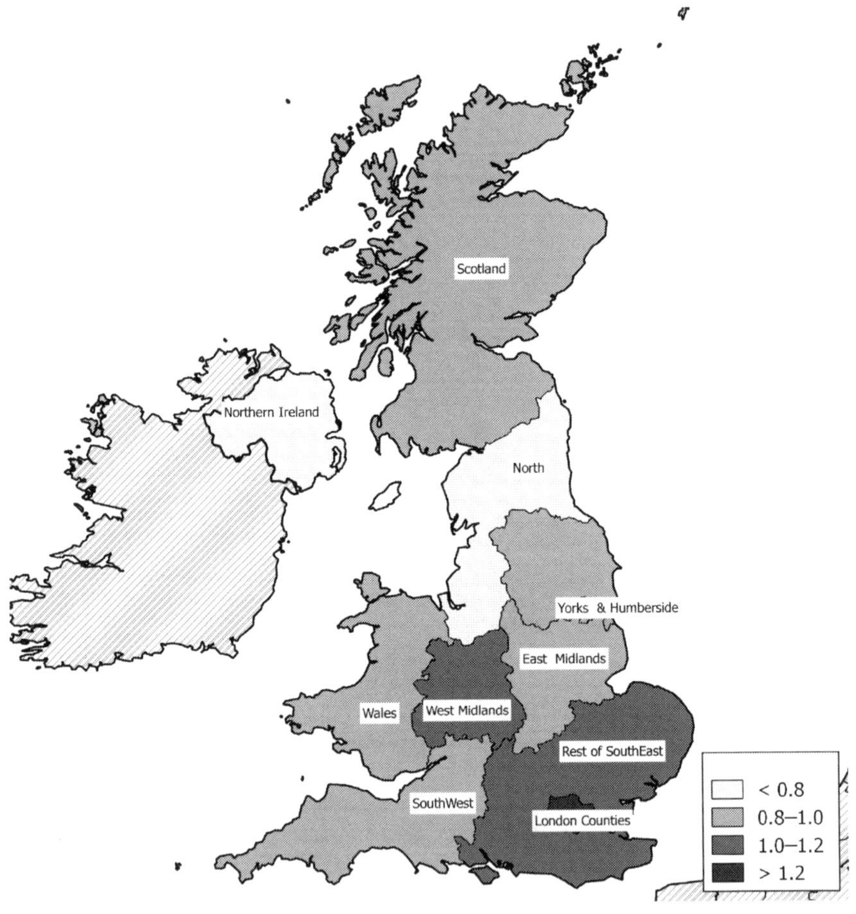

Map 3.14.4 Relative GDP per capita, 1938 (UK = 1)

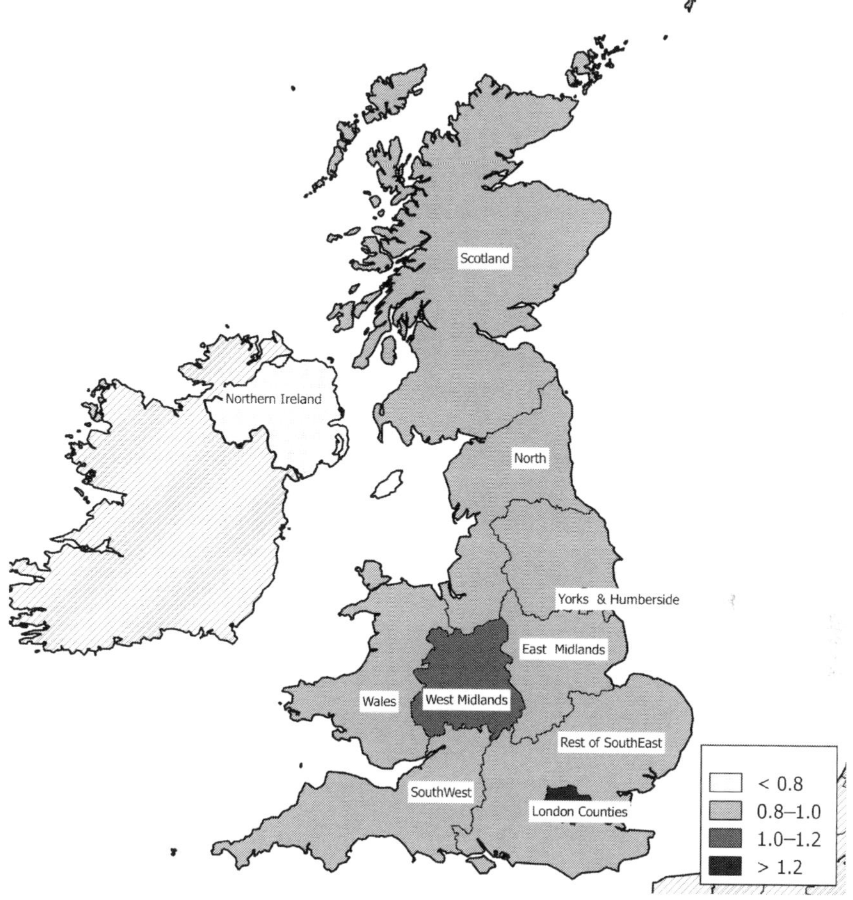

Map 3.14.5 Relative GDP per capita, 1950 (UK = 1)

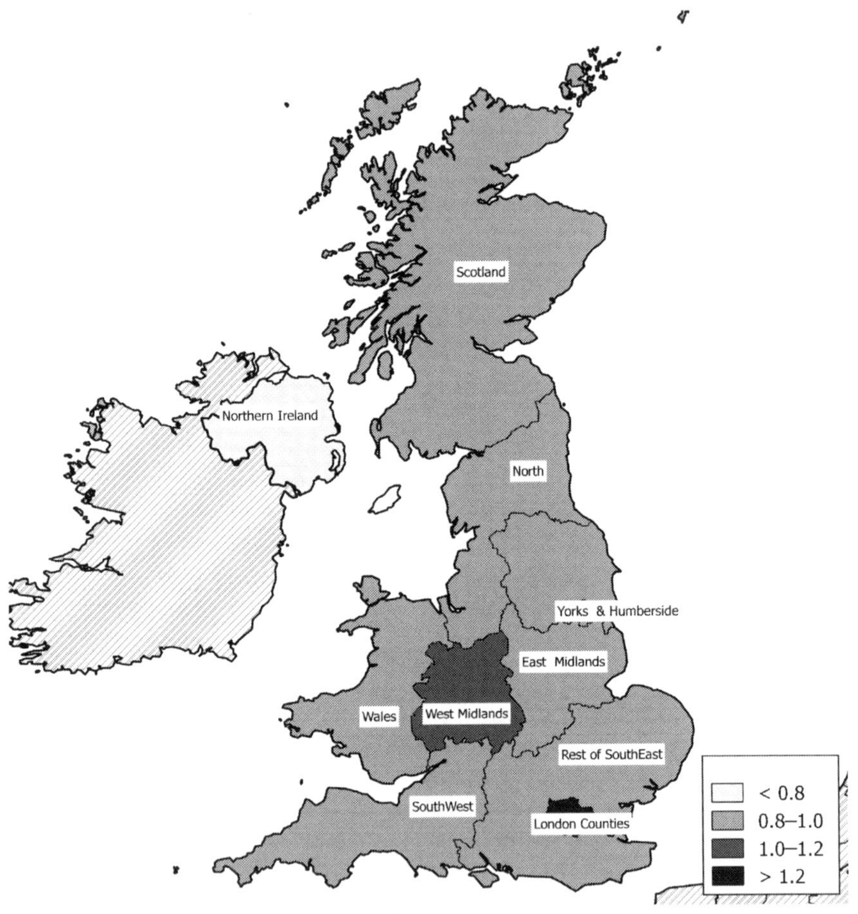

Map 3.14.6 Relative GDP per capita, 1960 (UK = 1)

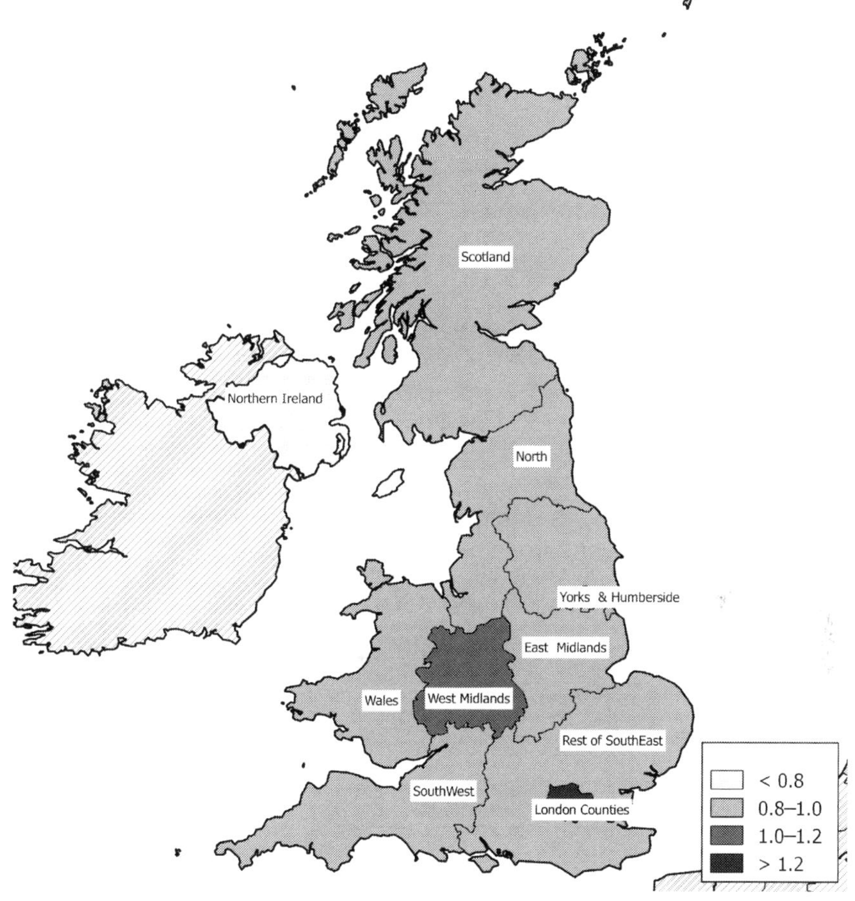

Map 3.14.7 Relative GDP per capita, 1970 (UK = 1)

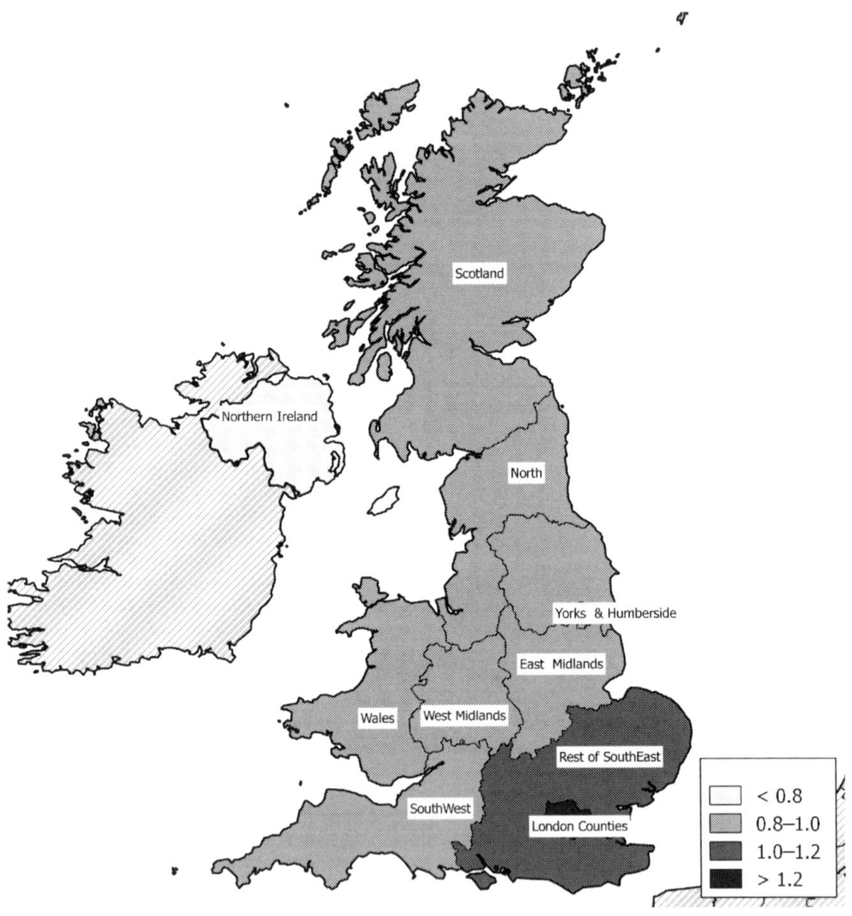

Map 3.14.8 Relative GDP per capita, 1980 (UK = 1)

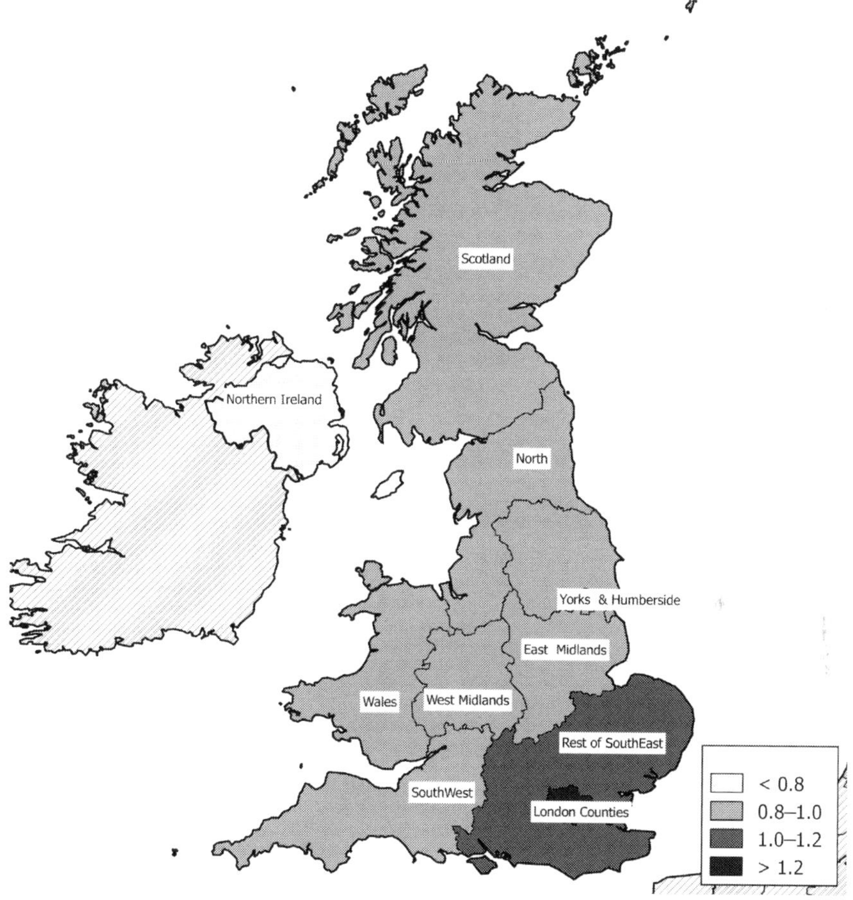

Map 3.14.9 Relative GDP per capita, 1990 (UK = 1)

Map 3.14.10 Relative GDP per capita, 2000 (UK = 1)

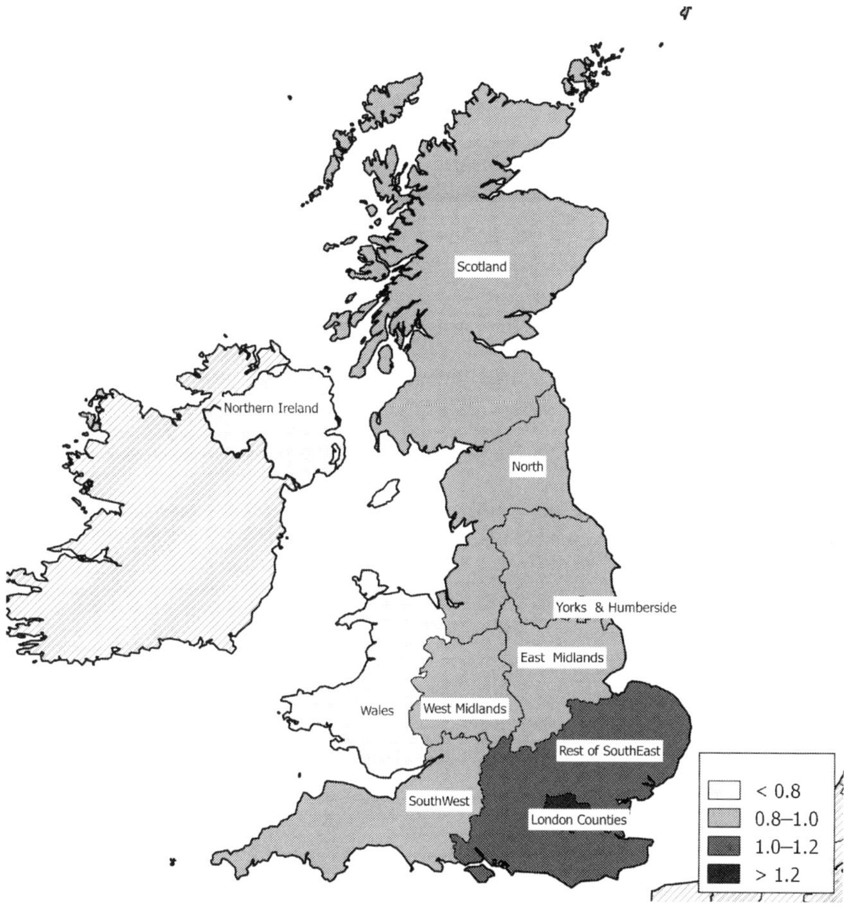

Map 3.14.11 Relative GDP per capita, 2010 (UK = 1)

Notes

1 Up to 1971, we define London as the counties of London (sometimes called Inner London), Middlesex and Surrey. For 1981 and after, we adopt the official definition of 'Greater London'. The official London GDP estimates first began in 1975. They are very comparable to our London Counties data.

2 The number of persons per worker varies across regions and years, so that ranking by GDP per head and GDP per worker is not always identical.

3 King Edward I of England colonized the principality of Wales between 1277 and 1283, and subsequent to the Glyndwr rebellion in the fifteenth century, a formal Act of Union was signed in 1536. Sixty-seven years later, James VI of Scotland also became King of England and Ireland – the union of three kingdoms. Parliamentary Acts of Union followed in 1707 between England and Scotland (i.e. Greater Britain) and finally with Ireland in 1800, at which point the official title the United Kingdom was first used. Periods of strife accompanied these changes, with the Civil War in

England (1639–1650), several military campaigns with Scotland culminating in the unsuccessful 1745 rebellion, while opposition to union in Ireland persisted, resulting in independence for 26 of the 32 Irish counties in 1922.

4 From the 'productivity gap' model of international price level determination in Kravis et al. (1978).

5 The data sources for the estimates are set out in detail in the appendices to Geary and Stark (2015, 2016).

6 Corresponding three sector-based estimates are available in Geary and Stark (2015). The difference in the GDP shares between three and four sector-based estimates disappear at whole-number level in 94 per cent (68) of the 72 observations over the six years, and in 92 per cent (66) are within 0.5 percentage points of each other. Only one observation exceeds a 1 percentage point difference (at 1.01 per cent).

7 A major change in the classification of distributive trades at the turn of the century forced Lee to compute two series – series A covering 1841–1911, and series B from 1901 to 1971.

8 Comparing estimates of regional GDP for 1901 and 1911 using both series gives average regional per cent difference (ARD) values of 2.57 for 1901 and 2.89 for 1911, so the change in employment classification does not have a strong effect in general. However, it does slightly reduce the share of the South East in GDP (see Geary and Stark 2015: Appendix B).

9 The 1901 and 1911 estimates for the six counties of Northern Ireland were extracted from the Irish census of population. There were, however, no censuses of population in 1921 and 1931 for the province. Instead, there were censuses in 1926 and 1937, only the former returning occupations. We projected the Northern Ireland populations for 1921 and 1931 from these two censuses and assumed the 1926 proportions of the industrial distribution of occupied and not occupied persons.

10 For 1951, we made extensive use of Deane's (1953) earnings data for 1948 combined with wage and net output data from the 1949 and 1951 censuses of production. We considered that the resulting almost 100 per cent coverage of all employees might offset any errors due to differences in timing in estimating the correct relatives for 1951.

11 European regional statistics define regions according to the EU's Nomenclature of Territorial Statistics for Units (NUTS). There are three NUTS levels in the UK: NUTS level 1 – Northern Ireland, Scotland, Wales and the nine GORs of England (a thirteenth 'region' known as Extra-Regio accounts for economic activity, mainly offshore oil and gas, which is not assigned to any specific region). NUTS level 2 consists of groupings of counties and local authorities (which, it might be argued, have no historical or administrative roots). In 2003, there were 37 NUTS 2 groupings; there are currently 40. NUTS level 3 consist of counties and groups of unitary authorities and council areas. Again, in 2003, there were 133 NUTS 3 areas; there are currently 173. The Republic of Ireland is a designated NUTS 1 region. There are a further two NUTS 2 groupings and eight NUTS 3 groupings.

12 Other major ports include Bristol, Liverpool, Glasgow and Newcastle.

13 We report the catch-up factor for London. A similar result is obtained when catch-up on the South East is measured.

14 Since the 1970s, Northern Ireland has received a net fiscal transfer from the UK central government that has accounted for between 15 and 30 per cent of its GDP.

15 Northern Ireland had a devolved government following the 1922 Ireland Act. In 1972, 'direct rule' was imposed and the devolved government was not re-established until 1998.

16 In 1976, the CSO decided that employment income from offshore oil and gas mining would be allocated to the region of residence of the employee. Non-employee income in turn was allocated to an area originally called the continental shelf and now designated as Extra-Regio. The early estimates dated back to 1968 and were interesting in that they were both extremely small and often negative. By 1981, however, the sums were large

and now defined to also include employee income that could not be allocated to a region of residence – foreign nationals presumably – a puzzling decision in that the base concept is a domestic as opposed to a national measurement. If we were endeavouring to measure from a geographical and output perspective, then a case could be made to allocate this output to specific regions. Scotland and the North East would be the obvious recipients, with Scotland getting the lion's share. In 1981, Extra-Regio income increased GDP by 6 per cent, 1.7 per cent in 1991 and 2001, and 2.3 per cent in 2011. If half of these amounts had, for example, been allocated to Scotland, then Scotland's GDP per head would have risen by 31 per cent in 1981, 10 per cent in 1991 and 2001, and 14 per cent in 2011, respectively, putting Scotland above the national average.

17 Geary and Stark (2016).

18 For discussion of Ireland's post-independence performance, see Cullen (1972), Kennedy et al. (1988) and Ó Gráda and O'Rourke (1996, 2000).

19 In Table 3.14.7, we present ratios of GDP per head between Ireland and the UK (and also Ireland and Northern Ireland). These are made both at current exchange rate prices and at PPP conversions. Ó Gráda and O'Rourke have drawn attention to the differences between Maddison's and the PWT PPP estimates, especially after 1970. It is for this reason that we present both series as well as recent Eurostat PPS estimates.

20 The IMF, the ECB and the UK.

21 The term is attributed by Findlay and O'Rourke (2007) to D.H. Robertson. It refers to the system of production and exchange by which the advanced economies produced manufactured goods that were exchanged for primary commodities produced by the rest of the world.

References

Aldcroft, D. (1973) *The Inter-War Economy: Britain 1919–1939*, London: Batsford.

Board of Trade (1930, 1935, 1948, 1949, 1950, 1954, 1958 and 1963) *Census of Production*, annual, various years, London: HMSO.

Board of Trade (later Dept. of Trade) (1950, 1957, 1961 and 1966) *Census of Distribution of Trade and Other Services*, annual, various years, London: Her Majesty's Stationery Office (HMSO).

Brunt, L. and Cannon, E. (2004) 'The Irish grain trade from the famine to the First World War', *Economic History Review*, Vol. 57 (1): 33–79.

Cullen, L.M. (1972) *An Economic History of Ireland since 1660*, London: Batsford.

Deane, P. (1953) 'Regional variations in United Kingdom incomes from employment, 1948', *Journal of the Royal Statistical Society*, Series A (General), Part II, Vol. CXVI.

Dunnell, K. (2009) 'National Statistician's article: measuring regional economic performance', *Economic & Labour Market Review*, Vol. 3 (1): 18–30.

Feinstein, C.H. (1972) *National Income and Expenditure and Output of the United Kingdom 1855–1965*, Cambridge: Cambridge University Press.

Findlay, R. and O'Rourke, K.H. (2007) *Power and Plenty*, Princeton, NJ: Princeton University Press.

Geary, F. and Stark, T. (2002) 'Examining Ireland's post-famine economic growth performance', *The Economic Journal*, Vol. 112 (482): 919–35.

Geary, F. and Stark, T. (2004) 'Trends in real wages during the Industrial Revolution: a view from across the Irish Sea', *The Economic History Review*, Vol. 57 (2): 362–95.

Geary, F. and Stark T. (2015) 'Regional GDP in the UK, 1861–1911: new estimates', *Economic History Review*, Vol. 68 (1): 123–44.

Geary, F. and Stark T. (2016) 'What happened to regional inequality in Britain in the twentieth century?', *Economic History Review*, Vol. 69 (1): 215–28.

Kennedy, K., Giblin, T. and McHugh, D. (1988) *The Economic Development of Ireland in the Twentieth Century*, London: Routledge.

Kravis, I.B., Heston, A.N. and Summers, R. (1978) 'Real GDP per capita in more than one hundred countries', *Economic Journal*, Vol. 88 (350): 215–42.

Law, C.M. (1980) *British Regional Development since World War I*, Exeter: David & Charles.

Lee, C.H. (1979) *British Regional Employment Statistics 1841–1971*, Cambridge: Cambridge University Press.

Lee, C.H. (1986) *The British Economy since 1700: A Macroeconomic Perspective*, Cambridge: Cambridge University Press.

McCann, G. (2011) *Ireland's Economic History: Crisis and Development in the North and South*, London: Pluto Press.

Maddison, A. (1995) *Monitoring the World Economy, 1820–1992*, Paris: OECD.

O'Donoghue, J., Goulding, L. and Allen, G. (2004) 'Consumer price inflation since 1750', *Economic Trends*, Vol. 604: 38–46.

Ó Gráda, C. and O'Rourke, K. (1996) 'Irish economic growth since 1945', in N. Crafts and G. Toniolo (eds), *Economic Growth in Europe since 1945*, Cambridge: Cambridge University Press, pp. 388–426.

Ó Gráda, C. and O'Rourke, K. (2000) 'Economic growth: performance and explanations', in J.W. O'Hagan (ed.), *The Economy of Ireland: Policy and Performance of a European Region*, Dublin: Gill & MacMillan, pp. 178–204.

O'Toole, F. (2010) *Ship of Fools: How Stupidity and Corruption Sank the Celtic Tiger*, London: Faber & Faber.

Richardson, H.W. (1967) *Economic Recovery in Britain 1932–1939*, London: Weidenfeld & Nicolson.

Sala-i-Martin, X. (1996) 'Regional cohesion: evidence and theories of regional growth and convergence', *European Economic Review*, Vol. 40 (6): 1325–52.

Scott, P. (2007) *Triumph of the South: A Regional Economic History of Early Twentieth Century Britain*, Aldershot: Ashgate.

4 Regional inequality in the United States

Long-term patterns, 1880–2010

Alexander Klein

1. Introduction

In the second half of the nineteenth century, the United States saw an unprecedented economic development that turned the country into the world's first economic power. The US began to outperform the economic leader of that time – Great Britain – and became the destination of millions of people looking for opportunities to improve their well-being. Ultimately, the US became a model of a successful economy soon to be studied by other countries. The economic development manifested itself by the rapid advance of existing industries, the dawn of new industries, and the creation of a large transportation and distributional network that gradually integrated the national market. This economic development, however, was not equally spread. On the contrary, regions with high concentration of industries emerged alongside regions with low industrial concentration. The first divergence of US regions occurred during the early phase of industrialization – manufacturing began to concentrate in the Northeast and Middle Atlantic, whereas the South remained largely agricultural. In the second half of the nineteenth century, industrialization spread across the Northeast, Middle Atlantic and Midwest regions, and formed the manufacturing belt, leaving the South predominantly agricultural. The twentieth century witnessed a convergence of regional income and industrial structure, though the process was uneven and can be viewed as mostly a post-Second World War development. Moreover, convergence lasted only until about the 1980s, when a slowdown began, and the process even stopped.

This chapter offers an overview of the main trends of regional economic development in the US between 1880 and 2010 at the state level. It first discusses data sources and a methodology used to estimate income per capita of US states before 1920. Various quantitative measures of regional inequality are then used to describe 130 years of regional development, attempting to provide a few stylized facts about US regional inequalities. After that, a discussion of the existing research offering insights into the determinants of unequal distribution of economic activities across the US is presented, followed by a conclusion.

2. Methodology and data sources

To analyse the long-term development of US regional inequality, time series of real income per capita figures for US states are needed.[1] First, I discuss the data sources for the nominal income per capita, then a price adjustment necessary to derive real income per capita, and finally an adjustment to construct an internationally comparable set of regional GDP per capita in 1990 GK$. Well-known figures of nominal total personal income per capita provided by the Bureau of Economic Analysis are used for the years 1930–2010.[2] Income per capita figures in 1920 come from Richard Easterlin (1957). Figures for 1880–1910 come from Klein (2013), where I followed the pioneering work of Richard Easterlin and, using his methodology, calculated states' nominal per capita income for 1890 and 1910, as well as improved his original figures for 1880 and 1900. The main idea of the methodology can be briefly described as follows.[3] For each state, a ratio of the state total personal income per capita relative to the US total personal income per capita is calculated. These ratios are then used to allocate US total personal income per capita among the states. The calculation consists of two main steps: estimation of the US total personal income per capita by type and industry, and estimation of a ratio of state total personal income per capita to the US total personal income per capita. The first stage provides US total personal income per capita, and US total personal income per capita by its type. There are two types of income: so-called service income, which includes wages, salaries and proprietor's income, and so-called property income, consisting of rental income, personal interest income and dividends. The second stage calculates state total personal income per capita relative to US total personal income per capita, which is done by summing state total service income per capita relative to US total service income per capita and state total property income per capita relative to US total property income per capita. The calculation of each of those ratios forms a complex system of mutually dependent equations and the result is total personal income per capita for each US state.[4]

To derive the real total personal income per capita of each US state, the nominal figures need to be adjusted for changes in price levels. This presents a challenge. Ideally, we would like to adjust the nominal figures across time as well as across space. However, we do not have price indices for each US state in 1880–2010. Two options are available. One is to use a US GDP deflator for the period 1880–2010; the other one is to use a spatial price adjustment developed by Mitchener and McLean (1999) for the years 1880, 1900, 1920, 1940, 1960 and 1980. I used the US GDP deflator from Johnston and Williamson (2018), adjusting the nominal figures only for temporal prices changes. Leaving spatial price adjustment out does present a problem, but, as shown by Mitchener and McLean (1999), it is not that severe. They have shown that even after spatial price adjustment, the trends in regional personal income remain unchanged, and the effect of differences in regional price levels is trivial by and after 1920 (Mitchener and McLean 1999: 1026). Since it is illuminating to compare and contrast US regional development with regional developments in other countries, an internationally comparable regional figure for GDP per capita is needed. In our case, a useful shortcut is to distribute US GDP in 1990 GK$ calculated by the Maddison Project among the US states using the shares of states' total personal income on the US total personal income. The usual caveats apply here, and I consider those figures to be a set of first-generation estimates suitable only for a comparative analysis of *long-run trends* of regional GDP inequalities between the US and other countries.

A more detailed calculation of an internationally comparable set of estimates of US regional GDP is an important agenda for future research. In addition to states' per capita income data, we use states' sectoral employment figures to provide further description of the main trends in regional inequality.[5]

3. Basic facts of regional inequalities

I will describe general trends in regional income inequality across US states in 1880–2010 along several dimensions: GDP per capita, sectoral employment, spatial Gini coefficient, and the concept of sigma-converge and beta-convergence. Furthermore, I will look at the states' real per capita personal income relative to the US, and I will consider patterns across US states as well as more broadly defined US regions. All of this will allow to us to shed some first light on an undoubtedly complex process of regional development over the course of 130 years.

Figure 4.1 presents trends of states' GDP per capita between 1880 and 2010. We see that the (population-weighted) average increased by about 850 per cent, with the largest increase occurring after the Second World War. Interestingly, the distance between the poorest and the richest US states was quite stable, beginning to widen considerably only since the 1980s.

As an example, the richest state in 1880 was the mining sector-driven Nevada and the poorest was North Carolina, while Mississippi was the poorest state in 2010 and Connecticut the richest one. Sectoral employment figures offer another angle when examining long-run regional inequality. Figure 4.2 plots the evolution of the sectoral employment shares between 1890 and 2010. The trends are clear: agriculture has been losing its dominant position at the expense of manufacturing and services.

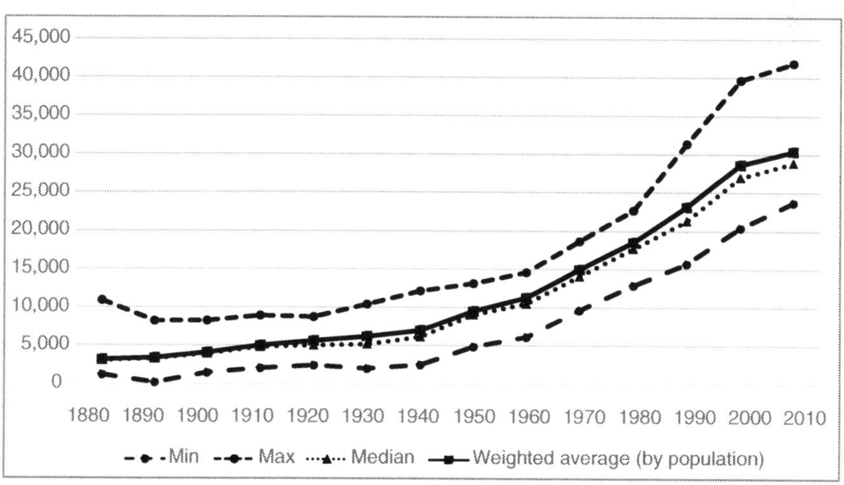

Figure 4.1 GDP per capita across US states, 1880–2010 (1900 GK$)

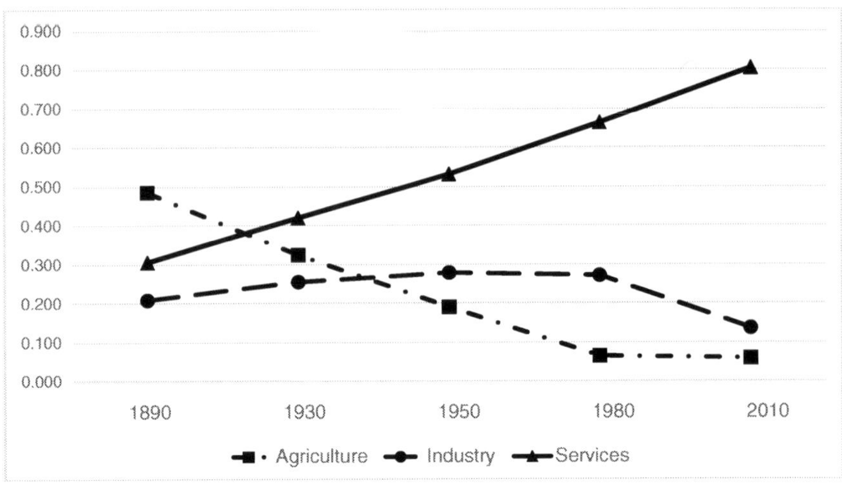

Figure 4.2 Sectoral employment shares across US states, 1890–2010

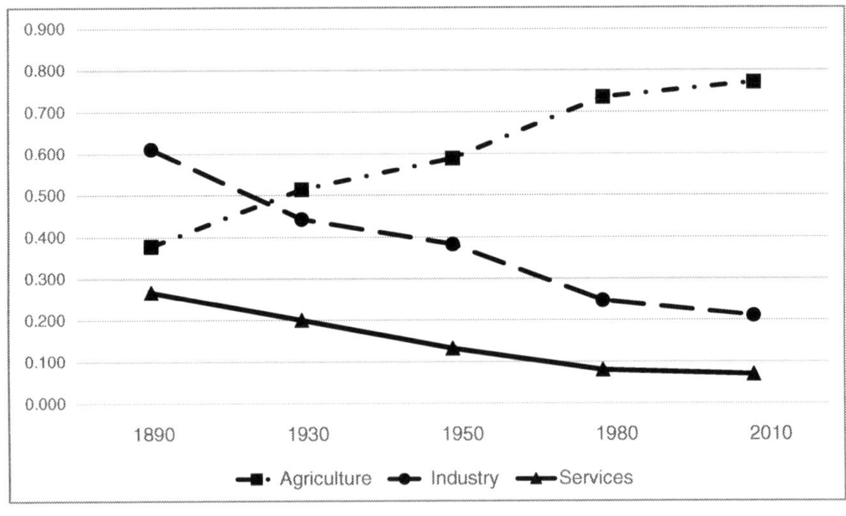

Figure 4.3 The coefficient of variation of location quotient of agriculture, industry and services across US states, 1890–2010

The service sector has been an important source of employment since the inter-war years, and Figure 4.2 strongly suggests that the structural change unfolding during the twentieth century has been as much a services story as it was an industry story. To get a better sense of the changes in the location of employment in those broad sectors across US states, Figure 4.3 presents the coefficient of variation of location quotients, as defined in Chapter 2 in this book.

We see that already in 1890, the industrial sector was quite regionally concentrated. The subsequent evolution of all three sectors shows a clear pattern of spatial localization of agriculture and dispersion of industry and services, respectively. All this is suggestive of spatially uneven development of the US economy over the past 130 years. This conjecture is confirmed in Figure 4.4, which shows the development of locational Gini coefficients measuring the extent of unequal distribution of GDP across US states.

We see an interesting picture of relatively stable regional inequalities when we compare the locational Gini coefficient at 1880 and 2010. In between, however, we see a sign of what can be broadly considered an inverted U-shape curve. This indicates a rise of regional inequalities until 1930s and their subsequent decline, though not enough to consider regional inequalities in 2010 being very less pronounced than in 1880. This, at first, might look to be at odds with the dispersion of employment across US states, as captured in Figure 4.3. However, while the dispersion of employment in industries and services might be an indication of the process potentially leading to more equal distribution of economic activities across US states, it might have been only related to the decline of regional inequalities since their peak in the 1930s.

The concepts of convergence arise from neoclassical models of economic growth. The concept of beta-convergence tells us that a poor region will have a tendency to grow faster than the average, enabling it to catch up with the rich and even out regional disparities. Here, we concentrate on beta-unconditional convergence.

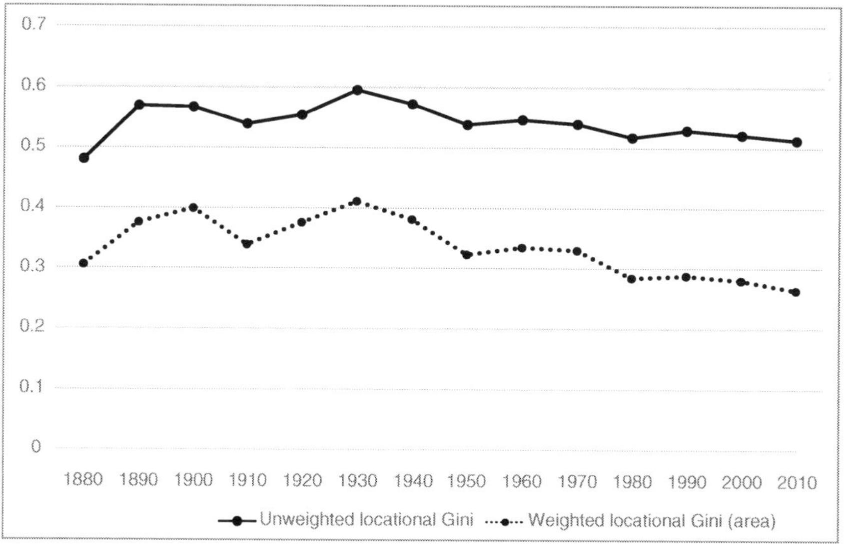

Figure 4.4 Locational Gini coefficients across US states, 1880–2010

Table 4.1 Sigma-convergence among US states, 1880–2010 (population-weighted coefficient of variation)

Region	*1880*	*1890*	*1900*	*1910*	*1920*	*1930*	*1940*	*1950*	*1960*	*1970*	*1980*	*1990*	*2000*	*2010*
All US	0.45	0.42	0.40	0.34	0.33	0.39	0.33	0.21	0.19	0.15	0.12	0.14	0.13	0.13
Less West	0.48	0.39	0.39	0.33	0.33	0.40	0.34	0.21	0.19	0.15	0.11	0.15	0.14	0.14
Less South	0.37	0.27	0.22	0.19	0.21	0.25	0.21	0.11	0.11	0.10	0.09	0.12	0.12	0.13

Source: See text.

The concept of sigma-convergence is related to the cross-sectional dispersion of regional income, and convergence occurs if the dispersion – measured by, for example, the standard deviation or the coefficient of variation of per capita income across regions – declines over time. Table 4.1 presents population-weighted coefficients of variation of GDP per capita across US states between 1880 and 2010.

The following basic facts emerge. Overall, regional inequality has a declining trend, though four sub-periods can be identified: 1880–1920, 1920–1940, 1940–1980 and 1980–2010. The first period shows a clear decline in regional inequality, while the interwar period (1920–1940) reversed this trend, and regional inequality actually increased by 1930. The post-Second World War period witnessed a rather strong regional convergence. This came to a halt by the 1980s, and since then regions began to diverge, something that was already visible in Figure 4.1, and can also be observed in Europe. Given the importance of the western regions and the South in the US regional development, I also calculated the coefficients of variation excluding those two regions, respectively (see Table 4.1). Looking at the pattern of regional inequality excluding the West, we see that the overall trend is preserved, and the post-1980 period suggests an even more profound increase in regional inequality. When we exclude the South, the overall trend is again preserved, though the coefficients of variation dropped considerably, much more than when excluding the West. An interesting feature emerges from the period 1940–1980. Unlike in the other two cases, the pattern of regional convergence, though still decreasing, is rather subdued, even flat in the 1950s and 1960s. This suggests, and quite strongly, that the South played a considerable role in diminishing regional inequalities in the post-Second World War area, as will be explored below.

The concept of beta-unconditional convergence can shed further light on the patterns and possible drivers of regional inequality and convergence.[6] Figures 4.5a–4.5d depict per capita average annual real growth rates against the logarithm of initial per capita values (both calculated using per capita figures in 1990 GK$) for the periods 1880–2010, 1880–1940, 1940–2010 and 1920–1940, respectively.

We see that in all but one period (1920–1940), regional convergence follows a well-known pattern of beta-unconditional convergence: US states with higher initial per capita income have lower growth rates than states with lower per capita income. Looking more closely at the differences between the figures, we can clearly observe the changing role of the western states in convergence over time. Specifically, Figure 4.5a shows that the states with the highest per capita income, and subsequently the lowest growth rates, in 1880–2010 are the western states.

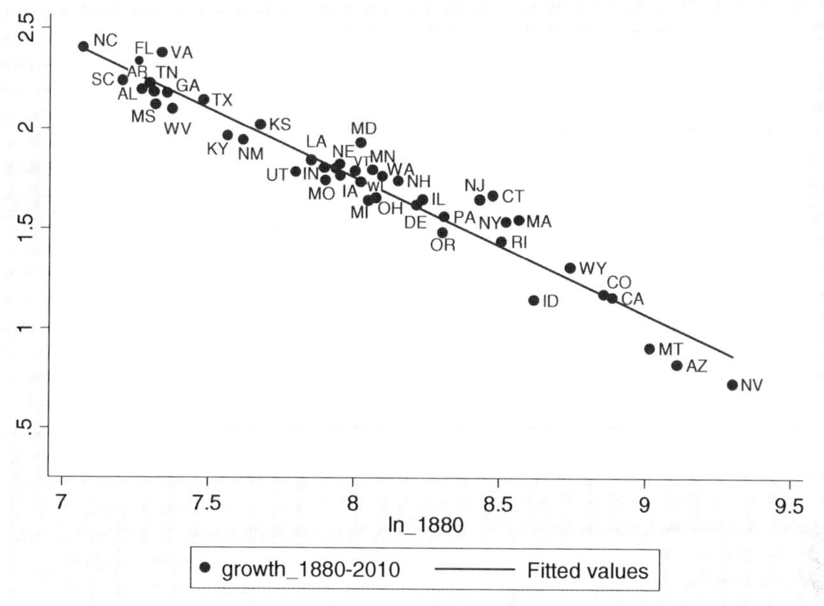

Figure 4.5a Beta-unconditional convergence among US states, 1880–2010

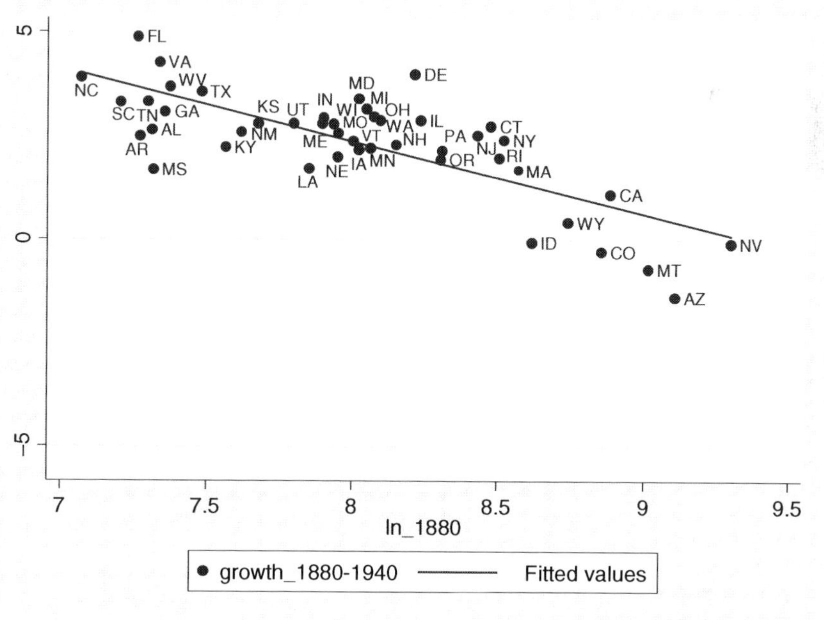

Figure 4.5b Beta-unconditional convergence among US states, 1880–1940

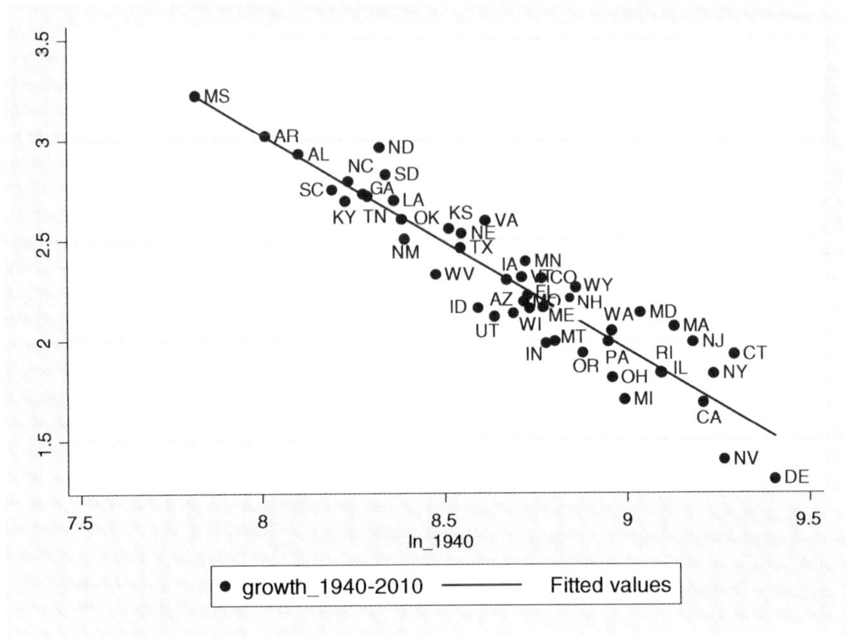

Figure 4.5c Beta-unconditional convergence among US states, 1940–2010

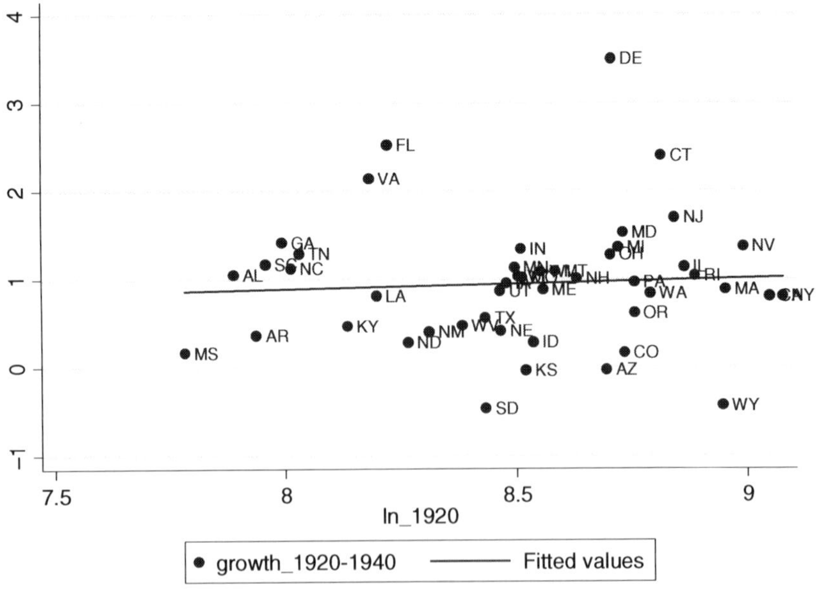

Figure 4.5d Beta-unconditional convergence among US states, 1920–1940

Figure 4.5b, depicting the period 1880–1940, makes the importance of the western states even more visible. Indeed, they create almost a separate cluster. That picture changes when we look at Figure 4.5c, showing beta-unconditional convergence for the period 1940–2010. We see that, as suggested in Table 4.1, the West 'loses' its dominant role in explaining the patterns of post-Second World War regional inequality, and it is only the states of California and Nevada that remain in the 'club' of high per capita real income. However, this time they are together with the states of Delaware, New York and Connecticut. The importance of the South can be also observed in those figures, most visibly in Figure 4.5c, where the southern states (together with North and South Dakota) are at the upper spectrum of US states with low initial per capita income but high subsequent growth rates.

The last piece of evidence helping us to describe (and also further fine-tune) basic patterns of regional inequality is the states' real per capita personal income relative to the US real per capita income, presented in Table 4.2.

The table presents not only figures for each US state in 1880–2010, but also for four US regions (Northeast, Midwest, South, West) and the manufacturing belt and the rest of the US.[7] The data are also illustrated in several maps (see Maps 4.1–4.6), each showing for each state the real GDP per capita relative to the US average, for 1890, 1920, 1930, 1950, 1980 and 2010, respectively.

Looking at the overall trends across regions in the period 1880–2010, we can distinguish convergence 'from above', 'from below' and no convergence. Northeast and West are the regions where per capita real income converged to the US average 'from above', meaning that their 1880 per capita income was higher than the US average. South exhibits convergence 'from below' as its per capita in 1880 income was only about 50 per cent of the US average. The performance of the Midwest region in terms of convergence was very stagnant, and even though there has been some signs of convergence to the US average in the twentieth century, as discussed below, overall the region started with 98 per cent of US average real per capita income in 1880 and ended with 95 per cent in 2010 – a sign of relative stability over the course of 130 years. It is interesting to look at the region of the manufacturing belt because its existence and its ultimate dissolution in the late decades of the twentieth century played a dominant role in the distribution of economic activities in the Northeast, Midwest and South. We see that despite some fluctuations in 1890 and 1910, the region held a very similar real per capita income relative to the US average in 1880–1940, declining until 1980, and then slightly increasing. The rest of the US witnessed an overall upward trend, though there was a significant drop in 1930.

What about the relative importance of the southern and western regions in explaining the patterns of convergence in 1880–2010? As for the West, the numbers in Table 4.2 clearly show that this region experienced a profound convergence to the US average real per capita income in the period 1880–1940, figures dropping from 92 per cent to 19 per cent above the US average.[8] Comparing that with the Northeast and Midwest, it is clear that the western states played a dominant position in diminishing US regional inequalities before 1940. Indeed, the Northeastern states exhibited only slight convergence to the US average per capita income, and the Midwestern states fluctuated around the US average during the entire period of 1880–1940. As for the South, the region showed only a

Table 4.2 Relative per capita total personal income of the US states (US = 1)

US state/US region	*1880*	*1890*	*1900*	*1910*	*1920*	*1930*	*1940*	*1950*	*1960*	*1970*	*1980*	*1990*	*2000*	*2010*
Alabama	0.47	0.49	0.43	0.50	0.48	0.43	0.47	0.60	0.68	0.73	0.78	0.81	0.79	0.84
Arizona	2.84	1.15	1.57	1.26	1.08	0.83	0.85	0.90	0.91	0.94	0.94	0.87	0.87	0.87
Arkansas	0.45	0.44	0.43	0.50	0.50	0.36	0.43	0.56	0.62	0.70	0.75	0.74	0.74	0.82
California	2.27	1.97	1.78	1.80	1.53	1.44	1.42	1.24	1.24	1.18	1.18	1.10	1.10	1.07
Colorado	2.20	2.08	1.55	1.34	1.12	0.92	0.91	1.01	1.03	0.99	1.06	1.00	1.12	1.06
Connecticut	1.50	1.44	1.44	1.21	1.21	1.49	1.55	1.25	1.23	1.24	1.22	1.35	1.38	1.37
Delaware	1.16	1.09	1.09	0.99	1.09	1.38	1.73	1.37	1.24	1.12	1.07	1.10	1.02	0.99
Florida	0.45	0.76	0.61	0.67	0.67	0.75	0.88	0.86	0.89	0.98	0.98	1.00	0.96	0.96
Georgia	0.49	0.53	0.43	0.48	0.53	0.49	0.56	0.70	0.74	0.83	0.83	0.91	0.94	0.87
Idaho	1.73	1.12	1.07	0.99	0.92	0.79	0.77	0.88	0.83	0.87	0.86	0.81	0.81	0.80
Illinois	1.18	1.25	1.27	1.34	1.27	1.30	1.27	1.22	1.18	1.12	1.09	1.08	1.08	1.05
Indiana	0.85	0.77	0.90	0.93	0.89	0.83	0.93	1.01	0.97	0.93	0.93	0.90	0.91	0.85
Iowa	0.96	0.95	0.97	1.13	0.87	0.81	0.83	1.02	0.91	0.95	0.95	0.90	0.90	0.95
Kansas	0.68	0.88	0.92	1.06	0.90	0.74	0.71	0.97	0.94	0.94	0.98	0.93	0.94	0.98
Kentucky	0.61	0.61	0.59	0.62	0.62	0.52	0.53	0.65	0.71	0.78	0.80	0.79	0.82	0.81
Louisiana	0.81	0.66	0.62	0.69	0.66	0.57	0.61	0.74	0.74	0.76	0.87	0.78	0.78	0.93
Maine	0.84	0.84	0.93	0.91	0.94	0.92	0.89	0.79	0.84	0.84	0.83	0.89	0.88	0.92
Maryland	0.96	0.97	1.00	0.96	1.12	1.15	1.20	1.09	1.04	1.12	1.11	1.17	1.14	1.23
Massachusetts	1.65	1.54	1.53	1.26	1.39	1.35	1.32	1.10	1.10	1.10	1.05	1.18	1.26	1.28
Michigan	0.98	0.87	0.91	0.96	1.10	1.06	1.15	1.14	1.07	1.03	1.02	0.97	0.97	0.87
Minnesota	1.00	1.01	1.02	1.09	0.88	0.88	0.88	0.95	0.94	0.99	1.01	1.02	1.08	1.07
Mississippi	0.47	0.45	0.41	0.46	0.43	0.32	0.35	0.51	0.54	0.64	0.69	0.68	0.71	0.78
Missouri	0.89	0.91	0.93	0.93	0.90	0.90	0.87	0.95	0.97	0.94	0.92	0.91	0.92	0.93
Montana	2.59	2.43	2.02	1.47	0.96	0.80	0.95	1.10	0.91	0.89	0.90	0.79	0.77	0.88
Nebraska	0.89	1.04	1.03	1.11	0.86	0.82	0.74	1.04	0.95	0.93	0.91	0.93	0.94	0.99
Nevada	3.43	2.22	1.95	1.73	1.45	1.34	1.51	1.32	1.29	1.21	1.16	1.04	1.02	0.92
New Hampshire	1.09	1.05	1.07	0.97	1.01	1.04	0.98	0.89	0.97	0.95	0.97	1.05	1.12	1.09

New Jersey	1.44	1.38	1.41	1.22	1.25	1.37	1.39	1.20	1.18	1.18	1.16	1.26	1.28	1.28
New Mexico	0.64	0.72	0.73	0.68	0.73	0.53	0.63	0.80	0.83	0.78	0.83	0.77	0.75	0.84
New York	1.57	1.58	1.53	1.50	1.58	1.67	1.47	1.23	1.24	1.19	1.09	1.23	1.14	1.21
North Carolina	0.37	0.33	0.35	0.41	0.54	0.46	0.54	0.71	0.71	0.80	0.81	0.89	0.92	0.88
North Dakota	–	1.03	1.04	0.93	0.70	0.50	0.59	0.92	0.82	0.80	0.78	0.82	0.84	1.07
Ohio	1.01	1.02	1.10	1.06	1.09	1.07	1.11	1.06	1.05	1.00	0.99	0.96	0.95	0.91
Oklahoma	–	0.05	0.47	0.75	0.77	0.59	0.62	0.76	0.84	0.85	0.94	0.83	0.81	0.89
Oregon	1.27	1.30	1.21	1.35	1.14	0.97	1.02	1.10	1.00	0.96	1.00	0.92	0.95	0.91
Pennsylvania	1.28	1.23	1.25	1.08	1.14	1.15	1.10	1.03	1.01	1.00	0.99	1.00	0.99	1.02
Rhode Island	1.55	1.47	1.48	1.23	1.30	1.28	1.27	1.03	1.00	1.00	0.96	1.02	0.97	1.05
South Carolina	0.42	0.40	0.36	0.42	0.52	0.39	0.52	0.61	0.63	0.75	0.77	0.82	0.83	0.81
South Dakota	–	0.74	0.90	0.95	0.83	0.57	0.60	0.86	0.83	0.80	0.80	0.83	0.87	0.99
Tennessee	0.46	0.50	0.50	0.54	0.55	0.52	0.57	0.68	0.72	0.78	0.82	0.86	0.88	0.88
Texas	0.56	0.71	0.67	0.79	0.83	0.66	0.73	0.90	0.86	0.89	0.98	0.89	0.94	0.94
Utah	0.77	1.02	0.90	1.01	0.85	0.80	0.80	0.89	0.90	0.83	0.84	0.77	0.81	0.81
Vermont	0.94	0.96	0.94	0.95	0.89	0.92	0.87	0.77	0.84	0.89	0.85	0.91	0.93	1.00
Virginia	0.48	0.51	0.55	0.59	0.65	0.62	0.78	0.83	0.84	0.93	1.00	1.05	1.04	1.11
Washington	1.03	1.67	1.39	1.47	1.18	1.06	1.11	1.14	1.07	1.03	1.07	1.01	1.07	1.07
West Virginia	0.50	0.50	0.59	0.73	0.79	0.66	0.68	0.70	0.73	0.76	0.80	0.75	0.73	0.80
Wisconsin	0.88	0.80	0.89	0.89	0.93	0.94	0.92	1.00	0.99	0.97	1.00	0.93	0.96	0.96
Wyoming	1.96	1.99	1.54	1.19	1.38	0.93	1.00	1.14	1.02	0.96	1.16	0.93	0.97	1.12
Northeast	1.42	1.39	1.39	1.27	1.33	1.40	1.31	1.13	1.14	1.12	1.07	1.16	1.15	1.18
Midwest	0.97	0.97	1.02	1.07	1.02	1.00	1.01	1.06	1.03	1.00	1.00	0.97	0.98	0.95
South	0.54	0.55	0.53	0.61	0.65	0.57	0.64	0.75	0.78	0.85	0.90	0.90	0.91	0.93
West	1.92	1.73	1.51	1.45	1.25	1.16	1.19	1.15	1.13	1.09	1.10	1.03	1.04	1.01
Manufacturing belt region	1.18	1.16	1.20	1.15	1.20	1.23	1.20	1.10	1.09	1.07	1.04	1.08	1.07	1.08
Rest of US	0.91	0.93	0.92	0.95	0.98	0.91	0.93	0.96	0.97	0.98	0.99	0.98	0.98	0.98

Source: See text.

Note: The calculation of locational Gini coefficients is based on GDP per capita in 1990 GK$.

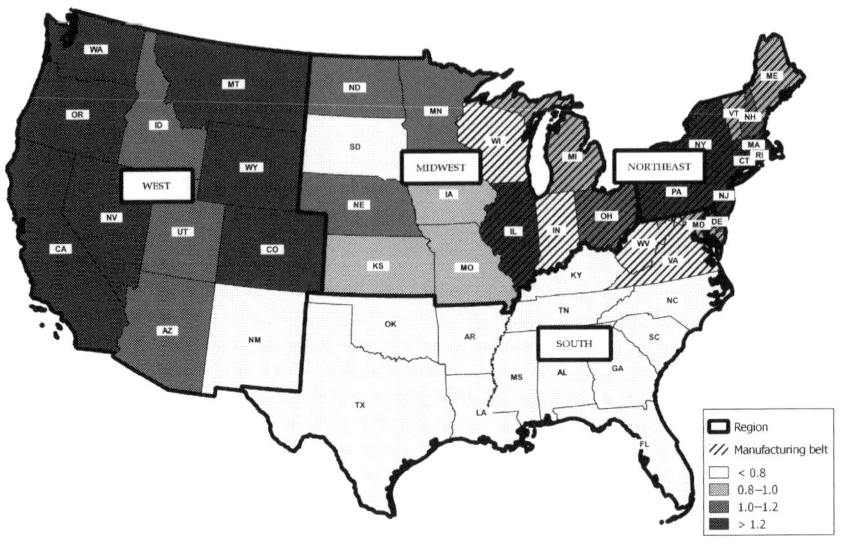

Map 4.1 Relative GDP per capita, 1890 (US = 1)

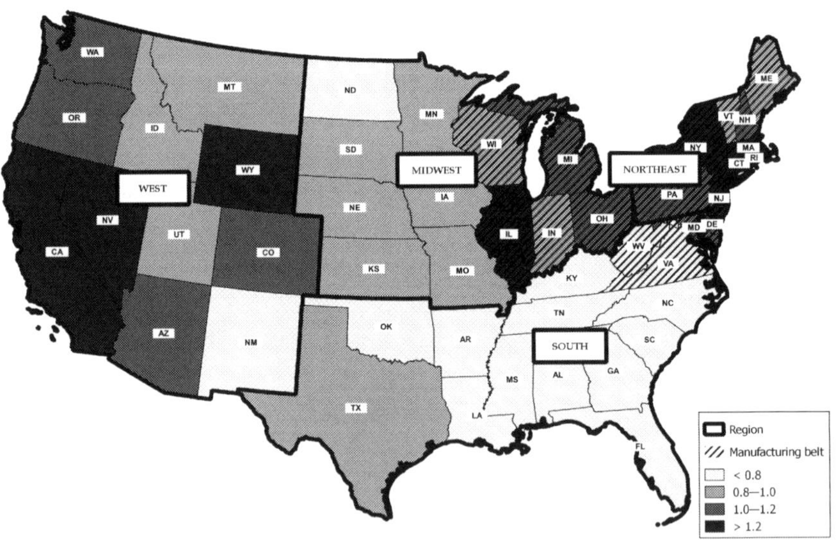

Map 4.2 Relative GDP per capita, 1920 (US = 1)

small increase in per capita income, which was still only 64 per cent of the US average in 1940.

The period after 1940 witnessed a retraction of the West as the main driving region of income convergence, and the South was the main region behind

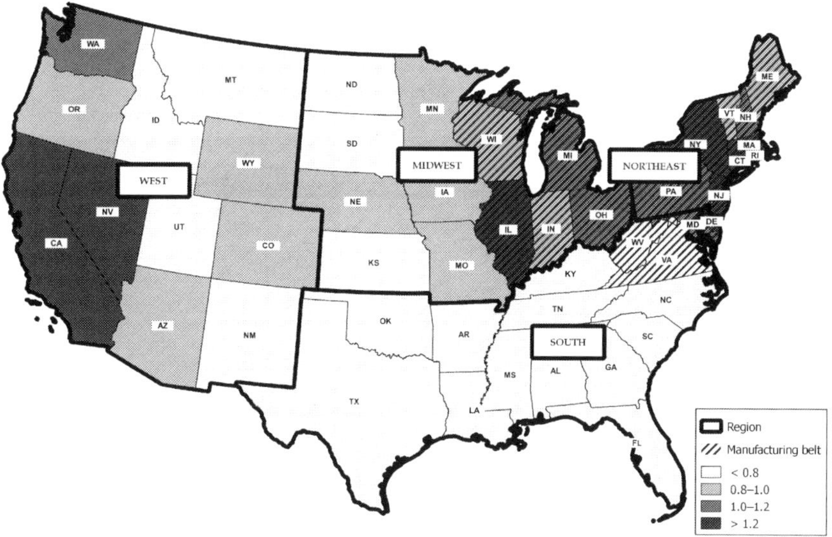

Map 4.3 Relative GDP per capita, 1930 (US = 1)

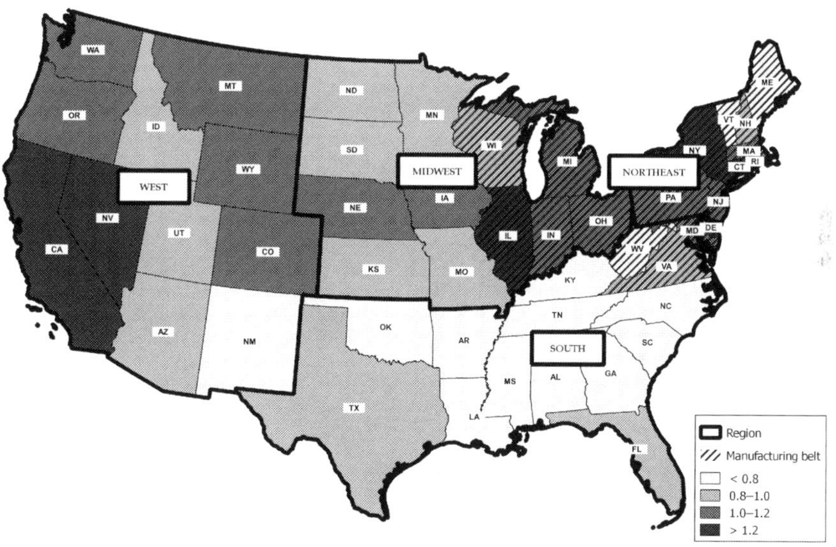

Map 4.4 Relative GDP per capita, 1950 (US = 1)

the post-Second World War regional convergence as its per capita real income raised from 64 per cent in 1940 to 93 per cent in 2010. The Northeast's per capita income embarked on the downward trend towards the US average, dropping from 31 per cent above the US average in 1940 to 18 per cent in 2010. The Midwest's

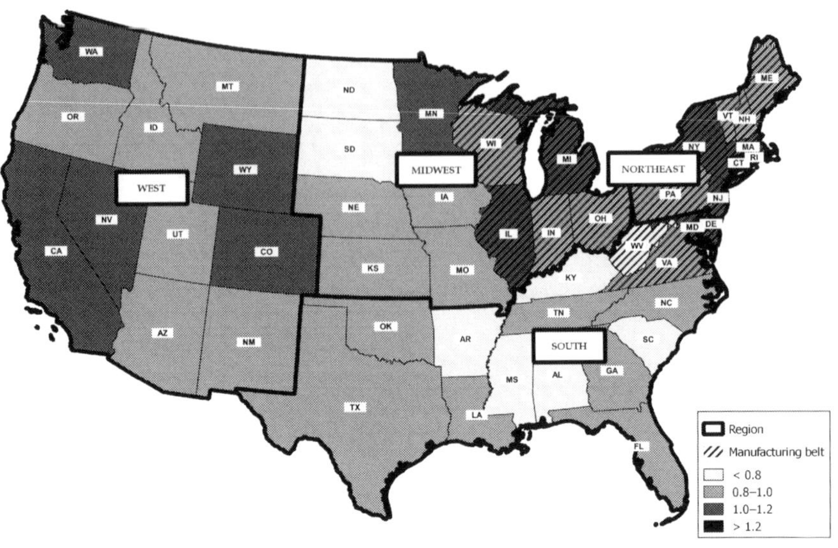

Map 4.5 Relative GDP per capita, 1980 (US = 1)

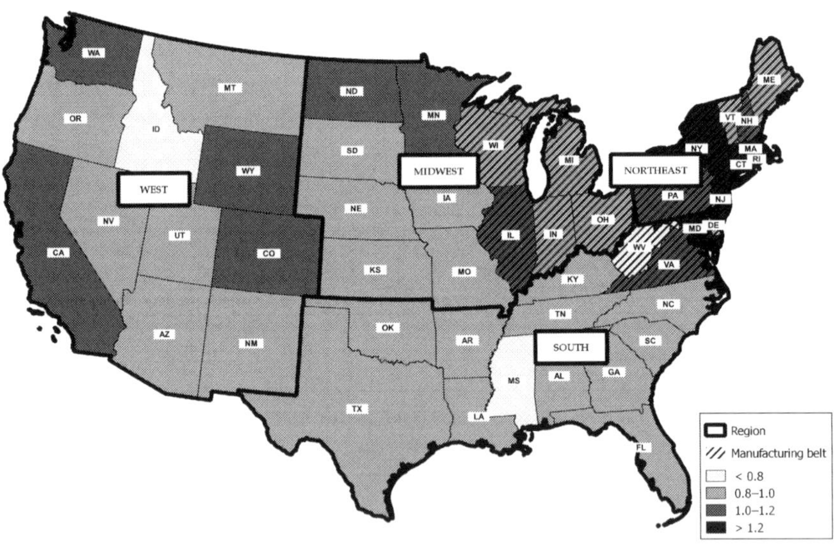

Map 4.6 Relative GDP per capita, 2010 (US = 1)

per capita income again fluctuated around the US average. It might be interesting to compare the manufacturing belt region with the Northeast and Midwest. It is a rather rough comparison since the manufacturing belt does include a few of the Midwest states, but it still reveals interesting points. In the post-Second World

War decades, per capita income of that region declines relative to the US average, but recovers from about the 1980s. This seems to be driven by the Northeastern states rather than the Midwest.

Before summarizing the main trends in regional inequality over the past 130 years, I will look at the evolution of per capita income relative to the US average of a few US states. Examining, for example, the state of Illinois, we can observe a pattern closely resembling an inverted U-shape. Indeed, Illinois reached its peak before the First World War, plateauing in the interwar period, and then declining after the Second World War. Michigan, arguably one of the core regions of the manufacturing belt, also exhibits something like an inverted U-shape pattern. Unlike Illinois, it peaked in 1940 and then experienced a steady decline. A contrast to those two states are the states of California and Nevada, which experienced a steady decline of their real per capita income relative to the US average over the entire period of 130 years. On the other hand, Florida and Virginia are examples of states with a gradual increase in their real per capita income relative to the US, even during the period 1880–1940, which was a period of laggard convergence among many Southern states. Lastly, despite convergence and diminishing regional inequalities over the course of the late nineteenth, twentieth, and early twenty-first centuries, some US states show a remarkable persistence. There are those that were among the richest in 1880 and remained so in 2010 – for example, Connecticut and Massachusetts – and there are some that were among poorest in 1880 and remained so in 2010 – for example, Mississippi and West Virginia.

Overall, the evolution of regional inequalities in the US since 1880 can be characterized as one of convergence, though not uninterrupted, accompanied by persistent regional inequalities. Indeed, one could even say that 130 years of US regional development were 130 years of 'unfulfilled convergence'. The period of 1880–1940 was dominated by the West converging to the US average from above while the convergence in the period 1940–2010 was driven by the South, which was converging to the US average from below. The period of 1920–1940 did not witness convergence – quite on the contrary (see Figure 4.5d) – and the post-1980 decades exhibit a considerable slowdown or even an end of convergence. It is important to note that though widespread, convergence was not universal, and we have US states that persistently missed out on convergence of their real per capita income to the US average. The locational Gini coefficient confirms that spatial inequalities were persistently high over the past 130 years and showed little or no sign of disappearing.

4. Regional inequality: determinants and causes

The basic facts about the evolution of regional inequality discussed in the previous section provide a springboard to review various explanations trying to understand the driving forces of convergence and divergence across US states over the course of 130 years.[9] These explanations, as will be seen below, are not mutually exclusive. On the contrary, putting them together offers us a story of the regional economic development, and even though it is very likely incomplete, its main characters and their contribution to that story have been quite clearly identified. There are a large number of studies investigating regional inequalities and causes related to them. Here, I will concentrate only on the studies that directly examine the forces behind regional development in the long run or focus on the sub-periods on which we are interested. There are two main ways to review this literature: one would be to focus on specific US regions; the other would be more guided by theory and centred around the type of explanation put forward by various studies. Here, I opt for the latter, since it allows me not only to summarize the main sources of long-run regional development, but also to identify future avenues of research more easily.[10]

Broadly, we can distinguish four different types of explanations that have emerged in the literature analysing *long-term* development in US regional income inequalities: factors of production, institutions, structural change, resource abundance and economic geography. Most generally, we can broadly distinguish between fundamental drivers of regional inequalities such as institutions and geographical characteristics, and factors that can be called 'proximate' sources of regional inequalities, such as factor prices, resource abundance and structural change.

4.1 Proximate sources of regional inequalities

4.1.1 Factors of production

Inputs of production, especially labour and human capital, received attention from scholars examining long-run regional inequalities. Mitchener and McLean (1999) put forward an explanation based on labour input and labour productivity in order to account for high levels of per capita income of the West in 1880, and its subsequent convergence to the US average from above, as well as the anaemic performance of the South. The decomposition of regional differences in per capita income relative to the US average revealed that the high income of the West in 1880 was not only due to the high level of productivity, but also due to the high level of labour input driven by a high percentage of males in the West and an age structure that favoured high labour force participation rates. This was complemented by the abundance of resources, allowing the West to achieve high productivity levels. The subsequent convergence of the West to the national average is less understood, and standard explanations of factor mobility or diffusion of technology are not entirely convincing (Mitchener and McLean 1999). It appears that the erosion of the favourable age structure, gender ratio and resource base might help to explain the rather rapid convergence of the West to the US average. As for the sluggish performance of the South, Mitchener and McLean (1999) found that the main reason was low productivity, while labour input does not help to illuminate the long and persistent underperformance of that region.[11] However, low levels of human capital, as measured by formal educational attainment, were found to be important in explaining the very slow convergence of the Southern states before 1950 (Connolly 2004).

The slowdown of convergence since the 1980s has recently drawn scholarly attention, and the role of labour migration, the demand for skilled labour and the housing market were examined. Research has observed that the income differences across US states have been increasingly capitalized into housing prices (e.g. Glaeser et al. 2005; Van Nieuwerburgh and Weill 2010). This, together with the fact that regional economic success after 1980 was connected to the rising importance of human capital and demand for high-skilled labour due to skill-based technological change (Autor and Dorn 2013), has led to an examination of the role of the housing market for rising regional inequalities. Ganong and Shoag (2017) show that the decline of income convergence can be explained in part by a change in the relationship between income and housing prices. Since housing prices began to account for a far greater proportion of the income differences across states after the 1980s, the return to living in productive areas has fallen for unskilled households, and their migration patterns diverge from the migration patterns of the skilled households. As a result, the US economy has shifted from one in which regional labour markets clear through net migration to one in which labour markets clear through skill-sorting – high-skilled workers move to high-income places, while low-skilled workers leave high-income places.

4.1.2 Structural change

Structural change has been viewed as one of the major forces of economic development.[12] Indeed, US economic development over 130 years witnessed, among other things, two structural changes: a 'first' structural change when agriculture was losing to manufacturing, and a 'second' structural change when manufacturing was losing to services. A study by Barro and Sala-i-Martin (1991) considers structural change as one of the explanations for the observed income convergence across US states. The effect of the differences in the sectoral composition of regions on regional income convergence and the process of narrowing those differences were examined by Kim (1998), who analysed them at broad SIC one-digit level. Even this rather crude measure of regional industrial structure has already yielded some valuable insights into the factors shaping US long-run development of regional inequalities. The disappointing performance of the South before 1940 can be attributed to the unfavourable industrial mix of that region focusing mostly on agriculture, while the rather spectacular convergence of the US economy from the 1940s until the 1980s can be partly attributed to the narrowing of differences in regional industrial structure. A study by Caselli and Coleman (2001) offers a valuable insight into the role of labour force reallocation in the convergence of US regions over the course of 100 years from 1880 to 1980. Their analysis focuses on the decomposition of convergence into sectoral labour reallocation effect, convergence of economy-wide agricultural wages to non-agricultural (so-called between-sector convergence), and convergence of Southern wages to Northern wages within sectors, respectively. Several important findings stand out. The Southern states' convergence to the Northern states before 1940 (or lack of it) was driven mostly by labour reallocation out of agriculture and convergence of agricultural to non-agricultural wages. Convergence of within-sector wages played a minor role before 1940. However, this was reversed thereafter, and the catching up of Southern wages with Northern wages within each sector was the main force behind post-Second World War convergence, accounting for about 40 per cent of it. This suggests that an important part of post-1950 catch-up of the South was an increase in labour productivity. Convergence of the Midwest to the North was largely because of agricultural outmigration. Interestingly, structural transformation played no role in regional convergence between the West and North before 1940, and only a small role after that. Structural change has also been a focus of a study by Bernard and Jones (1996), though it concentrates only on the period 1963–1989, which, from the point of view of long-run convergence, includes the decades of both rapid and stagnating regional convergence. Also, it does not discuss specifically the role of the South. Despite the limitation, the findings are illuminating, and suggest that structural change has contributed to about one-quarter of total aggregate convergence, though it argues that a shift from manufacturing to the service sector reduced productivity growth.[13] This is a potentially important finding since it implies a growth-inhibiting effect of labour reallocation towards services in the 1960s, 1970s and 1980s, known as Baumol's disease (Baumol 1967).[14]

Though we still lack studies thoroughly examining how labour reallocation from manufacturing to services impacted the evolution of regional convergence patterns, it is important to assess the effect of the rising service sector on regional income inequality given the growing importance of this 'second' structural transformation that started occurring, at least from the vantage point of labour productivity, in the middle of the 1990s. A recent study by Desmet and Rossi-Hansberg (2014) attempts, among other things, to link structural transformation to the regional distribution of economic activities. It shows a gradual increase in spatial concentration of services from the 1950s, as well as rising productivity of the service sector, which began in the mid-1990s. Though still far away from informing us about the causes of regional income differences, the study captures the shift of manufacturing activities from the manufacturing belt to the South, which will be discussed below, and argues for the replacement of manufacturing with service sector employment. The result of that study suggests that given the productivity advances of the service sector and the relocation of manufacturing employment from the Northeast and Midwest to the South, we can expect that the extent of regional income inequality will depend on how successful regions are in attracting high-productivity services and/or replacing manufacturing with the service sector.

4.1.3 Resource abundance

Another explanation of regional convergence patterns since 1880 that has drawn less attention from scholars is natural resources. This is not to say that the role of natural resources and their abundance did not play an important role in the explanations of US industrial success – quite the contrary (e.g. see Wright 1990; David and Wright 1997). However, little has been done when trying to account for the long-run convergence patterns of US regions, and especially the effect of resource abundance on rapid convergence of the West before 1940, as seen earlier. We can, however, gain some insights from a couple of studies attempting to shed some light on the long-run consequences of natural resources, even though they do not explicitly address the question of regional convergence. Mitchener and McLean (2003) examine the effect of the share of the workforce in mining in 1880 on the subsequent income per capita of US states, only to find a positive association until 1920. This is suggestive of natural resources playing a positive role in at least high initial per capita income of resource-abundant states in the West, possibly persisting until the interwar period. Michaels (2011) investigates the long-run impact of oil abundance in the South. The results are interesting and indicate that by the middle of the twentieth century, the oil sector increased per capita income and education in oil-abundant counties of the US South. That effect, however, dissipated by 1990. Hence, they suggest that oil extraction did not necessarily constrain the economic development of the South before 1940, but neither did it help to spur growth in the post-Second World War area. Altogether, both studies suggest a plausible story of natural resources having a positive impact on regional economic development in the late nineteenth century and possibly until about 1950, but a rather muted effect after that. Still, while highly suggestive and important, we do not yet know exactly the role of natural resources in the sluggish convergence of the South and rapid convergence of the West, as well as the transmission channels of their influence. A study by Papyrakis and Gerlagh (2007) is a rare case examining the effect of natural resources on gross state product (GSP) convergence across US states. Even though it focuses on a shorter time span, including the years of 1986–2000, those are the years that were identified earlier as the years of a stagnating regional convergence, which is suggestive of a potentially detrimental effect of natural resources on regional convergence. Their findings suggest that natural resources did not affect economic growth as such; hence, there is no evidence of natural resource course. However, natural resources had a negative impact on investment, schooling, R&D and openness, and increased corruption, which suggests that natural resources might be one of the reasons for economic underperformance of resource-abundant regions in the 1980s and 1990s.

4.2 Fundamental sources of regional inequalities

4.2.1 Institutions

Institutions are considered as one of the fundamental factors affecting long-run economic performance. Similarly, institutions can be considered as one of the fundamental causes of long-run regional inequalities. There is an extensive literature stressing the importance of specific Southern institutions on American economic development before and especially after the Civil War (e.g. Wright 1986, 2006). Indeed, the effect of the Civil War and the institution of slavery were considered as the primary reasons for the laggard performance of the Southern regions. It has been argued that the legacy of slavery, and especially dependence on large plantations, left the South vulnerable to the slow adoption of new technology and industrialization necessary to catch up to the rest of the US. In particular, the South witnessed low investment into physical capital and a lack of labour supply for prospective manufacturing industries. Factor markets did not play a favourable role either. Outmigration of the educated black population not only lowered human capital levels in the South, but also limited the intergenerational effect that a better-educated black population would have had, had it remained in the South (Margo 1988). Recently, a few studies have attempted to empirically test a link between slavery in the US South and regional inequalities at the end of the twentieth century. Nunn (2008) finds that all forms of slavery, not only large plantations, negatively affected economic development at the end of the twentieth century, though this adverse effect was not due to initial economic inequality. He finds that land inequality in 1860 is uncorrelated with income in 2000, and suggests that it can be due to the catch-up process that the South started in the 1940s. Bertocchi and Dimico (2014) examine the effect of slavery on income inequality across US counties and find a robust negative correlation. They also try to examine channels through which slavery affected inequality across US counties, and argue that an unequal educational attainment of blacks and whites is a crucial channel through which slavery is related to inequality across US counties.

4.2.2 Economic geography

As was discussed at the beginning of this chapter, US regions experienced a rather dramatic shift of manufacturing activities from the Northeast and Midwest, and specifically a region called the manufacturing belt, to the South (e.g. Holmes and Stevens 2004). Though dramatic in its scope, it was less dramatic in its speed as it took about a century for the manufacturing to start noticeably relocating to the Southern states. This affected the development of regional inequalities because in many states manufacturing was a dominant sector until the service sector started to gain importance from about the 1990s.

Our discussion has already pointed out the existence and potential importance of the manufacturing belt. This term has long been used to describe the remarkable spatial concentration of industry in the US that prevailed from the late nineteenth century to about the third quarter of the twentieth century. Indeed, in 1900, about four-fifths of American manufacturing output was produced in this part of the country, which comprised only one-sixth of its land area and a little over half its population (Klein and Crafts 2012). Another remarkable feature was its long persistence for almost a century. The causes of dominant concentration of manufacturing activities in the manufacturing belt for about a century have been a point of interest for many scholars, and it is clear that they most likely have a direct relationship to the causes of long-run regional inequalities. Various explanations have been put forward, including factor endowments, proximity to suppliers and purchasers of intermediate goods (forward and backward linkages, respectively), high market accessibility in the context of scale economies, and declining transport costs (Harris 1954; Perloff et al. 1960; Meyer 1983, 1989; Krugman 1991; Kim 1995; Healey 2014). A debate between factor endowment type explanation (Kim 1995, 1999) and market access type explanation revived by Krugman (1991) has yielded some robust conclusions. Klein and Crafts (2012) have tested the relative importance of both types of explanations by examining the persistence of the manufacturing belt in 1880–1920 using an empirical model that subsumes both market potential and factor endowment arguments. The results show that it was market potential that was at the heart of the existence of the manufacturing belt, that it mattered *more* than factor endowments, and that its impact came through interactions both with scale economies and with both forward and backward linkages. The market potential explanation is intimately linked to transportation costs, and we can better understand the development of regional inequalities if we consider an explanation advanced by proponents of the 'new economic geography' (notably Krugman 1991). This explanation, though stylized, offers valuable insights into a link between transportation costs and regional inequalities, and, as empirical evidence reviewed above suggested, should not be neglected. In the second half of the nineteenth century, when the US began a rapid industrialization, transportation costs began to fall dramatically, especially with the advancements of railroads, which were complementing the existing system of navigable rivers, coastal shipping and canals. The concentration of manufacturing activities in the Northeast and Midwest, which emerged in the first half of the nineteenth century, took advantage of it and locked in their initial advantage. Even though the West had an abundance of natural resources and a demographic structure favouring large labour supply, and even though the South abolished slavery, all this was not strong enough to pull manufacturing out of the manufacturing belt for about a century. As a result, the rise and persistence of the manufacturing belt from the second half of the nineteenth century to the second half of the twentieth century allowed the Northeast and Midwest to forge ahead of the Southern states, opening up a large north–south per capita income gap.

The dominance of the manufacturing belt started to erode noticeably from the 1970s with a relocation of the manufacturing sector to the South. Indeed, the Southern states experienced a boom in the decades after the Second World War, allowing them to catch up on per capita income with the rest of the US. The causes of this rather spectacular reversal of performance of the so-called 'Sun Belt' are still debated. As our earlier discussion would imply, structural change and factors of production were considered to be a very importance source of growing productivity in the South. However, amenities and housing supply were found to be important too (e.g. Glaeser and Tobio 2008). What about the role of transportation costs? Transportation costs continued to decline even further throughout the twentieth century as the transportation sector witnessed improvements in technology, organization of transport networks, the rise of trucking, and investment into new railroad infrastructure such as the interstate highway system (Glaeser and Kohlhase 2004). The implications of even lower transport costs for regional convergence are outlined by new economic geography models, which predict that in interaction with high factor costs in geographically concentrated areas, regional disparities will narrow as manufacturing activities relocate (e.g. Combes et al. 2008). That seems to be the story of the manufacturing belt – high wage costs and strong unions were pushing the costs of production up, very likely above agglomeration benefits such as access to intermediate goods offered by the manufacturing belt.

Once transportation costs had declined enough, industries began to relocate to the South, where the cost of labour was lower.

5. Conclusion

Overall, research on US regional activities has identified several channels that could explain the long-run development of regional income differences as presented earlier in this chapter. The narrowing down of regional disparities was due to structural change, a decline of transportation costs, and differences in resource endowments. At the same time, a lack of convergence of especially the South before 1940 could be attributed to the inner working of labour markets, and the specifics of the Southern institutions, notably several persisting effects of slavery. The slowdown of regional convergence since the 1980s was attributed mainly to rising housing prices, combined with a high demand for skilled labour, and even the abundance of raw materials. Certainly, other factors are at play to explain the dynamics of US regional development, and more work needs to be done regarding the role of infrastructure or state regulation to examine their effects on changing regional income inequalities.

Notes

1 Alaska and Hawaii are excluded.
2 The Bureau of Economic Analysis also provides real gross state product (GSP) figures, but they run from 1963 only.
3 Full details of the methodology are discussed in Klein (2013).
4 We do not have data for Oklahoma, North Dakota and South Dakota in 1880.
5 Employment figures for 1890 come from Perloff et al. (1960), and data for 1930, 1950, 1980 and 2010 come from the US censuses, and were generously provided by Alexandra Lopez Cermeno.
6 An extensive analysis of convergence across US states has been done by Barro et al. (1991) and Barro and Sala-i-Martin (1992).
7 At a disaggregated level, it is appropriate to demarcate the manufacturing belt in terms of counties. Our analysis is at the state level; states whose territory are wholly or predominantly in the manufacturing belt are Connecticut, Delaware, Illinois, Indiana, Maine, Maryland, Massachusetts, Michigan, New Hampshire, New Jersey, New York, Ohio, Pennsylvania, Rhode Island, Vermont, Virginia, West Virginia and Wisconsin.
8 The choice of the year 1940 might seem a bit imprecise given that the profound decrease on real per capita income relative to the US average ended in 1930. From the point of view of long-run trends in regional inequality, the dominant role of the western regions ended in the interwar period, and I opted to delineate it with the year 1940.
9 There is a large body of important studies focusing on the issues of the measurement of convergence, which are not reviewed here (e.g. Rey and Montouri 1999; Yamamoto 2007).
10 There is a large body of research analysing regional economic development in the US. Here, I focus mostly on the studies that attempted to account for a long-run pattern of US regional inequality, leaving out some studies with narrower time spans.
11 See Mitchener and McLean (1999: 1032, Table 3).
12 See, for example, Herrendorf et al. (2014).
13 Bernard and Jones (1996: 133).
14 A similar argument is put forward by Desmet and Rossi-Hansberg (2014).

References

Autor, D.H. and Dorn, D. (2013) 'The growth of low-skill service jobs and the polarization of the US labor market', *American Economic Review*, Vol. 103 (5): 1553–97.

Barro, R.J. and Sala-i-Martin, X. (1992) 'Convergence', *Journal of Political Economy*, Vol. 100 (2): 223–51.

Barro, R.J., Sala-i-Martin, X., Blanchard, O.J. and Hall, R.E. (1991) 'Convergence across states and regions', *Brookings Papers on Economic Activity*, 107–82.

Baumol, W. (1967) 'Macroeconomics of unbalanced growth: the anatomy of urban crisis', *American Economic Review*, Vol. 57 (3): 415–26.

Bernard, A.B. and Jones, C.I. (1996) 'Comparing apples to oranges: productivity convergence and measurement across industries and countries', *The American Economic Review*, Vol. 91 (4): 1216–38.

Bertocchi, G. and Dimico, A. (2014) 'Slavery, education, and inequality', *European Economic Review*, Vol. 70: 197–209.

Caselli, F. and Coleman, W.J. III (2001) 'The US structural transformation and regional convergence: a reinterpretation', *Journal of Political Economy*, Vol. 109 (3): 584–616.

Combes, P.P., Mayer, T. and Thisse, J.F. (2008) *Economic Geography: The Integration of Regions and Nations*. Princeton, NJ: Princeton University Press.

Connolly, M. (2004). 'Human capital and growth in the postbellum South: a separate but unequal story', *The Journal of Economic History*, Vol. 64 (2): 363–99.

David, A.P. and Wright, G. (1997) 'Increasing returns and the genesis of American resource abundance', *Industrial and Corporate Change*, Vol. 6 (2): 203–45.

Desmet, K. and Rossi-Hansberg, E. (2014) 'Spatial development', *American Economic Review*, Vol. 104 (4): 1211–43.

Easterlin, R.A. (1957) 'State income estimates', in E.S. Lee, A.R. Miller, C.P. Brainerd and R.A. Easterlin (eds), *Population Redistribution and Economic Growth United States, 1870–1950, Vol. I: Methodological Considerations and Reference Tables*, Philadelphia, PA: American Philosophical Society.

Ganong, P. and Shoag, D. (2017) 'Why has regional income convergence in the US declined?', *Journal of Urban Economics*, Vol. 102: 76–90.

Glaeser, E.L. and Kohlhase, J.E. (2004) 'Cities, regions and the decline of transport costs', in R.J.G.M. Florax and D.A. Plane (eds), *Fifty Years of Regional Science*, Berlin: Springer, pp. 197–228.

Glaeser, E.L. and Tobio, K. (2008) 'The rise of the sunbelt', *Southern Economic Journal*, Vol. 74 (3): 610–43.

Glaeser, E.L., Gyourko, J. and Saks, R.E. (2005) 'Why have housing prices gone up?', *American Economic Review*, Vol. 95 (2): 329–33.

Healey, R.G. (2014) 'Railroads, factor channelling and increasing returns: Cleveland and the emergence of the American manufacturing belt', *Journal of Economic Geography*, Vol. 15 (3): 499–538.

Harris, C. (1954) 'The market as a factor in the localization of industry in the United States', *Annals of the Association of American Geographers*, Vol. 64: 315–48.

Herrendorf, B., Rogerson, R. and Valentinyi, A. (2014) 'Growth and structural transformation', in P. Aghion and S.N. Durlauf (eds), *Handbook of Economic Growth, Vol. 2*, Amsterdam: Elsevier, pp. 855–941.

Holmes, T.J. and Stevens, J.J. (2004) 'Spatial distribution of economic activities in North America', in V. Henderson and J.F. Thisse (eds), *Handbook of Regional and Urban Economics, Vol. 4*, Amsterdam: Elsevier, pp. 2797–843.

Johnston, L. and Williamson, S.H. (2018) What was the U.S. GDP then? *Measuring Worth*, 2018.

Kim, S. (1995) 'Expansion of markets and the geographic distribution of economic activities: trends in U.S. regional manufacturing structure, 1860–1987', *Quarterly Journal of Economics*, Vol. 110: 881–908.

Kim, S. (1998) 'Economic integration and convergence: US regions, 1840–1987', *The Journal of Economic History*, Vol. 58 (3): 659–83.

Kim, S. (1999) 'Regions, resources, and economic geography: sources of U.S. regional comparative advantage, 1880–1987', *Regional Science and Urban Economics*, Vol. 29: 1–32.

Klein, A. (2013) 'New state-level estimates of personal income in the United States, 1880–1910', in C. Hanes and S. Wolcott (eds), *Research in Economic History*, Bingley: Emerald Group Publishing, pp. 191–255.

Klein, A. and Crafts, N. (2012) 'Making sense of the manufacturing belt: determinants of US industrial location, 1880–1920', *Journal of Economic Geography*, Vol. 12 (4): 775–807.

Krugman, P. (1991) 'History and industry location: the case of the manufacturing belt', *American Economic Review Papers & Proceedings*, Vol. 81 (2): 80–3.

Margo, R.A. (1988) 'Schooling and the great migration', *NBER WP* 2697.

Meyer, D.R. (1983) 'Emergence of the American manufacturing belt: an interpretation', *Journal of Historical Geography*, Vol. 9: 145–74.

Meyer, D.R. (1989) 'Midwestern industrialization and the American manufacturing belt in the nineteenth century', *Journal of Economic History*, Vol. 49: 921–37.

Michaels, G. (2011) 'The long term consequences of resource-based specialisation', *The Economic Journal*, Vol. 121 (551): 31–57.

Mitchener, K.J. and McLean, I.W. (1999) 'US regional growth and convergence, 1880–1980', *The Journal of Economic History*, Vol. 59 (4): 1016–42.

Mitchener, K.J. and McLean, I.W. (2003) 'The productivity of US states since 1880', *Journal of Economic Growth*, Vol. 8 (1): 73–114.

Nunn, N. (2008) 'Slavery, inequality, and economic development in the Americas', in E. Helpman (ed.), *Institutions and Economic Performance*, Cambridge, MA: Harvard University Press, pp. 148–80.

Papyrakis, E. and Gerlagh, R. (2007) 'Resource abundance and economic growth in the United States', *European Economic Review*, Vol. 51 (4): 1011–39.

Perloff, H.S., Dunn, E.S., Lampard, E.E. and Muth, R.F. (1960) *Regions, Resources, and Economic Growth*. Lincoln, NE: University of Nebraska Press.

Rey, S.J. and Montouri, B.D. (1999) 'US regional income convergence: a spatial econometric perspective', *Regional Studies*, Vol. 33 (2): 143–56.

Van Nieuwerburgh, S. and Weill, P.O. (2010) 'Why has house price dispersion gone up?', *The Review of Economic Studies*, Vol. 77 (4): 1567–606.

Wright, G. (1986) *Old South, New South: Revolutions in the Southern Economy since the Civil War*, New York: Basic Books.

Wright, G. (1990) 'The origins of American industrial success, 1879–1940', *The American Economic Review*, Vol. 80 (4): 651–68.

Wright, G. (2006) *Slavery and American Economic Development*, Baton Rouge, LA: Louisiana State University Press.

Yamamoto, D. (2007) 'Scales of regional income disparities in the USA, 1955–2003', *Journal of Economic Geography*, Vol. 8 (1): 79–103.

Data appendix

Table A.1 Regional nominal GDP (1990 international dollars, millions)

Country (current borders)	*NUTS codes*	*Region*	*1900*	*1910*	*1925*	*1938*	*1950*	*1960*	*1970*	*1980*	*1990*	*2000*	*2010*
Austria	AT11	Burgenland	457	545	520	582	636	1,017	1,540	2,278	2,879	3,839	4,652
Austria	AT21	Carinthia	632	798	790	903	1,243	2,592	4,293	6,104	7,349	9,764	11,298
Austria	AT12+AT13	Lower Austria	10,940	14,072	14,192	14,720	13,946	22,612	34,120	45,757	58,139	71,434	85,098
Austria	AT32	Salzburg	477	609	635	731	1,003	2,229	4,219	6,675	8,799	12,031	14,662
Austria	AT22	Styria	1,929	2,292	2,435	2,953	3,401	6,265	9,214	13,346	15,829	21,085	25,176
Austria	AT33	Tyrol	518	734	765	908	1,241	2,738	5,218	8,108	10,504	14,373	17,629
Austria	AT31	Upper Austria	1,927	2,288	2,370	2,758	3,525	6,928	11,389	17,060	21,351	27,820	33,545
Austria	AT34	Vorarlberg	333	424	451	498	708	1,526	2,792	4,545	5,628	7,532	9,409
Belgium	BE21	Antwerp	2,970	4,115	5,752	6,798	7,950	10,768	18,202	26,195	30,748	39,088	47,483
Belgium	BE10+BE24+BE31	Brabant	5,184	6,762	9,000	10,701	12,938	19,263	31,569	42,833	53,603	69,429	85,727
Belgium	BE25	West Flanders	2,023	2,466	3,273	3,963	4,193	5,831	9,692	14,663	17,786	21,853	25,667
Belgium	BE23	East Flanders	3,214	3,785	4,427	4,891	5,634	6,990	11,420	15,197	19,895	24,427	30,543
Belgium	BE32	Hainaut	5,158	5,911	5,780	5,735	6,300	7,368	11,115	14,576	15,705	17,558	20,020
Belgium	BE33	Liege	3,648	4,320	4,877	5,069	5,773	7,376	10,643	14,038	14,249	15,843	18,737
Belgium	BE22	Limburg	602	723	979	1,269	1,805	2,613	5,088	8,268	10,984	13,773	16,170
Belgium	BE34	Luxembourg	797	829	685	656	861	1,028	1,445	2,202	3,029	3,623	4,363
Belgium	BE35	Namur	1,446	1,562	1,391	1,388	1,680	2,128	3,091	4,461	5,389	6,390	7,957
Denmark	DK01	Hovedstaden	2,234	2,766	4,395	7,115	13,079	14,122	25,669	28,127	34,466	46,083	50,882
Denmark	DK02	Sjælland	1,377	1,821	2,454	3,034	3,427	5,158	7,594	10,488	10,969	13,545	14,042
Denmark	DK03	Southern Denmark	1,253	2,039	3,378	4,994	5,518	8,955	13,130	17,552	19,853	24,926	25,818
Denmark	DK04	Midtjylland	1,760	2,544	2,904	4,119	4,830	7,735	11,317	15,368	20,312	26,161	27,621
Denmark	DK05	Nordjylland	1,102	1,508	1,824	2,488	2,800	4,398	4,814	10,297	9,264	11,913	12,069
Finland	FI19	Länsi-Suomi	1,155	1,552	2,087	3,543	4,680	7,363	11,095	15,651	19,564	22,728	28,468

(continued)

Table A.1 (continued)

Country (current borders)	NUTS codes	Region	1900	1910	1925	1938	1950	1960	1970	1980	1990	2000	2010
Finland	FI1B	Helsinki-Uusimaa	958	1,129	1,756	3,267	4,252	6,582	12,065	17,335	27,005	37,977	48,347
Finland	FI1C	Etelä-Soumi	1,146	1,433	1,867	3,306	4,242	6,727	10,516	14,097	18,528	20,644	22,861
Finland	FI1D	Pohjois-ja Itä-Soumi	1,108	1,426	1,931	2,913	3,793	6,817	10,305	14,481	18,464	20,200	24,451
Finland	FI20	Åland	48	44	51	94	84	110	132	326	542	636	785
France	FR10	Île-de-France	26,210	27,297	42,120	49,209	63,954	100,635	164,171	220,313	293,506	362,145	419,249
France	FR21	Champagne-Ardenne	4,041	3,721	4,531	5,243	5,106	8,085	14,146	20,532	22,544	26,229	24,522
France	FR22	Picardie	4,466	4,023	4,857	5,947	5,910	9,823	18,231	23,294	27,901	31,865	31,200
France	FR23	Haute-Normandie	4,481	5,130	4,968	5,616	5,976	9,712	17,868	26,527	28,971	33,902	34,094
France	FR24	Centre	4,961	4,856	6,092	6,519	7,501	11,456	22,715	30,923	39,862	46,277	45,660
France	FR25	Basse-Normandie	3,229	3,089	3,696	4,231	4,925	7,802	13,473	16,667	20,759	24,190	24,495
France	FR26	Bourgogne	4,127	4,026	5,107	5,226	6,711	10,589	16,146	21,175	25,925	29,269	28,879
France	FR30	Nord-Pas-de-Calais	8,869	8,683	11,243	14,842	15,164	23,889	38,212	49,534	55,914	65,407	69,442
France	FR41	Lorraine	5,303	6,621	7,205	8,079	9,132	15,608	24,955	30,857	34,906	39,622	38,450
France	FR42	Alsace	3,201	4,109	4,918	5,950	6,087	9,216	16,629	24,055	30,092	36,165	36,043
France	FR43	Franche-Comté	2,241	2,877	3,307	2,930	4,111	6,807	10,749	14,064	17,162	20,390	19,741
France	FR51	Pays de la Loire	5,855	6,239	7,750	7,594	9,513	14,399	27,277	38,160	46,791	61,277	67,209
France	FR52	Bretagne	4,540	4,370	6,056	6,650	8,709	12,306	24,269	33,644	40,515	52,651	55,748
France	FR53	Poitou-Charentes	3,810	4,804	4,711	4,505	4,291	5,894	14,203	18,913	23,340	29,000	30,281
France	FR61	Aquitaine	6,081	6,583	7,711	8,161	9,756	14,302	25,181	37,099	44,223	54,882	60,623
France	FR62	Midi-Pyrénées	4,932	5,516	6,472	6,770	7,762	12,104	20,665	28,355	38,354	47,591	53,560
France	FR63	Limousin	2,055	2,460	2,755	2,535	2,775	4,091	7,377	8,440	10,770	12,096	11,848
France	FR71	Rhône-Alpes	10,094	10,604	14,713	16,008	19,516	32,597	52,400	73,291	98,965	121,721	132,636
France	FR72	Auvergne	3,366	3,256	4,350	4,707	5,396	8,197	12,765	15,540	20,376	22,743	22,856

France	FR81	Languedoc-Roussillon	3,969	4,000	5,260	6,141	5,287	8,078	16,191	22,687	30,265	37,961	43,434
France	FR82	Provence-Alpes-Côte d'Azur	5,607	6,436	10,728	10,537	12,276	17,940	33,110	56,944	71,847	88,579	99,087
France	FR83	Corse	350	429	563	562	635	1,080	1,658	2,750	3,504	4,300	5,508
Germany	DE11	Stuttgart, Regierungsbezirk	3,974	5,522	6,202	9,751	11,939	28,830	45,739	60,694	78,337	92,665	100,358
Germany	DE12	Karlsruhe, Regierungsbezirk	3,579	5,397	5,776	8,357	9,286	19,345	32,973	40,031	51,668	57,966	62,894
Germany	DE13	Freiburg, Regierungsbezirk	2,779	3,772	3,435	5,871	5,930	10,930	18,683	26,793	33,073	40,122	43,765
Germany	DE14	Tübingen, Regierungsbezirk	2,124	2,836	2,877	4,541	5,101	8,698	15,273	21,671	28,746	34,801	39,479
Germany	DE21	Oberbayern, Regierungsbezirk	3,898	4,887	5,869	9,144	10,681	23,342	44,526	67,229	92,511	109,821	123,170
Germany	DE22	Niederbayern, Regierungsbezirk	1,426	1,654	1,434	2,396	3,944	4,719	7,937	11,698	16,463	20,299	24,318
Germany	DE23	Oberpfalz, Regierungsbezirk	1,092	1,448	1,440	2,115	3,421	4,997	8,232	10,709	14,916	19,818	23,064
Germany	DE24	Oberfranken, Regierungsbezirk	1,525	2,036	2,275	3,921	5,067	7,406	11,252	13,489	18,004	18,842	20,709
Germany	DE25	Mittelfranken, Regierungsbezirk	2,381	3,445	3,779	5,521	5,563	10,771	17,833	22,994	30,074	34,415	37,966
Germany	DE26	Unterfranken, Regierungsbezirk	1,473	2,250	2,332	3,672	4,194	6,818	10,959	14,260	19,423	24,844	27,411
Germany	DE27	Schwaben, Regierungsbezirk	2,148	2,630	2,653	4,220	5,538	9,571	16,225	20,052	27,053	32,389	36,933
Germany	DE30	Berlin	11,095	18,322	22,122	32,741	13,103	24,782	35,590	46,250	41,751	61,987	67,016
Germany	DE40	Brandenburg	6,505	11,034	5,596	10,930	8,772	14,229	19,099	26,403	19,535	33,350	37,029

(continued)

Table A.1 (continued)

Country (current borders)	*NUTS codes*	*Region*	*1900*	*1910*	*1925*	*1938*	*1950*	*1960*	*1970*	*1980*	*1990*	*2000*	*2010*
Germany	DE50	Bremen	981	1,345	2,079	2,883	2,553	7,199	10,894	14,093	15,634	16,898	17,851
Germany	DE60	Hamburg	4,251	5,671	7,901	10,542	8,405	24,958	34,681	40,651	47,795	58,115	62,317
Germany	DE71+DE72	Darmstadt and Giessen	5,171	7,631	8,192	13,128	14,917	31,154	53,522	75,604	106,405	120,453	123,673
Germany	DE73	Kassel, Regierungsbezirk	1,924	2,804	2,975	4,522	3,810	7,957	12,597	16,327	21,254	22,802	24,153
Germany	DE80	Mecklenburg-Vorpommern	2,910	3,511	3,424	7,195	7,843	11,376	14,345	19,840	13,204	22,199	23,482
Germany	DE91+DE92	Statistische Regionen Braunschweig und Hannover	4,348	5,472	6,458	11,062	12,758	24,859	36,761	52,865	62,230	70,208	75,826
Germany	DE93	Statistische Region Lüneburg	2,165	2,581	2,506	4,263	5,852	9,614	15,298	15,169	18,694	23,458	24,437
Germany	DE94	Statistische Region Weser-Ems	2,373	2,653	3,377	6,285	6,814	13,184	17,367	27,383	33,897	41,103	45,673
Germany	DEA1	Düsseldorf, Regierungsbezirk	8,187	13,703	16,725	23,411	20,618	51,711	77,309	85,816	93,704	109,704	119,989
Germany	DEA2	Köln, Regierungsbezirk	5,332	7,710	8,982	12,009	11,126	27,285	42,572	60,486	70,412	90,342	97,155
Germany	DEA3	Münster, Regierungsbezirk	2,373	3,956	5,367	7,816	8,460	16,620	23,587	30,832	36,561	42,599	48,356
Germany	DEA4	Detmold, Regierungsbezirk	2,122	2,803	3,832	5,557	7,083	12,023	19,415	24,719	30,494	39,244	41,367
Germany	DEA5	Arnsberg, Regierungsbezirk	5,097	7,922	9,672	13,103	13,442	29,264	43,149	52,306	58,997	64,439	68,936
Germany	DEB1	Statistische Region Koblenz	2,712	3,837	3,757	4,961	4,714	7,564	12,724	16,446	19,716	24,951	26,887

Germany	DEB2	Statistische Region Trier	987	1,221	1,452	1,896	1,689	2,264	4,165	5,731	6,878	7,866	8,664
Germany	DEB3	Statistische Region Rheinhessen-Pfalz	2,785	4,155	5,013	7,481	6,193	11,201	21,867	27,173	31,333	36,445	39,408
Germany	DEC0	Saarland	1,590	2,613	3,031	3,997	3,503	7,691	11,021	14,048	16,419	18,954	20,163
Germany	DED2	Dresden, NUTS 2 region	4,369	5,987	8,082	12,081	5,870	11,462	15,277	19,722	13,175	22,006	24,591
Germany	DED4	Chemnitz, NUTS 2 region	5,574	6,984	8,765	11,928	7,573	12,848	17,554	21,900	10,679	20,596	22,198
Germany	DED5	Leipzig, NUTS 2 region	3,099	4,273	5,549	8,033	4,677	9,098	12,319	14,910	8,741	13,860	15,783
Germany	DEE0	Sachsen-Anhalt	6,427	7,708	9,334	17,078	10,734	19,287	25,238	33,049	19,449	32,040	34,319
Germany	DEF0	Schleswig-Holstein	3,402	4,146	4,389	7,229	8,752	15,155	23,696	33,681	40,232	47,922	49,131
Germany	DEG0	Thüringen	4,417	6,145	7,277	12,298	8,756	15,705	20,454	27,977	16,978	29,406	31,642
Italy	ITC1	Piemonte	6,982	9,250	12,705	16,251	18,276	31,049	55,160	71,149	82,068	93,493	89,455
Italy	ITC2	Valle d'Aosta/ Vallée d'Aoste	173	240	339	407	531	1,025	1,622	2,041	2,647	2,742	3,215
Italy	ITC3	Liguria	2,889	4,511	5,660	8,450	8,914	13,275	19,337	24,704	28,769	32,486	31,611
Italy	ITC4	Lombardia	9,510	13,519	19,033	27,333	34,867	63,937	113,198	151,689	192,693	223,980	237,080
Italy	ITH1+ITH2	Provincia Autonoma di Bolzano/ Bozen-Provincia Autonoma di Trento	767	1,040	1,807	2,233	2,730	4,752	8,840	15,447	19,587	23,655	24,856
Italy	ITH3	Veneto	3,854	6,104	7,607	9,948	13,180	22,021	39,228	62,442	80,495	99,496	104,465

(continued)

Table A.1 (continued)

Country (current borders)	*NUTS codes*	*Region*	*1900*	*1910*	*1925*	*1938*	*1950*	*1960*	*1970*	*1980*	*1990*	*2000*	*2010*
Italy	ITH4	Friuli-Venezia Giulia	1,341	1,919	3,196	4,782	4,647	6,400	11,765	16,397	20,698	25,194	25,775
Italy	ITH5	Emilia-Romagna	4,607	7,152	9,972	11,706	13,848	25,439	43,488	67,809	79,042	95,443	99,089
Italy	ITI1	Toscana	4,177	6,180	8,591	10,178	11,631	20,646	36,370	51,790	60,982	73,219	75,241
Italy	ITI2	Umbria	1,037	1,287	1,754	2,351	2,535	4,357	7,072	11,201	12,996	15,430	15,514
Italy	ITI3	Marche	1,595	2,136	2,702	3,366	4,063	6,813	11,525	18,750	22,253	27,523	29,348
Italy	ITI4	Lazio	3,985	5,611	8,178	10,783	12,723	26,535	50,466	69,553	95,796	109,996	121,189
Italy	ITF1	Abruzzo	1,223	1,687	2,233	2,266	2,489	4,680	8,188	13,376	17,911	20,122	20,824
Italy	ITF2	Molise	427	568	718	786	790	1,280	1,914	3,147	4,054	4,724	4,649
Italy	ITF3	Campania	4,944	6,893	8,517	10,164	10,417	19,675	33,413	46,030	60,964	69,751	69,786
Italy	ITF4	Puglia	3,351	4,478	6,383	6,465	7,285	13,661	23,311	34,806	42,876	50,149	50,922
Italy	ITF5	Basilicata	634	839	1,058	1,040	1,003	2,239	3,854	5,634	6,368	8,138	7,471
Italy	ITF6	Calabria	1,631	2,379	2,784	2,881	3,233	6,652	11,713	15,225	19,244	23,503	24,027
Italy	ITG1	Sicilia	5,680	7,597	8,797	9,687	8,980	16,539	29,559	45,310	56,576	61,527	61,821
Italy	ITG2	Sardegna	1,306	1,896	2,360	2,906	2,816	6,002	11,478	15,789	19,642	23,037	23,837
Netherlands	NL11	Groningen	874	1,096	1,606	2,006	2,512	3,807	6,969	16,921	11,827	14,024	19,225
Netherlands	NL12	Friesland	1,032	1,252	1,549	1,778	2,255	3,141	5,050	6,698	8,547	11,459	12,703
Netherlands	NL13	Drenthe	378	483	675	866	1,420	2,094	3,492	4,687	6,834	8,412	8,927
Netherlands	NL21	Overijssel	1,024	1,404	2,194	2,599	3,846	5,901	9,193	12,144	15,529	20,967	24,225
Netherlands	NL22	Gelderland	1,674	1,939	3,327	4,149	5,674	9,042	17,225	21,494	27,328	36,490	41,144
Netherlands	NL31	Utrecht	913	954	2,074	2,690	3,257	5,045	9,267	13,562	18,417	30,879	35,420
Netherlands	NL32	Noordholland	3,896	5,366	9,100	10,806	12,777	18,846	29,808	35,395	44,396	64,567	74,985
Netherlands	NL33	Zuidholland	4,614	5,633	10,444	12,812	16,223	24,652	41,191	49,917	60,720	77,098	85,434
Netherlands	NL34	Zeeland	669	840	986	1,231	1,522	2,189	3,615	4,976	6,704	7,172	8,944
Netherlands	NL41	Noordbrabant	1,683	2,234	3,111	4,149	6,676	11,517	20,001	27,520	37,543	53,630	60,471

Netherlands	NL42	Limburg	848	1,238	1,934	2,553	3,982	6,663	9,469	13,071	17,407	22,672	24,382
Netherlands	NL23	Flevoland (1960–)	–	–	–	–	–	–	676	1,596	2,841	5,171	6,963
Norway	NO01	Oslo og Akershus	1,076	1,278	2,416	3,946	4,946	7,242	10,218	13,169	22,201	27,964	33,584
Norway	NO02	Hedmark og Oppland	326	423	466	763	1,258	1,850	2,537	3,395	4,426	5,208	5,983
Norway	NO03	Sør-Østlandet	866	1,106	1,545	2,276	3,535	4,878	6,607	8,678	11,332	13,160	15,908
Norway	NO04	Agder og Rogaland	424	508	730	1,282	1,723	2,518	3,932	5,758	9,158	11,449	16,724
Norway	NO05	Vestlandet	590	732	1,170	1,620	2,530	3,569	5,366	7,305	10,792	13,954	18,355
Norway	NO06	Trøndelag	303	402	519	877	1,219	1,778	2,631	3,501	4,901	6,309	8,022
Norway	NO07	Nord-Norge	278	361	403	776	1,153	1,977	3,140	4,036	5,699	6,868	8,566
Portugal	PT11	Norte	3,081	2,767	3,477	4,906	5,625	8,456	14,633	24,344	33,779	43,314	51,437
Portugal	PT15	Algarve	267	300	318	519	531	696	1,054	2,491	4,035	6,109	7,654
Portugal	PT16	Centro	1,619	1,691	2,153	2,984	3,984	5,584	9,574	15,928	21,247	28,475	32,726
Portugal	PT17	Lisboa	1,530	1,782	2,589	3,662	5,888	10,169	21,828	32,241	44,570	59,233	72,285
Portugal	PT18	Alentejo	539	685	686	1,013	1,588	1,807	2,409	3,651	3,796	5,639	6,290
Spain	ES61	Andalucía	5,495	7,032	8,174	6,775	8,925	12,323	27,412	43,193	60,244	82,347	124,250
Spain	ES24	Aragón	1494	1707	2525	1916	2397	3532	7325	11587	15754	20131	29135
Spain	ES12	Principado de Asturias	1,053	885	1,697	1,445	2,241	3,276	6,770	10,380	12,243	14,538	20,407
Spain	ES53	Illes Balears	458	623	864	866	1,076	1,731	4,511	7,987	12,487	13,954	19,833
Spain	ES70	Canarias	386	548	879	757	1,509	2,313	6,412	12,124	18,047	24,645	36,178
Spain	ES13	Cantabria	485	512	867	787	1,026	1,566	3,262	4,930	6,022	7,986	12,146
Spain	ES42	Castile-La Mancha	2,128	2,251	2,899	2,279	3,338	4,133	7,971	11,714	16,273	21,192	30,289
Spain	ES41	Castile-León	3,362	3,583	4,518	3,465	5,853	7,206	14,064	20,715	27,510	35,152	50,048
Spain	ES51	Cataluña	6,469	7,574	11,516	8,944	10,955	18,575	43,048	68,090	92,315	117,652	172,587
Spain	ES52	Comunidad Valenciana	2,984	3,218	5,102	4,366	5,156	8,581	19,640	33,940	48,386	58,387	88,099

(continued)

Table A.1 (continued)

Country (current borders)	*NUTS codes*	*Region*	*1900*	*1910*	*1925*	*1938*	*1950*	*1960*	*1970*	*1980*	*1990*	*2000*	*2010*
Spain	ES43	Extremadura	1,039	1,226	1,493	1,287	1,773	2,431	4,229	6,151	8,859	10,546	15,807
Spain	ES11	Galicia	1,901	2,370	2,987	2,748	4,259	5,722	12,566	20,659	27,856	32,945	47,984
Spain	ES30	Comunidad de Madrid	2,252	2,525	5,086	4,773	5,953	11,728	31,124	55,615	77,921	113,602	178,627
Spain	ES62	Región de Murcia	634	779	1,207	1,072	1,273	1,850	4,347	7,108	10,461	14,868	23,546
Spain	ES22	Comunidad Foral de Navarra	457	515	864	649	987	1,463	3,372	5,189	7,407	10,934	16,393
Spain	ES21	País Vasco	2,202	1,971	3,440	2,803	4,137	6,788	16,281	22,909	28,903	41,477	60,138
Spain	ES23	La Rioja	365	312	368	324	570	812	1,637	2,605	3,626	4,763	7,080
Sweden	SE11	Stockholm	1,449	2,103	3,391	7,141	9,159	13,864	22,864	25,409	35,518	52,428	71,326
Sweden	SE12	Östra Mellansverige	1,868	2,552	3,267	5,369	7,469	10,570	17,347	20,494	23,695	26,318	33,646
Sweden	SE21	Småland med öarna	1,119	1,563	1,847	2,788	4,353	5,625	9,254	11,555	13,293	14,882	17,859
Sweden	SE22	Sydsverige	1,722	2,637	3,133	4,874	6,476	8,581	14,834	17,408	20,590	24,146	30,520
Sweden	SE23	Västsverige	1,988	2,609	3,922	6,384	9,437	12,067	20,553	24,410	30,571	35,016	45,005
Sweden	SE31	Norra Mellansverige	1,558	1,986	2,514	3,653	5,222	7,155	10,149	12,654	13,884	14,836	17,822
Sweden	SE32	Mellersta Norrland	892	945	1,303	1,839	2,522	3,667	4,414	5,601	6,349	7,051	9,058
Sweden	SE33	Övre Norrland	706	869	1,256	1,773	2,840	4,235	5,232	7,252	8,289	9,062	13,045
Switzerland	CH01	Région lémanique	2,137	2,730	3,480	4,217	6,662	11,190	18,236	21,044	26,922	30,009	38,088
Switzerland	CH02	Espace Mittelland	3,340	4,139	5,582	7,049	11,005	16,461	23,746	25,968	30,310	32,395	37,296
Switzerland	CH03	Nordwestschweiz	1,605	2,054	2,878	3,789	6,109	9,766	16,474	17,977	20,682	24,316	29,441
Switzerland	CH04	Zürich	1,996	2,566	3,694	5,092	8,250	13,590	22,126	25,609	31,363	34,897	42,458
Switzerland	CH05	Ostschweiz	2,194	2,953	3,253	3,926	6,104	8,974	13,772	15,380	18,761	20,627	22,772
Switzerland	CH06	Zentralschweiz	979	1,220	1,573	1,954	3,105	4,800	8,060	9,814	13,571	14,840	17,366
Switzerland	CH07	Ticino	398	516	606	755	1,310	2,013	3,522	4,118	5,292	6,162	7,479

United Kingdom	UKI	London Counties	38,821	41,420	50,338	72,063	69,829	90,169	116,077	114,967	142,099	209,363	297,249
United Kingdom	UKH+UKJ	Rest of South East	26,065	32,307	37,355	57,991	54,495	78,927	112,386	165,472	230,165	305,646	375,813
United Kingdom	UKK	South West	11,092	12,219	13,430	17,183	20,646	26,948	38,365	52,283	73,158	94,597	115,043
United Kingdom	UKG	West Midlands	11,831	13,461	16,409	26,455	32,094	42,716	56,668	61,591	80,152	97,432	109,408
United Kingdom	UKF	East Midlands	9,798	11,183	12,283	15,760	21,374	28,062	35,424	47,707	64,071	78,567	93,157
United Kingdom	UKC+UKD	North	34,569	39,556	43,427	40,955	65,707	79,778	101,145	117,118	140,899	164,085	189,958
United Kingdom	UKE	Yorkshire and Humberside	13,865	15,947	18,693	22,731	29,591	36,463	48,261	58,587	71,343	88,907	102,626
United Kingdom	UKL	Wales	7,579	9,112	10,815	13,559	15,394	20,684	26,074	30,528	40,501	46,532	53,409
United Kingdom	UKM	Scotland	18,671	19,881	23,608	29,220	31,756	40,019	52,300	64,469	81,486	98,011	120,881
United Kingdom	UKN	Northern Ireland	3,832	3,662	4,798	5,053	6,964	8,922	12,261	14,805	20,615	27,913	33,547
Ireland	IE0	Ireland	8,738	8,350	7,680	8,965	10,231	12,127	18,289	29,047	41,459	81,716	99,242
Luxembourg	LU00	Luxembourg	1,277	1,598	1,485	1,977	2,481	3,126	4,418	5,700	8,820	14,422	18,766

Source: See Rosés and Wolf in this book and country chapters for details.

Note: The data for Groningen (NL11) 1980 includes revenue from the exploitation of the large natural gas fields. However, this accrued to the national government, rather than the region (see Chapter 3.8 in this book).

Table A.2 Area (km^2)

Country (current borders)	*NUTS codes*	*Region*	*2010*
Austria	AT11	Burgenland	3,962
Austria	AT21	Carinthia	9,538
Austria	AT12+AT13	Lower Austria	19,601
Austria	AT32	Salzburg	7,156
Austria	AT22	Styria	16,401
Austria	AT33	Tyrol	12,640
Austria	AT31	Upper Austria	11,980
Austria	AT34	Vorarlberg	2,601
Belgium	BE21	Antwerp	2,867
Belgium	BE10+BE24+BE31	Brabant	3,358
Belgium	BE25	West Flanders	3,144
Belgium	BE23	East Flanders	2,982
Belgium	BE32	Hainaut	3,786
Belgium	BE33	Liege	3,862
Belgium	BE22	Limburg	2,422
Belgium	BE34	Luxembourg	4,440
Belgium	BE35	Namur	3,666
Denmark	DK01	Hovedstaden	2,473
Denmark	DK02	Sjælland	7,114
Denmark	DK03	Southern Denmark	12,100
Denmark	DK04	Midtjylland	12,823
Denmark	DK05	Nordjylland	7,843
Finland	FI19	Länsi-Suomi	58,304
Finland	FI1B	Helsinki-Uusimaa	9,131
Finland	FI1C	Etelä-Soumi	31,715
Finland	FI1D	Pohjois-ja Itä-Soumi	203,197
Finland	FI20	Åland	1,553
France	FR10	Île-de-France	12,012
France	FR21	Champagne-Ardenne	25,606
France	FR22	Picardie	19,399
France	FR23	Haute-Normandie	12,318
France	FR24	Centre	39,151
France	FR25	Basse-Normandie	17,589
France	FR26	Bourgogne	31,582
France	FR30	Nord-Pas-de-Calais	12,414
France	FR41	Lorraine	23,547
France	FR42	Alsace	8,280
France	FR43	Franche-Comté	16,202
France	FR51	Pays de la Loire	32,082
France	FR52	Bretagne	27,209
France	FR53	Poitou-Charentes	25,809
France	FR61	Aquitaine	41,309
France	FR62	Midi-Pyrénées	4,5348
France	FR63	Limousin	16,942

France	FR71	Rhône-Alpes	43,698
France	FR72	Auvergne	26,013
France	FR81	Languedoc-Roussillon	27,376
France	FR82	Provence-Alpes-Côte d'Azur	31,400
France	FR83	Corse	8,680
Germany	DE11	Stuttgart, Regierungsbezirk	10,558
Germany	DE12	Karlsruhe, Regierungsbezirk	6,919
Germany	DE13	Freiburg, Regierungsbezirk	9,357
Germany	DE14	Tübingen, Regierungsbezirk	8,918
Germany	DE21	Oberbayern, Regierungsbezirk	17,530
Germany	DE22	Niederbayern, Regierungsbezirk	10,329
Germany	DE23	Oberpfalz, Regierungsbezirk	9,690
Germany	DE24	Oberfranken, Regierungsbezirk	7,232
Germany	DE25	Mittelfranken, Regierungsbezirk	7,245
Germany	DE26	Unterfranken, Regierungsbezirk	8,531
Germany	DE27	Schwaben, Regierungsbezirk	9,994
Germany	DE30	Berlin	892
Germany	DE40	Brandenburg	29,484
Germany	DE50	Bremen	419
Germany	DE60	Hamburg	755
Germany	DE71+DE72	Darmstadt and Giessen	12,826
Germany	DE73	Kassel, Regierungsbezirk	8,289
Germany	DE80	Mecklenburg-Vorpommern	23,194
Germany	DE91+DE92	Statistische Regionen Braunschweig und Hannover	17,148
Germany	DE93	Statistische Region Lüneburg	15,495
Germany	DE94	Statistische Region Weser-Ems	14,971
Germany	DEA1	Düsseldorf, Regierungsbezirk	5291
Germany	DEA2	Köln, Regierungsbezirk	7365
Germany	DEA3	Münster, Regierungsbezirk	6,911
Germany	DEA4	Detmold, Regierungsbezirk	6,523
Germany	DEA5	Arnsberg, Regierungsbezirk	8,008
Germany	DEB1	Statistische Region Koblenz	8,073
Germany	DEB2	Statistische Region Trier	4,924
Germany	DEB3	Statistische Region Rheinhessen-Pfalz	6,851
Germany	DEC0	Saarland	2,569
Germany	DED2	Dresden, NUTS 2 region	7,931
Germany	DED4	Chemnitz, NUTS 2 region	6,524
Germany	DED5	Leipzig, NUTS 2 region	3,965

(continued)

Table A.2 (continued)

Country (current borders)	*NUTS codes*	*Region*	*2010*
Germany	DEE0	Sachsen-Anhalt	20,450
Germany	DEF0	Schleswig-Holstein	15,800
Germany	DEG0	Thüringen	16,173
Italy	ITC1	Piemonte	25,387
Italy	ITC2	Valle d'Aosta/Vallée d'Aoste	3,261
Italy	ITC3	Liguria	5,416
Italy	ITC4	Lombardia	23,864
Italy	ITH1+ITH2	Provincia Autonoma di Bolzano/Bozen-Provincia Autonoma di Trento	13,606
Italy	ITH3	Veneto	18,407
Italy	ITH4	Friuli-Venezia Giulia	7,862
Italy	ITH5	Emilia-Romagna	22,453
Italy	ITI1	Toscana	22,987
Italy	ITI2	Umbria	8,464
Italy	ITI3	Marche	9,401
Italy	ITI4	Lazio	17,232
Italy	ITF1	Abruzzo	10,832
Italy	ITF2	Molise	4,461
Italy	ITF3	Campania	13,671
Italy	ITF4	Puglia	19,541
Italy	ITF5	Basilicata	10,073
Italy	ITF6	Calabria	15,222
Italy	ITG1	Sicilia	25,832
Italy	ITG2	Sardegna	24,100
Netherlands	NL11	Groningen	2,325
Netherlands	NL12	Friesland	3,326
Netherlands	NL13	Drenthe	2,636
Netherlands	NL21	Overijssel	3,323
Netherlands	NL22	Gelderland	4,969
Netherlands	NL31	Utrecht	1,382
Netherlands	NL32	Noordholland	2,664
Netherlands	NL33	Zuidholland	2,806
Netherlands	NL34	Zeeland	1,784
Netherlands	NL41	Noordbrabant	4,914
Netherlands	NL42	Limburg	2,148
Netherlands	NL23	Flevoland (1960–)	1,413
Norway	NO01	Oslo og Akershus	5,372
Norway	NO02	Hedmark og Oppland	52,590
Norway	NO03	Sør-Østlandet	36,613
Norway	NO04	Agder og Rogaland	25,811
Norway	NO05	Vestlandet	49,163
Norway	NO06	Trøndelag	41,254
Norway	NO07	Nord-Norge	112,976
Portugal	PT11	Norte	28,784

Portugal	PT15	Algarve	4,960
Portugal	PT16	Centro	23,692
Portugal	PT17	Lisboa	7,825
Portugal	PT18	Alentejo	23683
Spain	ES61	Andalucía	87,598
Spain	ES24	Aragón	47,720
Spain	ES12	Principado de Asturias	10,604
Spain	ES53	Illes Balears	4,992
Spain	ES70	Canarias	7,447
Spain	ES13	Cantabria	5,321
Spain	ES42	Castile-La Mancha	79,462
Spain	ES41	Castile-León	94,226
Spain	ES51	Cataluña	32,113
Spain	ES52	Comunidad Valenciana	23,255
Spain	ES43	Extremadura	41,635
Spain	ES11	Galicia	29,574
Spain	ES30	Comunidad de Madrid	8,028
Spain	ES62	Región de Murcia	11,313
Spain	ES22	Comunidad Foral de Navarra	10,390
Spain	ES21	País Vasco	7,235
Spain	ES23	La Rioja	5,045
Sweden	SE11	Stockholm	6,519
Sweden	SE12	Östra Mellansverige	38,609
Sweden	SE21	Småland med öarna	33,332
Sweden	SE22	Sydsverige	13,982
Sweden	SE23	Västsverige	29,418
Sweden	SE31	Norra Mellansverige	63,987
Sweden	SE32	Mellersta Norrland	71,028
Sweden	SE33	Övre Norrland	153,439
Switzerland	CH01	Région lémanique	8,718
Switzerland	CH02	Espace Mittelland	10,063
Switzerland	CH03	Nordwestschweiz	1,959
Switzerland	CH04	Zürich	1,729
Switzerland	CH05	Ostschweiz	11,521
Switzerland	CH06	Zentralschweiz	4,483
Switzerland	CH07	Ticino	2,813
United Kingdom	UKI	London Counties	1,572
United Kingdom	UKH+UKJ	Rest of South East	38,215
United Kingdom	UKK	South West	23,800
United Kingdom	UKG	West Midlands	13,000
United Kingdom	UKF	East Midlands	15,627
United Kingdom	UKC+UKD	North	22,757
United Kingdom	UKE	Yorkshire and Humberside	15,420
United Kingdom	UKL	Wales	20,779
United Kingdom	UKM	Scotland	78,387
United Kingdom	UKN	Northern Ireland	13,843
Ireland	IE0	Ireland	70,273
Luexmbourg	LU00	Luxembourg	2,586

Source: See Chapter 2 in this book, and country chapters for details.

Table A.3 Population ('000s)

Country (current borders)	*NUTS codes*	*Region*	*1900*	*1910*	*1925*	*1938*	*1950*	*1960*	*1970*	*1980*	*1990*	*2000*	*2010*
Austria	AT11	Burgenland	292.426	292.007	288.1214	304.6225	276.1796	271.71	272.907	269.843	271.133	276.083	284.042
Austria	AT21	Carinthia	343.531	371.372	375.891	418.8435	474.839	494.4073	525.335	535.647	546.363	560.129	557.497
Austria	AT12+AT13	Lower Austria	3079.643	3508.868	3361.853	3391.798	3017.072	3003.989	3039.423	2964.116	2961.502	3088.502	3303.018
Austria	AT32	Salzburg	192.763	214.737	225.8725	255.2136	327.2837	346.71	399.596	439.079	476.289	513.853	527.114
Austria	AT22	Styria	889.017	957.61	986.055	1028.019	1109.51	1137.228	1192.522	1188.446	1170.631	1182.684	1205.514
Austria	AT33	Tyrol	266.374	304.713	318.4337	363.6581	427.5325	461.5354	539.484	583.569	621.28	669.479	704.976
Austria	AT31	Upper Austria	810.854	853.595	882.5902	912.1708	1108.895	1132.221	1225.008	1265.019	1304.058	1371.579	1410.014
Austria	AT34	Vorarlberg	129.237	145.408	141.9807	161.7674	193.6876	224.2197	272.81	303.714	326.594	349.257	368.894
Belgium	BE21	Antwerp	833.5817	968.677	1118.456	1243.529	1314.447	1431.131	1533.249	1567.248	1603.754	1644.845	1754.818
Belgium	BE10+BE24+BE31	Brabant	1281.144	1469.677	1624.8	1767.262	1838.318	1977.639	2176.373	2218.958	2248.342	2335.997	2567.189
Belgium	BE25	West Flanders	806.7407	874.135	894.645	962.2656	1011.564	1063.625	1054.429	1078.217	1106.145	1128.926	1162.167
Belgium	BE23	East Flanders	1034.694	1120.335	1141.914	1192.286	1228.805	1268.016	1310.117	1329.987	1337.256	1362.407	1439.079
Belgium	BE32	Hainaut	1136.683	1232.867	1260.785	1243.904	1229.915	1247.12	1317.453	1301.697	1283.162	1280.52	1313.582
Belgium	BE33	Liege	837.1234	888.341	951.1301	971.0598	972.2186	1000.639	1008.905	1000.098	1002.519	1020.151	1072.444
Belgium	BE22	Limburg	245.3799	275.691	342.1169	407.6383	482.8266	565.5869	652.547	712.2871	749.2557	792.1782	841.563
Belgium	BE34	Luxembourg	220.3469	231.215	223.45	222.3297	214.1957	216.6055	217.31	221.868	232.5166	247.9404	270.188
Belgium	BE35	Namur	351.0879	362.846	357.6729	355.9993	358.9078	368.4626	380.561	405.0762	423.1872	444.5658	474.558
Denmark	DK01	Hovedstaden	618.99	770.472	985.4794	1165.622	1396.528	1551.841	1645.42	1591.303	1547.873	1627.68	1691.28
Denmark	DK02	Sjælland	446.084	484.968	553.5424	552.9952	587.119	601.339	659.404	739.931	767.9265	796.8624	818.8884
Denmark	DK03	Southern Denmark	372.749	556.181	765.4531	948.7548	972.263	1033.307	1172.016	1241.312	1152.555	1177.642	1200.238
Denmark	DK04	Midtjylland	523.108	593.882	660.5317	674.0089	842.19	896.995	988.626	1068.184	1144.296	1196.881	1257.192
Denmark	DK05	Nordjylland	319.479	351.573	410.8263	441.3405	483.175	501.774	455.69	744.086	572.7143	578.8603	579.6397
Finland	FI19	Länsi-Suomi	814.051	827.043	874.1667	966.628	1177.732	1240.189	1237.4	1268.355	1300.085	1317.441	1357.6
Finland	FI1B	Helsinki-Uusimaa	202.015	262.046	333.7681	475.531	574.025	747.268	917.149	1025.733	1147.173	1304.595	1524.9
Finland	FI1C	Etelä-Soumi	601.271	671.305	721.5474	802.302	1008.7	1083.685	1132.88	1168.269	1204.764	1224.015	1156.1
Finland	FI1D	Pohjois-ja Itä-Soumi	777.455	805.092	905.3098	1026.342	1239.853	1354.331	1290.242	1305.951	1321.852	1309.288	1296.8

Finland	FI20	Åland	24.841	21.356	20.06079	21.196	21.69	20.981	20.666	22.5492	24.604	25.776	27.9
France	FR10	Île-de-France	4608.081	5264.963	6071.763	6924.845	7317.228	8470.015	9878.565	10073.06	10660.55	11030.99	11852.85
France	FR21	Champagne-Ardenne	1233.278	1212.756	1097.37	1136.376	1133.398	1205.836	1336.832	1345.935	1347.848	1341.788	1336.053
France	FR22	Picardie	1480.203	1461.666	1300.49	1370.836	1385.586	1481.41	1678.644	1740.321	1810.687	1862.917	1918.155
France	FR23	Haute-Normandie	1184.45	1199.517	1194.65	1233.953	1274.198	1397.786	1595.695	1655.362	1737.247	1785.494	1839.393
France	FR24	Centre	1895.487	1875.816	1726.109	1731.228	1757.735	1858.145	2152.5	2264.164	2371.036	2450.697	2556.835
France	FR25	Basse-Normandie	1235.512	1184.823	1094.392	1128.917	1164.713	1208.184	1306.152	1350.979	1391.318	1426.975	1475.684
France	FR26	Bourgogne	1629.164	1564.057	1412.877	1392.743	1374.509	1439.388	1570.943	1596.054	1609.653	1613.01	1642.734
France	FR30	Nord-Pas-de-Calais	2799.527	3009.64	2953.326	3286.803	3376.272	3660.314	3913.773	3932.939	3965.058	4000.697	4042.015
France	FR41	Lorraine	2337.327	2587.273	1759.712	1907.561	1956.039	2194.151	2330.822	2319.905	2305.726	2314.009	2350.657
France	FR42	Alsace	1141.341	1218.491	1153.632	1209.6	1217.581	1318.07	1517.33	1566.048	1624.372	1744.57	1852.325
France	FR43	Franche-Comté	924.8184	913.1388	843.5824	854.542	856.345	928.573	1060.317	1084.049	1097.276	1122.071	1173.44
France	FR51	Pays de la Loire	2345.684	2335.433	2167.781	2216.557	2320.177	2462.418	2767.163	2930.398	3059.112	3254.805	3601.113
France	FR52	Bretagne	2548.773	2596.857	2408.456	2367.193	2338.803	2396.582	2595.431	2707.886	2795.638	2933.229	3217.767
France	FR53	Poitou-Charentes	1486.642	1469.038	1344.739	1357.051	1392.853	1450.495	1528.118	1568.23	1595.109	1652.133	1777.773
France	FR61	Aquitaine	2272.011	2258.206	2139.119	2180.366	2208.898	2312.464	2550.346	2656.544	2795.83	2938.221	3254.233
France	FR62	Midi-Pyrénées	2269.423	2152.18	1943.09	1955.42	1975.391	2061.347	2268.298	2325.319	2430.663	2581.819	2903.42
France	FR63	Limousin	972.964	961.7575	834.2402	782.1507	739.929	733.955	738.726	737.153	722.85	713.627	741.072
France	FR71	Rhône-Alpes	3578.467	3580.083	3533.158	3646.368	3629.722	4018.598	4780.684	5015.947	5350.701	5700.637	6283.541
France	FR72	Auvergne	1511.237	1464.043	1325.735	1292.28	1246.711	1273.162	1330.479	1332.678	1321.214	1312.624	1350.682
France	FR81	Languedoc-Roussillon	1534.988	1530.637	1521.966	1517.579	1449.101	1554.646	1789.474	1926.514	2114.985	2327.395	2670.046
France	FR82	Provence-Alpes-Côte d'Azur	1773.88	1927.72	2097.771	2398.728	2414.978	2818.992	3675.73	3965.209	4257.907	4541.959	4916.069
France	FR83	Corse	295	290.961	287.9729	277.6352	246.995	180.862	225.562	240.178	250.371	264.7174	314.486
Germany	DE11	Stuttgart, Regierungsbezirk	1886.238	2095.911	2278.476	1827.637	3291.293	4105.496	4724.371	3476.4	3609.977	3917.305	4000.848

(continued)

Table A.3 (continued)

Country (current borders)	*NUTS codes*	*Region*	*1900*	*1910*	*1925*	*1938*	*1950*	*1960*	*1970*	*1980*	*1990*	*2000*	*2010*
Germany	DE12	Karlsruhe, Regierungsbezirk	1206.889	1469.691	1613.755	1294.443	1990.085	2293.486	2581.075	2392.4	2484.034	2676.257	2740.503
Germany	DE13	Freiburg, Regierungsbezirk	1296.295	1440.169	1511.491	1212.414	1809.13	2197.724	2524.413	1860.5	1934.781	2125.364	2196.018
Germany	DE14	Tübingen, Regierungsbezirk	1148.091	1254.936	1305.75	1047.383	1599.812	1889.635	2191.619	1506.4	1589.914	1757.006	1807.552
Germany	DE21	Oberbayern, Regierungsbezirk	1249.138	1467.001	1664.148	1815.76	2456.185	2754.704	3242.487	3642.6	3721.332	4033.643	4346.465
Germany	DE22	Niederbayern, Regierungsbezirk	682.4846	711.1844	755.769	824.6233	1081.052	961.593	1012.34	996.5	1057.436	1170.17	1189.194
Germany	DE23	Oberpfalz, Regierungsbezirk	556.5616	587.3111	629.282	686.6127	896.904	889.979	955.529	965.7	991.309	1074.338	1081.417
Germany	DE24	Oberfranken, Regierungsbezirk	673.5214	736.2698	757.515	826.5284	1115.793	1087.146	1116.345	1052.4	1055.822	1114.155	1076.4
Germany	DE25	Mittelfranken, Regierungsbezirk	787.3446	924.1447	998.386	1089.344	1284.269	1374.481	1484.619	1518.4	1566.07	1683.282	1710.145
Germany	DE26	Unterfranken, Regierungsbezirk	657.3886	714.6299	762.744	832.2338	1038.136	1089.61	1181.221	1192.7	1234.906	1333.803	1321.957
Germany	DE27	Schwaben, Regierungsbezirk	753.5326	825.4245	880.015	960.1887	1312.127	1357.966	1486.845	1528.7	1593.863	1745.576	1784.753
Germany	DE30	Berlin	2605.377	3632.074	4024.165	4321.521	3335.952	3269.183	3207.786	3051.429	3400.426	3386.667	3442.675
Germany	DE40	Brandenburg	2552.762	3373.285	1946.157	2186.361	2663	2626.318	2674.277	2707.386	2641.152	2601.207	2511.525
Germany	DE50	Bremen	221.8439	298.0413	410.911	445.067	558.619	706.366	722.732	694.6	673.68	663.065	661.716
Germany	DE60	Hamburg	969.1296	1255.932	1483.498	1698.388	1605.606	1832.345	1793.823	1648.8	1626.222	1704.735	1774.224
Germany	DE71+DE72	Darmstadt and Giessen	1791.01	2168.722	2316.618	2967.773	3062.847	3558.03	4032.708	4303.553	4472.92	4782.357	4837.21
Germany	DE73	Kassel, Regierungsbezirk	709.4323	789.5023	867.234	1110.996	1260.954	1256.353	1348.997	1400.532	1187.7	1269.109	1224.741

Germany	DE80	Mecklenburg-Vorpommern	1357.095	1431.255	1515.843	1772.639	2253	2106.704	2095.066	2100.594	1963.909	1789.322	1651.216
Germany	DE91+DE92	Statistische Regionen Braunschweig und Hannover	1676.2	1900.737	1977.388	2208.061	3274.481	3252.692	3362.615	3688.6	3646.604	3822.393	3759.16
Germany	DE93	Statistische Region Lüneburg	807.6935	915.6151	875.841	1110.115	1646.263	1534.058	1690.585	1450.8	1467.422	1660.653	1693.654
Germany	DE94	Statistische Region Weser-Ems	882.5786	1008.763	1161.736	1265.46	1876.635	1854.105	2028.958	2106.5	2169.774	2415.714	2476.001
Germany	DEA1	Düsseldorf, Regierungsbezirk	2517.703	3419.393	3866.119	4082.607	4301.897	5375.672	5625.893	5209.4	5167.713	5264.468	5172.839
Germany	DEA2	Köln, Regierungsbezirk	1557.542	1868.706	2123.412	2242.315	2443.262	3062.711	3428.638	3913.8	3963.108	4263.675	4383.044
Germany	DEA3	Münster, Regierungsbezirk	728.568	1018.851	1491.793	1598.436	1909.791	2259.344	2402.124	2412.4	2437.782	2608.779	2597.636
Germany	DEA4	Detmold, Regierungsbezirk	759.9338	879.2634	970.219	1152.065	1499.526	1606.031	1736.913	1814.3	1849.741	2048.62	2043.212
Germany	DEA5	Arnsberg, Regierungsbezirk	1721.076	2367.964	2512.855	3403.116	3041.7	3597.92	3720.55	3690.7	3685.24	3814.258	3676.032
Germany	DEB1	Statistische Region Koblenz	882.5575	973.8696	1006.045	1062.38	1139.663	1267.645	1354.269	1362.6	1377.003	1516.237	1490.711
Germany	DEB2	Statistische Region Trier	352.479	387.9451	417.135	440.493	428.774	459.282	482.412	470.6	477.962	511.548	513.794
Germany	DEB3	Statistische Region Rheinhessen-Pfalz	1059.953	1197.328	1315.923	1433.747	1436.315	1690.189	1808.756	1805.4	1846.692	2002.988	2008.17
Germany	DEC0	Saarland	543.2208	710.3502	805.049	823.978	955.413	1072.6	1119.742	1068	1064.907	1071.501	1022.585
Germany	DED2	Dresden, NUTS 2 region	1502.295	1778.254	1830.827	1901.609	1981	1885.214	1873.06	1806.401	2468.79	1724.703	1631.486
Germany	DED4	Chemnitz, NUTS 2 region	1830.444	2106.313	2162.97	2258.826	2334	2112.057	2047.854	1930.087	1183.302	1638.9	1540

(continued)

Table A.3 (continued)

Country (current borders)	NUTS codes	Region	1900	1910	1925	1938	1950	1960	1970	1980	1990	2000	2010
Germany	DED5	Leipzig, NUTS 2 region	1022.033	1229.517	1307.312	1357.854	1652	1518.693	1490.611	1412.037	1248.583	1096.1	997.2
Germany	DEE0	Sachsen-Anhalt	2672.48	2924.473	3058.253	3339.73	3641	3347.199	3242.599	3101.495	2964.971	2648.737	2356.219
Germany	DEF0	Schleswig-Holstein	1209.858	1387.507	1469.571	1538.888	2594.648	2317.441	2494.104	2605.2	2594.608	2777.275	2832.027
Germany	DEG0	Thüringen	1881.001	2116.362	1905.341	2034.454	2693	2519.619	2547.007	2529.009	2683.877	2449.082	2249.882
Italy	ITC1	Piemonte	3244.157	3353.554	3311.08	3417.361	3544.636	3906.575	4401.155	4468.793	4316.112	4233.815	4451.8
Italy	ITC2	Valle d'Aosta/Vallée d'Aoste	80.428	77.87	78.767	82.401	95.924	101.509	110.107	112.337	116.355	118.795	128
Italy	ITC3	Liguria	1077.806	1199.669	1329.336	1470.042	1573.79	1738.65	1856.756	1825.847	1695.674	1591.078	1616.4
Italy	ITC4	Lombardia	4286.094	4791.715	5104.327	5742.412	6518.421	7276.65	8376.23	8812.882	8859.334	9058.026	9872
Italy	ITH1+ITH2	Provincia Autonoma di Bolzano/ Bozen-Provincia Autonoma di Trento	515.887	558.629	687.346	687.804	739.394	778.352	840.552	892.219	925.04	949.615	1032.6
Italy	ITH3	Veneto	2539.512	2897.396	3235.55	3502.585	3834.857	3776.874	4097.872	4338.389	4407.173	4554.229	4925.1
Italy	ITH4	Friuli-Venezia Giulia	876.56	1109.814	1002.043	1127.245	1197.133	1168.689	1236.947	1264.846	1214.097	1186.095	1234.9
Italy	ITH5	Emilia-Romagna	2504.503	2747.184	3027.695	3283.666	3519.58	3615.911	3829.607	3967.397	3953.188	4048.293	4414
Italy	ITI1	Toscana	2493.765	2630.978	2760.312	2929.468	3165.016	3278.532	3480.831	3604.59	3590.946	3556.81	3740
Italy	ITI2	Umbria	571.223	583.622	629.858	716.284	803.762	780.835	773.707	805.772	820.575	845.198	903.6
Italy	ITI3	Marche	1059.769	1092.543	1147.661	1249.66	1348.812	1314.595	1346.907	1404.802	1430.345	1468.091	1562.4
Italy	ITI4	Lazio	1638.861	1765.762	2004.526	2642.109	3383.883	3932.433	4681.423	5029.491	5175.819	5187.981	5705.4
Italy	ITF1	Abruzzo	1010.179	1013.543	1028.346	1159.325	1227.791	1135.463	1121.256	1189.997	1234.932	1252.963	1340.6
Italy	ITF2	Molise	366.231	349.392	333.52	386.825	392.321	337.7	302.863	313.17	320.101	311.964	320
Italy	ITF3	Campania	2853.311	2991.546	3210.686	3638.749	4311.398	4628.326	4951.742	5363.873	5583.27	5688.534	5829.5
Italy	ITF4	Puglia	1980.644	2152.249	2319.802	2615.557	3193.164	3298.104	3479.561	3778.666	3959.081	3954.798	4087.6
Italy	ITF5	Basilicata	480.258	473.713	468.299	531.587	616.009	603.983	564.178	576.412	587.986	575.104	588.2
Italy	ITF6	Calabria	1368.934	1401.24	1511.482	1720.794	1982.473	1941.77	1868.978	1960.422	1988.074	1955.841	2010.4

Italy	ITG1	Sicilia	3526.517	3669.873	4059.208	3928.799	4440.936	4611.976	4580.987	4796.847	4912.895	4926.012	5047
Italy	ITG2	Sardegna	791.018	851.854	863.697	1024.518	1269.438	1361.923	1434.264	1562.584	1628.851	1610.987	1673.9
Netherlands	NL11	Groningen	299.6032	328.0463	377.2964	414.72	454.4368	474.657	517.305	551.315	553.862	562.646	576.668
Netherlands	NL12	Friesland	340.2634	359.5535	391.3293	414.72	455.405	478.206	521.751	578.203	599.151	624.5	646.305
Netherlands	NL13	Drenthe	148.5446	173.3187	214.1644	241.92	281.0427	311.196	366.59	415.978	441.028	469.806	490.981
Netherlands	NL21	Overijssel	333.3394	382.8816	473.5981	561.6	662.3603	770.848	920.882	1009.651	1020.424	1077.625	1130.345
Netherlands	NL22	Gelderland	566.5513	639.6046	771.8829	907.2	1066.506	1266.885	1505.76	1680.629	1804.209	1919.158	1998.936
Netherlands	NL31	Utrecht	251.035	288.5422	368.9557	466.56	568.6205	676.889	801.285	885.756	1015.515	1107.849	1220.91
Netherlands	NL32	Noordholland	968.135	1107.698	1385.641	1650.24	1810.52	2054.509	2244.456	2299.175	2376.015	2518.354	2669.084
Netherlands	NL33	Zuidholland	1144.453	1390.75	1790.937	2116.8	2335.869	2697.894	2968.67	3063.625	3219.839	3397.744	3505.611
Netherlands	NL34	Zeeland	216.2959	232.516	247.0865	250.56	260.0972	283.721	305.754	344.388	355.947	371.866	381.409
Netherlands	NL41	Noordbrabant	553.8443	623.0816	802.5396	1010.88	1232.754	1484.671	1787.783	2030.92	2189.481	2356.004	2444.158
Netherlands	NL42	Limburg	281.9352	332.0084	483.013	604.8	724.7525	882.386	998.57	1065.483	1103.96	1141.192	1122.701
Netherlands	NL23	Flevoland (1960–)	-	-	-	-	-	-	40.22	111.434	211.507	317.206	387.881
Norway	NO01	Oslo og Akershus	343.854	369.876	463.5361	536.7634	617.058	698.459	788.5914	821.545	872.867	974.519	1123.359
Norway	NO02	Hedmark og Oppland	242.462	253.791	287.0859	303.8835	333.488	343.936	352.1127	366.983	369.234	369.804	375.925
Norway	NO03	Sør-Østlandet	453.168	493.109	559.1801	571.8616	632.572	690.951	746.7856	793.603	822.87	862.841	928.852
Norway	NO04	Agder og Rogaland	289.094	299.563	326.1112	338.8744	384.126	421.819	468.9037	527.815	576.659	631.079	706.823
Norway	NO05	Vestlandet	433.181	457.535	508.2353	533.8819	600.01	651.02	694.8518	731.516	754.01	785.966	835.517
Norway	NO06	Trøndelag	218.815	233.254	263.384	278.2354	307.618	327.187	349.4749	368.942	377.202	389.96	422.102
Norway	NO07	Nord-Norge	259.458	284.654	322.9067	356.8656	403.674	437.182	455.6661	468.496	460.274	464.328	465.621
Portugal	PT11	Norte	2173.801	2410.565	2600.452	2960.192	3230.54	3392.392	3253.099	3602.016	3596.048	3654.307	3720.078
Portugal	PT15	Algarve	230.484	273.786	295.978	319.628	328.229	314.762	268.806	322.647	333.5423	374.9418	445.1529
Portugal	PT16	Centro	1301.444	1526.357	1721.719	1938.417	2103.326	2141.269	2016.725	2166.947	2340.418	2416.879	2463.569
Portugal	PT17	Lisboa	613.689	832.497	1138.105	1325.458	1549.208	1762.038	2048.887	2715.294	2672.517	2864.096	3083.928
Portugal	PT18	Alentejo	396.317	481.287	587.766	677.349	713.333	684.884	529.505	512.618	459.6754	438.2772	431.4716

(continued)

Table A.3 (continued)

Country (current borders)	*NUTS codes*	*Region*	*1900*	*1910*	*1925*	*1938*	*1950*	*1960*	*1970*	*1980*	*1990*	*2000*	*2010*
Spain	ES61	Andalucía	3549.337	3805.009	4395.163	4991.57	5613.166	5881.804	5987.387	6393.182	6959.406	7372.012	8393.235
Spain	ES24	Aragón	912.711	952.743	1014.211	1034.058	1083.763	1103.839	1147.401	1191.609	1198.803	1194.832	1346.114
Spain	ES12	Principado de Asturias	627.069	685.131	767.4133	832.2226	890.398	984.7388	1048.951	1120.176	1105.528	1075.943	1082.845
Spain	ES53	Illes Balears	311.649	326.023	351.9515	391.7275	417.096	446.3302	528.5692	642.5987	711.9749	862.129	1109.381
Spain	ES70	Canarias	358.564	444.016	504.0452	642.7125	802.899	942.452	1135.103	1353.992	1499.731	1748.822	2121.888
Spain	ES13	Cantabria	276.003	302.956	345.4268	384.9769	402.974	431.3344	466.6762	510.0123	530.1813	534.383	592.405
Spain	ES42	Castile-La Mancha	1386.153	1536.575	1733.813	1884.445	2047.23	1978.654	1745.086	1656.658	1673.663	1744.658	2105.941
Spain	ES41	Castile-León	2302.417	2363.118	2406.348	2626.776	2867.134	2853.909	2672.053	2585.575	2566.947	2479.274	2558.061
Spain	ES51	Cataluña	1966.382	2084.868	2558.28	2818.781	3199.174	3897.143	5019.536	5870.078	6098.287	6311.684	7523.817
Spain	ES52	Comunidad Valenciana	1587.533	1704.127	1819.556	2081.065	2295.319	2498.51	3039.296	3594.177	3875.134	4161.669	5111.737
Spain	ES43	Extremadura	882.41	990.991	1102.338	1200.721	1357.716	1372.266	1178.226	1077.952	1071.439	1071.401	1107.68
Spain	ES11	Galicia	1980.515	2063.589	2176.617	2488.08	2685.499	2637.3	2674.108	2796.128	2761.486	2732.414	2796.086
Spain	ES30	Comunidad de Madrid	775.034	878.641	1215.548	1496.102	1812.407	2570.141	3673.305	4602.28	4965.247	5288.921	6470.099
Spain	ES62	Región de Murcia	577.987	615.105	642.035	695.5213	751.289	798.263	834.5192	939.1842	1046.81	1169.853	1465.85
Spain	ES22	Comunidad Foral de Navarra	307.669	312.235	337.7842	352.1544	381.041	405.7334	461.4655	504.4579	522.3595	550.01	639.109
Spain	ES21	País Vasco	603.596	673.788	826.8863	913.3257	1033.192	1352.626	1827.155	2131.492	2125.876	2100.038	2180.978
Spain	ES23	La Rioja	189.376	188.235	198.2903	215.1485	229.616	230.6094	235.8058	251.5262	264.5481	267.289	322.518
Sweden	SE11	Stockholm	473.476	571.504	713.0454	878.163	1101.017	1271.014	1478.012	1528.2	1641.669	1823.21	2054
Sweden	SE12	Östra Mellansverige	913.935	963.859	1019.246	1042.903	1166.712	1248.424	1385.908	1422.804	1458.482	1492.078	1570
Sweden	SE21	Småland med öarna	642.566	655.765	674.5616	679.944	724.85	734.023	768.133	773.774	784.382	780.523	812
Sweden	SE22	Sydsverige	774.772	834.88	888.4006	923.394	987.157	1026.947	1137.352	1177.021	1219.151	1279.816	1396
Sweden	SE23	Västsverige	999.446	1057.47	1140.065	1206.58	1327.63	1420.296	1569.406	1637.301	1712.891	1786.294	1879

Sweden	SE31	Norra Mellansverige	710.04	747.8	795.325	790.308	833.411	870.367	855.203	865.058	861.471	832.524	827
Sweden	SE32	Mellersta Norrland	343.702	368.627	405.8564	414.196	427.813	425.475	398.699	402.869	396.881	376.469	370
Sweden	SE33	Övre Norrland	278.504	322.498	384.0419	435.944	473.239	501.421	488.503	510.91	515.703	511.878	508
Switzerland	CH01	Région lémanique	528.426	600.744	805.996	666.572	739.681	866.529	1050.013	1096.494	1230.823	1294.974	1462.21
Switzerland	CH02	Espace Mittelland	944.425	1035.632	1079.415	1153.813	1259.298	1397.166	1556.911	1538.724	1633.657	1656.109	1741.923
Switzerland	CH03	Nordwestschweiz	387.222	443.04	463.874	534.883	604.829	734.81	873.118	877.179	940.407	987.699	1060.753
Switzerland	CH04	Zürich	431.036	503.915	538.602	674.505	777.002	952.304	1107.788	1122.839	1179.044	1198.569	1351.297
Switzerland	CH05	Ostschweiz	610.669	706.927	705.56	699.252	752.487	821.359	902.552	907.017	987.52	1041.863	1094.202
Switzerland	CH06	Zentralschweiz	275.027	306.869	323.869	374.796	406.64	461.327	533.943	557.808	620.055	676.732	739.701
Switzerland	CH07	Ticino	138.638	156.166	155.7005	161.1524	175.055	195.566	245.458	265.899	282.181	308.498	335.72
United Kingdom	UKI	London Counties	5982.377	6440.685	6882.012	7627.588	7219.78	7171.422	7423.367	6688.422	6858.882	7277.321	8067.753
United Kingdom	UKH+UKJ	Rest of South East	5601.998	6273.539	6996.056	7793.114	9142.235	10273.98	11243.23	11978.34	11937.6	13101.1	14368.51
United Kingdom	UKK	South West	2601.376	2718.658	2806.072	2912.726	3312.081	3483.646	3847.798	4280.702	4571.629	4894.55	5251.731
United Kingdom	UKG	West Midlands	2984.465	3245.012	3595.579	3921.161	4422.511	4722.752	5073.199	5134.969	5093.467	5249.181	5567.462
United Kingdom	UKF	East Midlands	2274.252	2493.503	2686.299	2908.713	3196.447	3402.685	3613.83	3790.186	3908.171	4146.193	4495.754
United Kingdom	UKC+UKD	North	7713.507	8451.938	9050.916	9306.515	9516.863	9727.209	9939.681	9549.091	9198.798	9237.265	9607.903
United Kingdom	UKE	Yorkshire and Humberside	3356.992	3698.19	3961.242	4378.91	4349.296	4438.485	4613.254	4830.964	4802.236	4947.748	5250.943
United Kingdom	UKL	Wales	2012.876	2376.645	2631.035	2550.028	2598.675	2639.453	2722.359	2784.513	2809.721	2893.831	3047.028
United Kingdom	UKM	Scotland	4472.103	4731.204	4866.652	4815.509	5096.415	5170.991	5223.98	5140.474	4978.758	5051.935	5271.585
United Kingdom	UKN	Northern Ireland	1236.952	1249.166	1254.474	1281.874	1370.921	1419.535	1524.584	1512.489	1563.857	1673.366	1797.893
Ireland	IE0	Ireland	3221.823	3189.981	3142.808	2971.277	2962.157	2832.253	2961.857	3393.793	3517.4	3842.924	4508.345
Luxembourg	LU00	Luxembourg	235.954	259.891	270	299.5	295.587	313.968	339.15	364.15	383	439	498

Source: See Chapter 2 in this book, and country chapters for details.

Table A.4 Share of agriculture in total employment

Country (current borders)	*NUTS codes*	*Region*	*1900*	*1910*	*1925*	*1938*	*1950*	*1960*	*1970*	*1980*	*1990*	*2000*	*2010*
Austria	AT11	Burgenland	0.766	0.742	0.686	0.638	0.631	0.503	0.288	0.153	0.087	0.078	0.055
Austria	AT21	Carinthia	0.635	0.574	0.531	0.498	0.375	0.267	0.146	0.086	0.060	0.064	0.064
Austria	AT12+AT13	Lower Austria	0.233	0.208	0.198	0.190	0.215	0.158	0.107	0.070	0.050	0.049	0.037
Austria	AT32	Salzburg	0.522	0.478	0.445	0.420	0.313	0.231	0.131	0.076	0.052	0.047	0.037
Austria	AT22	Styria	0.645	0.602	0.540	0.491	0.433	0.333	0.215	0.131	0.090	0.077	0.059
Austria	AT33	Tyrol	0.635	0.561	0.476	0.412	0.365	0.263	0.127	0.067	0.043	0.046	0.049
Austria	AT31	Upper Austria	0.580	0.555	0.521	0.494	0.392	0.299	0.192	0.116	0.077	0.065	0.059
Austria	AT34	Vorarlberg	0.376	0.345	0.322	0.305	0.261	0.155	0.067	0.035	0.025	0.019	0.029
Belgium	BE21	Antwerp	0.258	0.176	0.156	0.137	0.094	0.055	0.027	0.022	0.018	0.016	0.011
Belgium	BE10+BE24+BE31	Brabant	0.246	0.174	0.140	0.117	0.078	0.046	0.024	0.018	0.011	0.008	0.005
Belgium	BE25	West Flanders	0.419	0.354	0.261	0.213	0.169	0.120	0.076	0.061	0.048	0.040	0.028
Belgium	BE23	East Flanders	0.361	0.293	0.242	0.208	0.155	0.111	0.065	0.051	0.032	0.027	0.018
Belgium	BE32	Hainaut	0.178	0.142	0.108	0.100	0.084	0.068	0.042	0.035	0.025	0.020	0.014
Belgium	BE33	Liege	0.157	0.117	0.113	0.113	0.092	0.070	0.046	0.034	0.023	0.018	0.012
Belgium	BE22	Limburg	0.544	0.489	0.405	0.330	0.204	0.119	0.052	0.035	0.038	0.032	0.022
Belgium	BE34	Luxembourg	0.542	0.461	0.437	0.406	0.358	0.281	0.174	0.120	0.078	0.060	0.042
Belgium	BE35	Namur	0.319	0.237	0.206	0.190	0.169	0.132	0.080	0.057	0.040	0.032	0.021
Denmark	DK01	Hovedstaden	0.106	0.053	0.061	0.064	0.038	0.039	0.020	0.006	0.010	0.009	0.004
Denmark	DK02	Sjælland	0.555	0.248	0.325	0.397	0.440	0.306	0.139	0.026	0.056	0.041	0.034
Denmark	DK03	Southern Denmark	0.486	0.219	0.293	0.356	0.391	0.281	0.155	0.029	0.078	0.057	0.041
Denmark	DK04	Midtjylland	0.534	0.238	0.318	0.373	0.398	0.295	0.169	0.029	0.077	0.054	0.036
Denmark	DK05	Nordjylland	0.594	0.267	0.363	0.433	0.475	0.351	0.188	0.034	0.088	0.058	0.049
Finland	FI19	Länsi-Suomi	0.702	0.799	0.767	0.689	0.498	0.384	0.233	0.150	0.061	0.013	0.010
Finland	FI1B	Helsinki-Uusimaa	0.378	0.483	0.355	0.260	0.168	0.100	0.047	0.098	0.111	0.116	0.093
Finland	FI1C	Etelä-Soumi	0.639	0.738	0.650	0.555	0.370	0.268	0.152	0.144	0.110	0.089	0.071
Finland	FI1D	Pohjois-ja Itä-Soumi	0.818	0.899	0.864	0.820	0.645	0.544	0.353	0.299	0.208	0.150	0.120
Finland	FI20	Åland	0.561	0.776	0.818	0.711	0.569	0.411	0.239	0.198	0.129	0.089	0.068

France	FR10	Île-de-France	0.079	0.067	0.044	0.028	0.032	0.018	0.012	0.009	0.004	0.004	0.002
France	FR21	Champagne-Ardenne	0.401	0.382	0.334	0.261	0.295	0.220	0.151	0.127	0.081	0.070	0.060
France	FR22	Picardie	0.368	0.396	0.310	0.284	0.317	0.211	0.127	0.103	0.051	0.040	0.029
France	FR23	Haute-Normandie	0.308	0.238	0.253	0.230	0.238	0.171	0.101	0.077	0.036	0.026	0.019
France	FR24	Centre	0.564	0.543	0.539	0.440	0.438	0.312	0.178	0.131	0.060	0.045	0.032
France	FR25	Basse-Normandie	0.560	0.537	0.543	0.481	0.492	0.414	0.277	0.230	0.099	0.071	0.050
France	FR26	Bourgogne	0.563	0.546	0.515	0.373	0.396	0.290	0.172	0.135	0.069	0.060	0.048
France	FR30	Nord-Pas-de-Calais	0.225	0.188	0.169	0.115	0.141	0.104	0.066	0.059	0.031	0.023	0.015
France	FR41	Lorraine	0.335	0.293	0.248	0.158	0.166	0.111	0.066	0.056	0.031	0.024	0.018
France	FR42	Alsace	0.387	0.373	0.318	0.197	0.249	0.151	0.072	0.050	0.023	0.020	0.020
France	FR43	Franche-Comté	0.541	0.488	0.450	0.355	0.333	0.224	0.122	0.093	0.049	0.038	0.027
France	FR51	Pays de la Loire	0.597	0.569	0.563	0.465	0.488	0.381	0.240	0.193	0.092	0.065	0.045
France	FR52	Bretagne	0.655	0.643	0.649	0.544	0.547	0.443	0.282	0.232	0.106	0.073	0.050
France	FR53	Poitou-Charentes	0.595	0.529	0.637	0.461	0.500	0.389	0.243	0.193	0.102	0.075	0.053
France	FR61	Aquitaine	0.599	0.582	0.573	0.409	0.464	0.344	0.214	0.171	0.090	0.071	0.051
France	FR62	Midi-Pyrénées	0.616	0.569	0.630	0.452	0.506	0.386	0.241	0.183	0.089	0.063	0.041
France	FR63	Limousin	0.665	0.659	0.683	0.517	0.564	0.441	0.287	0.224	0.100	0.075	0.056
France	FR71	Rhône-Alpes	0.458	0.434	0.397	0.268	0.292	0.187	0.102	0.070	0.033	0.026	0.017
France	FR72	Auvergne	0.628	0.597	0.606	0.436	0.474	0.358	0.226	0.175	0.090	0.069	0.053
France	FR81	Languedoc-Roussillon	0.513	0.515	0.527	0.354	0.413	0.317	0.202	0.147	0.076	0.056	0.040
France	FR82	Provence-Alpes-Côte d'Azur	0.354	0.324	0.227	0.241	0.205	0.122	0.079	0.064	0.033	0.027	0.016
France	FR83	Corse	–	–	–	–	0.536	0.455	0.300	0.190	0.080	0.051	0.029
Germany	DE11	Stuttgart, Regierungsbezirk	0.411	0.391	0.375	0.295	0.219	0.129	0.067	0.042	0.029	0.016	0.012
Germany	DE12	Karlsruhe, Regierungsbezirk	0.339	0.289	0.280	0.230	0.194	0.117	0.044	0.033	0.021	0.009	0.007
Germany	DE13	Freiburg, Regierungsbezirk	0.504	0.490	0.460	0.338	0.340	0.212	0.107	0.076	0.049	0.023	0.017
Germany	DE14	Tübingen, Regierungsbezirk	0.532	0.522	0.507	0.412	0.348	0.213	0.115	0.079	0.050	0.029	0.022
Germany	DE21	Oberbayern, Regierungsbezirk	0.396	0.398	0.330	0.267	0.232	0.145	0.085	0.060	0.039	0.023	0.018

(continued)

Table A.4 (continued)

Country (current borders)	*NUTS codes*	*Region*	*1900*	*1910*	*1925*	*1938*	*1950*	*1960*	*1970*	*1980*	*1990*	*2000*	*2010*
Germany	DE22	Niederbayern, Regierungsbezirk	0.683	0.704	0.662	0.596	0.490	0.394	0.260	0.178	0.108	0.059	0.046
Germany	DE23	Oberpfalz, Regierungsbezirk	0.629	0.636	0.575	0.508	0.404	0.279	0.172	0.121	0.077	0.042	0.032
Germany	DE24	Oberfranken, Regierungsbezirk	0.477	0.475	0.424	0.370	0.275	0.198	0.126	0.088	0.058	0.026	0.020
Germany	DE25	Mittelfranken, Regierungsbezirk	0.406	0.390	0.332	0.272	0.254	0.172	0.115	0.066	0.042	0.020	0.015
Germany	DE26	Unterfranken, Regierungsbezirk	0.580	0.587	0.543	0.472	0.388	0.262	0.135	0.097	0.058	0.026	0.020
Germany	DE27	Schwaben, Regierungsbezirk	0.512	0.535	0.507	0.439	0.342	0.235	0.154	0.106	0.067	0.042	0.031
Germany	DE30	Berlin	0.095	0.014	0.009	0.008	0.018	0.009	0.008	0.004	0.003	0.001	0.000
Germany	DE40	Brandenburg	0.319	0.260	0.407	0.309	0.341	0.252	0.185	0.145	0.147	0.032	0.029
Germany	DE50	Bremen	0.067	0.070	0.038	0.031	0.036	0.019	0.016	0.005	0.004	0.002	0.002
Germany	DE60	Hamburg	0.029	0.024	0.022	0.025	0.027	0.015	0.012	0.009	0.007	0.003	0.003
Germany	DE71+DE72	Darmstadt and Giessen	0.311	0.269	0.278	0.250	0.202	0.104	0.045	0.032	0.018	0.009	0.008
Germany	DE73	Kassel, Regierungsbezirk	0.464	0.462	0.440	0.405	0.343	0.232	0.122	0.085	0.049	0.025	0.019
Germany	DE80	Mecklenburg-Vorpommern	0.472	0.466	0.463	0.396	0.475	0.346	0.249	0.199	0.190	0.034	0.031
Germany	DE91+DE92	Statistische Regionen Braunschweig und Hannover	0.343	0.347	0.315	0.258	0.221	0.128	0.070	0.051	0.033	0.017	0.014
Germany	DE93	Statistische Region Lüneburg	0.541	0.541	0.575	0.503	0.391	0.263	0.148	0.126	0.082	0.043	0.043
Germany	DE94	Statistische Region Weser-Ems	0.517	0.520	0.508	0.432	0.373	0.257	0.144	0.109	0.075	0.039	0.038
Germany	DEA1	Düsseldorf, Regierungsbezirk	0.127	0.101	0.078	0.064	0.061	0.030	0.020	0.013	0.012	0.008	0.008
Germany	DEA2	Köln, Regierungsbezirk	0.253	0.217	0.183	0.151	0.136	0.063	0.031	0.018	0.015	0.008	0.007
Germany	DEA3	Münster, Regierungsbezirk	0.352	0.293	0.240	0.222	0.181	0.107	0.063	0.045	0.036	0.019	0.017
Germany	DEA4	Detmold, Regierungsbezirk	0.411	0.400	0.348	0.324	0.223	0.147	0.072	0.050	0.037	0.014	0.012
Germany	DEA5	Arnsberg, Regierungsbezirk	0.151	0.132	0.117	0.107	0.093	0.053	0.025	0.020	0.016	0.007	0.007
Germany	DEB1	Statistische Region Koblenz	0.481	0.487	0.469	0.417	0.373	0.222	0.098	0.065	0.044	0.019	0.016
Germany	DEB2	Statistische Region Trier	0.649	0.682	0.643	0.586	0.553	0.384	0.223	0.141	0.095	0.046	0.034

Germany	DEB3	Statistische Region Rheinhessen-Pfalz	0.379	0.373	0.340	0.297	0.298	0.170	0.085	0.061	0.044	0.027	0.025
Germany	DEC0	Saarland	0.229	0.197	0.134	0.145	0.150	0.084	0.024	0.022	0.013	0.006	0.005
Germany	DED2	Dresden, NUTS 2 region	0.108	0.077	0.085	0.075	0.178	0.116	0.095	0.078	0.074	0.021	0.016
Germany	DED4	Chemnitz, NUTS 2 region	0.231	0.201	0.199	0.148	0.099	0.083	0.066	0.058	0.051	0.023	0.017
Germany	DED5	Leipzig, NUTS 2 region	0.169	0.126	0.124	0.107	0.159	0.123	0.093	0.084	0.082	0.016	0.014
Germany	DEE0	Sachsen-Anhalt	0.372	0.364	0.331	0.279	0.266	0.199	0.145	0.118	0.118	0.026	0.022
Germany	DEF0	Schleswig-Holstein	0.355	0.332	0.333	0.293	0.254	0.161	0.094	0.072	0.047	0.027	0.027
Germany	DEG0	Thüringen	0.329	0.303	0.297	0.249	0.272	0.188	0.132	0.102	0.098	0.026	0.020
Italy	ITC1	Piemonte	0.612	0.555	0.488	0.421	0.356	0.281	0.141	0.106	0.064	0.040	0.054
Italy	ITC2	Valle d'Aosta/Vallée d'Aoste	0.768	0.720	0.638	0.586	0.567	0.392	0.237	0.125	0.099	0.052	0.044
Italy	ITC3	Liguria	0.425	0.358	0.298	0.253	0.264	0.205	0.119	0.076	0.039	0.032	0.034
Italy	ITC4	Lombardia	0.506	0.440	0.358	0.285	0.245	0.136	0.063	0.044	0.040	0.026	0.027
Italy	ITH1+ITH2	Provincia Autonoma di Bolzano/Bozen-Provincia Autonoma di Trento	0.682	0.631	0.571	0.502	0.503	0.407	0.198	0.148	0.102	0.075	0.070
Italy	ITH3	Veneto	0.626	0.602	0.573	0.527	0.505	0.326	0.172	0.122	0.081	0.051	0.047
Italy	ITH4	Friuli-Venezia Giulia	0.476	0.444	0.446	0.419	0.400	0.301	0.160	0.088	0.062	0.043	0.043
Italy	ITH5	Emilia-Romagna	0.630	0.586	0.606	0.586	0.497	0.312	0.175	0.136	0.102	0.062	0.053
Italy	ITI1	Toscana	0.578	0.516	0.510	0.475	0.425	0.282	0.134	0.115	0.055	0.033	0.038
Italy	ITI2	Umbria	0.741	0.700	0.680	0.645	0.567	0.455	0.220	0.151	0.098	0.047	0.042
Italy	ITI3	Marche	0.704	0.677	0.684	0.665	0.568	0.475	0.249	0.146	0.087	0.046	0.049
Italy	ITI4	Lazio	0.566	0.510	0.460	0.416	0.344	0.206	0.095	0.091	0.051	0.032	0.026
Italy	ITF1	Abruzzo	0.768	0.769	0.765	0.749	0.710	0.515	0.331	0.227	0.109	0.065	0.081
Italy	ITF2	Molise	0.792	0.781	0.759	0.727	0.691	0.688	0.486	0.328	0.158	0.086	0.112
Italy	ITF3	Campania	0.541	0.527	0.509	0.480	0.480	0.342	0.246	0.210	0.113	0.072	0.059
Italy	ITF4	Puglia	0.644	0.630	0.604	0.529	0.660	0.519	0.406	0.218	0.162	0.127	0.102
Italy	ITF5	Basilicata	0.779	0.768	0.759	0.752	0.763	0.637	0.420	0.330	0.166	0.107	0.121

(continued)

Table A.4 (continued)

Country (current borders)	*NUTS codes*	*Region*	*1900*	*1910*	*1925*	*1938*	*1950*	*1960*	*1970*	*1980*	*1990*	*2000*	*2010*
Italy	ITF6	Calabria	0.628	0.669	0.705	0.676	0.678	0.524	0.370	0.292	0.198	0.163	0.141
Italy	ITG1	Sicilia	0.533	0.528	0.555	0.510	0.578	0.433	0.301	0.202	0.146	0.106	0.086
Italy	ITG2	Sardegna	0.621	0.593	0.605	0.564	0.578	0.450	0.277	0.165	0.137	0.098	0.077
Netherlands	NL11	Groningen	0.393	0.352	0.285	0.234	0.180	0.164	0.015	0.014	0.011	0.028	0.039
Netherlands	NL12	Friesland	0.460	0.436	0.384	0.341	0.252	0.228	0.041	0.029	0.029	0.050	0.051
Netherlands	NL13	Drenthe	0.522	0.499	0.455	0.416	0.329	0.273	0.013	0.015	0.018	0.058	0.030
Netherlands	NL21	Overijssel	0.386	0.351	0.275	0.219	0.184	0.144	0.015	0.013	0.013	0.040	0.032
Netherlands	NL22	Gelderland	0.442	0.402	0.312	0.244	0.186	0.144	0.015	0.016	0.017	0.032	0.032
Netherlands	NL31	Utrecht	0.276	0.240	0.166	0.119	0.079	0.067	0.012	0.010	0.009	0.019	0.013
Netherlands	NL32	Noordholland	0.166	0.138	0.102	0.078	0.060	0.057	0.013	0.012	0.013	0.019	0.018
Netherlands	NL33	Zuidholland	0.198	0.166	0.124	0.095	0.073	0.076	0.025	0.019	0.022	0.033	0.028
Netherlands	NL34	Zeeland	0.537	0.502	0.439	0.387	0.259	0.231	0.031	0.025	0.024	0.026	0.032
Netherlands	NL41	Noordbrabant	0.443	0.418	0.307	0.228	0.148	0.107	0.010	0.011	0.015	0.031	0.032
Netherlands	NL42	Limburg	0.477	0.420	0.286	0.195	0.112	0.091	0.013	0.015	0.018	0.038	0.035
Netherlands	NL23	Flevoland (1960–)	–	–	–	–	-	0.501	0.278	0.072	0.058	0.060	0.034
Norway	NO01	Oslo og Akershus	0.168	0.171	0.099	0.094	0.081	0.051	0.027	0.017	0.013	0.008	0.006
Norway	NO02	Hedmark og Oppland	0.677	0.689	0.556	0.550	0.499	0.384	0.256	0.148	0.111	0.072	0.058
Norway	NO03	Sør-Østlandet	0.381	0.371	0.291	0.279	0.258	0.176	0.106	0.064	0.044	0.027	0.021
Norway	NO04	Agder og Rogaland	0.458	0.477	0.337	0.309	0.291	0.207	0.145	0.080	0.061	0.041	0.027
Norway	NO05	Vestlandet	0.595	0.576	0.401	0.360	0.326	0.245	0.182	0.101	0.080	0.051	0.034
Norway	NO06	Trøndelag	0.593	0.578	0.429	0.428	0.377	0.288	0.214	0.128	0.103	0.067	0.048
Norway	NO07	Nord-Norge	0.765	0.742	0.546	0.534	0.476	0.342	0.229	0.115	0.086	0.069	0.052
Portugal	PT11	Norte	0.665	0.638	0.590	0.553	0.497	0.458	0.366	0.241	0.180	0.089	0.079
Portugal	PT15	Algarve	0.663	0.641	0.629	0.617	0.629	0.585	0.451	0.251	0.207	0.087	0.047
Portugal	PT16	Centro	0.677	0.672	0.648	0.616	0.575	0.509	0.395	0.248	0.297	0.166	0.121

Portugal	PT17	Lisboa	0.325	0.301	0.273	0.247	0.232	0.178	0.110	0.054	0.086	0.007	0.011
Portugal	PT18	Alentejo	0.680	0.661	0.649	0.661	0.696	0.663	0.589	0.380	0.293	0.112	0.098
Spain	ES61	Andalucía	0.699	0.667	0.590	0.588	0.582	0.494	0.373	0.269	0.168	0.129	0.105
Spain	ES24	Aragón	0.732	0.754	0.604	0.578	0.589	0.447	0.346	0.211	0.128	0.089	0.075
Spain	ES12	Principado de Asturias	0.821	0.822	0.555	0.443	0.449	0.360	0.329	0.247	0.160	0.104	0.080
Spain	ES53	Illes Balears	0.705	0.639	0.384	0.436	0.417	0.334	0.208	0.124	0.040	0.033	0.029
Spain	ES70	Canarias	0.719	0.625	0.434	0.506	0.617	0.520	0.305	0.193	0.088	0.079	0.080
Spain	ES13	Cantabria	0.710	0.679	0.459	0.467	0.422	0.379	0.329	0.248	0.149	0.106	0.078
Spain	ES42	Castile-La Mancha	0.772	0.774	0.699	0.698	0.651	0.597	0.466	0.318	0.179	0.141	0.124
Spain	ES41	Castile-León	0.803	0.778	0.644	0.634	0.609	0.542	0.443	0.306	0.186	0.116	0.102
Spain	ES51	Cataluña	0.526	0.465	0.293	0.260	0.232	0.157	0.111	0.071	0.041	0.032	0.028
Spain	ES52	Comunidad Valenciana	0.703	0.676	0.536	0.517	0.512	0.388	0.260	0.153	0.090	0.056	0.052
Spain	ES43	Extremadura	0.800	0.777	0.694	0.751	0.732	0.634	0.525	0.376	0.239	0.182	0.141
Spain	ES11	Galicia	0.862	0.835	0.751	0.706	0.687	0.626	0.546	0.440	0.310	0.203	0.174
Spain	ES30	Comunidad de Madrid	0.342	0.363	0.120	0.107	0.095	0.059	0.030	0.018	0.010	0.004	0.004
Spain	ES62	Región de Murcia	0.768	0.532	0.567	0.607	0.561	0.446	0.310	0.234	0.154	0.138	0.125
Spain	ES22	Comunidad Foral de Navarra	0.719	0.702	0.564	0.597	0.529	0.403	0.280	0.163	0.076	0.068	0.054
Spain	ES21	País Vasco	0.506	0.455	0.280	0.304	0.284	0.158	0.105	0.074	0.043	0.041	0.036
Spain	ES23	La Rioja	0.677	0.645	0.562	0.554	0.528	0.477	0.381	0.232	0.139	0.117	0.094
Sweden	SE11	Stockholm	0.215	0.169	0.113	0.068	0.041	0.025	0.014	0.010	0.007	0.007	0.002
Sweden	SE12	Östra Mellansverige	0.529	0.486	0.402	0.305	0.199	0.128	0.080	0.051	0.041	0.038	0.017
Sweden	SE21	Småland med öarna	0.605	0.567	0.478	0.389	0.292	0.204	0.126	0.088	0.065	0.052	0.027
Sweden	SE22	Sydsverige	0.495	0.428	0.337	0.282	0.202	0.149	0.094	0.067	0.045	0.041	0.016
Sweden	SE23	Västsverige	0.553	0.492	0.372	0.277	0.204	0.135	0.085	0.059	0.038	0.030	0.013
Sweden	SE31	Norra Mellansverige	0.541	0.517	0.429	0.387	0.272	0.173	0.100	0.067	0.052	0.041	0.023
Sweden	SE32	Mellersta Norrland	0.573	0.590	0.484	0.459	0.318	0.213	0.120	0.077	0.058	0.052	0.029
Sweden	SE33	Övre Norrland	0.674	0.666	0.563	0.506	0.385	0.216	0.120	0.068	0.049	0.037	0.023

(continued)

Table A.4 (continued)

Country (current borders)	*NUTS codes*	*Region*	*1900*	*1910*	*1925*	*1938*	*1950*	*1960*	*1970*	*1980*	*1990*	*2000*	*2010*
Switzerland	CH01	Région lémanique	0.341	0.289	0.263	0.242	0.188	0.116	0.071	0.055	0.031	0.049	0.032
Switzerland	CH02	Espace Mittelland	0.339	0.303	0.273	0.243	0.122	0.088	0.099	0.085	0.054	0.076	0.059
Switzerland	CH03	Nordwestschweiz	0.241	0.204	0.172	0.144	0.102	0.066	0.045	0.037	0.025	0.033	0.025
Switzerland	CH04	Zürich	0.193	0.172	0.139	0.109	0.080	0.053	0.035	0.028	0.021	0.020	0.015
Switzerland	CH05	Ostschweiz	0.297	0.248	0.269	0.251	0.201	0.146	0.110	0.089	0.057	0.077	0.059
Switzerland	CH06	Zentralschweiz	0.401	0.357	0.333	0.296	0.248	0.182	0.133	0.102	0.074	0.084	0.063
Switzerland	CH07	Ticino	0.458	0.419	0.373	0.295	0.183	0.106	0.049	0.033	0.017	0.025	0.016
United Kingdom	UKI	London Counties	0.016	0.024	0.009	0.009	0.006	0.004	0.001	0.008	0.003	0.003	0.001
United Kingdom	UKH+UKJ	Rest of South East	0.152	0.137	0.125	0.070	0.088	0.058	0.040	0.023	0.024	0.017	0.009
United Kingdom	UKK	South West	0.158	0.158	0.144	0.105	0.108	0.079	0.056	0.044	0.035	0.027	0.017
United Kingdom	UKG	West Midlands	0.090	0.077	0.061	0.047	0.043	0.030	0.023	0.019	0.017	0.015	0.010
United Kingdom	UKF	East Midlands	0.103	0.112	0.098	0.078	0.077	0.052	0.039	0.030	0.023	0.019	0.012
United Kingdom	UKC+UKD	North	0.048	0.046	0.040	0.041	0.032	0.024	0.019	0.015	0.014	0.012	0.007
United Kingdom	UKE	Yorkshire and Humberside	0.057	0.054	0.045	0.045	0.037	0.029	0.020	0.022	0.012	0.016	0.010
United Kingdom	UKL	Wales	0.126	0.116	0.103	0.105	0.086	0.061	0.046	0.039	0.035	0.023	0.018
United Kingdom	UKM	Scotland	0.120	0.111	0.095	0.082	0.076	0.060	0.042	0.034	0.029	0.024	0.020
United Kingdom	UKN	Northern Ireland	0.340	0.328	0.260	0.260	0.178	0.133	0.083	0.057	0.043	0.031	0.023
Ireland	IE0	Ireland	0.525	0.505	0.525	0.537	0.411	0.364	0.268	0.174	0.140	0.074	0.049
Luxembourg	LU00	Luxembourg	0.432	0.432	0.354	0.287	0.230	0.148	0.075	0.051	0.028	0.017	0.013

Source: See Chapter 2 in this book, and country chapters for details.

Table A.5 Share of industry and mining in total employment

Country (current borders)	*NUTS codes*	*Region*	*1900*	*1910*	*1925*	*1938*	*1950*	*1960*	*1970*	*1980*	*1990*	*2000*	*2010*
Austria	AT11	Burgenland	0.123	0.147	0.194	0.237	0.245	0.321	0.443	0.466	0.413	0.321	0.252
Austria	AT21	Carinthia	0.191	0.221	0.257	0.286	0.371	0.400	0.412	0.399	0.356	0.314	0.260
Austria	AT12+AT13	Lower Austria	0.395	0.416	0.421	0.424	0.454	0.471	0.423	0.385	0.323	0.257	0.196
Austria	AT32	Salzburg	0.214	0.239	0.256	0.270	0.381	0.364	0.363	0.349	0.310	0.283	0.247
Austria	AT22	Styria	0.194	0.219	0.255	0.284	0.359	0.394	0.420	0.423	0.382	0.345	0.289
Austria	AT33	Tyrol	0.168	0.213	0.253	0.283	0.370	0.365	0.379	0.363	0.331	0.251	0.252
Austria	AT31	Upper Austria	0.235	0.248	0.278	0.302	0.367	0.429	0.465	0.472	0.427	0.361	0.321
Austria	AT34	Vorarlberg	0.461	0.464	0.454	0.445	0.508	0.563	0.586	0.549	0.489	0.436	0.356
Belgium	BE21	Antwerp	0.345	0.399	0.377	0.352	0.442	0.467	0.480	0.402	0.301	0.268	0.222
Belgium	BE10+BE24+BE31	Brabant	0.371	0.420	0.391	0.379	0.418	0.408	0.377	0.252	0.165	0.141	0.109
Belgium	BE25	West Flanders	0.267	0.362	0.374	0.388	0.450	0.479	0.497	0.444	0.321	0.299	0.260
Belgium	BE23	East Flanders	0.364	0.449	0.441	0.424	0.487	0.511	0.521	0.404	0.312	0.281	0.237
Belgium	BE32	Hainaut	0.571	0.618	0.589	0.543	0.581	0.548	0.499	0.368	0.259	0.170	0.207
Belgium	BE33	Liege	0.559	0.606	0.549	0.501	0.543	0.531	0.462	0.367	0.262	0.231	0.207
Belgium	BE22	Limburg	0.195	0.265	0.321	0.353	0.473	0.495	0.551	0.468	0.343	0.317	0.251
Belgium	BE34	Luxembourg	0.206	0.262	0.206	0.198	0.226	0.267	0.292	0.216	0.199	0.204	0.198
Belgium	BE35	Namur	0.390	0.465	0.401	0.369	0.396	0.396	0.389	0.274	0.184	0.173	0.154
Denmark	DK01	Hovedstaden	0.439	0.197	0.286	0.411	0.446	0.452	0.373	0.241	0.201	0.161	0.070
Denmark	DK02	Sjælland	0.236	0.115	0.182	0.273	0.257	0.360	0.404	0.309	0.260	0.240	0.106
Denmark	DK03	Southern Denmark	0.275	0.132	0.202	0.295	0.289	0.382	0.416	0.353	0.309	0.284	0.153
Denmark	DK04	Midtjylland	0.247	0.120	0.190	0.293	0.282	0.367	0.391	0.327	0.292	0.274	0.145
Denmark	DK05	Nordjylland	0.212	0.107	0.173	0.269	0.240	0.340	0.379	0.328	0.277	0.262	0.142
Finland	FI19	Länsi-Suomi	0.148	0.118	0.133	0.173	0.290	0.332	0.395	0.357	0.280	0.213	0.180

(continued)

Table A.5 (continued)

Country (current borders)	*NUTS codes*	*Region*	*1900*	*1910*	*1925*	*1938*	*1950*	*1960*	*1970*	*1980*	*1990*	*2000*	*2010*
Finland	FI1B	Helsinki-Uusimaa	0.245	0.239	0.271	0.321	0.384	0.390	0.371	0.360	0.334	0.334	0.299
Finland	FI1C	Etelä-Soumi	0.177	0.147	0.178	0.219	0.325	0.352	0.377	0.371	0.343	0.329	0.291
Finland	FI1D	Pohjois-ja Itä-Soumi	0.099	0.051	0.067	0.079	0.169	0.199	0.264	0.275	0.269	0.264	0.235
Finland	FI20	Åland	0.071	0.046	0.037	0.037	0.122	0.157	0.210	0.199	0.170	0.150	0.128
France	FR10	Île-de-France	0.467	0.526	0.493	0.403	0.440	0.443	0.400	0.445	0.260	0.173	0.136
France	FR21	Champagne-Ardenne	0.379	0.431	0.419	0.368	0.361	0.398	0.418	0.489	0.348	0.284	0.249
France	FR22	Picardie	0.408	0.388	0.447	0.357	0.346	0.409	0.444	0.519	0.363	0.286	0.237
France	FR23	Haute-Normandie	0.431	0.566	0.452	0.364	0.362	0.396	0.431	0.526	0.371	0.298	0.260
France	FR24	Centre	0.251	0.291	0.250	0.269	0.244	0.306	0.376	0.478	0.349	0.283	0.245
France	FR25	Basse-Normandie	0.241	0.276	0.238	0.255	0.200	0.235	0.304	0.411	0.319	0.272	0.249
France	FR26	Bourgogne	0.255	0.288	0.284	0.300	0.266	0.326	0.378	0.469	0.332	0.275	0.238
France	FR30	Nord-Pas-de-Calais	0.556	0.610	0.619	0.576	0.552	0.540	0.511	0.543	0.345	0.270	0.226
France	FR41	Lorraine	0.416	0.525	0.492	0.499	0.527	0.524	0.505	0.550	0.365	0.297	0.249
France	FR42	Alsace	0.365	0.374	0.428	0.453	0.428	0.458	0.474	0.543	0.388	0.282	0.038
France	FR43	Franche-Comté	0.290	0.354	0.357	0.393	0.391	0.462	0.509	0.575	0.415	0.345	0.308
France	FR51	Pays de la Loire	0.236	0.271	0.248	0.276	0.232	0.278	0.346	0.442	0.333	0.284	0.255
France	FR52	Bretagne	0.181	0.217	0.181	0.214	0.172	0.203	0.264	0.354	0.270	0.243	0.225
France	FR53	Poitou-Charentes	0.238	0.344	0.189	0.257	0.199	0.248	0.317	0.408	0.292	0.248	0.226
France	FR61	Aquitaine	0.223	0.257	0.231	0.265	0.224	0.278	0.318	0.387	0.265	0.214	0.200
France	FR62	Midi-Pyrénées	0.228	0.295	0.209	0.282	0.228	0.277	0.316	0.384	0.271	0.223	0.209
France	FR63	Limousin	0.210	0.225	0.188	0.256	0.193	0.248	0.312	0.395	0.289	0.246	0.212
France	FR71	Rhône-Alpes	0.355	0.383	0.394	0.440	0.403	0.460	0.467	0.525	0.353	0.283	0.244
France	FR72	Auvergne	0.226	0.261	0.233	0.319	0.250	0.311	0.365	0.459	0.325	0.274	0.242
France	FR81	Languedoc-Roussillon	0.262	0.288	0.250	0.292	0.232	0.269	0.288	0.345	0.223	0.174	0.169

France	FR82	Provence-Alpes-Côte d'Azur	0.313	0.392	0.299	0.378	0.292	0.338	0.333	0.377	0.234	0.176	0.167
France	FR83	Corse	.	.	.	.	0.091	0.115	0.138	0.252	0.192	0.151	0.169
Germany	DE11	Stuttgart, Regierungsbezirk	0.360	0.392	0.407	0.455	0.490	0.556	0.574	0.505	0.462	0.366	0.324
Germany	DE12	Karlsruhe, Regierungsbezirk	0.400	0.442	0.438	0.521	0.459	0.511	0.530	0.457	0.400	0.321	0.281
Germany	DE13	Freiburg, Regierungsbezirk	0.301	0.316	0.336	0.341	0.379	0.467	0.503	0.452	0.410	0.352	0.317
Germany	DE14	Tübingen, Regierungsbezirk	0.309	0.327	0.346	0.393	0.433	0.533	0.564	0.476	0.435	0.363	0.334
Germany	DE21	Oberbayern, Regierungsbezirk	0.291	0.276	0.329	0.332	0.364	0.417	0.433	0.355	0.318	0.249	0.215
Germany	DE22	Niederbayern, Regierungsbezirk	0.170	0.163	0.191	0.209	0.295	0.356	0.424	0.392	0.402	0.359	0.331
Germany	DE23	Oberpfalz, Regierungsbezirk	0.217	0.215	0.252	0.269	0.340	0.429	0.468	0.402	0.395	0.350	0.333
Germany	DE24	Oberfranken, Regierungsbezirk	0.358	0.362	0.411	0.420	0.478	0.537	0.557	0.488	0.454	0.375	0.323
Germany	DE25	Mittelfranken, Regierungsbezirk	0.367	0.386	0.426	0.437	0.430	0.491	0.508	0.431	0.390	0.316	0.279
Germany	DE26	Unterfranken, Regierungsbezirk	0.221	0.218	0.263	0.283	0.355	0.441	0.499	0.423	0.399	0.341	0.306
Germany	DE27	Schwaben, Regierungsbezirk	0.284	0.275	0.302	0.318	0.392	0.461	0.485	0.416	0.402	0.344	0.315
Germany	DE30	Berlin	0.468	0.537	0.509	0.475	0.491	0.508	0.450	0.347	0.343	0.177	0.125
Germany	DE40	Brandenburg	0.376	0.406	0.355	0.383	0.363	0.506	0.454	0.477	0.438	0.274	0.221
Germany	DE50	Bremen	0.426	0.425	0.395	0.459	0.416	0.415	0.378	0.333	0.294	0.239	0.192
Germany	DE60	Hamburg	0.393	0.407	0.376	0.384	0.385	0.395	0.358	0.283	0.229	0.169	0.130
Germany	DE71+DE72	Darmstadt and Giessen	0.393	0.429	0.425	0.431	0.426	0.482	0.500	0.391	0.342	0.246	0.204
Germany	DE73	Kassel, Regierungsbezirk	0.305	0.320	0.322	0.333	0.357	0.419	0.452	0.381	0.359	0.297	0.268
Germany	DE80	Mecklenburg-Vorpommern	0.257	0.260	0.240	0.261	0.243	0.382	0.334	0.365	0.338	0.234	0.189
Germany	DE91+DE92	Statistische Regionen Braunschweig und Hannover	0.391	0.392	0.406	0.402	0.412	0.474	0.480	0.400	0.352	0.283	0.236

(continued)

Table A.5 (continued)

Country (current borders)	*NUTS codes*	*Region*	*1900*	*1910*	*1925*	*1938*	*1950*	*1960*	*1970*	*1980*	*1990*	*2000*	*2010*
Germany	DE93	Statistische Region Lüneburg	0.259	0.273	0.243	0.261	0.301	0.388	0.423	0.301	0.271	0.244	0.207
Germany	DE94	Statistische Region Weser-Ems	0.261	0.268	0.239	0.249	0.317	0.382	0.415	0.359	0.324	0.282	0.256
Germany	DEA1	Düsseldorf, Regierungsbezirk	0.613	0.632	0.610	0.587	0.583	0.583	0.553	0.445	0.375	0.264	0.212
Germany	DEA2	Köln, Regierungsbezirk	0.457	0.489	0.470	0.461	0.488	0.508	0.484	0.399	0.339	0.239	0.189
Germany	DEA3	Münster, Regierungsbezirk	0.443	0.521	0.525	0.499	0.536	0.558	0.528	0.444	0.384	0.289	0.241
Germany	DEA4	Detmold, Regierungsbezirk	0.368	0.396	0.439	0.421	0.462	0.527	0.539	0.470	0.429	0.344	0.288
Germany	DEA5	Arnsberg, Regierungsbezirk	0.632	0.645	0.611	0.573	0.590	0.604	0.580	0.495	0.431	0.337	0.279
Germany	DEB1	Statistische Region Koblenz	0.300	0.308	0.306	0.312	0.335	0.406	0.439	0.376	0.341	0.295	0.265
Germany	DEB2	Statistische Region Trier	0.197	0.193	0.170	0.182	0.209	0.282	0.343	0.318	0.301	0.282	0.261
Germany	DEB3	Statistische Region Rheinhessen-Pfalz	0.373	0.389	0.423	0.420	0.414	0.479	0.507	0.432	0.386	0.301	0.256
Germany	DEC0	Saarland	0.561	0.577	0.591	0.524	0.554	0.542	0.517	0.449	0.390	0.319	0.279
Germany	DED2	Dresden, NUTS 2 region	0.700	0.723	0.706	0.675	0.506	0.656	0.571	0.572	0.539	0.296	0.255
Germany	DED4	Chemnitz, NUTS 2 region	0.493	0.506	0.524	0.522	0.668	0.732	0.642	0.629	0.595	0.348	0.315
Germany	DED5	Leipzig, NUTS 2 region	0.507	0.545	0.543	0.510	0.517	0.635	0.554	0.544	0.503	0.252	0.201
Germany	DEE0	Sachsen-Anhalt	0.381	0.394	0.413	0.425	0.437	0.578	0.514	0.520	0.484	0.288	0.254
Germany	DEF0	Schleswig-Holstein	0.308	0.324	0.323	0.318	0.351	0.393	0.372	0.302	0.269	0.227	0.195
Germany	DEG0	Thüringen	0.458	0.487	0.485	0.488	0.456	0.605	0.546	0.560	0.522	0.318	0.294
Italy	ITC1	Piemonte	0.226	0.273	0.299	0.349	0.387	0.425	0.513	0.446	0.385	0.349	0.272
Italy	ITC2	Valle d'Aosta/Vallée d'Aoste	0.091	0.121	0.184	0.243	0.264	0.330	0.321	0.307	0.258	0.221	0.235
Italy	ITC3	Liguria	0.262	0.317	0.310	0.355	0.297	0.316	0.327	0.275	0.232	0.214	0.194
Italy	ITC4	Lombardia	0.316	0.370	0.407	0.455	0.456	0.512	0.551	0.498	0.413	0.367	0.318

Italy	ITH1+ITH2	Provincia Autonoma di Bolzano/Bozen-Provincia Autonoma di Trento	0.152	0.169	0.181	0.222	0.213	0.236	0.285	0.262	0.255	0.236	0.240
Italy	ITH3	Veneto	0.198	0.213	0.222	0.250	0.245	0.341	0.420	0.428	0.398	0.378	0.344
Italy	ITH4	Friuli-Venezia Giulia	0.308	0.286	0.317	0.307	0.283	0.316	0.368	0.357	0.306	0.297	0.277
Italy	ITH5	Emilia-Romagna	0.200	0.239	0.199	0.210	0.231	0.339	0.407	0.386	0.355	0.338	0.307
Italy	ITI1	Toscana	0.244	0.301	0.265	0.286	0.300	0.376	0.424	0.392	0.336	0.314	0.270
Italy	ITI2	Umbria	0.149	0.172	0.177	0.196	0.210	0.268	0.361	0.406	0.327	0.307	0.278
Italy	ITI3	Marche	0.170	0.190	0.176	0.181	0.214	0.261	0.369	0.401	0.383	0.361	0.358
Italy	ITI4	Lazio	0.184	0.214	0.206	0.224	0.202	0.231	0.257	0.245	0.186	0.183	0.177
Italy	ITF1	Abruzzo	0.147	0.133	0.121	0.118	0.112	0.215	0.269	0.322	0.289	0.323	0.296
Italy	ITF2	Molise	0.120	0.120	0.128	0.145	0.166	0.141	0.188	0.256	0.287	0.280	0.273
Italy	ITF3	Campania	0.236	0.237	0.229	0.241	0.202	0.271	0.301	0.282	0.224	0.219	0.197
Italy	ITF4	Puglia	0.201	0.201	0.208	0.257	0.128	0.191	0.238	0.281	0.240	0.230	0.234
Italy	ITF5	Basilicata	0.124	0.128	0.132	0.129	0.104	0.172	0.252	0.260	0.257	0.281	0.247
Italy	ITF6	Calabria	0.259	0.211	0.162	0.159	0.146	0.221	0.257	0.246	0.160	0.164	0.173
Italy	ITG1	Sicilia	0.241	0.229	0.221	0.218	0.164	0.219	0.254	0.265	0.193	0.177	0.167
Italy	ITG2	Sardegna	0.181	0.206	0.178	0.200	0.170	0.221	0.256	0.286	0.221	0.189	0.181
Netherlands	NL11	Groningen	0.273	0.290	0.324	0.350	0.355	0.389	0.459	0.388	0.309	0.220	0.180
Netherlands	NL12	Friesland	0.226	0.239	0.259	0.275	0.302	0.349	0.429	0.373	0.311	0.264	0.208
Netherlands	NL13	Drenthe	0.269	0.300	0.304	0.306	0.325	0.382	0.469	0.387	0.336	0.255	0.223
Netherlands	NL21	Overijssel	0.395	0.420	0.472	0.512	0.460	0.507	0.521	0.415	0.374	0.276	0.217
Netherlands	NL22	Gelderland	0.292	0.311	0.367	0.411	0.395	0.434	0.442	0.345	0.294	0.235	0.189
Netherlands	NL31	Utrecht	0.342	0.346	0.376	0.393	0.378	0.391	0.372	0.268	0.208	0.134	0.128
Netherlands	NL32	Noordholland	0.371	0.372	0.377	0.377	0.381	0.386	0.370	0.277	0.229	0.162	0.132
Netherlands	NL33	Zuidholland	0.368	0.366	0.379	0.386	0.379	0.405	0.363	0.292	0.236	0.176	0.151
Netherlands	NL34	Zeeland	0.184	0.209	0.233	0.254	0.305	0.322	0.459	0.391	0.339	0.260	0.252

(continued)

Table A.5 (continued)

Country (current borders)	*NUTS codes*	*Region*	*1900*	*1910*	*1925*	*1938*	*1950*	*1960*	*1970*	*1980*	*1990*	*2000*	*2010*
Netherlands	NL41	Noordbrabant	0.341	0.347	0.425	0.482	0.470	0.521	0.548	0.438	0.379	0.276	0.221
Netherlands	NL42	Limburg	0.305	0.341	0.437	0.508	0.575	0.538	0.522	0.427	0.387	0.289	0.220
Netherlands	NL23	Flevoland (1960–)	–	–	–	–	–	0.168	0.392	0.296	0.217	0.188	0.157
Norway	NO01	Oslo og Akershus	0.462	0.437	0.340	0.309	0.427	0.395	0.314	0.220	0.177	0.137	0.111
Norway	NO02	Hedmark og Oppland	0.218	0.198	0.178	0.148	0.298	0.336	0.343	0.306	0.260	0.230	0.200
Norway	NO03	Sør-Østlandet	0.374	0.392	0.343	0.292	0.482	0.510	0.455	0.375	0.310	0.253	0.226
Norway	NO04	Agder og Rogaland	0.280	0.279	0.278	0.265	0.392	0.409	0.376	0.326	0.304	0.281	0.271
Norway	NO05	Vestlandet	0.225	0.221	0.233	0.216	0.375	0.391	0.354	0.315	0.278	0.263	0.243
Norway	NO06	Trøndelag	0.248	0.239	0.217	0.190	0.331	0.334	0.292	0.267	0.230	0.207	0.192
Norway	NO07	Nord-Norge	0.134	0.133	0.154	0.136	0.278	0.311	0.277	0.264	0.221	0.179	0.173
Portugal	PT11	Norte	0.182	0.198	0.206	0.217	0.275	0.311	0.366	0.427	0.446	0.466	0.379
Portugal	PT15	Algarve	0.138	0.150	0.156	0.188	0.194	0.224	0.249	0.273	0.196	0.209	0.179
Portugal	PT16	Centro	0.168	0.178	0.178	0.187	0.227	0.286	0.344	0.418	0.319	0.375	0.323
Portugal	PT17	Lisboa	0.271	0.287	0.274	0.256	0.283	0.328	0.332	0.344	0.293	0.257	0.186
Portugal	PT18	Alentejo	0.141	0.157	0.151	0.132	0.120	0.144	0.158	0.238	0.234	0.294	0.246
Spain	ES61	Andalucía	0.149	0.164	0.197	0.167	0.163	0.202	0.247	0.247	0.249	0.223	0.159
Spain	ES24	Aragón	0.116	0.102	0.188	0.178	0.182	0.257	0.297	0.336	0.348	0.332	0.278
Spain	ES12	Principado de Asturias	0.082	0.088	0.273	0.331	0.326	0.397	0.368	0.362	0.347	0.311	0.269
Spain	ES53	Illes Balears	0.149	0.192	0.339	0.267	0.280	0.271	0.265	0.230	0.210	0.191	0.143
Spain	ES70	Canarias	0.106	0.178	0.239	0.163	0.138	0.144	0.223	0.201	0.191	0.191	0.133
Spain	ES13	Cantabria	0.136	0.120	0.240	0.246	0.291	0.325	0.338	0.339	0.325	0.320	0.261
Spain	ES42	Castile-La Mancha	0.111	0.108	0.157	0.136	0.154	0.170	0.230	0.281	0.327	0.342	0.280
Spain	ES41	Castile-León	0.072	0.073	0.150	0.150	0.154	0.200	0.230	0.278	0.298	0.308	0.270

Spain	ES51	Cataluña	0.276	0.295	0.443	0.423	0.396	0.469	0.489	0.447	0.411	0.363	0.299
Spain	ES52	Comunidad Valenciana	0.151	0.165	0.246	0.254	0.262	0.288	0.356	0.382	0.368	0.360	0.297
Spain	ES43	Extremadura	0.102	0.112	0.154	0.081	0.077	0.142	0.165	0.185	0.223	0.238	0.205
Spain	ES11	Galicia	0.059	0.071	0.110	0.112	0.119	0.151	0.188	0.226	0.253	0.287	0.258
Spain	ES30	Comunidad de Madrid	0.207	0.195	0.324	0.290	0.294	0.347	0.361	0.319	0.274	0.236	0.195
Spain	ES62	Región de Murcia	0.095	0.284	0.209	0.137	0.180	0.253	0.304	0.303	0.308	0.303	0.231
Spain	ES22	Comunidad Foral de Navarra	0.111	0.117	0.195	0.159	0.208	0.302	0.393	0.418	0.442	0.432	0.399
Spain	ES21	País Vasco	0.264	0.274	0.356	0.349	0.397	0.477	0.506	0.470	0.423	0.395	0.342
Spain	ES23	La Rioja	0.151	0.168	0.214	0.200	0.201	0.269	0.324	0.383	0.405	0.386	0.337
Sweden	SE11	Stockholm	0.383	0.389	0.366	0.360	0.383	0.405	0.290	0.224	0.204	0.181	0.138
Sweden	SE12	Östra Mellansverige	0.304	0.319	0.357	0.418	0.492	0.523	0.464	0.399	0.346	0.323	0.245
Sweden	SE21	Småland med öarna	0.230	0.253	0.312	0.346	0.419	0.460	0.455	0.421	0.375	0.378	0.292
Sweden	SE22	Sydsverige	0.295	0.309	0.345	0.368	0.424	0.447	0.396	0.350	0.317	0.296	0.211
Sweden	SE23	Västsverige	0.235	0.275	0.338	0.387	0.438	0.473	0.426	0.372	0.331	0.317	0.242
Sweden	SE31	Norra Mellansverige	0.306	0.313	0.361	0.363	0.436	0.475	0.464	0.405	0.342	0.336	0.270
Sweden	SE32	Mellersta Norrland	0.279	0.239	0.294	0.263	0.346	0.376	0.362	0.305	0.292	0.259	0.206
Sweden	SE33	Övre Norrland	0.200	0.188	0.235	0.225	0.298	0.395	0.357	0.307	0.290	0.272	0.234
Switzerland	CH01	Région lémanique	0.354	0.351	0.348	0.349	0.372	0.415	0.392	0.302	0.234	0.202	0.193
Switzerland	CH02	Espace Mittelland	0.435	0.439	0.443	0.444	0.480	0.520	0.516	0.418	0.326	0.287	0.284
Switzerland	CH03	Nordwestschweiz	0.510	0.522	0.516	0.510	0.540	0.572	0.546	0.447	0.340	0.313	0.295
Switzerland	CH04	Zürich	0.529	0.522	0.496	0.469	0.476	0.495	0.447	0.350	0.263	0.199	0.172
Switzerland	CH05	Ostschweiz	0.513	0.535	0.470	0.454	0.487	0.544	0.525	0.447	0.368	0.330	0.330
Switzerland	CH06	Zentralschweiz	0.357	0.365	0.365	0.378	0.413	0.472	0.476	0.411	0.342	0.285	0.271
Switzerland	CH07	Ticino	0.336	0.320	0.338	0.365	0.429	0.453	0.426	0.316	0.248	0.273	0.261

(continued)

Table A.5 (continued)

Country (current borders)	*NUTS codes*	*Region*	*1900*	*1910*	*1925*	*1938*	*1950*	*1960*	*1970*	*1980*	*1990*	*2000*	*2010*
United Kingdom	UKI	London Counties	0.346	0.339	0.414	0.398	0.413	0.392	0.350	0.315	0.203	0.139	0.108
United Kingdom	UKH+UKJ	Rest of South East	0.295	0.273	0.283	0.268	0.375	0.410	0.401	0.402	0.285	0.218	0.177
United Kingdom	UKK	South West	0.344	0.325	0.349	0.284	0.350	0.365	0.378	0.334	0.281	0.224	0.189
United Kingdom	UKG	West Midlands	0.587	0.540	0.605	0.530	0.597	0.637	0.569	0.471	0.384	0.292	0.220
United Kingdom	UKF	East Midlands	0.440	0.503	0.552	0.496	0.550	0.494	0.516	0.409	0.376	0.279	0.229
United Kingdom	UKC+UKD	North	0.543	0.542	0.567	0.435	0.543	0.531	0.493	0.390	0.335	0.255	0.200
United Kingdom	UKE	Yorkshire and Humberside	0.579	0.573	0.605	0.505	0.577	0.564	0.523	0.426	0.347	0.264	0.212
United Kingdom	UKL	Wales	0.467	0.482	0.487	0.356	0.475	0.474	0.465	0.380	0.322	0.233	0.208
United Kingdom	UKM	Scotland	0.475	0.477	0.478	0.412	0.480	0.458	0.436	0.365	0.300	0.228	0.207
United Kingdom	UKN	Northern Ireland	0.364	0.346	0.396	0.396	0.435	0.431	0.436	0.330	0.267	0.239	0.197
Ireland	IE0	Ireland	0.177	0.168	0.128	0.136	0.227	0.244	0.303	0.321	0.277	0.277	0.194
Luxembourg	LU00	Luxembourg	0.384	0.384	0.389	0.381	0.405	0.428	0.428	0.329	0.292	0.238	0.201

Source: See Chapter 2 in this book, and country chapters for details.

Table A.6 Share of services in total employment

Country (current borders)	*NUTS codes*	*Region*	*1900*	*1910*	*1925*	*1938*	*1950*	*1960*	*1970*	*1980*	*1990*	*2000*	*2010*
Austria	AT11	Burgenland	0.111	0.112	0.120	0.125	0.123	0.176	0.269	0.380	0.500	0.601	0.693
Austria	AT21	Carinthia	0.175	0.205	0.212	0.216	0.253	0.333	0.443	0.515	0.584	0.622	0.676
Austria	AT12+AT13	Lower Austria	0.372	0.375	0.381	0.386	0.331	0.371	0.470	0.545	0.627	0.695	0.767
Austria	AT32	Salzburg	0.264	0.283	0.299	0.310	0.306	0.404	0.505	0.575	0.638	0.670	0.716
Austria	AT22	Styria	0.161	0.179	0.205	0.225	0.208	0.273	0.366	0.446	0.529	0.578	0.652
Austria	AT33	Tyrol	0.197	0.226	0.271	0.305	0.266	0.372	0.494	0.570	0.626	0.703	0.699
Austria	AT31	Upper Austria	0.185	0.196	0.201	0.204	0.241	0.272	0.344	0.412	0.496	0.574	0.620
Austria	AT34	Vorarlberg	0.163	0.191	0.223	0.250	0.231	0.282	0.347	0.416	0.486	0.544	0.615
Belgium	BE21	Antwerp	0.398	0.425	0.467	0.510	0.464	0.478	0.492	0.577	0.682	0.716	0.767
Belgium	BE10+BE24+BE31	Brabant	0.383	0.407	0.469	0.503	0.504	0.546	0.599	0.730	0.824	0.851	0.885
Belgium	BE25	West Flanders	0.315	0.284	0.366	0.399	0.381	0.401	0.427	0.495	0.631	0.660	0.713
Belgium	BE23	East Flanders	0.275	0.258	0.317	0.368	0.358	0.378	0.414	0.546	0.656	0.693	0.745
Belgium	BE32	Hainaut	0.250	0.240	0.303	0.357	0.335	0.383	0.459	0.596	0.715	0.810	0.779
Belgium	BE33	Liege	0.285	0.277	0.338	0.386	0.364	0.399	0.493	0.599	0.715	0.751	0.781
Belgium	BE22	Limburg	0.261	0.246	0.274	0.317	0.323	0.386	0.397	0.497	0.619	0.652	0.727
Belgium	BE34	Luxembourg	0.252	0.278	0.357	0.396	0.417	0.452	0.534	0.664	0.723	0.736	0.760
Belgium	BE35	Namur	0.291	0.297	0.393	0.442	0.435	0.472	0.531	0.669	0.776	0.795	0.825
Denmark	DK01	Hovedstaden	0.455	0.749	0.653	0.525	0.516	0.509	0.607	0.753	0.789	0.831	0.926
Denmark	DK02	Sjælland	0.210	0.637	0.493	0.330	0.303	0.333	0.457	0.665	0.684	0.720	0.860
Denmark	DK03	Southern Denmark	0.239	0.649	0.506	0.349	0.320	0.337	0.429	0.618	0.613	0.659	0.806
Denmark	DK04	Midtjylland	0.219	0.643	0.492	0.334	0.319	0.338	0.440	0.644	0.630	0.672	0.819
Denmark	DK05	Nordjylland	0.194	0.626	0.464	0.298	0.285	0.309	0.433	0.639	0.635	0.680	0.809
Finland	FI19	Länsi-Suomi	0.149	0.083	0.099	0.138	0.212	0.284	0.372	0.493	0.659	0.774	0.810
Finland	FI1B	Helsinki-Uusimaa	0.377	0.278	0.373	0.418	0.448	0.510	0.582	0.542	0.555	0.550	0.608

(continued)

Table A.6 (continued)

Country (current borders)	*NUTS codes*	*Region*	*1900*	*1910*	*1925*	*1938*	*1950*	*1960*	*1970*	*1980*	*1990*	*2000*	*2010*
Finland	FI1C	Etelä-Soumi	0.184	0.115	0.173	0.226	0.305	0.380	0.471	0.486	0.547	0.582	0.638
Finland	FI1D	Pohjois-ja Itä-Soumi	0.082	0.050	0.069	0.101	0.186	0.257	0.383	0.426	0.522	0.586	0.645
Finland	FI20	Åland	0.368	0.177	0.145	0.252	0.309	0.432	0.551	0.603	0.700	0.761	0.804
France	FR10	Île-de-France	0.454	0.406	0.463	0.569	0.528	0.539	0.588	0.546	0.736	0.823	0.862
France	FR21	Champagne-Ardenne	0.220	0.186	0.247	0.371	0.344	0.382	0.431	0.383	0.571	0.646	0.691
France	FR22	Picardie	0.225	0.216	0.242	0.359	0.337	0.380	0.429	0.378	0.586	0.674	0.734
France	FR23	Haute-Normandie	0.261	0.196	0.295	0.405	0.401	0.433	0.467	0.396	0.593	0.676	0.721
France	FR24	Centre	0.185	0.166	0.211	0.291	0.317	0.382	0.446	0.391	0.591	0.672	0.723
France	FR25	Basse-Normandie	0.199	0.187	0.219	0.264	0.308	0.351	0.419	0.359	0.582	0.657	0.701
France	FR26	Bourgogne	0.182	0.166	0.201	0.326	0.338	0.384	0.449	0.396	0.598	0.666	0.714
France	FR30	Nord-Pas-de-Calais	0.220	0.202	0.212	0.309	0.307	0.356	0.423	0.399	0.624	0.707	0.759
France	FR41	Lorraine	0.249	0.183	0.259	0.343	0.307	0.365	0.429	0.394	0.604	0.678	0.733
France	FR42	Alsace	0.248	0.253	0.254	0.350	0.323	0.391	0.454	0.407	0.590	0.699	0.942
France	FR43	Franche-Comté	0.169	0.157	0.193	0.252	0.277	0.314	0.369	0.332	0.535	0.617	0.665
France	FR51	Pays de la Loire	0.167	0.160	0.188	0.259	0.280	0.340	0.414	0.365	0.576	0.651	0.700
France	FR52	Bretagne	0.164	0.139	0.170	0.242	0.281	0.354	0.454	0.414	0.625	0.684	0.725
France	FR53	Poitou-Charentes	0.167	0.127	0.173	0.283	0.301	0.363	0.440	0.399	0.606	0.677	0.721
France	FR61	Aquitaine	0.179	0.162	0.196	0.326	0.312	0.379	0.468	0.441	0.645	0.715	0.749
France	FR62	Midi-Pyrénées	0.157	0.135	0.162	0.266	0.266	0.337	0.443	0.433	0.640	0.713	0.750
France	FR63	Limousin	0.125	0.116	0.129	0.227	0.244	0.311	0.401	0.381	0.611	0.680	0.732
France	FR71	Rhône-Alpes	0.187	0.183	0.210	0.292	0.306	0.352	0.431	0.405	0.614	0.691	0.739
France	FR72	Auvergne	0.146	0.142	0.161	0.245	0.276	0.332	0.409	0.367	0.586	0.657	0.705
France	FR81	Languedoc-Roussillon	0.226	0.197	0.224	0.354	0.356	0.414	0.510	0.508	0.701	0.769	0.792
France	FR82	Provence-Alpes-Côte d'Azur	0.333	0.285	0.474	0.381	0.504	0.540	0.588	0.558	0.733	0.797	0.817

France	FR83	Corse	.	.	.	.	0.373	0.429	0.562	0.558	0.727	0.798	0.801
Germany	DE11	Stuttgart, Regierungsbezirk	0.230	0.217	0.218	0.250	0.291	0.314	0.359	0.452	0.509	0.619	0.665
Germany	DE12	Karlsruhe, Regierungsbezirk	0.261	0.268	0.283	0.249	0.348	0.372	0.426	0.509	0.579	0.670	0.713
Germany	DE13	Freiburg, Regierungsbezirk	0.195	0.195	0.204	0.321	0.281	0.322	0.390	0.472	0.541	0.625	0.666
Germany	DE14	Tübingen, Regierungsbezirk	0.159	0.151	0.147	0.196	0.218	0.254	0.321	0.445	0.515	0.608	0.643
Germany	DE21	Oberbayern, Regierungsbezirk	0.313	0.325	0.340	0.401	0.404	0.438	0.482	0.585	0.643	0.729	0.767
Germany	DE22	Niederbayern, Regierungsbezirk	0.146	0.133	0.148	0.195	0.215	0.250	0.316	0.430	0.490	0.581	0.623
Germany	DE23	Oberpfalz, Regierungsbezirk	0.153	0.149	0.173	0.223	0.256	0.291	0.360	0.477	0.527	0.608	0.635
Germany	DE24	Oberfranken, Regierungsbezirk	0.166	0.163	0.165	0.210	0.247	0.266	0.318	0.424	0.488	0.600	0.657
Germany	DE25	Mittelfranken, Regierungsbezirk	0.227	0.224	0.243	0.291	0.316	0.337	0.377	0.503	0.568	0.664	0.706
Germany	DE26	Unterfranken, Regierungsbezirk	0.199	0.196	0.194	0.246	0.257	0.297	0.366	0.480	0.544	0.633	0.674
Germany	DE27	Schwaben, Regierungsbezirk	0.204	0.190	0.192	0.243	0.266	0.304	0.361	0.478	0.531	0.614	0.653
Germany	DE30	Berlin	0.436	0.450	0.482	0.517	0.490	0.483	0.541	0.649	0.654	0.822	0.875
Germany	DE40	Brandenburg	0.305	0.334	0.238	0.307	0.296	0.242	0.361	0.378	0.415	0.693	0.750
Germany	DE50	Bremen	0.507	0.505	0.567	0.510	0.548	0.566	0.606	0.663	0.702	0.759	0.806

(continued)

Table A.6 (continued)

Country (current borders)	*NUTS codes*	*Region*	*1900*	*1910*	*1925*	*1938*	*1950*	*1960*	*1970*	*1980*	*1990*	*2000*	*2010*
Germany	DE60	Hamburg	0.578	0.569	0.602	0.590	0.588	0.590	0.629	0.708	0.764	0.828	0.867
Germany	DE71+DE72	Darmstadt and Giessen	0.296	0.302	0.297	0.319	0.373	0.414	0.455	0.576	0.639	0.745	0.789
Germany	DE73	Kassel, Regierungsbezirk	0.231	0.218	0.238	0.262	0.301	0.349	0.426	0.535	0.592	0.678	0.713
Germany	DE80	Mecklenburg-Vorpommern	0.271	0.274	0.297	0.343	0.282	0.272	0.417	0.436	0.473	0.732	0.780
Germany	DE91+DE92	Statistische Regionen Braunschweig und Hannover	0.266	0.261	0.279	0.340	0.367	0.397	0.450	0.549	0.615	0.701	0.750
Germany	DE93	Statistische Region Lüneburg	0.200	0.186	0.181	0.236	0.308	0.349	0.429	0.574	0.647	0.713	0.750
Germany	DE94	Statistische Region Weser-Ems	0.222	0.212	0.252	0.319	0.311	0.361	0.441	0.532	0.600	0.680	0.707
Germany	DEA1	Düsseldorf, Regierungsbezirk	0.260	0.267	0.312	0.349	0.356	0.386	0.427	0.541	0.613	0.728	0.780
Germany	DEA2	Köln, Regierungsbezirk	0.290	0.294	0.347	0.388	0.377	0.428	0.485	0.583	0.647	0.754	0.804
Germany	DEA3	Münster, Regierungsbezirk	0.205	0.187	0.235	0.278	0.282	0.336	0.409	0.511	0.580	0.691	0.741
Germany	DEA4	Detmold, Regierungsbezirk	0.221	0.204	0.213	0.255	0.315	0.327	0.389	0.480	0.534	0.642	0.700
Germany	DEA5	Arnsberg, Regierungsbezirk	0.217	0.223	0.272	0.320	0.317	0.344	0.395	0.485	0.553	0.656	0.714
Germany	DEB1	Statistische Region Koblenz	0.218	0.206	0.224	0.271	0.293	0.372	0.464	0.559	0.615	0.687	0.720

Germany	DEB2	Statistische Region Trier	0.154	0.125	0.187	0.232	0.238	0.334	0.434	0.541	0.604	0.672	0.706
Germany	DEB3	Statistische Region Rheinhessen-Pfalz	0.248	0.238	0.237	0.283	0.288	0.351	0.408	0.507	0.571	0.672	0.718
Germany	DEC0	Saarland	0.210	0.227	0.275	0.331	0.296	0.374	0.460	0.529	0.598	0.676	0.716
Germany	DED2	Dresden, NUTS 2 region	0.192	0.200	0.209	0.250	0.316	0.227	0.335	0.350	0.387	0.683	0.729
Germany	DED4	Chemnitz, NUTS 2 region	0.276	0.293	0.277	0.331	0.233	0.184	0.292	0.313	0.354	0.629	0.668
Germany	DED5	Leipzig, NUTS 2 region	0.324	0.329	0.332	0.383	0.325	0.242	0.353	0.372	0.415	0.732	0.785
Germany	DEE0	Sachsen-Anhalt	0.247	0.242	0.255	0.296	0.297	0.223	0.341	0.362	0.398	0.687	0.724
Germany	DEF0	Schleswig-Holstein	0.337	0.344	0.344	0.389	0.395	0.447	0.534	0.626	0.683	0.747	0.778
Germany	DEG0	Thüringen	0.214	0.210	0.218	0.263	0.271	0.206	0.322	0.338	0.380	0.657	0.686
Italy	ITC1	Piemonte	0.162	0.172	0.213	0.230	0.257	0.295	0.346	0.448	0.551	0.611	0.674
Italy	ITC2	Valle d'Aosta/Vallée d'Aoste	0.141	0.158	0.178	0.172	0.169	0.278	0.442	0.568	0.643	0.726	0.721
Italy	ITC3	Liguria	0.313	0.325	0.392	0.392	0.439	0.479	0.554	0.649	0.729	0.754	0.772
Italy	ITC4	Lombardia	0.178	0.190	0.236	0.260	0.299	0.352	0.386	0.458	0.547	0.607	0.655
Italy	ITH1+ITH2	Provincia Autonoma di Bolzano/Bozen-Provincia Autonoma di Trento	0.166	0.200	0.249	0.277	0.284	0.357	0.517	0.591	0.643	0.689	0.690
Italy	ITH3	Veneto	0.176	0.185	0.205	0.223	0.250	0.333	0.408	0.450	0.521	0.571	0.609
Italy	ITH4	Friuli-Venezia Giulia	0.216	0.271	0.237	0.273	0.316	0.383	0.472	0.556	0.632	0.660	0.680
Italy	ITH5	Emilia-Romagna	0.170	0.175	0.196	0.205	0.273	0.348	0.418	0.478	0.542	0.600	0.641
Italy	ITI1	Toscana	0.179	0.183	0.225	0.240	0.276	0.342	0.442	0.492	0.609	0.653	0.692
Italy	ITI2	Umbria	0.110	0.128	0.143	0.158	0.223	0.277	0.419	0.442	0.576	0.646	0.680
Italy	ITI3	Marche	0.126	0.133	0.140	0.154	0.217	0.264	0.382	0.453	0.530	0.592	0.593

(continued)

Table A.6 (continued)

Country (current borders)	*NUTS codes*	*Region*	*1900*	*1910*	*1925*	*1938*	*1950*	*1960*	*1970*	*1980*	*1990*	*2000*	*2010*
Italy	ITI4	Lazio	0.250	0.276	0.334	0.361	0.454	0.563	0.648	0.664	0.763	0.785	0.797
Italy	ITF1	Abruzzo	0.085	0.097	0.114	0.133	0.178	0.270	0.400	0.451	0.602	0.612	0.623
Italy	ITF2	Molise	0.087	0.099	0.113	0.129	0.143	0.171	0.325	0.416	0.555	0.635	0.615
Italy	ITF3	Campania	0.222	0.236	0.261	0.279	0.317	0.387	0.452	0.508	0.663	0.709	0.744
Italy	ITF4	Puglia	0.156	0.168	0.188	0.214	0.211	0.290	0.357	0.501	0.598	0.642	0.665
Italy	ITF5	Basilicata	0.097	0.104	0.109	0.119	0.133	0.191	0.328	0.410	0.577	0.612	0.632
Italy	ITF6	Calabria	0.113	0.120	0.133	0.165	0.176	0.255	0.373	0.462	0.642	0.673	0.686
Italy	ITG1	Sicilia	0.226	0.243	0.224	0.272	0.258	0.349	0.445	0.532	0.662	0.717	0.747
Italy	ITG2	Sardegna	0.198	0.201	0.217	0.236	0.252	0.329	0.467	0.549	0.642	0.713	0.742
Netherlands	NL11	Groningen	0.333	0.358	0.391	0.416	0.465	0.447	0.525	0.598	0.679	0.752	0.781
Netherlands	NL12	Friesland	0.314	0.325	0.358	0.384	0.446	0.424	0.530	0.598	0.659	0.687	0.741
Netherlands	NL13	Drenthe	0.209	0.201	0.242	0.277	0.346	0.345	0.517	0.598	0.645	0.687	0.747
Netherlands	NL21	Overijssel	0.219	0.230	0.253	0.269	0.357	0.349	0.464	0.571	0.613	0.684	0.751
Netherlands	NL22	Gelderland	0.267	0.286	0.321	0.344	0.419	0.422	0.542	0.640	0.689	0.733	0.778
Netherlands	NL31	Utrecht	0.382	0.414	0.458	0.488	0.543	0.542	0.616	0.722	0.784	0.847	0.858
Netherlands	NL32	Noordholland	0.463	0.490	0.521	0.545	0.558	0.557	0.617	0.711	0.758	0.819	0.850
Netherlands	NL33	Zuidholland	0.434	0.468	0.497	0.519	0.548	0.519	0.612	0.689	0.742	0.791	0.821
Netherlands	NL34	Zeeland	0.279	0.289	0.328	0.359	0.436	0.447	0.510	0.584	0.637	0.714	0.716
Netherlands	NL41	Noordbrabant	0.215	0.235	0.268	0.290	0.381	0.372	0.442	0.551	0.606	0.693	0.747
Netherlands	NL42	Limburg	0.218	0.239	0.277	0.297	0.313	0.371	0.464	0.558	0.595	0.673	0.745
Netherlands	NL23	Flevoland (1960–)	–	–	–	–	–	0.331	0.329	0.632	0.724	0.751	0.809
Norway	NO01	Oslo og Akershus	0.370	0.392	0.561	0.597	0.492	0.554	0.659	0.763	0.810	0.855	0.884
Norway	NO02	Hedmark og Oppland	0.105	0.112	0.266	0.302	0.203	0.279	0.400	0.546	0.628	0.597	0.743
Norway	NO03	Sør-Østlandet	0.245	0.237	0.366	0.430	0.260	0.314	0.439	0.561	0.646	0.710	0.753
Norway	NO04	Agder og Rogaland	0.262	0.244	0.385	0.426	0.317	0.384	0.479	0.594	0.635	0.678	0.701

Norway	NO05	Vestlandet	0.181	0.203	0.366	0.424	0.299	0.364	0.464	0.584	0.643	0.686	0.722
Norway	NO06	Trøndelag	0.159	0.183	0.354	0.383	0.292	0.378	0.494	0.605	0.667	0.727	0.760
Norway	NO07	Nord-Norge	0.102	0.126	0.300	0.329	0.247	0.347	0.494	0.621	0.692	0.752	0.774
Portugal	PT11	Norte	0.153	0.163	0.203	0.230	0.229	0.231	0.269	0.332	0.374	0.445	0.542
Portugal	PT15	Algarve	0.199	0.209	0.215	0.195	0.177	0.191	0.300	0.476	0.597	0.704	0.774
Portugal	PT16	Centro	0.154	0.150	0.174	0.197	0.199	0.205	0.261	0.334	0.384	0.459	0.556
Portugal	PT17	Lisboa	0.404	0.412	0.454	0.498	0.484	0.494	0.558	0.602	0.621	0.735	0.804
Portugal	PT18	Alentejo	0.179	0.181	0.200	0.207	0.184	0.193	0.253	0.383	0.473	0.594	0.656
Spain	ES61	Andalucía	0.151	0.169	0.213	0.245	0.255	0.304	0.380	0.484	0.583	0.648	0.736
Spain	ES24	Aragón	0.152	0.144	0.208	0.244	0.229	0.296	0.357	0.453	0.524	0.579	0.648
Spain	ES12	Principado de Asturias	0.097	0.090	0.172	0.226	0.226	0.244	0.303	0.390	0.493	0.585	0.650
Spain	ES53	Illes Balears	0.146	0.169	0.277	0.297	0.304	0.395	0.527	0.646	0.749	0.775	0.828
Spain	ES70	Canarias	0.175	0.197	0.328	0.330	0.245	0.336	0.472	0.606	0.721	0.730	0.786
Spain	ES13	Cantabria	0.154	0.201	0.301	0.287	0.287	0.296	0.333	0.413	0.526	0.573	0.662
Spain	ES42	Castile-La Mancha	0.117	0.118	0.143	0.165	0.195	0.233	0.304	0.401	0.494	0.517	0.595
Spain	ES41	Castile-León	0.125	0.149	0.206	0.216	0.237	0.258	0.326	0.416	0.516	0.576	0.628
Spain	ES51	Cataluña	0.198	0.240	0.264	0.317	0.372	0.375	0.400	0.482	0.549	0.605	0.673
Spain	ES52	Comunidad Valenciana	0.147	0.159	0.217	0.229	0.225	0.324	0.384	0.465	0.542	0.584	0.651
Spain	ES43	Extremadura	0.098	0.112	0.152	0.168	0.191	0.224	0.310	0.439	0.538	0.580	0.654
Spain	ES11	Galicia	0.079	0.094	0.140	0.182	0.194	0.223	0.265	0.334	0.437	0.510	0.568
Spain	ES30	Comunidad de Madrid	0.451	0.442	0.556	0.602	0.610	0.594	0.610	0.663	0.716	0.761	0.801
Spain	ES62	Región de Murcia	0.137	0.184	0.224	0.256	0.259	0.301	0.386	0.463	0.538	0.560	0.644
Spain	ES22	Comunidad Foral de Navarra	0.170	0.181	0.242	0.244	0.264	0.295	0.327	0.419	0.482	0.500	0.547
Spain	ES21	País Vasco	0.230	0.272	0.364	0.348	0.319	0.365	0.389	0.456	0.534	0.564	0.621
Spain	ES23	La Rioja	0.172	0.187	0.224	0.246	0.271	0.254	0.295	0.385	0.456	0.498	0.568
Sweden	SE11	Stockholm	0.402	0.442	0.521	0.572	0.575	0.570	0.696	0.766	0.790	0.812	0.860
Sweden	SE12	Östra Mellansverige	0.167	0.195	0.241	0.276	0.310	0.349	0.455	0.550	0.613	0.638	0.738

(continued)

Table A.6 (continued)

Country (current borders)	*NUTS codes*	*Region*	*1900*	*1910*	*1925*	*1938*	*1950*	*1960*	*1970*	*1980*	*1990*	*2000*	*2010*
Sweden	SE21	Småland med öarna	0.165	0.179	0.210	0.264	0.289	0.337	0.419	0.491	0.560	0.570	0.681
Sweden	SE22	Sydsverige	0.210	0.264	0.317	0.350	0.374	0.403	0.510	0.583	0.638	0.663	0.773
Sweden	SE23	Västsverige	0.212	0.233	0.290	0.335	0.358	0.392	0.489	0.570	0.631	0.653	0.745
Sweden	SE31	Norra Mellansverige	0.153	0.170	0.210	0.250	0.291	0.351	0.436	0.528	0.606	0.624	0.707
Sweden	SE32	Mellersta Norrland	0.148	0.171	0.223	0.278	0.336	0.411	0.517	0.618	0.649	0.689	0.765
Sweden	SE33	Övre Norrland	0.125	0.146	0.202	0.268	0.317	0.390	0.523	0.624	0.661	0.691	0.744
Switzerland	CH01	Région lémanique	0.305	0.360	0.390	0.410	0.440	0.469	0.537	0.643	0.735	0.749	0.775
Switzerland	CH02	Espace Mittelland	0.226	0.258	0.284	0.314	0.398	0.392	0.385	0.496	0.620	0.638	0.657
Switzerland	CH03	Nordwestschweiz	0.249	0.274	0.311	0.346	0.358	0.362	0.409	0.516	0.635	0.655	0.680
Switzerland	CH04	Zürich	0.278	0.306	0.366	0.423	0.444	0.452	0.518	0.622	0.717	0.781	0.813
Switzerland	CH05	Ostschweiz	0.190	0.218	0.261	0.295	0.311	0.310	0.364	0.464	0.575	0.592	0.611
Switzerland	CH06	Zentralschweiz	0.242	0.278	0.303	0.325	0.339	0.347	0.392	0.487	0.583	0.631	0.666
Switzerland	CH07	Ticino	0.206	0.261	0.289	0.341	0.388	0.441	0.525	0.651	0.736	0.701	0.723
United Kingdom	UKI	London Counties	0.638	0.638	0.576	0.594	0.581	0.604	0.649	0.677	0.795	0.858	0.891
United Kingdom	UKH+UKJ	Rest of South East	0.552	0.589	0.592	0.662	0.537	0.531	0.559	0.576	0.692	0.765	0.814
United Kingdom	UKK	South West	0.498	0.517	0.507	0.611	0.542	0.556	0.566	0.622	0.684	0.749	0.793
United Kingdom	UKG	West Midlands	0.323	0.383	0.335	0.423	0.360	0.333	0.409	0.510	0.598	0.692	0.770
United Kingdom	UKF	East Midlands	0.457	0.385	0.349	0.426	0.373	0.454	0.445	0.561	0.601	0.702	0.759
United Kingdom	UKC+UKD	North	0.410	0.412	0.393	0.524	0.425	0.444	0.488	0.595	0.652	0.733	0.793
United Kingdom	UKE	Yorkshire and Humberside	0.364	0.373	0.350	0.450	0.386	0.408	0.457	0.552	0.641	0.721	0.778
United Kingdom	UKL	Wales	0.407	0.402	0.410	0.539	0.439	0.464	0.489	0.581	0.643	0.744	0.774
United Kingdom	UKM	Scotland	0.406	0.412	0.426	0.507	0.445	0.483	0.522	0.601	0.670	0.748	0.772
United Kingdom	UKN	Northern Ireland	0.296	0.326	0.343	0.343	0.387	0.435	0.482	0.613	0.690	0.730	0.780
Ireland	IE0	Ireland	0.298	0.327	0.348	0.328	0.361	0.391	0.428	0.505	0.582	0.649	0.757
Luxembourg	LU00	Luxembourg	0.184	0.184	0.257	0.332	0.366	0.424	0.498	0.620	0.680	0.744	0.785

Source: See Chapter 2 in this book, and country chapters for details.

Index

This index follows the structure of the chapters. Country specific entries can regularly be found under the country name entry. When country specific entries seem to be interesting for the broader picture, or might serve as a good example, they can also be found together with the main entry.